IT and the Development of Digital Skills and Competences in Education

Patricia Ordóñez de Pablos
University of Oviedo, Spain

Miltiadis D. Lytras
American College of Greece, Greece & Effat University, Saudi Arabia

Xi Zhang
Tianjin University, China

IGI Global
PUBLISHER of TIMELY KNOWLEDGE

A volume in the Advances in Educational Technologies and Instructional Design (AETID) Book Series

Published in the United States of America by
IGI Global
Information Science Reference (an imprint of IGI Global)
701 E. Chocolate Avenue
Hershey PA, USA 17033
Tel: 717-533-8845
Fax: 717-533-8661
E-mail: cust@igi-global.com
Web site: http://www.igi-global.com

Copyright © 2021 by IGI Global. All rights reserved. No part of this publication may be reproduced, stored or distributed in any form or by any means, electronic or mechanical, including photocopying, without written permission from the publisher. Product or company names used in this set are for identification purposes only. Inclusion of the names of the products or companies does not indicate a claim of ownership by IGI Global of the trademark or registered trademark.

Library of Congress Cataloging-in-Publication Data

Names: Ordóñez de Pablos, Patricia, 1975- editor. | Lytras, Miltiadis D., 1973- editor. | Zhang, Xi, editor.
Title: IT and the development of digital skills and competencies in education / Patricia Ordóñez de Pablos, Miltiadis D. Lytras, Xi Zhang, editors.
Other titles: Information technology and the development of digital skills and competencies in education
Description: Hershey, PA : Information Science Reference, 2021. | Includes bibliographical references and index. | Summary: "The book explores the new demands of labor markets in the digital economy, how educational institutions can respond to these new opportunities and threats, the development of new teaching and learning methods, and finally the development of digital skills and competences"-- Provided by publisher.
Identifiers: LCCN 2020018664 (print) | LCCN 2020018665 (ebook) | ISBN 9781799849728 (hardcover) | ISBN 9781799858324 (paperback) | ISBN 9781799849735 (ebook)
Subjects: LCSH: Education--Effect of technological innovations on. | Education--Effect of technological innovations on--Turkey. | Information technology--Study and teaching. | Information technology--Study and teaching--Turkey.
Classification: LCC LB1028.3 .I897 2021 (print) | LCC LB1028.3 (ebook) | DDC 371.3309561--dc23
LC record available at https://lccn.loc.gov/2020018664
LC ebook record available at https://lccn.loc.gov/2020018665

This book is published in the IGI Global book series Advances in Educational Technologies and Instructional Design (AE-TID) (ISSN: 2326-8905; eISSN: 2326-8913)

British Cataloguing in Publication Data
A Cataloguing in Publication record for this book is available from the British Library.

All work contributed to this book is new, previously-unpublished material. The views expressed in this book are those of the authors, but not necessarily of the publisher.

For electronic access to this publication, please contact: eresources@igi-global.com.

Advances in Educational Technologies and Instructional Design (AETID) Book Series

Lawrence A. Tomei
Robert Morris University, USA

ISSN:2326-8905
EISSN:2326-8913

Mission

Education has undergone, and continues to undergo, immense changes in the way it is enacted and distributed to both child and adult learners. In modern education, the traditional classroom learning experience has evolved to include technological resources and to provide online classroom opportunities to students of all ages regardless of their geographical locations. From distance education, Massive-Open-Online-Courses (MOOCs), and electronic tablets in the classroom, technology is now an integral part of learning and is also affecting the way educators communicate information to students.

The **Advances in Educational Technologies & Instructional Design (AETID) Book Series** explores new research and theories for facilitating learning and improving educational performance utilizing technological processes and resources. The series examines technologies that can be integrated into K-12 classrooms to improve skills and learning abilities in all subjects including STEM education and language learning. Additionally, it studies the emergence of fully online classrooms for young and adult learners alike, and the communication and accountability challenges that can arise. Trending topics that are covered include adaptive learning, game-based learning, virtual school environments, and social media effects. School administrators, educators, academicians, researchers, and students will find this series to be an excellent resource for the effective design and implementation of learning technologies in their classes.

Coverage

- Online Media in Classrooms
- Hybrid Learning
- Higher Education Technologies
- Educational Telecommunications
- Curriculum Development
- Web 2.0 and Education
- Classroom Response Systems
- Bring-Your-Own-Device
- K-12 Educational Technologies
- Adaptive Learning

IGI Global is currently accepting manuscripts for publication within this series. To submit a proposal for a volume in this series, please contact our Acquisition Editors at Acquisitions@igi-global.com or visit: http://www.igi-global.com/publish/.

The Advances in Educational Technologies and Instructional Design (AETID) Book Series (ISSN 2326-8905) is published by IGI Global, 701 E. Chocolate Avenue, Hershey, PA 17033-1240, USA, www.igi-global.com. This series is composed of titles available for purchase individually; each title is edited to be contextually exclusive from any other title within the series. For pricing and ordering information please visit http://www.igi-global.com/book-series/advances-educational-technologies-instructional-design/73678. Postmaster: Send all address changes to above address. Copyright © 2021 IGI Global. All rights, including translation in other languages reserved by the publisher. No part of this series may be reproduced or used in any form or by any means – graphics, electronic, or mechanical, including photocopying, recording, taping, or information and retrieval systems – without written permission from the publisher, except for non commercial, educational use, including classroom teaching purposes. The views expressed in this series are those of the authors, but not necessarily of IGI Global.

Titles in this Series

For a list of additional titles in this series, please visit:
http://www.igi-global.com/book-series/advances-educational-technologies-instructional-design/73678

Fostering Meaningful Learning Experiences Through Student Engagement
Despo Ktoridou (University of Nicosia, Cyprus) Elli Doukanari (University of Nicosia, Cyprus) and Nikleia Eteokleous (Frederick University, Cyprus)
Information Science Reference • © 2021 • 325pp • H/C (ISBN: 9781799846581) • US $195.00

Assessment Tools for Mapping Learning Outcomes With Learning Objectives
G. R. Sinha (Myanmar Institute of Information Technology, Mandalay, Myanmar)
Information Science Reference • © 2021 • 327pp • H/C (ISBN: 9781799847847) • US $185.00

Building STEM Skills Through Environmental Education
Stephen T. Schroth (Towson University, USA) and Janese Daniels (Towson University, USA)
Information Science Reference • © 2021 • 300pp • H/C (ISBN: 9781799827115) • US $180.00

Redesigning Teaching, Leadership, and Indigenous Education in the 21st Century
Leesha Nicole Roberts (University of Trinidad and Tobago, Trinidad and Tobago)
Information Science Reference • © 2021 • 350pp • H/C (ISBN: 9781799855576) • US $185.00

Advancing Online Course Design and Pedagogy for the 21st Century Learning Environment
Daniel Chatham (Middlebury Institute of International Studies at Monterey, USA)
Information Science Reference • © 2021 • 315pp • H/C (ISBN: 9781799855989) • US $195.00

Socioscientific Issues-Based Instruction for Scientific Literacy Development
Wardell A. Powell (Framingham State University, USA)
Information Science Reference • © 2021 • 359pp • H/C (ISBN: 9781799845584) • US $185.00

Fostering Communication and Learning With Underutilized Technologies in Higher Education
Mohammed Banu Ali (Institute of Management, University of Bolton, UK) and Trevor Wood-Harper (University of Manchester, UK)
Information Science Reference • © 2021 • 270pp • H/C (ISBN: 9781799848462) • US $195.00

Stagnancy Issues and Change Initiatives for Global Education in the Digital Age
Theresa Neimann (Oregon State University, USA) Jonathan J. Felix (RMIT University, Vietnam) Stacy Reeves (University of Southern Mississippi, USA) and Elena Shliakhovchuk (National Transport University, Ukraine)
Information Science Reference • © 2021 • 333pp • H/C (ISBN: 9781799849933) • US $185.00

IGI Global
PUBLISHER of TIMELY KNOWLEDGE

701 East Chocolate Avenue, Hershey, PA 17033, USA
Tel: 717-533-8845 x100 • Fax: 717-533-8661
E-Mail: cust@igi-global.com • www.igi-global.com

Editorial Advisory Board

Grisna Anggadwita, *Telkom University, Indonesia*
Giovanni Bronzetti, *University of Calabria, Italy*
Edgar Oliver Cardoso Espinosa, *Instituto Politécnico Nacional, Mexico*
María Trinidad Cerecedo Mercado, *Instituto Politécnico Nacional, Mexico*
Valentina Cillo, *Link Campus University, Italy*
Jésica Alhelí Cortés Ruiz, *Instituto Politécnico Nacional, Mexico*
Manlio Del Giudice, *Link Campus University, Italy*
Kadir Demir, *Dokuz Eylul University, Turkey*
Aquilino Adolfo Juan Fuente, *University of Oviedo, Spain*
Saarce Elsye Hatane, *Universitas Kristen Petra, Indonesia*
Dominga Ippolito, *Università della Calabria, Italy*
Ajeya Jha, *Sikkim Manipal Institute of Technology, India*
Ferry Jie, *Edith Cowan University, Australia*
Venetis Kanakaris, *Aristotle University of Thessaloniki, Greece*
Eleni Karakolidou, *Hellenic Open University, Greece*
Maria Pavlis Korres, *Hellenic Open University, Greece & Aristotle University of Thessaloniki, Greece*
Jose Emilio Labra Gayo, *University of Oviedo, Spain*
Piera Leftheriotou, *Hellenic Open University, Greece*
Domitilla Magni, *RomaTre University, Italy*
Pallavi Mathur, *Bhartiya Skill Development University, India*
Kapilan N., *Nagarjuna College of Engineering and Technology, India*
Hatice Ferhan Odabasi, *Anadolu University, Turkey*
Varvara Lemonia Oikonomou, *The University of Sheffield International Faculty, City College, Greece*
Eric Oktavianus, *Petra Christian University, Indonesia*
Beatrice Orlando, *University of Ferrara, Italy*
Vidhya P., *SRSMN Government First Grade College, India*
Nicole Palan, *University of Graz, Austria*
Rina D. Pasaribu, *School of Economics and Business, Telkom University, Indonesia*
Paschalia Patsala, *Arts and Humanities Research Council, UK*
Kristina Posavec, *Faculty of Education and Rehabilitation Sciences, University of Zagreb, Croatia*
Adhi Prasetio, *School of Economics and Business, Telkom University, Indonesia*

Maurizio Rija, *University of Calabria, Italy*
Andreas Schober, *University of Graz, Austria*
Amira Sghari, *University of Sfax, Tunisia*
Graziella Sicoli, *Università della Calabria, Italy*
Vandana Singh, *Bhartiya Skill Development University, India*
Josua Tarigan, *Petra Christian University, Indonesia*

List of Reviewers

Adilla Anggraeni, *Binus Business School, Bina Nusantara University, Indonesia*
Rajib Bhattacharyya, *Goenka College, Kolkata, India & University of Calcutta, India*
Som Sekhar Bhattacharyya, *National Institute of Industrial Engineering, India*
Anant Deogaonkar, *Shri Ramdeobaba College of Engineering and Management, India*
Mosharrof Hosen, *Universiti Tunku Abdul Rahman, Kampar Campus, Perak, Malaysia*
Md. Humayun Kabir, *East West University, Bangladesh*
Nilesh Kumar, *Amity University, Jharkhand, India*
Nishant Kumar, *Amity University, India*
Bruno Mascitelli, *Swinburne University of Technology, Australia*
Gaurav Nagpal, *BITS Pilani, India*
Biplob Kumar Nandi, *East West University, Bangladesh*
Sampada Nanoty, *M. S. University Vadodara Gujarat, India*
Muhamad Rusliyadi, *Polytechnic of Agricultural Development Yogyakarta Magelang, Indonesia*
Ahmad Setiawan, *Ministry of Communication and Information Technology, Indonesia*
Archana Shrivastava, *Jaypee Business School, JIIT University, India*
Ayuphita Tiara Silalahi, *Binus Business School, Bina Nusantara University, Indonesia*
Sachin Soonthodu, *Garden City University, India*
Shamila Rasanjani Wijesundara, *Uva Wellassa University, Sri Lanka*
Xi Zhang, *Tianjing University, China*

Table of Contents

Detailed Table of Contents

Thus far, digital transformation had a strong impact on business and society. The large-scale adoption of digital technologies changed social relationships and opened up to new opportunities for higher education. Currently, the interplay between innovation and digitalization become are among the most important assets for the educational system. In this light, this chapter aims to explore how digital skills and competencies modify the issue of co-creation in higher education. The authors use the case study analysis to explore such theme. The Little Genius International case is presented and discussed: an international alternative school in English for digital natives recognized as the best benefit corporation for the world. The main contribution of the chapter is that it outlines what are the new digital skills and competencies enabling a better understanding of the concept of students' co-creation in HEIs.

Today, companies manage increasing amounts of data. Companies that want to manage their data better must also adapt their information and reporting system to the current scenario of intelligent technologies. The market requires companies to have a financial communication that allows immediate comparison between the efficiency of reading the data and the effectiveness of the form in which they are presented. The information that the market requires is not only quantitative and temporal, but solutions that help speed up the extrapolation of the most strategic information to support business strategies. XBRL appeared in the beginning of the 21st century, and it represents one of the most important technological innovations in financial statement. On the basis of these premises, the idea of this work was born with which the authors analyze the importance of XBRL in the accounting environment of companies. The results of the study conducted allow us to conclude that XBRL can improve the quality of information of companies and at the same time can influence the choices of stakeholders.

The Hellenic Open University launched synchronous online group advisory meetings for the academic year 2016-17 through the Skype for Business videoconferencing platform. This chapter focuses on the extent to which interaction, immediacy, and collaborative learning are developed in this particular online learning environment, as well as on the skills required for an efficient adult e-tutor. Research conducted in 2019 has shown that learners scored high in terms of interaction, immediacy, and collaborative learning between each other and their tutor, especially when working in online workgroups, while the learning process was facilitated by immediate e-tutor feedback, which resolved queries, and the effective facilitation of the discussion. In terms of factors hindering the learning process, learners cited the lack of meaningful relationships with their peers as a leading one, e-tutors pointed to technical problems, while both agreed on the inadequate use of communication and collaborative tools in an online environment.

In the current scenario, many companies approached using a digital management system. For this reason, they must take into account an important issue: innovation. An essential strategic tool for management in current times. COVID-19 has imposed a reorganization of activities. There has been a sudden increase of digital systems, such as smart working and e-learning as regards the education system. The aim of the work is to illustrate how modern innovative technologies help the provision of services within universities. In an emergency, such as the spread of COVID-19, there is a sudden change in the use of educational services by the university structure. They are ready to delivery services based on Intelligent Technology. Through the administration of an on-line questionnaire, perception of the on-line education system is examined, gathering opinions of a sample of students in one of the most important Italian universities.

This chapter primarily provides information about digital literacy, which enables us to make basic use of today's technologies. In parallel with today's technological developments, high-level digital literacy skills expected from individuals are addressed. Definitions of digital fluency and studies on this subject are examined. The concept of digital fluency is redefined by the authors. It is based on theoretical foundations that are needed by authors on why digital fluency is needed in educational life. The authors point to the lack of a workforce with high-level digital literacy capabilities around the world.

Preface

Digital technologies are transforming societies and economies around the world. Education institutions experience the benefits of the use of IT to improve teaching methods and academic results. Markets demand new kinds of skills, especially digital skills and competences to adapt jobs to new economic scenarios and create new jobs. Thus it is essential to understand how information technologies can contribute to build human capital with the required skills and competences to live and work in the knowledge-based society and move to a life-long learning approach (Ordóñez et al., 2019), especially in the covid-19 scenario.

Developing a digitally skilled human capital is key for the creation of the Digital Single Market in Europe, for the building of an inclusive digital society and boosting competitive in Europe and internationally. In the case of Europe, there is a lack of workface with ICT skills to meet the requirements of jobs in many sectors of the economy (European Commission, 2020).

The pandemic has caused a global health emergency causing huge disruptions in citizens, societies and economies around the world. The Sustainable Development Goals proposed by United Nations can play a key role in the recovery of the world, working towards to greener, more inclusive and resilient economies (United Nations, 2020a). Among the 17 sustainable development goals (SDGs) proposed by United Nations, SDG4 "Quality Education" seeks to "ensure inclusive and equitable quality education and promote lifelong learning opportunities for all" (United Nations, 2020b).

The book explores the new demands of labor markets in the digital economy, how educational institutions can respond to these new opportunities and threats, the development of new teaching and learning methods, and finally the development of digital skills and competences to prepare young people for the digital economy.

Due to its innovative topic (digital skills and competences), geographical focus (Asia, Europe, Africa, Latin America) and approach (focus on empirical studies, case studies), the book can serve as a reference for academics, directors of schools, vice-chancellors, experts on education and IT, policy makers (in the field of Education and IT) and other relevant stakeholders. The book will offer readers a unique value, bringing new perspectives to understand the challenges and opportunities of the utilization of IT in the education sector around the world. It will present a valuable collection of chapters with empirical studies from leading researchers on these topics.

Target Audience

The book aims to be an international platform to bring together academics, researchers, lecturers, decision makers, policy makers, practitioners and non-profit organizations to share new theories, models, research findings, and case studies, to enhance understanding and collaboration in education (schools, higher education institutions).

Contents of the Book

The book presents a collection of 15 chapters that examine new and emerging topics in the field of education and information technologies:

Chapter 1, titled "Exploiting Digital Skills in Higher Education: A Case Study Analysis" (by Domitilla Magni, Beatrice Orlando and Manlio Del Giudice) states that digital transformation had a strong impact on business and society. The large-scale adoption of digital technologies changed social relationships and opened up to new opportunities for Higher Education. Currently, the interplay between innovation and digitalization become are among the most important assets for the educational system. In this light, this chapter aims to explore how digital skills and competencies modify the issue of co-creation in higher education. We use the case study analysis to explore such theme. The Little Genius International case is presented and discussed: an international alternative school in English for digital natives recognized as the best Benefit Corporation for the world (Best for the World 2018). The main contribution of the chapter is that it outlines what are the new digital skills and competencies enabling a better understanding of the concept of students' co-creation in HEIs.

Chapter 2, titled "XBRL and Smart Technologies" (by Maurizio Rija), observes that today, companies manage increasing amounts of data. Companies that want to manage their data better must also adapt their information and reporting system to the current scenario of intelligent technologies. The market requires companies to have a financial communication that allows immediate comparison between the efficiency of reading the data and the effectiveness of the form in which they are presented. The information that the market requires is not only quantitative and temporal, but solutions that help speed up the extrapolation of the most strategic information to support business strategies. XBRL appeared in the beginning of the 21st century and it represents one of the most important technological innovations in financial statement. On the basis of these premises, the idea of this work was born with which we analyze the importance of XBRL in the accounting environment of companies. The results of the study conducted allow us to conclude that XBRL can improve the quality of information of companies and at the same time can influence the choices of stakeholders.

Chapter 3, titled "The Need for (Increased) ICT-Skills in the Era of Digitalization" (by Nicole Palan and Andreas Schober) states that automation and digitalization have had profound effects on job losses as well as on skill requirements in advanced economies. This chapter analyzes the spatial distribution of ICT-skills requirements by analyzing some 73,000 job offers for the Austrian region of Styria. This region is characterized by a large variability of specialization patterns throughout its districts as well as differences regarding population density and infrastructure accessibility. The analysis allows to draw conclusions on the need for both basic and special ICT-skills for different education levels for 287 municipalities. The results also draw light on problems related to the new "digital divide" indicating the phenomenon that people have access to digital infrastructure but not yet acquired the digital competences to find work. One interesting conclusion is also that high-skill ICT-requiring jobs have the highest level of agglomeration – both compared with other skill-levels and with non-ICT related academic job positions.

Chapter 4, titled "Digital Learning Challenge in Indonesia" (by Adhi Prasetio, Grisna Anggadwita and Rina D Pasaribu), states that Industry Education Reform 4.0 was launched by the Indonesian government as one of nine Priority Agenda called Nawa Cita. The reform consists of two main programs:

First, to improve the quality of life of Indonesian people through improving the quality of education and training; Second, to revolutionize the nation's character through the policy of restructuring the national education curriculum. There are challenges though to implement those programs including Indonesian geographic, gap to access different level of education, and the gap to achieve the industrial revolution 4.0 skills. The aims of this chapter is to explore alternatives and solutions for access to education in Indonesia by utilizing technological advancements including the skills needed to face the current digital era. Education 4.0 is a good approach to answer those challenges. The use of internet technology for digital learning can provide access to students spread across the country. This approach requires skills set that are appropriate to Industry 4.0 by providing a flexible curriculum and online certification.

Chapter 5, titled "Women Empowerment Through ICT" (by Vandana Singh and Pallavi Mathur), proposes that ICT has the biggest potential today to become a key vehicle for the socio-economic advancement of women. There exists a plethora of opportunities for ICTs to improve women's economic activities in the field of trade, governance, education, health, crafts, employment in formal as well as informal sector. It can be used to fight many social issues and to empower weaker segments of society. The purpose of this chapter is to examine the opportunities which ICT can provide to improve the life of a woman in India. It will include the voices which speak of how women can fully participate and benefit from ICT and how ICT can be used as a tool to empower women. Women also should have an equal advantage of technology and the use of ICT should not be restricted to the upper section of the society. The aim here is to explore how women in India can improve their lives by using ICT. At last, it will also suggest ways on how all the segments of the female population can have benefited from technology.

Chapter 6, titled "The Training of the Digital Competence at the Postgraduate Level for a Knowledge-Based Economy" (by Edgar Oliver Cardoso Espinosa, Jésica Alhelí Cortés Ruiz and María Trinidad Cerecedo Mercado), aims to describe the main digital competences to be developed at the postgraduate level based on the characteristics established by the knowledge economy. It is a priority to evaluate, analyze and synthesize the information generated, in addition to communicating creatively and innovatively in a network environment. Thus, the postgraduate course has been constituted as a social community that develops innovation, scientific and technological projects as a substantial activity in which information is a fundamental resource in the development of the generation of new knowledge. To achieve this, it is necessary to carry out an investigation that involves a set of relevant processes such as identifying the problems; planning the search for information; selection of information sources; information processing, organization and storage, as well as the communication of results. The digital competence is defined as the set of capabilities focused on the use of ICT to obtain, store, organize, present and exchange information.

Chapter 7, titled "Investigating the Educational Needs of Elderly People Within the Scope of an Educational Program on the Use of Social Media Networks by Smartphones" (by Venetis Kanakaris and Maria Pavlis Korres), states that social media networks are becoming increasingly popular as a means for social interaction. A number of studies have found that elderly people have a difficulty in using social media platforms while exist a number of barriers that discourage them from using technology. This chapter investigates the educational needs of older people, who are members of two Elderly Care Centers in northern Greece, intending to attend an educational program on using smartphones as a communication tool to join social media networks. Research findings indicate that elderly women are more willing to attend an educational program than men and key areas of their interest include access to the internet e.g. online payments, how to create and use an e-mail account and how to join social media networks in order to feel less isolated by communicating with other individuals or groups with the same interests.

Chapter 8, titled "Facilitating the Educational Process in Synchronous Group Advisory Online Meetings in the Hellenic Open University" (by Eleni Karakolidou, Piera Leftheriotou and Maria Pavlis Korres), states that the Hellenic Open University launched Synchronous Online Group Advisory Meetings for the academic year 2016-17 through the Skype For Business videoconferencing platform. This chapter focuses on the extent to which interaction, immediacy and collaborative learning are developed in this particular online learning environment, as well as on the skills required for an efficient adult e-tutor. Research conducted in 2019 has shown that learners scored high in terms of interaction, immediacy and collaborative learning between each other and their tutor, especially when working in online workgroups, while the learning process was facilitated by immediate e-tutor feedback, which resolved queries, and the effective facilitation of the discussion. In terms of factors hindering the learning process, learners cited the lack of meaningful relationships with their peers as a leading one, e-tutors pointed to technical problems, while both agreed on the inadequate use of communication and collaborative tools in an online environment.

Chapter 9, titled "Innovative System for Education: The Advent of E-Learning in the University System in Pandemic Age" (by Eleni Karakolidou, Piera Leftheriotou and Maria Pavlis Korres), affirms that in the current scenario, many companies approached using a digital management system. For this reason, they must take into account an important issue: innovation. An essential strategic tool for management in current times. COVID-19 has imposed a reorganization of activities. There has been a sudden increase of digital systems, such as Smart Working and E-learning as regards the Education system. The aim of the work is to illustrate how modern innovative technologies help the provision of services within universities. In an emergency, such as the spread of Covid-19, there is a sudden change in the use of educational services by the university structure. They are ready to delivery services based on Intelligent Technology. Through the administration of an on-line questionnaire, perception of the on-line education system is examined, gathering opinions of a sample of students in one of the most important Italian universities.

Chapter 10, titled "The Importance of Digital Fluency in Terms of Disruptive and Emerging Technologies" (by Kadir Demir and Hatice Ferhan Odabasi), discusses information about digital literacy, which enables us to make basic use of today's technologies. In parallel with today's technological developments, high-level digital literacy skills expected from individuals are addressed. Definitions of digital fluency and studies on this subject are examined. The concept of digital fluency is redefined by the authors. It is based on theoretical foundations that are needed by authors on why digital fluency is needed in educational life.

Chapter 11, titled "How Does the Digital Transformation Affect the Job of University Teachers? Summary of the Required Skills of University Teachers" (by Amira Sghari), states that the use of digital devices, which is exponentially growing among students, requires universities rethinking teaching practices. Digital acceleration in the field of higher education is very important especially with the appearance of Modular Object-Oriented Dynamic Learning Environment, Massive Open Online Course and Small Private Online Courses phenomena. Thus, Digital pedagogy transforms the required digital skills of university teachers' teaching. Determining in detail the digital skills of university teachers was difficult. This article is based on some research works as well as on the repository of skills defined by the Virtual University of Tunis which provides training of university teachers to enhance their e-skills. This theoretical paper presents a synthesis of works dealing with the skills required by university teachers in a context of digital transformation. Such a synthesis will allow a good preparation of training programs for university teachers.

Chapter 12, titled "Using ICT in the Classroom for Acquiring Digital Competences: Three Case Studies From Croatian Primary School" (by Kristina Posavec), presents a research that explores the use of ICT tools in primary school and its impact on digital competences. What digital competencies can mean in this context and how they can be integrated into the primary school curriculum are some of the questions this chapter will explore. This chapter will present three case studies with three primary school teachers who participated with their students in CRISS project (CRISS is a project financed by the European Commission, through the Horizon2020 programme, ID:732489) during which all used CRISS platform and their experience with the process of students' digital competences evaluation, obstacles that they encountered during this process and how the use of ICT tools can improve primary school students' digital competences. The advantages and disadvantages of this type of learning method will emerge and be discussed.

Chapter 13, titled "New Trend in Intellectual Capital Disclosures of Higher Degree Institutions in Indonesia" (by Saarce Elsye Hatane, Eric Oktavianus, Josua Tarigan and Ferry Jie), explores the existence regarding the new method in disclosing intellectual capital called as web-based intellectual capital disclosure to overcome the limitation of traditional intellectual capital disclosures and also examine the determinant factors that may influence web-based intellectual capital disclosure of Indonesian universities such as autonomy, competitiveness, age, and size. A partial least-squares analysis is conducted to have an observation of 83 Indonesian higher education institutions. The results show that there is extensive use of intellectual capital disclosure through websites done by Indonesian universities, especially in internal capital, while the disclosure of external capital and human capital is still limited. Furthermore, autonomy gives the biggest impact toward web-based intellectual capital disclosure because autonomy provides freedom for universities in managing their institution especially in improving their web-based intellectual capital disclosure in order to attract more public and government fund.

Chapter 14, titled "Role of Virtual Laboratories in Teaching-Learning Process of India: Teaching Learning Process" (by Kapilan N. and Vidhya P.), proposes that the laboratory training and exercises provides hands-on experience to the students. However, the limitations in the laboratory facilities in the engineering colleges may affect the teaching and learning process of the future engineers. Hence government of India has started an initiate called as Virtual lab to overcome this issue. The premier institutions in India were funded and these institutes are the nodal centre in providing virtual lab facilities to colleges which do not have sophisticated laboratory facilities. The advancement in IT and internet facilities can no more hamper students and researchers in enhancing their skills and knowledge. Also, in a country such as India, costly instruments and equipment need to be shared with fellow researchers to the extent possible. This book chapter discusses and highlights the virtual lab initiatives and implementations.

Chapter 15, titled "The Integration of Educational Technologies in Foreign Language Education: Teachers' Practices and Attitudes in GREECE" (by Varvara Lemonia Oikonomou and Paschalia Patsala), studies the use of educational technologies in foreign language teaching in Greece. It explores whether FL teachers tend to integrate learning tools in their classroom, and if their implementation is affected by teachers' age, gender, level of confidence in using these tools, or any previous training they attended. The most popular technological tools employed in FL teaching are also presented, while the attitude of teachers towards the utilization of learning technologies is thoroughly investigated. A quantitative research method has been adopted with the usage of a web-based questionnaire. Based on the findings retrieved from the responses of a hundred FL teachers, they tend to integrate educational technologies extensively in their teaching practices, mainly to enhance learners' speaking and listening skills. Out of the variables examined, only teachers' confidence in using educational technologies seems to impact the integration of technology in their FL teaching.

After the summaries of the chapters included in the book, it is important to thank authors for their contributions to this book as well as members of the Editorial Advisory Board and reviewers for the time and efforts invested in choosing the best collection of chapters for this book. Thank you very much to all of you.

Patricia Ordóñez de Pablos
University of Oviedo, Spain

Miltiadis D. Lytras
American College of Greece, Greece & Effat University, Saudi Arabia

Xi Zhang
Tianjin University, China

REFERENCES

European Commission. (2020). *The digital skills and job coalition*. European Commission. https://ec.europa.eu/digital-single-market/en/digital-skills-jobs-coalition

Ordóñez de Pablos, P., Lytras, M. D., Zhang, X., & Chui, K. T. (2019). *Opening up education for inclusivity across digital economies and societies*. IGI Global. doi:10.4018/978-1-5225-7473-6

United Nations. (2020a). *The sustainable development goals: Our framework for covid-19 recovery*. United Nations. https://www.un.org/sustainabledevelopment/sdgs-framework-for-covid-19-recovery/

United Nations. (2020b). *Goals. Sustained Development Goals*. United Nations. https://sdgs.un.org/goals/goal4

Chapter 1
Exploiting Digital Skills in Higher Education: A Case Study Analysis

Domitilla Magni
Department of Business Studies, RomaTre University, Rome, Italy

Beatrice Orlando
Department of Economics and Management, University of Ferrara, Ferrara, Italy

Manlio Del Giudice
Department of Research, University of Rome Link Campus, Rome, Italy

ABSTRACT

Thus far, digital transformation had a strong impact on business and society. The large-scale adoption of digital technologies changed social relationships and opened up to new opportunities for higher education. Currently, the interplay between innovation and digitalization become are among the most important assets for the educational system. In this light, this chapter aims to explore how digital skills and competencies modify the issue of co-creation in higher education. The authors use the case study analysis to explore such theme. The Little Genius International case is presented and discussed: an international alternative school in English for digital natives recognized as the best benefit corporation for the world. The main contribution of the chapter is that it outlines what are the new digital skills and competencies enabling a better understanding of the concept of students' co-creation in HEIs.

INTRODUCTION

Rapid and continuous technological developments, favored by Information and Communication Technology (ICT), are causing disruptive changes from both the social and economic perspectives, thus encouraging the acceleration of scientific and technological knowledge (Scuotto, Ferraris, Bresciani, Al-Mashari, & Del Giudice, 2016; Santoro, Vrontis, Thrassou, & Dezi, 2018). Digital transformation has a substantial

DOI: 10.4018/978-1-7998-4972-8.ch001

Copyright © 2021, IGI Global. Copying or distributing in print or electronic forms without written permission of IGI Global is prohibited.

impact on all sectors of the economy, government, and social life. Through recognizing the variability of this emerging scenario, the attention of managers and researchers is focusing on how innovation can be supported for maximizing positive results (Del Giudice and Straub, 2011; Carayannis & Meissner, 2017).

The large-scale adoption of digital technologies changes relations in social life and opens up new opportunities for Higher Education Institutions (HEIs). Innovation and digitalization become one of the main assets for HEIs (Etzkowitz, 2003; Harryson, Dudkowski, & Stern, 2008). Universities must focus on exploring new knowledge through digitization processes and promote new forms of its dissemination in society. Following the Triple Helix model (Etzkowitz, 2008; Carayannis & Campbell, 2010; Leydesdorff, 2012), the University has an essential role in promoting an innovative environment. University, Industry, and Government formerly operated independently but nowadays tend to work together, generating different overlaps of communication networks. These interrelations continually reformulate structures, characteristics and objectives (Etzkowitz, 2008; Magni, Pezzi, & Vrontis, 2020). The model is used as a useful mechanism to trigger and sustain development dynamics based on innovation and technical progress (Lawton Smith, & Leydesdorff, 2014). Moreover, the Triple Helix model could be studied as a relational policy tool whose adoption aims to encourage the generation of an innovative firm (product, service, process) with the active presence of scientific talents, and research (University), managerial skills, and state financial support (central and local government) (Del Giudice, Carayannis, & Maggioni, 2017).

The intense connection between higher education institutions and industry provides for strengthening and reshaping the educational approach (Ahmad, Halim, Ramayah, Popa, & Papa, 2018). In this sense, a relevant aspect of the strategy of HEIs is the rapid development of advanced technologies and interactive tools aimed at improving the processes of knowledge transfer, coordination, and active students' involvement (Vargas-Vera, Nagy, & De Pablos, 2013; Del Giudice, Garcia-Perez, Scuotto, & Orlando, 2019; Magni et al., 2020).

Through the formation of knowledge and skills transferred to students, education takes place significantly in socio-economic and dynamic innovation development, and, at the same time, through the construction of a knowledge society (Martini & Vespasiano, 2015). The strategic relevance of these interventions confirms the importance of adopting new methodologies for the students' development, also contributing, as said by Mota and Scott (2014), to the training of professionals' skills and competencies for facing the challenge of innovative changes at an entrepreneurial level.

Besides, the development of dynamic innovations within the University 4.0 scenario helps the heterogeneity of knowledge to activate specific advantages on the education of new digitized educational system. Indeed, Del Giudice and Maggioni (2014) have highlighted that digitale tools are the fundamental basis for a new student-leadership approach.

University 4.0 is a new scenario that brings the concept of education into a fully automated and interconnected phase. The digitalization has a profound impact on data, computing power and connectivity (Cillo, Rialti, Bertoldi, & Ciampi, 2019). Another critical feature of University 4.0 is the management of analytics: the value of data is generated only when a University system has the ability to collect and analyze them (Ross, 2017). Nowadays, Universities use very few data (Dietz-Uhler & Hurn, 2013) and the interaction between people and technology, which involves increasingly widespread "touch" interfaces and augmented reality (Zhao, Qi, & De Pablos, 2014; Selwyn, 2012), is rarely implemented. Moreover, the University 4.0 scenario is based on the implementation of those marketing theories and models that were previously limited only to firms as a means to attracting, satisfying, and creating in-deep relationships with their students (Schlesinger, Cervera, & Iniesta, 2015). With the marketization of HEIs, Universities are permeated with marketing concepts and terms such as services, loyalty, satisfaction and co-creation (Zambon, Chatzkel, Sánchez, & Elena, 2006).

Also, the concept of digital enablers and value co-creation could be adapted to the field of education (Nicotra, Romano, Del Giudice, & Schillaci, 2018), through focusing mainly on the cooperative and constructive relationship between University and students (Gummesson, Mele, Polese, & Díaz-Méndez, 2012; Fagerstrøm & Ghinea, 2013; Judson & Taylor, 2014; Elsharnouby, 2015). Co-creation in education entails the creation of valuable experiences for people, together (Ramaswamy & Gouillart, 2010; Sang, Valcke, Van Braak, & Tondeur, 2010; Bowden & D'Alessandro, 2011). Methods used to foster collaboration, dialogue, and co-creation can be straightforward, such as the joint organization of events. However, the process can be more articulated, like the creation of hubs and other types of structured networks that involve students, staff, and teachers in an idea of joint development. While the distinction between value creation and value capture appears clear (Bowman & Ambrosini, 2000), the identification of mechanisms through which value is created, especially in the HEIs, is still incomplete. Accordingly, it is apparent that the real challenge for organizations is not so technology itself, but rather the organizational and cultural paths that define, guide, and communicate the digital conversation (Leonard-Barton, 1992; Judson & Taylor, 2014). This process works only if organizations develop the skills and knowledge necessary to manage this transformation.

In this contest, the radical transformation of the whole society - principally induced by the evolution of information and communication technologies - has significantly changed the learning process (Fagerstrøm & Ghinea, 2013; Hamid, Waycott, Kurnia, & Chang, 2015; Henderson, Selwyn, & Aston, 2017). However, while both HEIs and students are motivated to improve the experience of the students themselves, there are few paths to help them collaborate effectively, through digital enablers (Nicotra et al., 2018). The relational interaction between students and HEIs can be spurred on by digital technologies and innovations (Sang et al., 2010). Technological innovation inevitably has new educational and learning challenges (Martin et al., 2010). The debate on technologies in HEIs prefers a socio-technological approach in which technologies play a bridging role between different dynamics, not only those between learning and teaching, but also between immersion and distance, or between formal and informal learning (Selwyn, 2012). In this perspective, technologies become a third space where it is possible to merge different experiences and build reticular paths (Sang et al., 2010) under the teacher's guidance and due to the role of mediation carried out by technologies. The possibility of converging experiences deriving from the informal contexts guarantees a great personalization of the processes and great valorization of the student (Martin et al., 2010; Schlesinger et al., 2015).

This chapter aims to address how digital skills and competencies modify the issue of co-creation in higher education. To meet this aim, the Little Genius International case is presented and discussed: an international alternative school in English for digital natives recognized as the best Benefit Corporation for the world (Best for the World 2018). Little Genius is an international school, a certified B Corp, which stands out for its environmental and social results, through maintaining fair and transparent relationships with all its stakeholders, customers, suppliers or collaborators (McClure, 2018). The quality of services and transparency of the processes represent the distinctive features, together with a great attention to ethical, environmental, social, and technology aspects, also demonstrated by the propensity to develop digital and enabling technologies for the students.

The main aspects explored in this chapter, thanks to the analysis of the Little Genius International's strategies and activities, concern the role of the HEIs for economic, social and digital skills improvements, strategic orientation to sustainability and continuous innovation process as the driver of development.

As emerges from the analysis of the community engagement and of supply chain management activities, Little Genius International creates shared value. The prerequisite behind this new conceptualization is that organizations must take action to bring together the interests of all the shareholders, through the exploitation of digital skills and competencies.

Little Genius International case study helps to summarize and classify existing research. Also, it provides a better understanding of how digital co-creation could be accepted in the field of education. In University 4.0, all interested actors could achieve a competitive advantage if the knowledge is accessible and reusable (Campanella, Della Peruta, & Del Giudice, 2013). Therefore, University managers are also able to collect relevant information and exploit it through value co-creation. This way universities create an advantage for the whole environment (Foroudi, Yu, Gupta, & Foroudi, 2019).

The main contribution of the chapter is to outline the new digital skills and competencies that allow a better understanding of the concept of students' co-creation in HEIs.

The originality of the chapter lies with the fact that it attempts to bridge the literature gap in value co-creation in the field of education and achieve a categorization of digital skills and competencies in education. In particular, the aim of the chapter is the formalization of specific categories to promote students' digital skills in a digital era: i.e. interactive technology and digital enablement.

TECHNOLOGIES AND SOFT SKILLS FOR DIGITAL TRANSFORMATION

Emerging technologies as artificial intelligence (AI), cloud, augmented reality, and blockchain are shaping the current approach of living in a dynamic context. Today, change is disruptive, rapid, and continuous (Scuotto et al., 2016; Carayannis & Meissner, 2017). Digitization, digital skills, and new technologies impose a profound transformation at all organizational levels (corporate, social, and family) that is reflected in the renewed set of skills to be acquired and also in the renewal of the traditional approach to education and social life. The focus of the chapter is to examine the main aspects of this transformation, with a look at the impact on skills in social and education life.

New technologies arise continuously and have impact on society in terms of both simplification and replacement of processes (Nicotra et al., 2018; Ahmad et al., 2018). The current context is inserted in a scenario in which the speed of the changes requires organizations to have a digital mindset and an ability for an effective adaptation in order to activate digital transformation processes. Digital transformation is not only a firm-specific process, but it also occurs at institutional, educational, training, and social levels (Zhao et al., 2014; Pappas, Mikalef, Giannakos, Krogstie, & Lekakos, 2018). For example, in a few years, the distribution of multimedia has massively changed, switching from physical possession (videotapes, floppy discs, CDs), to digital files (iTunes), to cloud streaming (Spotify). New consumer trends and revolutionary business models have transformed the music distribution industry, allowing firms to compete globally, to reach more customers, and to create distinctive efficiencies (Spilker, 2017). Technology alone is not enough to gain a competitive advantage: digital skills must be developed to integrate technology with human resources and corporate culture.

The digital transformation suggests the opportunity to monitor and rethink the business processes and development paths of functional skills in the Fourth Industrial Revolution, such as Industry 4.0 (Skobelev and Borovik, 2017; Del Giudice et al., 2019). In other words, the paths of "adaptation to change", as well as those of forecasting future scenarios, can contribute to optimizing the effects of technological development itself, by rationalizing the elements of greater complexity such as the role of the human capital, the implications of technology on organizational, cognitive and behavioral processes, and the speed of technological innovations (McKnight, Maniam, & Robertson, 2019).

The current context is facing a revolution that, conceptually, has implications for the paradigm that connect human capital and skills to the multiple contexts (professional sphere, education and training systems, private life) in which it acts and with which it relates (Del Giudice & Maggioni, 2014). Digital transformation is also impacting on the use and exploitation of data and Big Data: their practical interpretation can bring concrete benefits to society in many areas, from health care to renewable energy, to IT security. Technological innovations characterizing Technological Revolution can generate a multiple effect on skills (Selwyn, 2012; Santoro et al., 2018): for example, it would be possible to develop digital technical skills including big data and analytics, cloud computing, digital security, and mobile application.

Technological Innovation and Soft Skills: Which Scenarios?

Digitization has a strong impact on society and individual skills (Skobelev & Borovik, 2017). In the new digital scenario, due to Industry 4.0, firms are starting to request specific technological skills and new competences (Manyika et al., 2013). The new skills of the digital scenario are "soft skills". Following Parente et al. (2012), "soft" skills are specific individual skills that each person, through experience and knowledge, manages to exploit day-by-day. The digital soft skills are those cognitive, emotional, and relational skills that allow people to be able to deal with the increasingly rapid changes brought by technological innovation. These characteristics are strictly connected with human nature and they cannot be acquired through exposure to coded knowledge (Hurrell, 2016). For this reason, soft skills are entirely different and at the same time complementary with what is defined as "hard" skills, which are technical skills inherent to professional ability (Hendarman & Cantner, 2018). Soft skills, in a scenario of digital transformation, are considered a precious resource at institutional, educational, and business levels.

Digital transformation is taking place rapidly in most public and private sector organizations, through the spread of the four "megatrends" of cloud, social, big data, and mobile technologies (Andersson et al., 2018). With their positive impact, these technologies are used not only to improve the efficiency of operational and decision-making processes, productivity, and customer service, but also to design new business models, to develop new services and products, to create new revenue streams by improving business performance, and to exploit new soft skills. The technological revolution has pushed firms to exploit and develop new soft skills (e-skills) (Van Laar, Van Deursen, Van Dijk, & De Haan, 2017) that allow human capital to operate in a highly dynamic contest. Many scholars (Van Laar et al., 2017; Andersson et al., 2018; Sousa & Rocha, 2019) have found a double interpretation on the role of the new soft skills needed in an Industry 4.0 contest. One refers to an optimistic approach, for what soft skills help a firm to synergistically and effectively manage technological transformations. The other interpretation refers to a pessimistic approach, predicting that digital revolution will have a destructive impact on the business scenario. These concerns about the economic impact of new technologies on soft skills are determined by the degree of instability of the environment and the degree of exploitation of resources by firms (Pappas et al., 2018).

In brief, scholars have analyzed two opposed visions related to the effects of new technologies on business. On one hand, there is a vision for what technology will generate a new era of prosperity with the creation of new professions and skills, able to "welcome" workers employed in tasks rendered obsolete by technology. In this regard, Sousa and Rocha (2019) show that, despite the disruptive impact of automation, it is plausible that new technologies can lead to the creation of new skills and types of work.

On the other hand, the second vision highlights negative expectations that indicate the risks associated with technological innovations and link them to the possibility of large-scale unemployment, which is challenging to remedy, with significant consequent on social and political impacts (McClure, 2018).

Starting from an analysis of strengths and weaknesses of technological innovations shown in table 1, it is useful to adequately exploit the opportunities made available by new technologies and to prevent potential threats. Technology generates new sectors, jobs, and areas of competence. Therefore, focusing on certain domains on which the effects of change have the most significant impacts, such as the labor market, social life, and education, it is possible to outline the main strengths and weaknesses and the related opportunities and threats to be observed.

Table 1. SWOT analysis of Technological innovations

Strengths	**Weaknesses**
• Application of new technologies in sectors with high social impact • Globalizing Digital System • Birth of new professions and explore of new soft skills • Self-learning • Multiplying effect of technologies for the propensity to innovation	• Risk of learning errors • Inadequate digital infrastructures • Digital immaturity • The substitution effect of human capital • Technology that requires a high initial investment • Social impact (privacy)
Opportunities	**Threats**
• New professional skills for highly qualified jobs • More significant business opportunities in highly specialized sectors (e.g., data-driven economy, big data analysis) • Creation of custom content • Adaptation to processes and user interaction • Social adaptation • Greater access to information sources	• Hack-able • Social exclusion of subjects who have less access to technology • Dissemination and inability to recognize fake news / fake profiles • Easily biased by large amounts of incorrect input

Source: authors.

The demarcation of opportunities and threats it's not very rigid. However, opportunities and threats are directly related to the challenges that need to be addressed to smooth out the mismatches and gaps in the education and training systems concerning the digital skills necessary for the development of talents and the up-skilling and reskilling of workers (Sousa & Rocha, 2019).

Despite the claimed and advertised advantages attributable to the phenomenon of digital transformation and technology innovation, many firms struggle to derive a real positive result from digitalization. Most of these firms have insufficient experience to drive change. Even in organizations where corporate leadership has shown that it can take charge, conduct and skillfully use digital transformation, it comes up against different strengths and challenges (Andersson et al., 2018). Thus, timely and robust response to digital change, on the other hand, if wisely guided by business leaders, creates an increase in operations, an intensification of new skills, and the emergence of new business models (McKnight et al., 2019). These new skills include in particular advanced-cognitive skills (such as problem-solving), socio-behavioral skills (such as teamwork), and a combination of traditional skills and e-skills.

Finally, following Cillo, Garcia-Perez, Del Giudice and Vicentini (2019) who confirm the importance of soft skills in Industry 4.0, the primary skills that manage to capture, more than others, the advantages and benefits of technological innovation in a digital transformations scenario are listed below:

- **Problem-solving**, it is undoubtedly one of the most essential soft skills and is required at every level and in many sectors. It is about the ability to face and solve problems of all kinds quickly and effectively, without being overwhelmed by the stress that sudden critical situations usually entail.
- **Critical Thinking**, functional illiteracy is the inability to process written thought, extract the information contained in a text such as newspaper articles or instructions in a manual: this problem lends itself to the side and triggers the phenomenon of the spread of fake news in a digital era.
- **Creativity,** the digital industry is still relatively young; many human resources are adapting to this technological revolution. For this reason, one of the most critical skills is creativity, that is, the ability to develop original, fresh, new ideas in a sector in constant evolution.
- **Knowledge networking**, it is the ability to combine individual knowledge and skills in achieving personal and business goals. It is the ability to access information by extracting it from the Web, creating value for the firm. So, it means navigating with intelligence and method, filtering the vast amount of information recognizing what has a value from everything that only creates volume.
- **Emotional intelligence and Team coordination**, resources must increasingly relate to customers, or establish a dialogue with other firms through increasingly advanced digital tools. The ability to empathize, to establish constructive and dynamic relationships, is appreciated mainly when firms cooperate in real-time and the responses must be quick and optimal. Coordination with other resources is also essential to avoid a waste of energy and time, optimizing everyone's skills given of the goal to be achieved.
- **Cognitive flexibility**, it is the ability to adapt to any working context, and therefore the attitude not to be overwhelmed by stress, caused for example by sudden changes in tasks or by unexpected situations that must be managed lucidly. Flexible resource become indispensable for a firm, as they are the only ones capable of bridging a technological gap when the working tools undergo an update, as happens in the case of digital transformation. Without these kinds of resources, the businesses' activities would become paralyzed.

It is precisely the presence of these new skills and soft skills that allow firms, society, and educational institutions to ride the digital wave in an optimal way (Sousa & Rocha, 2019).

TOWARDS DIGITAL SKILLS IN HIGHER EDUCATION INSTITUTES

In today's context of change, the education system would seem to be called to an unprecedented challenge. In particular, the HEIs and University should finally become aware of this paradigm transition that appears clearly (Magni et al., 2020). Educational systems should take on the need to train more (and better) e-skills and self-programming, because these are the needs of a system in digital transformation and which seeks its added value in innovation. Several scholars (Campanella et al., 2013; Mota, & Scott, 2014; Elsharnouby, 2015; Henderson et al., 2017; Ahmad et al., 2018; Magni et al., 2020) believe a more courageous organizational rethinking of educational institutions and HEIs. A profound rethinking of teaching methods, tools, and traditional teaching practices is needed (Dietz-Uhler & Hurn, 2013). The necessary renewal of teaching methods and school practices must take into account the attitudes and behaviors towards technologies of new generations of students. The debate on digital natives clarifies that there is room for educators to increase the awareness and digital "wisdom" of young people, first of all by defining the terms of a new digital literacy to be integrated into the formal education curriculum.

The recognition of the experiences of applying Web 2.0 tools to the educational context demonstrates the growing weight of participatory culture and informal learning (Grosseck, 2009). This confirms not only the potential but also the critical issues of a transition both the traditional educational setting and the role of the teacher in HEIs.

Cranfield and Taylor (2008) estimate that the digital revolution in HEIs revolves around the following pillars:

- **Infrastructure:** intended to increase the number of ICT devices, resources, and services available in the educational setting (from wireless communication to podcast lessons);
- **Contextual:** designed to make functional resources (time and space) more flexible to allow alternative solutions to traditional teaching/learning activities;
- **Curricular:** intended to update the curricular objectives or to accommodate new cultural tools or content typically related to New Millennium Learners (NML) (for example, to introduce personal student's portfolio sites);
- **Focused on the process:** designed to adapt the teaching/learning processes and activities to cognitive changes and communication practices of NML, including interpersonal communication and knowledge management, also to take advantage of their more extensive skills in ICT (most likely the most innovations challenging to introduce into the HEIs).

All these lines of intervention focus exclusively on creating the conditions useful for incorporating ICT in traditional teaching practices.

The technological environment in which HEI operates becomes increasingly complex, offering new opportunities, but also provoking new comparisons and challenges. In summary, the technological trends that are having a real impact on the education system are (De Freitas & Console, 2010): (1) the shift towards distributed network technologies; (2) the emergence of devices aware of the context and location; (3) different forms of representations and possible settings, increasingly differentiated; (4) the trend towards the use of more adaptive mobile devices; (5) a global technological infrastructure. Digital technologies, Artificial Intelligence, Augmented Reality, and Web 2.0 constitute the current scenario of continuous evolution, which is oriented in a direction that is not always easy to anticipate (Fagerstrøm & Ghinea, 2013).

Web 2.0: new Tools in the Educational System

Web 2.0 tools, to use the term introduced by Tim O'Reilly (2005), widely used also in educational fields, have entered the scene over the last few years. Expressions such as "social Web" have also been used, to indicate a shift towards more participatory Web tools and practices, and greater interaction between users. In recent years, much has been written about how these tools have changed the practices in HEIs of using the Web (Zambon et al., 2006; Cranfield & Taylor, 2008; Gummesson et al., 2012; Ahmad et al., 2018).

According to Dommett (2019), there are several ways in which the innovative tools can promote new forms of learning, including exploratory learning, new tools and forms of communication, and new forms of co-creation.

Web 2.0 technologies and practices make available new methods of exploratory and inquiry-based learning. New tools are emerging, accompanied by complex social and information environments to support research communities (Tchoubar, Sexton, & Scarlatos, 2018). From this point of view, Web 2.0 encourages users to familiarize themselves and become experts with new ways of scientific investigation (Grosseck, 2009; Chaka, 2010; Dalvi-Esfahani, Wai Leong, Ibrahim, & Nilashi, 2020). In these contexts, however, students and teachers must face new critical issues: on the one hand, the boundaries of control fade; on the other, issues relating to the legitimacy of information emerge (Lim & Newby, 2019). In a digital scenario, knowledge, sharing of ideas, and experiences are fundamental levers for the development of innovative educational skills (Magni et al., 2020). New forms of communication can come from the exploitation of social networks and between the contexts of formal communities (professional networks, formal learning contexts) in which new and collaborative knowledge develops (Gummesson et al., 2012; Ahmad et al., 2018). For example, in HEIs, social networks allow students to socialize with peers, helping each other and developing a shared dialogue in the forums. Similarly, Web 2.0 contexts encourage creativity and new forms of co-creation: the distributed nature of Web 2.0 technologies means that user who learns has easy access to the expertise of others (Lim & Newby, 2019).

The new digital tools allow to offer several opportunities for students to customize the learning process, in order to make it as accessible and very close to the needs of each student (Bowden & D'Alessandro, 2011). All the personalization activities of the students' path are the main objective for supporting growth and knowledge sharing in the University system (Vargas-Vera et al., 2013; Fagerstrøm & Ghinea, 2013; Hamid et al., 2015).

Lim and Newby (2019) analyze the use of Web 2.0, giving an indication of the level of adoption of these technologies in HEIs. Overall, these data suggest that the adoption of Web 2.0 technologies is an ongoing process, but that it is not yet an extensive phenomenon. Ali, Uppal and Gulliver, (2018) consider the obstacles to the adoption of technologies. In addition to this, there are also obstacles due to changes like privacy and intellectual property in technological environments. The practical implications on the adoption of technologies are still not understandable for some university components and, for this reason, negative attitudes towards a potential opening towards digital still persist (De Freitas & Conole, 2010; Ali et al., 2018). It is essential to identify and understand what the obstacles to wider adoption are, so that strategies can be designed to overcome them. Dommett (2019) focuses on three different approaches that analyze the benefits or difficulties in using the Web: (1) increase the digital awareness of teachers; (2) build capacity for a quality technological culture and (3) overcome disciplinary divisions. Strategies to overcome these problems should include mechanisms to give teachers the time to experiment with new technologies, as well as provide support and guidance to allow them to develop the new skills they need and target these new technologies with educational approaches more structured and reflective.

The greater the availability of teaching resources, the greater the encouragement to use digital technologies in HEIs (Butcher, 2015).

In a University 4.0 scenario, tools related to Web 2.0 are increasingly used to implement knowledge sharing and to offer new educational opportunities. Following Harris and Rea (2019), table 2 shows how some technological tools can be combined with different types of teaching and learning in HEIs, and what are the mail benefits for using them.

It is quite clear that Web 2.0 tools have characteristics that can be exploited in the educational context (Harris & Rea, 2019). As reported by several empirical studies (Dietz-Uhler & Hurn, 2013; Elsharnouby, 2015; Martini, & Vespasiano, 2015; Ahmad et al., 2018), all digital technologies help students and teachers to get in touch with each other for a more aware and immersive teaching (Campanella et al., 2013). Social policies must guarantee all enables capable of making new technologies available for University

Table 2. Digital tools in HEIs

Learning approach and digital tools	Benefits for using digital tools
In class learning	Use of classroom technologies to facilitate group learning and the sharing of dynamic and immersive experiences such as: IWB, digital tools for teamwork, apps, Internet, video projectors, laboratories.
Out of class learning	Use of experimental technologies in order to improve educational output and that make the student approach in a completely different way to study such as: connection with other students and with teachers on social networks, augmented reality, online resources.
In-deep learning	Use of digital tools for in-depth learning and to find lessons always "just a click": YouTube, blogs, SlideShare, digital repositories, records.

Source: authors.

4.0. While the adoption of Web 2.0 in teaching and learning is growing in higher education institutions, it is essential that these topics are addressed systematically.

EDUCATION 4.0: LITTLE GENIUS INTERNATIONAL CASE STUDY

In University 4.0, new technological opportunities permit students to establish digital student ecosystems to manage trigger innovative networks and relationships in the university system (Keser & Semerci, 2019). Precisely because of digital technologies and digital transformations, it is estimated that in the next future it will be necessary to explore new types of skills and abilities to exploit in peculiar activities still unknown to date (World Economic Forum, 2017). Having innovative types of knowledge permit the user to actively participate in social life, in labor market, and also in the University system (Keser & Semerci, 2019; Sousa and Rocha, 2019).

As emerges from the "Education at a Glance 2017" report of the Organization for Economic Cooperation and Development (OECD), the challenges that emerge from this scenario are mainly two:

1. Graduates from science-fields (Science, Technology, Engineering and Mathematics) are more likely to find employment faster than graduates from non-scientific disciplines.
2. Compared to recent years, adults and are generally more educated compared to the past.

To avoid a lack of skills, it is important to reshape educational system by linking it with digital transformation processes (Dalvi-Esfahani et al., 2020). In this sense, a relevant aspect of the Little Genius strategy is the rapid development of advanced technologies and interactive tools aimed at improving the processes of knowledge transfer, coordination, and active involvement of students. The "Infinite Child Evolution" (ICE®) methodology has a positive impact on society in all sectors, from the economic one by training to better skills in innovation in the Industry 4.0 era, to the social one by training aware people with an ethical and sustainable vision of the world.

The ICE® methodology, "Infinite Child Evolution", represents a teaching system that adapts to the environment in which it applies, going beyond traditional formal education methods. This teaching and learning methods lead to positive change, to develop innovative skills. According to the ICE® methodology, the use of a traditional approach limits the understanding and development of the basic knowledge of students and teachers, especially in learning areas such as digital skills, thus precluding the development of essential innovation skills for the professional future.

Little Genius International: International School for Digital Natives

The originality of the Little Genius International ICE® educational system lies in its dynamic-evolutionary nature which translates into the constant change of teaching methods, adapting them to new knowledge systems and to the individual characteristics of the child. In contrast, traditional systems remain static and they respond very slowly to developments in society. Interdisciplinary curricula are offered to children from an early age (Vásquez Macías, 2019). An environment that adapts to learning, in which new notions are made available to children in the form of texts, images, videos, and audio material, mainly, but not exclusively, through information technology (e-learning) aimed at amplification intelligence. This environment aims to extend the processing capacity of the human mind through distributed cognition (augmented learning).

The strategic relevance of these interventions confirms the importance of adopting new methodologies for the conscious development of students, also contributing, as pointed out by scholars Mota and Scott (2014), to the training of professionals capable of facing the challenges associated with a new scenario in which innovation and entrepreneurship are central priorities.

Starting from 2016, Little Genius International has been recognized as a Benefit Company by adopting a new corporate statute. The Benefit Companies, implemented in Italy in 2016, represent companies that excel in their environmental and social results, maintaining a relationship of fairness and transparency with all their stakeholders, customers, suppliers or collaborators (McClure, 2018).

For an institutional mission, benefit firms must: (i) have a positive impact on people and the environment; (ii) take into account the impact of its decisions on all shareholders; (iii) make their positive impact visible on society and the environment.

The first premise behind the new conceptualization is that educational field firms must take action to bring together the interests of the whole shareholders: create economic value or simultaneously co-create value for the HEI, responding at once to the needs of the firm and to the social needs. A new point of view concerning the enhancement of the HEI's know-how is the reconfiguration of relationships along the value chain. This approach therefore suggests that Little Genius International move towards those directions of intervention, which constitute areas of common interest with shareholders. Only in this way, the HEI can pursue the objectives of the whole shareholders (Vásquez Macías, 2019).

The shared value theory developed by Porter and Kramer (2006) does not conflict with social responsibility; in some ways, it represents its evolution. The relationship with stakeholders cannot be based just on the distribution of profits but on the integration of a common logic within the core strategies. This approach represents the point of contact of a hypothetical continuum of an imaginary line that sees classic social responsibility, on the one hand, and social innovation on the other.

Little Genius International entered the world top of B Corporations in 2016 with one of the highest scores, thus certifying its excellence in environmental and social results, as well as its ability to establish a relationship of trust and transparency with stakeholders.

Subsequently, the management of Little Genius International introduced alternative finance tools, through crowd funding campaigns and the entry of investment funds into the corporate structure (Vásquez Macías, 2019). The strategic objective of this choice is to create new products and services for the global diffusion of the teaching method, and the creation of a Campus for education innovation aimed at researching, training, and acceleration of innovative and sustainable business projects.

From this emerges a business development project based on continuous innovation that can allow the Little Genius International to take a strategic approach to the management of sustainable innovation (Elsharnouby, 2015; Pappas et al., 2018).

Little Genius International is also famous for:

1. annually donating/allocating a percentage share - defined according to demonstrable and specific needs - of its gross profit to non-profit associations or public and private organizations for the protection, for example, of education, health, environment, childhood, and cultural heritage where the gross profit on the balance sheet exceeds 250,000.00 euros;
2. aiming to promote local culture and economy through supply and subcontracting relationships with companies that have their headquarters within a radius of 350 km from the company's headquarters;
3. as a school that excels in educational programs, in particular for activities specifically aimed at "digital natives" (such as Fablab, co-working for parents, and the use of educational tools such as iPads, Lim, Leap Motion, etc.), but it is also a firm that has made its mission in social work and respect for the environment.

This approach is characterized by the search for innovative solutions to meet the expectations of one or more stakeholder groups, tending to make these solutions a factor of development of the corporate advantage. At the base, there is a correct balance between the social relevance and the corporate convenience of the actions taken which results from a summary assessment that has three determinants: (i) the relevance reported by management, (ii) the relevance attributed to the stakeholders, (iii) the relevance deriving from the degree of diffusion of a certain practice in the reference context. In strategic terms, the element that emerges from the analysis of the Little Genius International case is the choice to compete on innovation, sustainability, and the quality of the products and services offered. Quality is intended as a "dynamic response" to what stakeholders expect (Gummesson et al., 2012). Little Genius International's choice to operate with the high quality of products is supported by the necessary investments in research and development of products and processes. Investments in innovation and maintenance of the quality of products and services are accompanied by investments in the integration of the supply chain (to ensure quality throughout the process) and on the construction of a brand loyalty able to communicate the uniqueness offered (Ahmad et al., 2018).

The choice of promoting local culture and economy through supply and sub-supply relationships with Little Genius International and having their operational headquarters within a radius of 350 km, also stresses the importance of establishing collaborative and commercial relationships based on economy, and the minimization of the environmental impact. This strategy also exploits the importance of the construction of community bonds capable of increasing the relational capital of the firm (Scuotto et al., 2016). In the global economic competitiveness era, the need for collaboration between small and medium-sized enterprises (SMEs) has become a topic of primary importance (Andersson et al., 2018).

Collaboration and innovation have been widely considered as an important process of change capable of supporting business development in increasingly dynamic markets. For this reason, in recent years, a great deal of literature has emerged on collaboration strategies (Andersson et al., 2018; Dommett, 2019) and innovation (Carayannis & Campbell, 2010; Carayannis & Meissner, 2017).

Indeed, innovation is increasingly becoming a shared and collaborative process in society and firms (Lundberg & Andresen, 2012). As a result, there is a strong trend towards research and development partnerships and alliances (Cillo et al., 2019).

In this sense, Little Genius International's success is based on a widespread innovation strategy based on a hybrid organizational structure where all employees are called to contribute corporate success with innovations, through autonomous paths or specific employer engagement programs (Nicotra et al., 2018). As seen, a firm needs a large number of good ideas before starting revolutionary and successful initiatives (Andersson et al., 2018).

CONCLUSIONS

Due to a large network of relationships and a strong leadership, Little Genius International has acquired the ability to synergistically balance exploration and exploitation activities and become ambidextrous (Santoro et al., 2018). This was possible due to the creation of a network of relationships, which, at the same time, was possible to learn new knowledge to innovate and exploit the knowledge already present internally to maintain its profitable business model over time. Ambidextrousness has thus created a virtuous cycle in which the discovery and creation of the opportunity, the exploitation of present resources and the exploration of future are in a continuous cycle.

In conclusion, from the experience of the Little Genius International Benefit Company a clear trace emerges for the future of social innovation, in which the acceleration of progress passes solely through individual and social awareness. HEIs are organizations with the greatest potential for social and economic impact. They direct individuals and their social aggregations towards the progress and improvement of economic, scientific, and environmental life. In this direction, one of the strategies adopted for the improvement of its positive impact on society, the environment and the people of Little Genius International regards education for the sustainability of new generations and the community, pursued through both teaching and special initiatives or digital transformation.

University 4.0 and, more generally, education 4.0, are becoming increasingly important issues in the digital scenario. New approaches to integration and interaction between students encourage the entire University system to embark on a transition phase towards a digital and sustainable system (Buckler & Creech, 2014). Interconnection is the basis of the new phase of learning between students and the digital tools used in University 4.0 (Campanella et al., 2013; Zhao et al., 2014). Through exploitation of digital technologies over the past decade, the abundance of initiatives has grown at all levels of society.

University 4.0 trains students oriented towards sustainability, improving their active roles in an increasingly smart and digital society (Keser & Semerci, 2019; Santoro et al., 2018). It is from these challenges that Little Genius International has identified the importance of including digital technologies in an educational and experimental context as the solution to the enormous challenge of sustainability in digital era (Ahmad et al., 2018; Magni et al., 2020). Indeed, innovation can become a key factor for the quality of social life only if it considers and includes sustainability objectives, balancing the objectives of economic success with the constraints of environmental and social feasibility. Hence, innovation and sustainability should be combined and integrated into new education systems, helping to train a new generation of citizens capable of managing businesses and institutions along with these enormous challenges. It is known that sustainable innovation is based on the ability to break old paradigms through new skills and abilities.

New learning processes are also the key to succeed in today's massive global challenges (Mota & Scott, 2014). Little Genius International achieves success in training students who have specific digital and technical skills and knowledge useful to facilitate the student's future educational path and, more generally, to face further future technological changes and in the society. The 4.0 educational system takes into account the importance of the network between students and teachers and activates sustainable development processes that are also compatible with an environmental and social sustainability approach.

In this scenario, the role of the HEIs will therefore, contribute not only to economic development and competitiveness on local and global markets, but to the same awareness and sustainability of the processes of change for individuals and for the community.

REFERENCES

Ahmad, N. H., Halim, H. A., Ramayah, T., Popa, S., & Papa, A. (2018). The ecosystem of entrepreneurial university: The case of higher education in a developing country. *International Journal of Technology Management*, *78*(1-2), 52–69. doi:10.1504/IJTM.2018.093935

Ali, S., Uppal, M. A., & Gulliver, S. R. (2018). A conceptual framework highlighting e-learning implementation barriers. *Information Technology & People*, *31*(1), 156–180. doi:10.1108/ITP-10-2016-0246

Andersson, P., & Mattsson, L. G. (2018). Digital transformation supporting public service innovation–business model challenges and sustainable development opportunities. In P. Andersson & ... (Eds.), *Managing DigitalTransformation, The Stockholm School of Economics Institute for Research (SIR)*. Stockholm: Stockholm School of Economics.

Bowden, J. L. H., & D'Alessandro, S. (2011). Co-creating value in higher education: The role of interactive classroom response technologies. *Asian Social Science*, *7*(11), 35–49. doi:10.5539/ass.v7n11p35

Bowman, C., & Ambrosini, V. (2000). Value creation versus value capture: Towards a coherent definition of value in strategy. *British Journal of Management*, *11*(1), 1–15. doi:10.1111/1467-8551.00147

Buckler, C., & Creech, H. (2014). *Shaping the future we want: UN Decade of Education for Sustainable Development; final report*. UNESCO.

Butcher, N. (2015). *A basic guide to open educational resources (OER)*. Vancouver: Commonwealth of Learning (COL).

Campanella, F., Della Peruta, M. R., & Del Giudice, M. (2013). The role of sociocultural background on the characteristics and the financing of youth entrepreneurship. An exploratory study of university graduates in Italy. *Journal of the Knowledge Economy*, *4*(3), 244–259. doi:10.100713132-013-0157-4

Carayannis, E. G., & Campbell, D. F. (2010). Triple Helix, Quadruple Helix and Quintuple Helix and how do knowledge, innovation and the environment relate to each other? A proposed framework for a trans-disciplinary analysis of sustainable development and social ecology. *International Journal of Social Ecology and Sustainable Development*, *1*(1), 41–69. doi:10.4018/jsesd.2010010105

Carayannis, E. G., & Meissner, D. (2017). Glocal targeted open innovation: Challenges, opportunities and implications for theory, policy and practice. *The Journal of Technology Transfer*, *42*(2), 236–252. doi:10.100710961-016-9497-0

Chaka, C. (2010). E-learning 2.0: Web 2.0, the semantic web and the power of collective intelligence. In Handbook of research on practices and outcomes in e-learning: Issues and trends (pp. 38-60). IGI Global.

Cillo, V., Garcia-Perez, A., Del Giudice, M., & Vicentini, F. (2019). Blue-collar workers, career success and innovation in manufacturing. *Career Development International*, *24*(6), 529–544. doi:10.1108/CDI-11-2018-0276

Cillo, V., Rialti, R., Bertoldi, B., & Ciampi, F. (2019). Knowledge management and open innovation in agri-food crowdfunding. *British Food Journal*, *121*(2), 242–258. doi:10.1108/BFJ-07-2018-0472

Cranfield, D. J., & Taylor, J. (2008). Knowledge management and higher education: A UK case study. *Electronic Journal of Knowledge Management*, *6*(2).

Dalvi-Esfahani, M., Wai Leong, L., Ibrahim, O., & Nilashi, M. (2020). Explaining students' continuance intention to use Mobile web 2.0 learning and their perceived learning: An integrated approach. *Journal of Educational Computing Research*, *57*(8), 1956–2005. doi:10.1177/0735633118805211

De Freitas, S., & Conole, G. (2010). The influence of pervasive and integrative tools on learners' experiences and expectations of study. In R. Sharpe, H. Beetham, & S. de Freitas (Eds.), *Rethinking learning in the Digital Age*. Routledge.

Del Giudice, M., Carayannis, E. G., & Maggioni, V. (2017). Global knowledge intensive enterprises and international technology transfer: Emerging perspectives from a quadruple helix environment. *The Journal of Technology Transfer*, *42*(2), 229–235. doi:10.100710961-016-9496-1

Del Giudice, M., Garcia-Perez, A., Scuotto, V., & Orlando, B. (2019). Are social enterprises technological innovative? A quantitative analysis on social entrepreneurs in emerging countries. *Technological Forecasting and Social Change*, *148*, 119704. doi:10.1016/j.techfore.2019.07.010

Del Giudice, M., & Maggioni, V. (2014). Managerial practices and operative directions of knowledge management within inter-firm networks: A global view. *Journal of Knowledge Management*, *18*(5), 841–846. doi:10.1108/JKM-06-2014-0264

Del Giudice, M., & Straub, D. (2011). Editor's comments: IT and entrepreneurism: an on-again, off-again love affair or a marriage? *Management Information Systems Quarterly*, *35*(4), iii–viii. doi:10.2307/41409961

Dietz-Uhler, B., & Hurn, J. E. (2013). Using learning analytics to predict (and improve) student success: A faculty perspective. *Journal of Interactive Online Learning*, *12*(1), 17–26.

Dommett, E. J. (2019). Understanding student use of twitter and online forums in higher education. *Education and Information Technologies*, *24*(1), 325–343. doi:10.100710639-018-9776-5

Elsharnouby, T. H. (2015). Student co-creation behavior in higher education: The role of satisfaction with the university experience. *Journal of Marketing for Higher Education*, *25*(2), 238–262. doi:10.1080/08841241.2015.1059919

Etzkowitz, H. (2003). Innovation in innovation: The triple helix of university-industry-government relations. *Social Sciences Information. Information Sur les Sciences Sociales*, *42*(3), 293–337. doi:10.1177/05390184030423002

Etzkowitz, H. (2008). The triple helix: Industry, university, and government in innovation. *Social Sciences Information. Information Sur les Sciences Sociales*, *42*(3), 293–337. doi:10.1177/05390184030423002

Fagerstrøm, A., & Ghinea, G. (2013). Co-creation of value in higher education: Using social network marketing in the recruitment of students. *Journal of Higher Education Policy and Management*, *35*(1), 45–53. doi:10.1080/1360080X.2013.748524

Foroudi, P., Yu, Q., Gupta, S., & Foroudi, M. M. (2019). Enhancing university brand image and reputation through customer value co-creation behaviour. *Technological Forecasting and Social Change*, *138*, 218–227. doi:10.1016/j.techfore.2018.09.006

Grosseck, G. (2009). To use or not to use web 2.0 in higher education? *Procedia: Social and Behavioral Sciences*, *1*(1), 478–482. doi:10.1016/j.sbspro.2009.01.087

Gummesson, E., Mele, C., Polese, F., & Díaz-Méndez, M. (2012). Value co-creation and university teaching quality. *Journal of Service Management*, *23*(4), 571–592. doi:10.1108/09564231211260422

Hamid, S., Waycott, J., Kurnia, S., & Chang, S. (2015). Understanding students' perceptions of the benefits of online social networking use for teaching and learning. *The Internet and Higher Education*, *26*(1), 1–9. doi:10.1016/j.iheduc.2015.02.004

Harris, A. L., & Rea, A. (2019). Web 2.0 and virtual world technologies: A growing impact on IS education. *Journal of Information Systems Education*, *20*(2), 3.

Harryson, S. J., Dudkowski, R., & Stern, A. (2008). Transformation networks in innovation alliances–the development of Volvo C70. *Journal of Management Studies*, *45*(4), 745–773. doi:10.1111/j.1467-6486.2008.00768.x

Hendarman, A. F., & Cantner, U. (2018). Soft skills, hard skills, and individual innovativeness. *Eurasian Business Review*, *8*(2), 139–169. doi:10.100740821-017-0076-6

Henderson, M., Selwyn, N., & Aston, R. (2017). What works and why? Student perceptions of 'useful' digital technology in university teaching and learning. *Studies in Higher Education*, *42*(8), 1567–1579. doi:10.1080/03075079.2015.1007946

Hurrell, S. A. (2016). Rethinking the soft skills deficit blame game: Employers, skills withdrawal and the reporting of soft skills gaps. *Human Relations*, *69*(3), 605–628. doi:10.1177/0018726715591636

Judson, K. M., & Taylor, S. A. (2014). Moving from marketization to marketing of higher education: The co-creation of value in higher education. *Higher Education Studies*, *4*(1), 51–67. doi:10.5539/hes.v4n1p51

Keser, H., & Semerci, A. (2019). Technology trends, Education 4.0 and beyond. *Contemporary Educational Researches Journal*, *9*(3), 39–49. doi:10.18844/cerj.v9i3.4269

Lawton Smith, H., & Leydesdorff, L. (2014). The Triple Helix in the context of global change: Dynamics and challenges. *Prometheus*, *32*(4), 321–336. doi:10.1080/08109028.2014.972135

Leonard-Barton, D. (1992). Core capabilities and core rigidities: A paradox in managing new product development. *Strategic Management Journal*, *13*(S1), 111–125. doi:10.1002mj.4250131009

Leydesdorff, L. (2012). The triple helix, quadruple helix,..., and an N-tuple of helices: Explanatory models for analyzing the knowledge-based economy? *Journal of the Knowledge Economy*, *3*(1), 25–35. doi:10.100713132-011-0049-4

Lim, J., & Newby, T. J. (2019). Preservice teachers' Web 2.0 experiences and perceptions on Web 2.0 as a personal learning environment. *Journal of Computing in Higher Education*, *32*(2), 234–260. doi:10.100712528-019-09227-w

Lundberg, H., & Andresen, E. (2012). Cooperation among companies, universities and local government in a Swedish context. *Industrial Marketing Management*, *41*(3), 429–437. doi:10.1016/j.indmarman.2011.06.017

Magni, D., Pezzi, A., & Vrontis, D. (2020). Towards a framework of students' co-creation behaviour in higher education institutions. *International Journal of Managerial and Financial Accounting*, *12*(2), 119–148. doi:10.1504/IJMFA.2020.109129

Manyika, J., Chui, M., Bughin, J., Dobbs, R., Bisson, P., & Marrs, A. (2013). *Disruptive technologies: Advances that will transform life, business, and the global economy* (Vol. 180). McKinsey Global Institute.

Martin, W., Strother, S., Beglau, M., Bates, L., Reitzes, T., & McMillan Culp, K. (2010). Connecting instructional technology professional development to teacher and student outcomes. *Journal of Research on Technology in Education*, *43*(1), 53–74. doi:10.1080/15391523.2010.10782561

Martini, E., & Vespasiano, F. (2015). University Services to the Students: Analysis of the Main Satisfaction Indices. *Italian Sociological Review*, *5*(3), 293–321.

McClure, P. K. (2018). "You're fired," says the robot: The rise of automation in the workplace, technophobes, and fears of unemployment. *Social Science Computer Review*, *36*(2), 139–156. doi:10.1177/0894439317698637

McKnight, S. T., Maniam, B., & Robertson, J. (2019). Effects of Technology Innovations on Business. *Journal of Business and Behavioral Sciences*, *31*(1), 84–101.

Mota, R., & Scott, D. (2014). *Education for innovation and independent learning*. Elsevier.

Nicotra, M., Romano, M., Del Giudice, M., & Schillaci, C. E. (2018). The causal relation between entrepreneurial ecosystem and productive entrepreneurship: A measurement framework. *The Journal of Technology Transfer*, *43*(3), 640–673. doi:10.100710961-017-9628-2

O'Reilly, T. (2005). *What Is Web 2.0? Pattern Recognition*. Retrieved from https://www.oreilly.com/pub/a/web2/archive/what-is-web-20.html

Organization for Economic Cooperation and Development. (2017). *Education at a glance 2017: OECD indicators*. OECD.

Pappas, I. O., Mikalef, P., Giannakos, M. N., Krogstie, J., & Lekakos, G. (2018). Big data and business analytics ecosystems: Paving the way towards digital transformation and sustainable societies. *Information Systems and e-Business Management, 16*(1), 479–491. doi:10.100710257-018-0377-z

Parente, D. H., Stephan, J. D., & Brown, R. C. (2012). Facilitating the acquisition of strategic skills: The role of traditional and soft managerial skills. *Management Research Review, 35*(11), 1004–1028. doi:10.1108/01409171211276918

Porter, M. E., & Kramer, M. R. (2006). The link between competitive advantage and corporate social responsibility. *Harvard Business Review, 84*(12), 78–92. PMID:17183795

Ramaswamy, V., & Gouillart, F. (2010). Building the co-creative enterprise. *Harvard Business Review, 88*(10), 100–109. PMID:20929195

Ross, J. (2017). Speculative method in digital education research. *Learning, Media and Technology, 42*(2), 214–229. doi:10.1080/17439884.2016.1160927

Sang, G., Valcke, M., Van Braak, J., & Tondeur, J. (2010). Student teachers' thinking processes and ICT integration: Predictors of prospective teaching behaviors with educational technology. *Computers & Education, 54*(1), 103–112. doi:10.1016/j.compedu.2009.07.010

Santoro, G., Vrontis, D., Thrassou, A., & Dezi, L. (2018). The Internet of Things: Building a knowledge management system for open innovation and knowledge management capacity. *Technological Forecasting and Social Change, 136*(1), 347–354. doi:10.1016/j.techfore.2017.02.034

Schlesinger, W., Cervera, A., & Iniesta, M. Á. (2015). Key elements in building relationships in the higher education services context. *Journal of Promotion Management, 21*(4), 475–491. doi:10.1080/10496491.2015.1051403

Scuotto, V., Ferraris, A., Bresciani, S., Al-Mashari, M., & Del Giudice, M. (2016). Internet of Things: Applications and challenges in smart cities. A case study of IBM smart city projects. *Business Process Management Journal, 22*(2), 1–11. doi:10.1108/BPMJ-05-2015-0074

Selwyn, N. (2012). Making sense of young people, education and digital technology: The role of sociological theory. *Oxford Review of Education, 38*(1), 81–96. doi:10.1080/03054985.2011.577949

Skobelev, P. O., & Borovik, S. Y. (2017). On the way from Industry 4.0 to Industry 5.0: from digital manufacturing to digital society. *Industry 4.0, 2*(6), 307-311.

Sousa, M. J., & Rocha, Á. (2019). Digital learning: Developing skills for digital transformation of organizations. *Future Generation Computer Systems, 91*, 327–334. doi:10.1016/j.future.2018.08.048

Sousa, M. J., & Rocha, Á. (2019). Skills for disruptive digital business. *Journal of Business Research, 94*, 257–263. doi:10.1016/j.jbusres.2017.12.051

Spilker, H. S. (2017). *Digital music distribution: The sociology of online music streams*. Routledge. doi:10.4324/9781315561639

Tchoubar, T., Sexton, T. R., & Scarlatos, L. L. (2018, July). Role of digital fluency and spatial ability in student experience of online learning environments. In *Science and Information Conference* (pp. 251-264). Springer.

Van Laar, E., Van Deursen, A. J., Van Dijk, J. A., & De Haan, J. (2017). The relation between 21st-century skills and digital skills: A systematic literature review. *Computers in Human Behavior*, *72*, 577–588. doi:10.1016/j.chb.2017.03.010

Vargas-Vera, M., Nagy, M., & De Pablos, P. O. (2013). A framework for detecting and removing knowledge overlaps in a collaborative environment: Case of study a computer configuration problem. *Journal of Web Engineering*, *12*(5), 422–438.

Vásquez Macías, F. S. (2019). *Memoria del proceso de Design Thinking realizado en el modelo de negocios "Centro de educación inicial Little Genius"*. Universidad Casa Grande. Retrieved from http://dspace.casagrande.edu.ec:8080/handle/ucasagrande/1865

World Economic Forum. (2017). *The global competitiveness report 2016–2017*. Author.

Zambon, S., Chatzkel, J., Sánchez, M. P., & Elena, S. (2006). Intellectual capital in universities. *Journal of Intellectual Capital*, *7*(4), 529–548. doi:10.1108/14691930610709158

Zhao, J., Qi, Z., & De Pablos, P. O. (2014). Enhancing enterprise training performance: Perspectives from knowledge transfer and integration. *Computers in Human Behavior*, *30*, 567–573. doi:10.1016/j.chb.2013.06.041

ADDITIONAL READING

De Pablos, P. O. (2002). Evidence of intellectual capital measurement from Asia, Europe and the Middle East. *Journal of Intellectual Capital*, *3*(3), 287–302. doi:10.1108/14691930210435624

Harrang, K. J. (2007). Challenges in the Global IT Market: Technology, Creative Content, and Intellectual Property Rights. *Arizona Law Review*, *49*, 29.

Lai, K. W. (2011). Digital technology and the culture of teaching and learning in higher education. *Australasian Journal of Educational Technology*, *27*(8). Advance online publication. doi:10.14742/ajet.892

Lytras, M. D., Damiani, E., & de Pablos, P. O. (Eds.). (2008). *Web 2.0: The business model*. Springer Science & Business Media.

Singh, S. (2012). Developing e-skills for competitiveness, growth and employment in the 21st century. *International Journal of Development Issues*, *11*(1), 37–59. doi:10.1108/14468951211213859

Tay, H. L., & Low, S. W. K. (2017). Digitalization of learning resources in a HEI–a lean management perspective. *International Journal of Productivity and Performance Management*, *66*(5), 680–694. doi:10.1108/IJPPM-09-2016-0193

Thompson, P. (2013). The digital natives as learners: Technology use patterns and approaches to learning. *Computers & Education*, *65*, 12–33. doi:10.1016/j.compedu.2012.12.022

Zhang, X., De Pablos, P. O., & Xu, Q. (2014). Culture effects on the knowledge sharing in multi-national virtual classes: A mixed method. *Computers in Human Behavior*, *31*, 491–498. doi:10.1016/j.chb.2013.04.021

KEY TERMS AND DEFINITIONS

Digital Natives: Those who are used to using digital technologies from a very young age, being born in the internet era.

Digital Transformation: Set of mainly technological, cultural, organizational, social, creative and managerial changes associated with digital technology applications, in all aspects of human society.

Disruptive Technologies: Creates a new market or a new network of values.

E-Skills: Or electronic skills, include those needed to make use of Information and Communication Technologies (ICT) as well as those required to apply and develop them.

Higher Education Institutions: Universities, colleges, and further education institutions offering and delivering higher education.

Soft Skills: Personal and transversal characteristics different between than the technical skills.

Value Co-Creation: It is a form of market or marketing strategy that emphasizes the generation and realization of a firm value shared with the customer.

Chapter 2
XBRL and Smart Technologies

Maurizio Rija
University of Calabria, Italy

ABSTRACT

Today, companies manage increasing amounts of data. Companies that want to manage their data better must also adapt their information and reporting system to the current scenario of intelligent technologies. The market requires companies to have a financial communication that allows immediate comparison between the efficiency of reading the data and the effectiveness of the form in which they are presented. The information that the market requires is not only quantitative and temporal, but solutions that help speed up the extrapolation of the most strategic information to support business strategies. XBRL appeared in the beginning of the 21st century, and it represents one of the most important technological innovations in financial statement. On the basis of these premises, the idea of this work was born with which the authors analyze the importance of XBRL in the accounting environment of companies. The results of the study conducted allow us to conclude that XBRL can improve the quality of information of companies and at the same time can influence the choices of stakeholders.

INTRODUCTION

In the current market, intangibles become the main factor for the creation of corporate value. Among intangibles, knowledge is one of the assets in which to invest in order to gain new competitive advantages. Knowledge and innovation are strategic conditions for growth but also development tools that change the way companies communicate. To manage change well, companies must meet the new and different needs of stakeholders. It is necessary to implement a financial communication that allows an immediate comparison between the efficiency of reading the data and the effectiveness of the form in which they are presented, making decisions faster. In this context, corporate communication takes on a fundamental importance within the corporate strategy.

Communication becomes the imperative of every company, it is an indispensable tool for success, useful for improving one's image and bringing real consent closer to the necessary consent. As Cocozza argues, effective communication is able to give an important added value to the work and production activities of the company, up to representing a decisive source of competitive advantage (Cocozza, 2012).

DOI: 10.4018/978-1-7998-4972-8.ch002

Copyright © 2021, IGI Global. Copying or distributing in print or electronic forms without written permission of IGI Global is prohibited.

Companies implement not only a form of information communication, but also a wider communication that provides for greater market listening. The more the company communicates well, the greater the level of interaction it establishes with the internal and external environment, with a consequent increase in corporate value. The need therefore arises to create more detailed and punctual reports that help management to reduce information asymmetries (Healy & Palepu, 2001).

Training in digital skills improves corporate communication processes. Accounting is the language of the business as a language it has to communicate business and financial information to cater the need of all group of interested parties such as management, investors, employees, customers, regulatory authorities and the public at larger interest. To communicate business and financial information there is a necessity of a standardized mode which enables the firm to disclose entire accounting information of the business.

Thus, we are witnessing the development of specific technological tools such as XBRL (eXtensible Business Reporting Language), that is, a language for the electronic communication of financial and business information in general. XBRL offers the ability to exchange financial information globally through a digitalized global standard language.

It's an advanced technology and an extension to communicate corporate reporting in a structured manner in order to be understood and received across borders. XBRL manages to capture the needs of both businesses and the market. On the one hand, it guarantees the speed, accuracy and re-processing of information concerning the company's economic-financial communication, on the other, it ensures the containment of the related costs (Fradeani, 2005). XBRL reassures financial operators about the reduction of risk of error both in the re-typing of information and in its immediate transmission. All this creates advantages for companies which will tend to simplify and streamline the exchange of economic and financial information with the market. In addition, it is important to remember the important effects on the operation and functioning of the markets where at the same time the same information is requested by different subjects who find different reports in terms of content and timing

We can say that XBRL is used in financial information communication and as one major expected value of XBRL is the reduction of information asymmetry and an improvement to the quality of information (Yoon et al., 2011). Is a modern tool for the digitalized disclosure of business and financial information. XBRL, removes almost all pitfalls of traditional format of financial reports such as paper-based, pdf, HTML, word etc., these are static in nature not enable the preparers and users to easy comparison, analysis and re-using of previous reports for the preparation of current years reports. It also helps in cost savings, maintain greater efficiency and to improved accuracy and reliability of information being communicated to all stakeholders who are having both direct and indirect interest in the business operational and financial aspects. It is already being put to practical use in a number of countries and implementations of XBRL are growing rapidly around the world. Therefore, we can conclude that XBRL is a reporting standard which helps in harmonizing accounting standards and comply with business rules set by the regulatory authorities of the country. Of course, XBRL makes it necessary to expand roles, functions and responsibilities of all company actors if the transition to XBRL documents is to take place. On the basis of these premises, the idea of the present work originates which, after a brief analysis of the literature on the subject of the XBRL language, aims to analyze the importance of its use in the accounting environment of companies and the questions to which it tries to answer through the study of the existing literature are the following: can XBRL improve the quality of the information of the enterprises? Can the use of the XBRL language influence the choices of the stakeholders?

XBRL increases the transparency of financial information and therefore achieves a standardization in the archiving and storage of data, aimed at greater comparability over time and in the space of information externally, improving its accessibility by the many stakeholders involved (Hodge et al. 2004) from online book The advantages that the XBRL language offers to companies could induce them to provide more information more frequently, improving the understanding of the business realities of interest to all stakeholders.

XBRL and Corporate Communication

Economic-financial communication is the set of information concerning the management, results and on the income, financial and equity structure of the company. The doctrine has identified and proposed various classifications of economic-financial communication which vary in relation to the legislative constraints, the object, the frequency, the channels and the subjects of transmission and the recipients (Fellagara, 2008).The first distinction refers to the source of the information request and differentiates mandatory communication, which responds to legislative provisions and needs for general protection of the community, from voluntary communication, which has as its object additional needs to those required by law. Mandatory communication is particularly important because it responds to the satisfaction of a series of widespread interests, which are manifested by a multitude of subjects who come into contact with the company, who need a minimum level of corporate information. The insufficient production of information among stakeholders is one of the main reasons that led the legislator to impose minimum mandatory information from companies. Voluntary communication includes information not subject to legal constraints and, therefore, often arises as an opportunity that is offered to the company to provide additional information in addition to that provided by the legal system.

With reference to the object, the economic-financial communication is divided into operational, policy and institutional. As far as the frequency of communication is concerned, it is divided into initial, periodic, episodic and applied information. With regard to the main transmission channels of economic-financial communication, it distinguishes between direct communication and indirect or remote communication. The same distinction is made with regard to the transmitting subject; the latter classification refers to the recipient to whom the communication is addressed who can be internal to the company or external to it (financiers, potential investors, the community, analysts). Regardless of the proposed classification, it is appropriate to point out that economic-financial communication acts on the image of the company, influences its strategic and income credibility, increases trust and social legitimacy and contributes to creating value. Furthermore, it is precisely with reference to external recipients that the company size, performance levels and its listing on the markets are factors positively associated, on the one hand, with the intensity and on the other, with the quality with which the economic-financial communication is disseminated towards stakeholders.

The environment in which businesses operate today is extremely changeable and unpredictable. To remain competitive and develop a harmonious relationship with stakeholders, companies must enhance and intensify communication activities. It is important for each of them to implement an intense communication activity, capable of providing corporate interlocutors with information about the economic, financial and equity situation of the company. This consolidates the corporate image and allows for consent. A lack of transparency of the information conveyed by the company externally translates into a loss of consent and does not favour the creation and diffusion of value (Mishkin & Eakins, 2008). The new accountability needs, together with transparency and changing information needs of the financial markets, to increase the importance of the role of communication in the business economy. Careful and scrupulous communication is an indispensable means of remaining competitive. However, even today, there is no specific agreement on its content; there are those who promote communication projected to the future and there are those who, however, are satisfied with knowing data and results referring to the present. In any case, whenever it is necessary to disseminate news on the evolution of the income and assets of a company, the economic-financial communication is used which is the most important core of the corporate communication process. The most authentic expression of economic-financial communication is the financial statements. In addition to being a synthesis tool of the various areas of business management, it is the main means of dialogue with stakeholders and the market both in the top-down and bottom-up communication approach, that is, from the market to the company (Bushman et al, 2004).

Through the financial statements, the reader understands how the company has behaved, what results it has achieved and what is its state of health at a given time. In a single word, with the financial statements, stakeholders are informed about the ability of the company to create value (Herscovici, 2011). It is therefore no longer sufficient for "know-how" companies to perform but it is also necessary to make their skills known (make it known), to appreciate their distinctive skills, developing a high level of credibility on the market with all the tools that new forms of intelligent technology allow us to use (Khlifi & Bouri, 2007). Precisely for this reason, financial statements are the communication tool par excellence available to businesses. It is the main tool required by stakeholders, both internal and external to the company. The latter increasingly require timely and important accounting information. A simple and immediate reading of the results expressed in the financial statements offers investors significant opportunities in terms of correct assessment of the health of the company and above all its future prospects, as an adequate basis for making prudent investment decisions.

In the past thirty years, the advent of the internet has given birth to the subsequent real digital world. The do not appear simple and immediate to read. Hence the need to create a new, fully standardized language. Standardization should not be viewed as a negative aspect, as being approved or conforming to something. In the economic and financial field, standardization has a totally opposite value: it means facilitating the generation of reports, facilitating communication within and outside the company and the group, saving time and money.

The internationally established solution is the eXtensible Business Reporting Language (XBRL), a shared and unique computer language that, thanks to a universally usable protocol, facilitates transparency and the correct transmission of information (Southwell, 2005). Using the technology available today, XBRL allows solving the main problems inherent in the methods of disclosure of the economic-financial communication currently in use. The usual report in html, doc and pdf, is flanked by one encoded with the new elaborable electronic format (Fradeani, 2009). Electronic reporting was developed to overcome the disadvantages of communicating corporate information in the paper-based version, which ensures a lower cost of communication and transaction.

All this to avoid the burdens and risks of retyping. The standardization of the data allows, in fact, their reuse in subsequent applications, without having the problem of having to create the same documents several times. XBRL is, in summary, an evolution of corporate information systems. Analysts, companies and investors wanted to create this tool in order to be in step with the most advanced countries in terms of financial communication and transparency of corporate reporting. XBRL, in addition to filling the gaps in financial reporting, improves the transparency of the company, bringing about a substantial change in the way information is communicated, shared and analysed. To date, however, the technology supporting XBRL is complex, but major software developers are engaged in projects that will ease the conversion process for users.

This language is not only helps in disclosing the business information but also helps in following the international standards set for guiding the disclosure of financial and nonfinancial information i.e., IFRS an international accounting standards set by IASB to maintain the uniformity in accounting throughout the world.

If we want to summarize the main strengths and weaknesses of XBRL we can say that: the ability to store and subsequently process an increasing amount of financial information in a timely manner represents one of the main strengths that XBRL presents. In addition, another strong point is traceable in the fact that financial information is available in real time therefore it allows a more flexible and streamlined communication. XBRL is a tool that improves the comparability between the annual reports of different companies especially when they use universally accepted standards. The easy traceability of financial information allows investors to be more confident in creating corporate reporting. Furthermore, XBRL allows greater flexibility in updating and integrating data and the possibility of creating specific reports for particular categories of stakeholders. XBRL enables reported integrated information to be re-usable again and again without re-keying i.e., it avoids routine manual repetitive tasks. XBRL works with pre-coded integrated information templates that is taxonomy for integrated reporting which will works with greater accuracy with near zero defect i.e., 99.99966% level. XBRL also helps in preserving data structure and its context for the long period.

If on the one hand, XBRL provides information in real time, on the other, the risk of giving the public information that is not always correct increases. In fact, it is necessary to ensure that the information encoded in XBRL correctly represents the business reality. XBRL, being an innovative standard, is characterized by a certain level of technological uncertainty which is common to all innovations. The implementation requires continuous training of the personnel involved in the extraction of the data and the analyzes carried out on them. A critical aspect to highlight is also the greater ease of access to information which can lead to greater ease of misappropriation of company data. In addition, one of the main problems related to an XBRL document is the need to guarantee different levels of confidentiality for the data contained within the same instance of documents. Not all data have the same importance and the company will want some data to be made available to a very large audience, while more confidential data must remain hidden from most users. This makes us understand that a security system is needed to make the document secure. At this point it is clears that XBRL is a reporting standard which helps in harmonizing accounting standards and comply with business rules set by the regulatory authorities of the country.

XBRL: Review of the Empirical Literature

In recent years, new technologies have revolutionized the life of the company, have changed the way people work and have transformed the needs of accountability together with the information needs of the markets. In this context, the role of communication in the business economy has improved, which in order to be more effective presupposes essential conditions, that is, to be understandable, precise, fast and timely. The innovations related to the development of Information Technologies have contributed to simplifying the preparation of reports for management control which, thanks to the use of particular ICT languages and applications, have facilitated the internal decision-making process of companies and have improved relations with the market and stakeholders (Williams et al, 2006; Abu & Tsuji, 2012). Companies immediately realized that the success of company activity is caused by the availability and optimal use of information. Having the right information available at the right time can determine the success of a particular business strategy (Camussone, 2000). This is why the use of a universal classification and data protocol language such as XBRL (eXtensible Business Reporting Language) is very important.

Around the end of the 1990s, the Extensible Business Reporting Language – XBRL - appeared for the exchange of structured business information via the Web and was widely accepted by the international accounting community. Basically, the application of XBRL, which is often called the bar code for financial reporting is a sort of a solution to a pre-formulated problem, since this standard allows different operating systems to effectively bridge the gap in the exchange of business information, with a significant reduction in professional engagement.

XBRL is a language for financial and commercial reporting that uses XML technology (eXtensible Markup Language), that is, a set of rules that classify data during the insertion phase allowing anyone to be able to recognize and use the data entered by others. XBRL is one avenue that appears promising with respect to significantly improving accessibility to financial data. In 2004, the U.S. SEC tested a process for a limited number of public companies to voluntarily report XBRL data. This initiative is part of the Commission's broader effort to improve the quality of information available to investors and the marketplace. (SEC, 2005) Investors, analysts, business managers, researchers, students, and anyone who needs to access the financial data of organizations reporting through XBRL will be able to download that information directly into the spreadsheets and models of their choice. Thanks to the use of XBRL, financial operators are able to communicate company performance more easily and quickly.

Premuroso in his studies argues that the first mover companies in the voluntary implementation of the financial statements in XBRL format presented higher levels of governance, performance and transparency towards stakeholders, investors and other market participants compared to companies that had not yet adopted XBRL (Premuroso et al, 2008). Bakos also claims that the use of standard computer language makes companies strategically more competitive by overcoming competitors by improving business effectiveness and efficiency (Bakos et al, 1989). XBRL, by making accounting information timelier, reduces the costs of production, transmission, access and use of data (Elliott et al, 1997). Similarly, any authors (Bovee et al, 2002) believed that XBRL facilitates comparability and consistency of financial reporting through websites. The financial statements encoded in XBRL become tools accessible to all categories of users both inside and outside the company (Debreceny et al, 2005). XBRL allows all stakeholders to recognize the data entered and understand its meaning through the help of special labels that are a sort of conventional dictionary (taxonomy). The studies conducted by Hodge, Kennedy and Maines provide significant evidence on how the XBRL language provides evidence that such "search facilitating technology" reduces the likelihood that negative information would be overlooked when included as footnote disclosure, thus improving the overall transparency of the same reports. (Hodge et al, 2004). Even the empirical research conducted (Hodge et al. 2004) support the position of SEC Chairman, Cox, that interactive data serves to protect investors. Barry Melancon, American Institute of Certified Public Accountants (AICPA) President and CEO, also acknowledges that the breadth of information available and the speed with which users can extract the data they need will significantly enhance business reporting (Melancon, 2006). Studies have suggested that the development of XBRL is in line with the Financial Accounting Standard Board (FASB). For example, any authors believed that XBRL facilitates and ensures the availability of information (Baldwin et al, 2006).

Makhaiel and Sherer (Makhaiel & Sherer, 2018) found that political and economic reforms in Egypt had a negative impact on the quality of the financial statements. In addition, they analyzed and predicted that the role of auditors could be expanded with the introduction of the XBRL financial statements, thus advising them to acquire timely and in-depth knowledge of the implications of XBRL in auditing. Of course, it is plausible that XBRL will offer a strategic competitive advantage in the market. Oluic and Mamic Sacer (Oluic & Mamic Sacer, 2019) through the questionnaire concluded that XBRL information technology has significant effects on the quality of the financial reporting system ensuring the accuracy, timeliness and low cost of production accounting information. AICPA and XBRL-US (AICPA, 2017) conducted a study showing that there is a 45% drop in average financial reporting costs due to the XBRL initiative and also companies that have benefited from reaching more investors. All of this helps analysts for easy access to detailed financial reporting information. Yang (Yang et al, 2018) examined approximately 28,000 annual reports from 10 sectors for the period 2010-2014 and found a significant improvement in the structural comparability of financial statements. He also found that XBRL depots benefit regulators in providing suggestions for XBRL's continued development. Abhishek (Abhishek et al, 2019) analyzed the impact of XBRL on efficiency in the disclosure of integrated corporate information. He concludes that financial reports in XBRL format are more efficient than reports in non-XBRL format because of its beneficial benefits for all stakeholders. Yang (Yang et al, 2018) examined the impact of XBRL on the structural comparability of the financial statement during the post-XBRL implementation period in the United States and found a significant improvement in the structural comparability of the financial statements. The American Institute of Certified Public Accountants (AICPA, 2017) indicates the benefits and potential uses of XBRL in commercial relations and the exchange of information within all types of regulators (tax and financial authorities, central banks and governments), filing of loan reports and applications, credit risk assessments, authoritative accounting literature, which provides a standard way to describe the accounting documents provided by authoritative bodies.

Teller reports that XBRL should also bring four aspects to financial reporting: the production and publication of the information, information sharing and comparability; information checking and certification, gain in the analysis process (Teller, 2008). He concludes that XBRL is an optimal way for immediate dissemination of information. The taxonomy used by the XBRL language for coding the information contained in the reports makes the data homogeneous and immediately available, contributing to the preparation of databases on which analyses and comparisons can be made (Berkeley et al, 2009). Vasarhelyi, Chan and Krahel (Vasarhelyi et al, 2012) suggested that the relevant information selected by users determines the importance of the decision that is determined by the effectiveness of XBRL taxonomies. As Kull claims, XBRL greatly increases the speed of handling of financial data, reduces the chance of error, and permits automatic checking of information for validity, providing cost savings, greater efficiency and improved accuracy and reliability (Kull, 2007). Of course, the complete implementation process of XBRL takes some time, based on the complexity of the internal reporting system and especially on the company size (Bergeron, 2003).

XBRL: Implementation in Some International Contexts

XBRL is a universal markup language designed to optimize the preparation, analysis and electronic transmission of company information. With a relatively short history of less than two decades, XBRL has been used extensively worldwide since 1998, becoming the new international standard for electronic reports from companies around the world. At present, more than 60 countries implemented XBRL for business and financial reporting by the companies.

Among the first countries that have experimented with its adoption we remember China which already in 2004 formally asked public companies to standardize and elaborate their financial statements according to the new accounting language. It could be observed that in 2004, 50 companies listed on the Shanghai Stock Exchange were asked to present their annual reports in the XBRL format. In 2008, China opened a new phase for the use of XBRL through the use of an official website (http://www.xbrl-cn.org) to promote the use of XBRL and communicate to the world its development. China is having an increasing impact on the world economy, which suggests that IFRS adoption can have important practical implications for investors and academics alike. As mentioned by Liu different cultural and financial regulatory factors will influence the decision to adopt XBRL (Liu et al, 2011; Peng & Bewley, 2010).

Subsequently, several other countries have worked in the same direction. In India, XBRL emerged in 2007 when ICAI (Institute of Chartered Accountant of India) realized the importance of digital financial reporting to Indian scenario and MCA (Ministry of Corporate Affairs) was imposed reporting of business and financial information through XBRL.

Spain made the transition to XBRL coincide with the adoption of IFRS in July 2005. Korea developed a mandatory filing program in October 2007 as did Singapore which again in the same year provided for the adoption and filing of reports in XBRL format. Israel as well as Spain also made the transition to XBRL coincide with the adoption of IFRS in January 2008. In the same year, Belgium together with Luxembourg, Japan and India also moved to the filing of the reports in XBRL format. The United States SEC implemented a gradual process starting around 2009 until June 2011, the year in which all US public companies used XBRL. In 2009, the level of awareness was significantly lower in the Asia Pacific region and was highest in the US. Companies in Australia, China and Germany began using XBRL in July 2010. In 2011, however, both Denmark and the United Kingdom envisaged the adoption of XBRL for the preparation of corporate financial statements by assessing the impact on corporate communication processes. Italy was among the first countries to provide for the obligation of an electronic XBRL format for the presentation of financial statements as early as 2007. However, in the world, the mandatory adoption level of XBRL was sometimes considered disappointing with respect to initial forecasts. Consider, for example, countries such as Malaysia where the introduction has been quite slow (Ilias & Ghani, 2015). Also, Taiwan, which has planned to have reporting on XBRL format adopted to all companies listed on the stock exchange only starting from the first quarter of 2019. Recently, the desire to collect emerged from a work table carried out in Asia last June 2019. much more granular data in a timelier fashion than many of today‘s risk reports. This change would come about in order to increase regulatory awareness of fast-moving risks and to enhance the efficiency of data reporting and analysis. Korea plans to process reports in XBRL format, updating its taxonomies and improving them where necessary from 2020.

Regardless of the period chosen for the adoption envisaged by the individual States, the accounting data encoded in XBRL are available to all users, internal and external, who are interested in some processing necessary as a guide for company choices. XBRL allows them not only to recognize the data entered with any management software, but also to understand its meaning through special labels and through a sort of conventional dictionary (taxonomy). Faster and more rapid and efficient processing of information obtained with XBRL, increases the usefulness of decisions improves the consistency and comparability of data (Baldwin et al, 2006; Plumlee & Plumlee, 2008). The use of the XBRL taxonomy facilitates acquisition by users of all the information they need, making it recoverable and reusable at any time when decisions need to be made (Baldwin et al. 2006). XBRL allowing users to acquire the information they need, allows them to be able to evaluate the information acquired and to combine it to plan and program business decisions (Hogarth‘s 1980). Hunton and McEwen, argue that the accessibility of key information through the XBRL taxonomy allows users to more easily search for specific information throughout the decision-making process (Hunton & McEwen, 1997). The qualitative analysis of these studies allows confirmation of the first hypothesis, object of the work, namely that the quality of the information processed through the taxonomy of the XBRL language is better than the information obtained through traditional reports. In fact, the coding of financial statements in XBRL is less likely to alter the processes of information acquisition allowing a greater ability to connect different information elements useful to decision making.

The possibility offered by XBRL of finding the most important and necessary information for the implementation of certain company strategies and choices allows company dynamics to be monitored more easily (Fung et al, 2007), to control the market, to promote public interest and to ensure greater protection of the interests of financial investors (Koppell, 2005; Roohani et al, 2009). XBRL speeds up the availability of data and information and thus allows companies to satisfy a greater demand for transparency from stakeholders. Transparency entails truthful communication of government operation and performance (Koppell, 2005). Stakeholders possessing a higher quality of company information improve their decision-making process (Ettredge et al, 2005). These latest studies confirm the second hypothesis of our work, namely that the use of the XBRL language enhances the efficiency of the decision-making process by allowing stakeholders and the market to process data in the most convenient way in relation to the decisions to be made, reducing in the same time the risk. XBRL increases the transparency of financial information and therefore achieves a standardization in the archiving and storage of data, aimed at greater comparability over time and in the space of information externally, improving its accessibility by the many stakeholders involved from online book. The advantages that the XBRL language offers to companies could induce them to provide more information more frequently, improving the understanding of the business realities of interest to all stakeholders.

The professional literature but also the state of the market suggest that the XBRL standard has been accepted on a global scale and that it has very quickly assumed a dominant role in many economies. However, despite this being an era of software tools and techniques that we are constantly bombarded with by consulting companies and accounting software manufacturers. It is a fact that, unfortunately, the implementation of this standard has not yet come to life in some country and that there is a low level of knowledge in general about this standard.

CONCLUSION AND FUTURE DIRECTIONS

XBRL is a new technology for communicating business reporting for the purpose of disseminating information to stakeholders. The adoption of XBRL improves the effectiveness and efficiency of the company by making information to the market timelier and more transparent; the greater completeness and comprehensibility of the accounting data encoded in XBRL increases the quality of information and improves the expectations of stakeholders. The possibility of having information that can help monitor company behaviour improves the degree of adherence of information to the phenomena observed, thus allowing a quick, efficient and effective comparison among the various company areas. Furthermore, the high aptitude of XBRL for encoding data, thus making it homogeneous and readily available, facilitates decision-making while reducing the risk of decisions taken. In the future, we aim to assess the impact of adopting XBRL on different categories of stakeholders to understand how few classes of stakeholders are negatively affected by the transition to XBRL, compared to the many categories that we expect can, instead, benefit from them. On the basis of what has been said we can say eXtensible Business Reporting Language benefits both preparers and users in various ways such as in creation, analysis and disclosure of business and financial information. It also helps in cost savings, maintain greater efficiency and to improved accuracy and reliability of information being communicated to all stakeholders who are having both direct and indirect interest in the business operational and financial aspects. We can conclude that XBRL is a reporting standard which helps in harmonizing accounting standards and comply with business rules set by the regulatory authorities of the country. While this feature provides maximum flexibility, it can lead to challenges over the long term for financial statement comparability.

For this reason, in the future we aim to analyze the XBRL implementation in the international context where, to date, the analysis is still weak.

REFERENCES

Abhishek, N., & Ashok, M. L. (2019). Role of XBRL in promoting the integrated reporting in indian scenario. *Indian Journal of Accounting*, *51*(1).

Abhishek, N., Ashok, M.L., & Divyashree, M.S. (2018). A conceptual study on XBRL implementation in India: issues and challenges. *Open Journal of Economics and Commerce, 1*(4).

Abu, S. T., & Tsuji, M. (2012). The development of ICT for envisioning cloud computing and innovation in south Asia. In Grid and cloud computing: concepts, methodologis, tools and applications, IGI Global. doi:10.4018/978-1-4666-0879-5.ch207

AICPA. (2017). *Benefits and potential uses of XBRL*. Retrieved from https://www.aicpa.org/InterestAreas/FRC/AccountingFinancialReporting/XBRL/Pages/BenefitsandPotentialUsesofXBRL.aspx

Bakos, J. Y., & Treacy, M. E. (1989). Tecnologia dell'informazione e strategie aziendale. In R. Filippini (Ed.), Pianificare e gestire l'information technology. Tonino, Italy: Isedi.

Baldwin, A. A., Brown, C. E., & Trinkle, B. (2006). Xbrl: An impacts framework and research challenge. *Journal of Emerging Technologies in Accounting*, *3*(1), 97–116. doi:10.2308/jeta.2006.3.1.97

Bergeron, B. (2003). Essentials of Xbrl. Financial reporting in the 21st century. Wiley.

Berkeley A. R., Donahue D. F., Moyer P. D., & Bolgiano M. C. (2009). Xbrl reaches tipping point. *Journal of Securities Operations & Custody*, *2*.

Bonsòn, E. (2009). The role of Xbrl in Europe. *The International Journal of Digital Accounting Research*, *1*(2).

Bovee, M., Ettredge, M. L., Srivastava, R. P., & Vasarhelyi, M. A. (2002). Does the year 2000 Xbrl taxonomy accommodate current business financial-reporting practice? *Journal of Information Systems*, *16*(2), 165–182. doi:10.2308/jis.2002.16.2.165

Bushman, R., Chen, Q., Engel, E., & Smith, A. (2004). Financial accounting information, organizational complexity and corporate governance systems. *Journal of Accounting and Economics*, 37.

Camussone, P. F. (2000). *Informatica organizzazione e strategie*. McGraw-Hill.

Cocozza, A. (2012). *Comunicazione d'impresa e gestione delle risorse umane. Valorizzare le persone nelle imprese innovative e nelle pubbliche amministrazioni virtuose*. Franco Angeli.

Debreceny, R., Felden, C., Ochocki, B., & Piechocki, M. (2005). *Xbrl for interactive data. Engineering the information value chain*. Springer-Verlag.

Elliott, R. K., & Pallais, D. M. (1997). Know your market. *Journal of Accountancy*, 1.

Ettredge, M. L., Kwon, S. Y., Smith, D. B., & Zarowin, P. A. (2005). The impact of SFAS N. 131 business segment data on the market's ability to anticipate future earnings. *The Accounting Review*, *80*(3), 773–804. doi:10.2308/accr.2005.80.3.773

Fellagara, A. M. (2008). *Governo, controllo e informazione societaria nei gruppi aziendali*. McGraw-Hill.

Fradeani, A. (2005). *La globalizzazione della comunicazione economico-finanziaria. IAS/IFRS e Xbrl*. Giuffrè.

Fradeani, A. (2009). *Xbrl. Il presente e il futuro della comunicazione economico-finanziaria*. Giuffrè.

Fung, A., Graham, M., & Weil, D. (2007). *Full disclosure: the perils and promise of transparency*. Academic Press.

Healy, P. M., & Palepu, K. G. (2001). Information asymmetry, corporate disclosure, and the capital markets: A review of the empirical disclosure literature. *Journal of Accounting and Economics*, 31.

Herscovici, A. (2011). Economic Growth, technical progress and labor productivity: Knowledge economics and new forms of technical progress. *International Journal of Innovation in the Digital Economy*, 2.

Hodge, F. D., Kennedy, J. J., & Maines, L. A. (2004). Does search-facilitating technology improve the transparency of financial reporting? *The Accounting Review*, 79.

Hogarth, R. (1980). *Judgment and choice*. John Wiley & Sons.

Hunton, J.E., & McEwen, R., (1997). An assessment of the relation between analysts earnings forecast accuracy, motivational incentives and cognitive information search strategy. *Account Review*, *72*(3).

Ilias, A., & Ghani, E. K. (2015). Examining the adoption of extensible business reporting language among public listed companies in Malaysia. *Procedia Economics and Finance*, 28.

Khlifi, F., Bouri, A., (2007). Determinants of internet financial reporting. *Investment Research and Analysis Journal, 1*.

Koppell, J. G. S. (2005). Pathologies of accountability: ICANN and the challenge of multiple accountabilities disorder. *Public Administration Review*, *65*(1), 94–108. doi:10.1111/j.1540-6210.2005.00434.x

Kull, L., Miller, L. E., Clair, J. A., & Savage, M. (2007). Interactive data Xbrl: A revolutionary idea. *Journal of Government Financial Management*, 2.

Liu, C., Yao, L. J., Hu, N., & Liu, L. (2011). The impact of IFRS on accounting quality in a regulated market: An empirical study of China. *Journal of Accounting, Auditing & Finance*, *26*(4), 659–676. doi:10.1177/0148558X11409164

Makhaiel, N. K. B., & Sherer, M. L. J. (2018). The effect of political-economic reform on the quality of financial reporting in Egypt. *Journal of Financial Reporting and Accounting*, *16*(1), 245–270. doi:10.1108/JFRA-05-2016-0035

Melancon, B. (2006). *Testimony of Barry Melancon, President and CEO*. AICPA.

Miklos, A., Vasarhelyi, D.Y., Chan, J. P., & Krahel. (2012). Consequences of Xbrl standardization on financial statement data. *Journal of Information Systems*, *26*(1).

Mishkin, F. S., & Eakins, S. (2008). *Financial markets and Institutions. Boston, USA: Addison Wesley*. Cambridge University Press.

Oluic, A., & Mamic Sacer, I. (2019). Information technology and accounting information systems' quality in Croatian middle and large companies. *Journal of Information and Organizational Sciences*, *43*(2).

Peng, S., & Bewley, K. (2010). Adaptability to fair value accounting in an emerging economy: A case study of China's IFRS convergence. *Accounting, Auditing & Accountability Journal*, *23*(8), 982–1011. doi:10.1108/09513571011092529

Plumlee, R. D., & Plumlee, M. A. (2008). Assurance on XBRL for Financial Reporting. *Accounting Horizons*, 3.

Premuroso, R. F., & Bhattacharya, S. (2008). Do early and voluntary filers of financial information in Xbrl format signal superior corporate governance and operating performance? *International Journal of Accounting Information Systems*, 9.

Roohani, S., Furusho, Y., & Koizumi, M. (2009). Xbrl: Improving transparency and monitoring functions of corporate governance. *International Journal of Disclosure and Governance*, *6*(4), 355–369. doi:10.1057/jdg.2009.17

Southwell, G. (2005). *Global alliances and changes in financial reporting: how can XBRL help? In Fifth annual XBRL international academic competition 2004-2005*. State University.

Teller, P. (2008). The use of a formal representation of accounting standards. *International Journal of Computer Science and Applications*, *5*(3b).

Williams, S. P., Scifleet, P. A., & Hardy, C. A. (2006). On-line business reporting: An information management perspective. *International Journal of Information Management*, 26.

Yang, S., Zhu, X., & Liu, F.C, (2016). An exploratory study of financial reporting structures: A graph similarity approach using XBRL. *SSRN*, 9.

Yang, S., Zhu, X., & Liu, F.C, (2018). The impact of XBRL on financial statement structural comparability. *Lecture Notes in Information Systems and Organisation*, 1.

Yoon, H., Zo, H., & Ciganek, A. (2011). Does XBRL adoption reduce information asymmetry. *Journal of Business Research*, *64*(2), 157–163. doi:10.1016/j.jbusres.2010.01.008

KEY TERMS AND DEFINITIONS

Accounting: The skill or activity of keeping records of the money a person or organization earns and spends.

Corporate Communication: The way in which a company gives the public and its employees information about its aims and what it is doing.

Financial Statement: Financial documents showing a company's profits, debts, cash flow, etc. during a particular period, which are used by investors, banks, etc. to measure a company's performance before authorizing a loan, banks will review a company's financial accounts.

ICT: Information and communication technology, a school subject in which students learn to use computers and other electronic equipment to store and send information.

Stakeholder: A person such as an employee, customer, or citizen who is involved with an organization, society, etc., and therefore has responsibilities towards it and an interest in its success.

Taxonomy: A system for naming and organizing things, especially plants and animals, into groups that share similar qualities.

XBRL: eXtensible Business Reporting Language is a computer language that allows companies to collect financial information and share it electronically with others who need it.

Chapter 3
The Need for (Increased) ICT Skills in the Era of Digitalization

Nicole Palan
University of Graz, Austria

Andreas Schober
University of Graz, Austria

ABSTRACT

Automation and digitalization have had profound effects on job losses as well as on skill requirements in advanced economies. This chapter analyzes the spatial distribution of ICT-skills requirements by analyzing some 73,000 job offers for the Austrian region of Styria. This region is characterized by a large variability of specialization patterns throughout its districts as well as differences regarding population density and infrastructure accessibility. The analysis allows to draw conclusions on the need for both basic and special ICT-skills for different education levels for 287 municipalities. The results also draw light on problems related to the new "digital divide" indicating the phenomenon that people have access to digital infrastructure but not yet acquired the digital competences to find work. One interesting conclusion is also that high-skill ICT-requiring jobs have the highest level of agglomeration – both compared with other skill-levels and with non-ICT related academic job positions.

INTRODUCTION

The significant effects of automation and digitalization on labor markets are central in current policy debates in many advanced economies worldwide. This is because of the drastic effects of job destruction that the fourth industrial revolution is often projected to have: As put forth by Brynjolfson and McAffee (2014) in their book "Race Against The Machine", technological progress increases labor productivity and leads to many new innovations that unemployment as well as inequality within societies will rise. In combination with the structural transformation of countries towards knowledge economies, the skill requirements of job applicants are affected as well. The production of goods and services demands ever increasing specialized skills as well as more knowledge regarding information and communica-

DOI: 10.4018/978-1-7998-4972-8.ch003

Copyright © 2021, IGI Global. Copying or distributing in print or electronic forms without written permission of IGI Global is prohibited.

tion technology (ICT) related skills to handle production processes. In this respect, Goos et al. (2009, 2014) as well as Autor and Dorn (2013) show that routine tasks have been more and more taken over by machines, lowering not only the demand for unskilled labor but putting also under pressure the wages of this segment of workforce.

In this context, the Institute for Advanced Studies estimated that in Austria, one third of unskilled labor jobs are threatened by automation, as are 19 per cent of craftsmen and 11 per cent in the service sector (Nagl et al., 2017). Whereas it is undisputed that the future labor market requirements resulting from digital change cannot yet be assessed fully in detail, it seems clear that manual routine activities are increasingly streamlined away. Yet, it is also of central importance that digital technologies create new tasks such as the training of people, monitoring artificial intelligence, data analysis and the like. Moreover, digital technologies lead to the creation of new products, services and business models and thus lead to the creation of new jobs (Chun et al, 2015).

As such, it is of utmost importance to identify the skill requirements for these new jobs to provide potential job applicants with the proper training. Both labor market and education policy must address the effects of job losses as well as to tackle the changing demands on newly created jobs by adjusting education programs. Empirical research in this subject matter has however mainly focused on either the macroeconomic implications for entire countries with a special focus on the vulnerability of low-skill and low-wage workers or on the microeconomic impact on individual sectors (Frey and Osbourne, 2017).

One further important aspect that has not yet attracted as much attention, are the potential different implications of automation and digitalization at the regional level: Specialization patterns as well as different educational profiles of the workforce are likely to influence a region's vulnerability and the opportunities accompanied with increased automation and digitalization potential. For Austria, Firgo et al. (2018) studied the different effects of digitalization in rural areas in contrast to economic centers at the district level.

The aim of this chapter is to shed more light on the regional component of these digitalization effects. In contrast to many studies that focus on the destruction of jobs, the approach of this chapter adds to our understanding of the specific skill requirements needed to apply for new job offers. Thus, the authors concentrate the analysis on job advertisements; by doing this, we can gain a better understanding of the needs of the job market as well as a more detailed picture which regional profiles are more successful in creating a favorable economic environment for firms to create new jobs.

BACKGROUND

The broader public has first paid great attention to the labor market effects of digitalization when Frey and Osborne published their dramatic projections in a working paper in 2013 that has later been published in 2017. According to this Oxford study, almost half of all employees in the United States could be replaced by computers in the next 10 to 20 years with a probability of at least 70 percent (Frey and Osborne, 2017).[1] This fear of technological-induced unemployment is not a new phenomenon, however. In 1964, US-President Lyndon Johnson launched the *„BlueRibbon National Commission on Technology, Automation, and Economic Progress“* as concerns raised that automation would lead to higher job destruction not only in the manufacturing but also in the service sector (United States National Commission on Technology, 1966). The Commission however outlined that technological progress constantly destroys jobs – yet it does not destroy work as a whole and thus should rather be seen as a normal part of economic development. Moreover, the Commission suggested that (shifts in) the demand for goods and services affect both the level and length of unemployment by far more than efficiency gains and technological progress (Autor, 2015).

50 years later, Brynjolsson and McAffe (2014, p.11), dig deeper into the polarization effects on job creation and emphasize that *„there's never been a better time to be a worker with special skills or the right education, because these people can use technology to create and capture value. However, there's never been a worse time to be a worker with only 'ordinary' skills and abilities to offer, because computers, robots, and other digital technologies are acquiring these skills and abilities at an extraordinary rate.*"

This is also reflected in many studies which highlight the broad variation of automation probabilities for different sectors, jobs and tasks. In general, these probabilities are particularly high for low-skilled people in routine jobs as the demand for simple auxiliary activities is decreasing in all advanced economies. Additionally, it is becoming more and more apparent that computers or computer-controlled machines can increasingly take over routine tasks in the medium-educational segment as well. This implies that the assumption that higher education alone can guarantee greater job security is becoming outdated. Goos et al. (2009, 2014) in this respect introduce the term of „*job polarization*" as the demand for intermediate qualifications decline: Digitalization does not generally require higher skills among the workforce, but increases the demand for very specific skills. These particular skills, however, are often detached from the formal qualification level. Thus, digital technologies are capable of replacing mainly routine activities – regardless of whether they are carried out by low, medium or highly educated people. Yet, in general people with lower to medium qualifications are more affected by a possible loss of employment, as the proportion of routine work is higher and thus the probability that their main work can be automated. With increasing qualifications as well as with a higher degree of adaptability and flexibility, the possibility of automation through machines decreases (Nagl et al. 2017). Especially in the manufacturing sector and in general office work, a strong loss of manual (routine) activities has occurred and this development is likely to continue also in the future.

Moreover, it should not be forgotten that this development of job destruction is also counterbalanced by opportunities for new and complementary jobs. This means that digitalization can also act as a job engine – for example in knowledge-intensive service sectors. Joseph A. Schumpeter (1911, 1942) introduced the term "*creative destruction*", according to which innovations create new possibilities and new jobs in new firms and sectors. Creative destruction thus does not only lead to job losses, the destruction of firms and sectors but also has a positive effect on employment and can increase the competitiveness of countries and regions. In this chapter, the authors focus on job advertisements, i.e. on research questions related to the skills that new jobs require.

A further level of analysis is devoted to the geographical component of digitalization and the associated different development potential of regions. On the one hand, districts and municipalities are affected differently by automation probabilities due to different patterns of sectoral specialization. Peneder et al. (2019) point to the high spatial concentration of industries that are characterized by a high proportion of specialists in the information and communication technologies. On the other hand, digitalization can alter the influence of spatial advantages and disadvantages of economic areas. For example, the pull factors of economic centers could become less important, giving positive impetus to peripheral, rural regions and facilitate the reduction of the spatial digital divide. In this context, the public expansion of digital infrastructure in rural regions seems essential to achieve positive employment effects (Kolko, 2012). In this respect, the availability of fast and stable internet connections is of high importance and also became a highly discussed issue during the COVID-19 pandemic, when the percentage of people working from their homes increased significantly. For an overview of the numerous studies that provide evidence for the positive impact of copper- or coaxial cable-based broadband infrastructure on employment, productivity and economic growth in more general terms, see also Bertschek et al. (2016). In anticipation of these potential economic benefits, the European Commission (2010, pp.19) launched the Digital Agenda for Europe (DAE) already in 2010 that "*seeks to ensure that, by 2020, (i) all Europeans will have access to much higher internet speeds of above 30 Mbit/s[ec] and (ii) 50% or more of European households will subscribe to internet connections above 100 Mbit/s[ec]*" . In line with this, the Austrian government issued its own broadband strategy in 2014 and that had foreseen more differentiated coverage goals with (i) 70% of households should have access to at least 100 Mbit/sec until 2018 and (ii) 99% of households should have access to at least 100 Mbit/sec until 2020 (BMVIT, 2014). In 2018, however, only 97 per cent of the densely populated areas in Austria reached the access goal of 100 Mbit/sec whereas this was the case only for 28 per cent of the rural areas (BMVIT, 2019). The development of demand however confirms the need for bandwidths well beyond the 100 Mbit/s target already from 2025 onwards and thereby a new broadband strategy 2030 was issued by the Austrian Government by the end of 2019 (BMVIT, 2019).

The actual impact of the availability of fast internet connections on employment also appears to be of crucial importance for policy makers: Public broadband funding programs have been typically designed to supply coverage in non-profitable peripheral areas as also reflected in most national broadband plans (OECD, 2018). More and more governments have been inclined to see high-speed broadband infrastructure as a necessary policy tool to attract and retain more business and to increase employment in disadvantaged areas (Firgo et al, 2018).

Also, providing rural and peripheral regions with high-speed internet has become a central policy goal at the European level as the European Structural and Investment Funds as well as EU's rural policy agenda aim to accelerate economic growth in these regions and thereby achieve the goal of structural cohesion. Indeed, past and current public funding programs in the EU add up to two-digit billions of Euros. Public investment in the periphery is thus assessed to be crucial in the fight against the spatial digital divide that would even widen if the allocation is left to the free markets alone. Governments therefore have already invested vast sums into the expansion of (fast) broadband infrastructure. However, differences between economic centers and the periphery remain to exist – especially as in more rural areas with low population density the deployment costs compared to the benefits are much higher than for districts and municipalities with higher population and firm density and governments also face restrictions due to rising public debt levels.

MAIN FOCUS OF THE PAPER

In this chapter, the authors investigate the labor market of one Austrian region, namely Styria, and in more detail this region's districts and municipalities. As Styrian districts and municipalities differ widely regarding size, specialization patterns, accessibility to infrastructure and the degree of urbanization, this in-depth analysis can also shed light on the differences in job requirements and the attractiveness of districts to create jobs. The authors analyze the set of all 73,000 job advertisements. For each of these ads there is detailed information regarding the formal qualifications needed in the job (compulsory school / apprenticeship / university degree), the location of the company as well as details on the required ICT-knowledge. The authors use this rich dataset to contribute to the following research questions:

a) Which general and special ICT-skills do employers explicitly require from job applicants?
b) To which extent do also low-skilled workers need to have sufficient computer and digital skills to find a job?
c) What is the proportion of jobs for which expert knowledge is required?
d) How strong is the center-periphery gap in job advertisements? Is this gap stronger or weaker for ICT-based jobs than for the job market as a whole? Are there differences also between general ICT-skills and expert ICT-skills required in job advertisements?

Data and Method

Data for the following empirical analysis is provided by the Public Employment Service. The authors analyze the vast amount of information available on individual job offers with the help of a specially designed program code. Doing so, it is possible to examine the differences regarding ICT-requirements for different education levels as well as for individual districts and municipalities within Styria. Limitations of the data set must, however, be noted: According to estimates by the Statistical Office of Austria (2018), only about 60 per cent of all vacancies are actually advertised by the Public Employment Service – the remaining 40 per cent are advertised via internet portals, newspapers or word of mouth. In addition, occupations for which an academic education is required are generally not advertised as often with Public Employment Service as those at other levels of education (Figerl and Okropiridse, 2018). Yet, this underestimation of vacant jobs as well as the bias towards a higher rate of low-skilled jobs should however not influence the spatial distribution of job advertisements and thus not have an impact on the general conclusions we can draw from the analysis.

One caveat in this respect is that job profiles such as "smart service specialists", "digital project managers" or "IT manager for digital solutions" that have only recently developed, are not advertised by the Public Employment Service and therefore the latest trends cannot be identified with this large dataset.

Practitioners moreover point to another problem of the data set: companies tend to regularly advertise IT-positions – yet not because they aim to hire new people but rather to inform themselves about the current labor supply on the market – a job offer thus does not necessarily imply an open position in all cases. In addition, the same job can be advertised through different channels and repeatedly if no ideal candidate cannot be found. Thus, we opted to count identical advertisements from one and the same company only once in consecutive months to eliminate such bias.

In detail, the authors applied the following approach in the empirical analysis:

a) Each job advertisement was assigned to a municipality, which makes it possible to analyze job markets at the municipality level. The advantage is a highly disaggregated analysis that can shed light on the differences within labor market districts and increase the understanding about structural problems within districts. This approach can, however, also lead to distortions as the municipality is not necessarily the place where the work is carried out in all cases. Especially there is considerable risk of bias due to personnel search firms in and around the capital of Styria, Graz. This bias is particularly noticeable for the small town of Gössendorf, which is one of the towns surrounding Graz. The authors chose to take these shortcomings into account when interpreting the results.
b) A further bias may be present, since companies process their job advertisements via a central office, even if they have different locations. As this is a problem for all datasets and the fact that the Styrian job market is mainly characterized by small and medium-sized firms that do not spread

over too many municipalities, the authors did not take any further measures to counterbalance these data problems.

c) To identify the different levels of ICT-requirements in the job advertisements, the authors carried out a pre-analysis to identify important ICT-related keywords. Following this evaluation, the authors decided on running a test on several sets resembling ICT-knowledge. For low and general requirements, for example, one of the terms chosen was "IT" as it is general enough and a basic requirement that is absent in more specialized job advertisements. For medium ICT-requirements, the search focused on keywords such as "programmer/programming/programming". The search term "software" was chosen for job advertisements with a tendency towards more specialized jobs in the IT-sector. For each of these keywords, the search algorithm analyzes the occupation that the potential person should perform in which company and what the required educational level of the potential worker is. The data set distinguishes between 10 different educational levels – ranging from no completed training or compulsory schooling to technical college/university. Thereby the authors are also able to analyze whether more general ICT-requirements are linked to a certain education level in contrast to more specialized ICT-requirements and to which extent there is also a spatial component in these linkages.

A Descriptive Analysis of the Region

Styria is one of the nine federal states of Austria. In terms of size it is the second largest state of Austria, regarding population, it ranks fourth with 1.25 million inhabitants. There are about 520,000 employees, accounting for approximately 14 per cent of the Austrian workforce. In Styria, the total number of operating firms is about 40.000 – more than 80 per cent of which employ between one and nine people, whereas only 269 firms employ more than 250 people. However, these large firms are of utmost importance for the Styrian economy as they account for more than 40 per cent of all employees. The most important firms are Andritz AG, AVL List and Magna Steyr, which are located in the capital of Graz. The small businesses only account for 15 per cent of the Styrian labor force, yet they are of higher importance for peripheral districts and municipalities. Styria has undergone major structural change since the 1980s. Until then, the economy, especially in the region of Upper Styria, was characterized by large nationalized companies in the iron and steel sector. As a result of the international iron and steel crisis, a phase of restructuring as well as a gradual shift in specialization towards electronic engineering, the automobile industry as well as tourism have taken place.

Styria is divided into 13 districts, which consist of a total of 287 municipalities. Figure 1 maps the location of these districts. It should also be noted that the districts of Deutschlandsberg, Leibnitz and Südoststeiermark are neighbours to Slovenia, whereas all other districts have only borders to other regions within Austria. There is only one airport in Styria which is located 10km to the South of the capital: The airport Graz-Thalerhof is the third largest in Austria with almost one million passengers a year.

To understand the economic differences and challenges of the 13 Styrian districts, the authors present important demographic and economic data in Table 1. The strong agglomeration of the Styrian population in the provincial capital of Graz and in the surrounding municipalities are driving forces also for the tendencies of concentration in the Styrian labor market. Altogether, only three of the 287 municipalities have more than 20,000 inhabitants – Graz as well as Kapfenberg (district Bruck an der Mur) and Leoben (district Leoben). In Kapfenberg, the steel industry was a major job engine for decades – also nowadays Kapfenberg still hosts Voestalpine.

Figure 1. Spatial distribution of Styrian districts
source: www.info-graz.at

The university of applied sciences in Kapfenberg mainly focuses on offering programs in electronic engineering, IT-law, software design and industrial management, putting a clear focus on topics related to automation and digitalization. Leoben hosts a well-known and internationally competitive university with a special focus on petroleum, steel, and mineral resources.

Apart from these three exceptions, Styria is mainly characterized by small-scale towns: 222 of the 287 municipalities have between 1,000 and 5,000 inhabitants, only 13 have over 10,000. The size of the districts varies widely as does the population density and the average size of firms (for details see Table 1). These differences in endowment factors are crucial in understanding the spatial distribution of job offers and especially the distribution of jobs with ICT-requirements at different education levels.

The districts with exceptionally low population density are Murau and Liezen. Due to their high share of mountains and peripheral location, these districts have no single municipality with at least 10,000 inhabitants.

Regarding the importance of large firms for job creation a very heterogenous picture across Styria prevails as well: Whereas in the capital Graz more than 50 per cent of all workers are employed in large firms, the shares are above 40 per cent only in the rather centrally located districts of Graz-Umgebung, Leoben and Mürzzuschlag. These three districts are also characterized by a general good infrastructure being beneficial for the attraction of large firms. The share of large firms is below 25 per cent in the districts of Leibnitz and Hartberg-Fürstenfeld. The strong specialization towards the production of local

Table 1. Descriptive Analysis of Styrian Districts, own calculations

	Population	Population density	Share of population	Share of firms > 250 workers
Styria	1,242,635	76	-	-
Graz	28,995	2244	23.18	54.0
Graz-Umgebung	15,103	141	12.40	41.3
Liezen	79,905	24	6.43	34.7
Murau	27,689	20	2.23	26.5
Murtal	72,471	43	5.84	34.6
Leoben	60,151	57	4.84	46.1
Mürzzuschlag	99,437	46	8.02	44.1
Weiz	90,075	82	7.26	36.5
Hartberg-Fürstenfeld	90,452	74	7.29	23.4
Südoststeiermark	85,991	85	6.93	26.6
Leibnitz	82,469	113	6.64	22.3
Deutschlandsberg	60,805	70	4.89	33.3
Voitsberg	51,330	76	4.14	30.9

food products and day-tourism in both districts makes it also hard to increase the share of large firms in the market.

The Styrian job Market at the District Level

Before turning to the analysis of job advertisements, it is crucial to understand the specific characteristics of the 13 Styrian districts with respect to their industry specialization patterns, the education level of the inhabitants and their potential for creating new jobs in more detail:

In Graz, 33 per cent of all inhabitants have a university degree, double as many as in other districts of Styria. Employment in science, education, culture, health as well as administration are concentrated in the capital of Styria. Together with the Graz universities, the research- and technology-oriented leading companies are among the top innovators in Austria. Moreover, Graz is not only the administrative and spatial center of Styria, also the workforce is concentrated here: 38.4 per cent of all employed persons in Styria work in Graz. With 69.1 jobs per 100 inhabitants, the job density is not only the highest of all Styrian districts but also far above the Styrian average of 41.9 jobs per 100 inhabitants (WIBIS, 2020).

Together with the surrounding area called Graz-Umgebung, Graz forms both spatially as well as economically the central area of Styria. There is also an intensive interdependency between the two districts in terms of commuting. Moreover, the last decades were marked by a constant process of sub-urbanisation. The population development in Graz-Umgebung is extremely dynamic: More and more people tend to move to municipalities that offer lower living costs compared to the capital, yet still good job (and commuting) opportunities. The industrial focus of this district is on electrical and mechanical engineering as well as on the paper industry (WIBIS, 2020b).

The district Leibnitz is also economically closely intertwined with the central area of Graz as the good transport connections allow for intensive commuting. Leibnitz has a strong regional specialization in the (luxury) food industry. Its business structure is strongly shaped by small and medium-sized companies, which have over proportionally high demand for employees with apprenticeships and completed compulsory schooling. Highly qualified people rather tend to commute to Graz, where they find plenty of job opportunities (WIBIS, 2020c).

The district Leoben, which is centrally located in Upper Styria, is characterized by a high proportion of mountains and its long tradition of mining as well as its strong specialization towards the metal and steel industry. Additionally, Leoben is specialized into the electronic industry with AT&S being a major company. Leoben, like the other districts of the Mur-Mürz valley, experienced its population peak in the 1970s. Since then the population has been declining. An advantage of the district is its good connection to the high-ranking road and railwork networks that guarantee good regional and supra-regional accessibility. An advantage for the labor market is the high proportion of innovative, research-intensive companies, which also benefit from the University of Leoben and other research and competence centres. Thereby the district also offers attractive employment opportunities for highly educated people. Despite this fact, there is strong commute to the districts of Graz and Bruck-Mürzzuschlag. The situation is more disadvantageous in municipalities located in the north of the district, along the mountain barrier of the Eisenerz Alps and Hochschwab. These natural barriers make access to the southern part of the district, the regional economic centre, difficult and restrict job opportunities and also the access to digital infrastructure. The density of workplaces is thus below the Styrian average (WIBIS, 2020d).

Also located in Upper Sytria, Liezen is the largest of all Styrian districts. The region around the district's capital Liezen is industrially shaped with the metal industry and mechanical engineering as the two main sectors. In the rest of the district, tourism plays a major role with Schladming and Bad Aussee being the most well-known. Whereas the capital Liezen is well connected to the Austrian transportation network, major parts of this large district suffer from economic disadvantages stemming from the peripheral location in the middle of the Alps. Thus, many municipalities do not offer many job opportunities (aside from tourism) and the possibilities to commute to other districts is limited (WIBIS, 2020e).

Another district characterized by its peripheral, alpine location is Murau. The population has been decreasing as in particular young people have been leaving the region leading to a negative birth/death balance. Apart from tourism, the economy is mainly characterized by mechanical engineering, the timber industry and forestry. The low number of large enterprises and the low population density lead to a problematic economic environment – especially for highly educated the job market is in an unfavorable condition (WIBIS, 2020f).

In the district of Voitsberg, about half of the population lives in the three larger municipalities of Köflach, Voitsberg and Bärnbach. The district has a positive migration balance and a negative birth/death balance. The transport infrastructure is well developed, leading to many people commuting to Graz daily. Besides a long tradition in lignite mining and the glass industry, Voitsberg today is also specialized into the manufacture of metal products and vehicle construction (WIBIS, 2020g).

This share of people with a university degree is even lower in the district Murtal with only 9.3. per cent. The regional specialization is in the fields of mechanical engineering, metal production and processing, electrical engineering, and electronics. The area around Spielberg, where Formula 1 races take place, is relevant for tourism. With the several expressways and a motorway, the Murtal has a comparatively well-developed interregional road connection. Nevertheless, the central area of Graz is difficult to reach for many day commuters – especially from peripheries in valleys in the north of the district.

Consequently, the major part of employees based in Murtal also work in the district. As it is difficult for new firms to settle, young people tend to leave the area also due the low dynamic in job advertisements and the above average unemployment rate (WIBIS, 2020i).

Compared to Murtal, the accessibility in Bruck-Mürzzuschlag is extremely good. The transport infrastructure is highly developed regarding both public and private transport. The economic center is in the Mur-Mürz valley. About half of the inhabitants live in the three largest towns of the district: in Kapfenberg, in the district capital Bruck an der Mur and in Mürzzuschlag. The regional specialization has traditionally been in the metal production and processing, in the manufacture of metal products and in the building industry. As in all Upper Styrian industrial districts, the decline of the steel and metal industries was accompanied by a continuing decline in population (WIBIS, 2020j).

In contrast to the industrially dominated Upper Styrian regions, the manufacturing sector in the district of Weiz is generally more diversified. Weiz is characterized by its proximity to the central area of Graz. Together with the good accessibility in the south of the district, this leads to a large proportion of people commuting to Graz. Yet Weiz also attracts workers from the surrounding districts due to attractive job opportunities. The Weiz economy is characterised by a few large companies, among them MAGNA, ANDRITZ HYDRO and Siemens AG. The educational level of the population is characterized by a high proportion of people who have completed an apprenticeship or passed a master craftsman's examination as the highest level of education. In contrast, only 10.0 per cent of the population had a university or university of applied sciences degree compared to 16.1 per cent in Styria (WIBIS, 2020h).

The district Deutschlandsberg is a mainly industrial district with a specialization on electronics and vehicle construction. Therefore, more than 50 per cent of the workforce in this district works in the manufacturing sector, being the highest proportion among all Styrian districts. The service sector is comparatively small with tourism playing a major role. Interesting to note is the above-average number of people with an apprenticeship certificate – 45.6 percent of the working population in Deutschlandsberg, whereas only 10.6 percent have a university degree (WIBIS, 2020a).

For the district Hartberg-Fürstenfeld, tourism and the wood industry are of high importance. Work is created mainly by small and medium-sized firms as less than 25 per cent of firms employ more than 250 people. The favourable location of Hartberg-Fürstenfeld along the motorway keeps the district open in all directions leading to a high proportion of commuting. This occurs mainly to the central area of Graz, yet there are also many people commuting to the district from the neighboring region Burgenland. Hartberg-Fürstenfeld has been a tourist district since the 1990s at the latest – especially due to its orientation around thermal baths. Yet also the food and luxury food industry play an important role in the transition from an agricultural peripheral region to an important cornerstone of all-year-round tourism (WIBIS, 2020k).

The district Südoststeiermark is located in the southeast of Styria and has a very peripheral position within Styria, as there is no direct connection to the high-level transport network in the district itself. The economic structure is heterogeneous, but also traditionally focused on the food and luxury food production. Small enterprises are typical for the region. Leather industry products manufactured today are mainly upholstered furniture for the automobile and aircraft industry (WIBIS, 2020l).

In the next section, a detailed analysis of the job vacancies is carried out. As the data allows for a very disaggregated analysis, it can be shed light on the differences both between and within districts. Thus, also agglomeration tendencies at the municipal level can be detected and structural heterogeneities regarding ICT-skills can be identified.

The Market for ICT-related Jobs – a Spatial Analysis

In 2017, more than 73,000 job advertisements were placed for the entire region of Styria. The number of job offers differed widely with regard to education levels as well as with regard to the location of the individual job positions. Almost 30 per cent of all job advertisements were posted in the Styrian capital, where 23 per cent of the Styrian population live. The municipality with the second-most job advertisements is Hitzendorf in the district Graz-Umgebung. Comparing the almost 22,000 job offers posted in Graz with the 3,153 job offers posted in Hitzendorf, it becomes evident that Graz is *the* important job engine of Styria. The cities of Kapfenberg and Leoben –the municipalities with the second and third highest populations – only play a minor role, with 1,463 and 1,663 job offers, respectively. Almost half of all municipalities offered less than 50 jobs. As many municipalities have between 1,000 and 5,000 inhabitants only, this is not necessarily a sign of a stagnant labor market but can be explained by the seize of the municipalities.

Turning to the spatial distribution of ICT-related job advertisements in particular, Graz is again the single most important place for job offers, posting almost 46 per cent of all ICT-related jobs in Styria. At the other end of the spectrum lies the periphery district of Murau: All its 14 municipalities together only advertised 71 out of the 12,779 ICT-related jobs in Styria. Similar results could be reported for many other areas: About two thirds of all Styrian municipalities advertised less than ten jobs with an explicit reference to ICT-requirements and one third did not even post a single ICT-related job offer in the year 2017. As a result, two-thirds of all vacancies with ICT-requirements were concentrated in ten municipalities, although these account for only about 30 percent of the Styrian population and almost half of all vacancies in Styria.

To generalize results, the authors calculate and compare the concentration levels of job offers with the help of the Hirschman-Herfindahl-Index (Hirschman, 1958; Herfindahl, 1950). The result for the general job market was $HHI_{general} = 0{,}097$; for the ICT-related job market, this value almost doubled to $HHI_{ICT} = 0{,}170$, indicating that this job segment was spatially much more concentrated.

Moreover, there is a strong positive correlation between the education level required in a job and its spatial concentration: Whereas 65 per cent of all Styrian ICT-related jobs requiring a university degree were posted in Graz, this was the case for only 31 per cent of ICT-related jobs requiring only completed compulsory schooling. In general, the data show that more municipalities can offer jobs for people with lower levels of education that only require basic ICT-knowledge. For higher levels of education only few municipalities seem to have both the proper supply and demand for high-skill ICT-related jobs.

The results in Table 2 reveal the noteworthy differences between municipalities regarding the education levels that the job offers require, reflecting differences in both, specialization patterns and the educational background of the inhabitants. Liezen for instance is among the top municipalities offering jobs for people with low and medium educational background (i.e. completed compusory schooling and apprenticeship), however the number of jobs for people with university degrees is negligible. The opposite is true for Leoben, which ranges among the top municipalities in offering jobs for the highly educated but not for people with low and medium education levels.

In more detail, the results in Table 2 show that the municipalities Kapfenberg, Liezen, Leibnitz, Leoben, Weiz and Deutschlandsberg, all of which are district capitals, play an economically more prominent role than other (often smaller) municipalities. Gössendorf, Premstätten, Raaba and Wundschuh are located in Graz-Umgebung, thus benefting from the proximity to Graz. Ilz is part of the district of

Hartberg-Fürstenfeld and a small town only. However, it is located directly at the highway, with good infrastructure, and is thus favorable for firm settlement.

Table 2. Municipalities with High Numbers of ICT-related Job Offers, by Required Level of Education, own calculations

Total ICT Job offers	Compulsory school	Apprenticeship	University
Graz (5582)	Graz (838)	Graz (1871)	Graz (625)
Gössendorf (359)	Lannach (153)	Leibnitz (143)	Gössendorf (77)
Gleisdorf (319)	Raaba (135)	Gleisdorf (135)	Leoben (40)
Lannach (318)	Gleisdorf (82)	Kapfenberg (131)	Kapfenberg (35)
Kapfenberg (299)	Leibnitz (81)	Gössendorf (110)	Premstätten (22)
Raaba (282)	Liezen (69)	Liezen (105)	Lannach (19)
Leibnitz (265)	Ilz (69)	Lannach (98)	Deutschlandsberg (18)
Leoben (263)	Wundschuh (68)	Weiz (95)	Raaba (17)

To draw a more complete picture of the spatial distribution of job offers according to the required levels of education, Figures 2,3 and 4 provide information on all 287 municipalities. For the lowest level of education, all municipalities together posted a total of 2,689 job offers with explicit ICT-relevance. This documents that a remarkably high number of 2017 Styrian job offers explicitly required ICT-skills even for jobs for applicants with low levels of education. This is a relevant result also for economic policy and the design of education programs, as ICT-knowledge is becoming an ever more important prerequisite for the job market. The Hirschman-Herfindahl Index for the lowest level of education was $HHI_{ICTlow} = 0.111$, which is smaller than the general HHI_{ICT}. This shows that for the lowest level of education, concentration was lower than for the total number of ICT-related jobs. Thus, the preliminary results of a positive correlation between the level of education and spatial concentration can be supported also with the help of the concentration index. For a visualization of the spatial distribution of low-skill ICT-related job offers, see Figure 2:

Turning to ICT-relevant job offers for medium levels of education, Figure 3 shows the spatial distribution of the 4,612 jobs for all Styrian municipalities. It is interesting to note that 70 per cent more ICT-relevant jobs were posted for medium than for low education levels. Thus, it should be of high importance for education policy to increase both ICT-knowledge and the formal education level for people with only compulsory education in order to increase their job opportunities in the long run. As described in the literature review, both national and international studies have shown evidence that further processes of digitalization are likely to harm especially (1) those with low education levels, (2) those with a high proportion of routine tasks and (3) those who have not yet acquired enough ICT and digital skills.

Figure 3 also shows that the spatial distribution of ICT-related job offers for medium levels of education was more concentrated than that for the lowest level of education. This impression is confirmed by the higher Hirschman-Herfindahl-Index $HHI_{ICTmed} = 0{,}172$. The results moreover show that it is mainly the municipalities around Graz, some municipalities in the district of Liezen as well as the district capi-

Figure 2. Spatial Distribution of ICT-Jobs for Compulsory Education
source: own illustration

tals Bruck, Deutschlandsberg, Kapfenberg and Leoben that offer many job opportunities for medium education levels. More peripheral municipalities already lag behind in offering a sufficient amount of jobs for medium levels of education, leading to higher degrees of agglomeration. In analyzing the spatial distribution of the absolute numbers of job offers, the role of small municipalities can to some extent be underestimated. Small municipalities with inhabitants of 1,000 people are not able to offer as many new jobs as Graz with 280,000 inhabitants.

In contrast to the two levels of education discussed so far, ICT-relevant jobs for people with a university degree were mainly located in Graz. Other main municipalities offering high-skilled jobs were Kapfenberg and Leoben, which can be explained by the fact that universities and applied universities with a special focus on ICT-knowledge are located in these two towns. Additionally, many jobs were offered in Gössendorf and Premstätten, given the fact that job leasing firms and staffing companies are overrepresented in these two municipalities. These factors lead to a high degree of spatial concentration as also supported by the Hirschman-Herfindahl-Index. The value for high-skilled ICT-related jobs was $HHI_{ICThigh} = 0{,}441$, which also supports the results shown in Figure 4.

The results from this section thus support the central outcomes from other studies for Austria: Böheim et al. (2017) as well as Firgo et al. (2018) showed the importance of larger cities and their surrounding districts for the creation of high-skill, ICT-related jobs. These studies also described a pronounced center-periphery gap in ICT-specialists at the district level. Altogether, the results from this section are also relevant for the future development of peripheral areas: Under the current circumstances, it is rather unlikely that students from rural areas (once they finish their studies) return to their hometowns to work

Figure 3. Spatial Distribution of ICT-Jobs for Apprenticeship and Secondary Education
source: own illustration

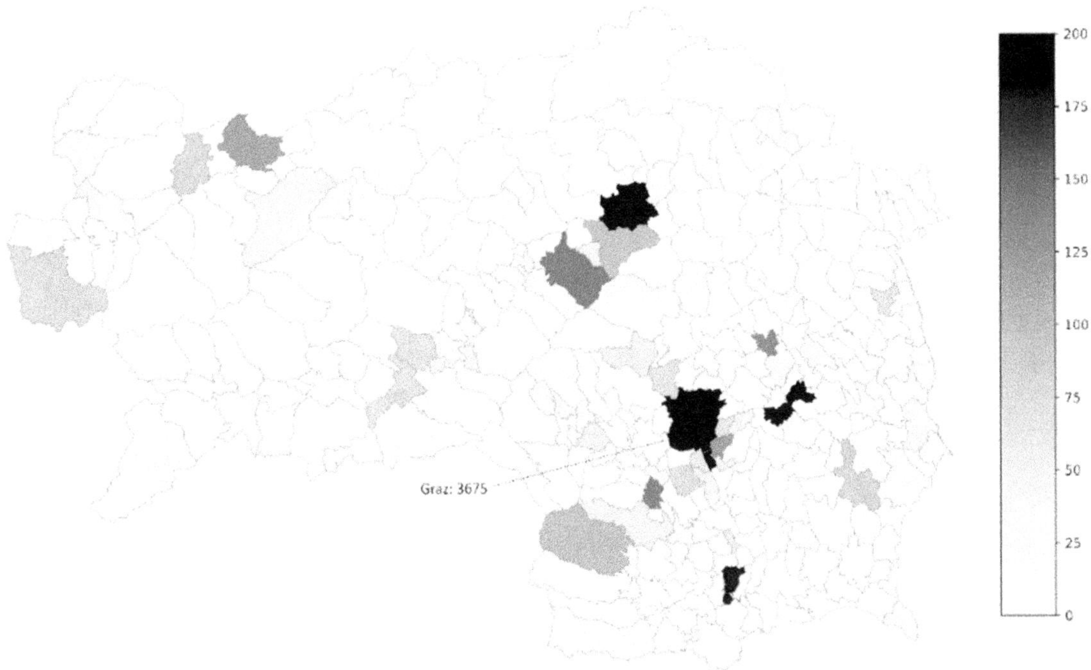

there. If there are hardly any desirable jobs for high-skill workers available in the more rural areas, this trend cannot be reversed.

Keywords in job Offers – Analyzing the Needs of the job Market

It could be argued that the number of ICT-related jobs is not as relevant as the total number of job advertisements for the economic development of a region (district or town). However, as digitalization and automation have been changing the job market and the requirements for job positions towards a higher level of ICT-relevant skills, it is of the utmost importance for a positive growth trend to identify the (present and future) needs of the job market.

Analyzing the full texts of job descriptions using data mining allows the researchers to determine keywords related to ICT-skills in job advertisements. First, the authors were able to identify large differences in the specific ICT-requirements depending on the level of education: While basic computer skills described by „knowledge in electronic data processing“ are explicitly required in 75 per cent of job advertisements for people who have only compulsory education, this is the case for about 50 per cent of the job offers for people with a completed apprenticeship and less than 30 per cent of the job offers for university graduates. This indicates that general computer skills are more often taken for granted in higher education and therefore are less frequently specified explicitly in job advertisements for high-skilled workers, especially for IT-specialists.

Figure 4. Spatial Distribution of ICT-jobs Universities and Applied Universities
source: own illustration.

In contrast, the words "programmer/programming" were particularly relevant for persons with an apprenticeship certificate and graduates of universities of applied sciences: About one quarter of all ICT-related jobs in the respective education segments were explicitly looking for programmers, while these kinds of jobs were almost entirely unavailable for people in the lower education segment. However, the authors also identified a clear disconnect between the requirement of ICT-knowledge and of formal education levels for this keyword, as almost 50 per cent of all job offers looking for people with „programming skills" did not specify a formal education level.

When it comes to keywords such as "SAP" and "software", firms on the one hand are mainly looking for people with vocational secondary education to execute tasks, and on the other hand are looking for people with degrees from applied universities and technical universities who would be employed in implementing SAP tools. Thus, the specific tasks associated with different education levels differ.

The analysis also identified interesting differences for tertiary education levels: Whereas firms looking for "web-" (i.e. web-design etc.), "android developers", and "social media managers" were by and large explicitly searching for graduates from applied universities, while offers including the keywords „data scientist" and „data manager" were mainly intended to attract graduates from technical universities.

In a last step, the authors map the spatial distribution for three different keywords. In Figure 5, the results for "Electronic Data Processing" are mapped at the municipality level. Results were again driven by the fact that Graz is the dominant economic center of Styria. Gleisdorf, Kapfenberg, Leoben, Liezen, Leibnitz, Raaba and Wundschuh were the municipalities in which overproportionally many firms offered jobs with these requirements. Moreover, many other municipalities also offered plenty of jobs for this keyword, leading to a rather modest level of concentration. As a point of reference, the Figure highlights the number of open jobs for Gleisdorf, which in 2017 was 154 for about 10.000 inhabitants. In comparison, Graz offered 2575, for about 280.000 inhabitants.

Figure 5. Spatial Distribution for the Keyword 'Electronic Data Processing'
Source: own illustration

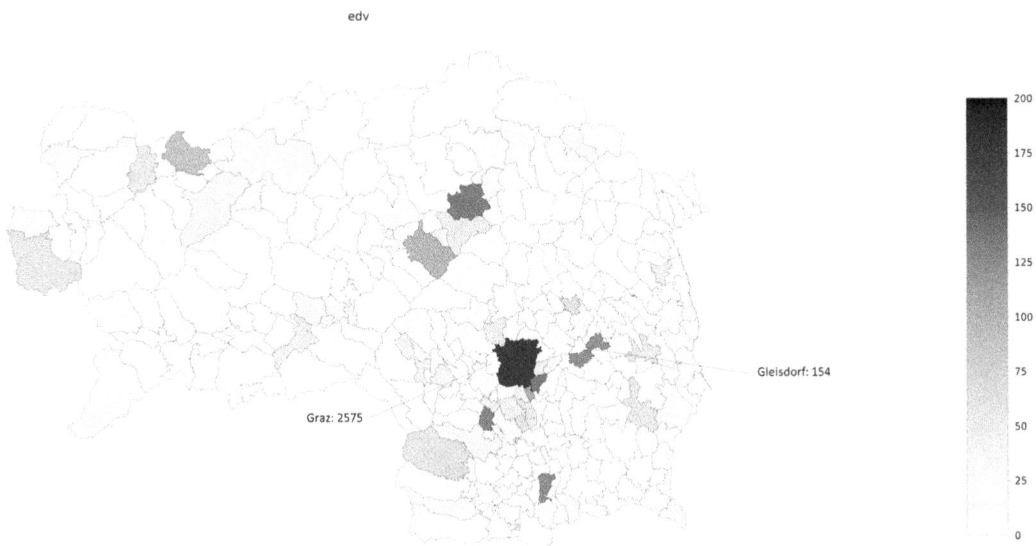

Turning to the keyword "Programmer/Programming", Figure 6 shows that the concentration was more pronounced than for the more general term „Knowledge in Electronic Data Processing". The more specific knowledge requirement also led to a higher concentration of job offers in larger municipalities and the municipalities surrounding Graz. Altogether, there were about half as many open jobs for specific programming requirements as for the more general IT-terms described above.

Analyzing the spatial distribution of the keyword "Software" in Figure 7 shows that Graz was by far the most dominant municipality offering jobs with this characteristic.

Deutschlandsberg, Deutschfeistritz, Gleisdorf, Leoben and Stainz were also offering jobs with these requirements – yet none of them more than 50, compared to 1567 in Graz. Thus, for software engineers, data scientists and software managers, there were hardly any other options but to work in Graz.

To reach policy conclusions, evidence-based policy recommendations, it is recommendable to not only rely on the absolute number of job offers but also on the relative terms. To be precise, ICT-related jobs should be measured both as a portion of total jobs and as a portion of inhabitants. Then it becomes evident that Gleisdorf offered more ICT-related jobs than Graz and this is also true for some other municipalities. When analyzing relative job offers, the market in many Upper Styrian municipalities, including Kapfenberg and Leoben are less favorable, indicating structural problems in creating new jobs.

Figure 6. Spatial Distribution for the Keyword "Programmer"
Source: own illustration

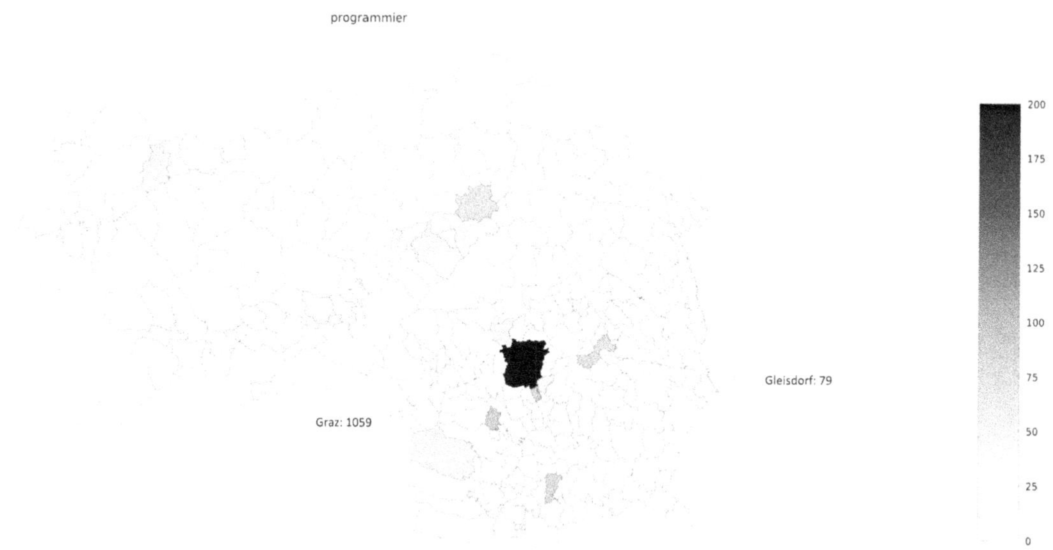

Figure 7. Spatial Distribution for the Keyword 'Software'
Source: own illustration

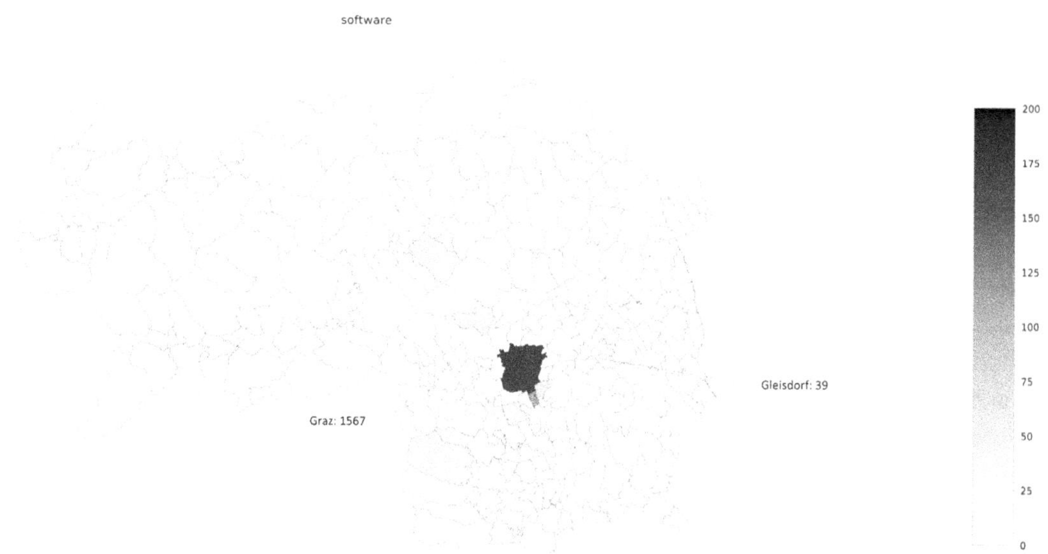

Thus, for reaching final policy conclusions, both the absolute and relative numbers of local job offers should be taken into account.

SOLUTIONS AND RECOMMENDATIONS

It is relevant for economic policy to gain a high level of understanding about which ICT-skills are relevant for job vacancies and how these requirements differ according to the level of education. Only with such insights can appropriate education tools for the unemployed, but also for schools and the tertiary sector be designed. Understanding the necessities of the job market and equipping workers with the proper qualifications can reduce the risks of unemployment and increase the competitiveness of entire municipalities and regions. In this context, the presented data should also make clear that education policy must not only mean „more education", but rather more education that allows people to participate in the job market of the future. This can be achieved by providing training in information and communication technologies in general and providing training for more specific requirements.

Furthermore, the spatial distribution of these vacancies is of great relevance with regard to the future development potential of individual communities and regions and could thus be relevant for regional economic policy as well. As outlined throughout this chapter, competences with respect to information and communication technologies and digital skills have become crucial for employability in many industries and at all educational levels. It has thus also become a key challenge for employees and job seekers, who may not have experience or confidence in their digital skills, to acquire and make use of the proper competencies (Centeno et al., 2019).

One advantage of the Austrian education system is the highly differentiated dual vocational training system (e.g. Bock-Schappelwein et al., 2017), which gives graduates a wide range of competencies and makes them suitable for use in many areas. This in turn reduces the probability of being affected by job losses for medium-skill levels. However, one factor that has to be given more emphasis is the regional access to (fast) digital infrastructure, where more peripheral regions are lagging behind. Economic policy making must ensure that rural areas are financially supported in expanding essential infrastructure in order to overcome economic push factors, i.e. disincentives affecting the settlement of firms in regions with low population density. As described in this chapter, some districts have already suffered during recent decades due to the lack of accessibility and the fact that high-skilled workers move to the center around Graz. It remains an open question whether the development towards a more digitalized labor market will increase or decrease the chances of peripheral regions. While digitalized jobs can more easily be created also in peripheral municipalities, these districts and municipalities may not be able to catch up as the costs to set up broadband internet coverage prove prohibitive.

CONCLUSION

This chapter analyzed the spatial distribution of job advertisements and the need for ICT-skills as demanded by firms in job vacancies. While many studies focus on the analysis of job destruction induced by automation and digitalization, this chapter aims to contribute to a deeper understanding of the fact that new technologies not only destroy jobs but also create jobs and change the requirements for existing jobs.

The results for Styria clearly show that the city of Graz serves as the main job engine – even more so for ICT-related jobs. This is true for IT professions in general and for high-skilled jobs such as software engineers in particular. Thus, the higher the level of education required, the more jobs tend to be concentrated in and around Graz (i.e. also in Graz-Umgebung) with high values also for parts of Upper Styria around Kapfenberg and Leoben. These latter two cities are regional centers since they offer high qualification at the University of Applied Sciences in Kapfenberg and the University of Leoben. In more general terms, 53 percent of all municipalities advertise ICT-jobs for persons with completed compulsory education, 47 percent for the intermediate education segment, but only 17 percent of the municipalities offer at least one job for the highest education segment. The Eastern and Southern Styrian districts exhibit below average potential. As some of these regions are highly specialized in tourism and local food production, this need not necessarily be a problem for their long-term economic development. However, these districts present the greatest challenges for labor market policies, especially when talking about retaining high-skilled workers in the region.

Altogether, the differences between the Styrian districts are remarkable and highlight the importance of region-specific factors for (the number and quality of) job offers also in a digitalized future. Whereas peripheral regions can benefit from faster internet connections (if they are available also in more remote places) and the fact that working from home will become ever more normal in workplaces, regional centers still have the advantage of preserving major pull factors such as critical mass for high-educated people, closeness to universities and public infrastructure as well as stronger forward and backward linkages in economic centers compared to more peripheral areas. It thus remains to be seen, which tasks will become extinct over the next decade, which new job requirements potential job applicants have to fulfill and whether the job market as a whole will become more spatially concentrated or whether the push factors will lead to higher job growth in more peripheral areas.

ACKNOWLEDGMENT

The authors are thankful for the financial support of the Styrian Government for the Project "(Un)Divided; Inequalities in the Digital Revolution: Regions, Labor Markets and Policy Responses.

REFERENCES

Autor, D. H. (2015). Why Are There Still So Many Jobs? The History and Future of Workplace Automation. *The Journal of Economic Perspectives*, *29*(3), 3–30. doi:10.1257/jep.29.3.3

Autor, D. H., & Dorn, D. (2013). The Growth of Low-Skill Service Jobs and the Polarization of the US Labor Market. *The American Economic Review*, *103*(5), 1553–1597. doi:10.1257/aer.103.5.1553

Autor, D. H., Levy, F., & Murnane, R. J. (2003). The Skill Content of Recent Technological Change: An Empirical Exploration. *The Quarterly Journal of Economics*, *118*(4), 1279–1333. doi:10.1162/003355303322552801

Bertschek, I., Briglauer, W., Hüschelrath, K., Kauf, B., & Niebel, T. (2016). The Economic Impacts of Broadband Internet: A Survey. *Review of Network Economics*, *14*(4), 201–227.

BMVIT. (2014). *Breitbrandstrategie 2020*. https://www.bmk.gv.at/.../breitbandstrategie2020_ua.pdf

BMVIT. (2019). *Breitbrandstrategie 2030, Österreichs Weg in die Gigabit-Gesellschaft*. https://www.bmk.gv.at/.../breitbandstrategie2030_ua.pdf

Bock-Schappelwein, J., Famira-Mühlberger, U., & Leoni, T. (2017), Labour market opportunities through digitization. WIFO study.

Böheim, M., & Firgo, M. (2018). Effects of digitisation on the development of economic areas. *WIFO-Monthly Reports*, *91*(12), 881–890.

Bonin, H., Gregory, T., & Zierahn, U. (2015). *Transfer of the study from Frey/Osborne (2013) to Germany*. ZEW Short Expert Report No. 57. https://www.bmas.de/DE/Service/Medien/Publikationen/Forschungsberichte/Forschungsberichte-Arbeitsmarkt/forschungsbericht-fb-455.html

Brynjolfsson, E., & McAfee, A. (2014). *The Second Machine Age: Work, Progress, and Prosperity in a Time of Brilliant Technologies*. W.W. Norton & Company.

Centeno, Cl., Vuorikari, R., Punie, Y., O'Keefe, W., Kluzer, S., Vitorica, A., Lejarzegi, R., Martinez de Soria, I., & Bartolomé, J. (2019). *Developing digital competence for employability: Engaging and supporting stakeholders with the use of DigComp, DigComp: The European Digital Competence Framework*. https://publications.jrc.ec.europa.eu/repository/bitstream/JRC118711/jrc118711_digcomp4empl_stakeholders_consultation_ws_report_v1.0_in_pubsy_final_v0.pdf

Chun, H., Kim, J.-W., & Lee, J. (2015). How does Information Technology improve aggregate Productivity? A new Channel of Productivity Dispersion and Reallocation. *Research Policy*, *44*(5), 999–1016. doi:10.1016/j.respol.2014.11.007

Dengler, K., & Matthes, B. (2018). The impacts of digital transformation on the labour market: Substitution potentials of occupations in Germany. *Technological Forecasting and Social Change*, *137*, 304–316. doi:10.1016/j.techfore.2018.09.024

European Commission. (2010). *A Digital Agenda for Europe*. https://www.kowi.de/Portaldata/2/Resources/fp/2010-com-digital-agenda.pdf

Figerl, J., & Okropiridse, A. (2018). *The job miracle on the labour market? A (long-term) look behind the scenes of the rapid increase in job vacancies at AMS*. A&W Blog. https://awblog.at/offene-stellen-beim-ams/

Firgo, M., Mayerhofer, P., Peneder, M., Grabmayer, P., & Reschenhofer, P. (2018). *Employment effects of digitisation in the federal states as well as in town and country*. Economic Research Institute. https://www.wifo.ac.at/jart/prj3/wifo/resources/person_dokument/person_dokument.jart?publikationsid=61633&mime_type=application/pdf

Frey, C. B., & Osborne, M. A. (2017). The future of employment: How susceptible are jobs to computerization. *Technological Forecasting and Social Change*, *114*, 254–280. doi:10.1016/j.techfore.2016.08.019

Goos, M., Manning, A., & Salomons, A. (2014). Explaining Job Polarization: Routine-Biased Technological Change and Offshoring. *The American Economic Review*, *104*(8), 2509–2562. doi:10.1257/aer.104.8.2509

Goos, M., Manning, A., & Solomons, A. (2009). Job polarization in Europe. *The American Economic Review*, *99*(2), 58–63. doi:10.1257/aer.99.2.58

Herfindahl, O. C. (1950). *Concentration in the Steel Industry* [Unpublished Ph. D. thesis]. Columbia University.

Hirschman, A. O. (1958). *The Strategy of Economic Development.* Yale University Press.

Kolko, J. (2012). Broadband and Local Growth. *Journal of Urban Economics*, *71*(1), 100–113. doi:10.1016/j.jue.2011.07.004

Nagl, W., Titelbach, G., & Valkova, K. (2017). *Digitisation of work: Substitutability of occupations in the course of automation by industry 4.0.* Studie des IHS im Auftrag des Sozialministeriums.

OECD. (2018). *Bridging the Rural Digital Divide.* OECD Digital Economy Papers No. 265. https://www.sipotra.it/wp-content/uploads/2018/03/BRIDGING-THE-RURAL-DIGITAL-DIVIDE.pdf

Peneder, M., Firgo, M., & Streicher, G. (2019). Digitalisierung in Österreich: Eine Standortbestimmung (Digital Transformation in Austria: A Status-Quo Analysis). *WIFO-Monatsberichte*, *92*(6), 447–457.

Schumpeter, A. (1942). *Capitalism, Socialism and Democracy.* Harper & Brothers.

Schumpeter, A. J. (1911). *Theorie der wirtschaftlichen Entwicklung. Eine Untersuchung über Unternehmergewinn, Kapital, Kredit, Zins und den Konjunkturzyklus.* Duncker & Humblot.

Statistik Austria. (2018). *Average annual job vacancies according to the Job Vacancy Survey and the Labour Market Service.* http://www.statistik.at/web_de/statistiken/menschen_und_gesellschaft/arbeitsmarkt/offene_stellen/118100.html (29.4.2019)

United States National Commission on Technology. (1966). *Automation and Economic Progress: America's industrial and occupational manpower requirements, 1964-1975.* U.S. Government Printing Office.

WIBIS. (2020). *Bezirksprofil Graz (Stadt).* https://wibis-steiermark.at/fileadmin/user_upload/wibis_steiermark/regionsprofile/2020-04/B601_PROFIL_2_Daten_17.04.2020.pdf

WIBIS. (2020a). *Bezirksprofil Deutschlandsberg.* https://wibis-steiermark.at/fileadmin/user_upload/wibis_steiermark/regionsprofile/2020-04/B603_PROFIL_2_Daten_17.04.2020.pdf

WIBIS. (2020b). *Bezirksprofil Graz-Umgebung.* https://wibis-steiermark.at/fileadmin/user_upload/wibis_steiermark/regionsprofile/2020-04/B606_PROFIL_2_Daten_17.04.2020.pdf

WIBIS. (2020c). *Bezirksprofil Leibnitz.* https://wibis-steiermark.at/fileadmin/user_upload/wibis_steiermark/regionsprofile/2020-04/B610_PROFIL_2_Daten_17.04.2020.pdf

WIBIS. (2020d). *Bezirksprofil Leoben.* https://wibis-steiermark.at/fileadmin/user_upload/wibis_steiermark/regionsprofile/2020-04/B611_PROFIL_2_Daten_17.04.2020.pdf

WIBIS. (2020e). *Bezirksprofil Liezen.* https://wibis-steiermark.at/fileadmin/user_upload/wibis_steiermark/regionsprofile/2020-04/B612_PROFIL_2_Daten_17.04.2020.pdf

WIBIS. (2020f). *Bezirksprofil Murau.* https://wibis-steiermark.at/fileadmin/user_upload/wibis_steiermark/regionsprofile/2020-04/B614_PROFIL_2_Daten_17.04.2020.pdf

WIBIS. (2020g). *Bezirksprofil Voitsberg*. https://wibis-steiermark.at/fileadmin/user_upload/wibis_steiermark/regionsprofile/2020-04/B616_PROFIL_2_Daten_17.04.2020.pdf

WIBIS. (2020h). *Bezirksprofil Weiz*. https://wibis-steiermark.at/fileadmin/user_upload/wibis_steiermark/regionsprofile/2020-04/B617_PROFIL_2_Daten_17.04.2020.pdf

WIBIS. (2020i). *Bezirksprofil Murtal*. https://wibis-steiermark.at/fileadmin/user_upload/wibis_steiermark/regionsprofile/2020-04/B620_PROFIL_1_FactText_24.04.2020.pdf

WIBIS. (2020j). *Bezirksprofil Bruck-Mürzzuschlag*. https://wibis-steiermark.at/fileadmin/user_upload/wibis_steiermark/regionsprofile/2020-04/B621_PROFIL_2_Daten_17.04.2020.pdf

WIBIS. (2020k). *Bezirksprofil Hartberg-Fürstenfeld*. https://wibis-steiermark.at/fileadmin/user_upload/wibis_steiermark/regionsprofile/2020-04/B622_PROFIL_2_Daten_17.04.2020.pdf

WIBIS. (2020l). *Bezirksprofil Südoststeiermark*. https://wibis-steiermark.at/fileadmin/user_upload/wibis_steiermark/regionsprofile/2020-04/B623_PROFIL_2_Daten_17.04.2020.pdf

ENDNOTE

1 By applying more suitable approaches, the Centre for Economic Research in Germany (ZEW) did not estimate labor saving potentials of entire sectors or occupation of people. In contrast to Frey and Osborne (2017), Bonin et al. (2015) apply the automation probabilities to individual areas of activity of jobs: This reduces the rationalization probabilities for the USA to 9 per cent and for Germany to 12 per cent. Dengler and Matthes (2018) make use of a task-based approach as well and highlight the fact that every occupation includes tasks that cannot be substituted by machines. They conclude that 15 per cent of jobs are at risk and that as a consequence of automation, employment growth is less rapid. The Institute for Advanced Studies comes to similar conclusions as it forecasts job losses of 9 per cent of Austria (Nagl et al., 2017).

Chapter 4
Digital Learning Challenge in Indonesia

Adhi Prasetio
School of Economics and Business, Telkom University, Indonesia

Grisna Anggadwita
https://orcid.org/0000-0003-1503-9146
School of Economics and Business, Telkom University, Indonesia

Rina D. Pasaribu
School of Economics and Business, Telkom University, Indonesia

ABSTRACT

Industry Education Reform 4.0 was launched by the Indonesian government as one of nine priority agendas called Nawa Cita. The reform consists of two main programs: first, to improve the quality of life of Indonesian people through improving the quality of education and training and, second, to revolutionize the nation's character through the policy of restructuring the national education curriculum. There are challenges though to implement those programs including Indonesian geographic, gap to access different level of education, and the gap to achieve the Industrial Revolution 4.0 skills. The aims of this chapter are to explore alternatives and solutions for access to education in Indonesia by utilizing technological advancements including the skills needed to face the current digital era. Education 4.0 is a good approach to answer those challenges. The use of internet technology for digital learning can provide access to students spread across the country. This approach requires skills set that are appropriate to Industry 4.0 by providing a flexible curriculum and online certification.

DOI: 10.4018/978-1-7998-4972-8.ch004

Copyright © 2021, IGI Global. Copying or distributing in print or electronic forms without written permission of IGI Global is prohibited.

INTRODUCTION

The rapid development of information and communication technology has influenced the spread and openness of information and knowledge by penetrating the boundaries of distance, place, space and time (Munir, 2017). Information and communication technology affects various fields of life and provides changes to the way of life and human activities, including in the education sector. The education sector has begun to change the digital-based learning system so that it can reach all levels of society. Although the benefits of information and communication technology have been recognized in advancing the education sector, the response to use in the teaching and learning process is still considered slow (Iswanto, 2016). The education sector is an important field because it has a function to prepare human resources in facing future challenges such as the industrial revolution. Higher education plays an important role in driving digital growth and innovation in the development of human resources (Permatasari & Anggadwita, 2019).

Higher education faces challenges in realizing digital-based education. Most programs to deal with these challenges are limited only to a subject that utilizes technology (Wedman & Diggs, 2001), rather than creating an actual or virtual learning environment where technology can develop and integrate with the learning process. Digital learning environments are central in efforts to design, develop and provide digital learning opportunities. The notion of a learning environment is associated with the constructivist movement (Wilson 1995), because the emphasis has moved from the individual, to the context, place and space around learning and teaching. The increasing use of digital technology in education gave rise to the idea of a digital learning environment.

This chapter introduces the reader to program initiatives in creating a digital learning environment through the industrial education reform program 4.0 with two main programs being to enhance the quality of life of the Indonesian people through improving the quality of education and training, and revolutionizing the nation's character through the policy of restructuring the national education curriculum. However there are challenges to implementing such programs including Indonesia's geography, gaps to access various levels of education, and gaps to achieve the skills of the industrial revolution 4.0. The purpose of this chapter is to explore alternatives and solutions for access to education in Indonesia by utilizing technological advancements including the skills needed to deal with the current digital era. Qualitative methods with descriptive and narrative approaches are used to explore answers in research questions.

This chapter is divided into five sections. The first section was an introduction to provide background on why the digital learning environment phenomenon is important to be explored further. The second and third sections contain a literature review on the digital learning environment and the role of education to build and create a digital learning environment. The fourth and fifth sections are discussions on digital learning programs in Indonesia and the challenges faced in implementing these activity programs. And, the last section contains the conclusions of this chapter.

DIGITAL LEARNING

Some scholars call today's young generation people who have grown up with computers, video games, the Internet, and cell phones, or so-called 'Digital Natives' (Gasser & Palfrey, 2008; Prensky, 2001; Burdick & Willis, 2011). This affects social practice, learning styles, and cognition, because of their initial and constant involvement with information technology. As a result, digital learning requires radical reworking of pedagogy to accommodate learners who are bricoleurs: they can gather information from various sources, intuitive visual communicators, have strong visual-spatial skills and learn best through inductive discovery (Burdick & Willis, 2011).

Although some studies show that not all digital natives have the skills to use the same technology and have different learning preferences and styles compared to previous generations (Bennett, Maton, & Kervin, 2008; Kvavik, Caruso & Morgan, 2004; Kennedy, Krause, Judd, Churchward & Gray, 2006; Oliver & Goerke, 2007), but in general the arguments for digital native concepts can still be used to provide solutions for students who have these characteristics. The argument for this is because although there are some digital natives who do not have uniform skills in the use of technology, this can be overcome by providing more equitable access to internet connectivity and adequate training. In addition, digital natives do have different characteristics from previous generations, but these differences do not make them completely incompatible with the approach taken in the world of education today. The challenge is how the world of education can adapt to these characteristics and differences (Bennett, Maton, & Kervin, 2008).

At present, initiatives in increasing digital literacy are developing rapidly in every educational institution with the aim of providing the necessary skills in the technology field. Learning in this context is no longer understood simply as absorbing and storing information in the classroom; instead focus on the ability to access information and contextualize it, and then use it in peer networks (Brown & Duguid, 2000; Ito et al., 2009; Jenkins et al., 2006; Burdick & Willis, 2011). The learning process is not only done in the classroom, but also informally and through social media tools that have a dialogic relationship with their culture. The generation raised in the media also needs literacy to understand this form of media. Digital learning is an innovation, so it raises knowledge in improving literacy, including digital literacy, multimedia literacy, information literacy and so on (Bawden, 2008; Jenkins et al., 2006; Lankshear & Knobel, 2008).

Successful efforts to reorganize education for digital students tend to manifest the quality of learning design thinking. Technological progress changes all the time, so educational institutions must always innovate to provide appropriate learning processes, such as digital learning. Some digital technology tools, such as films, radio and television can be positioned as important tools for school reform or transformation (Howard & Mozejko, 2015). The rationale for the integration of digital technology includes raising standards; increasing vocational relevance; contribute to the knowledge-based economy; enrich the learning experience; transforming pedagogy to be more student-centered, constructivist, and with a focus on high-level learning; and facilitating personalized learning (Fullan, 2013; Hammond, 2013; Somekh, 2007; Blundell, Lee, & Nykvist, 2016). Digital technology is also important to meet curriculum requirements and facilitate emerging trends (AiGroup, 2016; Baranyai et al., 2016).

The existence of an internet connection is important in digital learning, and Indonesia has the potential to use it because more than half the population has connectivity to the Internet (APJII, 2019). Although this penetration rate is still far below other developed countries such as Singapore, the development of Internet penetration in Indonesia is relatively fast. Other data from ITU shows that Indonesia still lags behind for the ICT Development Index with 111th rank in the world and 19th in the Asia Pacific (ITU, 2019). The use of the Internet in Indonesia for school-related activities shows a positive tendency because it already occupies the fourth position under chat, social media and looking for work-related information (APJII, 2019). This data indicates that despite the infrastructure readiness, Indonesia already has some proportion of digital literacy among students to support their learning activities. The use to find data related to this school has even been played online games, reading news, watching videos and music. This chapter discusses the context of the integration of digital technology and the challenges associated with implementing digital learning in developing countries, focusing on Indonesia.

THE ROLE OF EDUCATION INSTITUTION IN CREATING DIGITAL ENVIRONMENT

Schools and other educational institutions have laid the foundation in the education system by designing and creating digital-based learning. Technology plays a role in the transformation of education. Technology is able to empower everyone in the education ecosystem to maximize the resources they have. Education 4.0 is education that is influenced by the industrial revolution 4.0, characterized by education utilizing more digital technology (cyber systems) in the learning process. The use of this technology enables the learning process to take place indefinitely in space and time, meaning that the learning process is not only in the classroom and during study, but also anywhere and anytime we can access school learning materials.

Law of the Republic of Indonesia Number 20 of 2003 concerning the National Education System states the use of ICT in education through Distance Education that "(1) Distance education is carried out at all lines, levels and types of education, (2) Distance education functions to provide education services to groups of people who cannot attend face-to-face or regular education, (3) Distance education is organized in the form, mode and scope supported by learning facilities and services as well as an assessment system that ensures the quality of graduates in accordance with national education standards.

Groups, networks and communities are organizational structures that function in a digital learning environment. Some digital learning environments support certain types of organizational structures and create boundaries to maintain them (eg, LMS most often support and maintain groups). This is important because this type of organizational structure impacts learning and teaching in digital learning environments.

The importance of design for digital learning environments cannot be over-emphasized. Learning designers play an important role in working with faculty members, media developers, and researchers in the design and development of digital learning environments and need to carefully consider how to design digital learning environments to foster effective, meaningful and impactful learning experiences (Veletsianos, 2016). According to Wilson (2004), experience [learning] is mediated by technology, so an environmental design for e-learning is needed.

In the era of industrial technology 4.0, higher education institutions are required to create a digital environment in the learning process. Digital learning encourages academics to have digital competencies that illustrate technology-related skills. According to Kavalier and Flannigan (2008), digital literacy represents a person's ability to perform tasks effectively in a digital environment. Aviram and Eshet-Alkalai (2006) describe digital literacy as a combination of technical-procedural, cognitive and emotional skills. Digital fluency and digital literacy are interrelated competencies (White, 2013). Digital fluency as a body of competence and knowledge is needed to be critically involved with online content, while digital literacy is the ability to critically evaluate and understand various sources of online information (White, 2013). Thus, higher education institutions in Indonesia are required to provide a conducive digital environment by encouraging student competence in digital literacy and fluency.

One application in supporting digital learning environments is the distance learning process. LMS (Learning Management System) is one of the popular applications in higher education institutions in providing distance education because it allows institutional control over access. The digital environment most closely related to networks is social networking sites (eg Twitter, Facebook, Instagram, etc), which are defined by Boyd & Ellison (2007) as "web-based services that allow individuals to (1) build public or semi - public profiles in the system are bound, (2) articulate the list of other users with whom they share connections, and (3) view and traverse their list of connections and those made by others in the system. At this time, it is possible to hold distance learning by using internet media to connect between students and lecturers, see student grades online, check finances, view class schedules, send assignment files given by lecturers and so on.

The development and utilization of various kinds of ICT-based games for learning have become a trend in the education sector in the world, including in Indonesia. There have been many ICT practitioners, both independently and in collaboration with education people, developing various learning games. The challenge that arises is how to develop learning games that can truly facilitate student learning effectively. In addition, the development of concepts and technologies that enables mobile learning using information and communication technology devices such as smartphones, tablet computers, iPods, etc., to support the learning process.

Bransford, Brown, & Cocking (1999), summarize four perspectives that can guide the design of effective learning environments, including: Student-centered, where the learning environment must respect the experience, knowledge, attitudes, and culture that students bring to the environment; Knowledge-centered, the learning environment must enable students to become knowledgeable in a discipline and transfer their learning to a new domain, and emphasize common sense to enable students to make connections between goals and information so that they gain a holistic perspective from the discipline they are learning; Assessment-centered, the learning environment must provide assessment (both formative and summative) and feedback, trying to assess understanding and not just the recall of knowledge; and, Community-centered, the learning environment must understand the important role of the surrounding community in creating a learning environment that supports, reflects, and respects the reality, aspirations, and social norms of the community.

Meanwhile, the Ministry of Education and Culture of the Republic of Indonesia (2018), explained that there are five important elements that must be a concern to encourage economic growth and national competitiveness in the Industrial Revolution era 4.0:

1. Preparation of more innovative learning systems in high education, such as adjusting the learning curriculum, and improving students' abilities in terms of Data Information Technology (IT), Operational Technology (OT), Internet of Things (IoT), and Big Data Analytic, integrating physical objects, digital and humans to produce competitive and skilled college graduates especially in the aspects of data literacy, technological literacy and human literacy.
2. Reconstruction of higher education institutional policies that are adaptive and responsive to the industrial revolution 4.0 in developing the trans disciplinary knowledge and study programs needed. In addition, the Cyber University program has begun to be pursued, such as distance learning lecture systems, thereby reducing the intensity of lecturer and student meetings. Cyber University is later expected to be a solution for children of the nation in remote areas to reach high quality higher education.
3. Preparation of human resources, especially lecturers and researchers as well as responsive, adaptive and reliable engineers to deal with the industrial revolution 4.0. In addition, quality improvement through the rejuvenation and development of education, research and innovation infrastructure also needs to be done.

4. Breakthroughs in research and development that support the 4.0 Industrial Revolution and ecosystems to improve the quality and quantity of research and development in universities, R&D institutions, industry, and society.
5. Breakthrough innovation and strengthening innovation systems to increase industrial productivity and improve technology-based startups.

The education sector directly or indirectly will play a large role in the 4.0 industrial revolution. Thus, high education institution must dynamically make changes and adjustments to the education system to create an effective learning environment. According to the Ministry of Education and Culture of the Republic of Indonesia (2018), the education sector must prepare aspects of human resources (HR), which include lecturers, researchers, engineers, teachers, and instructors or tutors in the field of non-school education.

A GLANCE OF EDUCATION IN INDONESIA: INDUSTRY EDUCATION REFORM 4.0

The ministry of education and culture is one of the ministries that have the responsibility in developing Indonesia's human resources because it is a government representative especially in managing primary and secondary education. To elaborate the Nawa Cita program, the Ministry of Education and Culture has six priority programs in the 2015-2019 governance periods.

The Ministry's six priority programs are the Smart Indonesia Program (PIP = Program Indonesia Pintar), Strengthening Character Education (PPK = Penguatan Pendidikan Karakter), Revitalization of Vocational Education, Educational Zoning, Cultural Advancement, and School Digitalization. In general, the aim of these programs is to improve the quality and output of education in Indonesia and to provide access to more equitable education throughout Indonesia, including the frontier, outermost and disadvantaged regions which are often abbreviated as 3T (Terdepan, Terluar, Tertinggal) (Media Indonesia, 2019).

The Smart Indonesia Program is a program aimed at providing equal distribution of education to school-age children from disadvantaged and vulnerable families. With this program, children who become participants will get the opportunity to receive both formal and informal education. Meanwhile, the Character-Building Strengthening Program is a program that emphasizes improving the character of students by involving entities outside the school, namely the community and family. Strengthening the characters targeted by this program includes religious values, nationalism, independence and integrity.

In the field of vocational education, the government through the ministry of education and culture seeks to improve the ability of school graduation in the field of vocational education so that it can have the equivalent ability of graduates from other countries. The capacity building that is the focus of this program is in the areas of productivity and innovation that will lead to an increase in the nation's competitiveness. Indonesia has a huge demographic population at the age of high school education, so it needs to be prepared to face the challenges ahead in the era of the industrial revolution 4.0. These young populations need to improve their competitiveness and be revitalized so that it can become a demographic bonus in the future. Revitalization in the field of vocational education is intended to prepare a workforce that can compete, skilled and relevant to the demands of the world of work. Implementation of this program is carried out through revitalization of Vocational High Schools, various special education and training institutions.

To support the implementation of the Vocational High School revitalization program, the government issued Presidential Instruction No. 9/2016 on Vocational High School Revitalization. The presence of this presidential instruction is considered important to be published given the importance of the role of vocational schools as formal educational institutions in preparing workers who have skills and can compete with other countries. This program is carried out by making efforts to meet the number of productive teachers and increasing the competence of teachers by encouraging certification ownership in accordance with the respective areas of teachers expertise. This certification effort was carried out in collaboration with the National Professional Certification Board (BNSP = Badan Nasional Sertifikasi Profesi) to develop Vocational High School as a certification body. Other efforts to improve the competency of vocational high school graduates are made by forming a teaching factory. The teaching factory was developed by referring to the learning process in the Vocational High School which is based on production and according to standards.

Another problem that exists in the education system in Indonesia is that schools are perceived to be better than other schools in the same area. To overcome this, the government used the zoning approach when new students were recruited. This approach tries to give a higher weight to the distance of the student's house from the school so that it is hoped that students will tend to choose a school that is close to their homes rather than choosing a favorite school. Although this program has several negative impacts, including the small opportunity to get a school for prospective students who are located far from school, but this program has improved every year. The realization of the program in the field of culture is carried out by passing a law on the Advancement of Culture. The implementation of the program is the implementation of regional cultural mind diapers in all provinces.

The last program is an important program that seeks to bridge Indonesia's geographical condition in the form of an archipelago. The School Digitalization Program is a step taken by the government to prepare Indonesia's human resources in entering the era of the industrial revolution 4.0.

DIGITAL LEARNING CHALLENGES IN INDONESIA

Even though the ministry of education already has many programs, but there are challenges to implement Revitalization of Vocational Education and School Digitalization. Those challenges are Indonesian geographic challenge, access gap, and skill set definition for industrial revolution.

a. Indonesian Geographic

The first challenge is Indonesia's geographical location due to the diversity of geographical conditions in Indonesia. Indonesia is the world's largest island country and the 14th largest country by land area, at 1,904,569 square kilometers (735,358 square miles). Indonesia is a developing country consisting of approximately 269.9 million people (Central Statistics Agency, 2018a). The number of islands in Indonesia according to the Central Statistics Agency (2016) reaches 17,504 islands. The most islands are in the province of Riau Islands with the number reaching 2,408 islands, followed by West Papua which has 1,945 islands, North Maluku with 1,474 islands, Maluku with 1,422 islands, and East Nusa Tenggara with 1,192 islands. These geographical conditions have led to the spread of educational facilities in each region.

Indonesia also has massive and historically centralized education system that served well to unify the nation with a common language and a shared national identity (Heyward & Ed. D, 2011). This situation makes delivering equal national standard education become a challenging effort. Based on data from the Central Statistics Agency (2018b), in the 2017/2018 school year, the number of students at the elementary school level was 25.49 million people (56.26%), junior high schools reaching 10.13 million (22.35%), Senior High Schools reached 4.78 million people (10.56%), and Vocational High Schools as many as 4.9 million people (10.83%). The number of Indonesian students under the Ministry of Research, Technology and Higher Education in 2018 is 7 million. The number consists of 4.5 million students of private universities and 2.5 million students of public universities. Meanwhile, the number of school facilities spread across 34 provinces in Indonesia include: 72,237 elementary schools, 37,307 junior high schools, 16,696 senior high schools, 10,409 vocational schools, and 2,988 colleges. However, the distribution of school facilities differs by province, as the highest number of high educations is in West Java with 394 institutions.

In addition, indicators of the level of community education in an area can be seen from the Human Development Index (HDI) which was introduced by the United Nations Development Program (UNDP) in 1990 and published periodically in the annual Human Development Report (HDR) report. The HDI explains how residents can access the results of development in obtaining income, health, education, and so on (Central Statistics Agency, 2018c). HDI is formed by 3 (three) basic dimensions: Longevity and healthy living, Knowledge and Standard of living. Based on geographical location, the first rank of HDI in Indonesia is DKI Jakarta, second and third respectively is DI Yogyakarta and East Kalimantan. Meanwhile the last 3 ranks are the provinces of East Nusa Tenggara, West Papua and Papua. This shows that access to education in Indonesia based on geographical location is still uneven.

Indonesia's geographical position is one of the challenges in equitable access to education. This is the duty of the government in leveling the quality of education in each region; improving infrastructure is a priority to encourage the quality of Indonesian education. Advances in technology have an impact on the quality of education, moreover, now it has entered the digital era that enables digital learning. Information technology infrastructure is one of the key elements to realize Indonesia as a competitive and prosperous country from an economic standpoint.

Based on data from the 2018-2019 Global Competitiveness Index, Indonesia's competitiveness is ranked 50 out of 141 countries (World Economic Forum, 2019), with infrastructure ranked 72. The ranking has declined from the previous year which ranked 45th. Meanwhile, based on data from the IMD World Digital Competitiveness Ranking 2019, Indonesia ranked 56 out of 63 countries (IMD World Competitiveness Center, 2019). The measurement is based on 3 main factors which include knowledge, technology, and future readiness. This indicates that Indonesia's digital competitiveness is still low. Indonesia's internet speed averaged only 20.1 Mbps or the fourth lowest compared to more than 40 other countries. That speed is far below the world average (worldwide), which reached 73.6 Mbps (Hootsuite, 2020). Utilization of high-speed internet access is used to advance education as a strengthening of human resources.

In addition, Indonesia ranks 111th out of 176 countries in the Information and Communication Technology Development Index (IDI) (ITU, 2019). IDI is a standard measure that can describe the level of development of information and communication technology in a region, digital divide, and the potential for ICT development. IDI is compiled by 11 indicators consisting of 3 sub-indexes covering ICT readiness, ICT intensity, and ICT impact. The province with the highest IDI in 2018 is DKI Jakarta, while the lowest is Papua (Central Statistics Agency, 2019).

Some parts of Indonesia have geographical contours in the form of mountains and rivers. This geographical challenge causes obstacles to the development of physical infrastructure including telecommunications infrastructure. Therefore, the government must focus on improving information technology infrastructure to improve Indonesia's competitiveness and address the challenges of uneven education facilities in each region.

b. Access to Education

The second challenge is the gap to access different level of education for all children and its low completion rate. For primary schooling, around 96 per cent of Indonesian children already receive some primary schooling with 80 per cent completion rate primary (UNESCO, 2011). This number is getting lower along with the high level of education. Gross enrolment rates for secondary schooling are around 70 per cent and for higher education 20 per cent with net enrolments are around 50 and 10 per cent respectively.

Indonesia still experiences gaps in infrastructure, teaching staff, and access to technological literacy. This is an obstacle in the implementation of digital learning in Indonesia. Technology is one of the factors that support the educational process and can integrate ecosystems in education. Based on the data that has been explained above that internet access in Indonesia is still included in the low speed category. Indonesia still faces underdeveloped access to information technology, fundamentally due to: first, the operational mastery of teachers in information technology devices; second, not all schools have been able to meet the availability of information technology devices in providing adequate global information access (Lestari, 2015). Meanwhile, based on Hootsuit data (2020), the number of mobile connections in Indonesia reached 338.2 million or 124%. Thus, based on the device used, a smartphone is the main access device. Educational solutions that involve students, parents, teachers, schools, and administrative processes must be adapted to the smartphone platform. In addition, there is a collaborative platform, where all models of stakeholder interaction in the field of education, can be accommodated by technology-based educational platforms that include blended learning with supporting technologies such as Artifical Intelligent and Machine learning (Atmoko, 2020). The Indonesian network industry must strive, together with the application and content industry known as the creative digital industry, to integrally enhance the nation's competitiveness in supporting digital learning in higher education institutions (Pasaribu et al., 2012).

Currently, various educational platforms are widely available, including edtech which provides digital-based educational content with an easy-to-access platform by considering the factors of personalized learning experiences, measuring student performance, improving communication, and UI / UX that are easily accessed by users (Nadhifah, 2019). Another platform provider is Arkademi, a massive open online course (MOOC) platform. In addition, the challenge of access to education is the economic capacity of the people of Indonesia. Thus, digital education platforms are encouraged to be able to provide online-based education supported by the government, for example with online certification for expertise or skills.

c. Industrial Revolution 4.0 Skills

Preparing Industry 4.0 workforce like in the Revitalization of Vocational Education also has its own problem. The challenge is to build skill gap to achieve industrial revolution 4.0 skill that need to be delivered to students. Finding out the skill set for those workforces to meet the industry requirement requires a challenging process since no specific definitive skill set for industry 4.0. The challenges that exist in efforts to improve the ability of human resources in Indonesia require comprehensive problem solving. The concept of technology-based education can provide solutions in overcoming various problems that exist in the field of education in Indonesia. This concept of Education 4.0 is a candidate for a good approach to solve these problems.

Education 4.0 is a response to the needs of Industry Revolution 4.0 where human and technology are aligned to enable new possibilities (Hussin, 2018). Fisk (2017) conveys the need for a new learning vision to encourage students not only to stop learning the skills and knowledge needed but also so that they can identify sources for learning these skills and knowledge. The learning process is built around students by conveying about where and how they should learn and track their performance which is done through personal data-based customization. With this concept, learning with friends is a very important factor in their learning process because they will learn together and exchange information with each other. On the other hand, the role of the teacher turns to become a facilitator for their learning process. For this reason, the implementation of Education 4.0 needs to be supported and followed up with by increasing teacher competency.

Increased competence is needed, especially in the field of mastery of information and communication technology (ICT). Teachers can improve their competence by learning, both with instructors, independent learning, or learning with colleagues in teacher associations. In the concept of Education 4.0 the role of the teacher becomes increasingly important and vital because the teacher does not only teach, but must also understand and direct resources where children can learn. In other word, the teacher functions as a link between students and learning resources.

The role of the teacher as a facilitator makes the teacher must be able to facilitate, find relevant resource persons so that students can connect and learn from them, and facilitate the learning facilities needed by students. Given its role as a link with learning resources, on the other hand, the teacher must also be able to be a filter for existing learning information. The teacher must be able to filter out what information is needed and what information students should avoid.

The use of internet technology has become important in relation to the implementation of education 4.0. The use of the internet allows broad access for students in various places across the country. This opportunity arises by looking at the fact that the development of internet users in Indonesia already has better penetration. In 2018, more than 170 million Indonesians already have Internet access, which means that internet penetration in Indonesia is already more than 60% (APJII, 2019). The existence of this internet access increases the chance of using technology to solve existing problems. However, the availability of an internet connection only gives access and will not be useful without the availability of adequate learning facilities as an interface for students to learn material available through the internet.

The School Digitization Program is planned to be realized to 31,387 schools through the affirmation of school operational assistance and 5,987 schools through the performance of school performance assistance. Through this program, the Government will provide learning facilities in schools in the form of tablet computers to 1,753,000 students in grade VI, class VII, and class X throughout Indonesia, especially schools in the foremost, outermost and most remote areas. Indonesia internet user main proportion is in the age range of 15-19 with 91% of them already gaining access to the Internet. This is also a supporting factor for making internet-based technology solutions in Indonesia very potential to reach school age groups. This group is the main target of the capability and output improvement program for students from the Ministry of Education and Culture. Although internet penetration in Indonesia is getting better, it is still not optimal, especially for urban areas. Penetration of internet users still needs to be improved, especially in rural areas, which currently have a population of 38.4% that still do not have internet access. This condition is different from urban areas where the number of non-internet users is 25.9% smaller (APJII, 2019).

After fulfilling the access and user devices, the other thing that needs to be prepared is the learning content. Although the Indonesian government has provided a variety of learning content, there are significant challenges in creating this content. Research conducted by Agustina & Fajar (2018) shows that there are problems in the effectiveness of learning using the concept of Education 4.0 due to the lack of consistent student interest in learning the material. For this reason, content that interests learning is an important factor in the concept of Education 4.0. Students perform relatively independent learning activities together with other students in learning Education 4.0. This means that the role of content that can arouse interest in learning is very important.

Figure 1. Indonesian internet user penetration 2018 (based on age)
(Source: APJII, 2019)

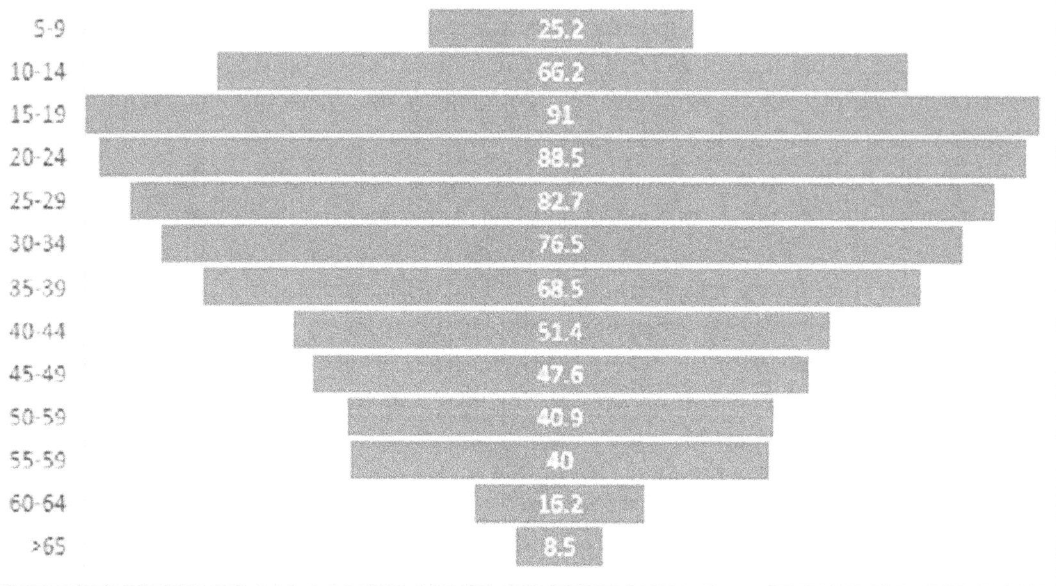

Source: APJII (2019)

One important factor in creating interesting learning content is the type of content. The APJII Survey (2019) shows that the main use of the internet is to communicate via messages or chat at 24.7% and followed by the use of the internet to carry out activities on social media at 18.9%. Social media also plays an important role for knowledge sharing (Sari & Prasetio, 2017; Eid & Al-Jabri;2016; Cevik, Aksel, Akoglu, Eroglu, Dogan, & Altunci, 2016; Prasetio, 2014) so it is important to use it in education. For this reason, learning content creators need to consider involving these channels in learning content. Another interesting fact revealed from the same survey, where the type of content that is widely accessed by internet users in Indonesia is related to the activity of watching movies / videos by 45.3% followed by playing games by 17.1%. By considering this situation, the content created needs to accommodate the type of video content in the form of storytelling and implementing gamification in the prepared learning content.

The issue of adjusting curriculum to industry needs has become a longstanding issue in the world of education since it will improve the quality of education to enhance economic development and better compete in a globalization (Haridza & Irving, 2017). The geographical condition of Indonesia, which is in the form of an archipelagic country, also increases the level of difficulty in creating curricula that are appropriate to the needs of each region and industry. Indonesia's unique geographical condition coupled with its very diverse economic potential requires an appropriate curriculum development approach in order to support the success of Education 4.0.

Samini (2018) offers the use of a concept proposed by King and Palmer (2010) as a solution. Vocational education needs to be adjusted to the potential that exists in the area where schools are located in order to be able to support one another. Vocational education institutions will find it easier to get partners where they do practical work and vice versa, the industry will get a workforce that suits their needs. The vocational education curriculum must have flexibility in modular and block form and can be integrated between formal and non-formal education. Furthermore, Samini (2018) offers a solution using Commodity-based vocational education development (CBVED) which is considered appropriate in the context of vocational education in Indonesia.

Another approach that needs to be developed is to increase the role and use of online certification bodies. Certification is an important factor in providing workers who have standards and meet certain criteria in accordance with their fields. Certification, along with education and experience is important for the industry (Earnhardt, Newcomer, Watkins, & Marion, 2014). With good certification, the industry can more easily find workers who have the special skills needed. Similar to the digital learning approach that has been discussed previously, the certification process needs to be encouraged so that more use of technology, especially the internet. With these approaches, it is hoped that educational institutions, both formal and non-formal, will be able to develop a curriculum that is more flexible and ultimately can improve the competitiveness of Indonesian workers in meeting the needs of Industry 4.0

CONCLUSION

Education in Indonesia faces many challenges. Among of them are, Indonesian geographic challenge caused by the diversity geographical condition in Indonesia, the gap to access different level of education for all children and its low completion rate and building skill gap to achieve industrial revolution 4.0 skill that need to be delivered to students. Education 4.0 is a good candidate approach to answer those challenges but need some important improvement to match the unique situation in Indonesia. The use of internet technology using digital learning could give access to widely spread students across the country, but the penetration still need some improvement especially in rural area. Creating content that is appropriate by using messages, channels, social media platforms, and formats that accommodate video storytelling and gamification are also important for the success of Education 4.0. Commodity-based vocational education development approach could deliver skill set that match local based industry 4.0 by delivering flexible curriculum and need to be supported by online certification.

REFERENCES

Agustina, D., & Fajar, D. A. (2018, July). Learner Autonomy as a Challenge in English Language Education 4.0 in Indonesia. *English Language and Literature International Conference (ELLiC) Proceedings*, *2*, 155–159.

AiGroup. (2016). *STEM programme index 2016*. Retrieved from http://www.chiefscientist.gov.au/wp-content/uploads/SPI2016_release.pdf

APJII. (2019). *Penetrasi & Profil Perilaku Pengguna Internet Indonesia*. https://www.apjii.or.id/survei

Atmoko, B. D. (2020). *Tantangan Transformasi Digital Dunia Pendidikan di Indonesia*. Retrieved from https://gizmologi.id/news/tantangan-transformasi-digital-dunia-pendidikan-di-indonesia/

Baranyai, K., Bowles, J., Hassan, S., Prinsley, R., Smith, P., & Walter, C. (2016). *Australia's STEM Workforce*. Retrieved from http://www.chiefscientist.gov.au/wp-content/uploads/Australias-STEMWorkforce_for-distribution.pdf

Bawden, D. (2008). Origins and concepts of digital literacy. *Digital literacies: Concepts, policies and practices, 30*(2008), 17-32.

Bennett, S., Maton, K., & Kervin, L. (2008). The 'digital natives' debate: A critical review of the evidence. *British Journal of Educational Technology*, *39*(5), 775–786. doi:10.1111/j.1467-8535.2007.00793.x

Blundell, C., Lee, K. T., & Nykvist, S. S. (2016). Digital learning in schools: Conceptualizing the challenges and influences on teacher practice. *Journal of Information Technology Education*, *15*, 535–560. doi:10.28945/3578

Boyd, D. M., & Ellison, N. B. (2007). Social network sites: Definition, history, and scholarship. *Journal of Computer-Mediated Communication*, *13*(1), 210–230. doi:10.1111/j.1083-6101.2007.00393.x

Brown, J. S., & Duguid, P. (2000). Balancing act: How to capture knowledge without killing it. *Harvard Business Review*, *78*(3), 73–73. PMID:11183980

Burdick, A., & Willis, H. (2011). Digital learning, digital scholarship and design thinking. *Design Studies*, *32*(6), 546–556. doi:10.1016/j.destud.2011.07.005

Central Statistic Agency. (2016). *Jumlah Pulau di Indonesia Menurut Provinsi.* Retrieved from https://databoks.katadata.co.id/datapublish/2018/10/16/berapa-jumlah-pulau-di-indonesia

Central Statistic Agency. (2018a). *Kependudukan*. Retrieved from https://www.bps.go.id/subject/12/kependudukan.html#subjekViewTab3

Central Statistic Agency. (2018b). *Pendidikan*. Retrieved from https://www.bps.go.id/subject/28/pendidikan.html#subjekViewTab3

Central Statistic Agency. (2018c). *Indeks Pembangunan Manusia*. Retrieved from https://www.bps.go.id/subject/26/indeks-pembangunan-manusia.html#subjekViewTab3

Central Statistic Agency. (2019). *Indeks Pembangunan Teknologi, Informasi, dan Komunikasi 2018*. Retrieved from https://www.bps.go.id/publication/2019/11/29/0328ba9a85b461816e917291/indeks-pembangunan-teknologi--informasi--dan-komunikasi-2018.html

Cevik, A. A., Aksel, G., Akoglu, H., Eroglu, S. E., Dogan, N. O., & Altunci, Y. A. (2016). Social media, FOAMed in medical education and knowledge sharing: Local experiences with international perspective. *Turkish Journal of Emergency Medicine, 16*(3), 112-117.

Earnhardt, M. P., Newcomer, J. M., Watkins, D. V., & Marion, J. W. (2014). An inquiry into the aviation management education paradigm shift. *International Journal of Aviation, Aeronautics, and Aerospace, 1*(4), 7.

Eid, M. I., & Al-Jabri, I. M. (2016). Social networking, knowledge sharing, and student learning: The case of university students. *Computers & Education, 99*, 14–27. doi:10.1016/j.compedu.2016.04.007

Fisk, P. (2017). *Education 4.0 … the future of learning will be dramatically different, in school and throughout life*. Retrieved from http://www.thegeniusworks.com/2017/01/future-education-young-everyone-taught-together

Fullan, M. (2013). *Stratosphere: Integrating technology, pedagogy, and change knowledge*. Pearson Canada.

Gasser, U., & Palfrey, J. (2008). *Born digital-connecting with a global generation of digital natives*. Perseus.

Hammond, M. (2014). Introducing ICT in schools in England: Rationale and consequences. *British Journal of Educational Technology, 45*(2), 191–201. doi:10.1111/bjet.12033

Haridza, R., & Irving, K. E. (2017). The Evolution of Indonesian and American Science Education Curriculum: A Comparison Study. *Educare (San José), 9*(2).

Heyward, M., & Sopantini. (2011). *Indonesia, the challenges of quality and equity in education*. doi:10.15730/books.7

Hootsuite. (2020). *Global Report: Indonesia*. Retrieved from https://hootsuite.com/id/pages/digital-2020

Howard, S. K., & Mozejko, A. (2015). Teachers: technology, change and resistance. *Teaching and digital technologies: Big issues and critical questions*, 307-317.

Hussin, A. A. (2018). Education 4.0 made simple: Ideas for teaching. *International Journal of Education and Literacy Studies, 6*(3), 92–98. doi:10.7575/aiac.ijels.v.6n.3p.92

IMD World Competitiveness Center. (2019). *IMD World Digital Competitiveness Ranking 2019*. IMD World Competitiveness Center.

Iswanto, Y. (2016). Menciptakan Lingkungan Pembelajaran yang Memperkuat Teknologi. In *Institusi Pendidikan Tinggi di Era Digital: Pemikiran, Permodelan dan Praktek Baik* (pp. 7–24). Universitas Terbuka, Tangerang Selatan.

Ito, M., Baumer, S., Bittanti, M., boyd, d., Cody, R., & Herr-Stephenson, B. (2009). Hanging out, messing around, and geeking out: Kids living and learning with new media. Cambridge: The MIT Press.

ITU. (2019). *ICT Development Index 2017.* Retrieved from https://www.itu.int/net4/ITU-D/idi/2017/index.html

Jenkins, H. (2007). *Reconsidering digital immigrants.* Message posted to http://www.henryjenkins.org

Kennedy, G. E., Judd, T. S., Churchward, A., Gray, K., & Krause, K. L. (2008). First year students' experiences with technology: Are they really digital natives? *Australasian Journal of Educational Technology*, *24*(1). Advance online publication. doi:10.14742/ajet.1233

King, K., & Palmer, R. (2010). *Planning for Teachnical and Vocational Skills Development.* Unesco International Institute for Educational Planning.

Kominfo. (2019). *Digitalisasi Sekolah Percepat Perluasan Akses Pendidikan Berkualitas di Daerah 3T.* https://kominfo.go.id/index.php/content/detail/22211/digitalisasi-sekolah-percepat-perluasan-akses-pendidikan-berkualitas-di-daerah-3t/0/artikel_gpr

Kompas. (2014). *"Nawa Cita", 9 Agenda Prioritas Jokowi-JK.* https://nasional.kompas.com/read/2014/05/21/0754454/.Nawa.Cita.9.Agenda.Prioritas.Jokowi-JK

Kvavik, R. B., Caruso, J. B., & Morgan, G. (2004). *ECAR Study Of Students And Information Technology 2004: Convenience, Connection, and Control.* EDUCAUSE Center for Applied Research. http://www.educause.edu/ir/library/pdf/ers0405/rs/ers0405w.pdf

Lankshear, C. J., & Knobel, M. (2008). *Introduction: digital literacies: concepts, policies and practices.* Peter Lang Publishing.

Lestari, N. T. (2015). *Tantangan Masa Depan Pendidikan di Indonesia dan Pendidikan Global.* Retrieved from https://www.kompasiana.com/noviana-trilestari/5511408ba333116642ba8084/a-tantangan-masa-depan-pendidikan-di-indonesia-dan-pendidikan-global

Media Indonesia, Enam Program Pendidikan di Nawacita Jadi Prioritas, Minggu 20 Oktober. (2019). https://mediaindonesia.com/read/detail/266451-enam-program-pendidikan-di-nawacita-jadi-prioritas

Ministry of Education and Culture of the Republic of Indonesia. (2018). *Pembiayaan Operasional Non Personalia untuk Optimalisasi Mutu Lulusan SMK. Directorate of Vocational High School Development.* Directorate General of Primary and Secondary Education, and Ministry of Education and Culture, Republic of Indonesia.

Munir. (2017). *Pembelajaran Digital.* Bandung: Alfabeta, CV.

Nadhifah, A. (2019). *Bagaimana Edtech Indonesia Mudahkan Akses Pendidikan bagi Pengguna.* Retrieved from https://id.techinasia.com/bagaimana-edtech-permudah-akses-pendidikan

Oliver, B., & Goerke, V. (2007). Australian undergraduates' use and ownership of emerging technologies: Implications and opportunities for creating engaging learning experiences for the Net Generation. *Australasian Journal of Educational Technology*, *23*(2). Advance online publication. doi:10.14742/ajet.1263

Pasaribu, R. D., Kartini, D., Oesman, Y. M., & Padmadisastra, S. (2016). The effect of customer demand and supplier performance in competitive strategy and business performance (Case of fixed broadband in Indonesia). *International Journal of Scientific & Technology Research*, *5*(2), 123–129.

Permatasari, A., & Anggadwita, G. (2019). Digital Entrepreneurship Education in Emerging Countries: Opportunities and Challenges. In Opening Up Education for Inclusivity Across Digital Economies and Societies (pp. 156-169). IGI Global.

Prasetio, A. (2014). Understanding knowledge sharing and social capital in social network sites. *International Journal of Science and Research*, *3*(3), 760–766.

Prensky, M. (2001). Digital natives, digital immigrants. *On the Horizon, 9*(5). http://www.marcprensky.com/writing/ Prensky-DigitalNatives,DigitalImmigrants-Part1.pdf

Samani, M. (2018, July). Vocational Education in the Era of Industry 4.0: An Indonesia Case. In *International Conference on Indonesian Technical Vocational Education and Association (APTEKINDO 2018)*. Atlantis Press. 10.2991/aptekindo-18.2018.10

Sari, P. K., & Prasetio, A. (2017). Knowledge sharing and electronic word of mouth to promote information security awareness in social network site. In *2017 International Workshop on Big Data and Information Security (IWBIS)* (pp. 113-117). IEEE. 10.1109/IWBIS.2017.8275111

Somekh, B. (2007). *Pedagogy and learning with ICT: Researching the art of innovation*. Routledge. doi:10.4324/9780203947005

United Nations Education Scientific and Cultural Organization (UNESCO). (2011). *EFA Global Monitoring Report 2011: Regional Overview East Asia and the Pacific*. http://unesdoc.unesco.org/images/0019/001917/191719E.pdf

Veletsianos, G. (2016). Digital learning environments. Wiley Handbook of Learning Technology, 242-260.

Wedman, J., & Diggs, L. (2001). Identifying barriers to technology-enhanced learning environments in teacher education. *Computers in Human Behavior*, *17*(4), 421–430. doi:10.1016/S0747-5632(01)00012-7

White, G. K. (2013). *Digital fluency: Skills necessary for learning in the digital age. Australian Council for Educational Research*. ACER.

Wilson, B. G. (1995). Metaphors for instruction: Why we talk about learning environments. *Educational Technology*, *35*(5), 25–30.

Wilson, B. G. (2004). Designing e-learning environments for flexible activity and instruction. *Educational Technology Research and Development*, *52*(4), 77–84. doi:10.1007/BF02504720

World Economic Forum. (2019). *The Global Competitiveness Report 2019*. Retrieved from http://www3.weforum.org/docs/WEF_TheGlobalCompetitivenessReport2019.pdf

Chapter 5
Women Empowerment Through ICT

Vandana Singh
Bhartiya Skill Development University, India

Pallavi Mathur
https://orcid.org/0000-0003-1019-4948
Bhartiya Skill Development University, India

ABSTRACT

ICT has the biggest potential today to become a key vehicle for the socio-economic advancement of women. There exists a plethora of opportunities for ICTs to improve women's economic activities in the field of trade, governance, education, health, crafts, employment in formal as well as informal sectors. It can be used to fight many social issues and to empower weaker segments of society. The purpose of this chapter is to examine the opportunities which ICT can provide to improve the life of a woman in India. It will include the voices which speak of how women can fully participate and benefit from ICT and how ICT can be used as a tool to empower women. Women also should have an equal advantage of technology and the use of ICT should not be restricted to the upper section of the society. The aim here is to explore how women in India can improve their lives by using ICT. At last, it will also suggest ways on how all the segments of the female population can have benefited from technology.

INTRODUCTION

Information and Communication Technologies (ICT) has the potential to expedite the process of women empowerment by facilitating access to education, information, occupational opportunities, market information, financial services, information about appropriate government programmes, health agencies and workers, feedback mechanism and support system and networking. Brown & Brown (2008) defines ICT as an umbrella term that includes all technologies like computers, smartphones, social media application which enable communication of information in the digital world. Scholars have identified ICT as a tool to facilitate women empowerment in emerging economies (Crittenden et al., 2019). In a developing na-

DOI: 10.4018/978-1-7998-4972-8.ch005

Copyright © 2021, IGI Global. Copying or distributing in print or electronic forms without written permission of IGI Global is prohibited.

tion, empowering women will improve household welfare, ensure better education, poverty reduction, and decreased violence. Cumulatively, this will have a positive impact on the social and fiscal health of the country. The rural population of India has not been able to reap the benefits of ICT to its full potential. However, urban India has had better access to the same. Though there have been considerable efforts in the recent past to facilitate empowerment through ICT, one need to explore the real impact on women, specifically in the rural areas in the Indian context. Efforts are being made by the government, civil society organizations and public/private agencies to empower women and girls through education, funding, participation and involvement in all spheres of activities for socio-economic development. ICT can facilitate the empowerment of women by ensuring their mainstreaming in the economic, political, technological and social environment. This paper discusses the economic empowerment of women through ICT in India and also explores the steps being taken by the government, non-government and other organizations, businesses, to empower them through ICT.

OBJECTIVE

The purpose of this paper is to indicate the relationship between ICT and the empowerment of rural women through secondary data. The aim is to study and analyze previous studies based on similar themes.

METHODOLOGY

In this study, secondary data has been collected from various sources, e.g. websites of various ministries of the Government of India, books, and journals, among others for analysis. Functional schemes of the Government that use multimodality and ICT for empowering minorities, especially women, have been taken for evaluation. We searched Scopus, Web of Science, Science Direct, Emerald, Taylor and Francis databases to search peer-reviewed literature. Google Scholar search engine was used for the literature review. Following keywords were used to search for the related articles - ICT*, Women*, Empowerment, Information and Communication Technology. The Boolean operator OR and AND were used to combine all the terms. Our Scopus search used the following keywords: Role*, Women empowerment*, and was combined with ICT to narrow our results. In both the databases, we limited our search to journals written in English.

LITERATURE REVIEW

Women empowerment through ICT has captured the imagination of various individuals, scholars, enterprises and development organizations across the globe. The aim of the present literature review is to provide readers with a discussion of studies that encompass the use of ICT to empower women as perceived from researchers and women perspective. The majority of these studies have investigated how digital technologies have improved the condition of women.

Abdulwaheed et al. (2016)_presented the role of ICT in agriculture knowledge management. The focus of this study is on the penetration of ICT in Nigeria and strategies to be adopted for enhancement of research and development in agriculture.

Hilbert (2011) analyzed whether there is a difference between men's and women's access to and use of ICT in developing countries. Data were analyzed from 12 Latin American and 13 African countries from 2005 to 2008. It revealed that in developing countries fewer women access and use ICT due to their unfavorable conditions to employment, education and income. If these variables are controlled, women turn out to be a more active user of digital tools than men. Also, it was found that digital technologies are tools that can improve living conditions, and tackle longstanding challenges of gender inequalities, including access to employment, income, education and health services.

Obayelu & Ogunlade (2006) analyzes the use of ICT for gender empowerment and poverty alleviation in Nigeria. They describe the roles that ICT has played in the lives of the poor and the untapped in Nigeria, and how ICT can assist women in addressing chronic issues of widespread poverty.

Hussain & Amin (2018) conducted a study in Afghanistan to explore how women empowerment is conceptualized in relation to ICT and also the use of ICT in processes to support empowerment. It was observed that women in Afghanistan have high hopes that ICT will be enabling and empowering. Although, the majority of women are of the view that ICT does not enable them to challenge patriarchal power relations. However, few are of the view that ICT can put a dent in patriarchal power, and support women empowerment.

Best & Maier (2007) conducted a study in the five villages of in Tamil Nadu to explore how women view and use ICT. Structured in-depth interview was conducted among women who use the internet and those who have never used it. The purpose was to systematically document the information and communication needs of women as expressed by women themselves. The research found that women found ICT useful. There were also gender-specific usage patterns and perceptions of ICT. The scholars found that the reasons for not using the internet were related to lack of time, location and illiteracy. It was concluded that ICTs had the potential for development and poverty reduction in south. However, in order to reap the benefits of technology, it is crucial to understand the specific need of women.

Mehra et al. (2004) presented the findings of three digital divide studies in their paper. One of the studies focused on African-American Women and aimed to understand how these women incorporate computers and the internet into their daily lives in a way that is meaningful to them. It was revealed that training black women to search for relevant health information on internet has proved to be empowering as they no longer depend on upon information specialists or librarians for carrying out the task. It has also helped them to upgrade their skills and be more confident.

Parveen & Gouda (2020) evaluated the various Government of India schemes oriented-towards the empowerment of females from the Muslim community and other minority groups. This study was conducted to evaluate these schemes and give valuable inputs for the policymakers engaged in minority upliftment. The authors concluded that though these schemes are theoretically sound, the challenge always lies in their proper implementation.

(Suvarna, (2020) analyzed how the digital transformation will help in the social and economic development of women. The purpose of this study was to focus on the current ICT development and its impact on women empowerment in India. It was observed that ICT, through e-learning tools, can be used to educate rural women to enhance their skill and to build their self-confidence. This is especially important as women in rural areas have certain skills, but because of their illiteracy or lack of knowledge about the demand for their product, they do not get an appropriate return for their product.

ICT INITIATIVES OF THE GOVERNMENT OF INDIA

Government of India has significantly contributed in the process of women empowerment through ICT. Few of the initiative by government of India are mentioned below:

(*Rajasthan Population (2019/2020*) Rajasthan is a state with a population close to 80 million. With its vast resources, diversity, strategic location, and entrepreneurial spirit of its people, Rajasthan has unlimited potential for development and growth. The major challenges include poverty, illiteracy, female foeticide, girl child marriage, caste prejudices, crimes against women and inadequate rural infrastructure. Despite these challenges, Rajasthan is rapidly becoming one of the leading agents of digital change in India. Today, the state is making considerable strides in digital transformation across sectors and cross-sections of society. While, on the one hand, it has emerged as a leading hub for startups in the country with iStart programme. On the other, it is driving e-governance at various levels, bringing digital technology where it really matters like women empowerment through Bhamashah Yojana and e-Sakhi and is helping employ local youth through *e-Mitra.*

Furthermore, at the cornerstone of these initiatives is the state government's Rajnet. This network is set to cover all 9,894 gram panchayats and 183 municipal areas along with all district and block headquarters in the state. The number of internet users in Rajasthan was the highest among rural areas in India at 7.3 million as of January 31, 2016 (6.47% share in all India) and second only to West Bengal, according to the Government Data ("Rural Subscriber Base of Internet Users as on 31.01.2016," n.d.)

In January 2017, the Rajasthan government partnered with global networking giant Cisco to facilitate video-enabled digital classrooms in women's colleges across the state to cover 10,000 women students by 2018. While this helped build a solid foundation for the progress of women in the state, the government also provided them with entrepreneurship opportunities.

E-SAKHI

E-Sakhi is a digital literacy programme initiated by the Department of Information Technology and Communication (DoITC), Government of Rajasthan, to make every individual in the state digitally literate. Under e-Sakhi, the government will leverage the state's "girl power", wherein young women in the age group of 20-35 will act as patrons in charting the course of a Digital Rajasthan. The Rajasthan Knowledge Corporation Limited (RKCL) centres had also conducted free basic computer training for women. As a part of the programme, approximately 31,398 women in Rajasthan were made digitally literate in 2016-17.

KRISHI VIGYAN KENDRA: EMPOWERING FARMERS WITH TECH AND DIGITAL TOOLS

Krishi Vigyan Kendra (KVK), are district-level institutions helping farmers with the latest agricultural technologies. Out of the 1,600 villages in and around Bharatpur, about 1,400 to 1,500 are in touch with the KVK. The center aspires to familiarize at least 10-15 farmers from each block with the Digital India mission. With a view to help farmers make the most of a farming season, the KVK sends voice and text messages regularly to farmers on best practices to grow crops, use of pesticides, climate information, etc. Digitalisation is a boon for even uneducated farmers who cannot read because they can watch videos to understand applications of technology in agriculture. The centre even has automated weather stations in place to help disseminate information about rain to the farmers in different areas. Apart from this, the centre also conducts sewing classes for women, and trains women and youth in horticulture, thus facilitating not only learning but also improving their chances of making a livelihood.

NATIONAL AGRICULTURE MARKET

National agriculture market initiative is an online trading platform for agricultural commodities in India. It has immensely helped farmers by eliminating middlemen and getting fair prices. Through this initiative, the farmers have also become aware of the prevailing prices of different produces in various *mandis*. This information enables them to sell their produce at the best price. The Rajasthan government is striving to empower each block with small-scale technologies, both software and hardware, so that farmers are updated on new farming techniques.

COMPUTERIZED MILK COLLECTION CENTERS

Managed by the Gujarat Cooperative Milk Marketing Federation (GCMMF), Amul is a nationally recognised brand name. The entity is a cooperative of over 3 million small farmers in the state of Gujarat. Over 80 per cent of the profits are received directly by farmers. While the whole region has benefited from the cooperative, women have especially profited from this venture. They have gained considerable economic independence that has not only empowered them but also allowed them to participate more actively in domestic matters and decision-making.

Most of the dairy-related activities are usually taken care of by the women of the state. According to a report, the number of female cooperative members had increased from 0.22 million in 1981 to 3.7 million in 2008. The cooperative movement has resulted in the empowerment of numerous women entrepreneurs by making them become contribute financially in their families. This also resulted in the improvement of the status of women and the male-female ratio. With subsequent infrastructural and educational advancement in the state, this business model was widely studied and appreciated. The use of ICT in rural areas by Amul has changed the operations of the dairy industry. While it has always been argued that investments related to ICT made in rural India are not effective, the case of Amul proves that "where there is a will, there is a way".

Amul has become rural India's flag bearer in the IT revolution. This system makes it easy for the farmers to get the cash payment as soon as the milk is delivered. The Amul experience indicates that, if properly designed and implemented, the rural poor can benefit from ICT platforms. Customisation of IT platforms for use in rural communities is emerging as a major opportunity for change. (Bowonder et al., 2005)

THE GYANDOOT PROJECT IN MADHYA PRADESH

The Gyandoot project was initiated in January 2000 at the Dhar district of Madhya Pradesh. It was established as an e-commerce and e-governance activity with the objective of providing useful information to people in rural areas and to act as an interface between the district government and citizens. It is an intranet project connecting 21 rural cybercafés called Soochanalayas. Each Soochanalayas provides services to about 10 to 15 gram panchayats, 20 to 30 villages, and 20,000 to 30,000 citizens. Women benefit from such interventions as now they have a greater understanding and control over the local processes. They may file complaints regarding common public grievances through the net, and an e-mail reply is assured within seven days. Provision of this basic information to the women communities ensures their greater awareness and interest about governance issues leading to their greater involvement. (Aggrawal et al., 2002)

FOOD INDIA

Foundation of Occupation Development (FOOD) India is a 35-year-old non-profit organisation conducting research on social development and implementing welfare programs in the field of water and sanitation, employment generation, poverty alleviation, cost-effective housing, education, health, energy conservation, ICTs, institutional and capacity building for women networks. FOOD implemented an e-Marketers project in partnership with CAPART (An autonomous society under the Ministry of Rural Development, Government of India).

The focus of this project is on e-commerce as a means to improve the economic condition of the rural artisans by marketing their products online. Towards this end, the project has established an e-commerce website to promote the sale of products made by rural artisans and cooperatives.

One more project, Inter-City Marketing Network of Women Entrepreneurs through a cell phone in partnership with infoDev establishes a closed group communication network for community-based women organisations to promote inter-city direct sales of products made by artisans and skilled workers. This is accomplished by providing the community-based organisations (CBOs) with communications links by way of cellular phones to enable them to network for marketing their products.

AKSHAYA PROJECT

The Akshaya project, first started in the rural Malappuram district of Kerala, India, and now implemented throughout the state, was the first district-wide e-literacy project in India, with a specific focus on female literacy and economic empowerment of women, and one of the largest known Internet Protocol (IP) based wireless networks in the world. In November 2002, the state government of Kerala put into place a project, piloted in Malappuram, with the goal of at least one person in every family to be computer literate in that district. Malappuram is now what is said to be India's First e-literate district. The mission continues with its efforts to make Kerala the first e-literate state in the country.

MEASURES ADOPTED BY VARIOUS ORGANISATIONS FOR EMPOWERMENT

With various initiatives aimed at using technology for women empowerment, the IT sector can be said to have marked the path. Several large IT companies have women-friendly policies encouraging women from various walks of life to achieve economic independence and self-identity. Infosys Technologies Limited, for instance, employs almost 33 per cent of the women in their workforce. They have a special women cell called IWIN (Infosys Women Inclusivity Initiative) to encourage women participation in the business operation. It also takes care of the welfare activities for women.

IBM India Pvt. Ltd. is one of the forerunners in introducing flexible working hours for women, including work from home facilities, extended maternity leaves and leadership councils. With the help of advanced technology, these working women can access their systems and information from anywhere and deliver their work targets. Considering that the family is generally an additional responsibility for women in India, this is certainly an empowering tool as they do not have to quit their jobs and can continue to work and even financially support their families.

Tel-Nek is an organisation based in Ramavaram, Bangalore Rural. It provides computer training to both women and men in the area. They aim to reduce rural-to-urban migration and empower disadvantaged groups through *emerging, innovative ICT models*. As an industrial belt surrounds the area of intervention, the training provided by Tel-Nek centres in locally adapted software has been extremely useful in ensuring that most women get jobs in administrative and data-entry positions, without having to migrate from their communities.

The progress in technology has also become a tool of social empowerment for women addressing their strongest concerns such as safety and timely help in the need of emergency. Such interventions are often a lifesaver during times of emergencies. Keeping in view the safety issues, many organisations have launched safety apps. Accenture, an IT giant, has launched safety apps for smartphones and dedicated services such as “Vahini” for women employees and 24X7 emergency helpline for women. The Government of India launched ‘Nirbhaya’ app some time ago for women as emergency support during distress. Needless to say that women safety is an important concern in India and ICT has played a major role in helping women during an emergency. Other mobile applications such as ‘Mysafetipin’ (a map-based safety app); Citizen COP (location-based safety app); Eyewatch SOS for Women have supported the cause of women safety and empowerment across the country.

FUTURE RESEARCH DIRECTIONS

There are immense study and research opportunities in the field of women economic empowerment through ICT. In future, empirical studies may be conducted to verify the validity of various government schemes, how successfully the various Govt. schemes have been implemented. In addition combination of both qualitative and quantitative study based on data retrieved through questionnaire and also from face to face interview from rural women may be conducted to reveal deeper motives, beliefs and thoughts.

CONCLUSION

Any country that wishes to attain holistic development goal cannot achieve its dreams without empowering its womenfolk. In the social fabric of India, women have a critical role to play. The socially, economically empowered women are the strongest base of a well-developed nation. In the Indian context, empowerment of women, particularly in rural areas is the necessity today. Basic human rights like education, nutrition and health are luxuries for millions of girls across the country. There are a plethora of girls in the rural areas who drop out from the school and end up in employment or doing household chores. Female feticide, domestic violence, early marriages, gender-based discrimination at workplace is some of the challenge's women face even today. When women are educated and empowered, families become happier. Employed women help their families in breaking the cycle of poverty. The ICT revolution is an essential vehicle for disseminating information and providing education and employment opportunities for the masses. Empowerment of women and girls through ICT is an integral part of this revolution. Awareness, training, skill development, funding and the scale of operation are the prerequisites for such an exercise. There are plenty of challenges which could easily be addressed with the usage of technology. A ray of hope is there as the general education level, and awareness level for ICT in women and girls is increasing by the day, and many organizations are actively taking part in this.

REFERENCES

Abdulwaheed, A., Paul, O. T., & Alu, F. (2016). The Complimentary Role of Information Communication Technology (ICT) in Agricultural Knowledge Management in Nigeria. *Journal of Agricultural Sciences*, *6*(5), 173–179.

Aggrawal, A., Dongre, A., Jafri, A., Shrivastava, S., Tripathi, V. N., & Overseas Development Institute. (2002). *Information communication technologies and governance: The Gyandoot experiment in Dhar District of Madhya Pradesh, India*. ODI. http://www.odi.org.uk/publications/wp160.pdf

Best, M. L., & Maier, S. (2007). Gender, Culture and ICT Use in Rural South India. *Gender, Technology and Development*, *11*(2), 137–155. doi:10.1177/097185240701100201

Bowonder, B., Prasad, B. R. R., & Kotla, A. (2005). ICT application in a dairy industry: The e-experience of Amul. *International Journal of Services Technology and Management*, *6*(3/4/5), 241.

Brown, W., & Brown, I. (2008). Next generation ICT policy in South Africa: Towards a human development-based ICT policy. In C. Avgerou, M. L. Smith, & P. van der Besselaar (Eds.), *Social Dimensions Of Information And Communication Technology Policy* (Vol. 282, pp. 109–123). doi:10.1007/978-0-387-84822-8_8

Crittenden, V. L., Crittenden, W. F., & Ajjan, H. (2019). Empowering women micro-entrepreneurs in emerging economies: The role of information communications technology. *Journal of Business Research*, *98*, 191–203. doi:10.1016/j.jbusres.2019.01.045

Gupta, P., Jain, S., & Vashishth, N. (2017). e-governance in India: A Case study of Leveraging Information & Communication technology (ICT) for Women empowerment under MgnRegA in the state of Rajasthan. *Journal of Governance & Public Policy*, *7*(1), 78–105.

Hilbert, M. (2011). Digital gender divide or technologically empowered women in developing countries? A typical case of lies, damned lies, and statistics. *Women's Studies International Forum*, *34*(6), 479–489. doi:10.1016/j.wsif.2011.07.001

Mehra, B., Merkel, C., & Bishop, A. P. (2004). The internet for empowerment of minority and marginalized users. *New Media & Society*, *6*(6), 781–802. doi:10.1177/146144804047513

Obayelu, A., & Ogunlade, I. (2006). Analysis of the uses of information communication technology (ICT) for gender empowerment and sustainable poverty alleviation in Nigeria. *International Journal of Education and Development Using ICT*, *2*(3), 45–69.

Parveen, B. (2020). Multimodality and ICT in empowering Muslim women. *An evaluation of Government of India Schemes*, *40*(48), 10.

Rajasthan Population (2019/2020). (n.d.). Retrieved June 20, 2020, from http://www.populationu.com/in/rajasthan-population

Rural Subscriber Base of Internet Users as on 31.01.2016. (n.d.). *Open Government Data(OGD) Community*. Retrieved April 29, 2020, from https://community.data.gov.in/rural-subscriber-base-of-internet-users-as-on-31-01-2016/

Suvarna, V. S. (2020). *Leveraging ICT for Intellectual Growth and For Women Empowerment*. Academic Press.

KEY TERMS AND DEFINITIONS

Bhamashah Yojana: Bhamashah Yojana is a scheme introduced by the Government of Rajasthan to empower the financial condition of women. It envisages transferring financial and non-financial benefits of governmental schemes directly to women recipients in a transparent way. The scheme was inaugurated by Chief Minister Vasundhara Raje on 15 August 2014. The Bhamashah card is access to- Scholarship for the education of the students including girl child. Loan for starting a new business. Free medical treatment at selected hospitals for certain diseases and operations. Identification of the beneficiaries for free and subsidized ration.

E-Sakhi: E-sakhi is a digital literacy programme initiated by the Department of Information Technology and Communication (DoITC), Government of Rajasthan, with the aim of making every individual in the state being digitally literate. Under eSakhi, the government will leverage the state's "girl power", wherein young women in the age group 20-35 will act as patrons in charting the course to a Digital Rajasthan. "A total of 1, 50,000 e-sakhis will be selected through an open competitive process who will work to make every Rajasthani digitally literate.

I-Start: iStart Rajasthan is the flagship program by the Department of Information Technology and Communication, Government of Rajasthan to foster innovation, create jobs and facilitate investment in the State. iStart is an integrated comprehensive platform, which is a one-of-its-kind, single window resource for startups, investors, incubators, accelerators, and mentors. The focus of this initiative is on idea stage, early stage, and startups with MVP (Minimal Viable Product). This initiative helps the startups minimize the bureaucracy associated with the initiation of startup operations.

Mandi: In India Mandi is a big wholesale market where crops, vegetables and other items are sold directly by manufacturers / farmers/ artisans at a fair price, generally in bulk.

Chapter 6
The Training of the Digital Competence at the Postgraduate Level for a Knowledge-Based Economy

Edgar Oliver Cardoso Espinosa
https://orcid.org/0000-0001-7588-9439
Instituto Politécnico Nacional, Mexico

Jésica Alhelí Cortés Ruiz
https://orcid.org/0000-0002-5459-4874
Instituto Politécnico Nacional, Mexico

María Trinidad Cerecedo Mercado
Instituto Politécnico Nacional, Mexico

ABSTRACT

The objective of the chapter is to describe the main digital competences to be developed at the postgraduate level based on the characteristics established by the knowledge economy. It is a priority to evaluate, analyze, and synthesize the information generated, in addition to communicating creatively and innovatively in a network environment. Thus, the postgraduate course has been constituted as a social community that develops innovation, scientific, and technological projects as a substantial activity in which information is a fundamental resource in the development of the generation of new knowledge. To achieve this, it is necessary to carry out an investigation that involves a set of relevant processes such as identifying the problems; planning the search for information; selection of information sources; information processing, organization, and storage; as well as the communication of results. The digital competence is defined as the set of capabilities focused on the use of ICT to obtain, store, organize, present, and exchange information.

DOI: 10.4018/978-1-7998-4972-8.ch006

Copyright © 2021, IGI Global. Copying or distributing in print or electronic forms without written permission of IGI Global is prohibited.

INTRODUCTION

Education has a relevant place because it improves the economic competitiveness of countries, as well as contributes to political culture and citizen participation. The nations that have achieved better economic performance have the fundamental characteristic of having made a growing and sustained investment in the education of their population at all levels, especially at the higher level, as well as the development of their own systems of science, technology and innovation (Lomelí, 2019).

In turn, the World Economic Forum (WEF, 2017) identified various disruptive technological changes that are transforming social relationships between humans and objects. So, there has been the widespread use of the Internet, the absolute use of mobile devices both personally and organizationally, the population census through *big data*, the collection of taxes through *blockchain*, as well as incorporating artificial intelligence in organization meetings.

In this sense, the integration of technologies has allowed the manufacturing industry to be potentiated with fully integrated, automated and optimized production processes, giving significant results in improving operational efficiency and organizational performance. This situation has generated an impact that is affecting the various areas of the company, from production and organization to research and development, coupled with inventory control, management and customer service (Cardoso, Cortés & Cuevas, 2018).

Consequently, a world of continuous alterations is glimpsed, where science and technology are at the base of the economic competitiveness of countries, where innovation plays a strategic role in competition, for which they are forced to cover a series of requirements to successfully compete in an increasingly globalized economy, including high investments in both education and research. With regard to organizations and individuals, the acquisition of new qualities is required to adapt to the rapid changes in the context, which implies continuous or permanent training. As long as countries, organizations or individuals fail to meet these requirements, they take the risk of being excluded from the knowledge society and, with it, from globalized economic competition.

Based on the above, innovative technologies will integrate different scientific and technological disciplines. The key forces will come together in a fusion of technologies that is blurring the lines between the physical, digital and biological spheres, that is, artificial intelligence is going to match the reach of human intelligence and even surpass it due to the continuous acceleration of information technologies (Schwab, 2015).

Hence, artificial intelligence is defined as the simulation of human intelligence in a machine in order to solve problems (Sosa, 2007). For its part, the European Commission (2018) indicates that this term refers to systems that are capable of analyzing their environment and taking action in order to achieve specific objectives. Thus, it ranges from a computer program to a variety of hardware devices.

The objective of artificial intelligence is the development of conceptual models and programming strategies in physical machinery for the most efficient and complete reproduction possible of the scientific-technical tasks of an organization (Mira, 2008). Its relevance is to represent diverse knowledge about the tasks, the means and the users that participate to provide active support to the processes of an organization (Barros & Verdejo, 2001).

In this way, the fusion of technologies goes beyond the combination because it creates new markets and new growth opportunities for each participant in innovation. In addition, the use of the Internet will allow the interconnection of networks of physical devices, which will result in advanced connectivity of devices, systems and services with a variety of applications. Therefore, the interconnection of these integrated devices is expected to lead to automation in almost all areas, while generating advanced applications such as an intelligent network with the ability to expand to areas such as smart cities (Gershenfeld & Vasseur, 2014).

Moreover, the Fourth Industrial Revolution is more than a change driven by technology because it is an innovation-oriented phenomenon to positively impact the central sectors of a country such as education, health and business. Specifically in the former, with previous industrial revolutions, the focus changed; now in the Fourth Industrial Revolution, technologies expand the modalities of training between face-to-face and virtual in various ways, thus requiring higher education to redefine its substantive functions considering new modes of curriculum and teaching, and consequently, to consider the various ways of learning; which has led to the relevance of designing alternative curricula (Jules, 2017).

In this context, it is decisive to identify the following perspectives based on the development of the digital economy as indicated by Becerra (2017) and which are stated below:

- Digital strategy: Oriented towards the modernization of the financial sector from the use of payment and collection processes based on the use of technology known as *fintech*. In this way, the banking sector is moving towards the realization of its credit and economic processes in digital form. In addition, multinational companies are investing in the development of digital strategies to carry out their operations in these means.
- Innovation: Considers that each organization establishes an innovation center to carry out the task of developing business mentality and philosophy, together with the design and implementation of innovative strategies based on the interpretation of the information databases related to each industry with the objective of measuring the competition in order to identify the various disruptive factors that may arise in the market.
- Artificial intelligence, robotics and automation: The use of automated robotics-based systems to achieve standardization and concentration of operations.
- Internet of Things: Refers to the fact that the various production, commercial and financial processes will have at least a digital support, which implies the gradual elimination of cash-based systems, as well as the digitization of purchases and sales by the companies, which is generating the phenomenon of business disruption.

This has led to the digitization of production processes with respect to the value chain of organizations, so it has impacted the following phases according to Katz (2015):

- In the inputs in which digitization has been incorporated through the use of platforms and information transmission systems to reduce transaction costs in purchasing, inventory management and logistics.
- In the processing of the transformation of inputs into products, automation of internal processes has been introduced, together with interaction with firms that provide services and/or components, so digitization addresses the inclusion of *business to business* platforms or the adoption of internal production planning systems such as ERP.
- For the distribution oriented to the sale and delivery of products to the market, digitization has been inserted in the adoption of new platforms for signaling prices (digital advertising), distribution and logistics costs (transport, storage, etc.).

Consequently, the massification of information and communication technologies (ICT), has caused that the generation of knowledge has a very high obsolescence, which is why human capital needs to be considered as a renewable resource, which means that it requires permanent updating and renewal with continuous learning, which will allow it to be given flexibility and responsiveness in an environment in which the only permanent thing is change. As mentioned by the OECD (1998:17):

Investment in human capital is at the core of countries' strategies to promote economic prosperity, full employment and social cohesion. Individuals, organizations and nations increasingly recognize that high levels of knowledge, skills and competences are essential to ensure a successful future.

In the same way, Barrios and Fajardo (2017:103) stated:

Young people in this digital space promote a virtual society scenario in which they establish meeting points, consolidate bonds of friendship and strengthen communication mechanisms, so that the digital biosphere becomes the information center, but in turn, in an agora of learning where the past is found, what has been learned and the specific data that is useful since it optimizes the search processes as well as determines that education has to transform in this new scenario.

In this way, the incursion of technologies has transformed the various spheres of human activity. The use of the Internet has revolutionized the concepts of interactivity; the empowerment of information has led to changes that imply transformations about how to interact with the world, which is why it is necessary to have an educational training oriented towards the management and use of digital resources and the virtualization of information (Levano, Sánchez, Guillén, Tello, Herrera & Collantes, 2019).

In this context, education plays a fundamental role in the development of a society, which is why educational systems require considering its needs and demands, as well as the interests of citizens and the goals that as a country they are intended to achieve. However, teachers face the challenge of educating people who are going to work in a society characterized by uncertainty, innovation and the circulation of information through the use of technological tools, which requires the training of new generations to live in this context (Bauman, 2008; Leymonié, 2015).

Therefore, the increasing influence of ICTs at all levels of the educational system is unquestionable, hence: "Faced with the technological revolution, higher education institutions (HEIs) behave like any other organization that cannot ignore and stop taking advantage of its benefits "(Marcovitch, 2002:87).

Thus, HEIs have to reinvent themselves, evolve and innovate towards the construction of flexible learning experiences in the student body in relation to the what, the where, the when and the how. In addition, they will be relevant because they will allow the elimination of barriers giving access to education without borders of time or space, so they will increase collaboration between people regardless of their geographical location, so generating information exchange networks (Castaño, Redecker, Vuorikari & Punie, 2014).

As noted by Ocaña, Valenzuela & Garro (2019:544):

The great challenge for HEIs of the new millennium is the urgent need to plan, design, develop and implement training processes based on the digital competence in order to achieve the training of better professionals that are fully capable of understanding and developing the technological environment in function of the needs of the labor sector.

To achieve this, Chou, Valdés & Sánchez (2017) mention that HEIs have implemented training processes together with ICTs such as:

- The development of technological and methodological tools in the teaching and learning process.
- The use of web 2.0 as a collective space that allows collaboration and creation of digital content.
- The generation of learning everywhere and at all hours and by all kinds of people using an integration of various sources and resources.
- The emergence of new areas of knowledge.
- Learning takes place permanently.

On the other hand, a new perspective of training for employment has been generated, focusing on the management of professional skills in relation to their development, linkage with the labor sector and decision-making, so that human talent is the fundamental element that allows generating innovative strategies in companies that allow responding to changing market conditions, as well as promoting not only economic but also comprehensive growth in organizations (UNESCO, 2010).

While the OECD (2012:15) has established that "competences transform lives and boost economies; without the right skills, people remain on the fringes of society, technological progress does not translate into economic growth, and countries cannot compete in today's economies."

Therefore, the objective of the chapter is to describe the main digital competences to be developed at the postgraduate level based on the characteristics established by the digital economy. Five axes of training at the postgraduate level are identified: technical practices, academic practices, training activities, content creation, as well as research management and dissemination.

BACKGROUND: DIGITAL COMPETENCE

The XXI century implies the challenge of using innovative teaching strategies focused on the student body, for which the teaching staff must incorporate technological resources to promote intellectual abilities, especially self-learning and that, at the same time, promote a broader comprehensive development (Varela & Valenzuela, 2020). The development of transversal competences in the use of ICTs is influenced by the dizzying changes that occur worldwide in education, as well as in the economic, political and social spheres, so that education must be transformed to be at the height of the challenges implied by global events, new economies, and scientific and technological advances in all areas of human endeavor (Mortera, 2016).

Besides, one of the consequences of economic globalization has been the use of ICTs as a tool that enables not only the exchange of knowledge but also a new way of interacting between individuals and organizations, both nationally and internationally. In this sense, higher education has integrated the use of ICTs as one of the competences to develop in its programs to face this new scenario established by the knowledge society (Hayes, 2010).

According to the United Nations Educational, Scientific and Cultural Organization (UNESCO, 2014), ICTs are conceived as tools to modernize the academic and administrative management processes of educational systems, as well as an opportunity for educational innovation, for which they have been established as means to contribute to the improvement of education and generate transformations in student learning, overcoming the traditional paradigm in which now greater autonomy is generated in the training process and in knowledge management accessing a diversity of information sources, making the development of the digital competence relevant.

In turn, the OECD (2005) defined that a competence is the ability of a person to face a complex situation in a particular context with the support and use of psychosocial resources (abilities, skills and attitudes). Meanwhile, Beneitone, Esqueti, González, Marty, Siufi, & Wagenaar (2007) conceptualize competences as a dynamic combination of knowledge, understanding, capacities and abilities, so that their generation and development is the purpose of educational programs. While Tobon (2008) considers that a competence is a complex process in which the cognitive and metacognitive components, personality qualities, motivation, social and professional experience of the subject are found.

Similarly, higher education has formulated strategies aimed at training professionals for the globalized world, one of them being (Tójar & Mena, 2015:611):

Implement the competency-based training model at the university, which integrates interdisciplinary knowledge, socioformation, research as a didactic strategy, innovation and the incorporation of new information and communication technologies in teaching-learning processes.

Meanwhile, digital competence according to Gutiérrez (2014) is the set of values, beliefs, knowledge and attitudes to adequately use technologies, including both computers and the different programs and the Internet that allow the search, access, organization and use of information in order to build knowledge. For their part, Esteve & Gisbert (2013) define it as the conjunction of various skills that are required by today's society and that include the ability to access and manage technological devices in order to search, store and use information in new professional and training environments.

While Gutiérrez & Tyner (2012) consider that the digital competence is the ability to access, understand, transform, use and share the information found on the network, which is why it includes the ability to process this information and turn it into knowledge, for which it is required to have skills in the use of technological devices and networks, including knowledge of the language related to what is sought.

Furthermore, the European Commission (2013) indicated that the digital competence is an interdisciplinary requirement for students to fully benefit from the new possibilities offered by technology for effective and inclusive learning. Thus, this ability is related to logical and critical thinking, as well as information management skills at a high level.

Also, Larraz, Espuny & Gisbert (2012) conceive it as knowing how to handle and understand the information found in the virtual world, which is a key factor in university life, and they even consider it a transversal competence that in today's society is fundamental for learning other skills and fields of study. In turn, these authors point out that digital competence is an essential factor for new professionals and that is demanded by companies within the characteristics of their employees so that they have excellent job performance.

On the other hand, Martin (2008) conceptualizes it as the ability of people to properly use digital tools in order to identify, access, manage, evaluate and synthesize digital resources, express themselves through multimedia resources and communicate with others in any context. Consequently, the digital competence is not only oriented towards ICTs management, but also includes the skills and attitudes to analyze, synthesize and evaluate the relevance and reliability of information in a productive way, making it one of the fundamental elements in which the permanent formation of the individual is based and that must have a high priority within an educational program (OECD, 2003b).

In this way, the digital competence has been recognized as a key factor for new professionals, which is why companies demand it within the characteristics of their employees, so that it has established itself as one of the main ones for training. Specifically, in higher education it has been positioned as a transversal type competence that in today's society is fundamental for learning other competences and fields of study because it enables the management and understanding of the information found in the virtual world.

In the same way, it has been determined that the development of the digital competence is decisive for the formation of skills such as logical and critical thinking, as well as metacognition, which in turn favor the acquisition of the resolution of problematic and language situations in the individual, as well as determine the use of reflection and the ability to discriminate useful information from that which is not.

According to Marza & Cruz (2018), the digital competence, in the training of citizens, will allow empowerment perspectives in relation to intrinsic social aspects such as politics, economy, and employability; as well as aspects of the new cultural and entertainment trends in the present century. On the other hand, Iordache, Mariën & Baelden (2017) propose that the digital competence be assumed as the most practical and measurable results of training processes in relation to digital literacy.

Thus, Ocaña, Valenzuela & Garro (2019); Durán, Gutiérrez & Prendes (2016) as well as Krumsvik (2011) established that the digital competence must be conceptualized under a holistic vision that integrates both knowledge and capabilities of a technological nature, which must be formed first in higher education and that, in addition, has as its support a network of high complexity in technological literacy but with a functional nature. This element has already been pointed out by Rangel & Peñalosa (2013) who stated that for the context of the knowledge economy, new competences, skills and attitudes are required, which will allow the person to mediate from the fact that HEIs implement a digital literacy process.

THE TRAINING OF HUMAN CAPITAL AT THE POSTGRADUATE LEVEL

The country with the largest stock of human capital always emerges as the technology leader and maintains its leadership as long as it maintains its advantage in human capital. Therefore, human capital constitutes one of the key factors in global competition to achieve preeminence in digital innovation. As Fernández, Leiva & López (2017:1) stated:

We live in a society that, due to its current dynamics, requires that educational systems around the world rethink the vision of future professionals who want to train according to global economic development and the demands of the ever-changing labor market; putting aside the traditional teaching model based on the transmission and memorization of knowledge, in favor of other methodologies that allow students to acquire a set of knowledge, skills, aptitudes and attitudes to apply them in a close and realistic work setting.

Given this panorama, it has originated that economies have to progressively transform considering high investments in education, training, research and development, as well as in information systems, in which now, they are characterized by their outstanding use of new ICTs, not only for communication between people, but also for the creation of new knowledge, which enables innovation. Organizations, communities and individuals have to acquire new qualities to be able to prosper in this world full of continuous changes. This concerns educational systems, labor markets, as well as the modes of organization of companies and markets.

UNESCO (2009), Ibarra (2000), as well as Balbo, Pacheco & Rangel (2015) consider that this panorama has led to the opening towards a global economy based on knowledge, motivating the rethinking of the knowledge that societies need to teach and learn together with the establishment of new demands that professionals have to satisfy in an increasingly competitive market both nationally and internationally; the increase in information processing that requires more complex techniques and methods for its analysis and systematization, in which the use of information and communication technologies (ICTs) has become a fundamental support to achieve this.

Consequently, a new technological paradigm has been generated that has led to global changes in countries where ICTs allow knowledge sources to multiply and spread through interconnected networks. Thus, it is no longer enough to teach reading and writing in the educational system, so the development of new skills such as critical thinking and information processing is required. In this way, it is relevant to develop digital and media literacy at all educational levels (Nazarenko, 2015; Sosa & Palau, 2018).

The above skills become extremely important at the postgraduate level because it is no longer enough for students to acquire the skills to use ICTs, as well as to write and to read both images and audiovisual messages. It is a priority to evaluate, analyze and synthesize the information generated, in addition to communicating creatively and innovatively in a network environment (Masanet, Contreras & Ferrés, 2013).

Based on Ocaña, Valenzuela & Garro (2019), the digital competence has to be developed under a holistic vision understood by knowledge and capabilities with technological and media support. For its complete and comprehensive training it is required that it be in higher education where it acquires the element of being functional for the student body.

In this way, the knowledge economy demands training in the appropriate use of digital technologies, so the development of the digital competence has been included in curricular proposals within the educational system (Matamala, 2014). According to Dardanou & Kofoed (2019), there are three primary scenarios for its development: School, family and relationships between equals.

In this context, HEIs are facing great challenges as a result of the paradigmatic transition in which society finds itself. Many of these transformations are related to the ability to produce new knowledge, develop innovative applications of these discoveries and transform their action plans and, ultimately, prepare students for a more global future (Vera, 2018).

Therefore, Area (2010) establishes the need to train university students in the digital competence because they must be able to access new information, train in search skills, develop their ability to build knowledge in interaction, know how to express themselves and communicate with new languages and tools and, finally, acquire skills for learning in spaces enriched and built with technologies.

In this sense, higher education has been considered as a transcendental component in the training of human capital for this 21st century, oriented towards the production of knowledge and its transfer, which allows the positioning of a country in the international sphere (Arrieta, Gaviria & Consuegra, 2017).

From this perspective, individual knowledge, experience, initiative and creativity are recognized as the unlimited resource of organizations and countries, thus recognizing that the talent of people is the basis of competitiveness and survival of organizations of any kind. Then, it is important to design and implement training strategies focused on knowledge management, be it people, organizations of all kinds and countries, regardless of size or weight in the world economy, what is known, what is to be known and what needs to be done to acquire the knowledge. So, the new educational framework in which the postgraduate level is located is characterized by giving priority not only to human capital but also to the management of new knowledge, innovation and the development of human capacities as sources of sustainable economic growth (ECLAC, 2008; Portnoi, Rust & Bagley, 2010).

Also, recognizing that among the essential competences in the knowledge economy, the digital is found, a training process that allows them to be used continuously, exchanging information and resources with a critical and reflective, autonomous, ethical and collaborative attitude is required (Castell, 2000; Marzal, 2010; Zempoalteca, Barragán, González & Guzmán, 2017).

In this sense, higher education, where the postgraduate degree is located, needs to redirect its training towards the generation of innovators who can increase the production of ICTs, as well as introduce the use of digital technologies as a fundamental axis in all programs. Thus, the new role of HEIs is their contribution to the development of innovation in the country, so they not only fulfill the function of research and teaching, but also actively create their own technologies, establish technology companies and are leaders as centers of creation of new industrial technologies.

In addition, the educational sector, having a social purpose, which mission is to train human talent with a set of fundamental competences that allow them to resolve the various labor and individual situations that they face, for which the formulation of a model that values the generation of human capital in the postgraduate course and so cover the quality criterion that has become an accrediting element of educational programs both nationally and globally (Cardoso & Cerecedo, 2011).

Also, when the individual has already had a training journey and is linked to work experience, then the need arises to expand and professionalize other skills such as personalization, collaboration, communication, informal learning, productivity and the creation of knowledge, which are essential elements that promote better professional performance.

Consequently, the postgraduate educational level has become the predominant space where professionals have the opportunity to complement their training to expand their development opportunities in the areas of teaching and research, as well as deepening into a specific field of knowledge; therefore, it offers three levels of training: specialization, master's and doctorate. For this reason, it has become responsible for promoting the generation of new knowledge through scientific, technological, humanistic and social research. Hence, it is essential that people who access this level acquire or strengthen a set of research-related competences that enable them to apply and generate scientific and technological knowledge in the productive, social and service sector with the continuous use of ICTs (Gekara & Snell, 2018; Carreño, 2011).

In this regard, the employee required by the digital economy is a university graduate with postgraduate training, highly trained in the knowledge and effective management of digital skills because they have become the key role in improving business performance. Companies with high ICT capabilities end up outperforming comparable companies in the same industry on a sustained basis. Investing in ICT appears to be profitable for some companies, but not for others, particularly due to organizational learning and ICT skills (Tippins & Ravipreet, 2003).

In this way, the innovation potential that graduates provide is a fundamental determinant both for success in their professional careers and for the total efficiency of production systems in different countries. Hence, postgraduate studies contribute to the development of competences focused on generating new knowledge and making decisions to put it to use, as well as for mobilizing the resources of the organization in which the digital competence has positioned itself as one of the training axes at the graduate level.

So, the postgraduate course has been constituted as a social community that develops innovation, scientific and technological projects as a substantial activity in which information is a fundamental resource in the development of the generation of new knowledge. To achieve this, it is necessary to carry out an investigation that involves a chain of relevant processes: identifying the problems; planning the search for information; selection of information sources; processing, organization and storage of information, as well as the communication of results (Rodríguez, Serra, Lasaga & Miranda, 2020).

The complexity of today's world increasingly requires the ability to know how to access, evaluate and use information (Trilling & Fadel, 2009). Information literacy has a truly transformative effect: it enables the acquisition of other fundamental competences for a prosperous life in the 21st century (Wan & Gut, 2011).

Then, digital literacy provides a framework for various forms of access, analysis, evaluation and creation of messages, leads to an understanding of the role of the media in society and strengthens the fundamental competences of inquiry and self-expression. Digital literacy is not just limited to interpretation, but also encompasses the ability to create messages for self-expression and to influence and inform others (Redecker & Punie, 2013).

In this sense, Cabra & Marciales (2009) mention that is required the understanding, use and appropriation of technologies of the following type:

- Operational focused on the management of hardware and software;
- Relevant informational that allow finding, selecting, processing and evaluating information according to specific needs;
- Strategic related to the use of sources and means to achieve objectives that allow the exercise of citizenship in the short and long term.

In addition, it is considered to have basic ICT knowledge oriented towards the ability to access, manage, integrate, evaluate and create information because technology alone cannot guarantee good results in the learning experience (Davies, Fidler & Gorbis, 2011).

In this regard, Larraz (2012) mentions that the digital competence is made up of informational, technological, multimedia and communicative literacy. The first is oriented towards the identification, location, organization and evaluation of information; the second is about hardware and software management; the third is focused on the elaboration and understanding of multimedia messages and the fourth is related to the presentation and dissemination of information to participate as a digital citizen.

To achieve this, it is important to consider at the postgraduate level the existence of the diversity of learning styles of the students that include a search and fluency in multiple sources of information, valuing each one for the types of communication, activities, experiences and expressions so that learning is carried out from the collective search in order to synthesize experiences instead of locating and absorbing information from a single source, which implies frequent opportunities for reflection through associative networks (Dede, 2005a).

Along these lines, the training of the digital competence has gained interest for its evaluation and certification, so different models have been developed that specify the contents and indicators (García & Tejedor, 2017). In Europe, the so-called DIGCOMP, which establishes the development of the digital competence in terms of knowledge, skills and attitudes in five areas: Information, Communication, Content Creation, Security and Problem Solving, with 21 sub competences that refer to key learning for citizen participation in the 21st century stands out (Ferrari, 2013; Enochsson, 2019).

Therefore, it is essential that academic training on the integral domain of ICTs be included in the postgraduate course, considering that technical knowledge is the basis and cuts across the digital competence (Prendes, Castañeda & Gutiérrez, 2010; Rodríguez, Serra, Lasaga & Miranda, 2020). As Ocaña, Valenzuela & Garro (2019) mention, the great challenge of the postgraduate of the new millennium is the incursion to plan, design, develop and implement academic processes for the digital competence in order to achieve the training of better professionals who are trained to understand, know, interact and develop the technological component in the organizations in which they work.

Thus, Table 1 shows the four dimensions of the digital competence training at the postgraduate level.

Table 1. Digital competence training dimensions at the postgraduate level

DIMENSIÓN	COMPETENCE
Technical practices	Knowledge of the computer and its most common peripherals Knowledge about the installation and uninstallation of computer programs Knowledge to store, organize, retrieve and select information Knowledge about the connection of audio equipment, video cameras and other devices
Academic practices	Development of multimedia presentations Use of word processor Use of browsers and search engines Use of spreadsheets Use of email Access and management of digital libraries Database management Use of organization and data analysis software Use of collaborative work tools
Training activities	Synchronous and asynchronous presentations On-site and online debates and discussion forums Search and consultation of specialized databases Sending documents by email Reading electronic files Organization of electronic evidence folders Research in digital libraries Access and use of simulators Sharing files between users Ability to assess the authorship and reliability of information on the Internet
Creation of content	Content development and integration Copyright and licenses Programming Innovation and creative use of technology
Research management and dissemination	Ability to create a research product with the support of technological tools. Ability to organize, analyze and synthesize information using tables, graphs or diagrams with the support of a computer program. Ability to analyze and integrate the information obtained by consulting databases. Ability to send an academic product on congress platforms, magazines and editorials.

Source: Elaborated based on Zempoalteca, Barragán, González & Guzmán (2017); Ferrari (2013) and Prendes, Castañeda & Gutiérrez (2010).

In this way, it is essential to generate educational processes that favor the acquisition of the digital competence by students and to design these processes from a comprehensive perspective, since it is not only learned by the presence and interaction with the media.

Thence, the incorporation of technological tools contributes to the educational field innovative aspects that allow a qualitative improvement in the ways of teaching and learning. In addition, for the postgraduate educational level, it enables the implementation of various teaching strategies with a multidisciplinary perspective due to the different profiles of the student body in terms of their work experience and academic training. So, the learning situations are varied, which allows the development of the digital competence, which includes communication, mediation, management and organization of information as relevant components to generate new knowledge.

Additionally, the digital competence is relevant as a strategic training element at the postgraduate level because the labor sector continually establishes requirements related to technological innovation processes, as well as constitutes a strength of the graduate of this educational level that will allow him to expand his employment opportunities or even greater positioning in the organization in which he works.

Hence, the development of the digital competence at the postgraduate level is important because one lives in a complex world that implies the establishment of various forms of interaction in the knowledge economy in which new technologies are constantly being generated that not only impact the economy of a country, but also the educational, political, social and cultural aspects.

FUTURE DIRECTIONS

Based on the dimensions of training of the digital competence at the postgraduate level, it is important to carry out research that allows identifying the levels of achievement in the student body of educational programs. Consequently, the impact assessment constitutes a fundamental process for decision-making at three points:

I. Initially, in order to shape the student's income profiles, the characteristics of their work context and their training needs.
II. Of process aimed at evaluating the educational actions of the program during its implementation with respect to the acquisition of the digital competence and,
III. Of products in order to determine the level of acquisition of the digital competence in students in each of the educational programs. Also, to identify the significance of the digital competence of the student body in the workplace. In addition, to analyze the impact of the digital competence in the face of the health contingency of COVID-19 on the academic training of postgraduate students.

CONCLUSION

Based on the requirements established by the knowledge economy regarding the generation of continuous information at the international level, it is necessary for HEIs to carry out various academic, organizational, humanistic and scientific transformations in order to face the new perspectives of systemic employment of the digital environment. Thus, the way in which the new digital education is approached will bring positive consequences for that society in the training of human capital, acquiring that related to the application of the digital competence, as well as the development of new technologies.

Thusly, it is necessary for teachers at the postgraduate level to incorporate into their teaching practice various learning resources based on the use of ICTs so that they can develop naturally in the new communication and collaboration spaces and thus provide quality training for students.

In this sense, the digital competence is not only oriented towards the management of ICTs, but also includes a systemic vision made up of both abilities, attitudes and skills oriented towards the analysis, synthesis and evaluation of the relevance and reliability of information in a productive way, which is why it is a fundamental component of the training of human capital and must have a high priority within an educational program of a superior type in which the postgraduate program is located.

Additionally, the postgraduate course is characterized by the generation of scientific and technological knowledge, so the educational training provided to students must systematically integrate the continuous use of the digital competence, so that its development must include five areas: technical practices, academic practices, training activities, content creation, as well as the management and dissemination of research.

Finally, in the face of the emergence of the COVID-19 pandemic at the international level, it is important to recognize that the use of digital technologies to provide the educational service constitutes an area of opportunity, which is why it is necessary to expand the information on its impact on academic training of the student body.

ACKNOWLEDGMENT

This research was supported by the Instituto Politécnico Nacional, México [SIP number 20200768].

REFERENCES

Area, M. (2010). ¿Por qué formar en competencias informacionales y digitales en la educación superior? *RUSC, Revista de Universidad y Sociedad del Conocimiento*, *7*(2), 2-5. Retrieved from http://rusc.uoc.edu/rusc/ca/index.php/rusc/article/download/v7n2-area/976-1011-1-PB.pdf

Arrieta-Reales, N., Gaviria-García, G., & Consuegra-Machado, J. (2017). Papel del capital intelectual en la calidad de las Instituciones de Educación Superior en Colombia. *Educación y Educadores*, *20*(3), 419–433. doi:10.5294/edu.2017.20.3.5

Balbo, J., Pacheco, M., & Rangel, Z. (2015). Medición de las competencias investigativas en los docentes adscritos al Departamento de Ciencias Sociales de la Universidad Nacional Experimental del Táchira. *Revista de investigación en administración e ingeniería*, *3*(2), 26 – 35. Retrieved from http://service.udes.edu.co/revistas/index.php/aibi/article/view/0302/030204.pdf

Barrios, A., & Fajardo, G. (2017). El ecosistema educativo universitario impactado por las TIC. *Anagramas*, *15*(30), 101–120.

Barros, B., & Verdejo, M. (2001). Entornos para la realización de actividades de aprendizaje colaborativo a distancia. *Revista Iberoamericana de Inteligencia Artificial*, *5*(12), 39-49. Retrieved from https://www.redalyc.org/pdf/925/92551205.pdf

Bauman, Z. (2008). *Los retos de la educación en la modernidad líquida.* Gedisa.

Becerra, J. (2017). *Innovación, estrategia digital y Cuarta Revolución Industrial.* México: Colegio de Contadores Públicos de México. Disponible en https://www.ccpm.org.mx/avisos/innovacion-estrategia-digital.pdf

Beneitone, P., Esqueti, C., González, J., Marty, M., Siufi, G., & Wagenaar, R. (2007). *Reflexiones y perspectivas de la educación superior en América Latina. Informe final–proyecto Tuning–América Latina 2004-2007.* Universidad de Deusto–Universidad de Groningen.

Cabra, F., & Marciales, G. (2009). Nativos digitales: ¿ocultamiento de factores generadores de fracaso escolar? *Revista Iberoamericana de Educación, 50*, 113–130. doi:10.35362/rie500665

Cardoso, E., & Cerecedo, M. (2011). Propuesta de Indicadores para Evaluar la Calidad de un Programa de Posgrado en Educación. *Revista Electrónica de Investigación Educativa, 13*(2), 68–82. http://redie.uabc.mx/vol13no2/contenido-cardosocerecedo.html

Cardoso, E., Cortés, J., & Cuevas, I. (2018). La formación de las competencias profesionales 4.0 a nivel posgrado. In M. González & J. Cortés (Eds.), *Tendencias de la cuarta revolución industrial* (pp. 171–200). Colofón.

Castaño, J., Redecker, C., Vuorikari, R. & Punie, Y. (2014). Open Education 2030: planning the future of adult learning in Europe. *Open Learning: The Journal of Open, Distance and e-Learning, 28*(3), 171-186.

Castell, M. (2000). *La era de la información. La sociedad red.* Alianza.

CEPAL. (2008). *Espacios Iberoamericanos: La economía del conocimiento.* CEPAL. Retrieved from http://www.cepal.org/publicaciones/xml/9/34459/EspacioIiberoIII.pdf

Chou, R., Valdés, A., & Sánchez, S. (2017). Programa de formación de competencias digitales en docentes universitarios. *Revista Universidad y Sociedad, 9*(1), 81-86. Retrieved from http:// rus.ucf.edu.cu/

Comisión Europea (2013). *Education and Training Monitor.* Bruselas: Oficina Publicaciones de la Comunidad Europea.

Comisión Europea (2018). *IA para Europa. Comunicación de la Comisión al Parlamento Europeo.* Bruselas: COM.

Dardanou, M., & Kofoed, T. (2019). It is not only about the tools! Professional digital competence. In G. Colette & I. Palaiologu (Eds.), *Early learning in the digital age* (pp. 61–76). SAGE Publications.

Davies, A., Fidler, D., & Gorbis, M. (2011). *Future Work Skills 2020.* Instituto de Investigación de la Universidad de Phoenix.

Dede, C. (2005a). Planning for neomillennial learning styles. *EDUCAUSE Quarterly, 28*(1), 7–12.

Durán, M., Gutiérrez, I., & Prendes, M. (2016). Análisis conceptual de modelos de competencia digital del profesorado universitario. *RELATEC: Revista Latinoamericana de Tecnología Educativa, 15*(1), 97–114. doi:10.17398/1695-288X.15.1.97

Enochsson, A. (2019). Teenage pupils' searching for information on the Internet. *Information Research, 24*(1). Retrieved from http://www.informationr.net/ir/24-1/isic2018/isic1822.html

Esteve, F., & Gisbert, M. (2013). Competencia digital en la educación superior: Instrumentos de evaluación y nuevos entornos. *Enl@ce Revista Venezolana de Información. Tecnología y Conocimiento, 10*(3), 29–43.

Fernández, E., Leiva, J., & López, E. (2017). Competencias digitales en docentes de educación superior. *Revista Digital de Investigación en Docencia Universitaria, 12*(1), 213–231. doi:10.19083/ridu.12.558

Fernández, E., Leiva, J., & López, E. (2017). Formación en competencias digitales en la universidad. Percepciones del alumnado. *Campus Virtuales, 6*(2), 79-89. Retrieved from http://uajournals.com/ojs/index.php/campusvirtuales/article/view/249/203

Ferrari, A. (2013). *DIGCOMP: A Framework for Developing and Understanding Digital Competence in Europe*. Joint Research Centre, Institute for Prospective Technological Studies., doi:10.2788/52966

García, A., & Tejedor, F. (2017). Percepción de los estudiantes sobre el valor de las TIC en sus estrategias de aprendizaje y su relación con el rendimiento. *Educación XXI, 20*(2), 137–159. doi:10.5944/educxx1.19035

Gekara, V., & Snell, D. (2018). Designing and Delivering Skills Transferability and Employment Mobility: The Challenges of a Markent-Driven Vocational Education and Training System. *Journal of Vocational Education and Training, 70*(1), 107–129. doi:10.1080/13636820.2017.1392996

Gershenfeld, N., & Vasseur, J. (2014). *As Objects Go Online: The Promise (and Pitfalls) of the Internet of Things*. Retrieved from https://www.foreignaffairs.com/articles/2014-02-12/objects-go-online

Gutiérrez, A., & Tyner, K. (2012). Educación para los medios, alfabetización mediática y competencia digital. *Comunicar, 19*(38), 31–39.

Gutiérrez, I. (2014). Perfil del profesor universitario español en torno a las competencias en tecnologías de la información y la comunicación. *Pixel-Bit. Revista de Medios y Educación, 44*, 51–65. doi:10.7821/naer.2016.1.152

Hayes, H. (2010). *Curriculum 21: Essential education for a changing world*. ASCD.

Ibarra, A. (2000). Formación de recursos humanos y competencia laboral. *Boletín Cinterfor, 149*, 95–107.

Iordache, C., Mariën, I., & Baelden, D. (2017). Developing Digital Skills and Competences: A Quick-Scan Analysis of 13 Digital Literacy Models. *Italian Journal of Sociology of Education, 9*(1), 6–30. doi:10.14658/pupj-ijse-2017-1-2

Jules, T. (2017). *Public Policy and Governance. The Global Educational Policy Environment in the Fourth Industrial Revolution: Gate, Regulated and Governed*. Emerald Group Publishing Limited.

Katz, R. (2015). *El ecosistema y la economía digital en América Latina*. Ariel – Telefónica.

Larraz, V. (2012). *La competencia digital a la Universitat*. Tesis: Universitat d'Andorra.

Larraz, V., Espuny, C., & Gisbert, M. (2012). *La presencia de la competencia digital en la universidad.* Retrieved from http://hdl.handle.net/123456789/3212

Levano, L., Sánchez, S., Guillén, P., Tello, S., Herrera, N., & Collantes, Z. (2019). Competencias digitales y educación. *Propósitos y Representaciones.*, *7*(2), 569–588. doi:10.20511/pyr2019.v7n2.329

Leymonié, J. (2015). Nativos e inmigrantes digitales: ¿cómo aprendemos y enseñamos? *Dixit*, *12*, 10–19.

Lomelí, L. (2019). Educación superior y desarrollo: Los desafíos de México. *Economía UNAM*, *16*(47), 3–11. http://www.economia.unam.mx/assets/pdfs/econunam/47/01Lomeli.pdf

Marcovitch, J. (2002). *La universidad (im)posible.* Cambridge University Press.

Marza, M., & Cruz, E. (2018). Gaming como Instrumento Educativo para una Educación en competencias Digitales desde los Academic Skills Centres. *Revista General de Información y Documentación*, *28*(2), 489–506. doi:10.5209/RGID.60805

Marzal, M. (2010). La evaluación de los programas de alfabetización en información en la educación superior: Estrategias e instrumentos. *Revista de Universidad y Sociedad del Conocimiento*, *7*(2), 28–37.

Masanet, M., Contreras, P., & Ferrés, J. (2013). Highly qualified students? Research into the media competence level of Spanish youth. *Communicatio Socialis*, *26*(4), 217–234.

Matamala, C. (2014). Factores predictivos de las competencias TIC en alumnos chilenos de secundaria. *Revista Iberoamericana de educación*, *67*(1), 121-136. doi:10.35362/rie671267

Mira, J. (2008). Aspectos conceptuales de la Inteligencia Artificial y la Ingeniería del Conocimiento. In J. Palma & R. Marín (Eds.), *Inteligencia Artificial* (pp. 72–85). Mc Graw Hill.

Mortera, F. (2016). Utilizar tecnologías de la información y de las comunicaciones: La alfabetización digital. In *J. R. Valenzuela (Comp.), Competencias transversales para una sociedad basada en conocimiento* (pp. 124–147). Cengage.

Nazarenko, A. (2015). Blended learning vs traditional learning: What Works? *Procedia: Social and Behavioral Sciences*, *200*, 77–82. doi:10.1016/j.sbspro.2015.08.018

Ocaña, Y., Valenzuela, L., & Garro, L. (2019). Inteligencia artificial y sus implicaciones en la educación superior. *Propósitos y Representaciones*, *7*(2), 536–568. doi:10.20511/pyr2019.v7n2.274

Ocaña-Fernández, Y., Valenzuela-Fernández, L., & Garro-Aburto, L. (2019). Inteligencia artificial y sus implicaciones en la educación superior. *Propósitos y Representaciones*, *7*(2), 17–28. doi:10.20511/pyr2019.v7n2.274

Organisation for Economic Cooperation and Development. (1998). Human Capital Investment. An International Comparison. París: OECD.

Organisation for Economic Cooperation and Development (2003b). *Los desafíos de las tecnologías de la información y las comunicaciones en la educación.* España: Ministerio de Educación, Cultura y Deporte. doi:10.1787/9789264103429-es

Organisation for Economic Cooperation and Development. (2005). La definición y selección de las competencias clave. Resumen ejecutivo. Retrieved from http://www.deseco.admin.ch/bfs/deseco/en/index/03/02.parsys.78532.downloadList.94248.DownloadFile.tmp/2005.dscexecutivesumm ary.sp.pdf

Organisation for Economic Cooperation and Development. (2012). Better Skills, Better Jobs, Better Lives: A Strategic Approach to Skills Policies. París: OECD. Retrieved from doi:10.1787/9789264177338-en

Portnoi, L., Rust, V., & Bagley, S. (2010). *Higher education, policy and the global competition phenomenon*. Palgrave MacMillan. doi:10.1057/9780230106130

Prendes, M., Castañeda, L., & Gutiérrez, I. (2010). Competencias para el uso de TIC de los futuros maestros. *Comunicar*, *35*(18), 175–182.

Rangel, A., & Peñalosa, E. (2013). Alfabetización digital en docentes de educación superior: Construcción y prueba empírica de un instrumento de evaluación. *Píxel-Bit. Revista de Medios y Educación*, *43*, 9–23. doi:10.12795/pixelbit.2013.i43.01

Redecker, C., & Punie, Y. (2013). The future of learning 2025: Developing a vision for change. *Future Learning*, *1*, 3–17.

Rodríguez, L., Serra, R., Lasaga, M., & Miranda, L. (2020). Impacto social del desarrollo de habilidades informacionales en doctorandos. *Universidad y Sociedad*, *12*(2), 38–47. https://rus.ucf.edu.cu/index.php/rus/article/view/1478

Schwab, K. (2015). *The Fouth Industrial Revolution: What It Means and How to Respond*. Retrieved from https://www.foreignaffairs.com/articles/2015-12-12/fourth-industrial-revolution

Sosa, M. (2007). Inteligencia artificial en la gestión financiera empresarial. *Pensamiento y Gestión*, *23*, 1-34. Retrieved from http://rcientificas.uninorte.edu.co/index.php/pensamiento/article/viewFile/3518/2252

Sosa, M., & Palau, R. (2018). Flipped Classroom para adquirir la competencia digital docente: Una experiencia didáctica en la educación superior. *Pixel-Bit. Revista de Medios y Educación*, *52*, 37–54. doi:10.12795/pixelbit.2018.i52.03

Tippins, M., & Ravipreet, S. (2003). IT competency and firm performance: Is organizational learning a missing link? *Strategic Management Journal*, *24*(8), 745–761. doi:10.1002mj.337

Tobon, S. (2008). *La formación basada en competencias en la educación superior. El enfoque complejo*. Magisterio.

Tójar, J., & Mena, E. (2015). Desarrollo de la competencia comunicativo – investigativa en la educación superior. Investigación con métodos mixtos y educación por competencias en Perú. In AIDIPE (Ed.), *Investigar con y para la sociedad*, (vol. 2, pp. 609 – 616). Cádiz: Bubok Publishing. Retrieved from http://avanza.uca.es/aidipe2015/libro/volumen2.pdf

Trilling, B., & Fadel, C. (2009). *21st Century Skills: Learning for Life in Our Times*. Jossey-Bass/John Wiley & Sons, Inc.

United Nations Educational Scientific and Cultural Organization. (2009). Conferencia Mundial sobre la Educación Superior. La nueva dinámica de la educación superior y la investigación para el cambio social y el desarrollo. París: UNESCO.

United Nations Educational Scientific and Cultural Organization. (2010). *Desafíos de la educación.* Buenos Aires: IIPE-UNESCO.

United Nations Educational Scientific and Cultural Organization. (2014). *Políticas TIC en los sistemas educativos de América Latina.* París: UNESCO.

Varela, S., & Valenzuela, J. (2020). Uso de las tecnologías de la información y la comunicación como competencia transversal en la formación inicial de docentes. *Revista Electrónica Educare, 24*(1), 1–20. doi:10.15359/ree.24-1.10

Vera, F. (2018). Percepción de estudiantes respecto de la calidad educativa y organizacional de la carrera de enfermería de una universidad privada chilena. *Revista Electrónica Educare, 22*(3), 1–25. doi:10.15359/ree.22-3.1

Wan, G., & Gut, D. (2011). *Bringing Schools into the 21 st Century. Explorations of Educational Purpose, 13. Dordrechet, (Países Bajos).* Springer. doi:10.1007/978-94-007-0268-4

World Economic Forum. (2017). *Project Plan Overwiew: 21st Century Curriculum Project.* Sydney: WSU.

Zempoalteca, B., Barragán, J., González, J., & Guzmán, T. (2017). Formación en TIC y competencia digital en la docencia de instituciones públicas de educación superior. *Apertura (Guadalajara, Jal.), 9*(1), 80–96. doi:10.32870/Ap.v9n1.922

KEY TERMS AND DEFINITIONS

Artificial Intelligence: Simulation of cognitive processes that are usually associated with human intelligence, corresponding to computer systems designed to interact with the world through functionalities (such as visual perception and voice recognition) and intelligent behaviors that we conceive as essentially human (for example, evaluate the available information and act in the most sensible way to achieve a certain objective).

Competence: Capacity that the person has in the being, knowing and knowing how to do in real situations, facing a new task, to solve problems, make decisions and develop projects, from an entrepreneurial and managerial vision.

Digital Competence: A set of capabilities focused on the use of ICTs to obtain, store, organize, present and exchange information together with participation in collaborative networks based on the internet.

ICT: Information and communication technologies cover all advanced technologies in manipulating and communicating information.

Internet of Things: Interconnection of everyday objects with the Internet so it uses objects equipped with embedded processors or sensors that are capable of transmitting information through the network. These connections allow remote administration, status monitoring, tracking and alerts.

Chapter 7
Investigating the Educational Needs of Elderly People Within the Scope of an Educational Program on the Use of Social Media Networks by Smartphones

Venetis Kanakaris
Aristotle University of Thessaloniki, Greece

Maria Pavlis Korres
Aristotle University of Thessaloniki, Greece

ABSTRACT

Social media networks are becoming increasingly popular as a means for social interaction. A number of studies have found that elderly people have a difficulty in using social media platforms while exist a number of barriers that discourage them from using technology. This chapter investigates the educational needs of older people, who are members of two elderly care centers in Northern Greece, intending to attend an educational program on using smartphones as a communication tool to join social media networks. Research findings indicate that elderly women are more willing to attend an educational program than men and key areas of their interest include access to the internet (e.g., online payments), how to create and use an e-mail account, and how to join social media networks in order to feel less isolated by communicating with other individuals or groups with the same interests.

DOI: 10.4018/978-1-7998-4972-8.ch007

Copyright © 2021, IGI Global. Copying or distributing in print or electronic forms without written permission of IGI Global is prohibited.

INTRODUCTION

Social media networks are becoming increasingly popular as a means for social interaction. Several studies have found that elderly people have a difficulty in using social media platforms, either due to a lack of technical knowledge and skills or because they feel intimidated to join them. Apart from these main barriers, there seem to be a few more reasons why third age people are discouraged from using this technology. Taking into consideration the challenges social media networks can pose to the elderly, as indicated by many studies, it appears that the key to overcome their negative attitudes towards technology, especially, towards social media networks, is the participation in educational programs that teach proper and safe use of communication technology and social media.

This chapter investigates the educational needs of older people intending to attend an educational program on the use of smartphones as a communication tool to join social media networks. The first section of the chapter includes an international literature review, with an emphasis on the reasons older people avoid using social media networks (Leist, 2013). Various factors, such as gender, family background, social status and education, appear to play an essential role in older people's use of Social Media Networks (Ma, Chan, and Chen, 2016). The literature has also shown that older women are more willing to join educational programs on the use of technology than their counterparts (Ramón-Jerónimo, Peral-Peral, & Arenas-Gaitán, 2013; Vošner, Bobek, Kokol, & Krečič, 2016). Moreover, the literature indicates that the use of social media helps older people to communicate with relatives and friends, while other studies suggest that participation in social media networks helps many older people to fight isolation (Delello & McWhorter, 2017; Jung, Walden, Johnson, & Sundar, 2017). On the other hand, other studies have shown that older people feel insecure in using social media, fearing that personal information may be disseminated to third parties, or that their accounts might get hacked (Hope, Schwaba, & Piper, 2014; Nef, Ganea, Müri, & Mosimann, 2013).

In the second section of the chapter, a research conducted in two Elderly Care Centers (E.C.C.) in Greece is presented. The research sample consists of older people, members of two E.C.C.s, sited in different cities in the region of Eastern Macedonia and Thrace. The aim of the research is to explore the educational needs of elderly people intending to participate in an educational program on using smartphones as a communication tool to join social media networks. Research findings suggest that elderly women are more willing to attend educational programs than men and the areas of their interest include learning how to get access to the internet so as to improve their daily lives e.g. online payments, how to create and use an e-mail account and how to join social media networks in order to feel less isolated by communicating with other individuals or groups with the same interests.

Additionally, elderly women intending to participate in such educational programs in both E.C.C.s requested to be trained on the use of smartphones and not PCs, because they claimed that even though they possessed these devices, they were unable to use them properly.

THEORETICAL APPROACH

Third Age Adult Learners

The term 'third age' refers to a particular age group within a population and, given that life expectancy is increasing, its characteristics are changing. In the present day, the third age group is showing an increased ability to actively participate in modern social activities, a fact that fuels a new and different urge for learning. Third age adult learning provides the elderly with the opportunity to set learning goals they were too busy to pursue in previous stages of their lives, to explore the world of communication and information technology and to utilize all the benefits that come along with it. One could say that the main idea of older adult learning is to provide people with the opportunity to undergo a constant process of personal development and redevelopment (Merriam, 2001).

The lives of the elderly are often linked to reduced social adaptability, which often creates ignorance around their ability to be educated (Baltes, 1992; Lehr, 2006). Therefore, it is vital that we support the possibility that older people become "active" again by participating in the educational process, focusing on the knowledge, experiences and skills they already possess.

According to Friebe and Schmidt-Hertha (2013, p.12)

The discourse on lifelong learning necessarily leads to questions concerning the impact of old age as a phase of life on the preservation of learning abilities and competencies. Research on lifelong learning shows that to achieve greater flexibility in life courses, new strategies for the construction and integration of knowledge are required. The prerequisites for this process of active competency development are not the same among older people. The age-based configuration of living environments, individual health, positive images of ageing, and a continuous participation in lifelong learning are important factors in enabling older men and women to maintain independent lifestyles.

Engelhardt, Buber, Skirbekk and Prskawetz (2010) conducted a study in 11 Europen countries and Israel in order to invstigate the relationship between cognitive performance, social participation and behavioural risks, taking into account age and educational attainment. They concluded that, for both men and women, all types of social involvement icrease cognitive function and that "investing in continued education and fostering social involvement at older ages may indeed help to sustain cognitive abilities at older ages, thus increasing the feasibility and practicability of increasing labour force participation into old age" (p. 803). Therefore, adult education is crucial to expand the capacities and motivation for social engagement in old age. Elderly people who take part in adult education programs increase healthy life years and reduce risk of social exclusion. Principi and Lamura (2009) stress that Lifelong Learning "should be promoted as a strategy not only to increase integration of people, (even older people of course), but to foster and increase their participation in society" (p.24). Education not only sets conditions for participation in a variety of areas of social life, but it also marks the beginning of an active ageing process.

Nevertheless, educational activities for older people are based on their differing biographic data and social conditions. Educational options and learning perspectives are influenced by previous schooling experiences, vocational training, and early adult education activities (Illeris, 2006). The opportunity to engage in formal and non-formal education has been and still is quite different for many generations and people with different social backgrounds (Greenhow & Lewin, 2016). Based on the above, one concludes that, aside from personal biography, the elements of formal education (school system, educational infrastructure, authoritarian teachers etc.) particular to every generation similarly affect both the eagerness to take part in lifelong learning and the learning competencies in older age. Unique generational experiences, as mentioned in the historical and cultural background (Carpentieri, Elliott, Brett, & Deary, 2017; Harrington, Bielby, & Bardo, 2014), are likely to shape individual conceptions of ageing, such as individual biographies and current living conditions. Self-perception and individual ageing processes are also significant indicators for learning activities (Cuddy, Norton, & Fiske, 2005; Levy, 2017). As Friebe and Schmidt-Hertha (2013, p. 12) point out "This complex interaction of social environment, individual resources, beliefs, attitudes, and educational behaviour cannot be explained in simple causalities; it rather requires an in-depth analysis that can be provided using a qualitative approach".

Also, research on perceptions of age suggests there is a relationship between negative stereotypes regarding ageing and self-perceptions in older age. "Depending on their perceptions of their own learning capabilities and their potential for personal development, adults are more or less open to new learning experiences and willing to get involved in educational processes. This further depends on their self-perception and whether they see themselves as active designers of their own environment or as powerless victims of their fate" (Friebe & Schmidt-Hertha, 2013, p.15). The relationship between prosperity, individual evaluation of health, and conception of ageing seems to be a mutual one. A similar interplay has also been observed between self-concept, self-perception, and perception of ageing.

Learning activities for elderly people are essential in the construction of three related concepts: active ageing, healthy ageing, and successful ageing. The concept of active ageing (WHO 2012) emphasizes opportunities for physical, social and mental well-being throughout the life course, in order to extend healthy life expectancy, productivity and quality of life in older age. According to Foster and Walker (2015, p. 84) "Active aging is concerned with facilitating the rights of older people to remain healthy (reducing the costs of health and social care), remain in employment longer (reducing pension costs), while also participating in community and political life." Healthy ageing, on the other hand, is related to the capability to be mentally, physically, socially and economically fully active (Cosco et al., 2014; Friebe & Schmidt-Hertha, 2013). Successful ageing includes active learning and social activities with the aim of decreasing health risk and gaining steady health status.

According to Manheimer (2007 as cited in Wolf, 2009) older adult education, is a sector of adult education that appeared during the middle of the twentieth century and is basically of the non-formal type. Programs are usually offered through a variety of organizations such as "colleges and universities, churches, synagogues and mosques, senior centers, public libraries, day health centers, hospitals, unions, and residential housing groups" (Manheimer, 2007 as cited in Wolf, 2009, p. 59).

Taking into consideration all the above literature, it is obvious that the content of the programs addressed to elderly people, does not appear to relate to vocational training, leaning more towards the general adult education aiming to personal development and social inclusion.

Barriers Third Age Learners Encounter

Older learners face the barriers mentioned in the adult education literature, along with some age-related ones. As with younger learners, we need to keep in mind that older people do not constitute a homogeneous group; they have social, economic and cultural differences, along with differences related to physical condition and health, which become more significant as individuals get older (Martin, 2009). Moreover, as far as new technology-related programs are concerned, it should be taken into account that the elderly are often digitally illiterate in a society that is digitally infused. As suggested by theorists, the term "literacy" should be redefined in today's society so as to include reading/writing and digital competencies (Tyner, 1998; Kress, 2003).

Adults as learners may face barriers which could render the whole learning process ineffective or cause its termination, if not dealt with appropriately by the designers and educators of a program. The literature highlights the importance of internal barriers as a factor which could hinder the learning process (Rogers, 2007). Knowles (1980) supports that the psychology of older learners might be linked with previous negative schooling experiences. It is commonly believed that such barriers are the most difficult to overcome.

Barriers related with adult education are a common theme in some of the models that describe the decision-making process of participation (Darkenwald & Merriam, 1982; Rubenson & Desjardins, 2009). In the literature concerning barriers or obstacles to learning, the Cross typology (1981) has been widely applied. According to Cross's classification, there are three categories of barriers: situational, institutional, and dispositional. **Situational** barriers, also referred to as human factors, arise from the personal and social situation of the learners. These barriers usually appear in financial, work and family related circumstances. **Institutional** barriers are related to the design, organization, and implementation of the educational programs, e.g. duration of the program, location and class schedule, tuition fees, conditions for acceptance. **Dispositional** barriers are based on attitudes, beliefs, past experiences, and psychology of learners, e.g. stress related to the fear of failure or criticism, negative educational experiences, biases regarding health and age.

Previous surveys have indicated that situational barriers are more intensely perceived by younger and elderly adults (Rubenson & Desjardins, 2009). Additionally, situational barriers refer to one's immediate life situation (family and work responsibilities), and, as such, they seem to be more often perceived by women compared to men. Education seems to have an impact on prevalence of institutional rather than situational barriers. People with low levels of educational attainment report that they are confronted with institutional barriers more often, mainly due to financial difficulties. In addition, people with lower or zero income may also feel more pressure by institutional barriers. Also, dispositional barriers are more prevalent among adults with lower education, low income and out of unemployment. This is brought about by previous negative schooling experience (Gorard & Smith, 2007). Upon investigating the barriers faced by older learners, Friebe and Schmidt-Hertha (2013) distinguished between exterior barriers –related to the existence of suitable educational institutions and programs for the elderly– and interior ones, such as the lack of motivation and self-confidence.

The Importance of Needs Analysis in an Educational Program

The investigation and analysis of the educational needs of potential learners is considered the most crucial step in the process of designing an effective educational program addressed to adults (Knowles, 1980; Caffarella 1988, 2002; Glynn et al., 1985; Moseley & Heaney, 1994; Pavlis Korres & Garcia Barriocanal, 2013). The identification of learners' educational needs enhances their effective participation and facilitates the fulfillment of the program's goals. According to Caffarella (1988, p. 74) "An educational need is usually defined as a discrepancy or gap between what presently is and what should be". Therefore, accurate identification of the educational needs of the potential learners shapes the content of the program, by way of filling the gap between the present situation and the desired one, while it also influences decisions regarding the program's schedule, duration or location of the courses. As far as the identification of the present situation of the target group is concerned, quantitative and/or qualitative data are being selected through a structure research procedure. To define, however the desired situation is a much more complex and difficult process, as it can be affected by personal assumptions and values of people involved in relation to the broader social context within which these are developed (Sork & Caffarella, 1989).

Identifying possible barriers for future learners through needs research is especially important for these barriers to be taken into account during planning stages. In this way, solutions can be found that will make it easier for learners to participate in and complete the program and prevent them from dropping out.

Literature Review on Educational Programs on New Technologies and the Use of Social Media for Third Age People

As observed in literature, research mostly focuses on recording and identifying factors that exclude the elderly from the use of new technologies, and on the cognitive, psychological and social benefits that arise when the elderly utilize new technologies and the internet (Czaja, Guerrier, Nair, & Landauer, 1993; Morrell, Mayhorn, Bennett, 2000; Lee, Godbey, & Sawyer, 2003; Ordonez, Yassuda, & Cachioni, 2011), as these contribute positively to their well-being and personal sense of empowerment and affect their interpersonal interactions (Shapira, Barak, & Gal, 2007). Especially in the last decade, with the accelerated development of new technologies and the rapidly aging global population, more and more research on the use of new technologies and social media by elderly people is being carried out (Castro et al., 2011). Van Deursen and Helsper (2015) investigated how useful it is for older people to learn how to use the internet, placing particular emphasis on each gender. Their research suggests that men are more adept at learning how to use technology compared to women, but only when they are trained in entertaining activities. On the other hand, women are more eager to learn new things, especially those that can be useful to them, but, compared to men, they have more difficulties in understanding them. A similar survey was conducted by Vošner et al. (2016), who found that older women use social media more than men, and that education plays a key role in the use of social media.

But what are the main motivations for older adults to use social media? According to Nef et al. (2013), elderly people are keen on learning how to use social media to be able to communicate with younger members of the family, thus bridging the generation gap. Also, Van Deursen et al.'s (2015) study suggests that the social environment plays an important role as well, since people want to share the same knowledge with their peers. Moreover, Wu and Koon (2012) dealt with the use of social networking media as a means of communication between elderly people and their caregivers. Also, some research findings showed that older people learn how to use social media both to connect with younger relatives (using video) and to alleviate feelings of social isolation (Jung, et al., 2017). Leist's (2013) study, demonstrated that the use of social media by older people can help them overcome loneliness and raise feelings of control and self-efficacy. Kobayashi et.al (2016), in an effort to make social media more accessible to older people, managed to create an automated message handling system to promote communication between elderly people and younger generation. Jung et al. (2017) and Delello et al. (2017) investigated the reasons older people use social media on portable touch devices (iPad). The first main factor cited by older people is pressure exerted by younger family members in order to learn how to make video calls and the second one is the alleviation from social exclusion feelings after learning how to use them.

However, other studies suggest that older people avoid using social media, fearing their accounts might get hacked and that personal information might get compromised (Hope et.al., 2014; Nef et. al., 2013).

Nguyen et. al. (2014) investigated how senior citizens learn new technologies and Internet use in developed countries and noted that most elderly people learn from younger members of their family. Also, Tirado-Morueta et al. (2016) found that it is better for the elderly to be trained by qualified educators than to use applications designed to make it easier for them to learn. This is also supported by the adult education principles which are primarily based on the role of the educator - namely the way they approach the learner (Knowles, 1980).

The literature also suggests there is a direct link between the socio-economic status of the elderly and their use of new technologies and smartphones. A survey by Ma Qi et al. (2015) showed that elderly people (around 65 years old) with higher education levels and good economic status were more likely to use smartphones. Pan and Jordan-Marsh (2010) conducted a study in China and found that, among other factors, it is very important to "make efforts by policy makers to remove those social and cultural obstacles that may negatively affect the Internet use among older adults" (p. 1118), as environmental barriers, such as lack of access and internet cost, are some of the financial concerns which Chinese older adults may have. Therefore, the cost of Internet use through the cellular network might be a critical factor influencing the intention of older people to use smartphones. Moreover, the cost of attending an educational program is undoubtedly one of the main problems older people who wish to engage with smartphones encounter. In a similar study conducted in Finland by Berenguer et al. (2017), it was observed that elderly people buy smartphones because they need to replace a previous device, but they cannot fully use them (for access to social media, online music and the internet), either due to their unwillingness to learn new "unnecessary" features or because most smartphone applications are aiming at younger ages.

RESEARCH CONTEXT AND METHODOLOGY

It is considered important to include some demographic data pertaining to Greece and more specifically to the target population of our research. According to the census of May 2011, the overall Greek population amounted to 10.8 million people with a mean age of 41.4 years (HSA, 2011). A steady process of ageing has taken place in the last six decades, since the ageing index rose from 38.7 in 1960 to 142.3 in 2016 (Dianeosis, 2019). In 2011, older people (over 65 years) represented more than a fifth of the total population (20.4%, around 2.3 million people), following an increasing trend. Indeed, they constituted a percentage of 12.9% in 1991, and 16.8% in 2001. According to the latest population predictions they should add up to 3.7 million people in 2050, that is, one third of the total population (Dianeosis, 2019; Eurostat 2019).

Educational programs for elderly people implemented in Greece have been few and far apart, although third age people are not excluded from participation in programs addressed to the general public. Since 2008 the thematic titled "Issues of Third Age", related to later life, has been added in a European Union funded program implemented by the General Secretariat of Long Life Learning, which is the strategic organization for adult education in Greece, titled "Schools for parents". During the educational period of 2011-2012 285 courses on this thematic have been implemented, in which 5.130 elders (4100 women and 1030 men) have participated.

During the same period (2011-2012) the Scientific Adults' Educators Association, a nonprofit organization, has also implemented a project on Later Life Issues, funded by the private sector aiming, among other subjects, to the familiarization of elderly people with ICTs. The results of the program showed that elderly people are willing to learn how to exploit new technologies (SAEA, 2012).

The present research has been conducted in the frame of a post doc focusing on the educational needs of elderly people, and, more specifically the design, implementation and evaluation of an educational program on the use of smartphones and the possibilities they offer in improving their daily lives and promoting communication and social networking. In order to design the educational program, the present study was conducted so as to determine its content and other elements regarding the way it will be implemented. The research was conducted in two Elderly Care Centers (E.C.C.), sited in different cities in the region of Eastern Macedonia and Thrace in Greece. The Elderly Care Center provides third age people with health care, fitness programs, and a variety of educational programs. The methodology that was chosen was the qualitative research approach (Cohen, Manion, & Morrison, 2013), which means that fundamental data was gathered using interviews as a research method. Sampling was convenient and the avalanche method was followed. The research sample is comprised of older people, members of the two E.C.C.s. In each Elderly Care Center, the research process lasted twelve days. The total sample is made up of 20 people. 12 of the interviews were conducted face to face in the E.C.C., while the remaining 8 were conducted via telephone. The interviews conducted in the premises of E.C.C. provided a familiar and cozy atmosphere to the participants and resulted in spontaneous and genuine responses. On the other hand, "impersonal" telephone communication deprived us of the benefits of face-to-face communication - which would have allowed us to directly interact and record non-verbal responses - and it seems that this had an impact on interviewees' responses as well.

The sample is not fully representative of elderly people, and thus no generalizations can be made, but it is interesting, in that it is self-representative and provides necessary and useful information for the design of an educational program that will be addressed to the elderly.

Research variables such as gender, age, education, previous working status and technology usage attitude were considered in the analysis regarding the educational needs of third age people within the scope of an educational program on the use of social media networks on smartphones.

The researcher conducted the interviews by specific appointment with each interviewee. Each interview was semi-structured, lasted between 15 to 20 minutes and consisted of open-ended questions (Cohen, Manion, & Morrison, 2013). Specific issues were investigated relating to the elderly's participation in educational programs, the barriers confronted, the role of the educational background, issues concerning the process - such as number of days per week participants could attend the educational program - possible location where classes could take place, reasons candidates may not participate in the program. Moreover, the benefits of learning how to use social media on smartphones were explained in the interview process, focusing on how smartphones and social media can be used by participants in their leisure time so as to promote communication of individuals and groups of specific interests and alleviate feelings of social isolation.

The main questions that we tried to get answers for through the interviews were the following: What are the educational needs of third age people in using new technologies? How can the use of new technologies and smartphones facilitate daily-life activities of third age people? How can third age people make the best use of their leisure time using smartphones? How can smartphones and social media be utilized to promote communication between third age people through social networking?

In order to analyze data, thematic analysis was applied, a well-recognized method for identifying, analyzing, and reporting themes within a qualitative data set (Braun & Clarke, 2006). The recorded interviews were transcribed and analyzed by researchers in a time period that could reduce researcher bias during the interpretation process (Noble & Smith, 2015). All participants were fully informed on the purpose of the research and consented to their involvement in the study. Participants were made aware that they could withdraw from the interview at any time.

RESEARCH RESULTS

In figure 1, information is provided on the age variation of the sample. The majority of the participants are aged between 61 and 65 years. Results reveal that 50% of the participants are aged between 61 and 65 years, 35% are aged between 66 and 70, while 15% are aged between 71 and 80 years.

Figure 1. Sample variation by age and gender

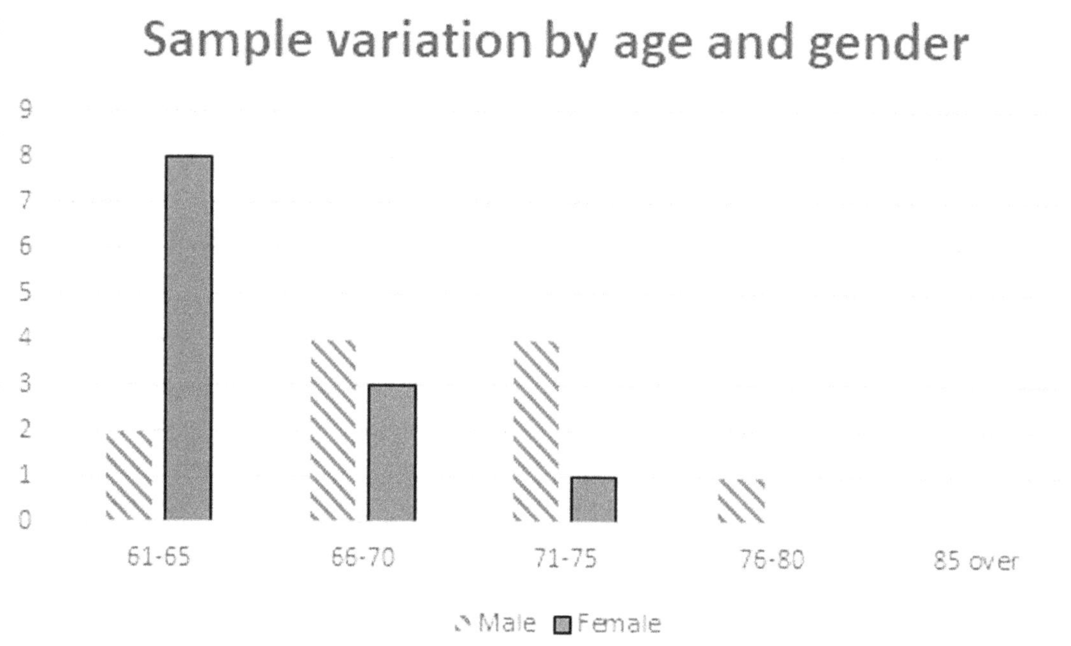

Figure 2 depicts information regarding the educational status of the investigated sample. The findings reveal that the educational status is almost equally spread by educational grade. 25% of the participants are elementary school graduates, 22.5% are high school graduates, 27.5% are Technical College graduates and 25% are University graduates. The findings also show that half of the women have had elementary education only, while men have had at least secondary education.

Another piece of information emerging from the research concerns the interrelationship between the profession of participants prior to retirement and technology. The profession of 60% of the study participants was technology related, while 40% had no connection to technology at all. Moreover, these results showed that 70% of those with technology-related jobs were men. These findings are in line with findings concerning the educational status of the sample, where men of high educational status make up nearly 70%.

The interviews also reveal that almost 95% of the study participants own a smartphone, 30% own a tablet and 25% own a laptop or a PC. Figure 3 presents the participant's preference on the educational medium for learning. A large majority of 70% prefer the smartphone, 20% the tablet and 10% laptops. Seeking the reasons participants favor smartphones over tablets and laptops, convenience and portability

Figure 2. Educational Status of the Sample

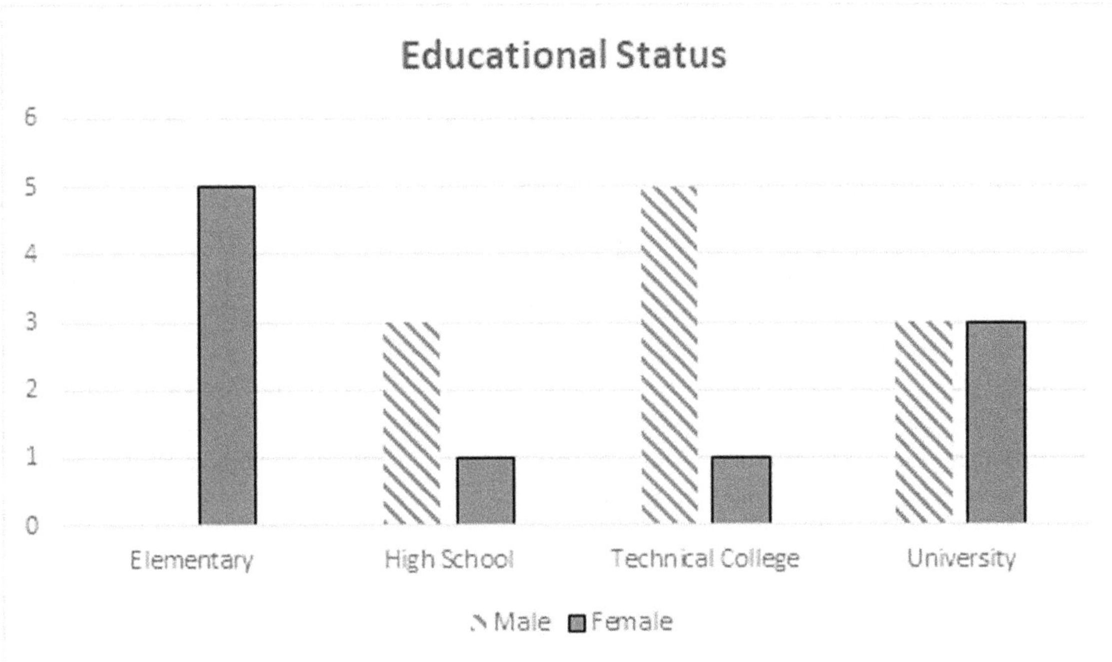

Figure 3. Choice of educational medium

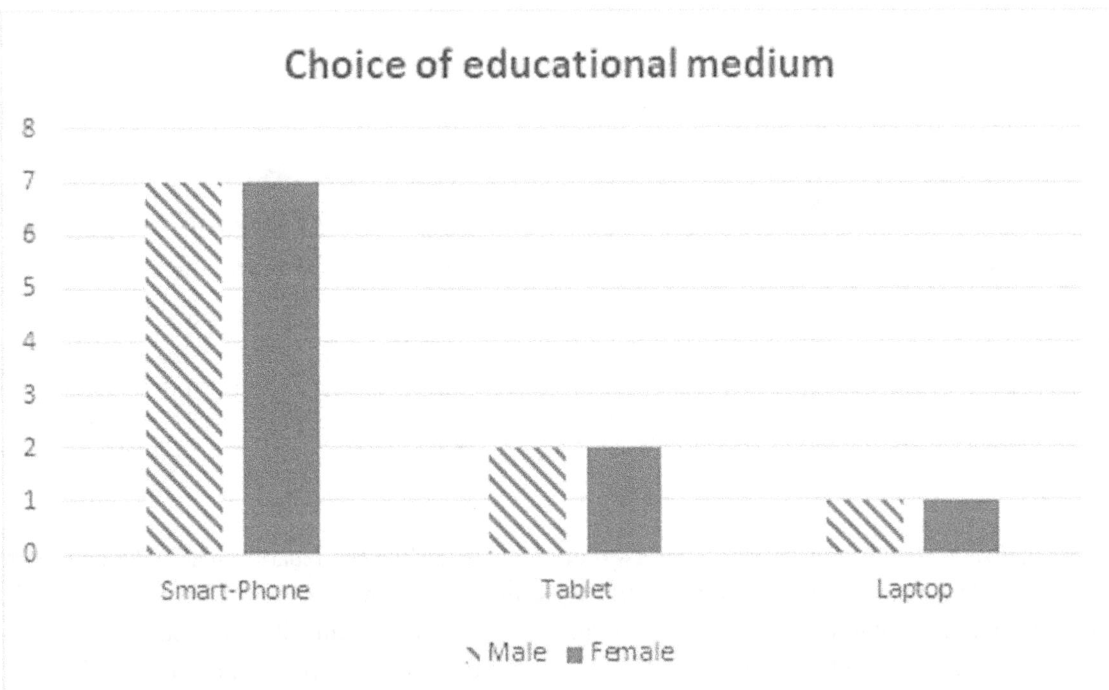

seem to be the determining factors. Additionally, participants claimed that there was no need to spend extra money on buying more equipment in order to attend the educational program. Furthermore, a woman stated that "*it is a great opportunity to take lessons on the use of smartphones and explore all the possibilities they offer*", another woman stated "*it is good for us to learn what else a smartphone can do*", while a male participant said "*yeah, let's find out how this....smartphone actually works*".

Figure 4 reveals the learning topics participants want to be educated on. The findings suggest that more than 65% of the participants prefer to be educated on the use of Internet, e-mail, Social Media and Instant Messaging applications (Viber, WhatsApp etc.). 80% of these were women and 40% were men. A remarkably interesting finding is that only women, and, indeed, the overwhelming majority (90%), wish to learn about e-banking and online shopping. For instance, a woman stated, "*I want to learn how to make online payments and avoid going to the bank*", while another one said, "*it is very good to know how to shop online*". Another interesting result that Figure 4 presents is the preference of some participants for learning how to use Google Apps (30% of them were women and 10% were men). Specifically, a male participant said, "*I want to learn how to share photos with my son*", while a female participant reported "*Google Maps will help me find new doctors*".

Figure 4. Preferred Learning Topics

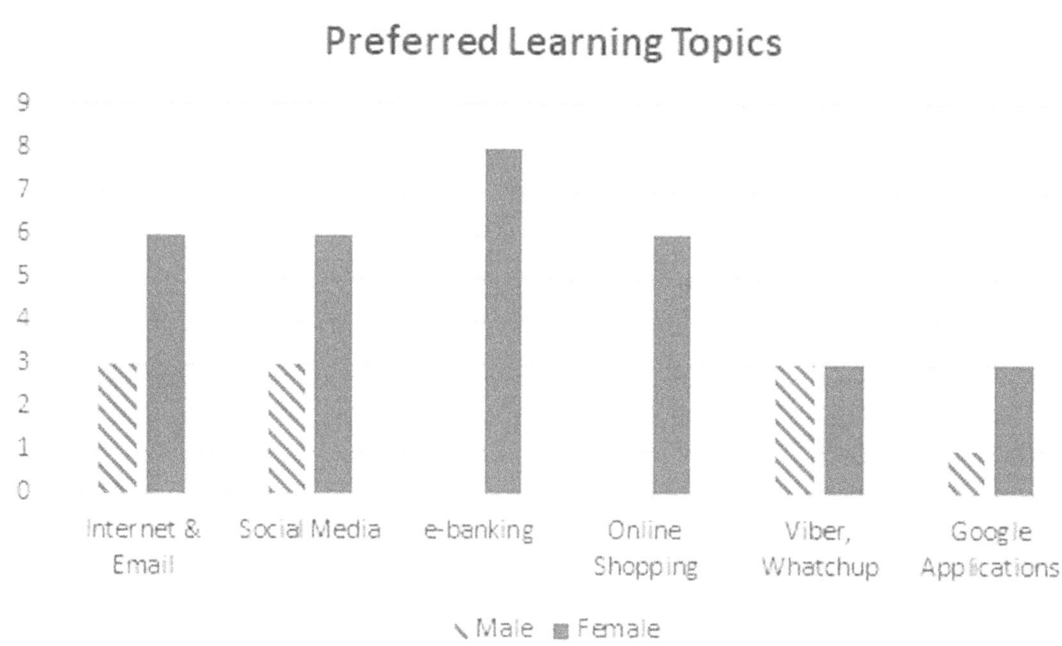

The interview also reveals the participants' preference regarding the location where the educational program could take place, i.e. in the E.C.C. (Elderly Care Center) premises or a different location. 70% of the participants want to attend the courses in the E.C.C premises, while 30% of them favour a different location. People who chose the E.C.C. premises seem to also attend fitness programs and a variety of other educational programs (painting, sculpture etc.), while some others live close to the E.C.C. and the location was very convenient to them. Interestingly, as two female participants pointed out "*It's not the classroom that matters, it is the educator who runs the program*", "*I believe that only the educator matters*".

Figure 5 provides information regarding the number of times per week participants are willing to attend lessons. 37% of them wish to attend once a week, 37% wish to attend twice a week, while 26% wish to attend lessons three times per week. The findings reveal that, for the majority of the participants - especially males ones – taking lessons more than once per week seems quite tedious, while women claim that they need to attend other courses as well or that they need to take care their grandchildren. To cite one example, a woman stated, "*it is very difficult for me to attend more than once a week because I have to look after my grandchildren*". Another one reported "*I have already enrolled in other classes and it is very difficult for me to attend this class more than once a week*", while a male participant said "*I would be bored to attend classes more than once a week*".

Figure 5. Frequency of participation preference

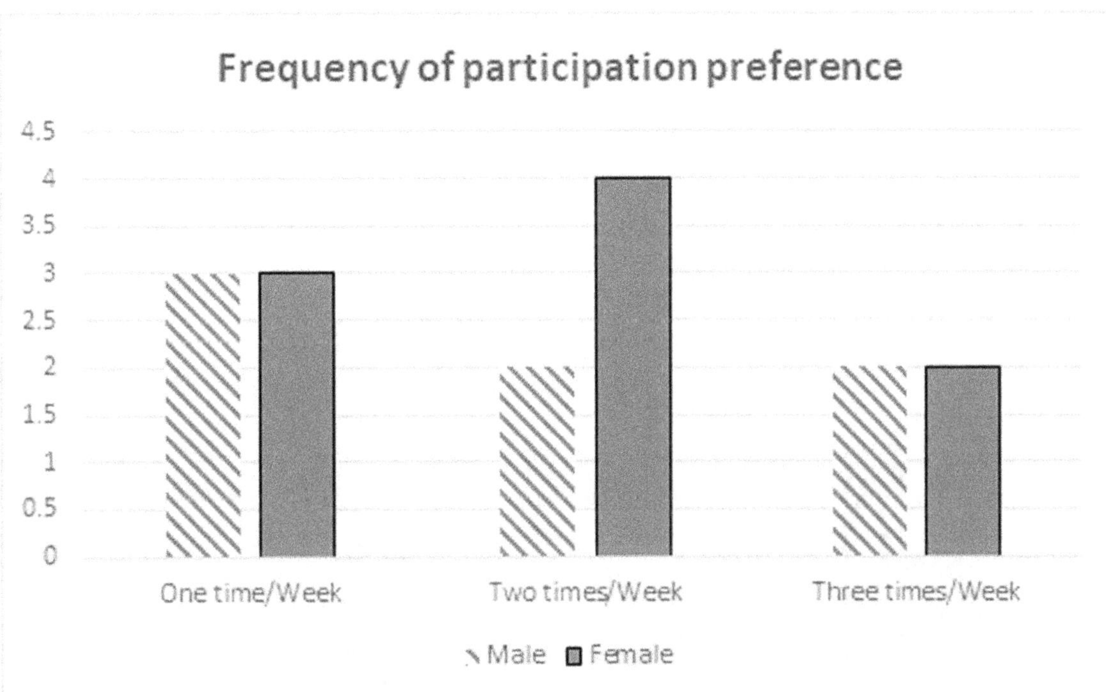

The findings presented in Figure 6 list the main reasons that people may abstain from courses. 44% of the participants cited personal reasons, 38% cited health reasons, 12% cited financial reasons, and 6% cited other reasons.

Figure 7 shows the preferences of participants on how to use the smartphone in their leisure time. 33% of them want to use smartphones in order to follow the news. 25% want to use smartphones as gateway to Social Media and another 25% intend to use the smartphone for connection with individuals through

Figure 6. Reasons for non-Participation

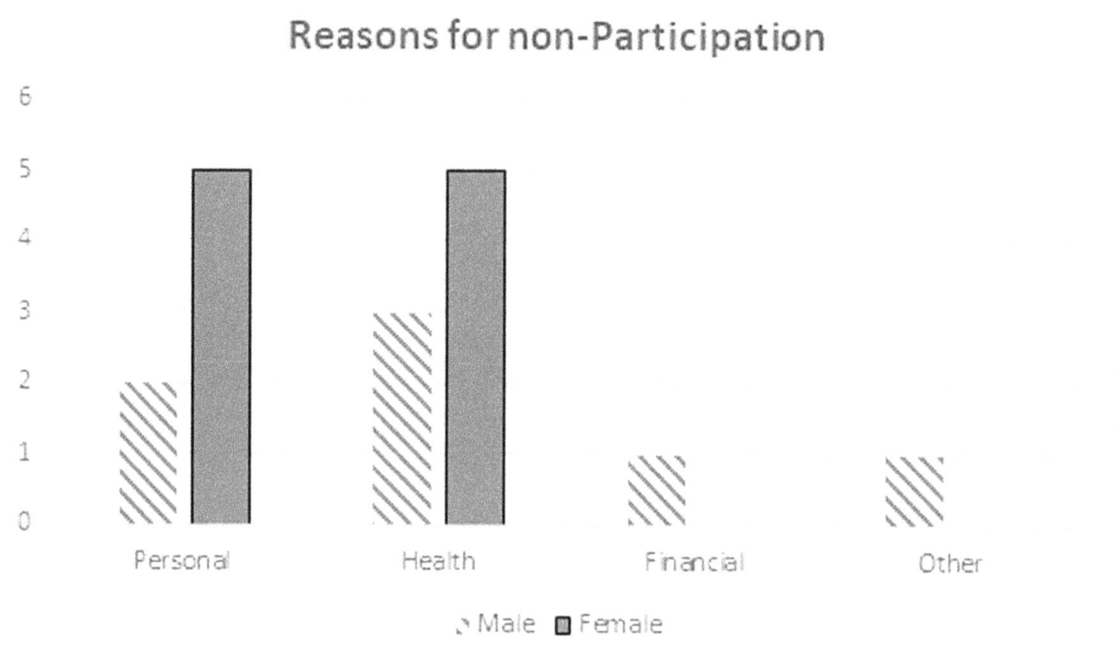

Figure 7. Preferable Use of the Smartphone

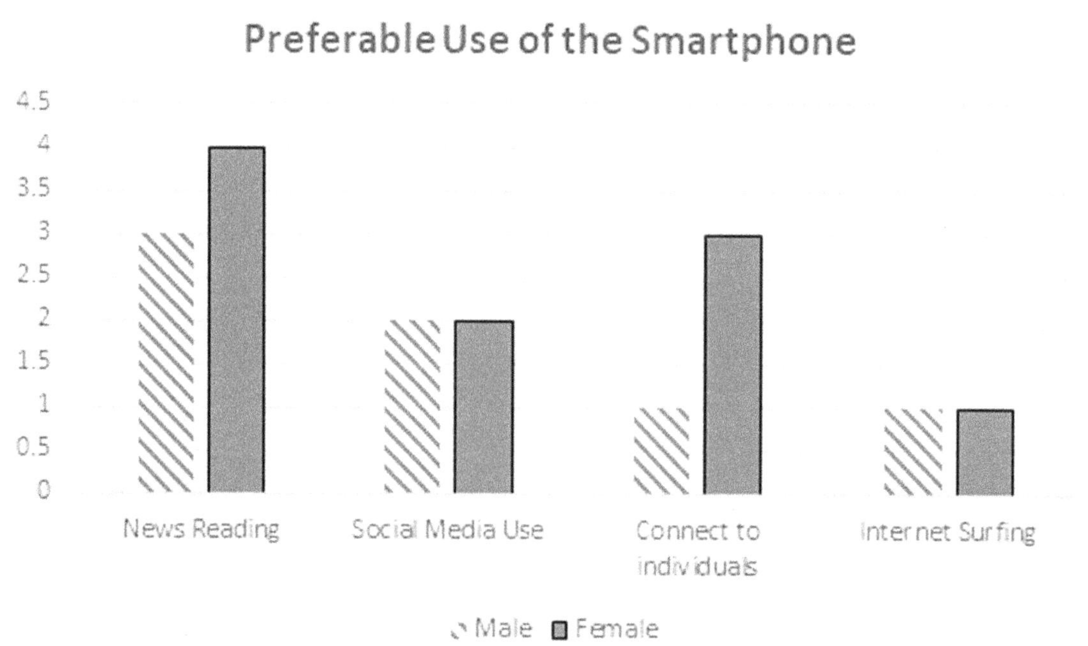

instant messaging apps (Viber, WhatsApp, Hangouts). Only 17% of the participants were willing to use smartphones for web browsing. To cite a few examples, a female interviewee stated "*I want to read the news*" while another woman said "*It would be nice to make video calls to my daughter*", while a man claimed he wanted "*To read the news on Facebook*".

The last figure (Figure 8) reveals information on how participants feel about the use of Social Media. 38% of them stated that if they knew how to use Social Media it would be easier for them to communicate with others. 31% insisted that they did not want to use them, either because they were afraid of them because they were reluctant to use something "new". 31% of the participants stated they already use Social Media to communicate with relatives and friends.

Figure 8. Participants' view on the use of Social Media

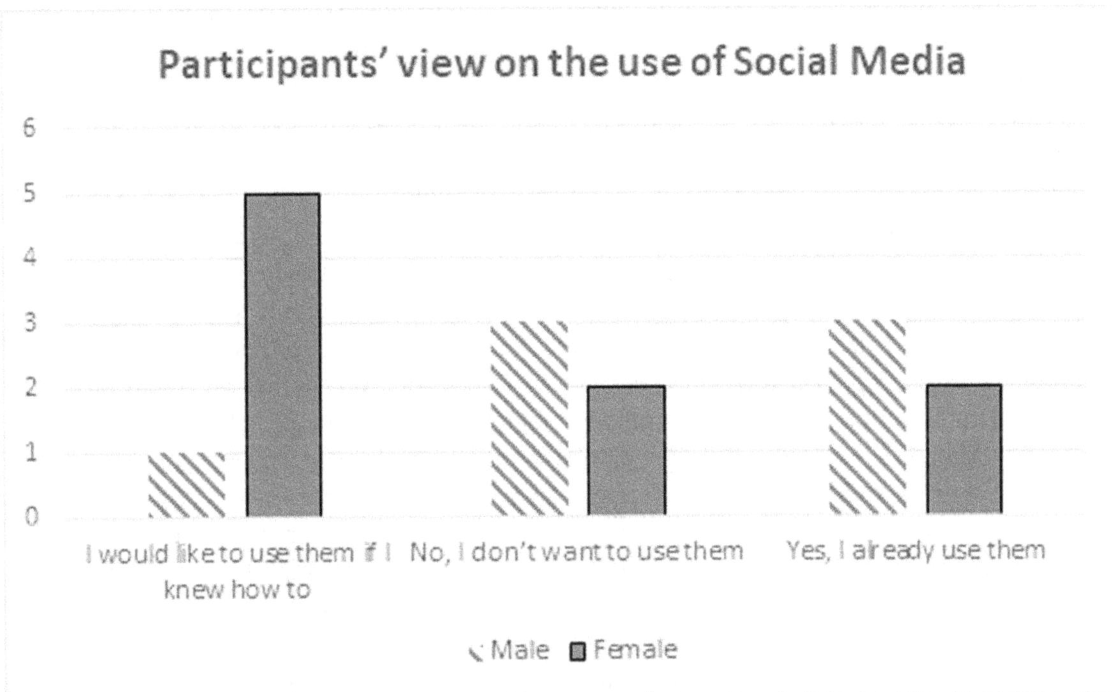

To give some examples, a female interviewee said "*I already use them and I have even found fellow students from elementary school, I am very happy*" while another woman said "*I have been using Facebook since 2018 and I have joined more than three knitting groups*".

DISCUSSION AND RECOMMENDATIONS

This study examined older people's educational needs and intention to participate in an educational program on the use of smartphones so as to gain access to the Internet, and use applications and social media networks.

Results suggest that the participants' gender, level of education and type of work determine their relationship with technology and affect their intention to attend an educational program on its use. Half of the women in the sample were elementary school graduates, while men had at least graduated from high school. The research also showed that technology-related professions were mainly practiced by men with a high level of education. The results are consistent with the literature on digital illiterates in a digitally-infused society (Tyner, 1998; Kress, 2003) and highlight the need to create programs aimed at the digital literacy of seniors in order for them to be able to function autonomously in modern society. Despite the fact that Presnky's (2001) theory on the importance of age in the relation of elders with new technologies and their classification as "digital immigrants" has been severely criticized, in the present research the sample appears to have all the characteristics of the "digital immigrants" and this is certainly related to their age, affecting their ability to take advantage of the digitally-infused society in the context of their daily life.

This study revealed that the educational medium chosen by virtually all participants was the smartphone, mainly due its convenience and portability, while a large percentage of the participants already own one. In addition, participants chose the smartphone not only due to its affordability compared to devices such as tablets or PCs, but also because it provides them with the opportunity to learn how to use all of its features. These findings are consistent with those of Berenguer et al. (2017), who report that the elderly are forced to buy smartphones due to a lack of "traditional" mobile phones, but are unable to use all of their features. The education of the elderly people on the use of smartphones is especially important, as these devices will be the interface through which they will interact with the educational content and the other learners, as well as other people in the social networks (Hillman, Willis, & Gunawardena, 1994).

The main topics participants wished to be educated on included the Internet, emails, Social Media and Instant Messaging applications (Viber, WhatsApp, etc.). Moreover, women were found to be more inclined to attend an educational program on these topics compared to men, which is consistent with the literature (Ramón-Jerónimo et al., 2013; Vošner et al., 2016). The findings are consistent with the literature on the online behavior of both genders, where women show a more social online behavior than men (Cuadrado-García et al., 2010) as they appreciate and welcome the interaction with their co-learners and the educator more than men (Patterson, 2012). Moreover, we should not forget what Jung (2012) points out, i.e. that learning is weaved directly in the social, cultural and financial canvas of womens' lives, their experiences and the gender differences, therefore all these must be taken into consideration on educational design.. Men justified their limited interest in participating in such programs, citing Internet, e-mail and social media familiarity as a reason.

A very interesting finding emerging from the research was that, apart from social media, women also expressed a desire to learn about e-banking and online shopping, as they wanted to avoid going to the bank and to be able to buy things online. These results are closely linked to Van Deursen et al.'s (2015) findings regarding differences between genders in learning new things; women seem to be keener on learning new topics regarding technology compared to men.

Another interesting finding concerns the emphasis some participants placed on the role and value of the adult educator in an educational program, an aspect that is consistent with theories on adult education (Cross 1981; Rogers, 2007; Knowles 1980), namely, with the significant role the educator is given in elderly people education (Tirado-Morueta et al., 2016).

Investigating participants' availability to attend an educational program also highlights the types of barriers seniors face. While it seems to be difficult for everyone to attend classes more than once a week, men's reluctance is due to the fact that they find it tedious to attend more classes and they have no interest in learning new things, whereas women cite lack of time due to family obligations as a reason. These findings are related to the dispositional and situational barriers that Cross (1981) described in relation to their impact on adult learning. They are also consistent with Smythe et al. (2017), Pavlis-Korres and Leftheriotou (2016) and Roosmaa and Saar (2011), who refer that situational barriers are the main reason adult learners usually abstain from most educational programs.

The study also revealed how participants would like to use smartphones in their spare time. Most older people want to use them as a tool to communicate with others on social media or instant messaging applications (Viber, WhatsApp, Hangouts), while a small portion of them claimed they wanted to use them for web browsing. Several of the participants reported having had the experience of using social media to communicate with family members and friends. As the literature suggests, the use of social media helps older people to communicate with relatives and friends, while other studies showed that participation in social media networks helped many older people to fight isolation (Delello & McWhorter, 2017; Jung et al., 2017). However, some male participants admitted to being afraid of using smartphones, whereas others were opposed to using something "new", a finding partly supported by the literature (Ramón-Jerónimo et al., 2013).

Research Limitations

Our findings were based on a small sample comprised of older people who are members of two Elderly Care Centers (E.C.C.) in Greece. The E.C.C.s were sited in different cities in the region of Eastern Macedonia and Thrace. More research with larger samples, from nearby prefectures and with different cultural and organizational context is needed so as to validate our findings. Additionally, the results of the present study do not allow broad generalizations to be drawn, as this is a qualitative research and, even though participants' actions were thoroughly investigated, the study is entirely dependent on the selected sample (Cohen, Manion, & Morrison, 2013).

CONCLUSION AND SUGGESTIONS FOR FUTURE RESEARCH

Third age is usually associated with lower levels of social adaptability and the assumption that older adults are unaware of their learning abilities (Boulton-Lewis, 2010; Lehr & Kruse, 2006). Hence, it is essential to provide older people with the opportunity to realize their full potential and become active through education by capitalizing on their own knowledge, experience, and skills.

The results of this study reveal that older people's preferences for smartphone use include more things than initially anticipated. Realizing that smartphones are not just devices for making phone calls, the first reason older people cite for their use is access to and use of social media, followed by the ability to make online payments, video calls, send/receive e-mails or messages through applications, succeeded by access to the internet and a variety of applications (online photo albums, Viber, WhatsApp etc.) that will entertain them in their spare time. The results of the research has led us to revise our initial planning for a program focused only on the use of social media networks, as set by the designers based on their own assumptions on defining the desired situation of the target group. The needs analysis raised the importance of the systematic and structure needs assessment of the target group, in order to define the educational needs and the development of the corresponding program (Sork & Caffarella, 1989). Moreover, the accurate definition of the program's content and the elements that will facilitate elderly people education are decisive factors in making the program interesting to the learners and cover their needs, while remaining within their capabilities so that learners will not be discouraged (Berlyne, 1960).

Elderly women are more willing to attend educational programs than men. Situational and dispositional barriers were highlighted by the participants who also stressed the important role of the educator in making educational courses more appealing and effective. Last but not least, the interview results showed that third age people are very keen on learning how to use social media, "if social media platforms offer all these things they say". They also believe that their use will provide them with the opportunity to fight isolation, by communicating with other individuals or groups with same interests.

These results could be the spark for further research in nearby regions with different cultural and organizational contexts, using larger samples. Moreover, the adoption of a mixed approach that incorporates both quantitative and qualitative data by using a Social Media platform as a medium for data collection, could trigger further research in all these directions.

REFERENCES

Baltes, P. B., Smith, J., & Staudinger, U. (1992). Wisdom and successful aging. In T. B. Sonderegger (Ed.), *Psychology and aging* (pp. 123–167). University of Nebraska Press.

Berenguer, A., Goncalves, J., Hosio, S., Ferreira, D., Anagnostopoulos, T., & Kostakos, V. (2017). Are Smartphones Ubiquitous? An in-depth survey of smartphone adoption by seniors. *IEEE Consumer Electronics Magazine*, *6*(1), 104–110. doi:10.1109/MCE.2016.2614524

Berlyne, D. E. (1960). *Conflict, arousal, and curiosity*. McGraw-Hill. doi:10.1037/11164-000

Boulton-Lewis, G. M. (2010). Education and learning for the elderly: Why, how, what. *Educational Gerontology*, *36*(3), 213–228. doi:10.1080/03601270903182877

Braun, V., & Clarke, V. (2006). Using thematic analysis in psychology. *Qualitative Research in Psychology*, *3*(2), 77–101. doi:10.1191/1478088706qp063oa

Caffarella, R. S. (1988). *Program Development and Evaluation: Resource Book for Trainers*. John Wiley and Sons.

Caffarella, R. S. (2002). *Planning programs for adults: A comprehensive guide* (2nd ed.). Jossey-Bass.

Carpentieri, J. D., Elliott, J., Brett, C. E., & Deary, I. J. (2017). Adapting to aging: Older people talk about their use of selection, optimization, and compensation to maximize well-being in the context of physical decline. *The Journals of Gerontology: Series B*, *72*(2), 351–361. PMID:28364519

Castro, M., Ruiz-Mezcua, B., Sánchez-Pena, J. M., Garcia Crespo, A., Iglesias, A., & Pajares, J. L. (2011). Tablets Helping Elderly and Disabled People. In *Partnerships for Social Innovation in Europe: Proceedings of the AAL Forum 2011 Lecce* (pp. 237–244). Lecce: Ambient Assisted Living Joint Programme Forum.

Cohen, L., Manion, L., & Morrison, K. (2013). *Research methods in education* (7th ed.). Routledge. doi:10.4324/9780203720967

Cosco, T. D., Prina, A. M., Perales, J., Stephan, B. C., & Brayne, C. (2014). Operational definitions of successful aging: A systematic review. *International Psychogeriatrics*, *26*(3), 373–381. doi:10.1017/S1041610213002287 PMID:24308764

Cross, K. P. (1981). *Adults as Learners: Increasing Participation and Facilitating Learning*. Jossey-Bass.

Cuadrado-García, M., Ruiz-Molina, M. E., & Montoro-Pons, J. D. (2010). Are there gender differences in e-learning use and assessment? Evidence from an interuniversity online project in Europe. *Procedia: Social and Behavioral Sciences*, *2*(2), 367–371. doi:10.1016/j.sbspro.2010.03.027

Cuddy, A. J., Norton, M. I., & Fiske, S. T. (2005). This old stereotype: The pervasiveness and persistence of the elderly stereotype. *The Journal of Social Issues*, *61*(2), 267–285. doi:10.1111/j.1540-4560.2005.00405.x

Czaja, S. J., Guerrier, J. H., Nair, S. N., & Landauer, T. K. (1993). Computer communication as an aid to independence for older adults. *Behaviour & Information Technology*, *12*(4), 197–207. doi:10.1080/01449299308924382

Darkenwald, G. G., & Merriam, S. B. (1982). *Adult education: Foundations of practice*. Harper & Row.

Delello, J. A., & McWhorter, R. R. (2017). Reducing the digital divide: Connecting older adults to iPad technology. *Journal of Applied Gerontology*, *36*(1), 3–28. doi:10.1177/0733464815589985 PMID:26084479

Dianeosis. (2019, January). *Low fertility in Greece, demographic crisis and family support policies*. Dianeosis-Research and Policy Institute. Retrieved from https://www.dianeosis.org/wp-content/uploads/2019/01/ekke_family_policies.pdf

Engelhardt, H., Buber, I., Skirbekk, V., & Prskawetz, A. (2010). Social involvement, behavioural risks and cognitive functioning among older people. *Ageing and Society*, *30*(5), 779–809. doi:10.1017/S0144686X09990626

Eurostat. (2018, August 17). *Proportion of population aged 65 and over*. Retrieved from https://ec.europa.eu/eurostat/tgm/table.do?tab=table&init=1&language=en&pcode=tps00028&plugin=1

Foster, L., & Walker, A. (2015). Active and successful aging: A European policy perspective. *The Gerontologist*, *55*(1), 83–90. doi:10.1093/geront/gnu028 PMID:24846882

Friebe, J., & Schmidt-Hertha, B. (2013). Activities and barriers to education for elderly people. *Journal of Contemporary European Studies*, *64*(1), 10–27.

Glynn, R. J., Bouchard, G. R., LoCastro, J. S., & Laird, N. M. (1985). Aging and generational effects on drinking behaviors in men: Results from the normative aging study. *American Journal of Public Health*, *75*(12), 1413–1419. doi:10.2105/AJPH.75.12.1413 PMID:4061714

Gorard, S., & Smith, E. (2007). Do barriers get in the way? A review of the determinants of post-16 participation. *Research in Post-Compulsory Education*, *12*(2), 141–158. doi:10.1080/13596740701387437

Greenhow, C., & Lewin, C. (2016). Social media and education: Reconceptualizing the boundaries of formal and informal learning. *Learning, Media and Technology*, *41*(1), 6–30. doi:10.1080/17439884.2015.1064954

Harrington, C. L., Bielby, D., & Bardo, A. R. (2014). *Aging, Media, and Culture*. Lexington Books.

Hillman, D. C., Willis, D. J., & Gunawardena, C. N. (1994). Learner-interface interaction in distance education: An extension of contemporary models and strategies for practitioners. *American Journal of Distance Education*, *8*(2), 30–42. doi:10.1080/08923649409526853

Hope, A., Schwaba, T., & Piper, A. M. (2014, April). Understanding digital and material social communications for older adults. In *Proceedings of the SIGCHI Conference on Human Factors in Computing Systems* (pp. 3903-3912). ACM. 10.1145/2556288.2557133

HSA. (2014, September 12). *Demographic and social characteristics of the Resident Population of Greece according to the 2011 Population - Housing Census revision of 20-3-2014*. Hellenic Statistical Authority. Retrieved https://www.statistics.gr/en/statistics/-/publication/SAM03/2011

Illeris, K. (2006). Lifelong learning and the low-skilled. *International Journal of Lifelong Education*, *25*(1), 15–28. doi:10.1080/02601370500309451

Jung, E. H., Walden, J., Johnson, A. C., & Sundar, S. S. (2017). Social networking in the aging context: Why older adults use or avoid Facebook. *Telematics and Informatics*, *34*(7), 1071–1080. doi:10.1016/j.tele.2017.04.015

Jung, I. (2012). Asian learners' perception of quality in distance education and gender differences. *The International Review of Research in Open and Distributed Learning*, *13*(2), 1. Advance online publication. doi:10.19173/irrodl.v13i2.1159

Knowles, M. S. (1980). The modern practice of adult education. New York: Cambridge.

Kress, G. (2003). *Literacy in the New Media Age*. Routledge.

Lee, B., Godbey, G., & Sawyer, S. (2003). SeniorNet, v. 2.0. *Parks & Recreation (Ashburn)*, *38*(10), 22–28.

Lehr, U., & Kruse, A. (2006). Verlängerung der Lebensarbeitszeit-eine realistische Perspektive? *Zeitschrift für Arbeits-und Organisationspsychologie A&O, 50*(4), 240-247.

Leist, A. K. (2013). Social media use of older adults: A mini-review. *Gerontology*, *59*(4), 378–384. doi:10.1159/000346818 PMID:23594915

Levy, B. R. (2017). Age-stereotype paradox: Opportunity for social change. *The Gerontologist*, *57*(suppl_2), S118-S126.

Ma, Q., Chan, A. H., & Chen, K. (2016). Personal and other factors affecting acceptance of smartphone technology by older Chinese adults. *Applied Ergonomics*, *54*, 62–71. doi:10.1016/j.apergo.2015.11.015 PMID:26851465

Martin, A. (2009). Digital literacy for the third age: Sustaining identity in an uncertain world. *eLearning Papers, 12*, 1–15. Retrieved from https://pdfs.semanticscholar.org/c7e3/ee4aee40aa07718a7f5d-1123ba074a604e78.pdf

Merriam, S. B. (2001). Andragogy and self-directed learning: Pillars of adult learning theory. In S. B. Merriam (Ed.), The new update on adult learning theory (pp. 3-13). New Directions for Adult and Continuing Education, No. 89. San Francisco: Jossey-Bass.

Morrell, R. W., Mayhorn, C. B., & Bennett, J. (2000). A survey of World Wide Web use in middle-aged and older adults. *Human Factors*, *42*(2), 175–182. doi:10.1518/001872000779656444 PMID:11022878

Moseley, J. L., & Heaney, M. J. (1994). Needs assessment across disciplines. *Performance Improvement Quarterly*, *7*(1), 60–79. doi:10.1111/j.1937-8327.1994.tb00617.x

Nef, T., Ganea, R. L., Müri, R. M., & Mosimann, U. P. (2013). Social networking sites and older users–a systematic review. *International Psychogeriatrics*, *25*(7), 1041–1053. doi:10.1017/S1041610213000355 PMID:23552297

Nguyen, H., Tapanainen, T., & Obi, T. (2014). A Review of Information Communication Technology (ICT) Training for Elderly People – Toward Recommendations for Developing Countries. *Proceedings of the Pacific Asia Conference on Information Systems (PACIS 2014)*, 267.

Noble, H., & Smith, J. (2015). Issues of validity and reliability in qualitative research. *Evidence-Based Nursing*, *18*(2), 34–35. doi:10.1136/eb-2015-102054 PMID:25653237

Ordonez, T. N., Yassuda, M. S., & Cachioni, M. (2011). Elderly online: Effects of a digital inclusion program in cognitive performance. *Archives of Gerontology and Geriatrics*, *53*(2), 216–219. doi:10.1016/j.archger.2010.11.007 PMID:21131070

Pan, S., & Jordan-Marsh, M. (2010). Internet use intention and adoption among Chinese older adults: From the expanded technology acceptance model perspective. *Computers in Human Behavior*, *26*(5), 1111–1119. doi:10.1016/j.chb.2010.03.015

Patterson, N. (2012). Distance education: A perspective from Women's Studies. *International Women Online Journal of Distance Education*, *1*(2), 1–14.

Pavlis-Korres, M., & Garcia Barriocanal, E. (2013). Promoting Multiculturalism in Technology Based-Education: A Framework for the Improvement of Compatibility between Educators of Special Groups and their Learners and a Case Study on Educators of Roma in Greece to Prove its Efficiency. In F. Garcia-Penalvo (Ed.), Multiculturalism in Technology Based Education: Case Studies on ICT-Supported Approaches (pp. 100-124). University of Salamanca. doi:10.4018/978-1-4666-2101-5.ch007

Pavlis Korres, M., & Leftheriotou, P. (2016). Building Interaction in Adults' Online Courses: A Case Study on Training E-Educators of Adults. In L. Kyei-Blankson, E. Ntuli, & C. Agyeman (Eds.), *Handbook of Research on Strategic Management of Interaction, Presence and Participation in Online Courses* (pp. 185–215). IGI-Global. doi:10.4018/978-1-4666-9582-5.ch008

Prensky, M. (2001). Digital Natives, Digital Immigrants. On the Horizon, 9(5).

Principi, A., & Lamura, G. (2009). Education for older people in Italy. *Educational Gerontology*, *35*(3), 246–259. doi:10.1080/03601270802611349

Ramón-Jerónimo, M. A., Peral-Peral, B., & Arenas-Gaitan, J. (2013). Elderly persons and Internet use. *Social Science Computer Review*, *31*(4), 389–403. doi:10.1177/0894439312473421

Rogers, A. (2007). *Teaching Adults* (3rd ed.). Open University Press.

Roosmaaa, E. L., & Saar, E. (2011). *Barriers to and in participation in lifelong learning*. Retrieved March 20, 2020 from http://lll2010.tlu.ee/folder.2006-02-22.7534376022/subproject-2/sp2-national-reports/sp2_nr_estonia_b-3.pdf

Rubenson, K., & Desjardins, R. (2009). The impact of welfare state regimes on barriers to participation in adult education: A bounded agency model. *Adult Education Quarterly*, *59*(3), 187–207. doi:10.1177/0741713609331548

SAEA. (2012). *Report on Educational Program for Third Age People*. Scientific Adults' Educators Association.

Shapira, N., Barak, A., & Gal, I. (2007). Promoting older adults' well-being through Internet training and use. *Aging & Mental Health*, *11*(5), 477–484. doi:10.1080/13607860601086546 PMID:17882585

Smythe, A., Jenkins, C., Galant-Miecznikowska, M., Bentham, P., & Oyebode, J. (2017). A qualitative study investigating training requirements of nurses working with people with dementia in nursing homes. *Nurse Education Today*, *50*, 119–123. doi:10.1016/j.nedt.2016.12.015 PMID:28043078

Sork, T., & Caffarella, R. (1989). Planning Programs for Adults. In Sh. Merriam & Ph. Cunningham (Eds.), *Handbook of Adult and Continuing Education* (pp. 233–245). Jossey-Bass.

Tirado-Morueta, R., Hernando-Gómez, Á., & Aguaded-Gomez, J. I. (2016). The capacity of elderly citizens to access digital media in Andalusia (Spain). *Information Communication and Society*, *19*(10), 1427–1444. doi:10.1080/1369118X.2015.1111401

Tyner, K. (1998). *Literacy in a Digital World*. Lawrence Erlbaum.

Van Deursen, A. J., & Helsper, E. J. (2015). A nuanced understanding of Internet use and non-use among the elderly. *European Journal of Communication*, *30*(2), 171–187. doi:10.1177/0267323115578059

Vošner, H. B., Bobek, S., Kokol, P., & Krečič, M. J. (2016). Attitudes of active older Internet users towards online social networking. *Computers in Human Behavior*, *55*, 230–241. doi:10.1016/j.chb.2015.09.014

WHO. (2002, April). *Active ageing. A policy framework*. World Health Organization. Retrieved from https://www.who.int/ageing/publications/active_ageing/en/

Wolf, M. A. (2009). Older Adulthood. In P. Jarvis (Ed.), *The Routledge International Handbook of Lifelong Learning* (pp. 56–64). Routledge, Taylor & Francis Group.

Wu, J., & Koon, L. C. (2012, July). Tangible social-media application for the elderly. In *Proceedings of the 6th International Conference on Rehabilitation Engineering & Assistive Technology* (article no 37, pp. 1-4). Singapore Therapeutic, Assistive & Rehabilitative Technologies (START) Centre.

KEY TERMS AND DEFINITIONS

Educational Needs: Educational needs is the gap between the learner's current level of knowledge, skills, and attitudes and the desired one, in order to adapt to a new situation which can be acquired through education.

Non-Formal Education: The educational process planned and organized outside of the formal educational system. It is flexible and often responds to the learning needs of specific groups of people.

Older Adult Learner: A third aged person voluntarily involved in learning and educational activities.

Smartphone: A modern mobile phone with a touchscreen interface, capable of performing communication and multimedia functions (e-mail, social media, internet access, camera, GPS) like a computer.

Social Media: A web-based communication platform where users form online communities and social networks share information and exchange personal messages.

Third Age People: People aged over 65 years, often in retirement stage, who may be facing physical and social limitations.

Chapter 8
Facilitating the Educational Process in Synchronous Group Advisory Online Meetings in the Hellenic Open University

Eleni Karakolidou
Hellenic Open University, Greece

Piera Leftheriotou
Hellenic Open University, Greece

Maria Pavlis Korres
Hellenic Open University, Greece & Aristotle University of Thessaloniki, Greece

ABSTRACT

The Hellenic Open University launched synchronous online group advisory meetings for the academic year 2016-17 through the Skype for Business videoconferencing platform. This chapter focuses on the extent to which interaction, immediacy, and collaborative learning are developed in this particular online learning environment, as well as on the skills required for an efficient adult e-tutor. Research conducted in 2019 has shown that learners scored high in terms of interaction, immediacy, and collaborative learning between each other and their tutor, especially when working in online workgroups, while the learning process was facilitated by immediate e-tutor feedback, which resolved queries, and the effective facilitation of the discussion. In terms of factors hindering the learning process, learners cited the lack of meaningful relationships with their peers as a leading one, e-tutors pointed to technical problems, while both agreed on the inadequate use of communication and collaborative tools in an online environment.

DOI: 10.4018/978-1-7998-4972-8.ch008

Copyright © 2021, IGI Global. Copying or distributing in print or electronic forms without written permission of IGI Global is prohibited.

INTRODUCTION

Advanced learning technologies have shaped a new reality in education, making distance education a feasible and effective process in teaching and learning, through which the accessibility of adult learners in education and learning is facilitated and increased (Seaman, Allen & Seaman, 2018; Gallagher, 2019; Legon, Garett, & Fredericksen, 2019). In present times, there is an abundance of e-learning programs offered in the context of both formal and non-formal education, aiming at the acquisition of qualifications and certifications. A number of programs are aiming to cope with the demands of the labour market, covering at the same time the educational needs of the workforce, seeking the convergence of existing skills with those required by the market (Stokes, 2015; Selingo, 2017). In contrast to the prevailing belief that e-learning programs are inferior to their respective live courses, they have proven to be just as good, if not better than the conventional courses (Bailey, Vaduganathan, Henry, Laverdiere, & Pugliese, 2018; Pavlis Korres, 2018). At the same time, there is also a change of attitude among employers who consider online degrees equivalent -to say the least- if not better than the conventional ones (Gallagher, 2019), reflecting the increasing popularity of those degrees.

The international literature indicates that all types of interaction increase, so does immediacy, whereas learning becomes more cooperative and social. Similarly, as learner satisfaction increases, so does the learning outcome. (Allen, Witt, & Wheeless, 2006; Schutt, Allen, & Laumakis, 2009). According to Dönmez et al. (2010), observing and studying interactions between learners can provide a variety of information regarding their characteristics, motivations and preferences, and each education system has to examine their individual characteristics (for example, gender, age and technological experience) in order to design appropriate educational/training programs.

However, the effectiveness of these programs is not based on proper and effective design (Song, Singleton, Hill, & Koh, 2004; Bonk & Zhang, 2006; Pavlis Korres, 2010). One of the serious criticisms levelled at e-learning is the lack of communication and interaction, due to geographical distance and time difference between educator and learner, which greatly impedes the creation of an effective learning environment (Anderson, & Garrison, 1998; Anderson, 2003; Muilenburg & Berge, 2005).

Therefore, the investigation of factors facilitating or hindering interaction, immediacy and collaborative learning in e-learning environments, is particularly important. E-learning environments adopt and combine asynchronous and synchronous e-learning modes, depending on the aim of the educational institutions and programs (Hrastinski, 2008). Among the educational institutions utilizing distance learning in Greece is the Hellenic Open University (HOU), the only University in the country offering distance learning for adults exclusively, through an asynchronous educational platform combined with face to face group advisory meetings. Since the academic year 2017-2018, HOU is offering alternative full online courses via Skype for Business, in which face to face meetings have been replaced by synchronous online ones, in order to overcome significant barriers in students' access to face to face meetings, especially those in remote areas of the country. These resulted in higher participation opportunity for learners, particularly in important meetings where support, feedback and further guidance is offered to the participants (Simpson, 2002).

This chapter focuses on the investigation of learners' and educators' views on educational process issues in the synchronous online group advisory meetings in HOU. In the first section of the chapter, the theoretical background is presented. In this context, the notions of interaction, immediacy and collaborative learning are clarified. The notion of collaborative learning is examined in relation to learning communities and social presence of the educator and the learners in an online educational environment

(Rovai, 2002; Salmon, 2004; Pallof & Pratt, 2005). Moreover, the role of the adult educator in an online environment, as well as the necessary skills required for the successful performance of their role, are defined.

In the second section of the chapter, the results of an empirical research carried out in 2019 on entirely online courses of two HOU postgraduate programs are presented; the research is conducted in the aid of both quantitative and qualitative data. A questionnaire concerning learners' views and interviews exploring educators' views were also applied as data collection tools.

The research focuses on the investigation of learners' and educators' views on educational process issues in the synchronous online group advisory meetings. Specifically, the degree of interaction, immediacy and student/student, student/educator collaborative learning are investigated, as well as the correlation between these factors, the effect of individual learner characteristics (such as gender, age, technological experience) on the above variables and the factors which facilitated or hindered the educational process in this courses.

THEORETICAL APPROACH

Interaction in an Online Environment

According to Pavlis-Korres & Leftheriotou (2016), it is necessary to incorporate adult education principles which have been shown to maximize educational benefits, reduce the feeling of isolation and lead to successful learning experiences in an e-learning environment. Investigating the needs of prospective learners, utilizing their preferred learning style, treating them as individuals with different desires and needs (Twigg, 2003), facilitating active, collaborative and interactive learning, developing high-order thinking skills (Huang, 2002; Ku, Tseng, & Akarasriworn, 2013) and acquiring new skills and knowledge that are in line with the learners' needs are essential elements in online adult education programs.

The integration of adult learning principles is crucial for quality e-learning (Pavlis Korres, Karalis, Leftheriotou, & García Barriocanal, 2009). The same holds for interaction, which has been extensively studied by many researchers (Thurmond & Wambach, 2004; Mutalib, Halim, & Yahaya, 2016; Tawfik et al., 2018; Oyarzun, Stefaniak, Bol, & Morrison, 2018) not only in terms of its various types, but also in terms of its quality. Interaction is defined as a dynamic process of communication in a learning environment between participants who modify their actions, behaviors and reactions to actions, behaviors and reactions of the interaction partners (Pavlis Korres, 2015, p. 175). Interaction is a multifaceted notion, its main characteristic being the mutuality of action and response (Simpson & Galbo, 1986, as cited in Chavdoulas, Pavlis Korres, & Leftheriotou, 2019).

Moore (1989) distinguished between three types of interaction: between learner and content, through which learners acquire new knowledge or enrich their knowledge, between peers, and between educator and learner. A fourth type of interaction was added by Hilman, Willis, and Gunawardena (1994) who introduced the learner-interface interaction, which presupposes digital literacy skills. This type of interaction affects the other three types as well and relates exclusively to e-learning, while the previous ones can be used in face to face learning environments with different quality characteristics. Anderson & Garrison (1998) mention three more types of interaction: teacher-teacher, teacher-content and content-content. The interaction between teachers is aimed at the mutual exchange of educational perceptions, teaching methods and more generally concerns that contribute to the improvement of the learning process and to their personal development as professionals (Ionita et al., 2015). Teachers can also interact with content as a result of their need to create conditions of active learning. Adding to the above types is the interaction between content and content, something that allows content to be updated and enriched with new data since it is able to "converse" with other types of content (Pavlis Korres, 2018).

In addition, Moore and Kearsley (1996), Soo and Bonk (1998), Hirumi (2002), Chou, Peng, and Chang (2010) and Pattnayak and Pattnaik (2016) also refer to the interaction between learner and self-interaction, given that, within an e-learning environment, learners are called upon to develop new skills, such as self-regulation and self-directed learning, creating a personalized learning environment. Finally, Sutton (2000) distinguishes between one more type of interaction, vicarious interaction, where "a student actively interacts with both students and the instructor" (p. 4).

Immediacy

Along with interaction, the relationships that develop within a synchronous and asynchronous e-learning environment play an important role in the educational process. For Thweatt and McCroskey (1996), immediacy is defined as those communicative behaviours that reduce perceived distance between people, whereas according to Mehrabian (1967), immediacy reflects the intensity of an interaction. Research by Woods and Baker (2004) demonstrates that the incorporation of verbal as well as non-verbal elements (e.g., facial expressions, body language) establishes an authentic intimacy between educators and learners.

Mehrabian (1971) and later Gorham (1988) asserted that verbal elements (e.g., using humour, using personal examples/experiences the teacher has had, posing questions, addressing students by name, initiating conversations) contribute to perceived immediacy and are linguistic choices that undoubtedly establish a sense of psychological closeness. At the same time, Mehrabian (1971) found that non-verbal elements, such as eye contact, head nods, voice expressiveness, gestures (Andersen, Andersen, & Jensen, 1979) enhance psychological closeness and create conditions that promote interaction and reduce the sense of isolation that learners may feel in an online class.

Butland and Beebe (1992) as well as Pavlis Korres and Leftheriotou (2016) recommend the timely establishment of immediacy in order to overcome space-time barriers and promote interaction more rapidly in the synchronous online environment. In fact, LaRose and Whitten (2000) illustrate how immediacy can be greater in an online educational environment compared to a conventional one. Through interface, personal greetings can be established when users connect, along with personal forms of communication with students, tutor guidance on online navigation, automatic praise and feedback responses, all of which can effectively contribute to enhanced immediacy. With the development of technology, non-verbal communication is also achieved through the use of devices like microphones and cameras, which promote audio-visual communication between participants, chat, which promotes interaction and immediacy, as well as the use of video conferencing, audio files, or videos in the forum (Finkelstein, 2006; Hrastinski, 2008).

Collaborative Learning

As educational technology is growing rapidly and communication and collaborative tools are being utilized in the learning process, the online learning environment is becoming a 'vehicle' that can strengthen the links between educators and learners, promote a community feeling and enhance the benefits of collaborative learning.

Based on research data, one can observe that, with the contribution of technology, learners develop collective forms of thinking through the joint construction of knowledge (Dillenbourg & Fischer, 2007; Masud, 2016), thus confirming the association between e-learning and collaborative learning (Dillenbourg & Fischer, 2007; Vuopala, Hyvönen, & Järvelä, 2016). In the same vein, Kupczynski et al. (2012) argue that collaborative groups gain more learning benefits in online classes than face to face ones.

However, despite the optimum results of the combination of e-learning and collaborative learning, not all technologies have been explored and harnessed sufficiently, including multi-user environments, the availability of digital tools, the creation of user groups according to common interests. etc. (Hrastinski, 2008; O'Neil et al., 2010), while in the last decade there has been a growing body of research exploring the role that popular social media platforms, such as Facebook, can play in collaborative learning. (Llorens & Capdeferro, 2011; Jumaat and Tasir, 2013; Tsovaltzi, Weinberger, Scheuer, Dragon, & McLaren, 2013; Prestridge, 2014; Mahmud & Wong, 2018). It is therefore evident that we still have a lot more to learn when it comes to quality elements of e-learning, which, despite having evolved, still remains largely unexplored (Wu, 2015; Esfijani, 2018).

A key factor in the achievement of collaborative e-learning is the educator, who moves away from being the "authority" in the traditional teacher-centred classroom and assumes the role of the designer and process facilitator (Goodyear, Salmon, Spector, Steeples, & Tickner, 2001). He or she is responsible for the overall coordination of a collaborative online environment that ensures the active participation of online group members (Gu,Shao, Guo, & Lim, 2015) by using online teaching techniques that enable learners to interact with educational material as well as with each other (Horton & Horton, 2003). More recent research (Sharan et al., 2013), however, indicates that cooperative activities might be limited due to teacher mentality and inadequate teacher training, an impediment to establishing collaborative learning at all levels of education. As reported by Vuopala et al. (2016), the role of effective interaction in the learning process should be understood by everyone involved, in order to achieve the desired collaborative learning.

The Adult Educator in the Online Environment

E-adult educators are crucial to the learning process in an online learning group, as they are required to possess a variety of skills in order for them to successfully perform their role. More specifically, the e-adult educator promotes interpersonal communication and collaboration with learners, facilitates all types of interaction, creates favourable learning conditions, and ensures the effective functioning of the online group. Central to establishing interaction is the smooth operation of the online group. In the first stage of its formation, students are welcomed by the educator, familiarized with the online environment and encouraged to participate actively. In the second stage, they get to know each other and build "the communication bridge". In the third, they utilize the educational material mainly individually and participate in activities that promote the exchange of ideas. In the fourth stage, they participate in group discussions and collaborative activities and, finally, in the fifth stage, they develop critical thinking around the subject matter, the e-learning process itself and the networking among group members (Salmon, 2004). Consequently, the operation of the online group promotes a friendly educational atmosphere, socialization of members and interaction between them, collaborative and self-directed learning, as well as the subsequent networking of group members, all of which is consistent with the basic principles of adult learning (Pavlis Korres, 2012; Pavlis-Korres & Leftheriotou, 2016). Therefore, it should be emphasized that interaction alone, without the creation of online groups, fails to develop a positive social dynamic that will prevent isolation among learners and lead to optimal learning outcomes in an online environment (Brown, 2001; Conrand & Donalson, 2004).

It is also necessary for the e-tutor to integrate the principles of adult learning and establish the conditions for effective adult learning in an e-learning environment (Pavlis Korres et al., 2009). This can be achieved when they plan appropriate individual and group activities (e.g. brainstorming, pair discussions, group work, group discussions facilitated by the use of microphones and cameras, "voting" and conducting "polls" on the platform) by utilizing active teaching techniques, (Cranton, 2000; Caffarella, 2002; Hrastinski, 2008). In addition to these activities, the e-tutor can contribute to the creation of Learning Objects Repositories that allow for improved e-tutor/content interaction, e-tutor/e-tutor interaction, and content/content interaction (Anderson, 2003).

Integrating adult education principles into an online learning environment can create conditions conductive to effective adult learning (Cranton, 2000) in order for learners to develop high order thinking skills, such as critical thinking (Huagn, 2002). At the same time, Huagn proposes collaborative, learner-cantered, authentic, interactive teaching as a guideline for adult educators. However, the role of the e-tutor becomes even more complex as they are required to help learners deal with constraints that can be caused by technology itself, regarding internet access, IT skills, familiarity with online communication, physical distance, isolation, lack of social interaction (Waltonen-Moore et al., 2006; Williams 2002; Karalis & Koutsonikos, 2003). E-tutors should also place particular emphasis on promoting interaction (Palloff & Pratt, 2003; Kearsley, 2000), understanding its nature, establishing a learning environment that enhances effective communication, and on their positive social presence (Klein & Eseryel, 2006; Rosen, 2009; Yang & Yuen, 2010; Pavlis-Korres & Leftheriotou, 2016), since all of the above can influence the effectiveness of the online class. The significance of these skills is corroborated by Denis's et al. research (2004), who found that the e-tutor must possess cognitive, pedagogical, communication and technological skills, while Salmon (2004) and Pavlis Korres (2010) include the educator's personal characteristics as well (positive attitude to online learning and training, ability to adapt to new roles, and to develop an online identity as an educator, etc.).

Further, in the context of e-moderating, the educator must promote and support learner autonomy, so that the learner is emotionally independent of the instructor (Moore, 2007), as the adult learner's need for autonomy stems from their maturation combined with the formation of their personal and social identity (Knowles, 1970). Along with the above roles, Salmon (2004) introduces the term "e-moderator" to refer to e-tutors, stressing their role as facilitators of communication and cooperation in the online classroom by organizing group activities and providing timely and objective feedback, which allows students to develop learning skills (Shepherd, 2000). Consequently, in order to achieve all of the above, "e-moderators" must effectively manage time, have excellent knowledge of their subject matter, possess technical and communication skills, be able to design, monitor and evaluate the online process (Jones et al, 2003; Berman, 2006), but also to adapt their teaching to the needs of online learners (Salmon, 2004). Therefore, e-educators have multiple and complex roles, since they need to combine characteristics of both adult and distance education.

EMPIRICAL STUDY

Research Methodology

The empirical research was conducted in 2019 at the Hellenic Open University (HOU), an educational institution aimed at providing undergraduate and postgraduate distance education and training, using appropriate educational material and teaching methods, as well as promoting scientific research and the development of technology and methodology in distance education. Until the academic year 2016-2017, this institution combined the methodology of asynchronous distance learning with five face to face Group Advisory Meetings (GAM). As of the academic year 2017-2018, and in response to the modern challenges and needs of students, it has been providing them the opportunity to choose between participating in face to face Group Advisory Meetings or online ones through the online Skype For Business teleconferencing platform. HOU has thus become the first Greek university to make such an essential step in e-learning, by creating Online Courses that combine asynchronous and synchronous education.

This research focuses on investigating learner and e-tutor views on the effectiveness of the learning process in two HOU postgraduate online courses. In particular, the views of students and e-tutors on the level of interaction, immediacy and collaborative learning that develops between learners and between learners and e-tutors were investigated, in relation to the individual characteristics of learners and the educator's "electronic" profile. In addition, the factors that facilitated or hindered the e-learning process were also examined. The research was conducted following both a quantitative and a qualitative approach and uses a questionnaire that investigates students' views as well as interviews exploring e-tutors' views as data collection tools (Cohen, Manion, & Morrison, 2000).

The questionnaire, which was handed out electronically via Google Forms, included 24 Likert scale questions that investigated the degree of interaction, collaborative learning, and immediacy among students in synchronous Group Advisory Meetings of the online course. It also included 15 questions exploring students' views on the immediacy, interaction, and collaborative learning developed between e-tutor and students. In addition, students identified two positive and two negative aspects of synchronous GAMSs through open-ended questions and made suggestions for further improvement of GAMs and the overall online course. Convenient non-probability sampling was used, as the 103 study participants were willing to provide useful information to answer the questions (Creswell, 2015). The questionnaire was forwarded to postgraduate students of online courses in HOU through their tutors and Facebook groups of HOU students. In terms of the reliability of the quantitative research, the Cronbach's reliability coefficient (Creswell, 2015) was used and the values were quite satisfactory (above 0.8). Version 20 of the SPSS statistical package was used to process the quantitative data.

The research included depth focus interviews with two e-tutors (Professors/Advisors) who were selected as a purposive sample, as these individuals could provide a wealth of information (Creswell, 2015) on the subject, given their teaching experience in adult education and online courses inside and outside HOU. The interviews were conducted online (via Skype) and included 18 open-ended questions that explored their views on the role of e-tutors in synchronous GAMs, along with their views on designing and conducting synchronous GAMs to promote interaction, immediacy, collaborative learning and the creation of online groups. Their views regarding their experience with online courses and their suggestions for further improvement of the learning process were also explored. In order to process the qualitative data and draw conclusions, thematic analysis was applied, whereas, through a combination of questionnaires and interviews, the triangulation of data (Creswell, 2015) was achieved.

RESEARCH RESULTS

Of the 103 respondents, 20% were men, 75% were aged between 25-45 years, 50% had previously attended e-learning courses outside HOU, 50% possessed advanced computer skills and 50% were introduced to workgroups through GAMs offered in HOU online courses.

The interaction between learners was considered satisfactory (Mean: 3.44), with significant room for improvement, as 50% of the students reported interaction values above 3.5 (Median: 3.5). The degree of immediacy among students had a mean of 3.84 and was found to be more satisfactory with little room for improvement, although there was a large variance, with a median of 4. Collaborative learning among learners had a mean of 3.44 with a median of 3.5 and was assessed as satisfactory, deeming the course successful in terms of collaborative learning. The interaction between learners and the educator had a mean of 3.73 and was considered positive with some room for improvement, although the median was 4, which indicated that 50% of the students scored above 4, which, in turn, was an indicator that interaction was facilitated by the educator. Immediacy between educator and learners was evaluated quite positively with little room for improvement (Mean: 3.82), while the evaluation of collaborative learning on the educator's part was marginally positive with vast scope for improvement (Mean: 3.59). Therefore, of the three variables concerning learners, immediacy was the characteristic that took on the highest value (see Table 1).

Table 1. Mean, standard deviation and median for the three scales relating to learners

	Mean	Median	Standard deviation
Immediacy	3,8447	4,0000	,91295
Collaborative learning	3,4414	3,5000	,80146
Interaction	3,4453	3,5000	,68510

Similarly, in terms of the three variables pertaining to the educator, immediacy was found to be the variable with the highest value (see Table 2).

Table 2. Mean, standard deviation and median for the three scales relating to the educator

	Mean	Median	Standard deviation
Interaction	3,7398	4,0000	1,02817
Immediacy	3,8214	4,0000	,88999
Collaborative learning	3,5900	3,8012	1,0021

Exploring whether interaction, immediacy, and collaborative learning between the educator and learners could affect interaction, immediacy, and collaborative learning that develops between learners, the Pearson correlation coefficient values (see Table 3) for the 6 variables ranged from moderate to slightly strong, as statistically significant correlations were obtained in all correlation pairs at a level of

Table 3. Pearson correlation coefficient values between Educator's Immediacy, Collaborative Learning and Interaction scales and Learner/Learner respective ones

	Learner/Learner Immediacy	**Learner/Learner Collaborative Learning**	**Learner/Learner Interaction**
Educator Immediacy	,499**	,540**	,643**
Educator Collaborative Learning	,460**	,563**	,588**
Educator Interaction	,476**	,586**	,661**

statistical significance of 99% (p-value = 0.01) (Creswell, 2015). More specifically, there was a positive correlation between learner/learner interaction and educator immediacy, which reveals a tendency for learner/learner interaction to be further facilitated when educator immediacy increases.

Regarding the impact of individual characteristics such as gender, age and proficiency in computer skills on immediacy, interaction and learner/learner and educator/learner collaborative learning, the analysis of variance (ANOVA) was used. The test did not indicate a statistically significant difference in age, education and computer skills. However, a statistically significant difference was found between the two sexes in terms of collaborative learning between learners ($p = 0.32$ $F = 4.751$). It is noteworthy, of course, that individuals with advanced computer skills or previous experience in e-learning within or outside HOU have shown higher rates of interaction, immediacy and collaborative learning, although these are not statistically significant (see Figure 1).

In addition, the analysis of variance (see Figure 2) regarding the creation of work groups during Group Advisory Sessions showed that this variable has a statistically significant impact on all research variables. Thus, it is clear and statistically documented that, in those online courses where work groups were created, all six variables took on higher values.

Regarding the factors that hindered the learning process in synchronous GAMs, learners underlined the lack of substantial relationships with their peers, while e-tutors pointed out the technical problems. Learners and e-tutors agreed that the underutilization of communication-collaborative tools in the online environment inhibited the educational process. In terms of the factors that facilitated the learning process, everyone agreed on the immediate feedback of e-tutors which resolved queries, as well as on the facilitation of the discussion through pertinent questions.

Thematic analysis of the e-tutors' interviews showed that the difficulties they encountered were mainly related to the limited capabilities of the platform in terms of the implementation of active educational techniques, especially in relation to the inability to create work groups. However, e-tutors tried to overcome this obstacle and to encourage students to actively participate during synchronous GAMs by enriching teaching, mainly with questions and answers, thus giving students the opportunity to freely express their opinion and also propose changes in relation to the structure of synchronous GAMs in order to adapt teaching to their own needs. Both e-tutors and learners considered learner/learner and learner/teacher interaction as necessary, which is why they exploited every possibility offered by the existing platform (e.g. using chat as a "board" where opinions are gathered, grouped and then discussed). Among the most significant difficulties identified during the coordination of an online group of students was the teacher's difficulty to perceive all students' needs and to effectively fulfill their own complex role (e.g. as coordinator and guide). Both e-tutors stressed that the preparation and design of synchro-

Figure 1. Grouped box plot testing the impact of familiarity with e-learning on the study's scales

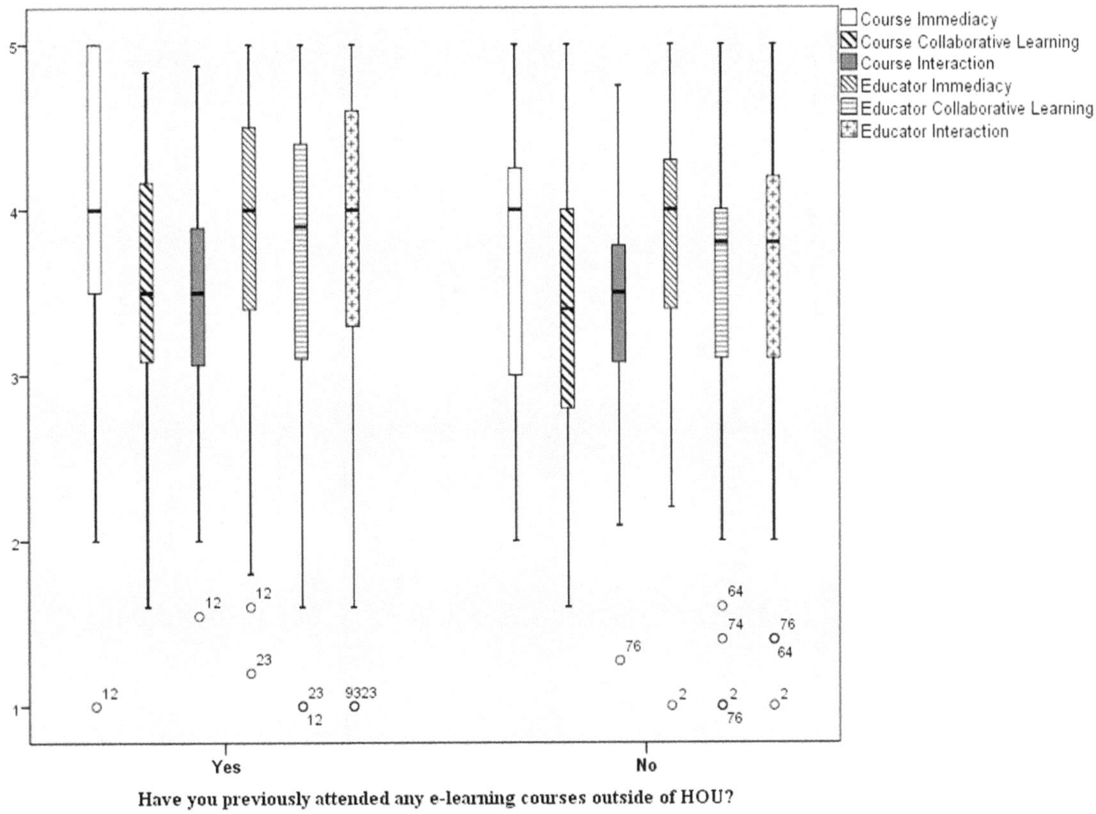

nous GAMs is more demanding and quite different to that of face to face ones. At the same time, they encouraged students to communicate with them and with each other outside of synchronous GAMs by using the asynchronous HOU platform, the internet (Skype, Messenger, Chat) and other offline media (e.g. telephone communication or face to face one, where possible). They also encouraged them to look for ways to create groups through social networks (e.g. Facebook groups), to which students responded positively. As for the role of the e-tutor, both educators agreed that it is demanding, as it includes creating an effective teaching plan, allotting extra time for activities and being closer to the students. Both educators stressed that synchronous GAMs offer students the opportunity to meet and collaborate with peers from different parts of the country, something that would not be possible otherwise, and they also pointed to GAMs' appeal, due to the fact that spatial and economic constraints are lifted. However, they also referred to issues that troubled them, such as the difficulty in building trust within the online group as a result of "faceless" communication or technical difficulties. When asked how HOU online courses could be further improved, they pointed out the need to upgrade the current platform by adding more communication and collaborative tools, the need for technical support to be more effective, and the need for students to be familiar with the platform beforehand. Finally, despite the problems they encountered, both had a positive attitude towards participating in an online course in the future, as they see it as a challenge and an opportunity for professional development.

Figure 2. Grouped box plot testing the impact of the creation of work groups on the study's scales

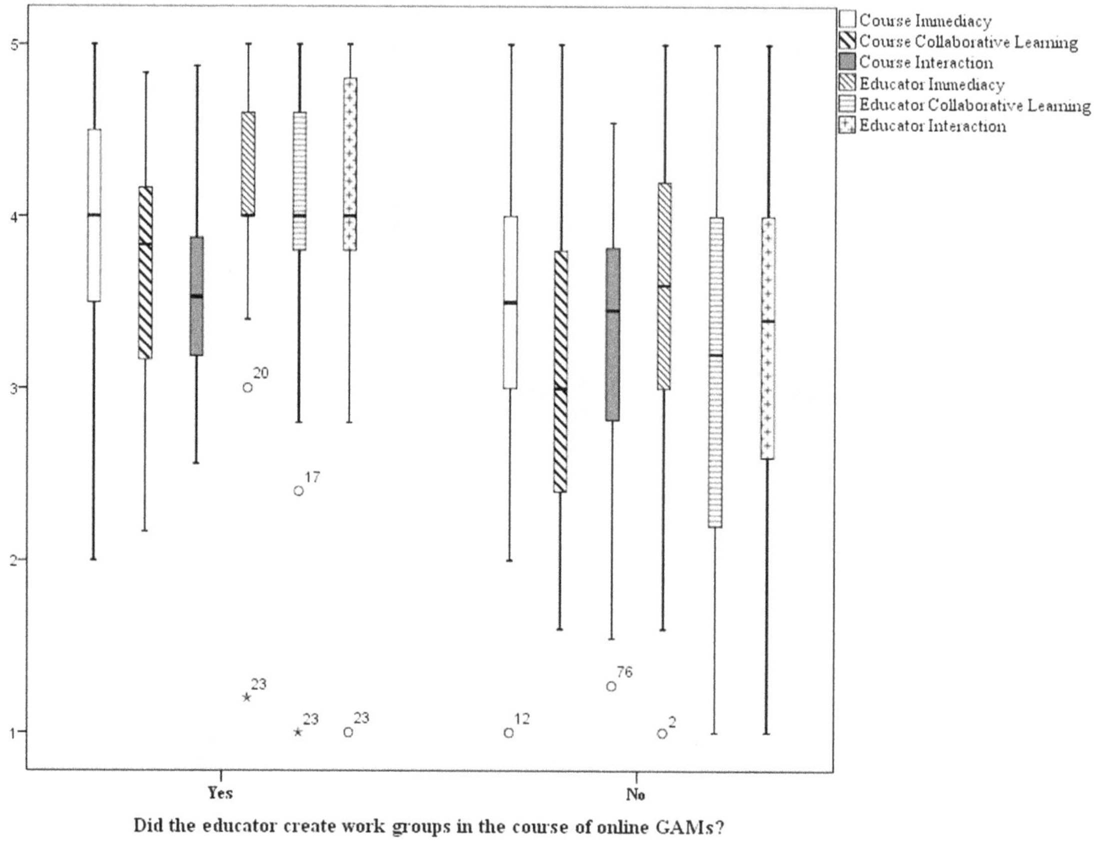

DISCUSSION AND RECOMMENDATIONS

The synthetically and comparatively obtained results from the quantitative and qualitative research data highlighted many interesting aspects of synchronous HOU Group Advisory Meetings. The satisfactory values of learner/learner and learner/teacher interaction that were derived from the questionnaires are reinforced by the interview data, as it seems that e-tutors tried to promote different types of interaction during their course in various ways. Thus, the interaction achieved led to an effective educational process (Berge, 2002). Learner/learner and teacher/learner interaction values, although satisfactory, can certainly be improved, which may arise from the fact that, due to technical problems participants faced, the interaction with interface was lesser, affecting at the same time other types of interaction as well (Hilman et el., 1994). Learner/learner and learner/teacher immediacy values were also quite satisfactory, a fact that is confirmed by quality findings. The constant feedback provided by e-tutors and the proper use of verbal and non-verbal communication technology create an affective climate which helps resolve communication problems individually or in groups (Gunter, 2007; Allen et al., 2006; Schutt et al., 2009). The immediacy that characterized synchronous GAMs may be a result of the timely immediacy behaviours that the professors/advisors exhibited and the establishment of an environment that encourages substantive discussions and free expression of views, either in writing or orally. Collaborative learning among students was at a high level, which, in turn, renders the course as successful in terms of collaborative learning, while the e-tutors' behaviours that promoted collaborative learning were marginally positive, with much room for improvement. Indicative of this is the finding that, in those synchronous GAMs where work groups were set up by educators, there was an increase in all six variables. A prerequisite for collaborative learning is the facilitation of group discussions, the public expression of students in the forum -rather than the exchange of personal e-mails- and more generally, the familiarization of students with each other along with the creation of groups with cohesive ties, regardless of differences in members' cultural and social learning backgrounds (Salmon, 2004; Misanchuk & Anderson, 2001). After all, according to Pavlis Korres (2012) the use of communication and collaborative tools facilitates self-regulated learning and contributes to the development of a dynamic community characterized by collaboration and learning as a social process (Klein & Eseryel, 2006; Rosen, 2009; Yang & Yuen, 2010). The behaviours exhibited by the two educators who participated in the study were also in this direction. By contrast, based on the participants' responses, the educators' behaviours promoting collaborative learning in synchronous GAMs were marginally positive. On the one hand, this was prompted by the fact that instructors often have conflicting feelings when they alternate between different teaching styles (Cranton & Carusetta, 2004), which affect their effectiveness. On the other hand, it is caused by the fact that different skills are required for e-tutors (Goodyear et al., 2001; Palloff & Pratt, 2003; Kearsley, 2000; Denis et al., 2004; Salmon, 2004; Pavlis Korres, & Leftheriotou, 2016). Comparing the variables of interaction, immediacy, and collaborative learning between learners, it is worth noting that immediacy takes the highest value. Similarly, upon comparing the same three variables among e-tutors, immediacy takes the highest value, while interaction is considered satisfactory and collaborative learning marginally positive.

A positive correlation was found in terms of interaction, immediacy, and collaborative learning between learners and between learners and educators, as, the more direct and collaborative the educator is, the greater the promotion of interaction between learners. The relationship between immediacy and the two other variables is also emphasized in the studies of Torun (2013), Allen et al., (2006) and Pavlis Korres and Leftheriotou (2016), according to which the high levels of educator immediacy act as interaction enhancers, especially when immediacy is manifested in a timely manner. The highest value of the correlation coefficient concerned interaction. By promoting and facilitating all types of interaction (Moore, 1989; Hilman et al., 1994), educators ensure the effectiveness of the online group, contributing greatly to the interaction between learners. Enhanced interaction is achieved both with the educator's effective communication and their positive social presence (Schutt et al., 2009). Research participants emphasize the importance of workgroups in an online learning environment, a finding that is consistent with the views of Conrand and Donalson (2004) and Pavlis Korres (2012), who hold that interaction alone - without the existence of an online group - is not enough to ensure quality teaching. It should be noted here that, along with setting up online groups, e-tutors cultivate active listening skills, online relationship development skills and online discussion management skills in an effective online learning environment where participants interact (Anderson et al, 2001; Kemshal-Bell, 2001). Therefore, e-tutor characteristics can contribute to establishing appropriate and desirable conditions for interaction, immediacy, and collaborative learning within the course.

Regarding the effect of individual learners' characteristics (gender, age, technological literacy) on interaction, immediacy and collaborative learning between learners and between learners and teachers, the analysis of quantitative data identified statistically significant differences between the sexes in relation to collaborative learning between learners. In particular, female students claimed that there was a collaborative atmosphere in the course's synchronous GAMs, which may be related to the fact that women approach the electronic classroom as an opportunity to collaborate and connect with other participants (Bostock, et al., 2005; Goldstein, et al., 2004; Gnanadass & Sanders, 2019). In terms of the remaining characteristics (age and technological literacy) no statistically significant difference was detected. However, technologically literate individuals with previous experience in e-learning tended to exhibit higher levels of interaction, collaborative learning, and immediacy.

As regards the factors hindering the learning process, students pointed out the lack of meaningful relationships with their peers. Numerous studies have identified loneliness and the lack of meaningful relationships in e-learning (Woods, 2002; Ludwig-Hardman & Dunlap, 2003; Berge & Huang, 2004; Pavlis Korres & Leftheriotou, 2016) as highly significant factors that may positively or negatively affect students' learning outcomes, but there seems to be an agreement among researchers on the fact that interaction and immediacy can actually eliminate the negative effects. For their part, e-tutors pointed out the technical problems, which, as reported in the literature, often discourage the instructor from making effective use of digital media and further exacerbate the problem of distance (Jones et al, 2003; Burrows, 2005). Both students and educators agree that the underutilization of communication and collaborative tools in the electronic environment obstructs the effectiveness of the learning process. Indeed, the use of active teaching techniques appropriately adapted to the digital environment enhances the effectiveness of e-learning (Cranton, 2000; Caffarella, 2002; Pavlis Korres, 2012). Regarding the factors that facilitated the learning process, educators and students referred to immediate e-tutor feedback which resolved queries, as well as the facilitation of the discussion through pertinent questions (Shepard, 2000; Jones et al, 2003). Their responses converge regarding e-moderator characteristics as described by Salmon (2004) and Jones et al, (2004) who highlighted the importance of providing timely feedback to online learners, and creating an atmosphere that is conducive to meaningful communication, and prevents the isolation learners may feel.

The contribution of this research is particularly significant as it explores the learning process in synchronous Group Advisory Meetings, a relatively new service the Hellenic Open University has been offering for two years. Its results can contribute to the improvement of the learning outcome and the operation of HOU online courses but can also prompt fruitful discussions and influence organizations offering online courses and adult e-tutors in Greece. In addition, as online education quality remains open to discussion internationally (Esfijani, 2018; Gallagher, 2019; Wu, 2015), the findings of this study can contribute to improving the quality of online courses that are being offered, since online learning has become a fundamental component of higher education. The findings of this research are in line with the findings of a research conducted in ten public and private universities in southern Taiwan. Findings presented remarkable correlations between e-learning and cooperative learning outcomes, as well as between e-learning and learning outcomes (Yeh & Fu, 2014). Additionally, the results of the research are relevant with those of a research implemented at a large public university in southern California aiming to determine the effects of instructor immediacy behaviours on participants' perception of the instructor's immediacy and social presence (Schutt et al., 2009). The results demonstrated that participants assigned to the high-immediacy sessions indicated significantly higher perception of instructor immediacy and social presence than participants assigned to the low-immediacy sessions.

Finally, research findings highlight the importance of the effective use of IT in education, but also the significance of cultivating digital skills/abilities so as to capitalize on opportunities that IT offers in the education sector.

Research Limitations

Among the research limitations is the fact that it was conducted in a single educational institution, the Hellenic Open University. However, HOU is the only university in Greece that offers only distance education programs addressed to adults, thus this specific study is subjected to the limitations of a case study. Additionally, convenient non-probability sampling was used and only two depth focus interviews were held. Due to these constraints, no safe general conclusions can be drawn. Moreover, the use of the Skype For Business platform, which is quite limited when used for pedagogical reasons, has created additional obstacles in the present research regarding the exploration of the utilization of advanced communication and collaborative tools along with their impact on the learning process.

CONCLUSION AND FUTURE RESEARCH DIRECTIONS

The present study highlights the correlation between interaction, immediacy and collaborative learning and their impact on the learning process, as well as the crucial role of the e-educator in promoting and developing them.

According to the research findings, learner/learner and learner/teacher immediacy has been developed at a high degree, while there has been a positive correlation between the six variables, i.e. interaction, immediacy, learner/learner and learner/teacher collaborative learning, with interaction taking on the highest value. As far as individual characteristics are concerned, differences between the two genders in learner/learner collaborative learning were found to be statistically significant. As regards the remaining individual characteristics (age and technological literacy), slight differences between learners with e-learning experience were identified, yet not statistically significant. These learners scored higher in interaction, collaborative learning and immediacy. In relation to the factors which hinder the learning process, learners maintained the lack of substantial relationships with their peers, while the educators prioritized the technical problems. Furthermore, both educators and learners pointed out the underutilization of communication and collaborative tools in the online environment. In relation to the factors which facilitated the learning process, both educators and learners pointed to immediate feedback provided by the educators on answering inquiries as well as the facilitation of discussion through pertinent questions. Additionally, a significant finding was that in all courses where the educator formed groups by integrating adult education principles, high values were recorded in all six variables.

Given the limitations of this research, it would be of interest to conduct a similar survey on a larger sample of students and educators, participating in both undergraduate and postgraduate online courses of HOU. Moreover, a comparative research between universities in different countries could be implemented focusing on the parameters affecting the online educational process, i.e. whether the university is public or private, undergraduate or postgraduate level, educational content etc. It would also be interesting to determine the specifications of an educational online platform, through which an effective online adult learning process could be achieved, based on the principles of adult education and online learning standards.

REFERENCES

Allen, M., Witt, P. L., & Wheeless, L. R. (2006). The Role of Teacher Immediacy as a Motivational Factor in Student Learning: Using Meta-Analysis to Test a Causual Model. *Communication Education*, *55*(1), 21–31. doi:10.1080/03634520500343368

Andersen, J. F., Andersen, P. A., & Jensen, A. D. (1979). The measurement of immediacy. *Journal of Applied Communication Research*, *7*(2), 153–180. doi:10.1080/00909887909365204

Anderson, L. W., Krathwohl, D. R., Airasian, P. W., Cruikshank, K. A., Mayer, R. E., Pintrich, P. R., Raths, J., & Wittrock, M. C. (Eds.). (2001). A taxonomy for learning, teaching, and assessing: A revision of Bloom's Taxonomy of Educational Objectives (Complete edition). New York: Longman.

Anderson, T. (2003). Modes of Interaction in Distance Education: Recent Developments and Research Questions. In M. G. Moore & W. G. Anderson (Eds.), *Handbook of Distance Education* (pp. 129–144). Lawrence Erlbaum Associates, Publishers.

Anderson, T., & Garrison, D. R. (1998). Learning in a networked world: New roles and responsibilities. In C. Gibson (Ed.), *Distance Learners in Higher Education* (pp. 97–112). Atwood Publishing.

Bailey, A., Vaduganathan, N., Henry, T., Laverdiere, R., & Pugliese, L. (2018). *Making digital learning work: success strategies from six leading universities and community colleges*. Arizona State University.

Berge, Z., & Huang, Y. (2004). A model for sustainable student retention: A holistic perspective on the student dropout problem with special attention to e-learning. *DEOSNEWS*, *13*(5).

Berge, Z. L. (2002). Active, Interactive and Reflective eLearning. *Quarterly Review of Distance Education*, *3*(2), 181–190.

Berman, P. (2006). *E-Learning Concepts and Techniques*. Bloomsburg University of Pennsylvania.

Bonk, C. J., & Zhang, K. (2006). Introducing the R2D2 Model: Online learning for the diverse learners of this world. *Distance Education*, *27*(2), 249–264. doi:10.1080/01587910600789670

Bostock, S., & Lizhi, W. (2005). Gender in Students' Online Discussions. *Innovations in Education and Teaching International*, *42*(1), 73–86. doi:10.1080/14703290500048978

Brown, R. E. (2001). The process of community-building in distance learning courses. *Journal of Asynchronous Learning Networks*, *5*(2).

Burrows, P. (2005). The role of the teacher-enactor and author-publisher. In M. Kalantzis & B. Cope (Eds.), *Learning by Design* (pp. 197–216). Victorian Schools Innovation Commission.

Butland, M. J., & Beebe, S. A. (1992). *A Study of the Application of Implicit Communication Theory to Teacher Immediacy and Student Learning*. Paper presented at the Annual Meeting of the International Communication Association, Miami, FL. Retrieved from ERIC database. ED 346 532.

Caffarella, R. S. (2002). *Planning programs for adult learners: A practical guide for educators, trainers, and staff developers* (2nd ed.). Jossey-Bass.

Chavdoulas, A., Pavlis Korres, M., & Leftheriotou, P. (2019). Investigating Asynchronous Interaction between MOOC Learners through Forum Use and Peer Review. In *P. Ordóñez de Pablos, M. D. Lytras, X. Zhang & K.T. Chui (Eds.), Opening Up Education for Inclusivity across Digital Economies and Societies*. IGI-Global. doi:10.4018/978-1-5225-7473-6.ch005

Chou, C., Peng, H., & Chang, C. Y. (2010). The technical framework of interactive functions for course-management systems: Students' perceptions, uses, and evaluations. *Computers & Education, 55*(3), 1004-1017. https://www.learntechlib.org/p/66863/

Cohen, L., Manion, L., & Morrison, K. (2000). *Research Methods in Education* (5th ed.). Routledge Falmer.

Conrad, R. M., & Donalson, J. A. (2004). *Engaging the online learner, Activities and resources for creative instruction*. Jossey-Bass.

Cranton, P. (2000). *Planning Instruction for Adult Learners* (2nd ed.). Wall & Emerson Inc.

Cranton, P., & Carusetta, E. (2004). Perspectives on authenticity in teaching. *Adult Education Quarterly, 55*(1), 5–22. doi:10.1177/0741713604268894

Creswell, J. W. (2015). *Educational Research. Planning, Conducting, and Evaluating Quantitave and Qualitatine Research*. Pearson Education Inc.

Denis, B., Watland, P., Pirotte, S., & Verday, N. (2004). *Roles and Competencies of the e-tutor.* Retrieved on 13 March, 2020 from https://orbi.uliege.be/bitstream/2268/12722/1/DENIS_WATLAND_PIROTTE_VERDAY_Roles_and_competencies_of_the_tutor_30_03_2009.pdf

Dillenbourg, P., & Fischer, F. (2007). Basics of Computer-Supported Collaborative Learning. *Zeitschrift für Berufs- und Wirtschaftspädagogik, 21*, 111-130.

Dönmez, O., Simsek, Ö., & Arikan, Y. D. (2010). How can we make use of learner interaction in online learning environments? *Procedia: Social and Behavioral Sciences, 9*, 783–787. doi:10.1016/j.sbspro.2010.12.234

Esfijani, A. (2018). Measuring quality in online education: A meta-synthesis. *American Journal of Distance Education, 32*(1), 57–53. doi:10.1080/08923647.2018.1417658

Finkelstein, J. (2006). *Learning in Real Time Synchronous Teaching and Learning Online*. Jossey-Bass.

Gallagher, S. (2019). *Online education in 2019: a synthesis of the data*. Center for the Future of Higher Education and Talent Strategy, Northeastern University.

Gnanadass, E., & Sanders, A. Y. (2019). Gender still matters in distance education. In M. G. Moore & W. C. Diehl (Eds.), *Handbook of distance education* (4th ed., pp. 70–90). Routledge.

Goldstein, J., & Sadhana, P. (2004). The Brink of Change: Gender in Technology-Rich Collaborative Learning Environments. *Journal of Science Education and Technology, 13*(4), 505–523. doi:10.100710956-004-1471-1

Goodyear, P., Salmon, G., Spector, J. M., Steeples, C., & Tickner, S. (2001). Competencies for online teaching. *Education Training & Development, 49*(1), 65–72.

Gorham, J. (1988). The relationship between verbal teacher immediacy behaviors and student learning. *Communication Education*, *37*(1), 40–53. doi:10.1080/03634528809378702

Gu, X., Shao, Y., Guo, X., & Lim, C. P. (2015). Designing a role structure to engage students in computer-supported collaborative learning. *The Internet and Higher Education*, *24*, 13–20. doi:10.1016/j.iheduc.2014.09.002

Gunter, G. A. (2007). The Effects of the Impact of Instructional Immediacy on Cognition and Learning in Online Classes. *International Journal of Social, Behavioral, Educational, Economic. Business and Industrial Engineering*, *1*(11), 729–735.

Hillman, D., Willis, D., & Gunawardena, C. (1994). Learner-Interface Interaction in Distance Education: An Extension of Contemporary Models and Strategies for Practitioners. *American Journal of Distance Education*, *8*(2), 30–42. doi:10.1080/08923649409526853

Hirumi, A. (2002). A framework for analyzing, designing, and sequencing planned e-learning interactions. *Quarterly Review of Distance Education*, *3*(2), 141–160.

Horton, W., & Horton, K. (2003). *E-learning Tools and Technologies: A consumer's guide for trainers, teachers, educators, and instructional designers*. Wiley Publishing.

Hrastinski, S. (2008). Asynchronous and synchronous e-learning: A study of asynchronous and synchronous e-learning methods discovered that each supports different purposes. *EDUCAUSE Quarterly*, *31*(4), 51–55. http://net.educause.edu/ir/library/pdf/EQM0848.pdf

Huang, H. M. (2002). Toward constructivism for adult learners in online learning environment. *British Journal of Educational Technology*, *33*(1), 27–37. doi:10.1111/1467-8535.00236

Ionita, A., Visan, M., Niculescu, C., & Popa, A. (2015). Smart Collaborative Platform for eLearning with Application in Spatial Enabled Society. *Procedia: Social and Behavioral Sciences*, *191*, 2097–2107. doi:10.1016/j.sbspro.2015.04.676

Jones, P., Packham, G., Miller, C., Davies, I., Jones, A., & Roberts, D. (2003). e-Retention: An Initial Evaluation of Student Withdrawals within a Virtual Learning Environment. In R. Williams, (Ed.), *Proceedings of the 2nd European Conference on E-learning (ECEL)* (pp. 239-248). Academic Conferences and Publishing International, Sonning Common.

Jones, P., Pickernell, D., & Welsh Enterprise Institute. (2004). *Student and tutor perspectives of online moderation*. Pontypridd: University of Glamorgan, Welsh Enterprise Unit.

Jumaat, N. F., & Tasir, Z. (2013). Students' types of online interaction through Facebook discussion. *Procedia: Social and Behavioral Sciences*, *97*, 353–360. doi:10.1016/j.sbspro.2013.10.245

Karalis, T., & Koutsonikos, G. (2003). Issues and Challenges in Organising and Evaluating Web based Courses for Adults. *Themes in Education, 4*(2), 177-188.

Kearsley, G. (2000). *Online education: Learning and teaching in cyberspace* (Vol. 91). Wadsworth.

Kemshal-Bell, G. (2001). *The Online Teacher. Final report prepared for the Project Steering Committee of the VET Teacher and Online Learning Project, ITAM, ESD*. TAFENSW.

Klein, J., & Eseryel, D. (2006). The Corporate Learning Environment. In M. Lytras & A. Naeve (Eds.), *Intelligent Learning Infrastructure for Knowledge Intensive Organizations A Semantic Web Primer* (pp. 1–38). Information Science Publishing. doi:10.4018/978-1-59140-503-0.ch001

Knowles, M. S. (1970). *The modern practice of adult education: Andragogy versus pedagogy*. New York Association Press.

Ku, H.-Y., Tseng, H. W., & Akarasriworn, C. (2013). Collaboration factors, teamwork satisfaction, and student attitudes toward online collaborative learning. *Computers in Human Behavior*, *29*(3), 922–929. doi:10.1016/j.chb.2012.12.019

Kupczynski, L., Mundy, M. A., Goswami, J., & Meling, V. (2012). Cooperative Learning in Distance Learning: A Mixed Methods Study. *International Journal of Instruction*, *5*(2), 81–90.

LaRose, R., & Whitten, P. (2000). Re-thinking Instructional Immediacy for Web Courses: A social cognitive exploration. *Communication Education*, *49*(4), 320–338. doi:10.1080/03634520009379221

Legon, R., Garrett, R., & Fredericksen, E. (2019). *The Changing Landscape of Online Education (CHLOE): Behind the Numbers*. Quality Matters. Retrieved from https://www.qualitymatters.org/qa-resources/resource-center/articles-resources/CHLOE-3-report-2019

Llorens, F., & Capdeferro, N. (2011). Facebook's Potential for Collaborative e-Learning. *Revista de Universidad y Sociedad del Conocimiento*, *8*(2), 197–210.

Ludwig-Hardman, S., & Dunlap, J. C. (2003). Learner support services for online students: Scaffolding for success. *International Review of Research in Open and Distance Learning*, *4*(1). Advance online publication. doi:10.19173/irrodl.v4i1.131

Mahmud, M. M., & Wong, S. F. (2018). Facebook and Collaborative Learning: An Empirical Study on Online Assessment. *International Journal of Learning and Teaching*, *4*(2), 107–113. doi:10.18178/ijlt.4.2.107-113

Masud, M. (2016). Collaborative e-learning systems using semantic data interoperability. *Computers in Human Behavior*, *61*, 127–135. doi:10.1016/j.chb.2016.02.094

Mehrabian, A. (1967). Orientation behaviors and nonverbal attitude communication. *Journal of Communication*, *17*(4), 324–332. doi:10.1111/j.1460-2466.1967.tb01190.x

Mehrabian, A. (1971). Nonverbal communication. *Nebraska Symposium on Motivation*, *19*, 107–161.

Misanchuk, M., & Anderson, T. (2001). Building Community in an Online Learning Environment: Communication, Cooperation and Collaboration. *Proceedings of the Annual Mid-South Instructional Technology Conference*. Retrieved from http://www.mtsu.edu/-itconf/proceed01/19.pdf

Moore, M. (1989). Three types of interaction. *American Journal of Distance Education*, *3*(2), 1–6. doi:10.1080/08923648909526659

Moore, M. G. (2007). The theory of transactional distance. In M. G. Moore (Ed.), *Handbook of distance education* (pp. 89–103). Lawrence Erlbaum Associates.

Moore, M. G., & Kearsley, G. (1996). *Distance education: A systems view*. Wadsworth Publishing.

Muilenburg, L. Y., & Berge, Z. L. (2005). Student barriers to online learning: A factor analytic study. *Distance Education*, *26*(1), 29–48. doi:10.1080/01587910500081269

Mutalib, M. A., Halim, N. D., & Yahaya, N. (2016). *Meta-analysis on Interaction in Online Learning.* Retrieved from https://www.semanticscholar.org/paper/Meta-analysis-on-Interaction-in-Online-Learning-Mutalib-Halim/1647b4ba14260089900ab06291cd5a76a153db45

O'Neil, S., Scott, M., & Conboy, K. (2010). A Delphi study on collaborative learning in distance education: The faculty perspective. *British Journal of Educational Technology*, *42*(6), 939–949. doi:10.1111/j.1467-8535.2010.01132.x

Oyarzun, B., Stefaniak, J., Bol, L., & Morrison, G. R. (2018). Effects of learner-to-learner interactions on social presence, achievement and satisfaction. *Journal of Computing in Higher Education*, *30*(1), 154–175. doi:10.100712528-017-9157-x

Pallof, R. M., & Pratt, K. (2005). *Collaborating online: learning together in community*. Jossey-Bass.

Palloff, R. M., & Pratt, K. (2003). *The virtual student: A profile and guide to working with online learners*. Jossey-Bass.

Pattnayak, J., & Pattnaik, S. (2016). Integration of Web Services with E-Learning for Knowledge Society. *Procedia Computer Science*, *92*, 155–160. doi:10.1016/j.procs.2016.07.340

Pavlis Korres, M. (2010). *Development of a framework for the e-education of educators of special groups aiming to improve their compatibility with their Learners* (PhD Thesis). University of Alcalá, Spain.

Pavlis Korres, M. (2012). The Role of the Communication Tools in the Development of the Learning Group in an Online Environment. *International Journal of Engineering Education*, *28*(6), 1360–1365.

Pavlis Korres, M. (2015). Promoting Interaction in an Asynchronous E-Learning Environment. In P. Ordonez, R. Tennyson, & M. Lytras (Eds.), *Assessing the Role of Mobile Technologies and Distance Learning in Higher Education* (pp. 154–175). IGI Global. doi:10.4018/978-1-4666-7316-8.ch007

Pavlis Korres, M. (2018). *Design and Implementation of E-Learning Programs*. Hellenic Open University.

Pavlis Korres, M., Karalis, Th., Leftheriotou, P., & García Barriocanal, E. (2009). Integrating Adults' Characteristics and the Requirements for Their Effective Learning in an E-Learning Environment. In M. Lytras (Ed.), *Best Practices for the Knowledge Society. WSKS* (pp. 570–584). Springer.

Pavlis Korres, M., & Leftheriotou, P. (2016). Building Interaction in Adults' Online Courses: A Case Study on Training E-Educators of Adutls. In L. Kyei-Blankson, E. Ntuli, & C. Agyeman (Eds.), *Handbook of Research on Strategic Management of Interaction, Presence and Participation in Online Courses* (pp. 185–215). IGI-Global. doi:10.4018/978-1-4666-9582-5.ch008

Prestridge, S. (2014). A focus on students' use of Twitter–their interactions with each other, content and interface. *Active Learning in Higher Education*, *15*(2), 101–115. doi:10.1177/1469787414527394

Rosen, A. (2009). *E-Learning 2.0 Proven Practices and Emerging Technologies to Achieve Results.* AMACOM.

Rovai, A. (2002). Building Sense of Community at a Distance. *International Review of Research in Open and Distance Learning, 3*(1). Retrieved 21/4/2020 from http://www.irrodl.org/index.php/irrodl/article/view/79/153

Salmon, G. (2004). *E-moderating. The Key to Teaching and Learning Online* (2nd ed.). Routledge Falmer. doi:10.4324/9780203465424

Schutt, M., Allen, B. S., & Laumakis, M. A. (2009). The Effects of Instructor Immediacy Behaviors in Online Learning Environments. *Quarterly Review of Distance Education, 10*(2), 135–148.

Seaman, J. E., Allen, I. E., & Seaman, J. (2018). *Grade Increase: Tracking Distance Education in the United States*. The Babson Survey Research Group.

Selingo, J. (2017). T*he future of the degree: how colleges can survive in the new credential economy.* Washington, DC: The Chronicle of Higher Education.

Sharan, S., Sharan, Y., & Tan, I. G. (2013). The Group Investigation approach to cooperative learning. In C. E. Hmelo-Silver, A. M. O'Donnell, C. Chan, & C. Chinn (Eds.), *The International Handbook of Collaborative Learning* (pp. 351–369). Taylor & Francis.

Shepard, L. (2000). The role of assessment in a learning culture. *Educational Researcher*, *29*(7), 4–14. doi:10.3102/0013189X029007004

Shepherd, C. (2000). *Competence Frameworks-Online tutors*. Institute of IT Training.

Simpson, O. (2002). *Supporting students in online, open and distance learning*. Kogan Page.

Simpson, R., & Galbo, J. (1986). Interaction and learning: Theorizing on the art of teaching. *Interchange, 17*(4), 37–51. doi:10.1007/BF01807015

Song, L., Singleton, E. S., Hill, J. R., & Koh, M. H. (2004). Improving online learning: Student perceptions of useful and challenging characteristics. *Internet and Higher Education, 7*(1), 59-70. https://www.learntechlib.org/p/102596/

Soo, K. S., & Bonk, C. J. (1998). *Interaction: What Does It Mean in Online Distance Education?* Retrieved from https://eric.ed.gov/?id=ED428724

Stokes, P. (2015). *Higher education and employability: new models for integrating study and work.* Harvard.

Sutton, L. A. (2000). *Vicarious Interaction: A Learning Theory for Computer-Mediated Communications.* Presented at American Educational Research Association Annual Meeting 2000. Retrieved 21/4 2020 from https://www.learntechlib.org/p/87645/

Tawfik, A. A., Giabbanelli, P. J., Hogan, M., Msilu, F., Gill, A., & York, C. S. (2018). Effects of success v failure cases on learner-learner interaction. *Computers & Education, 118*, 120–132. doi:10.1016/j.compedu.2017.11.013

Thurmond, V., & Wambach, K. (2004). Understanding Interaction in Distance Education, A review of the literature, *International Journal of instructional Technology & Distance Learning*. Available http://www.itdl.org/journal/Jan_04/article02.htm

Thweatt, K. S., & McCroskey, J. C. (1996). Teacher Nonimmediacy and Misbehavior: Unintentional negative communication. *Communication Research Reports, 13*(2), 198–204. doi:10.1080/08824099609362087

Torun, E. D. (2013). Synchronous Interaction in Online Learning Environments with Adobe Connect Pro. *Procedia: Social and Behavioral Sciences, 106*, 2492–2499. doi:10.1016/j.sbspro.2013.12.286

Tsovaltzi, D., Weinberger, A., Scheuer, O., Dragon, T., & McLaren, B. M. (2013). Collaborative learning in Facebook: Can argument structure facilitate academic opinion change? In N. Rummel, M. Kapur, M. Nathan, & S. Puntambekar (Eds.), Conference Proceedings Volume II of the *10th International Conference on Computer Supported Collaborative Learning (CSCL 2013)* (pp. 177-180). International Society of the Learning Sciences.

Twigg, C. A. (2003). Improving learning and reducing costs: New models for online learning. *EDUCAUSE Review, 38*(5), 28–38.

Vuopala, E., Hyvönen, P., & Järvelä, S. (2016). Interaction forms in successful collaborative learning in virtual learning environments. *Active Learning in Higher Education, 17*(1), 25–38. doi:10.1177/1469787415616730

Waltonen-Moore, S., Stuart, D., Newton, E., Oswald, R., & Varonis, E. (2006). From Virtual Strangers to a Cohesive Online Learning Community: The Evolution of Online Group Development in a Professional Development Course. *Journal of Technology and Teacher Education, 14*(2), 287–311.

Williams, C. (2002). Learning On-Line: A review of recent literature in a rapidly expanding field. *Journal of Further and Higher Education, 26*(3), 263–272. doi:10.1080/03098770220149620

Woods, R., & Baker, J. (2004). Interaction and immediacy in online learning. *The International Review of Research in Open and Distance Learning, 5*(2). Retrieved 10-1-2018 from http://www.irrodl.org/index.php/irrodl/article/view/186/268

Woods, R. H. (2002). How much communication is enough in online courses? Exploring the relationship between frequency of instructor-initiated personal email and learners' perceptions of and participation in online learning. *International Journal of Instructional Media, 29*(4), 377–394.

Wu, D. D. (2015). *Online learning in postsecondary education: a review of the empirical literature (2013-2014).* Ithaka S & R. doi:10.18665r.221027

Yang, H. H., & Yuen, C. Y. (2010). *Collective Intelligence and E-Learning 2.0 Implications of Web-based Communities and Networking*. Information Science Publishing. doi:10.4018/978-1-60566-729-4

Yeh, S.-P., & Fu, H.-W. (2014). Effects of Cooperative E-Learning Outcomes. *Eurasia Journal of Mathematics. Science & Technology Education, 10*(6), 531–536.

KEY TERMS AND DEFINITIONS

Adult Education: The entire body of organized educational processes, whatever the content, level, or method, whether formal or otherwise, whether they prolong or replace initial education in schools or colleges, and universities as well as in apprenticeship, whereby persons regarded as adults by the society to which they belong develop their abilities, enrich their knowledge, improve their technical or professional qualifications, or turn them in a new direction and bring about changes in their attitudes or behavior in the twofold perspective of full personal development and participation in balanced, independent, social, economic, and cultural development. (Definition by UNESCO, 1976. Records of the General Conference. Volume 1. Resolutions, "Annex I. Recommendation on the development of adult education. Content of adult education", resolution 19C/Annex I.I.1, p. 4)

HOU Group Advisory Meetings (GAMs): GAMs are four-hour meetings held five times during an annual HOU course. The purpose of the meetings is to promote communication and collaboration between educators-advisors and students, as well as between students, to clarify important concepts and elements of the subject and to provide guidance for students in terms of studying and writing. Participation in GAMs is optional. GAMs are conducted face-to-face, but synchronous online meetings have been taking place since 2017 as well. Students can choose the type of GAM they want to participate in at the beginning of the academic year.

HOU Online Courses: Courses offering the five synchronous group advisory meetings of the academic year on an online platform.

E-Educator: A teacher for adults who teaches online (in synchronous or asynchronous mode or a combination of both).

Educator of Adults: A teacher for adults. The term is used in order to define the different approach of the teacher, focusing on the dimensions of facilitation, co-learning, guiding and counseling.

HOU E-Tutor: Educator teaching in HOU online courses.

Chapter 9
Innovative System for Education:
The Advent of E-Learning in the University System in the Pandemic Age

Giovanni Bronzetti
University of Calabria, Italy

Graziella Sicoli
University of Calabria, Italy

Dominga A. Ippolito
University of Calabria, Italy

ABSTRACT

In the current scenario, many companies approached using a digital management system. For this reason, they must take into account an important issue: innovation. An essential strategic tool for management in current times. COVID-19 has imposed a reorganization of activities. There has been a sudden increase of digital systems, such as smart working and e-learning as regards the education system. The aim of the work is to illustrate how modern innovative technologies help the provision of services within universities. In an emergency, such as the spread of COVID-19, there is a sudden change in the use of educational services by the university structure. They are ready to delivery services based on Intelligent Technology. Through the administration of an on-line questionnaire, perception of the on-line education system is examined, gathering opinions of a sample of students in one of the most important Italian universities.

DOI: 10.4018/978-1-7998-4972-8.ch009

Copyright © 2021, IGI Global. Copying or distributing in print or electronic forms without written permission of IGI Global is prohibited.

INTRODUCTION

The world economic scenario has been hit by an unprecedented emergency: the spread of Covid-19. The first truly global crisis that has indiscriminately hit rich and poor countries and that requires the adoption of stringent measures that have brought about a sharp slowdown in the global economy. All sectors of the national and international production system have been put to the test as well as the world of work and education, which have suddenly suffered repercussions on a global scale. Governments around the world have tried to stem the effects of the pandemic with ad hoc financing instruments and incentives also dedicated to research and innovative projects in order to increase the efficiency and effectiveness of the system (Drnevich, Croson, 2013). The numerous investments in ICT (already unexpectedly increasing), have spontaneously given rise to a question: can emergencies turn into an opportunity to spread innovation? (Al-Fraihat, Joy, Masa'deh, Sinclair, 2020).

The timely adoption of new forms of intelligent technology to support business operations has made it necessary to reorganize their business strategies. Forms such as smart working, agile work, teleworking and home office / home working have quickly become concrete in organizations of all kinds, from public administrations to businesses. Each of these realities has had to decide with enormous effort and quickly how to continue operating. Thus, many of the things that until yesterday were done offline today are being done online, especially in the public sphere and in the world of education where technology has come to the aid as an enabling factor.

The education sector was suddenly catapulted from one day to the next, into the dimension of distance learning to give continuity to the training offer and the links of the "class" that has become virtual. Despite the many difficulties, technologies have proved to be a lifeline in combining innovation, education and inclusion. Consequently, education has stimulated the adoption of e-learning, which is the direct result of the integration of education and technology and is considered a powerful means of learning (Al-Fraihat, Joy, Sinclair, 2017) .Many IT players freely provided e-learning services. The latter were known in the last decade as one of the most efficient teaching methods (Gros, Garcia-Penalvo, 2016). In relation to the provision of digital education services, recent researches have focused specifically on the study of attitudes and interactions between students and teachers (vital interactions for the success of e-learning) (Cheng, 2011; Liaw, Huang, Chen, 2007; Selim, 2007; Al-Fraihat, Joy, Masa'deh, Sinclair, 2020).

In support of E-learning we find the main tools related to the use of the Internet: tablets, smartphone PCs and more. On the one hand, there is a school system that entrusts the network with the task of carrying out learning programs; on the other, there is the risk that economic and educational inequalities between families and young people will widen as statistical data (source: https://www.istat.it/it/archivio/240949). It turns out that thousands of families are poorly performing compared to the new needs that E-learning technology often requires due to the lack of a computer, a tablet and / or an internet line at home.

It is on the basis of these premises that the idea of work originates which, without being exhaustive, intends to understand how, in this moment of global crisis, students have understood the change; how they have adapted to using new forms of digital teaching; what is their opinion on the use of new IT platforms and on E-learning in general. To reach a summary judgment, a questionnaire was submitted to a sample of students enrolled at the University of Calabria to detect the degree of penetration of the "Teams" IT platform put in place by the University and implemented for educational use. The goal is to monitor both the status of the services offered and the level of perception of the same by users The work aims to highlight users' perception of the contribution that e-learnig has provided in the field of education; in particular, the perception takes into account the current global pandemic scenario that has brought about profound changes in people's way of life. It was necessary to refer to each type of innovative system to fill the problems related to work, education, and so on.

TECHNOLOGICAL INNOVATION: STATE OF THE ART

The competitive success of economic systems is closely linked to the ability to "innovate". But what is meant by innovation? The OECD (Organization for Economic Cooperation and Development) defines innovation as "the implementation of a product (good or service) or a process, new or considerably improved, of a new marketing method, or of a new organizational method with reference to commercial practices, the workplace and external relations ". Louis defines innovation as "taking something consolidated and introducing a new idea or method, which creates a new dimension of performance and adds value" (Slaper et al., 2011; Demircioglu, Audretsch, Sloper, 2019). At the basis of innovation is the knowledge that supports new and modern business models and feeds a process that produces continuous competitive advantages. (Chen, Huang, 2009; Sharbati, Jawad, Bontis, 2010). The evolution of innovation in a "technological" key has favored the spread of new forms of "intelligent technology" which applied to different areas of knowledge have led to important changes in an increasingly digital perspective. (Bharadwaj et al., 2013; Ghezzi et al., 2015). There is no doubt that technological innovations make it possible to make the most of a series of approaches that are part of agile working methods based on change in the interaction and collaboration of individuals. (Rigby et al., 2016; Cram, Newell, 2016; Paluch et al., 2017). Agility is the ability to accommodate and adapt to changes in a dynamic environment. Being agile means applying previous knowledge while learning from current experience in order to deliver high-quality products, under budget constraints and in short time frames (Jyothi, Rao, 2012). Agility hence encompasses the features of flexibility, velocity, learning and response to change and leanness (Conboy, Fitzgerald, 2004; Campanelli, Parreiras, 2015). The benefits for practice stemming from the application of agility methods have been widely recognized (De Cesare et al., 2010; Cram, Newell, 2016).

Innovation can help an organization to adapt to the environment, survive, and grow (Burns, Stalker, 1961; Thompson, 2010), enhance economic growth and performance, help to deal with grand challenges, climate change, and health (Kattel, Mazzucato, 2018). Overall, innovation is a driving force of firm productivity (Stojcic, Hashi, 2014) and "central to the growth of output and productivity" of firms and nations (Link and Siegel, 2007; Acs et al., 2017).

To resources knowledge, skills and human capital, a fourth factor is added: innovation in the digital environment that invests every activity, adapting to artificial intelligence mechanisms and interconnection (Hattinger, Eriksson, 2020). The perception of digital technology as a substitute for many physical and conceptual tasks of human beings must not lead us to think that human capital is no longer necessary (Brougham, Haar, 2018). Knowledge management practices are fundamental to encourage the creation of new ideas and knowledge to be developed within the company (Parly, Taylor, 2002).For instance, Nakamura explains how workers have been a key source of creativity and innovations for the last century. Additionally, research facilities and universities provide a source of knowledge and ideas underlying the development of many product and service innovations ((Nakamura, 2000; Carlino, 2001).

Europe has devoted considerable resources and effort to creating and analyzing systematic and comprehensive measurement of innovation activity. Most prominent are the Oslo Manuals, the European Union's Community Innovation Surveys (CIS) conducted in different European countries, the Maastricht

Economic and Social Research Institute on Innovation and Technology (MERIT) (Battisti, Stoneman, 2010; Bloch, Bugge, 2013).

Thanks to rapidly rising number of Internet users with smartphones and tablets around the world has supported the spread of e-learning, not only in higher education and vocational training but also in primary and secondary schools. E-learning and traditional distance education approaches share the emphasis on "any time, any place". This evolution has been made possible due to the technological platforms that support e-learning (Siemens, 2014).

ICT and e-Learning

Distance learning has spread widely in different academic contexts globally. In a "pandemic" climate, institutions have recently made a virtue of "necessity". Investing in technological innovation has become a primary necessity, although the problem of balancing the investment in research activities with that to be dedicated to educational innovation emerges (Gunn, 2010). The concept of e-learning has evolved parallel to the evolution of digital technology, from the introduction of computers to today's systems, favoring learning networks and the roots of connectivism (Siemens, 2005; Gros, Garcia-Penalvo, 2016) . Owing to the continuous evolution of technology, there is no unanimously shared definition of e-learning (Arkorful, Abaidoo, 2015).The immaturity of this relatively young phenomenon is reflected in an aggregation of terms that are often interchanged without meaningful definitions (Ali, Uppal and Gulliver, 2018). Lee, Hsieh, and Hsu defined e-learning as "an information system that can integrate a wide variety of instructional material (audio, video, and text mediums) conveyed through e-mail, live chat sessions, online discussions, forums, quizzes, and assignments (Lee, Hsieh, Hsu, 2011). The European Commission defines e-Learning as the use of new multimedia technologies and the Internet to increase learning quality by easing access to facilities and services as well as distant exchanges and collaboration (CE 2001).

Bearnish et. Al. (2002), define e-learning as a wide range of applications and processes associated with computer-based training and learning, such as online learning, virtual classrooms and digital collaboration (Bearnish et al 2002; Homan, Macpherson, 2005). A broader definition is provided by Sambrook (Sambrook, 2003) which defines e-learnig as any learning activity supported by information and communication technologies. E-learning can be considered a natural evolution of distance learning through a constant interaction between student and teacher (Ali et al., 2018).

E-learning is the direct result of the integration between education and technology (Al-Fraihat Joy, Sinclair, 2017; Al-Fraihat, Joy, Sinclair, 2020) and has allowed education at a time like the present to not stop, but rather to continue to be a continuous learning tool where students and teachers are involved in a virtual environment and have the opportunity to communicate with each other. Recently, there has been much debate about the evolution of innovation in academic systems, as there has been an important change in these "innovative ecosystems (Adkins, Foth, Summerville, Higgs, 2007; Aubusson, 2002; Crouzier, 2015) which can be traced back to the evolution of the education system and to the change of tools supporting distance learning. Most of the studies focus on the advantages of e-learning in terms of reducing training times, reducing costs and greater flexibility in simultaneously serving more users in distance learning, but none refers to the overall strategic contribution that e-learning brings to the organization (Rana, 2001).

In this regard, innovation is important in eduction because it encourages teachers to be more creative both in problem solving issues and weaknesses in teaching; these in order to make learning more interesting and engaging (Yahya, 2019)..

Nonetheless, most of the e-learning definitions found in the literature convey the idea that e-learning refers to the use of information and communication technologies to enable access to online learning/ teaching resources (Arkorful, Abaidoo, 2015).

Owing to the spread of Covid-19, the development of e-learning, and its use within universities, from what was a slow and niche process has become an urgent need. The emergency situation has required the redesigning of the courses in online mode through the use of the main web platforms. The "academic tribes" (Becher, Trowler, 2001) had to find ICT tools capable of guaranteeing didactic continuity and at the same time allowing the different disciplinary areas to adapt and redesign their educational offer based on new needs (Haywood, 2018). On the other hand, it has become necessary to introduce an easily-used technology. In fact, in order for a technological innovation to be successful, it must be accessible and usable by everyone. ICT have expanded the breadth and depth of opportunities within the institutions of learning everywhere in the world (James, 2019). User acceptance of technology (Davis et al., 1989) is the most widely adopted theory for measuring the success of new technologies in terms of consensus and use of technology itself (Surendran, 2012; Al-Fraihat, Joy, Masa 'deh, Sinclair, 2020). The research moves in the direction of also evaluating user satisfaction with regard to IT, in terms of effectiveness and therefore understanding the degree of success with respect to the innovation made and the technology introduced. Bikanga, et al (2017) in their recent research have found positive attitudes of teachers and students in the use of digital tools for learning and teaching purposes (Prihastuti, Wahyuni, Ramadhani, 2018). The improvement of students' skills and abilities are seen as the main advantages of the organization for e-learning (Waleed et. Al. 2019). The success of e-learning may require students to have a certain degree of "self-sufficiency" as regards the use of digital tools. This aspect can affect their level of satisfaction and their intention to continue using it. (Hayashi, Chen, Ryan, 2008). Despite of the benefits of ICT, researches have reported the low adoption of ICT in classroom teaching and delivery due to various reasons such as low self-efficacy and technological readiness (Goh, Sigala, 2020). Promoting innovation in schools and in the education sector in general, helps to build the digital transformation of the entity, improves its image and significantly affects the act of learning by making it more effective, accelerating collaboration and sharing. The innovation linked to e-learning allows the space-time barriers to be broken down, opening up the possibility of learning wherever there is an internet connection, thus expanding the concept of the right to study.

RESEARCH OBJECTIVE

Starting from the introductory research question: can the emergency turn into an opportunity to spread innovation? Through the administration of a questionnaire made available online to a sample of students of the University of Calabria, the work aims to understand the degree of penetration of the University's IT platform "Teams" put in place to deal with the COVID- 19 emergency for educational purposes and thus, monitor the status of the services offered in terms of E-learning by the University.

To support our analysis, we refer to Davis' studies which demonstrate that the success of an innovative investment is closely linked to the perception of the same by the users ((Davis et al., 1989).The questions to which the work wishes to answer are the following: **Hypothesis One: can an emergency situation become an opportunity to spread and invest in innovation and research?**

Hypothesis Two: does the innovative push undertaken by the University of Calabria during the "pandemic" period represent a successful innovation?

Methodology

The survey presented was carried out in April 2020, it was addressed to a sample of students from the University of Calabria, the aim was to detect the degree of penetration of the recent introduction of forms of online learning, through the Teams digital platform. The perception of students was also investigated, in relation to the quality of the service offered and the innovative perception linked to the activities undertaken by the University, to allow the continuity of the right to study.

With reference to the technological platform used for the creation of the questionnaire, reference was made to the Google Forms service, an online tool that made it possible to create the questionnaire and monitor responses in real time. In a second step, the survey was proposed to the students. To do this, the main social channels were taken into account, which put the students in contact with the student associations, proposing the survey to 1795 students .

Although the sample cannot be considered representative of the entire student universe, about 45% of the students contacted were respondents.

The questionnaire consisting of 29 multiple choice questions is divided into four sections of questions: socio-demographic aspects, student expectations, lesson planning and use of digital platforms, evaluation of the e-learning system and students' perceptions about the innovative activities of the university. In total, 819 responses were collected. The main information received is summarized in the search results.

Table 1. Socio-demographic aspects

SOCIO-DEMOGRAPHIC ASPECTS		No.	%
Gender	Male	203	24.8%
	Female	616	75.2%
Age	< 20	7	0.9%
	20 - 25	539	65.8%
	26 - 30	252	30.8%
	> 30	21	2.6%
Subscribed to	Bachelor's degree course	273	33.3%
	Master's Degree	546	66.7%
Having an adequate internet connection	Yes	679	82.9%
	No	140	17.1%
Possession of suitable digital devices	Yes	770	94%
	No	49	6%

Source: Our processing.

RESULTS

From the survey carried out, the first section of questions concerning socio-demographic data reveals preliminary aspects such as, gender, age, nationality, region of residence, as well as belonging to a three-year or master's degree course and possession of adequate instruments of e-learning support.

From the first section of questions administered, the predominance of female answers (75.2%) over male answers (24, 8%) emerges. The majority of students belong to an age group between 20 and 25 years (65.8%) and are enrolled in a master's degree course (66.7%). The majority of the students who answered the questionnaire are resident in the Calabria region and spent the restriction period due to Cov-19, in the place of residence (50.9%).

Figure 1. Percentage of students who spent the restriction period at the place of residence
Source: Our processing.

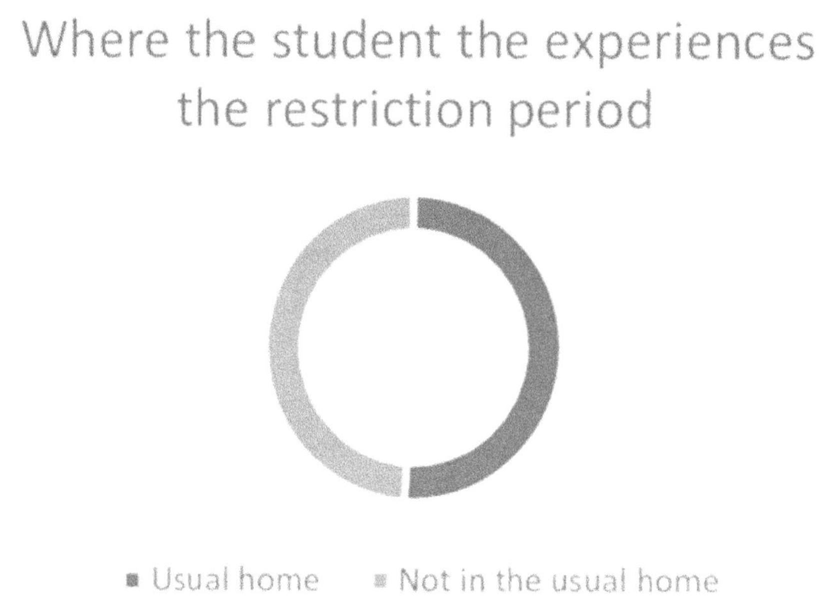

Even before investigating specific aspects related to online teaching, it was decided to evaluate whether each student is in possession of a suitable digital instrumentation (Computer, Tablet, adequate Internet connection, and so on). These instruments are fundamental for on line e learning. The survey showed that the majority of students have an adequate internet connection (82.9%) and a computer (94%). It is not to be overlooked, however, the albeit lower percentage of students who do not have adequate tools. 17.1% of students declare that they do not have an adequate internet connection and 6%, that they do not have an adequate tool to take advantage of online teaching. A series of investigations on this minority reveal an important aspect to reflect on: to date, Italy does not reach the total coverage of an adequate connection and / or digital instrumentation per family (obstacle to be able to use the right to study, in times of pandemic). In this sense, the institutions of competence are moving to be able to deal with this discomfort, giving obvious priority to compulsory schooling.

As regards the different aspects related to the use of the digital platform "Teams" and the relative organization of online lessons, important considerations emerged, as appears from the summary data expressed in Table 2.

Table 2. Planning of lessons and use of the digital platform

LESSON PLANNING AND USE OF THE PLATFORM		N.	%
Easy- to- use digital platform	Highly	322	39.3%
	Fairly	434	53%
	Scant	56	6.8%
	For nothing	7	0.9%
Online lesson organized in a comprehensive way	Highly	182	22.2%
	Fairly	525	64.1%
	Scant	70	8.5%
	For nothing	42	5.1%
Adequate online teaching material support	Highly	161	19.7%
	Fairly	413	50.4%
	Scant	210	25.6%
	For nothing	35	4.3%

Source: Our processing.

The Teams platform, adopted by the University of Calabria, is rated on average fairly (53%) or very (39.3%) simple to use by the majority of students who answered the questionnaire. For the organization of the lessons and the support of the same with adequate teaching materials, average positive summary data emerge (considering the recent introduction of the platform). Lessons are organized fairly comprehensively for more than half of the sample analyzed (64.1%). The same evaluation is given to the support material for online lessons by the majority of students (50.4%). In general, the negative responses related to the three aspects investigated by the second section of questions, register relatively low percentages (for example, only 0.9% of students negatively evaluate the ease of use of the e-learning platform).

In the third set of questions, we wanted to investigate the student's learning expectations. Subsequently, it was asked to evaluate a series of characteristics linked to the e-learning platform. The data emerged are summarized in Table 3. It should be noted that, in the second section of questions, the sample was asked to assign a score ranging from one to ten, starting from full insufficiency (vote 1) up to full excellence (vote 10). The scores assigned by the students were then reclassified, considering the score threshold that divides the sufficiency (6-10) from the insufficiency (1-5).

The organization of online courses is evaluated, overall, positively. In fact, the offer of the contents of the lessons (enough adequate for 68.4%) and the clear organization of the lessons (enough for 71.8%) are considered positively. The lessons arouse a lot of interest for 20.5% and enough interest for 53%.

Table 3. Student learning expectations and evaluation of the e-learning system

STUDENT LEARNING EXPECTATIONS AND EVALUATION E-LEARNING			
		N.	%
The online courses offer adequate learning content (skills, competences, etc.)	Highly	147	17.9%
	Fairly	560	68.4%
	Scant	105	12.8%
	For nothing	7	0.90%
Interest in the use of online courses	Highly	168	20.5%
	Fairly	434	53%
	Scant	175	21.4%
	For nothing	42	5.1%
Content of lessons organized clearly	Highly	133	16.2%
	Fairly	588	71.8%
	Scant	91	11.1%
	For nothing	7	0.90%

The evaluation of a series of characteristics related to e-learning, sees the possibility of assigning a score ranging from 1 to 10 (from full failure to excellence). The evaluation in this regard reported full sufficiency for each listed feature (audio quality, image quality and interaction allowed with colleagues and friends). A score from 6 to 10 is given to the connection by 86.3% of the students and the quality of the platform from 85.5%. Audio is adequate by 76.9% of students, together with images (82.9%) and digital interaction with teachers and students (64.1%).

The last set of questions tends to bring out the perceptions of the students regarding the innovative aspects promoted by the University of Calabria. Given the recent introduction of e-learning to face, from an academic point of view, the discomfort brought by the spread of Covid-19, it is interesting to examine

EVALUATION E-LEARNING SYSTEM		N.	%
Quality of internet connection	da 1 a 5	112	13,7%
	da 6 a 10	707	86.3%
Platform quality	da 1 a 5	119	14.5%
	da 6 a 10	700	85.5%
Image quality	da 1 a 5	140	17.1%
	da 6 a 10	679	82.9%
Audio quality	da 5 a 10	189	23.1%
	da 6 a 10	630	76.9%
Teacher support storytelling	da 5 a 10	105	12.8%
	da 6 a 10	714	87.2%
Digital interaction	da 5 a 10	294	35.9%
	da 6 a 10	524	64.1%

Source: Our processing.

the personal perceptions of the students. The data emerged from the students' answers are summarized below (Table 5).

Table 5. Student perceptions in relation to the innovative aspects of e-learning

STUDENT PERCEPTIONS AND INNOVATIVE ASPECTS		N.	%
Online course satisfaction compared to classroom courses	Highly	119	14.5%
	Fairly	350	42.7%
	Scant	189	23.1%
	For nothing	161	19.7%
Evaluation the validity of e-learning in the current emergency situation	Highly	252	30.8%
	Fairly	280	34.2%
	Scant	210	25.6%
	For nothing	77	9.4%
Is the innovative technology promoted by University to be considered a successful innovation?	Highly	287	35%
	Fairly	392	47.9%
	Scant	126	15.4%
	For nothing	14	1.7%

Source: Our processing.

The comparison of online lessons with those in the classroom, in terms of quality, is on average positive (14.5% of the students are very satisfied and 42.7% are quite satisfied). In this sense, only 19.7% of the total number of students gives a negative opinion. In the same way, students positively evaluate the introduction of e-learning in times of "pandemic" (very satisfied for 30.8% and quite satisfied for 34.2%). Finally, 35% and 47.9% of the students are respectively very and fairly convinced that the introduction of e-learning by the University of Calabria is a successful innovation. In general, the data emerging from the questionnaire reveal a positive acceptance sentiment towards the digitalization of the lessons. On average, students positively perceive the innovative push proposed by the University of Calabria, although the firm belief is maintained that this tool can be significantly improved over time, taking into account the different needs of the students.

FUTURE RESEARCH DIRECTIONS

The information received from the administration of the questionnaire to a sample of university students reveals an average positive perception of the introduction of online fingertips, although some limitations that research has found must be considered. The urgent need for an alternative solution to traditional teaching (due to the spread of Covid-19), calls for a second opinion to be considered in the medium-long term. In fact, the opinion of the students, only a month after the introduction of the Team's platform, is not fully mature and fully aware of the opportunities granted, although a first positive impression and evaluation is not negligible. It is also desirable to extend the administration of the questionnaire to a more significant sample of students than the one being studied. To do this, the authors propose to administer the questionnaire to all students regularly enrolled in the University of Calabria, transferring the assessment to a subsequent period.

CONCLUSION

The data that emerges from the analysis carried out, inherent in students' perception of e-learning technology, allows us to respond positively to the research hypotheses formulated. Online teaching finds consensus as an alternative means of learning to classroom teaching. This is considered a timely solution to traditional teaching, given the emergency situation that the academic world has found itself experiencing. Although this innovation cannot replace traditional teaching, to date it appears as a valid vehicle for dealing with emergency situations (such as the spread of Cov-19).

A good sample of students positively considers the innovative push of the University of Calabria. This "save school" strategy adopted by the entire National school system for almost a month, is gradually gaining first approval. To date, a large number of students believe that focusing on e-learning given the context can be considered a successful innovation. University poles are the first real engines of research and innovation at the national level. This is the starting point for the complex of ideas that, in the different and respective spheres of action, pushes to bring greater value to their innovative baggage. It is right that these ideas are shared and supported by the institutions and by their users.

The systemic expansion of distance learning facilitates maximum cooperation, collaboration and exchange between researchers in communicating the progress of research to classes of students not territorially defined. In an age of profound digitization, the education sector cannot afford to lag behind. In this regard, it is necessary for the universities of knowledge to be the first to promote innovation, seizing the right opportunities that the socio-economic scenario promotes. Too often it is thought that investing in technology and, specifically in the e-learning system, means focusing on information methods, surrogate for traditional classroom teaching. This thought is not shared today. The innovative drive towards the digitization of teaching should be understood as an added value contribution to traditional teaching; not only an alternative necessary to face a moment of crisis, but a starting point to be able to spread knowledge even more widely.

In this sense, there are still many limits. These mostly involve socio-economic aspects of families. In fact, not all families are adequately equipped with appropriate digital equipment (computer, tablet, internet connection) in order to welcome the e-learning experience well. To date, institutions cannot overlook this critical factor (albeit involving a minority), an objective barrier to the diffusion of the right to study.

REFERENCES

Acs, Z. J., Audretsch, D. B., Lehmann, E. E., & Licht, G. (2017). National systems of innovation. *The Journal of Technology Transfer*, *42*(5), 997–1008. doi:10.100710961-016-9481-8

Adkins, B. A., Foth, M., Summerville, J. A., & Higgs, P. L. (2007). Ecologies of innovation: Symbolic aspect of cross-organizational linkages in the design sector in an Australian innercity area. *The American Behavioral Scientist*, *50*(7), 922–934. doi:10.1177/0002764206298317

Al-Fraihat, D., Joy, M., Masa'deh, R., & Sinclair, J. (2017). Identifying success factors for e-learning in higher education. In *International conference on e-learning* (pp. 247-255). Academic Conferences International Limited.

Al-Fraihat, D., Joy, M., Masa'deh, R., & Sinclair, J. (2020). Evaluating e-learning system success: An empirical study. *Computers in Human Behavior*, *102*, 67–86. doi:10.1016/j.chb.2019.08.004

Ali, S., Uppal, M. A., & Gulliver, S. (2018). A conceptual framework highlighting e-learning implementation barriers. *Information Technology & People*, *31*(1), 156–180. doi:10.1108/ITP-10-2016-0246

Arkorful, V., & Abaidoo, N. (2015). The role of e-learning, advantages and disadvantages of its adoption in higher education. *International Journal of Instructional Technology and Distance Learning*, *12*(1).

Aubusson, P. (2002). An ecology of Science education. *International Journal of Science Education*, *24*(1), 27–46. doi:10.1080/09500690110066511

Battisti, G., & Stoneman, P. (2010). How innovative are UK firms? Evidence from the fourth UK community innovation survey on synergies between technological and organizational innovations. *British Journal of Management*, *21*(1), 187–206. doi:10.1111/j.1467-8551.2009.00629.x

Beamish, N., Armistead, C., Watkinson, M., & Armfiled, G. (2002). The development of e-learnig in UK/European corporate organization. *European Business Journal*, *14*(3), 105–115.

Becher, T., & Trowler, P. R. (2001). *Academic Tribes And Territories*. SRHE and Open University Press.

Bharadwaj, A., El Sawy, O., Pavlou, P., & Venkatraman, N. (2013). *Digital business strategy: Toward a next generation of insights*. Academic Press.

Bikanga Ada, M., Stansfield, M., & Bayter, G. (2017). Using mobile learning and social media to enhance learner feedback. *Journal of Applied Research in Higher Education*, *9*(1), 70–90.

Bloch, C., & Bugge, M. M. (2013). Public sector innovation—From theory to measurement. *Structural Change and Economic Dynamics*, 27.

Brougham, D., & Haar, J. (2018). Smart technology, artificial intelligence, robotics and algorithms (STARA): Employees' perceptions of our future workplace. *Journal of Management & Organization*, *24*(2), 239–257. doi:10.1017/jmo.2016.55

Burns, T. E., & Stalker, G. (1961). *The Management of Innovation*. Tavistock.

Campanelli, A. S., & Parreiras, F. S. (2015). Agile methods tailoring-A systematic literature review. *Journal of Systems and Software*, 110.

Carlino, J. (2001). Knowledge spillovers: cities' role in the New Economy. *Business Review*, *4*, 17- 26.

Chen, C.J. & Huang, J.W. (2009). Strategic human resource practices and innovation performance. The mediating role of knowledge management capacity. *Journal of Business Research*, *62*, 104-114.

Cheng, Y. M. (2011). Antecedents and consequences of e-learning acceptance. *Information Systems Journal*, *21*(3), 269–299. doi:10.1111/j.1365-2575.2010.00356.x

Commission of the European Communities. (2001). The eLearning Action Plan: Designing tomorrow's education. Brussels: Author.

Conboy, K., & Fitzgerald, B. (2004). Toward a conceptual framework of agile methods: A study of agility in different disciplines. *Proceedings of the 2004 ACM Workshop on Interdisciplinary Software Engineering Research*. 10.1145/1029997.1030005

Cram, W. A., & Newell, S. (2016). Mindful revolution or mindless trend? examining agile development as a management fashion. *European Journal of Information Systems*, *25*(2), 154–169. doi:10.1057/ejis.2015.13

Crouzier, T. (2015). *Science Ecosystem 2.0: how will change occor?* Luxemburg: Publications Office of the European Union.

Davis, F. D., Bagozzi, R. P., & Warshaw, P. R. (1989). User acceptance of computer technology: A comparison of two theorical model. *Management Science*, *35*(8), 982–1003. doi:10.1287/mnsc.35.8.982

De Cesare, S., Lycett, M., Macredie, R. D., Patel, C., & Paul, R. (2010). Examining perceptions of agility in software development practice. *Communications of the ACM*, *53*(6), 126–130. doi:10.1145/1743546.1743580

Demircioglu, M. A., Audretsch, D. B., & Sloper, T. F. (2019). Sources of innovation and innovation type: Firm-level evidence from the United State. *Industrial and Corporate Change*, *28*(6), 1365–1379. doi:10.1093/icc/dtz010

Drnevich, P. L., & Croson, D. C. (2013). Information technology and business – level strategy: Toward an integrated theoretical perspective. *MIS Quarterly*, *37*(2), 483–509. doi:10.25300/MISQ/2013/37.2.08

Ghezzi, A., Cortimiglia, M. N., & Frank, A. G. (2015). Strategy and business model design in dynamic telecomunications industries: A study on Italian mobile network operators. *Technological Forecasting and Social Change*, *90*.

Goh, E., Sigala, M. (2020). Integrating Information & Communication Technologies (ICT) into classroom instruction: teaching tips for hospitality educators from a diffusion of innovation approach. *Journal of Teching in Travel & Tourism*. doi:10.1080/15313220.2020.1740636

Gros, B., & Garcia-Penalvo, F.J. (2016). Future trend in the design strategies and technological affordances of e-learning. In M. Spector, B.B. Lockee, & M.D. Childress (Eds.), Learning and Technology. An International Compendoium of Theory, Research, Practice ad Policy (pp.1-23). Springer International Publishing.

Gunn, C. (2010). Sustainability factors for e-learning initiatives. *ALT-J: Research in Learning Technology*, *18*(2), 89–103. doi:10.1080/09687769.2010.492848

Hattinger, M., & Eriksson, K. (2020). Mind the Gap: a collaborative competence e-learning model between University and industry. *Proceedings of the 53rd Hawaii International Conference on System Sciences*. https://hdl.handll.net/10125/63750978-0-9981331-3-3

Hayashi, A., Chen, C., Ryan, T., & Wu, J. (2004). The role of social presence and moderating role of computer self efficacy in predicting the continuance usage of e-learning system. *Journal of Information Systems Education, 15*(2), •••.

Haywood, J. (2018). Leading innovation: digital education in a traditional university, Higher Education in the Digital Age. Edward Elgar Publishing.

Homan, G., & Macpherson, A. (2005). E-learning in the corporate university. *Journal of European Industrial Training, 29*(1), 75–90. doi:10.1108/03090590510576226

Hwang, H. G., Chang, I. C., Chen, F. J., & Wu, S. Y. (2008). Investigation of the application of KMS for diseases classifications: A study in A taiwanese hospital. *Expert Systems with Applications, 34*(1), 725–733. doi:10.1016/j.eswa.2006.10.018

James, S. A. (2019). Valuation of ICT proficiency of teachers in actualizing E-learning in home economics education, Ogun State, Nigeria. International Journal for Infonomics, 12(3).

Jyothi, V. E., & Rao, K. N. (2012). Effective implementation of agile practices - incoordination with lean Kanban. *International Journal on Computer Science and Engineering, 4*(1).

Kattel, R., & Mazzucato, M. (2018). Mission-oriented innovation policy and dynamic capabilities in the public sector. *Industrial and Corporate Change, 27*(5), 787–801. doi:10.1093/icc/dty032

Lee, Y. H., Hsieh, Y. C., & Hsu, C. N. (2011). Adding Innovation Diffusion Theory to the Technology Acceptance Model: Supporting Employees' Intentions to use E-Learning Systems. *Journal of Educational Technology & Society, 14*(4).

Liaw, S. S., Huang, H. M., & Chen, G. D. (2007). Surveying instructor and learner attitudes towardelearning. *Computers & Education, 49*(4), 1066–1080. doi:10.1016/j.compedu.2006.01.001

Link, A. N., & Siegel, D. S. (2007). *Innovation, entrepreneurship, and Technological Change*. Oxford University Press. doi:10.1093/acprof:oso/9780199268825.001.0001

Nakamura, L.I. (2000, July). Economics and the New Economy: the invisible hands meets creative destruction. *Federal Reserve Bank of Philadelphia Business Review.*

Paluch, S., Brettel, M., Hopp, C., Piller, F., Salge, & Wentzler, D. (2017). Innovation in the Digital Age: From Stage-Gate to an Agile Development Paradigm? *Journal of Business Research*. Available at: https://www.journals.elsevier.com/journal-of-business-research/call-for-papers/innovation-in-the-digital-age-from-stage-gate-to-an-agile-a

Parlby, D., Taylor, R. (2002). *The power of knowledge: a business guide to knowledge management.* Academic Press.

Prihastuti, A.H., Wahyuni, S., & Ramadhani, S.(2018). The use of social media as a learning media in improving students' motivation in the management accounting course. *International Journal of Education Best Practices, 2*(2).

Rana, E. (2001). Take initiative on online learning, trainers urged. *People Management, 25.*

Rigby, D. K., Sutherland, J., & Takeuchi, H. (2016). Embracing agile. *Harvard Business Review, 94*(5).

Sambrook, S. (2003). E-learning in small organization. *Education + Training*, *45*(8/9), 506–516. doi:10.1108/00400910310508892

Selim, H. M. (2007). Critical success factor for e-learning acceptance: Confirmatory factor models. *Computer Education*, *49*(2), 396–413. doi:10.1016/j.compedu.2005.09.004

Sharabati, A., Jawad, S., & Bontis, N. (2010). Intellectual capital and business performance in the pharmaceutical sector of Jordon. *Management Decision*, *48*(1), 105–131. doi:10.1108/00251741011014481

Siemens, G. (2005). Connectivism: A learning theory for the digital age. *International Journal of Instructional Technology and Distance Learning*, *2*(1), 3–10.

Siemens, G. (2014). *Digital Learning research network*. Retrieved from:www.elearspace.org/blog/2014/11/18

Slaper, T. F., Hart, N. R., Hall, T. J., & Thompson, M. F. (2011). The index of Innovation: A new tool for regional analysis. *Economic Development Quarterly*, *25*(1), 36–53. doi:10.1177/0891242410387592

Stojcic, N., & Hashi, I. (2014). Firm productivity and type of innovation: evidence from the community innovation survey 6. *Croatian Economic Survey*, *16*(2).

Surendran, P. (2012). Technology acceptance model: A survey of literature. *International Journal of Business and Social Research, 2*(4), 175-178.

Thompson, J. D. (2010). *Organizations in Action: Social Science Bases of Administrative Theory* (7th ed.). Transaction Publishers.

Walled, M.A., Yahaya, N., Aldraiweesh, A.A., Alamri, M.M., Aljarboa, N.A., Alturki U., & ALjerraiwi, A.A. (2019). Integrating technology acceptance model with innovation diffusion theory: an empirical investigation on students' intention to use e-learning system. *Integrating TAM with IDT, 7.*

Yahya, F. H. (2020). Teaching innovation with ICT. *Proceding Internasional Seminar of Primary Education*, *2*, 7–9.

KEY TERMS AND DEFINITIONS

Digital Interaction: Possibility to interact with users of a remote digital platform.

Digitalization: Corporate operations and activities carried out with the aid of digital tools.

E-Learning: Use of digital technologies for distance learning through the use of an internet connection.

Information Technology: Set of technological methods and tools for the processing and dissemination of information in a digital way.

Innovation: Set of innovative and creative ideas that have introduced something new and useful.

Platform: IT structure for the provision of tools and technological services for the distribution of digital services, free or paid.

Technology: Application and study of everything that can be functional to the resolution of practical problems and business strategies for achieving a goal.

Appendix 1

Table 6. Socio-demographic aspects

SOCIO- DEMOGRAPHIC ASPECTS		N.	%
Gender	Male	203	24.8%
	Female	616	75.2%
Age	< 20	7	0.9%
	20 - 25	539	65.8%
	26 - 30	252	30.7%
	> 30	21	2.6%
Subscribed to	Bachelor's degree course	273	33.3%
	Master's Degree	546	66.7%
Having an adequate internet connection	Yes	679	82.9%
	No	140	17.1%
Possession of suitable digital devices	Yes	770	94%
	No	49	6%

source: our processing.

Appendix 2

Table 7. Lesson Planning and Use of the Digital Platform

LESSON PLANNING AND USE OF THE PLATFORM		N.	%
Easy- to- use digital platform	Highly	322	39.3%
	Fairly	434	53%
	Scant	56	6.8%
	For nothing	7	0.90%
Online lesson organized in a comprehensive way	Highly	182	22.2%
	Fairly	525	64.1%
	Scant	70	8.5%
	For nothing	42	5.1%
Adequate online teaching material support	Highly	161	19.7%
	Fairly	413	50.4%
	Scant	210	25.6%
	For nothing	35	4.3%

source: our processing.

Appendix 3

Table 8. Student learning expectation and evaluation of the e-learning system

STUDENT LEARNING EXPECTATIONS AND EVALUATION E-LEARNING			
		No.	**%**
The online courses offer adequate learning content (skills, competences, etc.)	Highly	147	17.9%
	Fairly	560	68.4%
	Scant	105	12.8%
	For nothing	7	0.90%
Interest in the use of online courses	Highly	168	20.5%
	Fairly	434	53%
	Scant	175	21.4%
	For nothing	42	5.1%
Content of lessons organized clearly	Highly	133	16.2%
	Fairly	588	71.8%
	Scant	91	11.1%
	For nothing	7	0.9%

Appendix 4

EVALUATION E- LEARNING SYSTEM		No.	%
Quality of internet connection	da 1 a 5	112	13.7%
	da 6 a 10	707	86.3%
Platform quality	da 1 a 5	119	14.5%
	da 6 a 10	700	85.5%
Image quality	da 1 a 5	140	17.1%
	da 6 a 10	679	82.9%
Audio quality	da 5 a 10	189	23.1%
	da 6 a 10	630	76.9%
Teacher support storytelling	da 5 a 10	105	12.8%
	da 6 a 10	714	87.2%
Digital interaction	da 5 a 10	294	35.9%
	da 6 a 10	524	64.1%

Source: our processing.

Table 10. **Student Perceptions and Innovative Aspects** *of e-learning*

STUDENT PERCEPTIONS AND INNOVATIVE ASPECTS		No.	%
Online course satisfaction compared to classroom courses	Highly	119	14.5%
	Fairly	350	42.7%
	Scant	189	23.1%
	For nothing	161	19.7%
Evaluation the validity of e-learning in the current emergency situation	Highly	252	30.8%
	Fairly	280	34.2%
	Scant	210	25.6%
	For nothing	77	9.4%
Is the innovative technology promoted by University to be considered a successful innovation?	Highly	287	35%
	Fairly	392	47.9%
	Scant	126	15.4%
	For nothing	14	1.7%

source: our processing.

Chapter 10
The Importance of Digital Fluency in Terms of Disruptive and Emerging Technologies

Kadir Demir
Dokuz Eylul University, Turkey

Hatice Ferhan Odabasi
Anadolu University, Turkey

ABSTRACT

This chapter primarily provides information about digital literacy, which enables us to make basic use of today's technologies. In parallel with today's technological developments, high-level digital literacy skills expected from individuals are addressed. Definitions of digital fluency and studies on this subject are examined. The concept of digital fluency is redefined by the authors. It is based on theoretical foundations that are needed by authors on why digital fluency is needed in educational life. The authors point to the lack of a workforce with high-level digital literacy capabilities around the world.

INTRODUCTION

The transition from industrial to information society accelerates with the effect of internet technology. The term 'information society' refers to a society that develops mainly due to scientific and technological development (Pinho and Lima, 2013). Today, knowledge is becoming more and more important. Societies that have knowledge and determine the right place, time and reason for using it are increasingly economically strengthened. Today, it is stated that mankind has more knowledge than ever had. Due to the developments in scientific research and Information and Communication Technologies (ICT) in the 21st century, the increase of knowledge in a doubling manner is considered as an "information explosion" (Sagasti, 2001). The validity of the information is becoming shorter and constantly updated (Odabaşı, 2000). It is important for individuals to constantly improve and renew their knowledge and skills as a precaution against the rapid obsolescence and out-of-date of knowledge. It is stated that the

DOI: 10.4018/978-1-7998-4972-8.ch010

Copyright © 2021, IGI Global. Copying or distributing in print or electronic forms without written permission of IGI Global is prohibited.

task of education is to prepare students for their own future, not for the past (OECD, 2018). According to the 2017 Future Human/Machine Association report, 85% of the occupations that will exist in 2030 have not yet been discovered (Institute for the Future for Dell Technologies, 2017). Teachers who prepare students for professions that are not yet known should be to equip their students with basic digital competencies. In this chapter, the main goal is to give the importance of digital fluency in terms of disruptive and emerging technologies.

BACKGROUND

Today's technological developments have made digital tools an indispensable element of our lives. Digital tools that radically change the way we communicate carry us into a future where machines communicate with each other. Digitization brings together individuals, cities, countries and continents to increase individual and social potential. It leads us to live in a more complex and more uncertain world (OECD, 2018). It is stated that specialization has become a special form of abstraction by detaching information from its context (Morin, 2003). Specialization isolates knowledge takes it out of context and makes a blackout between concrete events. We can adapt this to information technologies with the following example: Instead of expecting an accountant to use word processor and spreadsheet programs at a level as competent as expert software developers, he will be able to facilitate his work and solve complex problems in the context, time and appropriate purposes, when necessary. It makes more sense to expect it to use easily.

Each new technology makes it compulsory to have different skills and knowledge. For example; mobile devices must be used at a basic level when it is necessary to work with virtual reality technologies. If it is desired to develop original content with these technologies, three-dimensional modeling is among the skills that should be known. An individual who is an expert in three-dimensional modeling can transfer this knowledge for the use of different technologies and can also use it with, for example, three-dimensional printers. Computer programming and computational thinking transform society and encourage innovation, entrepreneurship, teamwork and creative thinking. Having only reading, writing and arithmetic skills does not seem sufficient for the individual in developing economies. Computer science determines the meaning of being a world citizen and being literate in the 21st century (Harel, 2016). In this context, the concept of digital literacy stands out as an important competence area.

MAIN FOCUS OF THE CHAPTER

Digital Literacy

Today, many institutions have started to provide services in electronic environment in order to speed up their service. The concept of knowledge-based labor has emerged instead of labor based on muscle strength through the transition from rural to urban and industrial society to information society. The concepts of robots, artificial intelligence, big data and the Internet of Things are gaining more and more space in our lives every day. This situation threatens the knowledge-based labor force that existing professions move towards automation (OECD, 2016). In the face of these uncertainties, digital competencies have taken place among the basic skills required by business life with the development of information processing technologies. In order to receive education, to have a job and to fulfill the civic duties, it is necessary to have basic digital competencies. Being able to take part in the digitalizing world and in the society makes digital literacy knowledge compulsory for individuals.

In order for the individual to be digitally literate, he or she must first be literate. Traxler (2018) defines digital literacy as "skills, abilities and attitudes that allow people and communities to survive, develop and grow in an increasingly digital environment". In order to better understand digital literacy, firstly, the concept of literacy should be considered. Kurt et al. (2013) stated literacy as being able to explain what is meant by symbols and to understand correctly what is explained through symbols. UNESCO (2006) defines literacy as having the ability to read, write and calculate to allow an individual to participate in all activities requiring literacy in society. With the proliferation of information and communication technologies, in addition to basic skills such as reading, writing and computing, information processing is a skill to be learned (Astrachan, Hambrusch, Peckham and Settle, 2009). Digital literacy is not seen only as the ability to use software and digital devices. It includes the capabilities that users need to effectively participate in digital environments (Eshet-Alkalai, 2004). Merchant (2009) defines digital literacy as reading and writing with new technologies. Jones and Flannigan (2006) describe digital literacy as the ability to use and understand information that is available through computers and accessed from different sources in various formats. Individuals with effective digital content creation, collaboration and communication processes are considered to be digital literate (Hague & Payton, 2010). Martin (2005) states digital literacy as defining, accessing, managing, integrating, evaluating, analyzing and synthesizing digital resources in a way that structures social events in the context of daily life. Digital literacy should not be seen as merely technical skills. Thanks to their literacy, individuals are able to live their lives in a better quality in the community. The concept of digital literacy cannot resist the rapid changes in technology due to its easy ability to lose its resilience to time. As technology changes, individuals are expected to adapt to new situations. Individuals who have received adequate training during formal education are forced to continue their skills gain after graduation. At this point, the concept of 'digital fluency' is preferred instead of 'digital literacy' in order to express high-level competencies (National Research Council, Committee on Information Technology Literacy, 1999).

Digital Fluency

Digital fluency is also expressed in field writing as technology fluency, information technology fluency, ICT fluency. In this study, the concept of digital fluency will be preferred. Spencer (2015) states that the word fluency derives from the word flow and expresses flexibility, accuracy, effectiveness and appropriateness in any context.

Digital fluency is a concept against the digital native-digital immigrant dilemma put forward by Prensky (Garrick, Pendergast & Geelan, 2017). According to this statement, not every individual expressed as digital native can also have equal technological means and knowledge. It has been suggested that it may be more appropriate to use the concept of digital fluency, which can be influenced by specific and subtle variables, in order to express this situation. There are many definitions in the field literature on digital fluency. Hsi (2007) defines digital fluency as individuals gaining and demonstrating the actions of acquiring, designing, evaluating, criticizing, synthesizing and developing digital media contents, messages and other electronic expressions using digital tools. It is defined as the competences, applications, awareness and strategic expertise that the learners have developed for these purposes. According to another definition, digital fluency is a combination of critical thinking and information literacy skills

(Miller ve Bartlett, 2012). Similarly, Pinho and Lima (2013) stated that digital fluency is a dynamic and variable competence that is expressed as being able to adapt to the transformations in technology in order to gain new information that will be encountered throughout life. Liu, Li, and Ye (2018) state that digital fluency involves critical thinking, knowledge comprehension skills, and the use of specific knowledge. According to Demir et al. (2015, p.3), digital fluency requires the ability to know when and where to use technology. Information technology fluency is defined as the ability of individuals to use information technologies productively in their personal and professional lives and to recognize the situations in which information technologies will work (National Research Council, Committee on Information Technology Literacy, 1999). In another definition that emphasizes the social aspect of digital fluency, digital fluency is defined as the ability to use social and mobile technologies for communication, collaboration and connection with people (Ross, 2015). Digital fluency is not just sharing using social media and social networking apps; understand complex issues such as identity management and digital participation (Savin-Baden, 2015). According to Briggs, and Makice (2011), digital fluency is the ability to reliably achieve the desired results through technology. Briggs, and Makice (2011) considered digital fluency as a journey of four stages. They state that each stage can be gained by gaining knowledge and skills. These four stages are as follows:

- **Anti-Literate:** Although an anti-literate individual has no experience of any technology and does not fully understand the benefits and limitations of the existing technology, he rejects it.
- **Pre-Literate:** An individual who is a literate person has the potential and curiosity to develop knowledge, skills and understanding of an existing technology.
- **Literate:** The literate individual has the basic skills to fully utilize digital technologies. They are individuals who know what they can do with digital tools.
- **Fluent:** Fluent individuals are aware of when it is appropriate to use digital tools. They know why these tools should be used. They can use digital tools very easily. They have made using automated tools an automated skill. As technology changes, they adapt to new situations.

According to Spencer (2015), digital fluency consists of the following components:

- **Digital competence**: To be able to understand, select and use different technologies or technologies.
- **Digital literacy:** Cognitive and intellectual competencies, reading, creating, evaluating and judging by applying technical skills.
- **Social competence:** To be able to communicate effectively with other individuals.

According to the American National Research Council, digital fluency requires three types of information. (National Research Council, Committee on Information Technology Literacy, 1999). These types of information:

- **Intellectual abilities:** Apply information technologies to complex and sustainable situations, including high-level thinking.
- **Information technology concepts:** Basic principles and ideas of computers and networks.
- **Information technology skills:** Ability to use computer applications of that period.

It has been stated that modern skills may change over time, but the basic concepts of mental abilities and information technologies will not change. However, the change in technology today shows that the basic concepts of information technologies are also changing radically. The National Research Council (Committee on Information Technology Literacy, 1999) lists ten priority points for each type of information as follows:

Intellectual Capabilities

1. Engage in sustained reasoning.
2. Manage complexity.
3. Test a solution.
4. Manage problems in faulty solutions.
5. Organize and navigate information structures and evaluate information.
6. Collaborate.
7. Communicate to other audiences.
8. Expect the unexpected.
9. Anticipate changing technologies.
10. Think about information technology abstractly.

Information Technology Concepts

1. Computers
2. Information systems
3. Networks
4. Digital representation of information
5. Information organization
6. Modeling and abstraction
7. Algorithmic thinking and programming
8. Universality
9. Limitations of information technology
10. Societal impact of information and information technology

Information Technology Skills

1. Setting up a personal computer
2. Using basic operating system features
3. Using a word processor to create a text document
4. Using a graphics and/or artwork package to create illustrations, slides, or other image-based expressions of ideas
5. Connecting a computer to a network
6. Using the Internet to find information and resources
7. Using a computer to communicate with others
8. Using a spreadsheet to model simple processes or financial tables
9. Using a database system to set up and access useful information

10. Using instructional materials to learn how to use new applications or features

According to Miller and Bartlett (2012), digital fluency has three main components:

Net-savviness: It means understanding how the Internet works. For example, if you're in the way search engines produce results, the design and installation of Web sites, and how to publish images and videos.

Critical evaluative techniques: Know and use simple controls, techniques and principles to assess the accuracy and reliability of information contained on the Internet. Both critical thinking skills (accuracy control, diversifying resources, understanding the nature of evidence, reaching the main source) as well as special online skills (knowing how filtering programs work, Wikipedia peer to know the editing process).

Diversity: It relates to the extent to which users' online content consumption is comprehensive, varied and diverse.

According to Sparrow (2018), digital fluency; the ability to use technology to create new knowledge, to deal with new challenges and new problems, and the ability to solve these skills with critical thinking, complex problem solving and social intelligence. Digital fluency consists of, but is not limited to, the different types of fluency detailed below (Sparrow, 2018).

Curiosity Fluency: Includes a passion for having questions and answering them. It instills the awareness that students grow up to be able to develop their own answers to questions, not just as individuals who find answers to questions using Google.

Communication Fluency: The ability to communicate new knowledge between different communities and to choose a suitable and effective environment for a specific audience. Using virtual reality and augmented reality to tell the story can change not only how technology works, but also its impact on the reader and how this tool can be told to understand the truth.

Creation Fluency: Deep understanding how information is created and developed to produce something new. These production contents can be developed in a physical or virtual environment and may include three-dimensional printing and programming.

Data Fluency: The ability to push the boundaries of what technology can do to process data to ask new questions, along with the capacity to use information sets to make informed decisions.

Innovation Fluency: It involves recognizing that failure is a valuable part of the learning process. In order to innovate, students need to take risks, fail, learn from failures and repeat the process with different ideas.

Wang, Myers and Sundaram (2012) proposed a model for the concept of digital fluency (Figure 1). According to this model, seven factors explain digital fluency. These factors and the determinant variables of each factor are:

Organisational Factors: University/school, science/ subject/ faculty, type of university study, computer-aided learning.

Demographic characteristics: Age, gender, socio-economic status, race/nationality/country, geography (urban/rural), language (ability or disability to speak foreign languages) and home size.

Psychological factors: Interest, personality, computer anxiety, aging anxiety, perceived technology use ability.

Social influences: Family and peer influence, use of teachers, ability and influence.

Behavioural intention to use: Behavioral intent to use, attitude towards technology.

Opportunity: Accessibility, home access, access location, year of computer ownership.

Use of technology: General technology experience, custom technology experience, exercise (application-oriented), type of technology used, user profiles/ groups.

Figure 1. Conceptual model of digital fluency (Wang, Myers, ve Sundaram, 2012)

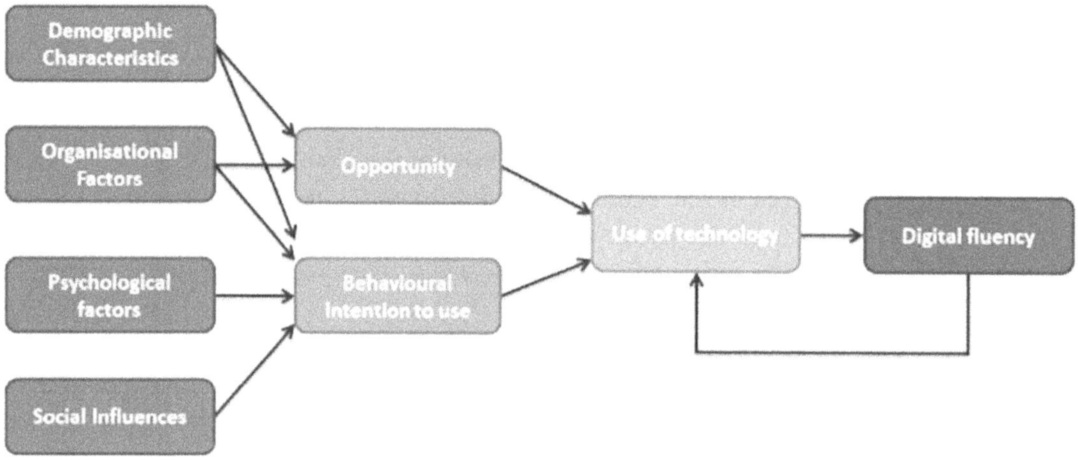

Digital fluency enables us to communicate more effectively, enriches learning and connectivity, and creates a stronger culture and commitment (Ross, 2015). In light of technological developments, newer digital tools are being used for different purposes every day. Individuals who grow up in environments with different digital tools have different attitudes towards new technologies (Williams, Crittenden, Keo and McCarty; 2012). Today, to be digitally fluent, it is necessary to have more skills than before (Briggs, and Makice, 2011). In such an environment, digitally fluent individuals are expected to become lifelong learners (National Research Council, Committee on Information Technology Literacy, 1999). A digitally fluid individual should be able to examine the information and content he/she encounters on the Internet from a critical point of view and use secure and reliable resources. They must keep their knowledge up to date by finding new digital tools through research and discovery, (Pinho and Lima, 2013). Digital fluency should not be seen as a static gain. Acquired capabilities become less useful over time without new experiences (Briggs, and Makice, 2011). Digitally fluid individuals need to learn more and adapt to changing technology in order to use digital tools effectively in personal and professional contexts throughout their lives (National Research Council, Committee on Information Technology Literacy, 1999). Kuhn (2017) states that progress must be made in three key areas in order to increase digital fluency. These areas include; attitude towards technology, the skill required for effective use to learn about technology capacity in academic environments and technology. It is thought that it will contribute to the continuous practice of individuals through trial and error in order to be proficient in this regard. It is anticipated that an individual will not be able to specialize in a digital tool within a few days (OECD, 2016). Being able to create and sustain digital fluency is a lifelong process. Personal experience is seen as the best way to develop knowledge, skills and understanding to develop digital fluency skills. Similar to fluency in language or music, digital fluency is also developed and sustainable through practice (Briggs, and Makice, 2011). Pinho and Lima (2013) have expressed a special definition of digital fluency for teachers. According to this definition, teachers should be able to manage the complexity of teaching through technology. Together with technology, they need to have the knowledge, skills and attitudes to plan, create, carry out tasks and evaluate student performance and skills.

In the learning model created by Burch in the 1970s, four stages known as "The Four Stages of Competence" in which individuals acquire a new skill are shown in Figure 2 (Kavis, 2015).

The stages in the hierarchy of competence are described below from the lower level to the top:

Figure 2. Hierarchy of competence (Kavis, 2015)

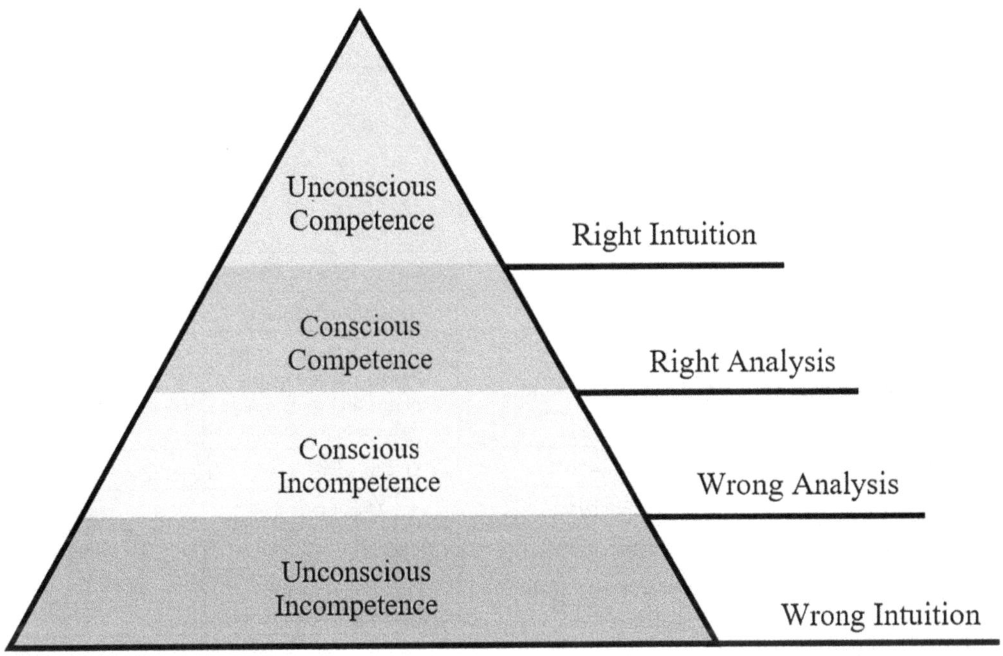

Unconscious Incompetence: The individual does not understand or know how to do something and is not aware of his condition.

Conscious Incompetence: The individual does not understand or know how to do something but is aware of his condition.

Conscious Competence: An individual understands or knows how to do something, but he needs to focus when showing his or her skills or knowledge.

Unconscious Competence: The individual understands or knows how to do something and is not aware of it. Until the individual reached this stage, he had experience and practice disassociates of such skills or knowledge many times.

The Unconscious Competence phase, the highest level learning phase in the Hierarchy of. Competence model proposed by Burch, meets the expression of high-level skills in many definitions of digital fluency (Kavis, 2015). After examining the concepts in the field literature by the researchers, a more inclusive definition of digital fluency has been tried to be created by synthesizing (Briggs, & Makice, 2011; Demir et al., 2015; Hsi, 2007; Liu, Li, & Ye, 2018; Miller & Bartlett, 2012; National Research Council, Committee on Information Technology Literacy, 1999; Pinho & Lima, 2013; Ross, 2015; Savin-Baden, 2015; Sparrow, 2018; Spencer, 2015; Wang, Myers & Sundaram, 2012). According to this definition, digital fluency; To be able to think critically about ICT concepts and applications, to be able to use ICT effectively and efficiently, to have quality ICT experiences, to manage complexity, to produce solutions, to think abstractly about ICT, to adapt quickly to technological transformation to be able to provide, to be able to run appropriate skill sets to work, and to use ICT flexibly for different purposes (Demir & Odabasi, 2016). After this section where digital fluency definitions and frameworks are discussed, digital fluency studies in the literature are examined in the light of this information.

Literature of Digital Fluency

In this section, from studies on digital fluency in the field literature, research type is included. Related research is shown in Table 1.

Table 1. Digital fluency studies

Author/ Authors	Participants	Research Design/ Method	Data Collection Tool
Parahita (2017)	Adults (n=189)	Quantitative/Survey	Questionnaire
Bose, Pakala, & Grover (2017)	Undergraduate students (n=53)	Mixed/ Pretest-posttest quasi-experimental study design Focus group interview	Questionnaire / Focus group interview questions
Accenture (2016)	Adults (n=5000)	Quantitative / Survey	Questionnaire /Data logs
Lubbe (2016)	Academicians	Quantitative	Questionnaire
Pinho & Lima (2013)	Teachers (n=25)	Qualitative / Case studyı	Forum content
Kim, Chung, & Yu (2013)	Secondary school students (n=149)	Pretest-posttest quasi-experimental study design	Test
Wang, Wiesemes, & Gibbons (2012)	Undergraduate students (n=6)	Qualitative / Content analysis	Interview, Monthly group meeting notes
Miller & Bartlett (2012)	Teachers (n=>500)	Quantitative / Survey	Questionnaire
Costa, Prado, Oliveira, Peres, Massarollo, Fernandes, ... & Freitas (2011)	Undergraduate students (n=51)	Quantitative / Survey	Questionnaire
Kaminski, Switzer, & Gloeckner (2009)	Undergraduate students (n=2494)	Pretest-posttest quasi-experimental time series study design	Scale
Gayol & Boubsil (2009)	Faculty members (n=53)	Quantitative / Tarama	Questionnaire
Bologa, Lupu, Sabau, & Bologa (2007).	Undergraduate students (n=25)	Pretest-posttest quasi-experimental study design	Portfolio evaluation/Rubric
Glewa & Bogan (2007)	Primary school students	Qualitative / Content analysis	Reflective diary
Green (2005)	Adults (n=334)	Mixed/ Survey and content analysis	Scale and story analysis

When the studies in Table 1 are examined, the participants of the digital fluency studies are mostly university students. Only one study included faculty members, 98% of whom were educated at doctoral level. When the studies conducted in terms of research methods are examined, it is observed that quantitative research methods are used predominantly.

In a study focused on the relationship of adults with digital disinformation, research was conducted with 189 adults belonging to different age, gender, religious ethnicity, belief type, education and level and income level in Jakarta, Indonesia (Parahita, 2017). Data were collected from 189 adults in a survey model. The questionnaire used for the research consists of eight main topics. These titles include trust, creativity, action, ethics, privacy, skills, personal development and criticality. According to the inferences obtained from the study, gender, age, religion and belief type are not among the variables predicting digital fluency. It is concluded that income level and education level have a meaningful relationship with digital fluency. It is stated that the higher the income level and education level, the more likely it is to experience experiences that will increase the digital fluency of the individual.

Accenture (2016) aims to better understand and define the role of digital fluency in terms of gender equality in the workforce. The sample of the research included 5000 female and male participants from 31 countries. Participants are asked which devices (from smartphones to wearable devices), when and how they use them, their educational level and career status, whether they take a virtual course from an online university, a questionnaire has been conducted with questions such as how they use digital collaboration, instant messaging and internet cameras for business purposes, and whether the female employees of the company they work for are preparing to make senior managers. In addition, internet usage information has been obtained from international communication agencies for each country in which its participants are involved. The Accenture Digital Fluency Model has been developed as part of this research. This model not only compares men to men in terms of digital fluency, but also reveals the positive contributions of digital fluency in terms of education, work experience and promotion in the workplace. According to the research results, digital fluency contributes positively to the career cycle. Digital fluency, on the other hand, has a greater impact on women than men. Digital fluency has been found to contribute significantly to gender equality at work in participating countries. It has been stated that men have higher digital fluency than women and are more willing to learn digital skills.

In the study conducted by Bose, Pakala and Grover (2017), students used their mobile learning strategies and devices to help ensure that they have effectively increased their communication and digital skills, and that to determine its impact in Idaho, United States of America. The students participating in the engineering course were given tablet computers in order to communicate with their friends and faculty members. Students borrowed these tablet computers for use in the fall and spring. At the beginning and end of the fall semester 2016, anonymous questionnaires were applied to the students. In light of data from surveys conducted in fall 2016, recommendations have been established on how students can improve their digital fluency and communication using tablet computers. At the end of spring 2017, qualitative data were collected by conducting a focus group meeting. As a result of the research, students receiving learning support using tablet computers have increased their perceived digital fluency.

An experimental study conducted by Bologa, Lupu, Sabau, and Bologa (2007) investigated whether there was a correlation between the digital fluency of university students and their ability to use the necessary computer applications in everyday life in Bucharest, Romania. It is aimed to measure their digital fluency by giving students the chance to use tools to demonstrate their digital fluency. For this purpose, SCRATCH software, which is one of the block-based programming software, has been preferred. Participants were selected on a voluntary basis among university students enrolled in elective web development at Romania's largest universities. A digital fluency formula was developed by researchers to determine the digital fluency of participants on Scratch. Information on this formula is below:

Digital Fluency Level (DAL) = MF + AF + IF + DS + SOF

MF = Number of Scratch motion features used

AF= Number of Scratch audio features used
IF = Number of Scratch interaction features used
DS = Number of Scratch data structures used
SOF = Number of Scratch other features used

The digital fluency level indicator score formulated in the figure above was calculated and the students' digital fluency levels were evaluated by the researchers. According to this formula, students' projects were evaluated after 14 weeks of education. According to the results of the analysis, there is a correlation between the digital fluency levels of university students and their ability to use the necessary computer applications in everyday life.

Reporting the first phase of the three-year project conducted by Lubbe (2016) to enable students to acquire the necessary special skills and qualifications in their online teaching and work subject matter in Pretoria, South Africa. The aim of the project is to evaluate the digital fluency of academicians working at the Open Distance Education and Learning Institution. In the study, which was patterned as quantitative research, the data were collected by means of questionnaire. The results show that academicians are willing to use new teaching technologies but perceive their own skills as inadequate.

A study to determine the fluency of university students in information technology included 2012 students who had just started university in 2001 and 482 students who graduated in 2005 in Colorado, United States of America (Kaminski, Switzer, & Gloeckner, 2009). Using the perception of information technology fluency scale, students' basic knowledge and skills about more complex applications, such as word processing, presentation software and digital audio software, were measured. According to the results obtained using the "Perceived information technology fluency scale" that the change in information technology fluency of university students over the intervening four years, students' presentation and web browser while there is an increase in information; database, web animation, programming, desktop publishing, digital video and audio software information is significantly declined (Kaminski, Switzer, & Gloeckner, 2009). Another study that sees digital fluency as a technical skill is aimed at revealing the perception and personal experience of the use of mobile devices in the research of PhD students (Wang, Wiesemes & Gibbons, 2012). Semi-structured interviews and monthly group meetings were conducted and according to the results of the research, it was concluded that using mobile devices did not make an important contribution to doctoral studies. These studies differ from other studies by seeing digital fluency only as technical skills. Digital fluency requires social skills as well as technique. A study conducted in this direction investigated how well young people are equipped to distinguish good information from bad information (Miller & Bartlett, 2012). For this purpose, more than 500 teachers were surveyed to obtain their opinions about their students. Teachers; sees the digital fluency of its students as weak. Teachers state that 95% of the students' information source is online, but they think that their students cannot critically evaluate the information on the internet. Similarly, in a study conducted with 51 nursing undergraduate students in order to describe the digital fluency, knowledge, skills and interests of nursing undergraduate students, students do not consider themselves to be fluent in digital level. In this study, it is stated that students perceive themselves as moderate because they use computers since childhood and adolescence (Costa et al., 2011). In another study conducted to describe the digital fluency of the participants, the digital fluency of faculty members is considered to be open to development in Santa Barbara, United States of America (Gayol & Boubsil, 2009). These studies aiming at describing digital fluency treat digital fluency as a technical or social skill as different concepts. The factors that predict the concept of digital fluency in these studies are not clearly defined. In another study, sociological and emotional factors of digital fluency; openness to innovation, extroversion, adaptability, technology skills, intelligence, childhood memories and positive technology memories (Green, 2005).

In a study conducted to examine the perceptions of pre-service and in-service teachers about digital fluency and pedagogical use of digital technologies in foreign language learning and teaching, a questionnaire was applied and the contents of the forum were analyzed by the teachers. According to the results obtained; it is stated that digital fluency is a factor that increases motivation in foreign language teaching, it is a competence needed to create more attractive and dynamic courses and it is important to give institutional support to teachers to become digital fluent (Pinho & Lima, 2013). In another study aimed at improving digital fluency, it was aimed to develop an educational program to develop creative problem solving skills through programming (Scratch) and to increase students' digital fluency. The study was conducted with 149 secondary school students, 30 of whom needed special education, and a test was developed to measure creative problem solving ability. At the end of the study, it was concluded that digital fluency of students increased. It is concluded that digital fluency will increase if creative problem solving skills are developed with programming tools (Kim, Chung & Yu, 2013). Similarly, a research conducted to encourage students to become digitally fluent individuals through the use of blogs in the classroom concluded that writing awareness by using technology-based tools in students increased awareness in Florida, United States of America (Glewa & Bogan, 2007).

In the theoretical study conducted by White (2013), the topics related to Digital Fluency course which should be taught in primary, secondary and high schools are suggested. These topics are listed below:

- Acceptable behavior
- Collaboration, communication, problem solving and research strategies
- Community involvement
- Critical thinking
- Design skills
- Digital rights and copyright
- Digital fluency
- Ethics
- Internet history
- Identity and privacy
- Project management
- Security
- Technology concepts

It is said that digital fluency alone is not the most important factor in learning. Digital fluency is seen as an aid in having the knowledge, skills and behaviors necessary for a successful and secure digital life (White, 2013). In line with the studies examined in the field literature, it is observed that students and teachers are mostly involved as participants in digital fluency studies. In this context, it can be said that more research is needed with prospective teachers who have the potential to directly affect primary, secondary and high school students. Therefore, the importance of digital fluency for education is discussed in the next section.

Importance of Digital Fluency in Education

The need for digital fluency, called displaying high-level digital literacy skills, is growing day by day in the educational world. The report, published by the EEF and focusing on the use of digital technology for the purpose of improving learning, contains four key recommendations (Education Endowment Foundation, 2019):

- Schools should consider how technology will improve teaching and learning before introducing it.
- Using technology to improve the quality of explanations and modelling.
- Technology should be used to improve the impact of pupil practice.
- Technology should play a role in improving assessment and feedback.

Given these recommendations; technology seems to play an important role in learning and teaching environments, qualified content development, student skills enhancement, measurement, evaluation and feedback. In addition to these points, technology is being put into work for school administrators and student parents for school management and student monitoring. Large-scale educational technology projects have been implemented by countries, especially in the belief in the transformative power of education with the widespread development of technology. In a study focusing on Japan, USA, China, Italy and Germany, educational technology trends and perspectives in these countries are discussed in the STEEP (social, technological, economic, environmental, and political) framework (Mao, Ifenthaler, Fujimoto, Garavaglia, & Rossi, 2019). According to the results of the study, longitudinal research is needed in Japan and Germany to measure the effectiveness and efficiency of educational technology in learning and teacher environments. China needs better trained and informed experts in both education and technology. Basic digital skills and competencies have spread with the spread of technology. Expectations of students also change day by day. While the use of technology was seen as sufficient in the 2000s, today the ability to produce media, content, etc. using technology comes to the fore. Students are expected to realize their ideas through current technologies.

The basic standards expected from students and teachers published by the International Society for Technology in Education (ISTE) are below (Figure 3).

According the ISTE standarts (ISTE, 2019), students should interact technology in ways that are safe, legal and ethical. Each standard addresses students' interaction with technology from a different perspective.

Empowered Learner: In order to become a strengthened student, students should use technology to improve learning processes and learning outcomes. Especially the empowered student should be able to transfer existing knowledge to discover current technologies.

Digital Citizen: In order to become a digital citizen, students must establish their digital identities. Students should behave ethically, safely and legally during their social interaction.

Knowledge Instructor: Students should have the basic skills of critical digital literacy and media literacy. In this way, students can obtain meaningful connections and results with the information they produce by obtaining data from digital sources.

Innovative Designer: Students should be able to develop, test and improve design by selecting appropriate digital tools for the cyclic design process. Students should be able to produce innovative solutions to identify existing problems and find solutions to these problems.

Figure 3. ISTE Standards for Students

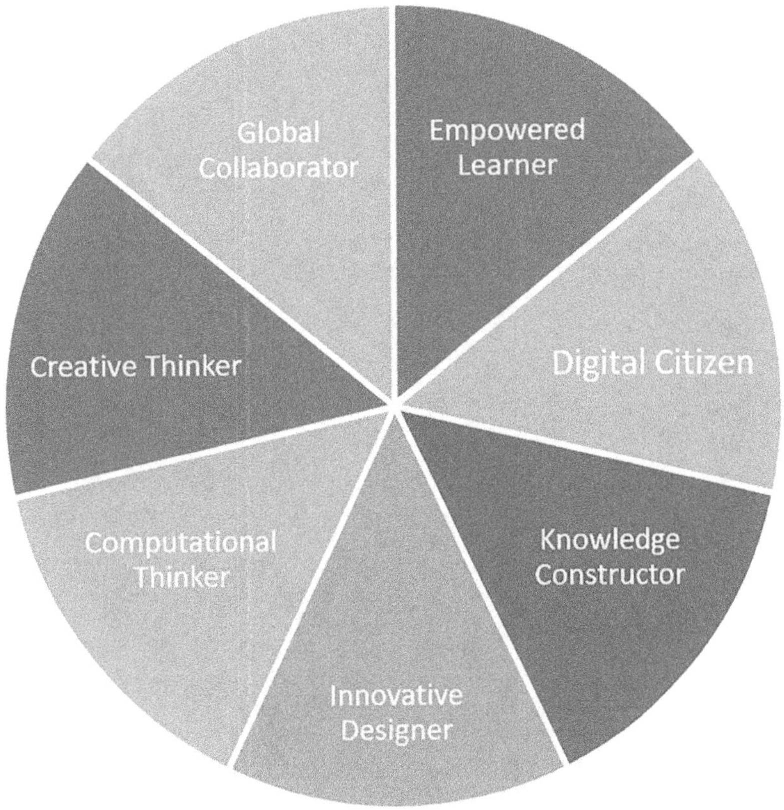

Computational Thinker: Students should be able to solve existing problems with data analysis, abstract modeling, pattern recognition and algorithmic thinking. Students should be able to use digital tools to collect, analyze, present and visualize data appropriate to the solution, and automate solutions.

Creative Communicator: Students should be able to select appropriate digital platforms and tools to express themselves. Students should be able to present their ideas through visualization, modeling or simulating using digital tools.

Global Collaborator: Students should be able to develop collaboration with students locally and globally to develop mutual understanding and learning by using collaborative technologies. Students should be able to reach solutions using collaborative technologies.

Learner: Educators should learn pedagogical approaches that will increase their productivity using technology. Educators should continue their professional development by being involved in local and global learning networks.

Leader: Educators should take initiatives to improve students' learning experiences with technology. Educators should ensure that students have access to educational technologies, digital content and learning opportunities tailored to their different needs. Educators should be role models in using digital resources and tools for learning.

Figure 4. ISTE Standards for Teachers

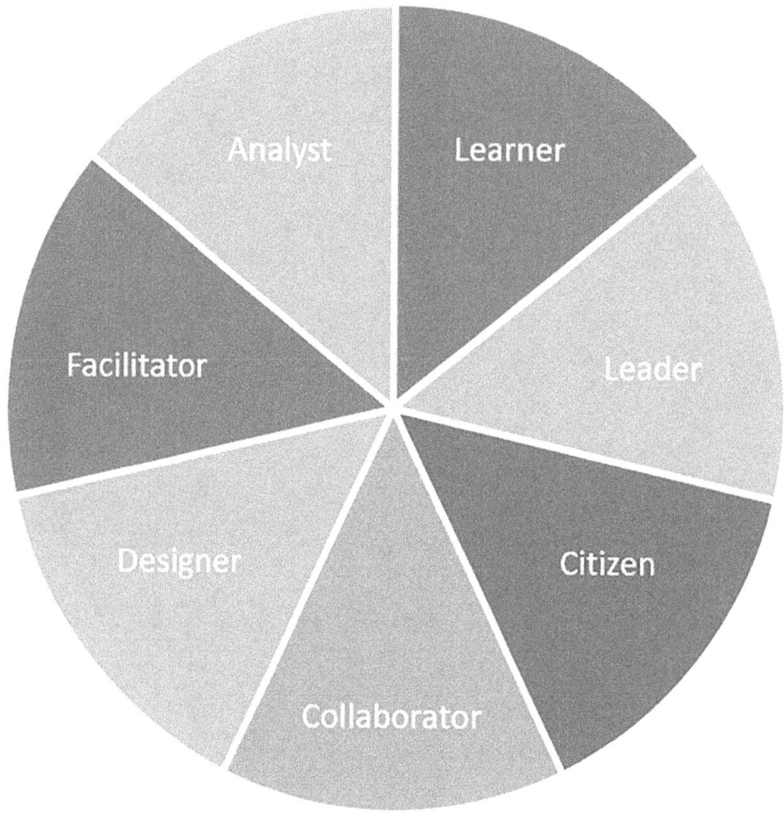

Citizen: Educators should encourage students to participate in the digital world. Educators should create an online learning culture for students. Educators should be mentoring to protect students' digital rights.

Collaborator: Educators should come up with ideas about how they can use technology as facilitators for learning in collaboration with students and educators. Educators should enable students to communicate with relevant experts using collaborative digital tools.

Designer: Educators should be able to design learning environments with a personalized learning experience with digital tools and resources. Educators should increase learning efficiency by using digital tools and resources.

Facilitator: Educators should manage strategies that enable students to use technology more effectively on digital platforms and makerspace environments.

Analyst: Educators should support the student to collect and learn digitally his / her data. Educators should be able to perform learner needs, feedback and assessments by collecting data through technology.

When the ISTE standards developed for students and educators are examined in detail, it is seen that high-level digital literacy skills are needed to fulfill the roles given to both groups. Digital fluency is seen not only as part of a lifetime of education, not just throughout school life. From a theoretical point of view, these basic competencies are needed for learning and teaching.

In the light of technological developments, more and more digital tools are being used for different purposes. Educational technologies that have been thought of in recent years and are now used in many learning environments include learning management systems, e-books, virtual and augmented reality, robotics, mobile devices and applications, smart boards, wearable technologies and cloud applications. This section will focus on technologies that are becoming more and more common in the near future and are potentially becoming more and more common, rather than detailed information about these technologies that have already been assimilated. These technologies and digital tools include mixed reality, three-dimensional printing technologies and artificial intelligence. Mixed Reality (MR) means that the user interacts with the virtual objects in the real object while interacting with the real object (Loup-Escande, Frenoy, Poplimont, Thouvenin, Gapenne, & Megalakaki, 2017). Especially in medical education, students have the opportunity to experience a realistic experience in diagnosis, treatment and consultation thanks to the mixed reality (Karaca, Demir & Caliskan, 2018). Although three-dimensional printing technology is still a technology that has not yet entered the end-users' homes, it is becoming more and more widespread in the corporate sense. When it comes to three-dimensional printing technologies, three-dimensional printers come to mind first. In addition to three-dimensional printers, three-dimensional scanning and three-dimensional modeling and slicing software are important and complementary components of this ecosystem (Demir et al, 2016).

Artificial intelligence is defined as information processing models developed to perform the tasks that human beings can perform in its simplest form (Skilton, & Hovsepian, 2017). According to another definition, artificial intelligence is the combination of algorithms and computer software to realize cognitive processes (Cross, & Lucas, 2019). Artificial intelligence, which has started to directly affect the transportation (Bösch, Becker, Becker, & Axhausen, 2018), health (Sitterding, Raab, Saupe, & Israel, 2019), agriculture (Elahi, Weijun, Zhang, & Nazeer, 2019), production (Gelmereanu, Morar, & Bogdan, 2014), banking (Tavana, Abtahi, Di Caprio, & Poortarigh, 2018) areas has also started to affect the education area. In the field of education, many tools and technologies including artificial robots, intelligent robots, adaptive learning systems have been introduced (Chassignol, Khoroshavin, Klimova, & Bilyatdinova, 2018). The concept of Artificial Intelligence, which is an umbrella concept, consists of a combination of sub-disciplines and methods such as neural networks, machine learning, voice, image and text recognition and robotics. Machine learning is the use of computer systems for pattern recognition and prediction. Deep learning is a sub-discipline of machine learning. With deep learning, deep artificial neural networks based on complex algorithms, computers can learn from large amounts of data as they reach new levels of accuracy (Touger 2018).

As the digital tools that come into our lives and the tasks that can be accomplished with these tools become more complex, we need to update our digital skills. To adapt to the transformations in technology in order to gain new knowledge throughout life, and to facilitate the transfer of our existing knowledge to new situations, which are expressed as dynamic competence potential (Lima, 2013). One of the main goals of the education is the transfer of the gains obtained to the workplace.

Importance of Digital Fluency in Workplace

Having the digital competencies to use digital technologies that have the potential to deeply affect, transform, eliminate and create new sectors has taken its place among the basic requirements of business life. What is expected of today's modern people is to become information producers instead of being consumers of data. 350,000 highly skilled technical experts are needed in the fields of artificial intelligence, data analytics and cybersecurity, the report said, adding that the European Union will ensure that the future workforce will have advanced digital skills between 2021 and 2027. 700 million Euros budget allocated to ensure (European Commission, 2018a). It is important that many countries and international unions attach importance to this issue and it is important for those who work to be aware of the direction in which their professions evolved.

To give an up-to-date example, radiology is one of the sectors deeply influenced by artificial intelligence technology. There are many scientific studies about how artificial intelligence affects medical education and its predictions and expectations about this situation (Wartman, & Combs, 2018; Wartman, & Combs, 2019). One of the fields in which artificial intelligence is successfully applied in the field of medicine is the field of radiology. Despite this situation and the increase in artificial intelligence studies in the field of radiology, there is a lack of awareness and knowledge among the employees (Waymel, Badr, Demondion, Cotten, & Jacques, 2019). The field of artificial intelligence and radiology is a small part of the iceberg that appears in digital technologies. It is necessary to look at the big picture to examine the importance of digital competences in business life.

Importance of Digital Fluency in Real World Scenario

Importance of digital competences in life has become more vital than ever before in 2020 with a global pandemic in these days. Nowadays, when main concern is to protect human health, digital fluency states such as South Korea and Singapore have sought ways to survive a global pandemic with minimal damage by employing digital skills. Digital fluency levels of citizens have become a decisive factor in this process where solutions such as digital patient tracking, global location monitoring, remote physician treatment, remote disease testing have been developed. In this environment where a global pandemic spreads, another danger that looks as dangerous as the virus was data pollution. Digital fluency consists different types of fluency such as data fluency which has become more important in this environment. Data fluency is the ability to push the boundaries of what technology can do to process data to ask new questions, along with the capacity to use information sets to make informed decisions (Sparrow, 2018). Individuals with digital fluency made decisions in real life situations using their data literacy skills. In the controlled social life experienced in global quarantine days and beyond, it has become imperative to take advantage of the features of digital technologies in every area of life. In order to use these advantages, it is important to develop digital competencies and to have digital fluency.

CONCLUSION

In the 21st century, many business sectors have become data-driven. According to the results of a systematic literature review, the 21st century skills that employees should have as knowledge workers were revealed such as information, communication, collaboration, critical thinking, creativity, and problem-solving skills (Van Laar, Van Deursen, Van Dijk, & De Haan, 2017). Digital literacy skills can be employed in order to have basic competencies in these skills areas which can be described as continuation of teacher and student standards. In order to make a difference in working environments, to become an in-house entrepreneur and to reach different career goals, digital fluency skills are required. Digital fluency has many characteristic features, but the intelligence is seen as core item of this features. Among the digital fluency features are studies that include intelligence and social intelligence (Green, 2005; Sparrow, 2018).

Digital fluency has been handled by different researchers with different aspects. Many frameworks have been created due to the fact that a clear agreement has not yet been reached on the concept and the very broad features of the concept. These frameworks become more complex as the age of the target audience increases. It should not be forgotten that the main goal of digital fluency is to turn individuals into individuals who can do what they think in the digital age we feel today.

FUTURE RESEARCH DIRECTIONS

In this study, importance of digital fluency in terms of disruptive and emerging technologies emphasized. In addition, the studies that focus on digital fluency mentioned above. There are many variables such as age, gender, technology skills, intelligence; the relationship of which is investigated with the concept of digital fluency. There are many variables that is investigated with the concept of digital fluency such as age, gender, technology skills, intelligence (Green, 2005; Kaminski, Switzer, & Gloeckner, 2009; Parahita, 2017). Future researchers are suggested to conduct research examining the relationship between intelligence and digital fluency. The concept of digital fluency is a concept that should be handled as applied theoretically as well. It may not be enough for individuals to know only in order to be able to exist and adapt to the changing digital world. Their ability to do so is also of great importance. Considering this situation, it is recommended to use digital application environments in order to reach more objective results in the researches to be conducted.

ACKNOWLEDGMENT

This study is a part of the first author's Ph.D. dissertation, which is supervised by the second author. This study was supported by the Anadolu University Scientific Research Projects Commission [grant number 1702E041].

REFERENCES

Accenture (2016). Getting to equal: How digital is helping close the gender gap at work. *Digital Fluency Indonesia Report.* Retrieved from https://www.accenture.com/t20160506T060137__w__/id-en/_acnmedia/Accenture/Conversion-Assets/DotCom/Documents/About-Accenture/PDF/3/Accenture-IWD-2016-Digital-Fluency-Indonesia-Report.pdf

Astrachan, O., Hambrusch, S., Peckham, J., & Settle, A. (2009). The present and future of computational thinking. In *Proceedings of the 40th ACM Technical Symposium on Computer Science Education - SIGCSE '09* (pp. 549–550). New York, NY: Association for Computing Machinery. Retrieved from 10.1145/1508865.1509053

Bologa, R., Lupu, A. R., Sabau, G., & Bologa, A. (2007). Digital fluency and its importance in educating young students for the knowledge age. In L. Congyan (Ed.). *Proceedings of the 7th WSEAS Int. Conference on Distance Learning and Web Engineering* (pp. 354-457). Stevens point, WI: World Scientific and Engineering Academy and Society (WSEAS).

Bösch, P. M., Becker, F., Becker, H., & Axhausen, K. W. (2018). Cost-based analysis of autonomous mobility services. *Transport Policy*, *64*, 76–91. doi:10.1016/j.tranpol.2017.09.005

Bose, D., Pakala, K., & Grover, L. (2017). *Learner perceptions of increase in digital fluency after participation in a living learning community based mobile learning community: A progress report.* Pacific North West American Society for Engineering Education (PNW-ASEE). Retrieved from https://www.researchgate.net/publication/318470232_Learner_perceptions_of_increase_in_digital_fluency_after_participation_in_a_Living_Learning_Community_based_Mobile_Learning_Community_A_progress_report

Briggs, C., & Makice, K. (2012). *Digital fluency: Building success in the digital age.* Sociolens. Retrieved from http://www.socialens.com/blog/wp-content/uploads/downloads/2012/01/SociaLens_Digital_Fluency_Sample1.pdf

Chassignol, M., Khoroshavin, A., Klimova, A., & Bilyatdinova, A. (2018). Artificial Intelligence trends in education: A narrative overview. *Procedia Computer Science*, *136*, 16–24. doi:10.1016/j.procs.2018.08.233

Costa, P. B., Prado, C., Oliveira, L. D. F. T. D., Peres, H. H. C., Massarollo, M. C. K. B., Fernandes, M. D. F. P., ... and Freitas, G. F. D. (2011). Digital fluency and the use of virtual environments: the characterization of nursing students.*Revista da Escola de Enfermagem da USP, 45*(SPE), 1589-1594.

Cross, A., & Lucas, E. (2019). *Getting into Medical School 2020 Entry*. Trotman Education.

Demir, E. B. K., Çaka, C., Tuğtekin, U., Demir, K., İslamoğlu, H., & Kuzu, A. (2016). Üç boyutlu yazdırma teknolojilerinin eğitim alanında kullanımı: Türkiye'deki uygulamalar. *Ege Eğitim Dergisi*, *17*(2), 481–503. doi:10.12984/egeefd.280754

Demir, K. & Odabaşı, H. F. (2016). Dijital akıcılık kavramına eleştirel bir bakış. In *4. Uluslararası Öğretim Teknolojileri ve Öğretmen Eğitimi Sempozyumu* (pp. 373-376). Elazığ. Retrieved from http://www.ittes2016.org/belge/oku/37

Demir, K., Aydin, B., Ersoy, N. S., Kelek, A., Tatar, I., Kuzu, A., & Odabasi, H. F. (2015). Visiting digital fluency for pre-service teachers in Turkey. *World Journal on Educational Technology, 7*(1), 01-08.

Education Endowment Foundation. (2019). *Using digital technology to improve learning.* https://educationendowmentfoundation.org.uk/public/files/Publications/digitalTech/EEF_Digital_Technology_Guidance_Report.pdf

Elahi, E., Weijun, C., Zhang, H., & Nazeer, M. (2019). Agricultural intensification and damages to human health in relation to agrochemicals: Application of artificial intelligence. *Land Use Policy*, *83*, 461–474. doi:10.1016/j.landusepol.2019.02.023

Eshet-Alkalai, Y. (2004). Digital literacy: A conceptual framework for survival skills in the digital era. *Journal of Educational Multimedia and Hypermedia*, *13*(1), 93.

European Commission. (2018). *Digital Transformation 2021-2027.* https://ec.europa.eu/commission/sites/beta-political/files/budget-june2018-digital-transformation_en.pdf

Garrick, B., Pendergast, D., & Geelan, D. (2017). *Theorising personalised education: Electronically mediated higher education.* Springer. doi:10.1007/978-981-10-2700-0

Gayol, Y., & Boubsil, O. (2009). Digital fluency of faculty at distance education university. In Y. E. Ioannidis, D. L. Lee, & R. T. Ng (Eds.), *Proceedings of the ICDE: International Conference of Open and Distance Education.* Shanghai, China: IEEE Computer Society. Retrieved from https://www.ou.nl/Docs/Campagnes/ICDE2009/Papers/Final_Paper_396Gayol.pdf

Gelmereanu, C., Morar, L., & Bogdan, S. (2014). Productivity and cycle time prediction using artificial neural network. *Procedia Economics and Finance*, *15*, 1563–1569. doi:10.1016/S2212-5671(14)00626-1

Glewa, M., & Bogan, M. B. (2007). Improving children's literacy while promoting digital fluency through the use of blogs in the classroom: Surviving the hurricane. *Journal of Literacy and Technology*, *8*(1), 40–48.

Glewa, M., & Bogan, M. B. (2007). Improving children's literacy while promoting digital fluency through the use of blogs in the classroom: Surviving the hurricane. *Journal of Literacy and Technology*, *8*(1), 40–48.

Green, R. M. (2005). *Predictors of digital fluency [Yayımlanmamış doktora tezi]*. Northwestern Üniversitesi.

Hague, C., & Payton, S. (2010). *Digital literacy across the curriculum.* Bristol: Futurelab. Retrieved from https://www.nfer.ac.uk/publications/FUTL06/FUTL06.pdf

Harel, I. (2016). *American schools are teaching our kids how to code all wrong.* Retrieved from https://qz.com/691614/american-schools-are-teaching-our-kids-how-to-code-all-wrong/

Hsi, S. (2007). Conceptualizing learning from the everyday activities of digital kids. *International Journal of Science Education*, *29*(12), 1509–1529. doi:10.1080/09500690701494076

Institute for the Future for Dell Technologies. (2017). *The next era of human/machine partnerships: Emerging technologies' impact on society and work in 2030.* Retrieved from http://www.iftf.org/fileadmin/user_upload/downloads/th/ SR1940_IFTFforDellTechnologies_Human-Machine_070717_readerhigh-res.pdf

ISTE. (2019). *ISTE Standards for Students.* Retrieved from September 22, 2019 from https://www.iste.org/standards/for-students

Jones, B., & Flannigan, S. L. (2006). Connecting the digital dots: Literacy of the 21st century. *EDUCAUSE Quarterly*, *29*(2), 8–10.

Kaminski, K., Switzer, J., & Gloeckner, G. (2009). Workforce readiness: A study of university students' fluency with information technology. *Computers & Education*, *53*(2), 228–233. doi:10.1016/j.compedu.2009.01.017

Karaca, O., Demir, K., & Caliskan, S. A. (2018). Virtual, Augmented and Mobile Learning in Health Education. In Computer-Mediated Learning for Workforce Development (pp. 168-195). IGI Global.

Kavis, M. (2015). *The four stages of cloud competence.* Retrieved from https://www.forbes.com/sites/mikekavis/2015/10/21/the-four-stages-of-cloud-competence/#2fb55322183a

Kim, S., Chung, K., & Yu, H. (2013). Enhancing digital fluency through a training program for creative problem solving using computer programming. *The Journal of Creative Behavior*, *47*(3), 171–199. doi:10.1002/jocb.30

Kühn, C. (2017). Are students ready to (re)-design their personal learning environment? The case of the e-dynamic. space. *Journal of New Approaches in Educational Research*, *6*(1), 11–19. doi:10.7821/naer.2017.1.185

Kurt, A.A., Dönmez, F.İ., Ersoy, M., Dindar, M., Mısırlı, Ö. ve Akçay, T. (2013). Teknoloji ışığında okuryazarlıklar. *Eğitim Teknolojileri Araştırmaları Dergisi (ETAD)*, *4*(2).

Liu, A., Li, Y., & Ye, H. (2018). *Digital fluency and social media use: An empirical ınvestigation of WeChat use. In Proceedings of the 51st Hawaii International Conference on System Sciences | 2018.* Curran Associates. Retrieved from https://scholarspace.manoa.hawaii.edu/bitstream/10125/49952/1/paper0065.pdf

Loup-Escande, E., Frenoy, R., Poplimont, G., Thouvenin, I., Gapenne, O., & Megalakaki, O. (2017). Contributions of mixed reality in a calligraphy learning task: Effects of supplementary visual feedback and expertise on cognitive load, user experience, and gestural performance. *Computers in Human Behavior*, *75*, 42–49. doi:10.1016/j.chb.2017.05.006

Lubbe, J. C. I. (2016). Digital fluency of faculty members at an ODL institution. *Progressio*, *38*(2), 63–83.

Mao, J., Ifenthaler, D., Fujimoto, T., Garavaglia, A., & Rossi, P. G. (2019). National Policies and Educational Technology: A Synopsis of Trends and Perspectives from Five Countries. *TechTrends*, *63*(3), 284–293. doi:10.100711528-019-00396-0

Martin, A. (2005). DigEuLit – a European framework for digital literacy: A progress report. *Journal of ELiteracy*, *2*, 130–136.

Merchant, G. (2009). Literacy in virtual worlds. *Journal of Research in Reading*, *32*(1), 38–56. doi:10.1111/j.1467-9817.2008.01380.x

Miller, C., & Bartlett, J. (2012). 'Digital fluency': Towards young people's critical use of the internet. *Journal of Information Literacy*, *6*(2), 35–55. doi:10.11645/6.2.1714

Morin, E. (2003). *Geleceğin eğitimi için gerekli 7 bilgi*. İstanbul Bilgi Üniversitesi Yayınları.

National Research Council, Committee on Information Technology Literacy. (1999). *Being fluent with information technology*. National Academies Press.

Odabaşı, H. F. (2000). Akademik eskimişlik ve sürekli mesleki gelişim. *Anadolu Üniversitesi Eğitim Fakültesi Dergisi*, *10*(2), 161–166.

OECD. (2016). *Trends shaping education spotlight15: A brave new world: technology & education.* Paris: OECD Publishing. Retrieved from http://www.oecd.org/education/ceri/Spotlight-15-A-Brave-New-World-Technology-and-Education.pdf

OECD. (2018). Emerging trends, challenges and opportunities. In *Valuing our teachers and raising their status: How communities can help*. OECD Publishing. doi:10.1787/9789264292697-3-

Parahita, G. D. (2017). Mapping digital fluency in diverse socio-economic status of citizens of DKI Jakarta 2017. *INFORMASI*, *47*(2), 213–228. doi:10.21831/informasi.v47i2.16224

Pinho, I. D. C., & Lima, M. D. S. (2013). Teacher's digital fluency: A new competence for foreigh language teaching. *Revista Brasileira de Lingüística Aplicada*, *13*(3), 711–739. doi:10.1590/S1984-63982013005000014

Ross, P. (2015). Digital fluency, social enterprise and why they are important for HR. *Huffpost Business*. Retrieved from http://www.huffingtonpost.com/pam-ross/digital-fluency-social-en_b_7148050.html

Sagasti, F. (2001). *The knowledge explosion and the knowledge divide*. United Nations Development Programme: Human Development Reports. Retrieved from http://hdr.undp.org/sites/default/files/sagasti-1-1.pdf

Savin-Baden, M. (2015). *Rethinking Learning in an Age of Digital Fluency: Is Being Digitally Tethered a New Learning Nexus?* Routledge. doi:10.4324/9781315718910

Sitterding, M. C., Raab, D. L., Saupe, J. L., & Israel, K. J. (2019). Using Artificial Intelligence and Gaming to Improve New Nurse Transition. *Nurse Leader*, *17*(2), 125–130. doi:10.1016/j.mnl.2018.12.013

Skilton, M., & Hovsepian, F. (2017). *The 4th Industrial Revolution: Responding to the Impact of Artificial Intelligence on Business*. Springer.

Sparrow, J. (2018). Digital fluency: Preparing students to create big, bold problems. *New Horizons*. Retrieved from https://er.educause.edu/articles/2018/3/digital-fluency-preparing-students-to-create-big-bold-problems

Spencer, K. (2015). *What is digital fluency?* Retrieved from https://www.blog.core-ed.org/blog/2015/10/what-is-digital-fluency.html/

Tavana, M., Abtahi, A. R., Di Caprio, D., & Poortarigh, M. (2018). An Artificial Neural Network and Bayesian Network model for liquidity risk assessment in banking. *Neurocomputing*, *275*, 2525–2554. doi:10.1016/j.neucom.2017.11.034

Touger, G. E. (2018, August 3). *What's the Difference between Artificial Learning (AI), Machine Learning, and Deep Learning?* Prowesscorp. Retrieved from www.prowesscorp.com/whats-the-difference-between-artificial-intelligence-ai-machine-learning-and-deep-learning

Traxler, J. (2018). Digital literacy: A palestinian refugee perspective. *Research in Learning Technology*, 26.

United Nations Educational, Scientific and Social Cultural Organization (UNESCO). (2006). *Education for all: Literacy for life. Global monitoring report 2006*. Retrieved from http://unesdoc.unesco.org/images/0014/001442/144270e.pdf

van Laar, E., van Deursen, A. J., van Dijk, J. A., & de Haan, J. (2019). Determinants of 21st-century digital skills: A large-scale survey among working professionals. *Computers in Human Behavior*, *100*, 93–104. doi:10.1016/j.chb.2019.06.017

Wang, E., Myers, M. D., & Sundaram, D. (2012). Digital natives and digital immigrants – Towards a model of digital fluency. *Proceedings of the European Conference on Information Systems (ECIS 2012)*. Retrieved from https://aisel.aisnet.org/ecis2012/39

Wang, R., Wiesemes, R., & Gibbons, C. (2012). Developing digital fluency through ubiquitous mobile devices: Findings from a small-scale study. *Computers & Education*, *58*(1), 570–578. doi:10.1016/j.compedu.2011.04.013

Wartman, S. A., & Combs, C. D. (2018). Medical education must move from the information age to the age of artificial intelligence. *Academic Medicine*, *93*(8), 1107–1109. doi:10.1097/ACM.0000000000002044 PMID:29095704

Wartman, S. A., & Combs, C. D. (2019). Reimagining medical education in the age of AI. *AMA Journal of Ethics*, *21*(2), 146–152. doi:10.1001/amajethics.2019.146 PMID:30794124

Waymel, Q., Badr, S., Demondion, X., Cotten, A., & Jacques, T. (2019). Impact of the rise of artificial intelligence in radiology: What do radiologists think? *Diagnostic and Interventional Imaging*, *100*(6), 327–336. doi:10.1016/j.diii.2019.03.015 PMID:31072803

White, G. K. (2013). *Digital fluency: Skills necessary for learning in the digital age*. Australian Council for Educational Research.

Williams, D. L., Crittenden, V. L., Keo, T., & McCarty, P. (2012). The use of social media: An exploratory study of usage among digital natives. *Journal of Public Affairs*, *12*(2), 127–136. doi:10.1002/pa.1414

KEY TERMS AND DEFINITIONS

Digital Fluency: Ability to reliably achieve the desired results through technology.

Digital Literacy: Being able to explain what is meant by symbols and to understand correctly what is explained through symbols.

Digital Skill: Digital skills include awareness and ability to recognise information needs from digital technology sources and to make effective use of digital resources and facilities.

Chapter 11
How Does the Digital Transformation Affect the Job of University Teachers?
Summary of the Required Skills of University Teachers

Amira Sghari
Laboratory PRISME (LR18ES24), Faculty of Economics and Management, University of Sfax, Tunisia

ABSTRACT

The use of digital devices, which is exponentially growing among students, requires universities rethinking teaching practices. Digital acceleration in the field of higher education is very important especially with the appearance of modular object-oriented dynamic learning environment, massive open online course, and small private online courses phenomena. Thus, digital pedagogy transforms the required digital skills of university teachers' teaching. Determining in detail the digital skills of university teachers was difficult. This chapter is based on some research works as well as on the repository of skills defined by the Virtual University of Tunis, which provides training of university teachers to enhance their e-skills. This theoretical chapter presents a synthesis of works dealing with the skills required by university teachers in a context of digital transformation. Such a synthesis will allow a good preparation of training programs for university teachers.

INTRODUCTION

The development of Information and Communication Technologies (ICT) such as Big Data, robotics and self-learning neural networks is disconcerting organizations. The use of digital devices particularly is growing exponentially among students and is encouraging universities to lead the organizational changes and teaching practices that result from them. According to Göktalay and Özeke (2015, p.100), "This generation speaks the language of technology from birth". Therefore, the teacher's traditional pedagogy

DOI: 10.4018/978-1-7998-4972-8.ch011

Copyright © 2021, IGI Global. Copying or distributing in print or electronic forms without written permission of IGI Global is prohibited.

of exposing knowledge in the form of lectures is no longer effective. New generations of learners need new pedagogical approaches to stay motivated (Prensky, 2001). In the context, teachers must be familiar and comfortable using digital technology in order to keep up with both an ever-changing technology context and students who no longer process information sequentially (Lambert and Cuper, 2008).

Digital acceleration in the field of higher education is very important especially with the appearance of phenomena of Modular Object-Oriented Dynamic Learning Environment (MOODLE), Massive Open Online Course (MOOC) and Small Private Online Courses (SPOC). Thus, digital pedagogy transforms teachers' as well as students' lives. This transformation is primarily social based on the changing dynamics of relationships and human organizations. Research in this context deals with the mobilization of serious games in education (Rumeser and Emsley, 2018), the determinants of the intention to use e-learning systems (Zainab et al., 2017; Weng, et al., 2018) and the determinants of its use continuity (Wu and Chen, 2017). However, research on digital skills to be acquired by university teachers remains relatively rare. According to Claro et al. (2018), in addition to the teaching skills, teachers acquire a new set of skills related to the use of ICT. It is very important to identify the skills required by university teachers. Indeed, their determination will make it possible to properly prepare teacher training programs (Instefjord and Munthe, 2017; Gegenfurtner, 2019). "Systems of education and training for teachers need to provide them with the necessary opportunities. All this makes the field of teacher professional development a growing and challenging area, and one that has received major attention during the past few years" (Lopukhova and Makeeva (2019, p. 516).

This theoretical chapter presents a synthesis of works dealing with the skills required by university teachers in a context of digital transformation. Such a synthesis will allow a good preparation of training programs for university teachers.

BACKGROUND

The digital transformation affects higher education by the emergence of educational technologies that encourage universities to lead changes in teaching practices. Thus, university teachers always keep the basic skills of their profession, namely communication, problem solving, coordination, etc. However, with the development of educational technologies, new skills are added to those required for this job. These skills are designated in recent works as "technical skills" or "digital skills". Few research studies present in detail these skills. The purpose of this chapter is to present a summary of the skills required by university teachers with a description of digital skills. This will help define the professional development programs of university teachers, which are, according to Lopukhova and Makeeva (2019, p. 514), a field which is receiving major attention during the past few years.

This chapter is divided into two parts. In the first one, the job of university teacher is defined and the teaching skills are presented. While The second part deals with the development in higher education field associated with the evolution of ICT and the digital skills required by university teachers.

JOB OF A UNIVERSITY TEACHER

"Teach means to impart knowledge to or instruct (someone) as to how to do something; or to cause (someone) to learn or understand something by example or experience; or to encourage someone to accept (something) as a fact or principle (Soanes and Stevenson, 2003, p. 1809). Teacher is a "professional who is qualified for theoretically profound and critical analysis of educational phenomena, processes in the teaching his study subject" (Blašková et al., 2014, p.458). It designs the educational policies and procedures in a way that leads to the educational objectives creating optimal condition for the students' moral development and their self-development (Valica and Rohn, 2013, p. 866). According to Samson and Vyjayanthi (2013, p. 92), creating a warm classroom climate, promoting enthusiasm and motivation as well as maintaining an interactive classroom are an effective teacher's responsibilities.

In order to succeed in his responsibilities, the university teacher requires professional competences. "The definition of a higher education teachers' competences profile cannot be separated from its three main professional functions (teaching, research and management), neither its professional scenarios (society, institution and classroom)" (Pozos Pérez and Mas Torelló, 2012, p. 1114). These skills are seen as capacities of excellence (Slavík et al., 2012, cited in Blašková et al., 2014) having a significant effect on the students' performance (Lopukhova and Makeeva, 2019).

Initial research emphasizes teaching competencies which are "a group of teaching acts or behaviours intended to facilitate pupil's learning directly or indirectly" (Passi, 1976). Gray and Gerrand (1977) recommended sixteen competencies, stressing classroom behaviour and personal adjustment. Shulman, (1986) highlights the importance of four skills relating to knowledge, diagnosing students understanding levels, classroom monitoring and management and ability to differentiate curriculum. Teachers must develop the required abilities and skills of teaching for making the education "qualitiful" (Mehta, 2011). According to Adediwura and Tayo (2007), the teacher should possess essential teaching skills as to promote order and learning in the classroom. Indeed, teaching skills constitute a vital link necessary to translate the teachers' theoretical knowledge to the students thereby promoting effective learning by the students (Pandey, 2011; Samson and Vyjayanthi, 2013). Effective teaching skills affect the teaching and learning process, quality of a teacher (Samson and Vyjayanthi, 2013) and student performance (Laut, 1995; Adediwura and Tayo, 2007).

Several authors emphasize the importance of the skills such as communication, didactic and pedagogical skills, adaptability skills, evaluation skills (Nath, 2009; Maria, 2011; Valica and Rohn, 2013). In his analysis of the general framework of teachers' competencies, Selvi (2010) propose many aspects, namely: field competence, research competence, life-long learning, communication competencies, curriculum, socio-cultural competencies, emotional competencies and environmental competencies. Later, Pozos Pérez and Mas Torelló (2012) determine the professional profile of a university teacher in Europe. In the same vein, Blašková et al. (2014) develop a competency model of university teachers based on student feedback. Recently, Lopukhova and Makeeva (2019) have developed the 21st Century Competencies Model based on a survey of 90 teachers working at Samara State Technical University and Samara State University of Social Sciences and Education from 2014 till 2017.

Educational Profile of a University Teacher of Pozos Pérez and Mas Torelló (2012)

According to Pozos Pérez and Mas Torelló (2012), the educational profile of a university teacher in Europe contains several skills presented in Table 1 below.

In Table 1 above, Pozos Pérez and Mas Torelló (2012) suggest pedagogical competences. Among the Competence Units (CU) of "Tutoring student' s learning process promoting activities to achieve more autonomy "is" using virtual tutoring strategies "which were moved from the table to be presented

Table 1. Pedagogical competences associated to the teaching functions (Pozos Pérez and Mas Torelló, 2012, p. 1114)

Pedagogical Competences (PC)	Competence Units (CU)
1. Designing the Teaching Guide according to student needs, context and professional profile, in coordination with other professionals	1.1. Characterizing the learning group.
	1.2. Assessing student needs.
	1.3. Defining learning objectives according to the competences defined in the professional profile.
	1.4. Describing and arranging disciplinary contents in sequence.
	1.5. Designing of methodological strategies to meet student diversity and specificity of context.
	1.6. Selecting and designing didactical media and resources according to learning strategies.
	1.7. Developing content into didactical units.
	1.8. Designing the learning evaluation plan and the necessary assessment tools.
2. Conducting the learning process fostering individual and collaborative learning opportunities	2.1. Applying a variety of methodological strategies according to the learning outcomes.
	2.2. Using diverse didactical media and resources in the learning process.
	2.3. Managing the didactical interaction and the relations with students.
	2.4. Establishing the optimal conditions to generate a positive social climate in the learning and communication processes.
	2.5. Using ICT to combine face to face and distance learning.
	2.6. Managing resources and infrastructure provided by the institution.
	2.7. Managing virtual learning environments.
3. Tutoring student' s learning process promoting activities to achieve more autonomy	3.1 Planning tutoring activities, considering learning outcomes and student characteristics, to improve the learning process.
	3.2. Creating a favorable climate to foster a positive communication and interaction with students.
	3.3. Guiding student' s knowledge construction processes (individually or collaboratively) providing guidelines, information, resources,... to foster the development of professional competences.
4. Evaluating the learning process	4.1. Applying the evaluation device according to the established evaluation plan.
	4.2. Reviewing students learning achievement.
	4.3. Evaluating the components of the learning process.
	4.4. Using and fostering self evaluation techniques and instruments among students.
	4.5. Making decisions based on the obtained information.
	4.6. Getting involved in co-evaluation processes.
	4.7. Tackling duties and ethical dilemmas of the evaluation process.
5. Contributing actively for the improvement of teaching	5.1. Participating with other professionals in the conceptual definition and development of new instruments, materials and didactical resources to improve professional competences.
	5.2. Keeping relationships with the socio-professional environment in a systemic and periodical way for teacher updating and improvement.
	5.3. Participating actively in innovation activities oriented to optimization of the learning process.
	5.4. Applying techniques and instruments for teacher' s self-assessment.
	5.5. Self-assessment of training needs for teaching improvement
6. Participating actively in the academic and organizational dynamics of the institution (University, Faculty, Area, Department, program...)	6.1. Participating in working groups.
	6.2. Participating in multi-disciplinary teaching commissions.
	6.3. Fostering and participating in working groups regarding course planning.
	6.4. Participating in the planning of training actions and modules.
	6.5. Promoting the organization and participation of academic seminars, debates, round tables,...
	6.6. Participating in the development of the new curricula following the directions, descriptors,... provided by the competent bodies.

in the second part dedicated to digital skills. In the following subsection, the typology of Blašková et al. (2014) is presented.

Competency Model of University Teachers of Blašková et al. (2014)

Table 2. Competence model of university teacher (Blašková et al., 2014, p. 464)

Competence	Competence determination
Professional competence	The person is a qualified and recognised specialist in the field of his/her teaching and research; has excellent professional skills and competences; rightly serves as a proficient expert, able to combine theoretical knowledge with practical knowledge and experience; he/she masters and knows how to apply the principles, methods, benefits as well as restrictions of all professional terms, elements and the links between them.
Educational competence	The person is an excellent teacher; can define the key terms and elements of any topic and explain them to students understandably; uses and greatly combines various educational methods and elements, always with regard to the topic that he/she teaches; uses both formative and summative evaluation of knowledge, skills and competences of students, and always maintains objectiveness and impartiality towards any student.
Motivational competence	The person motivates others through each of his/her action, every lecture or seminar; sees motivation as the key element of any process, work, effort or relationship; respects the dynamics of the motivation of individuals (students, colleagues) as well as groups (study groups, departments); identifies and strictly eliminates any demonstrations of his/her as well as someone else's unethical, dishonest and demotivational behaviour; has the self motivating and self-keeping ability and the ability to surmount obstacles, to draw and deliver energy in a beneficial manner.
Communicational competence	The person has great communication skills, notably assertiveness, empathy, active listening, persuasion and metacommunication; appropriately combines those communication skills and uses them in his/her educational activities; prevents communication misunderstandings (with students and colleagues alike); his/her written as well as spoken language is always distinguished and fair; he/she sees and uses communication as an instrument to build trust.
Personal competence	The person is a mature, highly creative, inventive, resourceful and courageous personality; is always tolerant, empathic, accommodating and helpful to others (students and colleagues alike); sees his/her mission as the accomplishment of his/her personal qualities, and permanently strives to cultivate them; educates students and colleagues in close participation with them, respecting and developing their personalities.
Science & research competence	The person is a zealous, responsible, relentless, resourceful and highly competent scientist and researcher, either at the level of a cooperating solver or an owner/guarantor of scientific projects; his/her scientific efforts and creative research contribute to knowledge development; he/she reveals and subsequently provides others with knowledge and outputs that are always up-to-date, true, useful and inspirational; sees science and research as the driver and concurrently as the inevitable determinant of good higher education and of the progress of society; refines his/her competence in carrying out valuable scientific research in his/her scientific field.
Publication competence	The person publishes his/her outputs (publications) in such quality, periodicity and originality that these do the author valuable credit, being of high scientific, social and educational significance (both local-language and foreign-language monographs; higher education textbooks drawing from national as well as international authors; articles in domestic and foreign journals and at scientific conferences); as an author, he/she always maintains absolute fairness and high quotation discipline.

Following an empirical study, Blašková et al. (2014) analyse the professional-personal profile of university teachers and the competences they should have. These competences are presented in Table 2 below.

Table 2 above summarizes the results of the study of Blašková et al. (2014) dealing with the skills required of university teachers. In the following sub-section, the typology of Lopukhova and Makeeva (2019) is presented.

21st Century Competencies Model of Lopukhova and Makeeva (2019)

In their research, Lopukhova and Makeeva (2019) elaborate the 21st Century Competencies Model. According to this model, ten most actual skills can be organised into four groups presented in Table 3 below.

Table 3. 21st Century Competencies Model (Lopukhova and Makeeva, 2019, p. 524)

Groups	Skills	Activities
Ways of Thinking	Creativity and innovation	· Modelling creative habit; · appreciate the critical importance of questions; · treat mistakes as learning opportunities; · give yourself sufficient time to complete the project; · participate in the discussion in professional forums
	Critical thinking, problem solving, decision making	· using the Six Steps to Effective Thinking and Problem Solving (IDEALS)
	Learning to learn, Meta cognition	· self-educating; · be an active member in scientific and/or academic communities; · publishing in scientific journals; · participating in training programs.
Ways of working	Communication	· participating in foreign academic and other internships and scholarships; · participate in scientific conferences; · replacing strict criticism by providing supportive feedback; · learning when it is appropriate to listen and when to speak
	Collaboration (teamwork)	· working in interdisciplinary projects; · receiving feedback from the colleagues at the department; · coaching and consulting experienced educational authorities; · conducting collaborative research.
Tools for Working	Information literacy	· learning where to find information; · selecting key points from retrieved information; · using high-quality content and reflect evaluative thinking; · developing new insights or theories.
Living in the World Citizenship – local and global		· developing teachers' leadership

In "Tools for Working" group exist the skill "ICT literacy" which were moved from the table to be presented later in the second section dedicated to digital skills.

In an era of rapid change of technologies, the job of university teacher has evolved and required new skills especially digital ones.

DIGITALIZATION AND THE JOB OF THE UNIVERSITY TEACHER

The development of ICTs has led to the emergence of reflections on educational innovations. In this context, the emergence of new educational formats such as MOOCs (Massive Open Online Courses) and SPOCs (Small Private Online Courses) shake up fundamentally higher education institutions. Thus, the educational environment is characterized by the emergence of online distance learning in which the pedagogical material is planned and prepared by educational institutions (Kaplan and Haenlein, 2016). This process is facilitated by firms such as Coursera and Udacity (Kaplan and Haenlein, 2016).

The e-learning courses are designed in order to satisfy the educational needs of students and the implementation of a new educational approach based on ICT (Spivakovskiy et al., 2017). Shift in higher education induced by digital transformation requires new skills for university teachers. Thus, it is necessary for university teachers to follow professional training programs in order to improve their teaching skills (Al-Hattami et al., 2013; Spivakovskiy et al., 2017). The teachers' training to organize and conduct distance or blended learning, the use of web 2.0 services and blended learning technologies are the important part of the educational process (Kukharenko, 2007; Cho, 2011; Spivakovskiy et al., 2017). In this context, there is a lack of research on the digital skills of university teachers. Previous studies suggest the importance of technical skills (Magana, 2009), information technology usage (Selvi, 2010) and technology handling (Nath, 2009; Maria, 2011; Valica and Rohn, 2013) without detailing these skills.

Pozos Pérez and Mas Torelló (2012) focus on one skill, namely: "Using virtual tutoring strategies". Later, Morze and Kocharyan (2014) propose a standard of development of ICT competence of university teachers that describes the levels of activities: understanding the role of ICT and education and its use, ICT, educational work, research activities and advanced training. Recently, Lopukhova and Makeeva (2019) propose the skill "ICT literacy" which includes the following activities:

- applying technology effectively;
- using digital technologies;
- creating interactive e-course books and online courses;
- working with MOOCs, shared online courses.

This paper, would try to identify the digital skills of university teachers. First, the digital profile of a university teacher in Europe is presented. Subsequently, we present the digital skills defined by the Virtual University of Tunis (VUT).

Digital Competences Pozos (2010)

Pozos (2010 cited by Pozos Pérez and Mas Torelló, 2012) determine the digital profile of a university teacher in Europe which contains several skills presented in Table 4 below.

In addition to the skills proposed by Pozos (2010 cited by Pozos and Mas, 2012), the areas of digital skills defined by the VUT are presented in the following sub-section.

The Areas of Digital Skills According to the Virtual University of Tunis

The Virtual University of Tunis (VUT)[1] was founded in 2002 to support higher education development efforts by providing free quality education and training to students and teachers in Tunisian universities

Table 4. Digital Competences associated to the teaching, research, management and social responsibility functions (Pozos, 2010, p. 161)

<table>
<tr><th rowspan="2">Digital Competences (DC)</th><th>Basic Knowledge</th><th>Knowledge Deepening</th><th>Knowledge Generation</th></tr>
<tr><th colspan="3">78 Competence Units (Instrumental, methodological, personal and participative competences…)</th></tr>
<tr><td>1. Planning and designing of learning experiences in face-to-face, blended and virtual environments.</td><td rowspan="7">Basic digital competences in the knowledge and use of ICT for:
ü Solving problems in basic learning situations in face-to-face environments with the use of ICT,
ü Managing of the basic professional activities in teachers development with the support of ICT,
ü Socially participating in immediate contexts, ...
Allowing teachers to be INTEGRATED in the Knowledge Society as citizen and teaching professionals.</td><td rowspan="7">Digital competences for knowledge deepening and integration ICT in all teachers' professional activities for:
ü Solving problems in complex learning situations, in face-to face, blended and virtual environments,
ü Managing, communicating and collaborating through networks for improving professional development,
ü Participating and demonstrating social commitment through the creation of improvement proposals for community and society development,...
Allowing teachers to adequately DEVELOP themselves and socially CONTRIBUTE as teaching professionals in the Knowledge Society in a reflexive and critical way.</td><td rowspan="7">Advanced digital competences in the integration and use of ICT for:
ü Building broader capacities and abilities for new knowledge construction, knowledge management and innovation,
ü Developing a strong commitment for applying new knowledge in the continuous improvement of the teaching profession and the society, ...
Allowing teachers to GENERATE, APPLY AND SHARE new knowledge in a critical and responsible way in multiple contexts within the Knowledge Society.</td></tr>
<tr><td>2. Developing and conducting collaborative learning experiences in face-to-face, blended and virtual environments.</td></tr>
<tr><td>3. Tutoring and assessment of knowledge construction processes in face-to-face, blended and virtual environments.</td></tr>
<tr><td>4. Managing of growth and professional development with the support of ICT.</td></tr>
<tr><td>5. Pedagogical research, development and innovation with/for ICT in education.</td></tr>
<tr><td>6. Diversity, ethics and responsible use of ICTs in teachers' professional development.</td></tr>
<tr><td>7. Environmental concerns, labour health and safety in the use of ICT in the teaching profession.</td></tr>
</table>

and higher education institutions. It was initially established to spread distance-education and foster ICT integration in the higher education sector.

VUT is gradually spreading e-learning in priority disciplines. It is committed to improving the quality of education through the use of interactive and innovative tools, encouraging and supporting online curriculum design for higher education training.

Tunisia's virtual university has invested in a state of the art infrastructure in order to work on promoting online learning. It has 234 well-equipped access centres in various universities throughout the country. They are mainly used to support the use of online courses designed by VUT pedagogic teams and hosted in the Virtual Learning Environment ().

To achieve its mission of disseminating knowledge, Tunisia's virtual university is constantly developing and implementing new programmes and innovative learning tools. Online Training Engineering (OTE) is a training program for university teachers on the new skills required by this environment and characterized by the invasion of digital tools.

The VUT proposes a blended learning in Online Training Engineering (OTE) divided into seven areas of expertise. This training program enables teachers to engage in an active professional development approach by reinforcing their deployment of ICT in the university environment. At the end of this training, the participants will be able to mobilize, in the development of an online or hybrid educational device and in pedagogical arguments, knowledge about:

- Added values of learning technologies.
- The design of an effective pedagogical device (coherence between learning objectives, activities and evaluation)
- Learning activities and tools of Learning
- The modes of management of the trained interactions
- Online tutoring

The Online Training Engineering (OTE) program is based on a skills framework that responds to the need for training university teachers who want to integrate educational ICT into their teaching and research activities. The aim is to ensure pedagogical renovation with a view to promoting an education focused more on exchanges between the various actors involved.

The skills framework is based on four areas related to the integration of educational ICT in the different components of the job of the university teacher:

- Documentation: research, treatment and scientific and didactic exploitation of the various available resources;
- Production: the design of learning sequences and the preparation of the necessary means for their implementation;
- Communication: support for learning through the active and participative involvement of all actors in training; by promoting several types of interactions between them;
- Evaluation: The implementation of a strategy for assessing learners' prior learning, both in terms of certification and monitoring and coaching.

The professional skills to be acquired are established with reference to the tasks of the job of the university teacher. It is a coherent set of skills needed for the development and implementation of a training plan using educational ICT in its various stages. Each skill is broken down into specific objectives as shown in tablc 5 bclow.

CONCLUSION

The development of Information and Communication Technologies (ICT) among students encourages universities to change the teaching practices. The new generations of learners need new pedagogical approaches to stay motivated. This explains the appearance of the phenomenon of the Modular Object-Oriented Dynamic Learning Environment (MOODLE), Massive Open Online Course (MOOC) and SPOC (Small Private Online Courses). Thus, the job of university teacher has evolved and requires new skills especially technical ones. In order to meet the digital challenges, training programs for university teachers on new skills are needed.

In Tunisia, Ministry of Higher Education gives importance to the use of digital devices in the students' university courses. In this context, the Virtual University of Tunis (VUT) provides the training of univer-

Table 5. The area of skills required by the university teacher (VUT)

Skills	Objectives
Pedagogy and Technology	- Reflect on teaching practices to improve learning; - Know the principles of active pedagogy and adopt them to his/her needs; - Discover and identify the different techno-educational devices; - Improve his/her skills in finding information and resources and their organization.
Master the strategies of research and exploitation of Free Educational Resources (FER)	- Improve his/her teaching by using Free Educational Resources - Contribute to the development of the movement by developing Free Educational Resources
Screenwriting an online course	- Master the general concepts on the educational screenwriting. - Design an online training device that takes advantage of the added value of ICTs by applying the main stages of the online course educational screenwriting - Design innovative learning activities. - Develop an educational structure of an online course.
Mediatization of an online course	- Produce a teaching-learning situation using educational ICT - Mediatise a teaching-learning situation using educational ICT - Transpose the scenario conceived in skill area 3 using digital tools; - Mediate the different activities of the educational path; - Prepare the deployment of an online training sequence
Teach with Moodle	- Know the main techno-educational devices and the modalities of an online training - Identify the actors and associated functionalities in a techno-educational device - Put online a course on a techno-educational device
Evaluate the learning online	- Make Appropriate the basic knowledge of evaluation - Conduct an assessment of learners' prior learning - Regulate the teaching-learning process - Review the achievements of learners
Tutor an online course	- Understand the value of social interactions in distance training - Distinguish interactions modalities - Foster interaction among and with learners - To deepen the tutorial functions - Animate an online teaching-learning situation

sity teachers to enhance their e-skills, raise awareness and encourage them to use digital technologies. This chapter has presented a summary of the skills required by university teachers. Determining digital skills in detail has been difficult. We are based on some research work as well as on the repository of skills defined by the VUT.

REFERENCES

Adediwura, A. A., & Tayo, B. (2007). Perception of teachers' knowledge, attitude and teaching skills as predictor of academic performance in Nigerian secondary schools. *Educational Research Review*, *2*(7), 165–171.

Al-Hattami, A. A., Muammara, O. M., & Elmahdi, I. A. (2013). The need for professional training programs to improve faculty members teaching skills. *European Journal of Research on Education*, *1*(2), 39–45.

Blašková, M., Blaško, R., & Kucharcíková, A. (2014). Competences and Competence Model of University Teachers. *Procedia: Social and Behavioral Sciences, 159*, 457–467. doi:10.1016/j.sbspro.2014.12.407

Chehidi, T. (2012). *Tunisia's ICT in education policy: Engaging teachers.* Retrieved from http://siteresources.worldbank.org/EDUCATION/Resources/TarekChehidi_TunisiasICTinEducationPolicyEngagingTeachers.pdf

Claro, M., Salinas, A., Cabello-Hutt, T., San Martín, E., Preiss, D. D., Valenzuela, S., & Jara, I. (2018). Teaching in a Digital Environment (TIDE): Defining and measuring teachers' capacity to develop students' digital information and communication skills. *Computers & Education, 121*, 162–174. doi:10.1016/j.compedu.2018.03.001

Gegenfurtner, A. (2019). Reconstructing goals for transfer of training in faculty development programs for higher education teachers: A qualitative documentary method approach. *Heliyon, 5*(11), 1–7. doi:10.1016/j.heliyon.2019.e02928 PMID:31844771

Gibbs, G., & Coffey, M. (2004). The impact of training of university teachers on their teaching skills, their approach to teaching and the approach to learning of their students. *Active Learning in Higher Education, 5*(1), 87–100. doi:10.1177/1469787404040463

Göktalay, S. B., & Özeke, S. (2105). Essential for 21st Century Teachers in Turkey: Uludag University Example. *An Independent Scientific Journal for Interdisciplinary Research in Pedagogy, 19*(6), 100-121. doi:10.5507/epd.2015.020

Gray, W., & Gerrand, B. (1977). *Learning by doing: Developing teaching skills.* Addison-Wesley Publishing Company.

Instefjord, E. J., & Munthe, E. (2018). Educating digitally competent teachers: A study of integration of professional digital competence in teacher education. *Teaching and Teacher Education, 67*, 37–45. doi:10.1016/j.tate.2017.05.016

Kaplan, A. M., & Haenlein, M. (2016). Higher education and the digital revolution: About MOOCs, SPOCs, social media, and the Cookie Monster. *Business Horizons, 59*(4), 441–450. doi:10.1016/j.bushor.2016.03.008

Lambert, J., & Cuper, P. (2008). Multimedia technologies and familiar spaces: 21st century teaching for 21st Century Learners. *Contemporary Issues in Technology & Teacher Education, 8*(3), 264–276.

Laut, J. T. (1995). *The identification of critical teaching skills and their relationship to student achievement: A quantitative synthesis* (Doctoral dissertation). The Ohio State University. Retrieved from https://search.proquest.com/docview/304199329/142656967665CED9957/1?accountid=38885

Lopukhova, J., & Makeeva, E. (2019). University Teacher Professional Development in the Digital World. In The Challenges of the Digital Transformation in Education. ICL 2018. doi:10.1007/978-3-030-11935-5_49

Mangal, S. K., & Mangal, U. (2009). *Essentials of educational technology.* New Delhi, India: PHI Learning Private Limited

Maria, L. (2011). The professional competence of teachers: Which qualities, attitudes, skills and knowledge contribute to a teacher's effectiveness? *International Journal of Humanities and Social Science, 1*(21), 66–78.

Mehta, D. M. (2011). Comparative study of teaching competancy of c.b.s.e & g.b.s.c higher secondary school teacher. *International Referred Research Journal, 3*(31), 23–24.

Morse, N. S., & Kocharian, A. (2014). Model Standard of ICT Competence of University Teachers in the Context of Improving the Quality of Education. *Information Technologies and Learning Tools, 43*(5), 27–39.

Nath, B. K. (2009). *Revising teaching skills for professional empowerment*. Retrieved from https://files.eric.ed.gov/fulltext/ED507652.pdf

Passi, B. K. (1976). *Becoming Better Teacher: Microteaching Approach*. Sahitya Mudranalaya.

Pozos, K. V. (2010). La competencia Digital del Profesorado Universitario para la sociedaddel Conocimiento: Aproximacion a un Model y Validacionde unCuestionario de Necesidades de Formcion Continua. Bellaterra: Departamento de Pedagogia Aplicada- UAB. (Unpublished)

Pozos Pérez, K. V., & Mas Torelló, O. (2012). The digital competence as a cross-cutting axis of higher education teachers' pedagogical competences in the European higher education area. *Procedia: Social and Behavioral Sciences, 46*, 1112–1116. doi:10.1016/j.sbspro.2012.05.257

Prensky, M. (2001). The games generation: How learners have changed. In *Digital game-based learning*. McGraw-Hill.

Rumeser, D., & Emsley, M. (2018). A systematic review of project management serious games: Identifying gaps, trends, and directions for future research. *Journal of Modern Project Management, 6*(1), 48–59.

Samson, V., & Vyjayanthi, S. (2013). Pre-University Teachers' Teaching Skills. *Journal of Education and Practice, 5*(4), 90–96.

Selvi, K. (2010). Teachers' Competencies Culturass. *International Journal of Philosophy of Culture and Axiology, 7*(1), 167–175. doi:10.5840/cultura20107133

Shulman, L. S. (1986). Those Who Understand: Knowledge Growth in Teaching. *Educational Researcher, 15*(2), 4–14. doi:10.3102/0013189X015002004

Soanes, C., & Stevenson, A. (2003). *Oxford Dictionary of English* (2nd ed.). Oxford University Press.

Spivakovskiy, O., Kushnir, N., Kushnir, N., & Vinnyk, M. (2017). ICT Advanced Training of University Teachers. *13th International Conference on ICT in Education, Research and Industrial Applications: Integration, Harmonization and Knowledge Transfer*, 176-190.

Valica, M., & Rohn, T. (2013). Development of the Professional Competence in the Ethics Teachers. 4th International Conference on New Horizons in Education. *Procedia: Social and Behavioral Sciences, 106*, 865–872. doi:10.1016/j.sbspro.2013.12.099

Weng, F., Yang, R. J., Ho, H. J., & Su, H. M. (2018). A TAM-Based Study of the Attitude towards Use Intention of Multimedia among School Teachers. *Applied System Innovation*, *1*(36), 1–9. doi:10.3390/asi1030036

Wu, B., & Chen, X. (2017). Continuance intention to use MOOCs: Integrating the technology acceptance model (TAM) and task technology fit (TTF) mode. *Computers in Human Behavior*, *67*, 221–232. doi:10.1016/j.chb.2016.10.028

Zainab, B., Bhatti, M. A., & Alshagawi, M. (2017). Factors affecting e-training adoption: An examination of perceived cost, computer self-efficacy and the technology acceptance model. *Behaviour & Information Technology*, *36*(12), 1261–1273. doi:10.1080/0144929X.2017.1380703

KEY TERMS AND DEFINITIONS

Digital Education: Innovative use of digital tools and technologies during teaching and learning.

Digital Literacy: Individual's ability to find, evaluate, and compose clear information through writing and other media on various digital platforms.

Teacher: Professional who is qualified for theoretically profound and critical analysis of educational phenomena.

Teaching Competencies: Group of teaching acts or behaviours intended to facilitate pupil's learning directly or indirectly.

Virtual University of Tunis: Public establishment support higher education development efforts by providing free quality education and training to students and teachers in Tunisian universities and higher education institutions.

ENDNOTE

1 The presentation of the VUT is taken from its website: https://www.uvt.rnu.tn/about-as

Chapter 12
Using ICT in the Classroom for Acquiring Digital Competences:
Three Case Studies From Croatian Primary Schools

Kristina Posavec
https://orcid.org/0000-0003-0449-6325
Faculty of Education and Rehabilitation Sciences, University of Zagreb, Croatia

ABSTRACT

This research will explore the use of ICT tools in primary school and its impact on digital competences. What digital competencies can mean in this context and how they can be integrated into the primary school curriculum are some of the questions this chapter will explore. This chapter will present three case studies with three primary school teachers who participated with their students in CRISS project (CRISS is a project financed by the European Commission, through the Horizon2020 programme, ID:732489) during which all used CRISS platform and their experience with the process of students' digital competences evaluation, obstacles that they encountered during this process, and how the use of ICT tools can improve primary school students' digital competences. The advantages and disadvantages of this type of learning method will emerge and be discussed.

INTRODUCTION

In the digital era, the use of computers, tablets, laptops, smartphones, applications and software has become an integral part of every segment in life. Education is one of such segments where hardware and software are used to transform the educational system and modify the learning process. Use of information and communication technologies (ICT) and their tools in education, especially in primary and secondary education can motivate students to be more independent in their learning process, they can become researchers, e.g. take more active role in learning process (Suryani, 2010; Corr, 2006; Ghavifekr, Rosdy, 2015; Leko, 2019). In addition, ICT can "provide the tools for the creation, collection, storage

DOI: 10.4018/978-1-7998-4972-8.ch012

Copyright © 2021, IGI Global. Copying or distributing in print or electronic forms without written permission of IGI Global is prohibited.

and use of knowledge as well for communication and collaboration" (Pérez-Escoda, Rodríguez-Conde, 2015, p. 355).

This research will give insight on how combination of different types of learning, i.e. collaborative learning (CL) and project-based learning (PBL) with use of teaching scenarios, ICT tools and digital technology contributed and form the process of acquiring digital competences for primary school students in three Croatian schools. This type of learning method was applied in 535 primary and secondary schools in 6 European countries as part of European Commission's Horizon2020 project CRISS. This research is focusing exclusively on primary school teachers and students which main aim is to determine whether the process of acquiring, evaluating and certifying digital competences is applicable to primary education level and under which terms. Used methodology in this research is semi-structured interviews conducted with teachers during the school year 2018/2019 and relies on teachers' personal attitudes, perceptions, views and experience with teaching and evaluating digital competences of primary schools students.

First learning model, PBL, De Graaf and Kolmos (2003) describes as "an educational approach whereby the problem is the starting- point of the learning process" (p. 658). They are pointing out that problem which is put in front of the students needs to be based on real-life situations "which have been selected and edited to meet educational objectives and criteria" (De Graaf, Kolmos, 2003, p. 658). This segment of PBL is important because its goal is "to engage students in real-world tasks" (Bell, 2010, p. 42). This type of learning method is "student-driven, teacher-facilitated approach to learning" (Bell, 2010, p. 39) where learning is "organized around project" (Thomas, 2000, p. 1).

Second learning model which is mentioned in this chapter is collaborative learning which is defined as "an educational approach to teaching and learning that involves groups of learners working together to solve a problem, complete a task, or create a product" (Laal, Laal, 2012, p. 491). Pluta, Richards and Mutnick (2013) are pointing that CL refers to "any learning activity that includes the coordinated engagement of two or more learners for the purpose of completing tasks (e.g., solving cases) that lead to desired learning outcomes (e.g., developing deep content knowledge)" (p. 9). Kreijns et.al. (2007) are referring to computer-supported collaborative learning (CSCL) and describing it as an environments that "can be characterized as functional environments because they focus on functional, task-specific support, often disregarding explicit support for the social (emotional) aspects of learning in groups" (p. 176).

Third factor, which is important for this study are teaching scenarios that students used during their PBL and CL educational approach. At Ryerson University teaching scenarios are defined as "a collection of tasks you may want to achieve in the classroom or while managing your course. Each teaching scenario is paired with a technology-based solution on how to achieve that task" (Ryerson University, 2020). In addition, Massey University defines this type of learning as scenario-based learning (SBL) where students "uses interactive scenarios to support active learning strategies such as problem-based or case-based learning" (Massey University, 2020). Mariappan (2004) is stating that SBL "is based on the understanding that in order for a learner to acquire and retain skills & knowledge, the learner must be placed in a scenario where his/her decisions affect, or alter subsequent events leading to new events, just like in real life" (p. 2). Combination of these learning approaches was supported and accompanied by use of various ICT tools and digital technologies, which enabled students to acquire their digital competences during school year 2018/2019.

THEORETICAL BACKGROUND

Digital competences are an important segment of society, in general this term is used "to describe or explain the ability (of a citizen, a student, a teacher, etc.) to use information technology (IT) in a specific context" (Rizza, 2014, p. 1614). However, the use of ICT tools in terms of digital competences lies in acquiring skills and knowledge on how to use electronic devices (e.g. computers, laptops, tablets, etc.) with purpose to gain, search, produce, assess, evaluate, store, present, share information and establish collaborative online working environment (Ilomäki, Kantosalo, Lakkala, 2011). Calvani and his colleagues (2008) describe and define digital competence as the ability to "explore and face new technological situations in a flexible way, to analyze, select and critically evaluate data and information, to exploit technological potentials in order to represent and solve problems and build shared and collaborative knowledge, while fostering awareness of one's own personal responsibilities and the respect of reciprocal rights/obligations" (p. 186). Ferrari (2013) states that "digital competence can be broadly defined as the confident, critical and creative use of ICT to achieve goals related to work, employability, learning, leisure, inclusion and/or participation in society" (p. 2). Additionally, School Educational Gateway (2020) and European Commission define digital competences as one of the eight key competences which refers to the confident and critical usage of the full range of digital technologies for information, communication and basic problem-solving in all aspects of life.

The research will describe and analyse the use of ICT tools in primary schools in Croatia for certifying digital competences of primary school students. In school year 2018/2019, eight primary schools from Croatia participated in the European Commission's Horizon2020 project CRISS[1]. The main goal of the project was for students to acquire, evaluate and certify their digital competences under teachers' guidance. Teachers and students who participated in the project used the CRISS platform[2], which was crucial for the process of certification. The CRISS platform was "designed to track students while they work on their assigned activities and collect relevant information" (Guàrdia, Maina, Julià, 2017, p.80). It is cloud based platform where student and teachers could work, communicate and collaborate in real time which enabled "sharing of digital content and provide easy access to shared documents and various apps, thus facilitating work of virtual teams" (Blau, Shamir-Inbal, 2017, p. 773). Teachers conducted the evaluation process. During the project, students' obligation was to upload solutions of tasks to platform and when teachers evaluated it, students instantly could see their results and track their progress. As a part of the project, the team of experts from University of Catalonia (UOC) developed a framework for acquiring, evaluating and certifying digital competences which was based on "The European Digital Competence Framework"[3] (DigComp) developed by European Commission. The CRISS framework consists out of five areas and 12 sub-competence areas in which each of them contains a group of performance criteria, which are connected to the group of indicators that are used to evaluate students' competences (Guàrdia, Maina, Julià, 2017). Guitert, Romeu and Baztàn (2017) are stating, "sub-competences refer to the competences embedded into an Area, and Performance Criteria specify what the student should be able to demonstrate" (p. 80). Digital competence that were evaluated and certificated consist of five areas, digital citizenship, digital communication and collaboration, search and manage digital information, digital content creation and digital problem solving. First area named digital citizenship includes three sub-competences creating and managing digital identity with privacy, health and well-being (1), protecting data and digital systems and be ethical and responsible when using digital technology (2), engaging in citizenship while using digital technologies (3). Second area named search and manage digital information includes two sub-competences communicating through digital technologies (1) and collaborating through digital technologies (2). Third area named search and manage digital information includes sub-competences planning, searching and critically selecting data, information and digital content (1) and managing data, information and digital content (2). Fourth area named digital content creation includes sub-competences developing digital content (1) and developing creativity using digital technologies (2). Fifth area named digital problem solving includes sub-competences applying digital solutions to identified needs (1), solving technical problems (2) and programming and configuring digital tools, applications and devices (3). Detailed description and overview of complete digital framework is available on https://www.crissh2020.eu/booklet/. According to authors this framework "is flexible enough to integrate digital competence development and assessment into different disciplines or subject matters, thus adapting to different curricula and organizational structures" (Guàrdia, Maina, Julià, 2017, p.81).

Evaluation of digital competences was conducted through a set of eleven teaching scenarios, named Competence Assessment Scenario (CAS)[4] that teachers used in their classrooms. CASs were developed by project partners (Croatia, Italy, Romania, Greece, Sweden and Spain) and validated by University of Catalonia. Guàrdia and colleagues (2017) state that CASs are "designed on the basis of advanced instructional approaches where the learner or learners are required to solve problems, develop projects or search for solutions in realistic contexts and meaningful situations" (p. 4). These scenarios are modular which means they could be used or adapted for any subjects or educational level (Guàrdia, Maina, Julià, 2017; Guàrdia, Maina, Baztán, 2018). In addition, Guàrdia, Maina and Julià (2017) states that "the CAS proposes a set of activities and tasks that allow one or more performance criteria to be assessed" (p.80). In the research conducted in Croatia, teachers used original scenarios and some of the scenarios they adapted to their needs and curricular requirements.

List of CASs which were included in the project are: Improve employee competence – company, Was Oliver Twist a son of the Industrial Revolution?, How could you promote your county or region?, My Internet, We welcome our guests, Publish an electronic school newspaper, Reach 20 First, Tips to become a responsible digital citizen, Alice Through the Screen and What Alice Found There, Locked-in and Our Virtual Museum.

All scenarios cover subjects as history, computer science, literacy, first and second language subjects, mathematics, etc. and are available on Croatian, English, Greek, Italian, Romanian, Spanish and Swedish languages. Materials are under Creative Common license in open access for use as teaching materials on international level in primary and secondary schools.

All involved teachers and students had initial education trainings before using scenarios, platform and ICT tools. Trainings were held face to face in a form of workshops. Frist set of workshops were for teachers, were facilitators explain and demonstrated functionalities and use of CRISS platform, explain methodology behind the project, presented all CASs and evaluation process. In addition, all teachers were familiarize with process of CAS adaptation, e.g. how to modify scenarios to their specific needs regarding the subject they are teaching, how to upload additional teaching materials, how to assign tasks and activities to their students, how to monitor progress of their students and how to evaluate students tasks. Second set of workshops were for involved students which goal was to teach students how to use platform, upload materials, browse through tasks and activities which teachers assign to them, how to communicate with teachers using the platform and how to send materials, homework and solutions of the tasks for evaluation to their teachers. All schools and teachers had system of help and support during the whole school year on national level. Use of ICT in primary education has various advantages for students as Frydrychova Klimova (2012) and Hlasna, Klímová and Poulova (2017) claims that learning process is tailored to students' needs, can be conducted from anywhere (classroom, home, etc.), develops critical thinking, and it is more diverse and dynamic for students. In addition, technology can stimulate "a collective, participative and active perspective" (Perez-Escoda, Castro-Zubizarreta, Fandos-Igado, 2016 p. 78) for students.

PURPOSE OF THE STUDY

Research will describe the whole process that the teachers underwent with their students and how they managed to certify students' digital competences. Additionally, author will provide information about the teaching materials used in the process, methods of teaching, evaluation process and the process of CAS adaptation for their respective subjects. This chapter will present three case studies with three primary school teachers who participated with their students in CRISS project during which all used CRISS platform. In addition, research will describe and explore teachers' experience with the process of evaluating students' digital competences, obstacles they encountered during this process and how the use of ICT tools can improve digital competences of primary school students. Teachers who participated in the research were selected due to their advanced experience with the use of ICT in the classroom. Furthermore, these teachers were selected due to the fact they do not teach IT subjects like Computer Science or Informatics. The teacher selection will provide insight into how ICT tools can be used in non-IT subjects (e.g. L1 or L2 language subjects, Mathematic, Geography, Media Culture, Literacy, etc.) for acquiring digital competences in primary schools. More specifically, the chapter describes and analyses in detail (1) how teachers experienced the process of evaluating students' digital competences and weather that was an appropriate approach for primary school students; (2) how important is the process of acquiring digital competences at primary educational level; (3) what are the advantages and disadvantages of introducing ICT tools in education curriculum with the goal of certifying digital competences of primary school students. Through monitoring process and interviews with primary school teachers, conclusion were made about these three research questions. The case studies will provide valuable insight how digital competences could be implemented into national curriculum and classroom teaching within subjects, which are not related with ICT. Based on teachers' attitudes, perspective and experience author will present practical information and conclusions about importance of digital competences for students' future education and knowledge. In addition, this research will try to answer the question, do integration of digital competences in primary school education rise students' motivation for specific subject, from teachers' point of view.

CRISS pilot project was conducted in 6 countries (Croatia, Greece, Italy, Romania, Spain and Sweden) with 535 primary and secondary schools during which more than 27 000 users tested the platform, students created 274 000 evidences, e.g. digital materials that were uploaded on CRISS platform and more than 44 000 of these materials were sent to teachers for evaluation. Out of that, 37 738 evidences (materials that students produced during the pilot project) were evaluated by teachers and 64% of students reached certification level in one or more sub-competences.. All information about CRISS project and its results is available at https://www.crissh2020.eu/resources-2/. CRISS was a large-scale project that produced methodology framework for evaluating, acquiring and certifying digital competences for students in primary and secondary schools in Europe. In addition, during the project all project partners and some teachers produced teaching scenarios that are in open access and could be used in further teaching on international level.

METHOD

Research was conducted during the school year 2018/2019 with three teachers in three different primary schools in Croatia (Primary school Horvati, Primary school Ivo Andrić and Primary school "dr. Franjo Tuđman" Šarengrad). Teachers who participated in this research are teachers of the Croatian language, Mathematics and one of them is a teacher generalist teaching in lower primary classes. In Croatia, primary school lasts for 8 years and it is divided into lower and upper primary. Lower primary begins with the age of 6/7 and lasts for four years. One teacher (teacher generalist) teaches all subjects in lower primary classes. Upper primary school begin with the age 10/11 and it lasts for additional four years. Every subject in upper primary has its own teacher. Overall primary school in Croatia lasts for 8 years and students' age is between 6/7 in first grade of lower primary and 14/15 in eight grade (last grade) in upper primary school.

This empirical research is based on three case studies where qualitative methodology is used to interpret teachers' responses, thoughts, attitudes, perspectives and emotions. It is important to investigate teachers' point of view about the use of ICT tools in the process of acquiring, evaluating and certifying students' digital competences so that this process could be integrated in a school curriculum. Digital competences are not just about the use of ICT tools and developing digital skills, as they also enable students to develop "social and emotional aspects for using and understanding digital device" (Ilomäki, Kantosalo, Lakkala, 2011, p 2.). Due to this social and emotional component, it is important to gain insight into teachers' perspective as they are the ones that work directly with students and have the best understanding of students needs and their emotional state, in other words, teachers are the closest link to subjects whom the policy recommendations on the use of ICT will concern the most.

The methods that were used for this research are semi-structured interviews that were conducted with teachers during the school year 2018/2019. Teachers were provided with open-ended questions that were followed by how and why questions (Newcomer, Hatry, Wholey, 2015). This approach was selected because it can provide valuable insights and information in which measure, if any, could digital competences be incorporate in primary school curriculum based on teachers' practical experience gained through CRISS project. During the interviews, teachers were asked to provide answers to 18 questions about their experience and impressions regarding use of ICT for purpose of acquiring digital competences in primary school environment based on their experience teaching within CRISS project. Questions were divided into three main categories related to teachers' perception about teaching materials and process of adaptation (1), perception of students' experience and motivation during the process of acquiring and certifying digital competences (2) and teachers personal perception about project goals and used methods of teaching and evaluating students digital competences (3). First category (1) of questions aimed to investigate teachers' opinion, thoughts and perception based on their teaching experience and knowledge about provided teaching materials for acquiring digital competences. In addition, teachers were asked to describe their process of adopting existing teaching materials (CASs) to their subject if there was a need for adaptation. Second category (2) was related to teachers' perception of students' experience with project based and collaborative learning. In addition, teachers provided their viewing of students' motivation level during the process of acquiring and certifying digital competences. Teachers provided valuable insight into classroom atmosphere among primary school students. Third category (3) had intention to provide answers how did teachers experienced whole project, what were the advantages and disadvantages regarding teaching and evaluating digital competences of their students and is this approach applicable for primary school students. All answers were examined and conclusions were made based on personal views of teachers regarding the whole process of teaching and evaluating digital competences of their students as part of their regular subjects in primary schools.

During the CRISS project in school year, 2018/2019 all teachers were contacted on monthly base and some teacher even more frequently to report on their progress. Throughout whole process facilitators offered teachers help and support and gather their impressions about project activates, students' motivation and interest. All impressions, perceptions and attitude of three teachers were collected during this period through face-to-face interviews and email conversations. Final interview was conducted with three primary school teachers who were selected because of their experience with ICT tools and excellent results they archived during the CRISS project on the national level.

For the purpose of the research, all three teachers will remain anonymous and will be named as follows: Mathematics teacher = MT (upper primary), Croatian language teacher = CLT (upper primary), teacher generalist = GT (lower primary). All teachers have full time teaching jobs in three primary schools in Croatia and rich experience in teaching and working on various projects that are related with use of ICT for education purpose.

FINDINGS

Finding and interpretation of the research results will be presented in three sections where each refers to case study for one of the teachers and their students. Each case study presents approach, which teachers conducted in the classrooms with their students during the project and how did teachers perceive process of teaching digital competences through their subjects. In addition, study will present how did teachers experienced whole process of teaching and evaluating digital competences, how did teachers perceive emotional state of their students during the project and level of students' motivation for use of ICT tools.

Table 1 shows total number of involved students in CRISS project in three schools where teacher MT, CLT and GT are teaching. Primary school 1 in which teacher MT is teaching had total of 170 students registered on platform, out of that 163 students were active which means they worked on platform, and 138 students certify their digital competences is one or more sub-competences area.

Primary school 2 in which teacher CLT is teaching had total of 122 students registered on platform, out of that 95 students were active which means they worked on platform, and 76 students certify their digital competences is one or more sub-competences area.

Primary school 3 in which GT is teaching had 13 students registered on platform, all 13 students were active which means that they worked on platform, and 12 students certify their digital competences in one or more sub-competences area.

Table 1. Number of involved students in CRISS project for three primary schools

Primary School	No. of registered students	No. of active students	No. of certificates
School 1	170	163	138
School 2	122	95	76
School 3	13	13	12

Table 2 shows number of classes and students which teachers MT, CLT and GT lead during the CRISS project. Additionally, data in last column refers to number of students who gain certificates during the project.

Table 2. Number of students in classes of teachers MT, CLT and GT

	No. of classes	No. of students	No. of certificates
Teacher MT	6	138	128
Teacher CLT	2	41	41
Teacher GT	1	3	3

During the CRISS pilot project, teacher MT was working with 6 primary classes where 4 classes were from upper primary (7A, 7B, 7C, 8A) and 2 classes were from lower primary (4A, 4B). Student age was between 10 to 15. Class 7A had 24 students, class 7B had 22 students, class 7C had 24 students, class 8A had 17 students, class 4A had 24 students and class 4B had 27 students. Number of students that certified at least one sub-competence in total was 128. Teacher CLT was working with 2 classes (8A and 8B) from upper primary, age 14 to 15. Class 8A had 21 students, class 8B had 20 students, and number of students that certified at least one sub-competence in total was 41. Teacher GT was working with one class from lower primary (4), age 8. Class had 3 students and all of them certified one sub-competence.

Case 1: Croatian Language Teacher (CLT) in Upper Primary School

Teacher CLT is teaching Croatian language in upper primary school where student age is between 11 and 15 years. During the CRISS project teacher CLT lead 2 classes, 8A and 8B. Class 8A had 21 students and class 8B had 20 students.

Teacher CLT described process of evaluating digital competences as clear, precise and meaningful because students received feedback on the tasks, in a way that they fully understood the positive and / or negative aspects of their work. In addition, the part of the platform which was used for evaluation of students was optimally developed. The biggest challenge regarding the evaluation for teacher CLT was the time factor because he had to spend a lot of time to evaluate a large number of tasks.

The biggest advantage of this certification process is the fact that during regular school activities, digital competencies can be learned and tested, because they are not generally evaluated. Digital competences usually are not goals but a means to achieve other goals. Nevertheless, they are all important competencies that should be recognized and valorised, according to his experience.

The advantages of incorporating ICT tools into the curriculum aimed at certification of students' digital competences in primary schools are the modernization of teaching methodology and new possibilities for developing creativity. The disadvantages of this kind of education are in correlation with some school systems that are not prepared for this type of teaching, as well as the rigid national curricula of different countries.

Teacher CLT experienced the whole process as challenging but this experience led him to ponder about adapting his own established way of working. He stresses: "It was not stressful, but it was gruelling and time consuming" (Teacher CLT)

Teacher CLT would give maximum freedom to the users, e.g. teachers to modify content of scenarios within the platform as long as they leave intact the essential part of platform that relates to the digital competencies. His opinion is that it would be better if the teaching scenarios were more generic and less related to specific topics.

Is it possible to incorporate certifying digital competences into primary school curriculum was one of the questions of this research. Based on experience in CRISS project teacher CLT perception is that it could be done through a cross-curricular topic, which are related with digital technology that would clearly identify learning outcomes that would match with the digital framework used in this project.

Teachers CLT Perception about Teaching Materials

Teacher CLT adapted all teaching scenarios that he used during the project. He describes his process:

I adapted all the scenarios that I used because the topics of scenarios did not fit into the annual plan and program (national curriculum) which we must follow. From certain scenarios, I choose activities and tasks depending on which digital competencies they were referring. I would keep the part related to digital competencies and adapt the context of the tasks to the topics from the annual plan and program in my teaching process (Teacher CLT).

Attitude of Teacher CLT regarding the use and level of appropriateness of scenarios for primary school students is as follows:

The scenarios are generally appropriate for upper primary school students, perhaps not always in the context of a complete scenario with respect to the topics they are addressing, but always with respect to the digital component, that is, the use of digital tools and other aspects of technology use for learning purposes (Teacher CLT).

Teacher CLT did not stray from subject curriculum and it was easy for him to incorporate tasks in his teaching plan and program. He describes whole process:

I did not move too far from my curriculum because I adapted CRISS materials to my teaching plan and program. It was not difficult to include tasks from scenarios, but it was difficult to organize classes since my school has only one IT classroom. In addition, the high level of students' digital competencies helped me to transfer part of the activities from classroom assignments to home assignments (Teacher CLT).

Teacher CLT fully adapted one CAS named "Publish an electronic school newspaper" to "Publish vlog about animated movie". This scenario is available in Croatian language on the following link https://www.crissh2020.eu/booklet/. Goal of the original CAS was for students to create and manage school newspaper in online form but teacher CLT recreate whole scenario but kept indicators and structure of digital competences form the CAS. In his scenario students needed to create and design vlog[5] about various Croatian animated movies and their producers.

Teacher CLT Perception of Students' Experience and Motivation

Teacher CLT attitude and perception about motivation and experience of his students with project-based learning is positive, he states that for his students it was not difficult to learn in this way. For the most part, students solved tasks together through collaborative and peer learning and they were highly motivated. The part that was most appealing to the students was the digital component, which each task contained. For example, using different types of ICT tools like G-Suite and programs for creating mind maps and interactive posters. The students preferred working together on documents and presentations using G-Suite. Except CRISS platform teacher and students mostly used emails and online clouds to share content on the Internet, e.g. Google Drive and for collaboration they used, e.g. Google Slides. Use of variety of different ICT tools for learning motivated students to successfully complete tasks. Teacher CLT points that more different tools there were, the greater the level of motivation was because students perceived each of them (ICT tools) as a challenge and that raised students' motivation for learning. In addition, students were also motivated by the opportunity to receive certificates because certificates represent a clear acknowledgment for work, they have done.

Emotional state of students during the process of acquiring, evaluating and certifying digital competences in the classroom for teacher CLT was satisfying. He states that evaluation process aroused interest and anticipation among students and acquired certificates for different sub-competences resulted in clear satisfaction.

Case 2: Mathematics Teacher (MT) In Upper Primary School

Teacher MT is teaching Mathematics in upper primary school where students age is between 11 and 15 years. During the CRISS project teacher MT lead 6 classes, 4 from upper primary and 2 from lower primary.

Teacher MT describes her experience with process of evaluating digital competences as excellent because the students were delighted to work on platform and to learn and acquire new digital competencies. She emotionally experienced the process without stressful impacts, she emphasis: *"The whole process was not stressful but it was a challenge from which I came out enthusiastic and happy because I learned something new and because my students learned something new" (Teacher MT).*

She would not change anything except evaluation part of process so that teachers can individually select what they want to evaluate, i.e. what digital competences they would like to teach and include in their subject. With experience that she gained, she would use even more ICT tools in her work in classroom with students because it showed her that use of different ICT tools motivates students to their best and learn more.

For Teacher MT the biggest challenge was question how to integrate some of the tasks with the indicators for the evaluation of digital competences. She states: *"At first it was a little stressful but afterwards it went smoothly" (Teacher MT).*

The biggest advantage was the fact that platform and all materials were free for use for teachers and students. Secondly, in addition to learning content, students acquired digital competences from which they will greatly benefit in their future education and development. The only downside was the inability for teachers to independently select the criteria, e.g. what digital competences will be evaluated in a particular task of the scenarios.

Teacher MT perspective and attitude about advantages and disadvantages of introducing ICT tools in education curriculum with goal of certifying digital competences in primary school is as follows:

In my opinion, there are more advantages than disadvantages. A disadvantage would be a poor internet connection, inability to connect to a platform. The benefits are learning something new, combining ICT and classic teaching, breaking the monotony of everyday work, exploratory learning. Important prerequisites for successful inclusion of ICT into teaching process are teacher education about ICT tools, facilitating good internet connection in classrooms, availability of computers in every classroom for every student (Teacher MT).

Teacher MT states that certification of digital competences is possible to incorporate into primary school curriculum but in a way that the scenarios are adapted to the curriculum, or it must be allowed to the teachers to tailor the scenarios to their needs.

Teachers MT Perception about Teaching Materials

Teacher MT adapted each scenario according to the students' age and all levels of 4 upper primary and 2 lower primary school classes.

She adapted CAS named "Was Oliver Twist son of industrial revolution?" and developed her own scenario that is about Pythagoras theorem. She altered content of all tasks and assignment but left indicators for evaluating digital competences. This scenario is available in English and Croatian language on the following link https://www.crissh2020.eu/booklet/. Original scenario was not related to Mathematics, it was intended for subjects History and English as a Foreign Language, but teacher MT saw potential and recreated whole scenario for her subject. She kept indicators and digital competencies but altered the whole content and create teaching scenario for Mathematics that can be used in any primary school.

Teacher MT did not move away from her curriculum. She describes the whole process:

I took my plan and program and looked where I could incorporate the work on the CRISS platform. After that, I looked (go through the scenarios) at available scenarios and tasks and looked at what I could use in my teaching process. I adapted the tasks from the scenarios to my curriculum and everything worked without any problems. The students worked on the curriculum (that is mandatory) but they learned how to use different ICT tools by working on the CRISS platform (Teacher MT).

Teacher MT Perception of Students' Experience and Motivation

Teacher MT attitude about whole process is extremely positive, she states that her students had no problems with tasks from scenarios and: *"They did them very well and we were learning some new things together. Students were very happy with the work they have done" (Teacher MT).*

Her students were positive and excited about project-based learning and use of ICT tool, she points: *"Students were very motivated, and they could not wait for their diploma (that's what they called the certificates)" (Teacher MT).*

During the project, Teacher MT used various ICT tools, like Google Drive, Office 365 for schools, Canva, Kizoa, Liveworksheets, etc., with her students and this approach raised their motivation for subject (Mathematics) and learning. Teacher MT points that students who in the past years did not regularly fulfilled their obligations, during this project did it regularly and with more motivation and satisfaction. According to teacher MT from all ICT tools students, love the most Canva and Mind maps because they were simple and interesting for them. Students used them in every almost segment, from learning new teaching units to repetition of learned materials.

Emotional state of students during the process of acquiring, evaluating and certifying digital competences in the classroom for teacher MT was extremely positive. She points: *"Students were impatient and happy to see that they had done everything right. Great excitement for them was the moment when they saw the increment of the percentage after the work they have done on platform" (Teacher MT).*

Case 3: Teacher Generalist (GT) in Lower Primary School

Teacher GT is teacher generalist in lower primary school where students' age is between 6 and 10 years. During the CRISS project teacher GT lead one class with three students. She is teaching all subjects from first until fourth grade.

Her experience with process of evaluating digital competences was excellent in which she and her students enjoyed working on. The whole process was not stressful, but different in positive way. She did not move away from her curriculum, she had picked tasks and activities from scenarios that were appropriate for younger children in lower primary class.

During the project teacher GT, except CRISS platform, used various ICT tools, like Office 365 for schools, shared slides and documents, etc. for which she considered it would be appropriate for her students. Because of her special circumstances in the classroom, she had more time to work intensively with her students on projects activities and tasks.

She shares her thoughts and attitudes toward the process of integrating certification of digital competences into primary school curriculum with Teacher MT and CLT. Her opinion is that this is possible, and it would be useful for students but certification process must be in compliance with the national curriculum for primary schools and content of scenarios must be adapted for younger students.

Regarding the evaluation process Teacher GT states that it was not difficult nor stressful, the whole process was intuitive and easy to understand. Because this was the pilot, sometimes the platform for evaluation and certification did not worked correctly and this was the one disadvantages but at the end, all worked fine, and all students gained their certificates.

Teachers GT Perception about Teaching Materials

Teacher GT worked with younger students, so she adapted all the scenarios to her curriculum. Some tasks she could use in her teaching but for most tasks, she needed to adapt content so it would be appropriate for her students. This process was time consuming but after the first scenario, she got a hang of it. Students were delighted with teaching scenario named "My Internet" in which they learn how they must act on the Internet and in online communication.

Teacher GT Perception of Students' Experience and Motivation

Students were enthusiastic about CRISS project and they loved to work on the platform and with different ICT tools. They were in the category of younger students that participated in the CRISS pilot project, but they were very successful. All students get their certifications for one or more digital sub-competences.

According to teacher GT, students did all tasks without any problems and at the end of the year they had certification ceremony which was organized by teacher GT.

This teacher had unique situation because she had only three students in her classroom and she could devote hers and their time to project activities. She had proven that even the youngest students could participate in activities devoted to gaining digital competences.

Emotional state of students during the process of acquiring, evaluating and certifying digital competences in the classroom according to teacher GT was positive and students had positive attitude towards the scenarios and ICT tools. Students were very motivated and interested to learn something new.

CHALLENGES

During the CRISS pilot project there were many challenges that teacher had to overcome and deal with. When interviewing teachers all had similar or same statements and thoughts about low points of the project and disadvantages. Challenges could be classified into three main categories, technical (1), curriculum (2), and time (3).

Majority of challenges that teachers reported were correlated with technical difficulties and this was the first and most common challenge (1). One of the most common challenges was CRISS platform, which was unstable at the beginning of the piloting phase. There were periods when platform did not work, what was challenging for teachers and students because this break occurred during the teaching classes with students. Other times when technical problems occurred was during the evaluation process when teachers evaluated students' tasks or when students did their homework and they could not send it on time due to errors on platform. All teachers that participated in the project had complains about slow working platform, errors on platform during the classes and evaluation process, analytics that was not accurate and not in real time. This factor caused the decrement of motivation with teachers and students because they could not perform what they planned for the class. In addition, teachers' emphasis that one of the problems was insufficient technical equipment of schools, many schools (like this from the research) have one IT classroom with computers so it was difficult for them to organized classes.

Second challenge (2) that teachers cope with were predefined teaching scenarios, i.e. CASs which they had to use during the project. Eleven modular scenarios were available through CRISS platform. Majority of scenarios did not fit to national curriculum for primary schools in Croatia and teachers struggled with it. All teachers from this research adapted tasks and activities from scenarios to their subjects. They replaced existing content with their learning materials. As it is described in Case 2 and 3, Teacher MT and CLT created their own teaching scenarios based on topics they had to teach students as part of their subjects.

Third challenge (3) that teachers pointed relates to time, the project tasks were time consuming especially for teachers who did not have many experiences working with ICT in their teaching practices as Cvetković and Stanojević (2018) states "the greatest obstacle to the integration of digital technologies into teaching process are poor competencies on the part of teachers, that is, insufficient training of teachers to apply digital technologies in the classroom" (p. 1220). This was not the case with teachers CLT, MT and GT but some of other teachers had problem during the project. Nevertheless, it is important that teachers who are teaching digital competences have adequate level of digital literacy which "means that a person can be called digitally literate if they possess the knowledge of where and how they can get information and if they possess the ability to virtually manipulate data, i.e. this is a person who knows how to save or send information and create and display information with the use of digital technologies" (Cvetković, Stanojević, 2018, p. 1222).

In addition, adaptation of scenarios to national curriculum was time consuming for teachers, as preparation for classes in which teachers worked on CRISS platform. For almost every class, teachers conducted special preparation and adapted almost every task and activity to their needs so that students could learn mandatory educational content and certify digital competences.

Nevertheless, teachers manage to respect national curriculum and conduct project activities with their students.

DISCUSSION AND CONCLUSION

This research has emerged few conclusions and remarks regarding the implementation of digital competences in primary school teaching process.

Collective learning was a successful teaching method, students enjoyed learning together in groups especially creating, developing, and resolving tasks in shared documents, spreadsheets and presentations. Students' motivation level was hight during the use of different ICT tools and platform, but it also decreased when students experienced technical difficulties. There were times when CRISS platform and other ICT tools did not work correctly and in this period student motivation was low and students did not want do use that tool anymore or they did not want to do tasks from project. The greatest motivation for students during the project was ability to monitor their progress. CRISS platform had functionality, which enabled students to see in which measure, e.g. percentage they are proceeding to certifying digital competences. After teacher evaluated students' tasks, students could see results in real time in form of percentage. On the platform, there was a circle that indicated amount of percentage student had acquired. All teachers form this study agreed that this was a big motivation factor for their students. When students saw their results after few completed tasks, their motivation was on high level and they asked teachers for more tasks and homework. Additional motivation factor for students' success was collaboration because "peer pressure contributes to the accomplishment of ongoing group tasks throughout the learning process and the culmination of a successful final product" (Bell, 2010, p. 40). In this way "the learners are challenged both socially and emotionally as they listen to different perspectives, and are required to articulate and defend their ideas" (Laal, Laal, 2012, p. 491).

Teacher MT pointes that their students made competition out of the process of acquiring digital competences, due that, their students had better performance criteria, better grades and their interest in Mathematics has risen. When students can see or visualise their progress, which is not only described with grades, they have better motivation and their interest in subject is higher, consequently they learn more and are more satisfied with themselves.

Three main research question were evaluated and analysed during this research, (1) how teachers experienced the process of evaluating students' digital competences and weather that was an appropriate approach for primary school students; (2) how important is the process of acquiring digital competences at primary educational level; (3) what are the advantages and disadvantages of introducing ICT tools in education curriculum with the goal of certifying digital competences of primary school students. Based on three case studies it can be concluded that all involved teachers had positive experience when teaching digital competences to their students in primary schools. They all stated that digital competences are important segment of primary school education, but it needs to be implemented in national curriculum and adapted to students' age and content of teaching subject. During the process of acquiring digital competences, students are preparing themselves for further education, labour market and they are developing needed skills for digital society and virtual environment. As Bell (2010) states "PBL promotes social learning as children practice and become proficient with the twenty-first-century skills of communication, negotiation, and collaboration" (p. 40). In addition, Hsu and Liu (2005) points that "project-based learning can motivate students to integrate and formulate the multi-disciplinary knowledge previous learned into a real-world embedded system project development" (p. 362). These statements are in correlation with teachers' attitudes and perceptions of teaching digital competences based on PBL in primary schools.

The biggest challenge with introducing digital competences in primary schools is adequate surroundings, e.g. technical equipment of classrooms, education of teachers, e.g. teachers' level of digital competences and support of school and national administration, e.g. competent authority for the education and curriculum development. As Blau and Shamir-Inbal (2017) states when referring to digital competences of students and its integration to school curriculum "its development in the education system requires the development of digital competence by teaching staff and school ICT leaders" (p. 770). In addition, Blau and Peled (2012, 2017) points that some of the factors that influence on successful integration of ICT tools in schools are teachers' abilities, attitudes, and beliefs. Process of evaluating digital competences is important "first step to reach an acceptable level in these competences, if they are assessed they can be recognized, and if recognized, then, they can be required and integrated in the curriculum from the elementary school to the higher education" (Pérez-Escoda, Rodríguez-Conde, 2015, p.359).

This research has shown that integration of digital competences in primary schools is possible, but it needs be organized on national level so it could be implemented in school curriculum for most of the primary school subjects. In addition, teachers must undergo adequate trainings on how and with what ICT tools they can teach digital competences within their subjects. Use of different ICT tools is not that much of the problem for teachers, but how to incorporate them into their subjects is still a divisive issue that needs attentions and further research.

REFERENCES

Bell, S. (2010). Project-based learning for the 21st century: Skills for the future. *The Clearing House: A Journal of Educational Strategies, Issues and Ideas*, *83*(2), 39–43. doi:10.1080/00098650903505415

Blau, I., & Shamir-Inbal, T. (2017). Digital competences and long-term ICT integration in school culture: The perspective of elementary school leaders. *Education and Information Technologies*, *22*(3), 769–787. doi:10.100710639-015-9456-7

Calvani, A., Cartelli, A., Fini, A., & Ranieri, M. (2008). Models and Instruments for assessing Digital Competence at School. *Journal of e-Learning and Knowledge Society, 4*(3), 183-193. Retrieved February 7, 2020 from https://www.learntechlib.org/p/43442/

Corr, A. C. (2006). *Children and Technology: A Tool for Child Development*. Barnardos' National Children's Resource Centre.

Cvetković, B. N., & Stanojević, D. (2018). Integrating digital technologies into teaching process. *TEME: Casopis za Društvene Nauke, 12*(4).

De Graaf, E., & Kolmos, A. (2003). Characteristics of problem-based learning. *International Journal of Engineering Education, 19*(5), 657–662.

Digital competence: the vital 21st-century skill for teachers and students. (2020, January 17). Retrieved February 13, 2020, from https://www.schooleducationgateway.eu/en/pub/resources/tutorials/digital-competence-the-vital-.htm

Ferrari, A. (2013). *DIGCOMP: A framework for developing and understanding digital competence in Europe*. Academic Press.

Frydrychova Klimova, B. (2012). Impact of ICT on foreign language learning. *AWER Procedia Information Technology and Computer Science, 2*, 180–185.

Ghavifekr, S., & Rosdy, W. A. W. (2015). Teaching and learning with technology: Effectiveness of ICT integration in schools. *International Journal of Research in Education and Science, 1*(2), 175–191. doi:10.21890/ijres.23596

Guàrdia, L., Maina, M., & Baztán, P. (2018). Digital competence assessment framework for primary and secondary schools in Europe: the CRISS project. *Towards Personalized Guidance and Support for Learning*, 229.

Guàrdia, L., Maina, M., & Julià, A. (2017). Digital competence assessment system: supporting teachers with the CRISS platform. In *Central European Conference on Information and Intelligent Systems* (pp. 77-82). Faculty of Organization and Informatics Varazdin.

Guitert, M., Romeu, T., & Baztàn, P. (2017). Conceptual framework on digital competences in primary and secondary schools in Europe. *Proceedings of ICERI, 2017*, 5081–5090. doi:10.21125/iceri.2017.1336

Hlasna, P., Klímová, B., & Poulova, P. (2017). Use of information and communication technologies in primary education–A case study of the Czech Republic. *International Electronic Journal of Elementary Education, 9*(3), 681–692.

Hsu, R. C., & Liu, W. C. (2005, June). Project based learning as a pedagogical tool for embedded system education. In *ITRE 2005. 3rd International Conference on Information Technology Research in Education, 2005*, 362–366.

Ilomäki, L., Kantosalo, A., & Lakkala, M. (2011). What is digital competence. Linked portal. Brussels: European Schoolnet (EUN), 1-12.

Kreijns, K., Kirschner, P. A., Jochems, W., & Van Buuren, H. (2007). Measuring perceived sociability of computer-supported collaborative learning environments. *Computers & Education, 49*(2), 176–192. doi:10.1016/j.compedu.2005.05.004

Laal, M., & Laal, M. (2012). Collaborative learning: What is it? *Procedia: Social and Behavioral Sciences, 31*, 491–495. doi:10.1016/j.sbspro.2011.12.092

Leko, A. (2019). Learning and evaluation with the support of digital technologies in the Science and Society subject in Croatia. In K. Bilić Meštrić & A. Mudrinić (Eds.), *Teachers and head teachers as the agents of change in their own educational contexts: action research on new technologies as a challenge, stimulation and support to learning and teaching* (pp. 72–106). CARNET.

Mariappan, J., Shih, A., Schrader, P. G., & Elmore, R. (2004, January). Scenario-based learning and multimedia in improving engineering education. In *ASME 2004 International Design Engineering Technical Conferences and Computers and Information in Engineering Conference* (pp. 521-525). American Society of Mechanical Engineers Digital Collection. 10.1115/DETC2004-57704

Massey University. (2016). *Scenario-based learning*. Retrieved March 3, 2020, from https://www.massey.ac.nz/massey/fms/AVC%20Academic/Teaching%20and%20Learning%20Cenrtres/Scenario-based-learning.pdf

Newcomer, K. E., Hatry, H. P., & Wholey, J. S. (2015). Conducting semi-structured interviews. Handbook of practical program evaluation, 492.

Perez-Escoda, A., Castro-Zubizarreta, A., & Fandos-Igado, M. (2016). Digital Skills in the Z Generation: Key Questions for a Curricular Introduction in Primary School. *Comunicar. Media Education Research Journal, 24*(2).

Pérez-Escoda, A., & Rodríguez-Conde, M. J. (2015, October). Digital literacy and digital competences in the educational evaluation: USA and IEA contexts. In *Proceedings of the 3rd International Conference on Technological Ecosystems for Enhancing Multiculturality* (pp. 355-360). 10.1145/2808580.2808633

Pluta, W. J., Richards, B. F., & Mutnick, A. (2013). PBL and beyond: Trends in collaborative learning. *Teaching and learning in medicine, 25*(sup1), S9-S16.

Rizza, C. (2014). Digital Competences. Encyclopedia of Quality of Life and Well-Being Research, 1614-1619.

Ryerson University. (n.d.). *Teaching Scenarios*. Retrieved March 14, 2020, from https://www.ryerson.ca/digital-media-projects/teaching-scenarios/

Suryani, A. (2010). ICT in education: Its benefits, difficulties, and organizational development issues. *Jurnal Sosial Humaniora, 3*(1), 13–33. doi:10.12962/j24433527.v3i1.651

Thomas, J. W. (2000). *A review of research on project-based learning*. The Autodesk Foundation. https://tecfa.unige.ch/proj/eteach-net/Thomas_researchreview_PBL.pdf

ADDITIONAL READING

Calvani, A., Ranieri, M., & Fini, A. (2009). Assessing Students' Digital Competence in Schools. In T. Bastiaens, J. Dron & C. Xin (Eds.), *Proceedings of E-Learn 2009--World Conference on E-Learning in Corporate, Government, Healthcare, and Higher Education* (pp. 852-859). Vancouver, Canada: Association for the Advancement of Computing in Education (AACE).

Freiman, V., Godin, J., Larose, F., Bourgeois, Y., LeBlanc, M., Léger, M., Robichaud, X., Chukalovskyy, R., Cormier, D., & Pelletier, W. (2015). Towards the construction of a theoretical and methodological framework to study partnership development for digital competences within the CompéTICA network. In *Proceedings of Global Learn Berlin 2015: Global Conference on Learning and Technology* (pp. 351-356). Berlin, Germany: Association for the Advancement of Computing in Education (AACE).

Hollow, D., & Masperi, P. (2009, April). An evaluation of the use of ICT within primary education in Malawi. In *2009 International Conference on Information and Communication Technologies and Development (ICTD)* (pp. 27-34). IEEE. 10.1109/ICTD.2009.5426707

Kawade, D. R., & Kulkarni, S. N. (2012). *Use of ICT in primary school.* Pioneer Journal.

Konstantinos, T., Andreas, A., & Karakiza, T. (2013). Views of ICT Teachers about the Introduction of ICT in Primary Education in Greece. *Turkish Online Journal of Educational Technology-TOJET, 12*(1), 200–209.

Kreijns, K., Kirschner, P. A., Jochems, W., & Van Buuren, H. (2007). Measuring perceived sociability of computer-supported collaborative learning environments. *Computers & Education, 49*(2), 176–192. doi:10.1016/j.compedu.2005.05.004

Lim, C. P., & Oakley, G. (2013). Information and communication technologies (ICT) in primary education: Opportunities and supporting conditions. In *Creating Holistic Technology-Enhanced Learning Experiences* (pp. 1–18). Brill Sense. doi:10.1007/978-94-6209-086-6_1

Zurita, G., & Nussbaum, M. (2004). Computer supported collaborative learning using wirelessly interconnected handheld computers. *Computers & Education, 42*(3), 289–314. doi:10.1016/j.compedu.2003.08.005

KEY TERMS AND DEFINITIONS

Collaborative Learning: The main aim of this type of learning is to motivate students to work together on problem solving. This is an educational approach in which two or more student are working together with the aim to resolve given task, activity, or problem.

Digital Competence: According to European Commission digital competence is one of the eight key competences and refers to the confident and critical usage of the full range of digital technologies for information, communication and basic problem-solving.

Evaluation Process: In this research evaluation process is referring to evaluating students tasks for purpose of acquiring, certifying and assessing digital competences of students.

ICT Tools: Term is referring to various digital tools, e.g. software, applications that can be used for different purpose. Each ICT tool has it own purpose, e.g. tools for editing images, digital drawing and creating illustration, developing mind maps, etc. They are used in education process as assets for enrichment of the teaching process.

Information and Communication Technology (ICT): Term refers to the hardware, software and all communication technologies, services and components that enables users to manage, use, store and secure information.

Project-Based Learning: This learning approach is based on projects. During the specified period, students are working on tasks and activities, which are part of the project. Main aim of this approach in education is for students to gain new knowledge, experience and produce materials for wider public.

Teaching Scenarios: Teaching materials which intent is to be used during the education process in classrooms or in virtual environment for specific subject, training, course, etc.

ENDNOTES

1 CRISS is a project financed by the European Commission, through the Horizon2020 programme (ID:732489, 2017-2019) https://www.crissh2020.eu/criss-project/

2 MyDocumenta designed the CRISS platform, more about the company is available at: http://www.mydocumenta.com/

3 The European Digital Competence Framework is available at: https://ec.europa.eu/jrc/en/digcomp/digital-competence-framework

4 All CASs are available on https://www.crissh2020.eu/booklet/ .

5 Term refers to a video blog: a record of your thoughts, opinions, or experiences that you film and publish on the internet. Definition is available on: https://dictionary.cambridge.org/dictionary/english/vlog

Chapter 13
New Trends in Intellectual Capital Disclosures of Higher Degree Institutions in Indonesia

Saarce Elsye Hatane
https://orcid.org/0000-0002-3797-1623
Petra Christian University, Indonesia

Eric Oktavianus
Petra Christian University, Indonesia

Josua Tarigan
Petra Christian University, Indonesia

Ferry Jie
Edith Cowan University, Australia

ABSTRACT

This study aims to investigate the existence regarding the new method in disclosing intellectual capital called as web-based intellectual capital disclosure to overcome the limitation of traditional intellectual capital disclosures and also examine the determinant factors that may influence web-based intellectual capital disclosure of Indonesian universities such as autonomy, competitiveness, age, and size. A partial least-squares analysis is conducted to have an observation of 83 Indonesian higher education institutions. The results show that there is extensive use of intellectual capital disclosure through websites done by Indonesian universities, especially in internal capital, while the disclosure of external capital and human capital is still limited. Furthermore, autonomy gives the biggest impact toward web-based intellectual capital disclosure because autonomy provides freedom for universities in managing their institution especially in improving their web-based intellectual capital disclosure in order to attract more public and government fund.

DOI: 10.4018/978-1-7998-4972-8.ch013

Copyright © 2021, IGI Global. Copying or distributing in print or electronic forms without written permission of IGI Global is prohibited.

INTRODUCTION

In maintaining their existence, organizations must take several things into consideration such as tangible factors and even the intangible factors owned by the organization. One of an important intangible asset factor is intellectual capital (IC) (Siboni et al., 2013). Nowadays, the intensity of competition is getting higher causes the role of IC to become more crucial in an organization. In this current condition, organization that can survive is the one that is able to be adaptive and innovative (Low et al., 2015).

Study of intellectual capital has become more crucial for an organization especially a not-for-profit organisation such as university. Universities is known as an organization with high degree of intangibility since their primary outputs are intangible services, hence making a strong requirement of intellectual capital disclosure (Secundo et al., 2016). Another scholar also stated that the fact about the main purpose of the university is producing and disseminating knowledge or which is the main assets of university, then an intellectual capital disclosure is an important thing to be done by higher education (Ramírez-Córcoles et al., 2016).

Although the intellectual capital disclosure for university is crucial, the study about this important matters is still limited (Dumay and Guthrie, 2017). Traditionally, several researchers use annual report of university as the primary source to obtain intellectual capital information and they claim that annual report is not created for intellectual capital disclosure and therefore the information is not reliable and limited (Dumay and Cai, 2015). Thus, a new method in disclosing intellectual capital need to be done to give accurate information about intellectual capital (Edvinsson, 2013).

Based on Rossi et.al. (2018), several researchers were trying to explore new way of intellectual capital disclosure through website. The existence of website provides greater transparency, reliability and accessibility in disclosing any information with minimum cost (Gallego-Alvarez et.al, 2011). Universities could focus to use website for disseminating information and publication or research for external users for annual, quarterly, theoretical periods and real time. The university official website may become a tool to improve intellectual capital disclosure (Gallego-Alvarez et.al., 2011).

The main focus of this paper is to investigate the existence of intellectual capital disclosure through website done by Indonesian universities and examine the influence of determinant factors towards web-based IC disclosure from the previous researches. This paper indicates four determinant factors: autonomy, competitiveness, age, and size

Therefore, this paper is the first study to reveal the new data source about intellectual capital information being disclosed through website done by Indonesian universities and providing evidence of determinants factors affecting the intellectual capital disclosure in Indonesian higher education institution. Furthermore, the amount of research on web-based intellectual capital disclosure of universities in Indonesia is still few and it also rarely examines the relationship between intellectual capital and determinants factor that influence the disclosure of intellectual capital information.

This study is conducted on Indonesian universities that have A accreditation from period 2018. An accreditation means the best accreditation issued by Indonesian National Education Accreditation Body for Indonesian campuses that that have exceeded national accreditation standards, thus proving the performance of institutions that are already excellent (Indonesian National Accreditation Body, 2017). Based on Webometrics, not all Indonesian universities own official website except higher education institutions with an accreditation, thus these universities are expected to be able to disclose information about intellectual capital comprehensively on their sites. The result of this research may overcome the limitation of traditional intellectual capital information disclosure method done by Indonesian universities and give new strategy to help Indonesian universities in promoting their performance towards the stakeholders through web-based intellectual capital disclosure.

BACKGROUND

Intellectual capital is considered as one of the most vital intangible assets for enhancing the value of an organization (Morariu, 2013; Marr et al., 2015; Cricelli et al., 2018). It was also being emphasized by Marr et al. (2015) that intangible resources and intellectual capital are the keys for firms to develop a competitive advantage; it also empowers the organization to run its operation. Correspondingly, Edvinsson and Malone (2013) portrayed intellectual capital as "intellectual materials that can be changed over into values". Intellectual Capital is the total value of an organization that describes the intangible assets of a company that comes from three pillars, namely human capital, organizational (internal capital), and relational (external capital) (Cricelli et al., 2018).

The past observational examinations on ICD tends to be more focused on the companies (Low et al., 2015), with less of focusing on public or non-profit organisation, whereas university is one of the example from non-profit organization that utilize great extent intangibles resources such as knowledge (Bezhani, 2010; Low et al., 2015; Secundo et al., 2015). In higher education institution, IC refers to all intangible assets owned by the institution, including processes, capacity of innovation, patents, knowledge possessed by its members, talent, skills, recognition from the public, cooperative networks and others (Ramírez Córcoles et al., 2011, Cricelli et al., 2018). IC reporting is an approach that is used to measure intangible assets to describe the results of knowledge-based activities because the stakeholders of universities emphasize the need for IC information to make the right decisions, so that the transparency of universities in intellectual resources is needed (Rossi et al., 2018).

However, previously, numerous IC scientists have communicated a problem arise from exploring ICD solely through annual reports, asking for more research inspecting other potential IC dispersal channels (Abeysekera, 2006; Dumay and Cai, 2015; Dumay and Guthrie, 2017). It is because all of these files are arranged yearly and don't exclusively concentrate on IC. Hence, a few investigations tending to university revelations have featured that the site can be an increasingly valuable device to improve correspondence with the university's stakeholders (Ismail and Bakar 2011; Bisogno et al., 2014). Based on past research and following a proposal by several researchers (Edvinsson, 2013; Guthrie, 2014; Dumay and Guthrie, 2017), this study expects to examine online ICD through official website owned by universities and, going past conventional orders, to look for logical factors behind this disclosure. The examination does not concentrate on the management viewpoint, rather it supports the data's need for external stakeholders who request more prominent responsibility about the colleges' significant resources, for the most part including IC. In doing as such, this investigation investigates another approach to unveiling IC and potential determinants influencing this disclosure.

Autonomy and Web-based Intellectual Capital Disclosure

The existence of autonomy possessed by higher education institutions provides a broad range of freedom for universities to run their institutions in order to develop the intellectual capital which can be used to attract and manage government funds and public funds (Sánchez, 2009; Ramírez Córcoles et al., 2011). The purpose of such disclosure is to give positive signal toward the stakeholders that universities have been managed well. Therefore, by giving information regarding the universities' performance toward stakeholders, it is in line with signaling theory (Cornelly et.al. 2011).

The disclosure of intellectual capital becomes a signal that can increase the knowledge of stakeholders with the main resources possessed by universities (Rossi et.al. 2018). In attracting public and government fund, universities should provide a highly reliable information. However, based on previous researches numerous IC scientists (Abeysekera, 2006; Dumay and Cai, 2015; Dumay, 2016) have stated that conducting traditional ICD through annual reports will cause the emergence of unreliable information, because annual report is not designed to concentrate exclusively on IC reporting. An unreliable source may create a misleading information for the stakeholders. Therefore, by using web-based disclosure, university can provide greater transparency, reliability and accessibility in disclosing intellectual capital information with minimum cost (Gallego-Alvarez et.al. 2011). Increased funds obtained by universities and the presence of autonomy have increased the flexibility of universities in managing and improving the institutions (Serrano-Cinca et al., 2009). Based on the background, the hypothesis one is higher education autonomy has a positive effect on web-based disclosure of intellectual capital information on the official university website.

Competitiveness and Web-based Intellectual Capital Disclosure

Intellectual capital can improve organizational performance and competitiveness because intellectual capital existence drives higher education institutions to focus on managing their resources so they can survive in a knowledge-based environment that is rapidly changing (Secundo et al., 2016). Knowledge, innovation, and Intellectual capital is very closely related to universities and it is used as a tool to build sustainable competitive advantages.

The claim supports research that higher education institutions rankings which determines the competitiveness of the universities are related to perceptions of intellectual capital (Chen and Chen, 2013). Based on some of the previous studies, higher education institutions will continue to develop their intellectual capital publications to maintain and raise the rank obtained by higher education institution beforehand (Siboni et al., 2013). Therefore, by doing intellectual capital publication, universities have applied signaling theory (Bergh et.al, 2014). Signaling theory has strong correlation with disclosure of intellectual capital which should be done by universities (Connelly et al., 2011 and Ramírez-Córcoles et al., 2016).

Furthermore, university in Indonesia does not only facing domestic competition but also internationally. In the new learning economy, higher education will try to fulfil international standards to enlist the fittest understudies and analysts by offering them the opportunity to find out about different societies and access advanced education in other nations, thus increasing competitiveness (Kim, 2009). This kind of competition drives universities to give more information about their performance, tending to worldwide understudies and scientists also (Ramírez-Córcoles et al., 2016). Therefore, the usability and accessibility from web-based ICD will support universities to disseminate intellectual capital information globally (Gallego-Alvarez et al., 2011). Based on the explanation above, the second hypothesis is the universities' competitiveness contributes a positive effect on web-based disclosure of intellectual capital information.

Age and Web-based Intellectual Capital Disclosure

According to Ismail and Bakar (2011), in their investigation on an example of Malaysian state higher education institutions, found older universities unveil more information about their institution performance both in their yearly reports and on their sites than new colleges. By disclosing those information, universities have implemented signaling theory (Bergh et.al, 2014). The underlying reason is that older organizations have more experience in publishing information and organizations with more experience will know more about the need from stakeholders for organization information (Connelly et al., 2011).

In contrary, a few researchers underline how newly established higher education institutions are increasingly innovative and bound to receive new advancements to enhance their operations compared to older universities, which may tend to reject changes (Saxton and Guo, 2011). Despite of the positive relationship stated by Ismail and Bakar (2011) and the other researcher, in the contrary Gallego-Alvarez et al (2011) and Bisogno et al. (2014) stated that there had not found any correlation between university age and web-based intellectual capital disclosure. Based on the explanation above, the third hypothesis is there is a correlation between university age and the web-based disclosure of intellectual capital information.

Size and Web-based Intellectual Capital Disclosure

A few investigations on open part straightforwardness and exposure feature that bigger public organization will in general reveal more data through innovative and imaginative devices (sites) than smaller organizations, since they have more assets and are exposed to a more prominent interest for accountability by a bigger number of stakeholders in order to maintain their institution reputation (Serrano-Cinca et al., 2009; Rossi et al., 2018). Another supporting supposition originates from Gallego-Alvarez et al. (2011) that expressed organization size has been one of the factors most utilized so as to clarify the disclosure of data.

Along these lines, from the point of view of the signaling theory perspective, a site can be a stable and a proficient vehicle of correspondence to satisfy responsibility in terms of information dissemination to higher education institutions' stakeholders (Bisogno et al., 2014). In addition, bigger public entities and colleges specifically are more politically noticeable and are liable to more prominent outer impact from their stakeholder network (for example citizens, governments, understudies), so they are driven to uncover more data, particularly on the web, to diminish political expenses and get more noteworthy authenticity (Gallego-Alvarez et al., 2011; Garcìa-Sànchez et al., 2013; Rossi et al., 2018).

Furthermore, taking into record these contentions most past research has discovered that schools' and colleges' size impacts the measure of voluntary information uncovered on sites and site page navigability (Serrano-Cinca et al., 2009; Gallego-Alvarez et al., 2011; Garcìa-Sànchez et al., 2013; Rossi et al., 2018). Based on previous studies, University's size was only being measured from the number of student owned by the higher education institution (Rossi et al., 2018). However, the author also uses number of lecturer to enrich the explanation regarding universities size and its relationship with web-based intellectual capital disclosure. By adding number of lecturer which reflects the worker of universities it means that this paper also adds one more factors that are needed to measure the size of an organization (Garcìa-Sànchez et al., 2013). Therefore, the author split the hypothesis regarding the correlation between size and web-based intellectual capital disclosure to give evidence in regards of the existence of relationship between numbers of lecturer toward web-based intellectual capital disclosure. Based on the explanation above, the fourth hypotheses are:

H4a: There is a positive correlation between numbers of student with the web-based intellectual capital disclosure.

H4b: There is a positive correlation between numbers of lecturer with the web-based intellectual capital disclosure.

RESEARCH METHODOLOGY

To conduct the test of this research, Partial Leas Squares (PLS) analysis through WarpPLS software is used to analyses the correlation between the variables. The data collection is categories as secondary data and the sample are Indonesian universities in the year of 2018. Moreover, the universities chosen as the sample must possess an accreditation and official website. The data were found from the universities' official website, QS World University Ranking, and Indonesian Directorate General of Higher Education website. Accordingly, the Table 1 contain the description regarding the total sample observed, which 83 universities are for 1 year, thus in total there are 400 observations.

Table 1. Summary of the sample observed

Sampling Criteria	No. of Observations
All Indonesian universities that have official websites during 2018 period	2149
Less with Indonesian universities with accreditation besides A	(2064)
Less with Indonesian universities that not stated the data about number of lecturer and students	(2)
Universities used as sample	83
Research period (2018)	1
Total sample	83

Web-based intellectual capital disclosure have 25 items of ICD from Tripartite Classification of Intellectual Capital Disclosure Items (Low et al., 2015). In addition, this study combines the ICD with 17 items of web accessibility item, adopted from Bisogno et.al. (2014). Scoring system is deployed, 1 if it is disclosed in universities' website and 0 if it is not disclosed. Furthermore, from table 2, can be concluded that the overall score from ICD and web accessibility items will be combined and calculated by using GICD index (Rossi et.al, 2018).

$$\text{GICD index} = \frac{\sum_{k=1}^{n} d_i}{n} \quad (1)$$

$\sum_{k=1}^{n} d_i$ is the score obtained by incorporated all the 42 items from ICD items and Web Disclosure Index items and n the maximum score obtainable while taking into account all the items. Autonomy given to the university is divided into 3 types, Legal Entity state universities, Public Service Agency state university, and private universities (Indonesian Law No. 12 of 2012 concerning higher education) which is measured by using dummy variable. Score 2 if it is stated as Legal Entity state universities, 1 for private universities, and 0 for Public Service Agency state university. Competitiveness is measured according to the name of Indonesian university that are stated in the QS World University Ranking 2018. Based on the data acquired from QS World Ranking Universities in 2018, there are only 9 Indonesian universities listed in the QS ranking database (Sheeja et.al. 2018). Therefore, the measurements of the variable are using dummy scale with a score of 1 if the name of the university is stated in QS World

University ranking and 0 if vice versa. Data on higher education institutions age obtained based on the data from the internet as well as official university sites and news released by the university's sample sites. While, the data on higher education institutions number of students obtained from the website of Indonesian Directorate General of Higher Education for the year 2018. Indonesian Directorate General of Higher Education website is the official Indonesian higher education database.

Table 2. Variable definitions and data source

Variable(s)	*Definitions*	*Data Source*
Web-based ICD	GICD Index: total combined score of IC items (adopted the Tripartite Classification of Intellectual Capital Disclosure Items by Low et al. (2015)); and Web accessibility items	University websites
Autonomy	Dummy variables of whether: included as Legal Entity state universities (Score 0) or Public Service Agency state university or private universities	University websites
Competitiveness	Dummy variables of whether: the name of the university is stated in the QS World University Ranking 2018 or not	QS World University Ranking (http://www.webometrics)
Age	Number of years since the established year	University websites
Size	Number of student and lecturer	Indonesian Directorate General of Higher Education website

This paper focuses the variables relationship namely, Autonomy, Competitiveness, Age, Size as the determinant factors toward Web-based intellectual capital disclosure. Because the model uses more than two independent variables, thus this study utilize a multivariate analysis called as the multivariate regression model (Wijnhoven et al., 2014). Based on the theoretical model, the following is regression models.

$$\text{Web-based ICD}_{i,t} = \beta 0 + \beta 1(\text{Autonomy})_{i,t} + \beta 2(\text{Competitiveness})_{i,t} + \beta 3(\text{Age})_{i,t} + \beta 4(\text{Size})_{i,t} + \varepsilon_{i,t} \quad (1)$$

Where Web-based ICD is the global intellectual capital disclosure index of university; β0 is the constant; β1–β4 is the coefficient of the determinants variables (Autonomy, Competitiveness, Age, and Size); ε_i is the error or disturbance terms of university. According to Wijnhoven et al. (2014), multivariate regression model can be tested by using Warp PLS, therefore Warp PLS will be utilised in this paper.

RESEARCH RESULTS AND ANALYSIS

Validity and Reliability Test

In Table V the relationships among variables with square root of AVE are shown diagonally and the numbers that are showed in the diagonal section should be the biggest among the other coefficient correlation of latent variables (Kock, 2015). Moreover, the VIFs must be lower than 3.30 or 10 for the relax criteria (Kock, 2015). Table 3 and Table 4 below show that all variables already fulfilled the validity and reliability test.

Table 3. Correlations among Variables with Square Root of AVE

Variable	ICD	AUT	COM	AGE	Lect	Std
ICD	0.842	0.612	0.354	0.168	0.324	0.372
AUT	0.612	1.000	0.489	0.146	0.225	0.174
COM	0.354	0.489	1.000	0.190	0.497	0.412
AGE	0.168	0.146	0.190	1.000	0.420	0.370
Lect	0.324	0.225	0.497	0.420	1.000	0.825
Std	0.372	0.174	0.412	0.370	0.825	1.000

Table 4. Collinearity Values

	Web-based ICD	*Aut*	*Com*	*Age*	*Lect* Size*	*Std*Size*
Full collinearity VIFs	**1.824**	**1.958**	**1.669**	**1.225**	**3.637**	**3.367**

Analysis Result

Table 5 demonstrates the overall information regarding the analysis result of web-based intellectual capital disclosure. As to intellectual capita item classes specifically, in average, every higher education institution unveils 16.71 intellectual capital items (67% of absolute intellectual capital items) on its site, with an exceptional focus on internal capital (88% of the overall internal capital items uncovered, in average, by each higher education institution) and trailed by external capital (58 percent) and human capital (56%).

In addition, as it can be seen in Table 5, the average mean value of ICD index is 0.67 which is considered as high. This indicate that most of the intellectual capital disclosure item has been disclosed in the main website own by Indonesian universities which can also be seen in Table 6. In the perspective of the presentation which is reflected through web accessibility item, in average, each of the Indonesian higher education university disclose 67.7% from the total of web accessibility items or about 11.69 items being disclosed by each of Indonesian university, where it is dominated by technology items (79% of total technology items is presented on average), followed by interactivity with user items (67%) and navigability (52%). The finding is in line with Rossi (2018) and shows how higher education institutions utilize the potential offered by sites for disclosing intellectual capital information, thus, it can enhance the accessibility and understandability of stakeholders.

Table 6 describes the results of web-based intellectual capital disclosure for each item. In terms of intellectual capital disclosure item, the highest disclose intellectual capital item are "Brand identity"; "Brand Merchandising"; "Post-graduation"; and "high education and specialisation programs" in external

Table 5. Web-based Intellectual Capital Disclosure Analysis Result

	Total Items	Mean	%	Min	Max
Human Capital	8	4.47	56%	0	7
Internal Capital	8	7.06	88%	4	8
External Capital	9	5.18	58%	3	8
Total ICD (content)	**25**	**16.71**	**67%**	8	23
Technology	4	3.17	79%	2	4
Navigability	9	4.67	52%	3	5
Interactivity with user	4	3.84	67%	3	4
Total Web Accessibility Item (presentation)	**17**	**11.69**	**67.7%**	8	13
Total GICD	**42**	**28.40**	**67.6%**	18	36
Indices of Disclosure					
ICD Index		0.67		0.31	0.92
GICD Index		0.68		0.43	0.86

capital criteria, and "Higher education culture"; "Management philosophy"; and "Infrastructure facility" in internal capital criteria. It can be seen that all 83 universities fully disclosed this items (100%).

Furthermore, the highest disclosed item in human capital criteria is "Information about PhD courses" with 76 out of 83 (92%) universities disclosed this item. In addition, the lowest disclosed item is coming from "Students information" from external capital criteria with only 4 universities (5%) disclosed it, followed by "Graduate student's information" that is also included in external capital criteria and "Information about PhD students" that is included in human capital criteria.

From the perspective of web accessibility item, the result in technology criteria show that all of the official websites (100%) owned by Indonesian universities provide fast download speed and incorporated imaged and graphs inside their websites. In navigability criteria, 100% of the universities has provided help button, possibility in changing text size and visible content menu in their websites to improve the convenience in accessing the websites. Meanwhile, 100% of the universities also provide access and link on social and cultural activities and information about higher education activities in their websites to enhance the interactivity with users. Contrarily, in navigability criteria, all of the 83 universities don't provide glossary of terminology, option to change into higher readability mode, table of content and Multilanguage option. Furthermore, in technology criteria, only 17% of the total university sample provide sound file in their official websites. Table 7 below showed the descriptive analysis of each of the variable, including minimum, maximum, mean, and standard deviation.

In Table 7, it shows that number of student (Std) has a minimum and maximum value of 342 and 60,750 respectively, with a mean value of 19,302.550, while the number of lecturer has a minimum and maximum value of 27 and 2,616, with a mean value of 811.397. Both has a standard deviation value of 12,815.950 and 582.385 respectively. Meanwhile, autonomy (AUT) which has a minimum and maximum value of 0 and 2, and a mean value of 0.698, with a standard deviation value of 0.694. The next variable is age (AGE) that has a minimum and maximum value of 9 and 73 respectively, with a mean value of 49.626 and has a standard deviation value of 16.061. Next is the last independent variable which is competitiveness (COM) which has a minimum and maximum value of 0 and 1 respectively and a mean

Table 6. Web-based Intellectual Capital Disclosure Analysis Result for Each Item

Intellectual Capital Item Disclosure		% of higher education institutions	0	1	Frequency
External Capital					
1	Brand identity	100%	0	83	83
2	Brand Merchandising	100%	0	83	83
3	Student satisfaction	10%	75	8	8
4	Mobility programs for students	78%	18	65	65
5	Post-graduation, high education and specialisation programs	100%	0	83	83
6	University third mission-spin off	48%	43	40	40
7	University third mission research consortia and cluster	71%	24	59	59
8	Students information	5%	79	4	4
9	Graduate students information	6%	78	5	5
Internal Capital					
1	Patent rights	57%	36	47	47
2	Publications	95%	4	79	79
3	Higher education culture	100%	0	83	83
4	Management philosophy	100%	0	83	83
5	Infrastructure facility	100%	0	83	83
6	ICT Infrastructure	88%	10	73	73
7	National research project	96%	3	80	80
8	European and international research project	77%	19	64	64
Human Capital					
1	Information about Lecturers	54%	38	45	45
2	Information about PhD students	14%	71	12	12
3	Information about PhD courses	92%	7	76	76
4	Information about Research colleagues	80%	17	66	66
5	Staffs' mobility programmes	27%	61	22	22
6	Information about staff administration	59%	34	49	49
7	Internationalisation of lecturers	76%	20	63	63
8	Training programmes	47%	4	39	39
Web Accessibility Item		**% of higher education institutions**	**0**	**1**	**Frequency**
Technology					
1	Download speed of the main website (<10s)	100%	0	83	83
2	Images and Graphs	100%	0	83	83
3	Sound files usage	17%	69	14	14
4	Video files usage	99%	1	82	82
Navigability					
1	Help button	100%	0	83	83
2	Glossary of terminology	0%	83	0	0
3	Readability (option to change into higher readability mode)	0%	83	0	0
4	Text size (Possibility to change text size)	100%	0	83	83
5	Table of content	0%	83	0	0
6	Internal search engine	72%	23	60	60
7	English language option	95%	4	79	79
8	Multilanguage option (other International language besides English)	0%	83	0	0
9	Visible content menu	100%	0	83	83
Interactivity with User					
1	Access and link on library	88%	10	73	73
2	Access and link on social and cultural activities	100%	0	83	83
3	Information about other higher education services, physical exercise, etc.	100%	0	83	83
4	Access to social network	96%	3	80	80

Table 7. Web-based Intellectual Capital Disclosure Analysis Result for Each Item

Variable	Min	Max	Mean	Std. Deviation
ICD	0.43	0.83	0.707	0.086
AUT	0	2	0.698	0.694
AGE	9	73	49.626	16.061
COM	0	1	0.108	0.312
Std (Size)	342	60,750	19,302.550	12,815.950
Lect (Size)	27	2,616	811.397	582.385

that have value of 0.108 with a standard deviation value of 0.312. Furthermore, the dependent variable of this paper which is web-based intellectual capital disclosure (ICD) has a minimum and maximum value of 0.43 and 0.83, with a mean of 0.707 and has a standard deviation value of 0.086.

Figure 1. Structural model

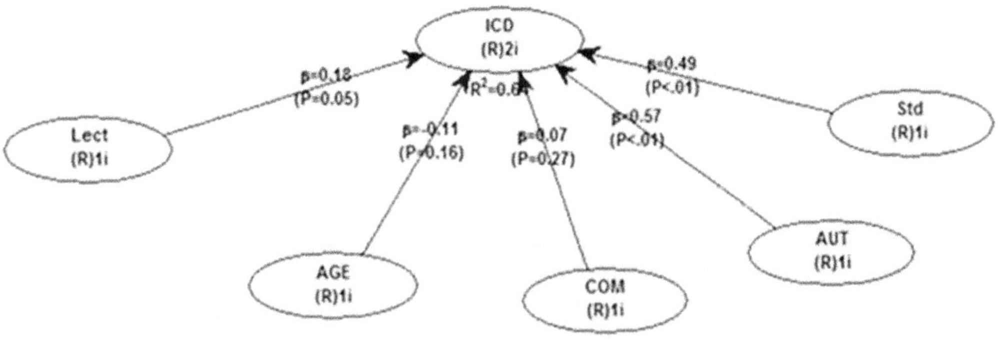

Figure 1 shows the result of direct effect of age (AGE), competitiveness (COM), autonomy (AUT), and size which is reflected as number of student (Std) and number of lecturer (Lect) to web-based intellectual capital disclosure (ICD). Both number of student and number of lecturer as the measurement of size, have significant positive effect towards the GICD index as the indicators of web-based intellectual capital disclosure with the coefficient of 0.49 (p-value<0.01) and coefficient of 0.18 (p-value=0.05) respectively. Furthermore, autonomy also has significant positive effect towards web-based intellectual capital disclosure, with the coefficient of 0.57 (p-value<0.01). However, age and competitiveness has no significant effect toward web-based intellectual capital disclosure, with coefficient of -0.11 (p-value=0.16) and coefficient of 0.07 (p-value=0.27) respectively.

Table 8. Web-based Intellectual Capital Disclosure Analysis Result for Each Item

Independent Variable	Dependent Variable	Effect Size
Autonomy	Web-based ICD	0.358
Competitiveness	Web-based ICD	0.023
Age	Web-based ICD	0.029
Size (number of student)	Web-based ICD	0.224
Size (number of lecturer)	Web-based ICD	0.061

As seen in the table 8, it can be seen that the effect of autonomy to web-based ICD is big, since the size of autonomy effect to web-based ICD is 0.358, which is higher than 0.35. In addition, the effect of number of student toward web-based ICD is medium, since the size of number of student to web-based ICD is 0.224, which is higher than 0.15 and lower than 0.35. Meanwhile, the effect of competitiveness to web-based ICD; the effect of age and web-based ICD; the effect of number of lecturer and web-based ICD are weak since the size is equal to 0.023, 0.029, and 0.061 (above 0.02 and under 0.15).

Table 9. Web-based Intellectual Capital Disclosure Analysis Result for Each Item

		Aut	Com	Age	Size*Std	Size*Lect
Direct Effect	Web-based ICD	0.574***	0.065	-0.110	0.494***	0.177**
Total Effect	Web-based ICD	0.574***	0.065	-0.110	0.494***	0.177**

* p<0.10 (weakly significant); **p<0.05 (significant); ***p<0.01 (highly significant).

Based on Table 8 and Figure 1, the hypothesis and research result shows there are 3 hypothesis that are accepted in this paper such as, autonomy toward web-based ICD, number of student toward web-based ICD and number of lecturer toward web-based ICD

SOLUTIONS AND RECOMMENDATIONS

Autonomy and Web-based ICD

Autonomy is found to have positive impact toward web-based intellectual capital disclosure. It means the higher the level of autonomy. The result is in line with the previous studies (Sánchez et al., 2009, Rahayuningtas and Triana, 2017), the greater the autonomy possessed by a college, it will increase the willingness of the high institution to make disclosure of intellectual capital. With the existence of autonomy, universities have the flexibility to manage their institution to encourage higher education institutions to seek more funds that can be obtained from stakeholders, one of which is through the disclosure of intellectual capital. University that possess the highest level of autonomy have the highest degree of freedom in managing their institution especially in terms of developing better intellectual capital disclosure which can be used to attract and manage government fund and public funds (Sánchez, 2009). Furthermore, in order to acquire those funds, university need provide a highly reliable information. Based on previous researches numerous IC scientists (Abeysekera, 2006; Dumay and Cai, 2015; Secundo et al., 2016) have stated that conducting traditional ICD through annual reports will cause the emergence of unreliable information, because annual report is not designed to concentrate exclusively on IC reporting. By using web-based disclosure, university can provide greater transparency, reliability and accessibility in disclosing intellectual capital information with minimum cost (Gallego-Alvarez et al., 2011).

Competitiveness and Web-based ICD

The result of this research shows that competitiveness gives no significant influence toward web-based intellectual capital disclosure. Thus, the result of this research is in contrary with the result of previous study (Chen and Chen, 2013). This may be cause by the awareness for Indonesian universities to compete globally is still low. The number of Higher Education Institution in Indonesia in 2018 has been increased to 4,270, consisting of universities, polytechnics, academies and institutes (Director General of Higher Education, 2014). However, based on QS World University Ranking, since 2015 until 2018 period, the number of Indonesian universities that are recognised as higher education that has fulfilled international standard are still 9. Based on the college rankings released by the QS World University Ranking, in 2018 the best ranking that universities were able to achieve in Indonesia was ranked only 277 achieved by the University of Indonesia (UI), even in 2019, the ranking achieved actually declined to rank 292. This indicate that an increase in the number of tertiary institutions in Indonesia has not been followed by awareness of Indonesian universities to increase their competitiveness. It can be concluded that Indonesian universities don't use web-based intellectual capital disclosure as the primary tool in maintaining or even rise the university's quality that is recognised internationally, because of the low awareness in increasing the competitiveness in global manner still exist among Indonesian universities.

Age and Web-based ICD

From the statistical point of view, the result of this research shows that age give no significant influence toward web-based intellectual capital disclosure, which indicate that this research is in line with the result of previous study (Gallego-Alvarez et al., 2011; Bisogno et al., 2014; Rossi et al., 2018) which stated that age has no significant effect toward web-based intellectual capital disclosure. This inconsistent result are caused by two things, namely: (1). Age is not a mirror of experience and understanding in intellectual capital disclosure, the longer the age of the company does not mean the better level of understanding and experience related to intellectual capital will be achieved, resulting in capital disclosure intellectuals cannot be optimal. (2) Age cannot be used as benchmarks for the extent of intellectual capital disclosure because the functions and roles of government that are less than optimal are generally occur in developing countries like Indonesia, that is indicated by higher of corruption, collusion and nepotism, ineffective policies and efficient, and bureaucratic malfunctions.

Size and Web-based ICD

Size which is reflected in number of student give highly positive significant influence toward web-based intellectual capital disclosure which indicate that this research is in line with the result of previous study (Gallego-Alvarez et al., 2011;) which stated that size reflected as the number of student has significant effect toward web-based intellectual capital disclosure. Furthermore, the new indicator in measuring size that is reflected as the number of lecturer show the similar result as size that is reflected as the number of student which is positive significant relationship exist between number of lecturer toward web-based intellectual capital disclosure with coefficient value of 0.177 and p-value of 0.046. This means the result is in line with the statement of Garcìa-Sànchez et al. (2013) that said number of customer and organizational worker should be included as the indicator in measuring size. If it is related to university perspective, number of student is the customer and number of lecturer is the organizational worker. Therefore, it can be concluded that the more number of student and lecturer own by university the higher education do more web-based intellectual capital disclosure. The reason is because larger universities possess a wider number of audience and resulting in the needs of maintaining their institution images through intensive disclosure on the internet (Gallego-Alvarez et al., 2011). In addition, bigger public entity more politically noticeable and are liable to more prominent outer impact from their stakeholder network, for example citizens, governments, understudies (Gallego-Alvarez et al., 2011; Garcìa-Sànchez et al., 2013; Rossi et al., 2018)

CONCLUSION

The purpose of this research is to find out the existence regarding the new method in disclosing intellectual capital called as web-based intellectual capital disclosure to overcome the limitation of traditional intellectual capital disclosure and also examine the determinant factors that may influence web-based intellectual capital disclosure of Indonesian universities such as autonomy, competitiveness, age, and size. The sample used in this research comes from Indonesian higher education institution which have A accreditation and have official websites. The total number of sample that fulfil the sampling criteria are 83 Indonesian universities. The observation period is 1 year which is 2018 period.

Independent variables that are incorporated in this research are autonomy (divided into three levels which are legal entity state university, public service agency state university, and private university), competitiveness (QS World University Ranking), age, and size (number of student and number of lecturer). The dependent variable that is used in this paper is web-based intellectual capital disclosure (intellectual capital disclosure item and web accessibility item).

In addition, the result of this research show that there is an evidence about the usage of web-based intellectual capital disclosure done by Indonesian universities. Furthermore, autonomy and size give positive impact toward web-based intellectual capital disclosure, while age and competitiveness give no significant effect to web-based intellectual capital disclosure. Based on the statistical result, autonomy give the highest contribution regarding the impact toward web-based intellectual capital disclosure among other determinant factors displayed through the effect size of autonomy to web-based intellectual capital disclosure. The reason is because autonomy provide freedom for universities in managing their institution in order to develop better intellectual capital (core competitiveness for university) resulting in attracting more government and public fund.

This paper also provide suggestion for university management to utilize autonomy in increasing disclosure of intellectual capital through websites resulting in attracting more public and government fund and displaying the information regarding university's size through the number of student and lecturer that can also enhance web-based intellectual capital disclosure that can help university to gain more students and lecturer. For the stakeholders of university, intellectual capital disclosure done through website can increase the understanding and reliability regarding the information about the performance of university. Furthermore, through website it can enhance the accessibility and presentation regarding the information about intellectual capital disclosure done by higher education institution.

There are some limitations that might affect the study of the research, these limitations are described to improve further studies in the future. First limitation of this study is regarding the R Square. The R Square number is considered to be low, showing that there are other variables that have an effect but not included in the study. In addition, the number of samples used is still too small compared to the number of universities in Indonesia. Another limitation of this study is that it only covers Indonesian universities as the sample for the research. Future studies could be improved by do benchmarking with universities in the other country. When this is included, a better comparison can be drawn up too in terms of comparing universities based on its reputation and how it impacts towards web-based intellectual capital disclosure in global scope. Suggestion for further research are the process of reviewing the web-based intellectual capital item on the official website of higher education should be conducted by more than one person, to enhance the reliability of the data acquired. In addition, testing new variables obtained through a more in-depth study and increase the amount of research sample should be done in for the future study.

REFERENCES

Abeysekera, I. (2006). The project of intellectual capital disclosure: Researching the research. *Journal of Intellectual Capital*, *7*(1), 61–77. doi:10.1108/14691930610639778

Bergh, D. D., Connelly, B. L., Ketchen, D. J. Jr, & Shannon, L. M. (2014). Signalling theory and equilibrium in strategic management research: An assessment and a research agenda. *Journal of Management Studies*, *51*(8), 1334–1360. doi:10.1111/joms.12097

Bezhani, I. (2010). Intellectual capital reporting at UK universities. *Journal of Intellectual Capital*, *11*(2), 179–207. doi:10.1108/14691931011039679

Bisogno, M., Citro, F., & Tommasetti, A. (2014). Disclosure of university websites. Evidence from Italian data. *Global Business and Economics Review*, *16*(4), 452–471. doi:10.1504/GBER.2014.065365

Business Dictionary. (2019). *Research methodology. Web Finance*. Retrieved from http://www.businessdictionary.com

Chen, I-S., & Chen, J-K. (2013). Present and future: a trend forecasting and ranking of university types for innovative development from an intellectual capital perspective. *Quality and Quantity*, *47*(1), 335-352.

Connelly, B. L., Certo, S. T., Ireland, R. D., & Reutzel, C. R. (2011). Signalling theory: A review and assessment. *Journal of Management*, *37*(1), 39–67. doi:10.1177/0149206310388419

Consejo Superior de Investigaciones Científicas (CSIC). (n.d.). *Ranking Web of Universities*. Retrieved from http://www.webometrics.info/en

Cricelli, L., Greco, M., Grimaldi, M., & Dueñas, L. P. (2018). Intellectual capital and university performance in emerging countries. *Journal of Intellectual Capital*, *19*(1), 71–95. doi:10.1108/JIC-02-2017-0037

Dumay, J., & Cai, L. (2015). Using content analysis as a research methodology for investigating intellectual capital disclosure: A critique. *Journal of Intellectual Capital*, *16*(1), 121–155. doi:10.1108/JIC-04-2014-0043

Dumay, J., & Guthrie, J. (2017). Involuntary disclosure of intellectual capital: Is it relevant? *Journal of Intellectual Capital*, *18*(1), 29–44. doi:10.1108/JIC-10-2016-0102

Edvinsson, L. (2013). Reflections from 21 years of IC practice and theory. *Journal of Intellectual Capital*, *14*(1), 163–172. doi:10.1108/14691931311289075

Gallego-Alvarez, I., Rodríguez-Domínguez, L., & García-Sánchez, I. M. (2011). Information disclosed online by Spanish universities: Content and explanatory factors. *Online Information Review*, *35*(3), 360–385. doi:10.1108/14684521111151423

García-Sánchez, I., Frías-Aceituno, J., & Rodríguez-Domínguez, L. (2013). Determinants of corporate social disclosure in Spanish local governments. *Journal of Cleaner Production*, *39*, 60–72. doi:10.1016/j.jclepro.2012.08.037

Indonesian Constitution. Law No. 12 of 2012 concerning Higher Education Institutions. Retrieved January from https://unnes.ac.id/wp-content/uploads/uu-12-2012/

Indonesian National Accreditation Body. (2017). *National Higher Education Accreditation System*. Indonesian University National.

Ismail, S., & Bakar, N. B. A. (2011). Reporting practices of Malaysian public universities: The extent of accountability disclosure. *African Journal of Business Management*, *5*(15), 6366–6376.

Kock, N. (2015). *WarpPLS 5.0 User Manual*. Script Warp Systems. Retrieved from http://www.scriptwarp.com/warppls/UserManual_WarpPLS_V3_Redirect.pdf

Low, M., Samkin, G., & Li, Y. (2015). Voluntary reporting of intellectual capital: Comparing the quality of disclosures from New Zealand, Australian and United Kingdom universities. *Journal of Intellectual Capital*, *16*(4), 779–808. doi:10.1108/JIC-03-2015-0022

Marr, B., Schiuma, G., & Neely, A. (2015). Intellectual capital – defining key performance indicators for organizational knowledge assets. *Business Process Management Journal*, *10*(5), 551–569. doi:10.1108/14637150410559225

Ministry of Education and Culture. (2019). *Coordination of Private Universities Edition XII*. Retrieved from: https://www.kemdikbud.go.id/main

Ministry of Research, Technology and Higher Education of the Republic of Indonesia. (2019). *Higher Education Institution*. Retrieved from: https://ristekdikti.go.id

Morariu, C. M. (2013). The determinants of intellectual capital disclosure: Evidence from Romania. *Research in Accounting in Emerging Economies*, *13*, 163–186.

Online Indonesian Dictionary. (2019). *Autonomy Ministry of Education and Culture*. Retrieved from: https://kbbi.kemdikbud.go.id

Rahayuningtas, D. P. A., & Triana, E. (2017). Intellectual capital and higher education competitiveness. *Journal of Accounting and Investment*, *16*(1), 154–157.

Ramírez Córcoles, Y., Santos Peñalver, J., & Tejada Ponce, A. (2011). Intellectual capital in Spanish public universities: Stakeholders' information needs. *Journal of Intellectual Capital*, *12*(3), 356–376. doi:10.1108/14691931111154689

Ramírez-Córcoles, Y., Tejada, A., & Manzaneque, M. (2016). The value of disclosing intellectual capital in Spanish universities: A new challenge of our days. *Journal of Organizational Change Management*, *29*(2), 176–198. doi:10.1108/JOCM-02-2015-0025

Rossi, F. M., Nicolò, G., & Polcini, P. T. (2018). New trends in intellectual capital reporting. *Journal of Intellectual Capital*, *19*(4), 814–835. doi:10.1108/JIC-09-2017-0119

Sánchez, M. P., Elena, S., & Castrillo, R. (2009). Intellectual capital dynamics in universities: A reporting model. *Journal of Intellectual Capital*, *10*(2), 307–324. doi:10.1108/14691930910952687

Saxton, G. D., & Guo, C. (2011). Accountability online: Understanding the web-based accountability practices of non-profit organizations. *Voluntary Sector Quarterly*, *40*(2), 270–295. doi:10.1177/0899764009341086

Secundo, G., Dumay, J., Schiuma, G., & Passiante, G. (2016). Managing intellectual capital through a collective intelligence approach: An integrated framework for universities. *Journal of Intellectual Capital*, *17*(2), 298–319. doi:10.1108/JIC-05-2015-0046

Secundo, G., Elena-Perez, S., Martinaitis, Ž., & Leitner, K. H. (2015). An intellectual capital maturity model (ICMM) to improve strategic management in European universities: A dynamic approach. *Journal of Intellectual Capital*, *16*(2), 419–442. doi:10.1108/JIC-06-2014-0072

Serrano-Cinca, C., Gutiérrez-Nieto, B., & Molinero, C. M. (2012). Social and financial Efficiency of Microfinance Institutions. In B. Armendariz & M. Labie (Eds.), *The Handbook of Microfinance*. World scientific publishing.

Sheeja N.K., Susan, M. K., & Cherukodan, S. (2018). Impact of scholarly output on university ranking. *Global Knowledge, Memory and Communication*, 1-8.

Siboni, B., Nardo, M. T., & Sangiorgi, D. (2013). Italian state university contemporary performance plans: An intellectual capital focus? *Journal of Intellectual Capital*, *14*(3), 414–430. doi:10.1108/JIC-03-2013-0033

Solimun, F.A.A.A., & Nurjannah. (2017). Multivariate Statistics Method - Structural Equation Modelling (SEM) WarpPLS Approach. Indonesia: UB Press.

Symonds, Q. (n.d.). *QS World University Ranking*. Retrieved from: https://www.topuniversities.com

Widyaningdyah, Y. A. U., & Aryan, A. (2015). Intellectual capital and competitive advantage. *Journal of Accounting and Finance*, *15*(1), 3–5.

Wijnhoven, F., Amrit, C., & Dietz, P. (2014). Value-Based file retention. *Journal of Data and Information Quality*, *4*(4), 1–17. doi:10.1145/2567656

Chapter 14
Role of Virtual Laboratories in Teaching Learning Processes of India

Kapilan N.
Nagarjuna College of Engineering and Technology, India

Vidhya P.
SRSMN Government First Grade College, India

ABSTRACT

Laboratory training and exercises provide hands-on experience to the students. However, the limitations in the laboratory facilities in the engineering colleges may affect the teaching and learning process of the future engineers. Hence, Government of India has started an initiative called Virtual Lab to overcome this issue. The premier institutions in India were funded and these institutes are the nodal centre in providing virtual lab facilities to colleges which do not have sophisticated laboratory facilities. The advancement in IT and internet facilities can no more hamper students and researchers in enhancing their skills and knowledge. Also, in a country such as India, costly instruments and equipment need to be shared with fellow researchers to the greatest extent possible. This chapter discusses and highlights the Virtual Lab initiatives and implementations.

INTRODUCTION

The development of any country depends upon the skilled manpower and educated population. The education increases productivity and creativity of the people and also and promotes technological advancement. It plays a crucial role in country's economic growth and social progress. India's educational policy focuses on improvement in literacy rate and a number of initiates were taken to promote primary and higher education. The importance is given in science and engineering education to improve employability and to meet demand of the industries. The effectiveness of teaching and learning process is very important to impart necessary knowledge to the students (Lynette, et al. 2010). The younger population

DOI: 10.4018/978-1-7998-4972-8.ch014

Copyright © 2021, IGI Global. Copying or distributing in print or electronic forms without written permission of IGI Global is prohibited.

is high in India and it can be educated for the development of the country (Mohan Gautam, 2016). The employability of educated population increases with the skill set. The candidate may be under employment if lacks necessary knowledge and skill set (Nadar, 2018). The higher education system in India faces many challenges due to faculty shortage, poor curriculum, untrained staff etc. Hence state and central governments have taken many steps to improve educational quality (Anubhav, 2015).

In the laboratory, students follow standard laboratory protocol and perform experiments to meet the pre-determined outcome. The teaching and learning process in science and engineering education may be augmented with the laboratory classes. The laboratory classes help the students to understand the concept and hence play a key role in understanding the theoretical concept, collection and interpretation of data and report writing etc. Also students' observation capability, results and analyzing skills are improved. Hence it is suggested that the laboratory components may be introduced in each subject for better understanding (Lyle, et al., 2005). The development of innovative design oriented laboratory will engage the students in laboratory activities and students spend long time in the laboratory (Dunne & Ryan, 2010). This will enhance the students' learnability (Kirschner & Meester, 1988). The well maintained equipments, competent instructors and faculty members are essential for this (Edward, 1983). The learning of theory subjects may be improved with the help of laboratory experiments (Gian et al. 2018). The students get practical experience in the laboratory and also understand laboratory safety guidelines, safety labels, storage and handling of hazard materials (Romklao, 2012). Both the theoretical and experimental knowledge is important for the students (Lyle et al. 2005). The course syllabus and teaching methodology affects the learnability (Wallace & Kang, 2004). The prior knowledge on laboratory experiments and experimentation procedure help the students to understand the concept effectively (Julia & Kilian, 2016).

It is reported that the students face problems in understanding the content knowledge and instructions in the laboratory class (Ayse, et al. 2017). The qualitative research work carried out reveals the problems related to laboratory, staff members and fellow students (Özlem & Murat, 2013). The students will be motivated in learning process if the laboratory has latest laboratory equipments and instruments (Romanas et al. 2007). The students' learnability can be improved if they come prepared for the laboratory (Rodgers, et al., 2020). It is reported that the students lack team activities in the laboratory environment as they do not perceive team roles as a key parameter in success and productivity (Laura, et al. 2018). The students' critical thinking to perform the experiments and deep learning is low in the conventional teaching and learning process. One of the best methods in improving learning process of the students is virtual laboratories (VLs). The objective of this book chapter is discuss about VLs, types of VLs, review of success of VLs, advantages and limitations of the VLs.

BACKGROUND

The conventional teaching methods is teacher centered and in this method students are taught and learn through recitation techniques, memorization etc. The students demonstrate their knowledge based on the information absorbed in the class. The teachers adopt different techniques such as questioning, demonstrating, collaborating etc, which provide multiple learning styles to the students in understanding the subjects. However it is not developing students' problem solving, critical thinking and decision making skills. The e-learning is getting popularity in recent years and particularly in mathematics and engineering courses. The learners' knowledge can be tested based on their level of understanding (Gurudeo,

2018). It is necessary to indentify new methods of motivating students. The questions aligned with the learning outcomes may be asked in examination and prompt feedback may be given with suggestions to improve their learning level (Arturo, 2018). The development in information technologies is significant and teachers should be trained in this area so that they can effectively use this technology for teaching and learning process. The teacher should be given academic freedom in using information communication technology (ICT) tools in class rooms (Valbona & Mimoza, 2017).

It is reported that ICT integration has positive impact on both students and teachers. This technology will be successful if the teachers are well equipped with ICT tools and their preparation in handling the ICT tools in class room. The regular teachers training on ICT tools will play a key role in developing the skill-set of the teachers and it will ensure quality learning of the students (Ghavifekr & Rosdy, 2015). The ICT tools help the students in active learning and have great potential in augmenting teaching and learning process. Also it helps to introduce innovation in teaching and overcome barriers in learning (Neha, 2019).

India's higher education system consists of educational programs such as diploma, under graduation, post graduation, doctoral etc. The large numbers of this type of educational institutions offering these programs are owned by private entities. The facilities such as class rooms, laboratories, library, etc and well qualified teachers helps to attain program specific outcomes. However, inculcating knowledge among students and their professional competencies and further studies is important (Debarun, 2018).

The virtual laboratory (VL) is the virtual teaching and learning environment and provide interactive environment for carrying out the virtual experiments. This e-learning resource improves the accessibility of experimental setups providing a distance teaching framework. The remote triggered VL experiments enhance both theoretical and practical learning experience using real time data streaming and analysis (Rathod & Kalbande, 2016). The students learning experience in VLs can be supplement to the conventional laboratories. For the effective VLs, expertise and novelties are important. Most of the VLs are free and also helps the students to do independent evaluation (Rossiter et al. 2018). The VLs can play a key role in vocational education as the institutions offering this program lack latest instruments or equipments. The famous VLs are MIT OCW, HHMI Biomedical Interactive labs and the VLs Media Library at Summit, Stanford.

MAIN FOCUS OF THE CHAPTER

The number of educational institutions in India is increasing every year due to increase in enrollment of students in higher educations. However, few institutions do not have expensive equipments or devices in the laboratory and also do not have qualified and experienced faculty members. These issues affect the learning of the students and also affect the employability of the fresh graduates. The educational institutions have funding problems to upgrade the laboratory facilities to meet the requirements of the industries due to lower fee, poor admission in traditional branches etc. The industries say that the fresh graduates do not have skill sets and suggest imparting effective hands-on training in institutions to fill the gap between institutions and industries. Hence it is necessary to equip educational institutions with necessary laboratory facilities with well qualified faculty and staff members. Hence government of India has taken several initiatives to improve the learning process of the students. One of the solutions suggested is the introduction of VLs in educational institutions which are developed by the premier

Figure 1. Simulation based VL

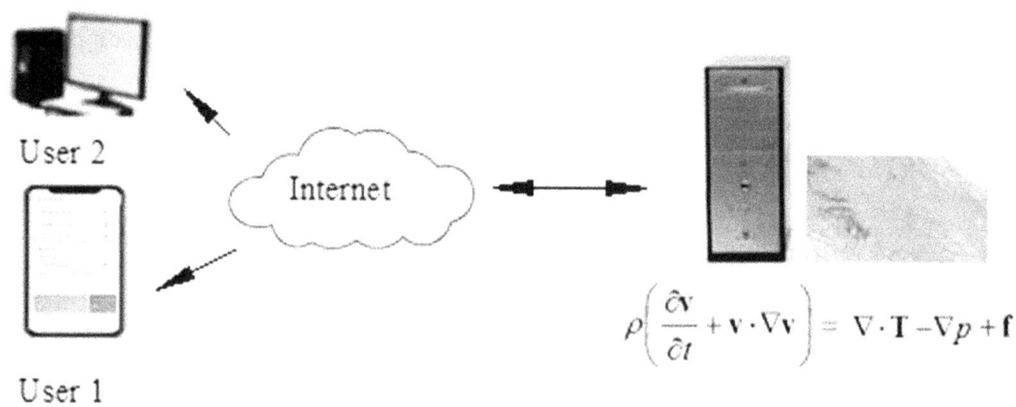

institutions such as Indian institute of technologies (IITs) and Universities. Different types of VLs are developed to meet the effective learning process of different branches of students.

SOLUTIONS AND RECOMMENDATIONS

The VLs is divided into three categories such as simulation type, measurement type and remote triggered type VLs. The mathematical equations are used in the experiment modeling of simulation type VLs. It shows hypothetical environment on a computer and the user carryout the simulation experiments and understands the working principle. This VL also helps to predict the behavior of the system. The experiments can be repeated several times, till the students acquire technical skills (Banks, 2001). Figure 1 shows the simulation based VL experiments.

The measurement laboratory is similar to the simulation VLs and helps the students to perform experiments related to measurements. Figure 2 show the measurement based VL experiments.

The remote triggered VL experiments are remotely conducted on the real time laboratory experiments through the Internet. The user performs the real time experiments and gets the experimental results and videos of the experimentation through internet. The experimental results are given in form of table as well as charts for better analysis (Petros et al. 2012). Figure 3 shows the remote triggered VL experiments.

Impact of Virtual Laboratories

An evaluation work conducted on VL at university of Hong Kong suggests that the VLs can be used as a supplement to the conventional laboratory to enhance the students' knowledge (Cecilia & Wilton, 2009). The study carried out in Denmark reports that the VL allows interactive learning, understanding the operation of equipments and also to analyze the results of the experiments. The students are comfortable

Figure 2. Measurement type VL

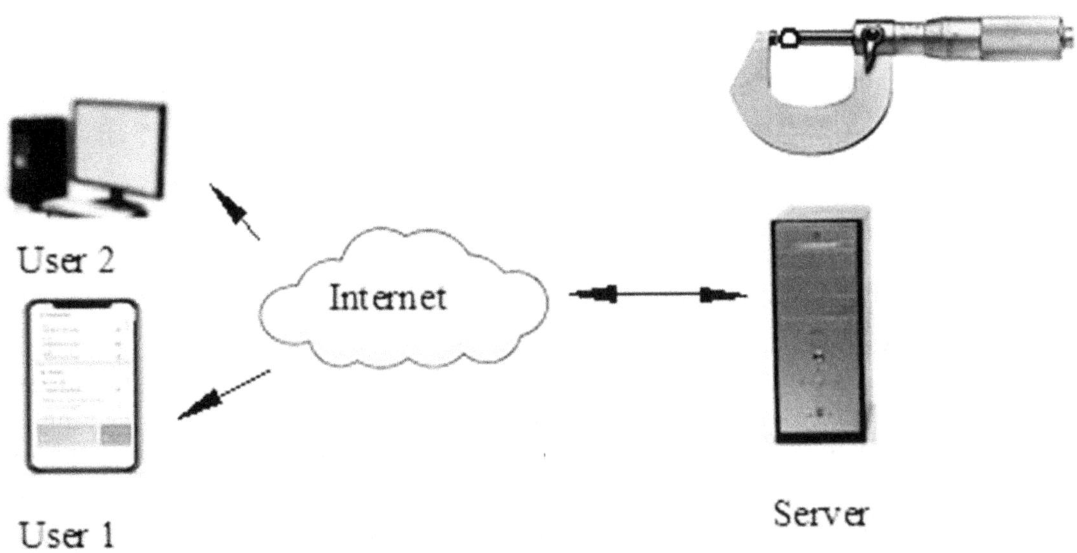

in handling laboratory equipment and also actively engaged in laboratory work with confident after attending VLs. The staff members said that the students had good interaction with them (Nadia et al. 2016).

The study carried out at China shows that the VL can be used as a new pedagogical tool for undergraduate students to prepare for the laboratory and suggest that blended laboratories are the best laboratory (Rong et al. 2018). The work carried out at Taiwan shows that VLs can improve students understanding and also to enrich students' knowledge (Wen, 2010). The work carried out at Spanish university

Figure 3. Remote triggered VL

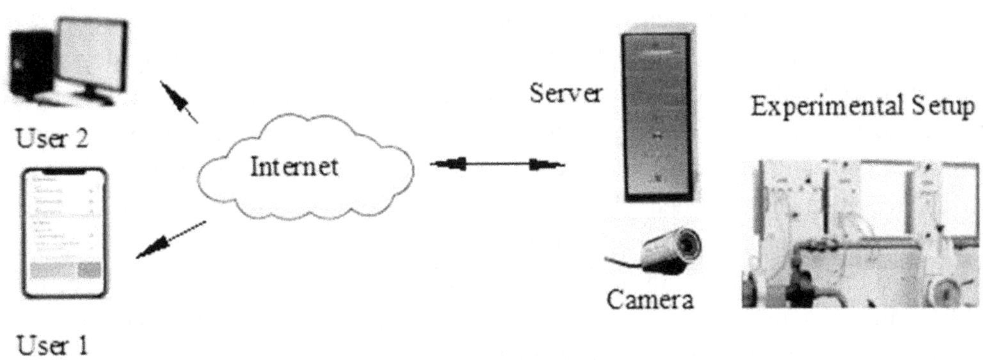

reveals that the VLs can open new perspectives for higher education sustainability (Esther et al. 2018). The outcome of the study carried out at Indonesia suggested that the VL has higher efficiency than the conventional laboratory in vocational training. The students became independent learner and used VL in flexible manner and reported that the VLs are economical as compared to conventional laboratory (Wisnu et al. 2019). The VL activities play a key role in supporting scientific learning fields and also to obtain practical skills. It also gives a chance for better understanding of the laboratory content as per the survey conducted at Saudi Arabia (Khulood et al. 2018). The study carried out at Slovenia shows that VL helps in better understanding of knowledge acquisition (Nataša, 2016).

Virtual Laboratories in India

The Ministry of Human Resource Department (MHRD) has established several VLs in premier institutions and universities in India, under the scheme national mission on education through ICT with an initial budget of about five billion Indian currency values. The aim of this scheme is to provide remote access to laboratories to the students of different engineering institutions. The VLs were setup for different engineering and science branches, at all levels starting from under graduate to research level. The additional web resources, video lectures, self evaluation using quizzes and demonstration using animation were also included in the VLs. In the remote triggered VLs helps to conduct hands-on experiments on costly experimental setup and the expenses can be shared by the institutions which use the VLs facilities. Presently, the remote triggered VLs established in the government institutions do not charge any fee as these laboratories were established with the grant give by the government of India. The government of India has established VLs in premier Indian Institutes such as IIT Bombay, IIT Madras, IIT Delhi, IIT Kanpur, IIT Kharagpur, IIT Roorkee and IIT Guwahati, Amrita University, IIIT Hyderabad, Dayalbagh University, NITK Surathkal and College of Engineering, Pune. These institutions and universities offers VL experiments in various engineering branches such as mechanical engineering, computer science and engineering, chemical engineering, biotechnology engineering, electronics and communications, electrical engineering and civil engineering. The VLs offered in science branches are physics; chemistry, mathematics and biology (Wikipedia, 2020). For example, Amrita University with the support of government of India offers VLs in 23 biotechnology discipline with 211 experiments.

In India, the VL experiments were prepared based on the syllabus of university grants commission and all India council for technical education. The VLs experimental protocol was first standardized based on journal articles, codes and text book references. The software development is carried out in the next step to carryout modeling and to present the results in animated mode with results. The virtualization steps of the VLs make the VL experiment close to real laboratory scenario. The theory sections are included in the VLs to provide few basic concepts related to the experiments. The step by step procedures with figures are provided to perform the experiments easily. The additional literatures related to experiments are given in the VLs for further reading of the user. The user can attend quiz to do self evaluation. A set of questions are given in the assignment section as a part of VL examination. The actual experimentation is video recorded and uploaded for better understanding and also to provide visual experience. The user can give suggestions about VLs in the feedback section to enhance the quality of VL experiments. The user has to login into the VL through internet, to access the VLs as it helps to track the number of users. The simulation and measurement type VLs can be performed anytime and anywhere. The two dimensional Adobe Flash player is used in the simulated VL experiments as it faster and reduces server issues. However, prior booking is necessary to perform the remote triggered VL experiments as it is a real experimentation and needs manual interventions. The remote triggered VLs are expensive as it uses real equipments and needs proper instrumentations and controls. Also the operating and maintenance cost of this type of VLs are higher than the other types of VLs. Few institutions are having this type of VLs (Indian, 2020).

In India, VLs help the educational institutions to expand their academic reach, to reach academic excellence, reduce their operating cost and for effective training. The online courses help the working professional to continue their education as it is flexible. Few academic institutions offer online courses and uses VLs to give laboratory practice (Makransky, 2019). The government of India has taken several steps to improve teaching and learning by mobilizing the resources and introduced a number of initiatives. The establishment of VLs helps the educational institutions in remote and rural areas to adopt new teaching pedagogy. Also it helps to increase the enrollment of students in higher education as the admission to higher education depends upon the locality and may depends upon household decision. Also the VLs enhance the learning independence and the ability to understand concepts (Walid et al. 2014).

More than 300 department heads, teaching and non-teaching staff members of more than 52 educational institutions attended the VLs training. More than 20 nodal centers have been established in different locations in India to meet the need of a particular region.

The pilot phase of VL was started in India during 2009 and 20 VLs were established as proof of concept and main phase was started in 2010. The number of VLs is gradually increased and presently more than 80 VLs were established. The effectiveness of the VLs is improved based on the feedback received from the user and stake holders. The nodal centers of VLs are started in recent years which take care of the local and regional needs. The nodal centers conduct awareness workshop on VLs. The remote triggered VLs increase the collaboration between researchers of various institutions as the researchers can share their research facilities (Eletsonline. 2010). The research work carried out at IIT Bombay can help other institutions for joint research collaboration through VLs (Sandipan et al. 2012). The effectiveness of the VL is evaluated based on the students' performance in the examination (Anita et al. 2016). The self assessment can be done through quizzes and assignments. It is suggested that the limitations of the conventional education system can be improved with ICT and VL will supplement it (Diwakar et al. 2015).

Roles of Virtual Laboratories

The introduction of ICT in educational sectors have generated opportunities to the under developed and developing countries to augment the teaching and learning process. The advancement in information technology and infrastructure makes the VLs as one of the tool to improve the teaching and learning process and also helps to overcome constrains in the educational sector. In the technical education system, practical knowledge is as important as theory courses. The VL assists the technical institutions to overcome the problems and issues associated with the laboratory classes as the VLs assist the students to familiarize with laboratory procedures and also to conduct the laboratory experiments remotely without any direct contact with the laboratory equipment (Seiler et al. 2015). The VL is a cost effective as the expenses can be shared by several institutions and also it is a sustainable educational tool in providing a hands-on laboratory experiment. It is boon to financially depressed institutions to overcome their problems associated which their institution's laboratories and also complement to conventional laboratories (Chan & Fok, 2009). The effectiveness of the VLs laboratories associated with mechanical engineering was measured using a model and it reveals that the user have a realistic understanding of the experiments and reports that VLs are comparable to conventional laboratories in problem solving (Jeffrey et al. 2007). The outcome of the hybrid learning with virtual chemistry laboratory reveals improvement in students learning and also helps to resolve the limitation (Solikhin et al. 2019). The roles of VLs in teaching and learning processes are discussed below.

1. Student engagement and academic performance

The students' zeal on practical courses may reduce if the students face several hurdles in conventional laboratory practice. The VLs have several challenges such as limited equipment, time constraint, lack of safety equipments and supporting staff, etc, which affects the students' interest in laboratory and learning process. Few studies reported that a significant percentage of students discontinue their courses due to lack of interest; however VL increases student engagement and excitement. Few studies show that introduction of VLs augment students' performance in examination (Cecilia & Wilton, 2009).

2. Critical Thinking

The critical thinking is an intentional and reflective way of looking at things and to find creative solutions to the problem. It is reported that the VL helps in increasing the critical thinking, creativity and conceptual understanding of the students in the class room. It was suggested that the teachers have to use VLs to improve teaching quality and students' learning outcomes (Firman & Irwanto. 2017).

3. Problem Solving Skill

The results of the work carried out at Mataram University shows that the problem solving skills of the students can be improved with VL. It is also suggested that the experimental group has better planning and implementing problem solving skill as compared to control group (Gunawan et al. 2017). It is suggested that the ability to do networking and problem solving is important (Hämäläinen et al. 2015).

4. Distance learning

The distance learning mode is picking up and most of the working professionals join distance learning course due to flexibility in timing and cost. In spite of several advantages, this type of learning process is not effective. The integration of VLs and distance learning will enable distance learning students to develop skills and provides a virtual hands-on experience. It is suggested that the VL can facilitate distance learning programs in educational fields without compromising quality (Dongfeng et al. 2015).

5. Students' Learnability

Few studies shows that the students prefer to participate in VLs as compared to conventional laboratories. The results also show that students perceived higher learning gains due to their participation in VLs as compared to conventional laboratories (Veljko et al. 2016).

6. Curriculum Development

Few studies show that the poor quality of fresh graduates is due to poor curriculum, lack of knowledge and confidence. The curriculum should be modified based on the need of industries to make the fresh graduate employable. The curriculum of the universities should be flexible and should adopt newer technological changes. The VLs can be introduced without much expense as the institutions can share the investment and operating costs with other institutions (Inés et al. 2019).

7. Academic Performance

The VL can enhance the students learning process and attitude as compared to conventional learning method. The outcome of few case studies shows that the students understanding of concepts are better in VL over conventional methods. Few studies suggested that the VL can be used to prepare students for practical experience and also to improve their self-confidence to solve real problems (Abdulla et al. 2018).

8. Safety Issues

The safety in conventional laboratories which use radioactive materials, concentrated acids, highly flammable materials, high voltage equipments etc are important. The VL eliminates risks associated with these types of experiments. The VL is an ideal platform which gives an exposure to students before attending this type of experiments and improves safety concerns (Romklao, 2012).

9. Sustainability

The simulation type of VL does not wear out, requires lower operating cost and has longer life. The cost of science, technology engineering and mathematics (STEM) VLs is cheap and the students can repeat experiment anytime and anywhere without the help of the staff members. The VLs are web-based and any additional requirement in infrastructure may be added without much investment. The maintenance, servicing and operating cost of the VLs are low and hence VLs are sustainable.

10. Anytime and Anywhere Facility

The VL is accessed through internet and hence it can be used anytime and anywhere so as not to interfere with the lesson (Hidayat & Utomo, 2015). In recent day's online learning has become popular throughout the world due to COVID-19 and also it reduces the temporal and spatial problems associated with this form of education. Most of the educational institutions successfully used online educations and students are getting adjusted to this system. The online learning is also beneficial to students because it can be learned by the students on their own.

Advantages of Virtual Lab

The major advantages in VLs are as follows

1. No limitation on number of users

In simulation type VLs, any number of students from different institutions can perform the experiments without any restriction. The student can perform the experiments with their friends and compare and discuss the results with their classmates for better understanding.

2. Easy accessibility with any time and from any place

The VLs gives flexibility to the students to perform the VL experiments any time from any place. This will be useful to the students when they are preparing for the examination.

3. No restrictions on number of repetitions

The students are permitted to repeat the VLs any number of times without any restrictions. This helps the students to familiarize with the working principle and concept. Also it improves their confidence in performing the experiments on their own without much supervision.

4. Better safety and security

The safety guidelines should be strictly followed while performing real laboratory experiments and most of the time laboratory instructor perform the experiments and students note down the readings, if the experimental setup is expensive. Also in real laboratory setup, equipment or device may be damaged or misplaced by the students. These types of problems are totally eliminated in VLs.

5. Lower operating and maintenance cost

The experimental setup used in real laboratory needs consumables such as work piece / fuel etc, to conduct the experiments. Also regular maintenance work / servicing has to be carried out as per the service manual. The maintenance cost is generally high if the equipment is expensive. If the institute is using VLs, then the operating and maintenance cost is reduced drastically.

6. Lower initial cost and easy to setup

The institute has to invest only on computers, internet connectivity, UPS, furniture to setup computer laboratory for the VLs facility. Hence, the initial cost to setup VLs in institute is low and also it is easy to setup.

7. Student centered teaching method

The VLs are developed to meet the requirements of slow and fast learners. The animation and videos related to VLs are available in the VLs. Hence, VL is student centric and will be very much useful to the students.

8. Comfortable and relaxed learning environment

In the real laboratory environment, the students may be uncomfortable due to faculty strictness and disturbance by their classmates during the conduction of experiments. However, in VLs, there is no control or supervision on the students and also the students can repeat the experiments any number of time and till he or she understand the concepts.

9. Greater familiarity with laboratory procedures

The conduction of the VL experiments makes the students to understand the laboratory experimental procedures effectively and get familiarize with the experimental procedures.

10. Improvement in teaching and learning process

The students can perform the experiments after studying the VL materials such as theory, animation and step by step procedure which helps the students to understand the concepts and perform the experiments without any difficulties. The laboratory mistakes such as overloading of the equipments or device will not be problem in simulation type of VLs. Hence students can do experiments on its own which helps in improvement in its learning process.

Limitations of Virtual Lab

The limitations of VLs are as follows

1) Faculty members may not be serious when students performing experiments

In the VL experiments, step by step procedure is given and hence students can do experiments on their own. Hence the faculty members may not be serious in monitoring the learning process of the students. Hence, it is necessary for the faculty members shall ask questions related to VL experiments in regular classes to evaluate level of understanding among students.

2) Distraction in learning

When the students are conducting the virtual lab experiments outside the class, they may be disturbed by their friends or family members at home. Hence the learning process may not be effective in some cases.

3) Lack of hands-on training

The simulation type of experiments will not give hands-on training and students may not know the experimental errors related to the experiments. Also the students may have lack of knowledge in safety procedure and precautions, which should be taken in-case of emergency.

4) Few students do not take it seriously

Few students think that simulation VL experiments are games and do not conduct the experiments with seriousness. They may conduct the VL experiments and may not understand the concept of doing the experiments. It may affect their learning process.

5) Knowledge of information technology is important

The students should have minimum basic computer knowledge so that he can do the VL experiments effectively without any problems.

6) Information Technology infrastructure

The VLs needs good information technology infrastructure and internet connectivity so that the students can perform the experiments. However, in rural and remote areas, internet connectivity is poor and few students may have basic mobile and may not have computer.

7) Limitations of Remote triggered VLs

The remote triggered VLs needs advance booking to perform the experiments. Also this type of VLs cannot be performed by any number of students at any time due to limitations in the preparation of the specimen, loading and unloading of the specimens etc.

FUTURE RESEARCH DIRECTIONS

The present features in the VLs in India are not updated and this has affected the learning process of the students. This problem may be solved by introducing new concepts with augmented reality. Hence further research work can be carried out to include latest technologies for the development of VLs. The challenges in the information and communication technologies may be identified and best solutions can be implemented.

The VLs should be designed with a clear idea about purpose of the VL experiments and context. Appropriate technology should be selected to ensure good level of realism considering quality of the end users. Also suitable learning guides should be provided before and after the VL session. The desktop application architecture and web server should be user friendly. Also it is affordable and requires lower maintenance cost.

If the remote triggered or simulation based VLs breaks down due to major fire or earth quake etc, then alternative arrangement should be readily available so that it will not affect learning process of students. Also this alternative arrangement should be affordable.

The simulation should be simple and easy for the students to understand and remember. Appropriate low cost technology has to be developed to ensure efficient design, realism and media usage. The remote triggered VL experiments are conducted one person at a time. However this facility may be given to any number of students in remote triggered VLs without the possibility to control. However the students can watch and attend to real events mimicked by the virtual surrounding (Pascalis et al. 2020).

The VLs should have the facilities for the under graduate engineering students to carry out their project work (Michae, 2016). The VL should have the facilities to solve real time engineering problems with high environmental relevance as it gives the students a real time industrial experience (Juan et al. 2020). Also the mobile VLs may be developed to meet the requirements of the students (Adrián et al. 2018).

CONCLUSION

The Industry 4.0 needs skilled manpower to meet the expectations of the industry. The VL, which is a web-based platform improves teaching and learning approaches and introduces safe and interactive lab environment. The higher educational institutions which do not have the sophisticated laboratory may have negative impact on students learning process. The students who graduated from these types of institutions may not have any technical and hands-on experience. The VLs offer many features that can be optimized to support more effective and efficient learning. The academic stakeholders appreciate the introduction of VLs in learning process as it helps the institutions to meet industrial revolution 4.0.

Different types of VLs are developed to meet the requirements of the students and the educational institutions. The remote triggered VLs may help the students to get a hands-on experience on the real machine. But the booking of these VL experiments is difficult and students may not able to get a chance to do real time experiments. There are many advantages in using VLs in learning process. However there are few limitations and it can be overcome by the involvement of all the stake holders who are involved in teaching and learning process. The advancement in IT technologies and IT infrastructure helps to implement VLs easily in rural areas. However this facility cannot be accessed by the students who are in remote areas due to internet connectivity issues.

Several studies reported that the VLs benefits students and faculty members in teaching and learning process. Few studies show that the students' critical thinking and problem solving skills improved in VLs. Also it is suggested that the students' performance in conventional laboratory can be improved with the help of VLs. However, VLs have few challenges which have to be addressed. The VLs helps to save cost, time and effort as compared to conventional laboratory and play a key role in the teaching and learning process.

ACKNOWLEDGMENT

This research received no specific grant from any funding agency. This research work was supported by Virtual Lab nodal centre of NCET, India.

REFERENCES

Afacan, Ö., & Demirbaş, M. (2013). The problems that science and technology teachers face in science laboratory. *Balkan Physics Letters*, *21*(211006), 51–64.

Aljuhani, K., Sonbul, M., Althabiti, M., & Meccawy, M. (2018). Creating a Virtual Science Lab (VSL): The adoption of virtual labs in Saudi schools. *Smart Learning Environments*, *5*(1), 1–13. doi:10.118640561-018-0067-9

Ambusaidi, A., Al-Mosawi, A., Al-Balushi, S., & Al-Balushi, K. (2018). The impact of virtual lab learning experiences on 9th grade students' achievement and their attitudes towards science and learning by virtual lab. *Journal of Turkish Science Education, 15*(2), 13–29.

Artdej, R. (2012). Investigating Undergraduate Students' Scientific Understanding of Laboratory Safety. *Procedia: Social and Behavioral Sciences, 46*, 5058–5062. doi:10.1016/j.sbspro.2012.06.385

Axaopoulos, P. J., Moutsopoulos, K. N., & Theodoridis, M. P. (2012). Engineering education using a remote laboratory through the Internet. *European Journal of Engineering Education, 37*(1), 39–48. do i:10.1080/03043797.2011.644764

Balid, W., Abdulwahed, M., & Alrouh, I. (2014). Development of an educationally oriented open-source embedded systems laboratory kit: A hybrid hands-on and virtual experimentation approach. *International Journal of Electrical Engineering Education, 51*(4), 340–353. doi:10.7227/ijeee.0006

Balliu, V., & Belshi, M. (2017). Modern Teaching versus Traditional Teaching-Albanian Teachers between Challenges and Choices. *European Journal of Multidisciplinary Studies, 2*(4), 20–26. doi:10.26417/ejms.v4i4.p20-26

Banks, J., Carson, B. N., & Nicol. (2001). Discrete-Event System Simulation. Prentice Hall.

Brüggemann & Bizer. (2016). Laboratory experiments in innovation research: a methodological overview and a review of the current literature. *Journal of Innovation and Entrepreneurship, 5*, Article number 24.

Chakraborty, D., Dhara, S. K., & Santra, A. (2018). Effectiveness of ICT in Strengthening the Process of Higher Education System in India, *Amity. Journal of Management Research, 3*(1), 40–53.

Chan, C., & Fok, W. (2009). Evaluating learning experiences in virtual laboratory training through student perceptions: A case study in Electrical and Electronic Engineering at the University of Hong Kong. *Engineering Education, 4*(2), 70–75. doi:10.11120/ened.2009.04020070

Chan, C., & Fok, W. (2009). Evaluating learning experiences in virtual laboratory training through student perceptions: A case study in Electrical and Electronic Engineering at the University of Hong Kong. *Engineering Education, 4*(2), 70–75. doi:10.11120/ened.2009.04020070

Diwakar, Kumar, Radhamani, Nizar, Nair, & Sasidharakur. (2015). Role of ICT-enabled virtual laboratories in biotechnology education: Case studies on blended and remote learning. *International Conference on Interactive Collaborative Learning (ICL)*, 915-921. 10.1109/ICL.2015.7318149

Diwakar, A. S., & Noronha, S. B. (2016). The Effectiveness of Virtual Labs in Engineering Education-what do we Measure? *Journal of Engineering Education Transformations, 30*(1), 73. doi:10.16920/jeet/2016/v30i1/97425

Dyrberg, N. R., Treusch, A. H., & Wiegand, C. (2016). Virtual laboratories in science education: Students' motivation and experiences in two tertiary biology courses. *Journal of Biological Education, 21*, 1–17.

Eletsonline. (2010). *Digital Learning*. https://digitallearning.eletsonline.com/2012/02/virtual-labs-project-launched-by-mhrd-under-nmeict/

Ernst, E. W. (1983). A New Role for the Undergraduate Engineering Laboratory. *IEEE Transactions on Education*, *26*(2), 49–51. doi:10.1109/TE.1983.4321598

Firman Ramadhan, M., & Irwanto. (2017). Using virtual labs to enhance students' thinking abilities, skills, and scientific attitudes. In *Proceedings of International Conference on Educational Research and Innovation*, (*vol 1*, pp 494-499). Academic Press.

Gautam, M. (2016). Education System in Modern India. *International Journal of Scientific Research and Education*, *4*(1), 4876–4879.

Ghavifekr, S., & Rosdy, W. A. W. (2015). Teaching and learning with technology: Effectiveness of ICT integration in schools. *International Journal of Research in Education and Science*, *1*(2), 175–191. doi:10.21890/ijres.23596

Gian Paolo Cimellaro, & Domaneschi. (2018). Development of Dynamic Laboratory Platform for Earthquake Engineering Courses. *Journal of Professional Issues in Engineering Education and Practice*, *144*(4), 18–26.

Goldberg, L. R., Parham, D., Coufal, K., Maeda, M., Scudder, R. R., & Sechtem, P. R. (2010). Peer Review: The Importance of Education for Best Practice. *Journal of College Teaching and Learning*, *7*(2), 71–84. doi:10.19030/tlc.v7i2.91

González. (2018). Turning a traditional teaching setting into a feedback-rich environment, *International Journal of Educational Technology in Higher Education*, *15*, Article number: 32.

Gunawan Gunawan, Sahidu, & Herayanti. (2017). Virtual laboratory to improve students' problem-solving skills on electricity concept. *Journal Pendidikan IPA Indonesia*, *6*(2), 257-264.

Gupta. (2019). Role of ICT on the Teaching and Learning Process. *Paripex - Indian Journal of Research*, *8*(4), 49-50.

Hämäläinen, R., De Wever, B., Malin, A., & Cincinnato, S. (2015). Education and Working Life: Vet Adults' Problem-Solving Skills in Technology- Rich Environments. *Computers & Education*, *88*(1), 38–47. doi:10.1016/j.compedu.2015.04.013

Herga, N. R. (2016). Virtual Laboratory in the Role of Dynamic Visualisation for Better Understanding of Chemistry in Primary School, *Eurasia Journal of Mathematics. Science & Technology Education*, *12*(3), 593–608.

Hidayat, A., & Utomo, V. G. (2015). Virtual Laboratory Implementation to Support High School Learning. *International Journal of Computers and Applications*, *120*(16), 14–18. doi:10.5120/21310-4283

Indian Institute of Technology Delhi. (2020). *Virtual Labs.* http://www.vlab.co.in/

Julie, D., & Barry, R. (2010). Improving the Undergraduate Laboratory Learning Experience Through Redesigned Teaching and Assessment Strategies Integrating Transferable Skills and Focusing on Feedback. Learning, Teaching & Technology Centre, Dublin Institute of Technology, Paper 21, 1-8.

Kirschner, P. A., & Meester, M. A. M. (1988). The laboratory in higher science education: Problems, premises and objectives. *Higher Education*, *17*(1), 81–98. doi:10.1007/BF00130901

Krivickas, R. V., & Krivickas, J. (2007). Laboratory Instruction in Engineering Education, *Global. Journal of Engineering Education*, *11*(2).

Liu, D., Valdiviezo-Díaz, P., Riofrio, G., Sun, Y.-M., & Barba, R. (2015). Integration of Virtual Labs into Science E-learning. *Procedia Computer Science*, *75*, 95–102. doi:10.1016/j.procs.2015.12.224

Lyle, Feisel, & Rosa. (2005). The Role of the Laboratory in Undergraduate Engineering Education. *The Research Journal for Engineering Education*, *94*(1), 121-130.

Makransky, G., Mayer, R. E., Veitch, N., Hood, M., Christensen, K. B., & Gadegaard, H. (2019). Equivalence of using a desktop virtual reality science simulation at home and in class. *PLoS One*, *14*(4), e0214944. doi:10.1371/journal.pone.0214944 PMID:30973900

Murphy, M. D. (2016). A modular virtual laboratory quadrotor control simulation. *IFAC-Papers on Line*, *49*(6), 93–98. doi:10.1016/j.ifacol.2016.07.159

Nadar, R. N. (2018). Contemporary Issues and Challenges In The Indian Education System. *Journal of Business and Management*, 86–91.

Nickerson, J. V., Corter, J. E., Esche, S. K., & Chassapis, C. (2007). A model for evaluating the effectiveness of remote engineering laboratories and simulations in education. *Computers & Education*, *49*(3), 708–725. doi:10.1016/j.compedu.2005.11.019

Ott, L. E., Kephart, K., Stolle-McAllister, K., & La Course, W. R. (2018). Students' Understanding and Perceptions of Assigned Team Roles in a Classroom Laboratory Environment. *Journal of College Science Teaching*, *47*(4), 83–91. doi:10.2505/4/jcst18_047_04_83 PMID:29681667

Peidró, A., Tendero, C., Marín, J. M., Gil, A., Payá, L., & Reinoso, Ó. (2018). m-PaRoLa: A Mobile Virtual Laboratory for Studying the Kinematics of Five-bar and 3RRR Planar Parallel Robots. *IFAC Papers on Line*, *51*(4), 178–183.

Potkonjak, V., Gardner, M., Callaghan, V., Mattila, P., Guetl, C., Petrović, V. M., & Jovanović, K. (2016). Virtual laboratories for Education in Science, Technology and Engineering: A Review. *Computers & Education*, *95*, 309–327. doi:10.1016/j.compedu.2016.02.002

Ram'ırez, J., Soto, D., Lopez, S., Akroyd, J., Nurkowski, D., Botero, M. L., Bianco, N., Brownbridge, G., Kraft, M., & Molina, A. (in press). A. (2020). Virtual Laboratory to support Chemical Reaction Engineering courses using real-life problems and industrial software. *Education for Chemical Engineers*.

Rathod, S. S., & Kalbande, D. R. (2016). Improving Laboratory Experiences in Engineering Education. *Journal of Engineering Education Transformations*, *29*(4), 51–60.

Ray, S., Koshy, N. R., Diwakar, S., Nair, B., & Srivastava, S. (2012). Sakshat Labs: India's Virtual Proteomics Initiative. *Journal of Engineering Education Transformations*, *10*(7), e1001353. PMID:22802723

Rodgers, T. L., Cheema, N., Vasanth, S., Jamshed, A., Alfutimie, A., & Scully, P. J. (2020). Developing pre-laboratory videos for enhancing student preparedness. *European Journal of Engineering Education*, *45*(2), 292–304. doi:10.1080/03043797.2019.1593322

Rossiter, & Pasik-Duncan, Dormido, Vlacic, Jones, & Murray. (2018). A Survey of Good Practice in Control Education. *European Journal of Engineering Education, 18*, 1–22.

Salmerón-Manzano, E., & Manzano-Agugliaro, F. (2018). The higher education sustainability through virtual laboratories: The Spanish University as case of study. *Sustainability, 10*(11), 1–22. doi:10.3390u10114040

Sasongko, W. D., & Widiastuti, I. (2019). Virtual Lab for Vocational Education in Indonesia: A Review of the Literature. *AIP Conference Proceedings, 2194*, 020113. doi:10.1063/1.5139845

Seiler, S., Ptasik, D., & Sell, R. (2011). Remote and Virtual Labs in a Distance Learning Environment. In *Proceedings of 22nd International Daaam Symposium* (vol. 22, no. 1, pp. 1-12). Academic Press.

Shyr, W. J. (2010). Multiprog virtual laboratory applied to PLC programming learning. *European Journal of Engineering Education, 35*(5), 573–583. doi:10.1080/03043797.2010.497550

Singh, A. (2015). Challenges in Indian Education Sector. *International Journal of Advance Research in Commerce and Management, 1*(3), 54–58.

Solikhin, F., Ikhsan, J., & Sugiyarto, K. H. (2019). A need analysis in developing virtual laboratory according to the chemistry teachers, IOP Conf. Series. *Journal of Physics: Conference Series, 1156*, 012020. doi:10.1088/1742-6596/1156/1/012020

Tejado, I., González, I., Pérez, E., & Merchán, P. (2019). Introducing systems theory with virtual laboratories at the University of Extremadura: How to improve learning in the lab in engineering degrees. *International Journal of Electrical Engineering Education, 20*, 1–26.

Trentsios, P., Wolf, M., & Frerich, S. (2020). Remote Lab meets Virtual Reality – Enabling immersive access to high tech laboratories from afar. *Procedia Manufacturing, 43*, 25–31. doi:10.1016/j.promfg.2020.02.104

Tularam, G. A. (2018). Traditional vs Non-traditional Teaching and Learning Strategies – the case of E-learning! *International Journal for Mathematics Teaching and Learning, 19*(1), 129–158.

Wallace, C. S., & Kang, N. H. (2004). An investigation of experienced secondary science teachers' beliefs about inquiry: An examination of competing belief sets. *Journal of Research in Science Teaching, 41*(9), 32–41. doi:10.1002/tea.20032

Wang, R., Liu, C., & Ma, T. (2018). Evaluation of a virtual neurophysiology laboratory as a new pedagogical tool for medical undergraduate students in China. *Advances in Physiology Education, 42*(4), 704–710. doi:10.1152/advan.00088.2018 PMID:30431325

Wikipedia. (2020). *Virtual Laboratory*. https://en.wikipedia.org/wiki/Virtual_Labs_(India)

Yalcin-Celik, A., Kadayifci, H., Uner, S., & Turan-Oluk, N. (2017). Challenges faced by pre-service chemistry teachers teaching in a laboratory and their solution proposals. *European Journal of Teacher Education, 40*(2), 210–230. doi:10.1080/02619768.2017.1284792

ADDITIONAL READING

Academy. (2020). *Virtual Labs*. https://academy.3ds.com/en/lab/virtual-laboratories

Alphonse, J., & Diwakar, S. (2020). Deploying a Web-based Electroencephalography Data Analysis Virtual Laboratory. *Procedia Computer Science*, *171*, 2420–2425. doi:10.1016/j.procs.2020.04.261

Ballu, A., Yan, X., Blanchard, A., Clet, T., Mouton, S., & Niandou, H. (2016). Virtual metrology laboratory for e-learning. *Procedia CIRP*, *43*, 148–153. doi:10.1016/j.procir.2016.02.110

Grodotzki, J., Ortelt, T. R., & Tekkaya, A. E. (2018). Remote and Virtual Labs for Engineering Education 4.0. *Procedia Manufacturing*, *26*, 1349–1360. doi:10.1016/j.promfg.2018.07.126

Indian Institute of Technology Delhi. (2020). *Virtual Labs*, http://www.vlab.co.in/

Labster. (2020). *Virtual Lab*, https://www.labster.com/

Praxilabs. (2020). *3D Interactive Virtual Labs*, http://praxilabs.com/

Ucalgary. (2020). *The Virtual Laboratory Environment*. https://pages.cpsc.ucalgary.ca/~pwp/bmv/vlab-for-linux/html-docs/environment.html

Chapter 15
The Integration of Educational Technologies in Foreign Language Education:
Teacher Practices and Attitudes in Greece

Varvara Lemonia Oikonomou
CITY College, International Faculty of the University of Sheffield, Greece

Paschalia Patsala
https://orcid.org/0000-0002-4875-3066
Arts and Humanities Research Council, UK

ABSTRACT

The aim of this chapter is to examine the use of educational technologies in foreign language teaching in Greece. It explores whether FL teachers tend to integrate learning tools in their classroom, and if their implementation is affected by teachers' age, gender, level of confidence in using these tools, or any previous training they attended. The most popular technological tools employed in FL teaching are also presented, while the attitude of teachers towards the utilization of learning technologies is thoroughly investigated. A quantitative research method has been adopted with the usage of a web-based questionnaire. Based on the findings retrieved from the responses of a hundred FL teachers, they tend to integrate educational technologies extensively in their teaching practices, mainly to enhance learners' speaking and listening skills. Out of the variables examined, only teachers' confidence in using educational technologies seems to impact the integration of technology in their FL teaching.

DOI: 10.4018/978-1-7998-4972-8.ch015

Copyright © 2021, IGI Global. Copying or distributing in print or electronic forms without written permission of IGI Global is prohibited.

INTRODUCTION

The integration of technology in foreign language (FL) teaching and the necessity to enhance teachers' and students' digital skills have become even more prominent issues of great educational significance during the past decades due to the rapid advances in technology. In a digital era that is characterized by huge technological progress, it is imperative that language teaching conforms to the current trends in order to promote innovative classroom environments and help abandon certain old-fashioned practices of the past. A significant number of studies has been conducted to analyze the integration of educational technologies in FL teaching, as well as the role that teachers' stance towards their implementation plays (see, for example, Abdykhalykova, 2019; Al-Awidi & Ismail, 2014; Albirini, 2006; Alizadeh et al., 2019; Bensalem, 2019; Chen, Chan, & Beck, 2019; Egbert et al., 2002; Liu et al., 2004; Loewen, Isbell, & Sporn, 2020; Ndyay, Nguyen, & Grunina, 2020; Park & Son, 2009; Russell, 2020; Shaffer, 2013; Taguchi, 2020, and others).

Amid a context of controversial findings, which will be discussed in detail in the next section, the current study is oriented towards filling a void by investigating whether Greek teachers of foreign languages integrate educational technologies in their teaching, as well as whether the use of learning technologies is affected by their gender, age, level of confidence in using Information Technology (IT) tools, or any training they have received on how to employ them. Also, this study attempts to reveal which educational technologies are the ones more frequently used in FL teaching in Greece. Finally, it focuses on the attitude that FL teachers hold towards the integration of IT tools and whether their attitude is affected by their gender, age, level of confidence in using them, or training received.

The current research aims to offer valuable insights based on the responses received by a hundred Greek FL teachers. Also, due to the constant development of technological tools, its originality and significance lies in the fact that it highlights whether education remains up-to-date with contemporary technological evolution which frequently necessitates, though, a number of adjustments in the teaching process. In addition, to the best of the authors' knowledge, only a few similar studies have been conducted in relation to the integration of technological tools in the FL classroom focusing on the educators' perspective. This is a reason why the exploration of educational technologies in the Greek context is expected to provide valuable knowledge which could contribute to the educational reform in language teaching attempted in Greece, and also inspire other studies exploring whether, and to what extent, FL teachers both in Greece and abroad employ educational technologies.

More precisely, the research questions that this chapter attempts to address are the following:

RQ1: Do Greek FL teachers integrate educational technologies in their teaching?
RQ2: Is the use of learning technologies affected by teachers' age, gender, previous training, or their level of confidence in using educational technologies?
RQ3: Which educational technological tools do FL teachers in Greece employ?
RQ4: What is the overall attitude of Greek teachers towards the integration of IT tools in the foreign language classroom?
RQ5: Is the attitude of Greek FL teachers towards the integration of educational technologies affected by their age, gender, level of confidence in using them, or any prior training?

Regarding the structure of the chapter, the following section constitutes a review of some key studies related to the implementation of educational technologies, also accounting for the reasons that led to the design and implementation of the present study. This part also resumes some findings associated with the integration of educational technologies in FL teaching; it primarily discusses studies that refer to the use of technological tools as perceived by both learners and teachers. Then, the methodological decisions that were made in this research are presented, emphasizing in particular the quantitative methodological approach followed, the participants' profile, the data collection process, as well as how ethical issues were efficiently addressed. Then the findings that were derived from the data analysis of the variables examined and the relations that were explored are presented and discussed. Undoubtedly, one could not omit referring to the limitations and implications of the current research, and the directions for future research. Finally, conclusions are drawn in relation to the research questions posed by the authors.

BACKGROUND

The integration of technology in education has gradually evolved into a critical issue of discussion and concern that has attracted the interest of a remarkable number of scholars and educators over the past decades. As a result, the present section aims to provide readers with a discussion of studies that relate to the use of educational technologies in a wide array of educational contexts, and discuss the benefits these offer. Moreover, it presents various researches that encompass the use of technological tools in FL teaching and learning from diverse perspectives. Prior scholarly work that elaborates on teachers' point of view are analyzed and classified according to their attitudes towards educational technologies, the obstacles that they have reportedly encountered in the use of technological tools in their class, and the role training plays in their approach to IT tools in education. The majority of these studies have investigated the impact of the use of technological tools on the language learning process and learners' performance. On the other hand, other researches have focused on students' perceptions about educational technology's implementation into the classroom and how this affects language learning.

Overall, the integration of learning tools by FL teachers has been found to offer a wide variety of advantages to FL learning and teaching. A number of scholars and researchers (Jauregi et al., 2012; Yamauchi, 2009) have associated the benefits of technology in the language learning process with the enhancement of motivation. For example, according to Jauregi et al. (2012), the increase of motivation is due to the innovative character of technology and the reduction of stress, while for Yamauchi (2009) motivation stems from the pleasant and interactive environment that is fostered through the implementation of technology in classroom. Also, the integration of technological practices in the classroom enhance motivation which in turn facilitates language learning, improves linguistic competence and intensifies learners' willingness to acquire knowledge (Hussein, 2011). In addition, it has been found that computer-mediated communication enhances student communication skills and benefits holistically the learning process (Lee, 2000). Based on findings, the integration of technology in the classroom supports the development of speaking, listening, writing and reading skills by engaging learners more actively in classroom activities (Anderson and Speck, 2001). Within this framework, Van Deusen-Scholl et al. (2005) examined how the use of chat improves accuracy of grammar; in addition, Kiernan and Aizawa (2004) explored how the use of mobile phones facilitates the acquisition of vocabulary, while Sun and Dong (2004) conducted a study on how technology-based tasks and videos improve learners' pronunciation. Moreover, Lee (2005) investigated web-based instruction in relation to the enhancement of the writing skill. Along similar lines, Gruba (2004) revealed how videotext can boost learners' listening skill.

In these and other studies, it is widely recognized that educational technologies can contribute to the facilitation of the learning process and function as an effective and beneficial tool for language teachers.

This is the reason why it has been widely claimed that teachers should adjust to the novel needs and demands evoked by technological advancements, and overcome any possible obstacles in the integration of learning technologies in classroom. It should be noted that prior research highlights that the use of technology in classroom is influenced by teachers' personal perspective regarding the benefits it offers to their students (Kim, 2002; Lam, 2000). Consequently, their attitude can function either as a facilitator, or an obstacle to the implementation of technological tools in language teaching. Similarly, it has been observed that the successful integration of technology in language teaching depends on teachers' concerns and attitudes (Liu et al., 2004), as well as on their willingness to utilize them (Park and Son, 2009), which makes their role fundamental in bringing educational technologies into effect. In a study focusing on flipped learning and peer feedback (Brown, 2020), for example, the L2 writing teachers characterized the teaching process as being "specific, actionable and feasible for real-life teaching, which also leaves sufficient freedom for teachers to make adjustments" (p.1); yet, they did highlight that the size of the together with teachers' competence should be seriously taken into consideration when digital tools are employed. Similarly, the advantages of—and barriers to—integrating Social Network Sites (SNSs) in the teaching and learning process, from teachers' perspective, have also been well evidenced in the literature (see, for instance, Baföz, 2016; Faizi, 2018; Gruzd et al. 2018; Kabilan et al., 2010; Manca & Ranieri, 2016; Prasojo et al. 2017).

However, opposing views have been expressed as well, supporting that teachers' attitude towards new technologies does not imply or coincide with their ability to use them and, therefore, it cannot guarantee their successful integration (Egbert et al., 2002). Apart from teachers' own viewpoints, there are also other, equally significant, reasons that may affect FL teachers in implementing IT in their classroom and teaching. For example, lack of training is considered to be a major obstacle to educators' use of learning technologies in FL teaching (Shaffer, 2013; Yang and Chen, 2007), as well as lack of equipment or the provision of inappropriate equipment that can prevent teachers from integrating IT in their class and teaching practices (Shin and Son, 2007). Time constrains also appear in the relevant literature as a significant obstacle that discourages teachers from incorporating technologies in their curriculum (Park and Son, 2009). Thus, it has been suggested that the integration of technology in education, and more specifically in the FL teaching process, requires a change or adjustments in teachers' role and considerations, and it necessitates that teachers should alter their teaching practices and the way they view classroom life in a manner that should reflect contemporary IT developments (Lam and Lawrence, 2002).

Educational Technologies in Language Learning: Learners' Perspective

Exploring the impact of the use of educational technologies on language learning, their integration is an inter-temporal phenomenon whose value is acknowledged in a considerable number of studies. Literature has a lot to offer in relation to how students view the use of technology in classroom as well as the role that teachers play in its successful, or not, implementation. Mathew and Alidmat (2013), for instance, investigated the significance of audiovisual aids, such as PowerPoint presentations, as well as audio and visual clips, in the FL classroom and its relation to effective instruction. The study was carried out with fifteen undergraduate students in Saudi Arabia who responded positively towards the implementation of technological tools in the classroom, as they believed that language teaching enhanced by technology appeared to be effective and stimulating. The integration of technology created an interactive, productive, and pleasant environment that inspired learners.

Moreover, Jauregi et al. (2012) examined the use of computers in video-web communication. The participants of the study were thirty five beginners and intermediate students and the study was carried out in Netherlands. The results showed that video-web communication offered learners the opportunity to interact with native speakers and experience language learning in an innovative, pleasant and constructive way. Learners' anxiety was reduced, while their self-confidence augmented considerably. Although this study clearly indicates the positive impact of technology on students' motivation in class, it questions whether it was the use of computer or the meaningful interaction the main factor that facilitated language learning.

Yang and Wu (2012) conducted a survey to explore digital storytelling as an educational tool and how it affects motivation, critical thinking as well as academic achievement. The one hundred and ten participants, all of whom high school learners of English in Taiwan, were invited to create digital narratives which generated positive impacts on language learning. Due to the authenticity and the creative character of the tasks they performed, the interest of the learners was triggered significantly. Due to the valuable effects of technology in learning a foreign language, Yang and Wu (2012) recommended that language teachers should be encouraged to integrate educational technologies in class since these stimulate active learning and their utilization as a teaching practice is crucial.

In a rather different setting, Hussein (2011) conducted a research aiming to examine seven hundred undergraduate students' attitude towards the integration of technology in the FL classroom in North Cyprus. Surprisingly, the results demonstrated that, in general, participants did not respond positively and appeared to be resistant towards technological tools in the process of language learning. On the one hand, negative attitude and tension was triggered by the use of Overhead Projectors, projectors, slides, CDs and DVDS, while, on the other, they demonstrated positive reactions towards PowerPoint presentations. Hussein (2011) emphasizes the importance of how educational technologies are used in order to offer valuable educational results. The findings unveiled that the infrequent and insufficient use of technological tools by teachers decreases learners' motivation and tends to confuse them; as a result, the role of teachers seems to be extremely crucial in whether an educational tool may evoke positive or negative effects to learners.

In a similar study, Yang and Chen (2007) investigated Internet technology in FL learning, and more particularly the use of e-mails, video-conferencing, web-based courses, English homepage design, group e-mailing, chat room discussion and writing programs. The subjects (i.e. forty-four high school students and their teacher) who came from Taiwan portrayed the positive side of multimedia technology in the FL classroom. The study findings demonstrated technology-enhanced teaching appealed to students whose motivation increased due to the variety in instruction and authenticity, as well as due to stimulating students' curiosity. Nonetheless, Yang and Chen (2007) also concluded that teachers lacked appropriate training which reduced the effectiveness of the integrated technological materials and tools, and that further assistance and guidance should be provided to them in relation to the equipment.

Educational Technologies in FL Teaching: Teachers' Conceptions

Given that teachers' attitude towards the integration of educational technologies in FL teaching is the chapter's focal point, a number of studies with findings related to the integration of educational technologies in FL teaching are presented in the following subsections. Bolandifar (2013), for example, examined Malaysian teachers' attitude towards the integration of technology in teaching English as a second language by conducting a qualitative study. The randomly selected participants were interviewed, and despite the fact that they were only five in number, interesting results emerged. The Malaysian teachers showed a positive attitude toward the integration of educational technologies (and more specifically the use of Internet) in the classroom due to the fact that such educational tools can motivate students, make the learning process more enjoyable, and provide rich opportunities for authentic language use. However, it was found that the teachers who took part in the study used technology rarely. Consequently, despite the fact that the teachers may be in favor of educational technologies, their implementation is not defined only by teachers' attitude. Among the obstacles reported one may find the lack of equipment and of internet access and time, as well as teachers' limited computer skills.

Along similar lines, Shaffer (2013) attempted to examine the integration of educational technological tools in Korean EFL classrooms as well as how frequent its use was in FL teaching. 124 teachers were questioned about how frequently they used digital devises, such as mobile phones, CD players, online and offline computer as well as recordkeeping software and material-creating tools. The results showed that although teachers were positive towards the use of technology due to its efficiency and the enhancement of learners' motivation, they were not though in favor of using them frequently because of the unavailability of the required equipment or its malfunctioning. Thus, despite the fact that technological applications were considered attractive and productive by the participants in the study, their implementation was not successful due to the lack of the appropriate equipment and training that could make teachers more confident in the use of digital tools. Another study, conducted by Shin and Son (2007), focused on Internet-assisted language teaching among English language teachers in a secondary school in Korea. The one-hundred teachers who took part indicated the factors that influenced the integration of the Internet in language teaching. More specifically, the majority of the participants appeared to use the Internet in order to prepare teaching material, while others exploited it for activities delivered in the classroom. The attitude of the Korean EFL teachers' towards Internet was positive, and they perceived it as an effective teaching tool that motivates students. However, the study indicated certain obstacles in its use, such as time constrains, poor computer facilities, improper size of the class, restricted technical support, as well as sudden internet connectivity failures. Therefore, this study also suggests that the role of teachers' attitude in decision making regarding the integration of educational technologies in the FL classroom is not the only determining factor.

Albirini (2006) also investigated educational tools integration in relation to FL teachers' attitude in Syria. According to the author, the teachers' viewpoint is the key to its use; 326 teachers that took part expressed a positive attitude towards technology use in classrooms. However, the difficulties they faced were interwoven with the curricula, the class-time limitations as well as the unavailability of proper equipment. It was also suggested that teachers should be offered training opportunities to become more competent in the use of computers and new technologies. In addition, Lawrence (2000) explored computer-mediated language learning and teachers' attitude towards it. The participants, who were English as Second Language teachers, exhibited favorable attitude towards the integration of computer technology and considered it a useful educational tool although they did not integrate it on a daily basis. Results showed that teachers who used computers on a weekly basis had a more positive attitude towards technology enhanced language learning. Interestingly enough, it was found that the more experienced the teachers were, the more resistant they were towards adopting technological practices in their teaching. Also, it is worth mentioning that the participants were against the use of computers in lab but in favor of their use in an instructor-driven way. Lastly, Jung (2001) examined teachers' beliefs towards the integration of technology, and more specifically Internet and computers, in teaching the English language in Korea from 1999 to 2001. Teachers' attitude appeared to be positive and favorable overall; the findings also showed that over the years teachers' preference in using CD ROM and video decreased, while it remained positive towards incorporating Internet. In addition, it was found that the availability of technological tools in Korean schools increased in 2001. Moreover, teachers tended to prefer attending training emphasizing on how to use computers and Internet applied to their teaching of English, rather than acquiring knowledge on computers and the Internet in general.

Among the various topics discussed in the literature, teacher training seems to occupy a prominent place. Kessler (2007), for instance, carried out a study to examine TESOL teachers' attitude towards computer-assisted language learning (CALL) in association with their CALL training with the participation of 108 graduates from TESOL Master's programmes. The findings showed a relation between teachers' attitude and training, while it was found that TESOL graduates' attitude is influenced by informal rather that formal training. Yunus (2007) also explored ESL teachers' decisions in relation to the integration of Information Technologies in Malaysia. 444 Malaysian teachers participated in the survey by responding to a questionnaire, while 35 of them were interviewed so that more information is collected. Participants expressed a positive attitude towards the integration of ICT. However, they mentioned a number of obstacles they encountered related to insufficient training, lack of computer resources, and limited access to appropriate equipment. Against this context, Martins et al. (2004) conducted a survey at FL schools in Brazil, and explored the factors that influence teachers' use of educational technologies. In almost half of the language schools Internet was used as a teaching tool, while the majority of the participants claimed to lack appropriate training. Interestingly, the integration of technology in teaching was influenced by teachers' appeal to their managers to make educational technologies more accessible and offer them with training opportunities. Another study by Egbert et al. (2002) explored whether CALL courses influenced language teachers in integrating technology in their classroom. Twenty language teachers who had attended the same CALL course were recruited; participants claimed that lack of time and resources, as well as rigid curricular or administrative restrictions, were among the most prevalent reasons that prevented them from integrating technology in their teaching. Moreover, it was shown that, after their completing the CALL program, the main resource for discovering new activities was input from colleagues and web browsing. Although the study was based on a small number of participants, it offers valuable findings and highlights the importance of educators' being offered opportunities to reinforce their skills and use educational technologies.

Although literature has to exhibit a rich number of studies related to the integration of technology in FL teaching and learning, from the above critical review it becomes evident that there is no study to examine the integration of educational tools in language teaching from teachers' perspective in the Greek educational context, examining the parameters that are under investigation in the present research (i.e. gender, age, level of confidence and prior training). Therefore, in this chapter the attitude of Greek FL teachers is examined in relation to specific variables that may affect their attitudes and teaching practices.

MAIN FOCUS OF THE CHAPTER

Research Methodology: Issues and Challenges

Research Method and Tool

Aiming to shed light on the research questions explored in this chapter, a questionnaire-based quantitative methodology has been selected as the most appropriate method, since it could offer measurable data based on responses gathered from a great number of participants. Although quantitative methods have been criticized for dealing with average concepts, they do occupy a significant place in research due to the fact they yield data that can be generalized through statistics, while also remaining systematic and rigorous (Dörnyei, 2007). In addition, quantitative studies use "numerical data and, typically [...] structured and predetermined research questions, conceptual frameworks and designs" (Punch, 2005, p.28). The decision to follow a quantitative method as the most suitable for this study is also attributed to the fact that variables and their relations, a central point of the current work, can be assigned numbers and "a logical scale of values" (Dörnyei, 2007, p.26) and thus be analyzed faster and more straightforward. Similarly, the numbers which are contextualized under specific categories have a strong validity owned to their connection with mathematics, which in turn has made quantitative methods occupy a dominant position in Applied Linguistics (Lazaraton, 2000).

The survey tool that has been employed in this study for data collection was a web-based questionnaire designed by the authors in the format of a Google form. Questionnaires have been described as "a series of questions or statements to which they react either by writing out their answers or by selecting from among existing answers." (Aarons et al, 2001 p.6); these statements or questions can be answered at a short time and the participants are safeguarded against tiring or stressful research conditions. In addition, they are adaptable and can help researchers gather, in a rather fast mode, easily processed information (Dörnyei, 2003). As far as data collection via the Internet is concerned, this exhibits many advantages, such as low-cost surveys, not requiring researchers' presence, participants' answers being recorded automatically in spreadsheets, anonymity, while it also offers the possibility to recruit sample populations from various areas (Birnbaum, 2004). In this study, the online process led to recruiting one hundred respondents and it was designed to identify the most frequently technological tools used in Greece and to examine Greek language teachers' stance towards the integration of technological tools in teaching. The questionnaire was released by posting a link on Greek FL teachers' Facebook groups, inviting Greek FL teachers to provide the researchers with their input on their personal teaching practices and conceptions. When the prospective subject clicked on the link, they could read the Information Sheet including a detailed description of the study, as well as read and complete the Consent Form. Once they agreed with its terms, they were allowed to fill the questionnaire in. All subjects participated voluntarily in this study, providing actual and valuable knowledge about the use of educational technologies in FL teaching in Greece.

The questionnaire designed was divided in two parts. The first part of the questionnaire involved eight "classification questions", namely questions related to the respondents' overall profile. These items contributed to gathering the demographic attributes of the subjects and also functioned as variables to be further examined. These questions referred to the participants' gender, age, degree of education, years of experience, current teaching affiliation, level and numbers of students, as well as teaching hours per week. In the second part, participants were invited to answer "behavioral questions" (Dörnyei, 2003) focusing on what they do or have done in relation to the integration of educational technologies in classroom. In particular, they were enquired about whether and how often they used technological tools in foreign language teaching, which educational technologies they tended to integrate, rating also which skills they attempted to primarily enhance through the integration of educational technologies in their teaching. In addition, they were asked how confident they felt about the use of technologies and whether they had received any particular training in how to use them or whether they had participated in relevant development activities. Furthermore, participants were invited to answer "attitudinal questions" expressing their opinion towards educational technologies' integration, as well as the reasons that may inhibit them from using educational technologies in teaching a foreign language. In order to avoid collecting questionnaires with missing information in case the respondents skipped questions, the settings of the online questionnaire were such that answering every question was compulsory.

Participants and Sampling Procedures

With respect to the participants, the study was addressed to Greek teachers who taught foreign languages, both in language schools and institutes and through private lessons. The target group authors aimed at was FL teachers, both males and females, of any age group/level of education/teaching experience, who worked at various educational settings (i.e. state schools, private schools, private teaching, etc.). The rationale behind this approach without strict selection criteria was a more holistic approach to examining the behavior of Greek foreign teachers in general, and not comparing the characteristics of specific groups of FL teachers. The participants of the study were recruited via Internet, through a random selection by posting a link on a wide range of Greek foreign language teachers' Facebook groups. Although the basic weakness of random sampling is that a systematic strategy cannot be followed, the specific choice aimed at attracting participants from various areas, possessing different teaching experiences and working with diverse teaching affiliations, as, according to Dörnyei (2007), random sampling eliminates chances of subjectivity and biased choices.

Regarding ethical issues, in order to ensure that the research would be executed without any risk for the participants, approval was sought by the University of Sheffield Research Ethics Committee. A detailed description of the study's aims, objectives, methodological approach and tools, along with the individual Information Sheet, Consent Form and the proposed questionnaire were submitted to the Committee, and permission was granted. The individual Information Sheet revealed to all potential participants the aims and rationale of the survey and made them aware of the procedures that would follow. Participants were asked to fill in a Consent Form, which clearly stated that all personal data would be treated as confidential, that the questionnaires were anonymous, while they were also reassured that no physical or mental harm would be caused to them through their participation in the present study.

RESEARCH FINDINGS AND DISCUSSION

In the present section, the findings based on the primary data that collected from the multiple-choice online questionnaire will be illustrated in an attempt to shed light on the research questions articulated. The data collection took place in the academic year 2017-2018 and 100 foreign language teachers took part in the study. Firstly, the population's demographic attributes will be presented, and then frequencies and percentages of the responses provided by the participants will be illustrated. At this point it should

Figure 1. Participants' educational level

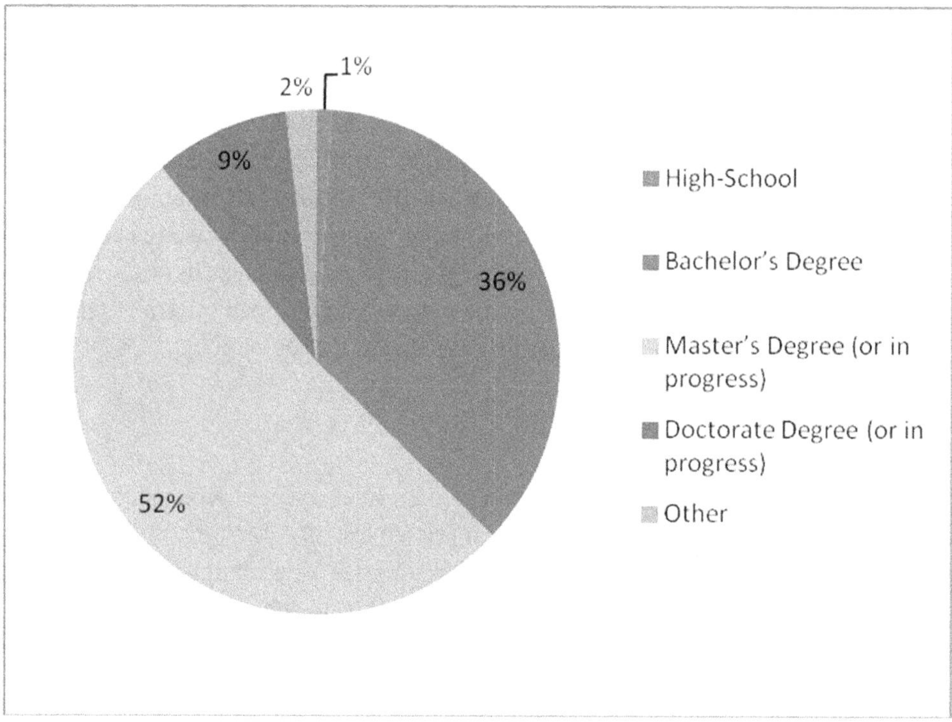

be mentioned that all of the completed questionnaires were valid, and thus the frequency and percentage values coincide. In addition, correlation tests that were carried out among the examined variables will be showcased to demonstrate any dependency relations that emerged. More specifically, correlation tests were carried out between the integration of educational technologies in FL teaching and teachers' attitude with the subjects' gender, age, level of confidence and training.

With respect to the analysis of the data collected, this was conducted with the use of the SPSS 24 statistical tool kit. SPSS software allows the analysis of numerical data, and will enable the authors to provide answers to the research questions posed above—mainly through frequencies and correlation tests. In order to process the findings that emerge, descriptive statistics will be employed to provide frequencies and percentages (Cohen et al., 2011), while tables and graphs will also visually depict findings.

Participants' Demographics

To begin with, regarding the percentage of male and female FL teachers that comprised the population of the study, males occupied only 10% and females 90%. This outcome was anticipated by the authors on the grounds that female FL teachers outweigh in number their male colleagues. The age groups 21-30 and 31-40 occupied the same percentage (i.e. 32%). 26% of the subjects belonged to the age group 41-50, whereas the age group 51-60 occupied only 10%. No participants were identified within the 61+ age group.

Concerning participants' level of education, Figure 1 demonstrates that the majority of the respondents (52%) held a Master's degree, 36% a Bachelor's degree, while only 9% possessed a PhD. Moreover, the option 'Other' (covering primarily Proficiency Certificate holders) occupied 2%, with High School degree having been selected only by one participant.

Table 1 below provides information about the teaching experience the study participants possessed. Specifically, 23% of them had gained more than 20 years of experience, 21% had 6-10 years of experience and 20% of them had been teaching for 11-15 years.

Table 1. Participants' teaching experience

Teaching experience in years	Percentage (%)
1-5	18
6-10	21
11-15	20
16-20	18
21+	23

With respect to teaching affiliation, due to the fact that the participants could provide multiple answers, dummy dichotomous variables were created. As Table 2 reveals, private teaching (55%) and private language centers (53%) are the two affiliations that the majority of participants declared. Also, 13% of the

Table 2. Participants' teaching affiliation

Affiliation	Percentage (%)
Private Teaching	55
Private Language Center	53
State School	13
Private School	9
Higher Education (other)	7
Not-for-profit organizations	3
Research Center	1

Table 3. Level of students the study participants taught

Level of students	Percentage (%)
Beginner	59
Elementary	70
Intermediate	72
Upper-Intermediate	69
Advanced	62
Proficient	52

respondents stated that they worked at state schools, while lower percentages appear for private schools (9%), Higher Education institutions (7%), not-for-profit organizations (3%), and research centers (1%).

Dummy dichotomous variables were also applied to the level of students FL teachers instruct, as participants were allowed to provide more than one answer. More specifically, the intermediate level occupies the highest percentage (72%), while the elementary stands for 70% and the upper-intermediate for 69%. In addition, as Table 3 demonstrates, 62% of the respondents taught advanced classes, 59% beginners, and 52% proficiency-level students.

Table 4. Number of students the study participants taught

Student No.	Percentage (%)
1-5	32
6-10	42
11-15	14
15+	12

Table 4 below indicates the number of students by average paticipants taught in their classes. The majority of them (42%) instructed groups of 6-10 students, whereas 32% taught groups of 1-5 students.

Lastly, regarding the question as to how many hours per week respondents used to teach, as projected in Table 5, 40% tended to teach 21-30 hours per week, whereas 37% delivered sessions for 11-20 hours per week.

Table 5. Number of hours the study participants taught

Teaching hours/week	Percentage (%)
1-10	9
11-20	37
21-30	40
31-40	9
40+	5

Participants' Responses on the Integration of Educational Technologies in FL Teaching

Having presented the demographics of the study, the focus of the current section lies in whether Greek FL teachers integrate educational technologies in their sessions. Regarding RQ1, the vast majority of them (99 out of 100 subjects) gave a positive reply about incorporating learning technologies in their teaching practices. Based on previous literature, the authors' initial hypothesis was that Greek language teachers integrate educational technologies to a rather limited extent. This hypothesis though was not

Table 6. Technological Tools employed

Digital Tool	Percentage (%)
Video projection (e.g. from YouTube etc.)	83
Audio play (e.g. recordings available online, CDs)	73
Interactive Boards (in-class installed boards with specific interactive software)	66
Online exercises (e.g. ready-made Multiple-choice Questions from websites etc)	64
Online Games	51
Video screencasts prepared by the Teacher (e.g. PowerPoint presentations etc.)	35
Social media (e.g. Twitter, Facebook etc.)	30
Online exercises developed by the teacher (e.g. tools to create MCQ etc.)	27
Blogs and Discussion Boards (e.g. texts posted on line by the teacher or their students etc.)	18
e-Assessment (e.g. track changes, comments on documents etc. or using online assessment tools)	16
Story boards (e.g. tools to create cartoon stories etc.)	16
Animation Software (e.g. using tools to create animated stories)	13
Virtual Classroom (e.g. teleconferencing with students etc.)	12
Speech-to-text software (e.g. online dictation tools etc.)	11
Audio podcasts developed by the Teacher (e.g. self-recorded audio)	9
Other (Digital school activities, Tablets, Online platforms like Quizlet, Edpuzzle, Quizalise, Web 2.0 tools, LMS)	5

confirmed, and Greek FL teachers seem to integrate educational technologies at the percentage of 99%, irrespective of the barriers they may encounter.

In the question about how often subjects integrate technology in their FL teaching, 57% use educational technologies in all their classes, 35% use educational technologies once/twice per week, 6% employ educational tools once/twice per month and only 2% use them once/twice per year. The option "never" was not selected by any participant.

With respect to RQ3, i.e. *which educational technological tools foreign language teachers in Greece employ*, dummy dichotomous scales were employed since multiple correct answers could be provided. Based on participants' responses (Table 6 below), the use of video projection was rated first (83%) as the most frequently used tool in FL teaching. Second is the use of audio play (73%), followed by interactive boards (66%), while online exercises and online games were rated at 64% and 51% respectively.

Regarding the question where subjects had to rate from 1-4 the language skills they attempt to enhance by integrating educational technologies, it was found that these are mostly employed to cultivate and enhance primarily students' Speaking and Listening skils; as Table 7 shows, Reading is the next in piority skill they aim at strengthening, while Writing is rated last.

The literature examined has a lot to offer on the use of technology on developing specific skills. Anderson and Speck (2001) discussed the development of all skills by integrating educational technologies in clasroom. Literature has also demonstrated that videotext was integrated in order to boost the listening skills (Gruba, 2004) and computer-assisted language learning was used to enhance both speaking and listening (Kessler, 2007). Also, web-based instruction was implemented to enhance learners' writing skills (Lee, 2005). Chen (2008) recommended the use of technology to enhance Reading and Listening,

Table 7. Skills enhanced through educational technologies

Skill	1	2	3	4
Speaking	38	31	15	16
Listening	37	30	19	14
Writing	16	14	26	44
Reading	9	25	40	26

while Al-Awidi and Ismail (2014) investigated on the use of CALL to reinforce students' reading skills. Consequently, although the present study revealed that Greek FL teachers use educational technologies in order to develop mainly learners' Speaking and Listening skills, literature portrays controversial findings.

In an ettempt to address RQ4, which is associated with the overall attitude Greek teachers hold towards the integration of IT tools in the FL classroom, in addition to the questionnaire item that explicitly addressed this question, participants were also invited to evaluate their confidence in the use of learning technologies, and comment on the the relevant training they may have attended. Within this framework, they were asked to make reference to the hidrances they have faced while incorporating technological tools in their teaching. More precisely, 91% of the participants hold a positive attitude towards the integration of educational technologies in FL teaching, while only 9% declared being neutral in their approach to digital tools. Interestingly enough, though, no respondent was negative towards the use of educational technologies. These findings are completely aligned with previous studies that clearly depict the positive attitude of FL teachers towards educational technological tools due to the benefits they offer in teaching and learning of foreign languages (see, for instance, Bolandifar, 2013; Park and Son, 2009; Shin and Son, 2007; Yunus, 2007).

When asked how confident they feel about the use of educational technologies in their teaching, the majority of them stated that they are moderately confident (57%). Only, 30% of the respondents felt extremely confident; 11% of them replied that they are somewhat confident and only 2% feel slightly confident.

Examining whether participants had received any particular training on educational technologies in teaching, the results revealed that 60% of the participants had been trained on educational technologies, whereas 40% of them had not received any relevant training. Regarding the training specifics, Figure 2 illustrates the developmental activities subjects had attended or additional training they attended. The majority of them (86%) invested in conferences and seminars, while 68% attended online tutorials, and 59% had studied relevant literature. Only 42% had enrolled in Unit(s) of Bachelor's and Master's programmes to enhance their knowledge on educational tools, and 37% had participated in online courses such as MOOCs.

When inquired about the obstacles they had faced in incorporating learning technologies, as Table 8 projects, FL teachers classified the lack of resources as the main barrier to technology integration (48%). Moreover, lack of time and lack of confidence follow with 48% and 30% respectively. Other barriers such as schedule conflicts with existing training sessions (8%), as well as lack of professional development activities on educational technologies (4%) occupied lower percentages. A very small number of participants (3%) stated that there is no specific reason for not using technological tools; 2% expressed that they are not interested in using learning technologies, and 2% opted for 'Other' without specifying any further. What should be highlighted here is that the afore-mentioned barriers do not prevent Greek

Figure 2. Training Activities

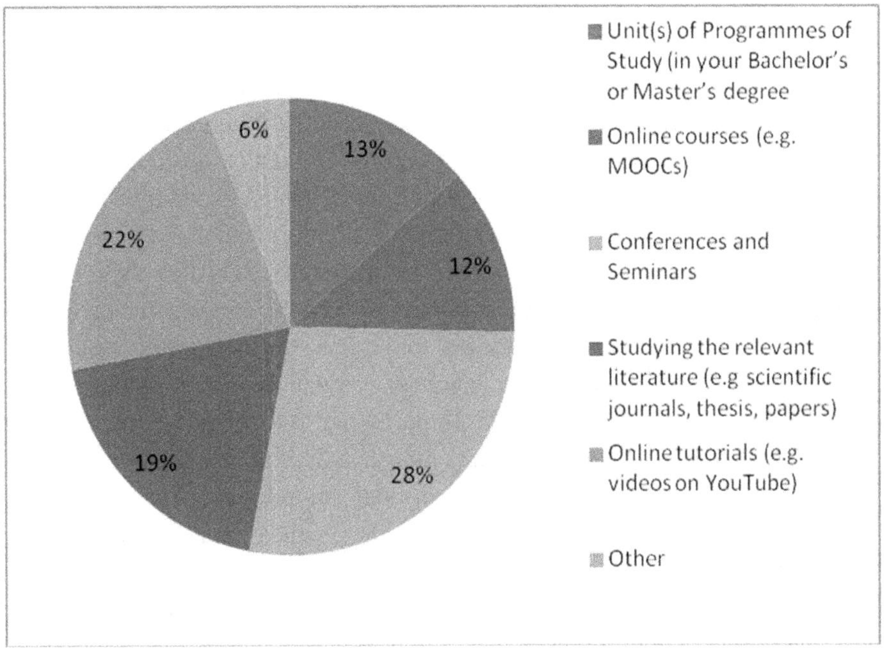

FL teachers from using educational technological tools in their teaching. Contrary to the findings of the current study, prior studies suggest that these and similar obstacles tend to inhibit the implementation of educational technologies in the classroom (see Bolandifar, 2013; Shaffer, 2013; Shin and Son, 2007).

Dependency Tests: Correlation

As already stated, in order to answer Research Questions 2 and 5 below:

RQ2: *Is the use of learning technologies affected by teachers' age, gender, previous training, or their level of confidence in using educational technologies?*

Table 8. Barriers in technology integration in their teaching

Barriers identified	Percentage (%)
Lack of time	62
Lack of resources	48
Lack of confidence	30
The training development sessions conflict with my work schedule	8
There are no professional development activities offered on Educational Technologies	4
No reason	3
Not interested	2
Other	2

RQ5: *Is the attitude of Greek FL teachers towards the integration of educational technologies affected by their age, gender, level of confidence in using them, or any prior training?*

the authors had to perform correlation tests, so as to assess relations of dependency among the various variables examined. The first variables that were tested with correlation was whether teachers integrate educational technologies in their teaching and the frequency of their implementation, which were tested against participants' gender, age, level of confidence and training. Findings demonstrated that the implementation of technology in FL teaching by Greek teachers has a dependency relation only with the confidence factor, but not with any of the other variables. Based on the results retrieved, educational technology integration and the frequency of the integration appears to be related to the variable of the confidence in using educational technological tools. The confidence levels teachers feel about the use of educational technologies demonstrate a dependency relation with the integration of educational technology with approximate significance 0,093. In particular, this relation demonstrates that the more confident FL teachers are, the more frequently they integrate digital tools in their teaching. Also, confidence was related to the frequency in the use of educational technologies with approximate significance 0,022 and value 0,229. This value shows that the integration of educational technologies is more frequent when the FL teacher is more confident about their use. Although literature discusses a relation between training and the integration of technology in foreign language teaching, rather surprisingly, the current findings suggest that these are not interdepended. Contrary to the majority of prior studies (Darus and Luin, 2008; Kessler, 2007; Egbert et al., 2002; Jung, 2001) which associate teachers' training to the use of learning tools in FL teaching, based on the present study this is not a determining factor.

The last variable that was examined for dependency relations was the attitude of teachers; correlation tests were carried out between subjects' overall stance towards the integration of educational technologies and demographics as well as other variables. As the following table illustrates, there is a dependency relation between the attitude of FL teachers and their age. More specifically, the approximate significance was 0,093 and the direction of this relation is negative with value -0,169. As previously, what is noticeable in these results is the fact that any training FL teachers may have received does not impact on their attitude towards the use of technological tools. A number of previous studies (Bolandifar, 2013; Shaffer, 2013; Albirini, 2006; Jung, 2001) indicated training as a significant factor that affects FL teachers' attitude towards the implementation of technology in their teaching. Consequently, the results of the present study are in contrast with the anticipated findings regarding teachers' training.

Table 9. Pearson's R for age and level of confidence with attitude

Variables	Value	Approximate Significance	N of Valid Cases
Age	***-0,169***	,093[c]	100
Confidence	**0,376**	,000[c]	100

*relation significant at p-value<0.1

Value in **bold demonstrates a positive relation

Value in ***bold italics demonstrates a negative relation

FUTURE RESEARCH DIRECTIONS

Considering the fact that, as with all studies, there are certain limitations in the present research, there is a lot of ground available for future research opportunities in the field of digital skills and their use in FL education. Firstly, it is recommended that a future study should be carried out with a larger number of participants, so as to verify—or challenge—the validity of the findings of the current chapter. In addition, a combination of a quantitative and qualitative approach based on data retrieved not only through questionnaires, but also via face-to-face interviews, could offer more thorough insights in FL teachers' attitudes and practices and it might also reveal deeper motives, beliefs and thoughts. In addition, employing interviews as a supplementary survey tool would eliminate the risk of potential lack of integrity in subjects' responses or hasty completion of a survey questionnaire.

Furthermore, taking into consideration that the vast majority of the specific participants were females due to the nature of the profession, future studies that encompass a balanced number of male and female participants may lead to a diverse viewpoint or potentially to some significant variation in how technological tools are employed by the different genders. Another intriguing suggestion for future research would the examination of the use of technology by an equal number of teachers of a spectrum of foreign languages taught, so as to explore any differentiating behaviors that could relate to the nature of each language or the educational background of teachers. Lastly, the implementation of educational technologies in FL teaching should be examined not only in relation to teachers' gender, age, level of confidence in using learning tools, or any previous training, but also considering other parameters as well, such as the teaching environment they work and the length of their professional experience. This could ultimately unveil other factors which may have an impact on the integration of educational technologies in FL teaching in Greece or abroad.

CONCLUSION

The present chapter is centered around a study carried out in order to explore the perspective of Greek foreign language teachers on the use of educational technologies in their teaching. This is an issue of great interest that has not been investigated extensively—neither in Greece nor in other European countries—and, thus, its findings are considered to be valuable not only for the field of Language and Linguistics, but also for Educational studies in general. Also, the subject of this research deems to be closely interwoven with the contemporary digital era and is expected to attract a lot of scholar attention due to the constant advances of technology and its benefits to education.

The focus of this work was to investigate the teaching practices and attitudes of a hundred Greek foreign language teachers regarding the use of educational technologies, while addressing the following five research questions:

RQ1: Do Greek foreign language teachers integrate educational technologies in their teaching?
RQ2: Is the use of learning technologies affected by teachers' age, gender, previous training, or their level of confidence in using educational technologies?
RQ3: Which educational technological tools do foreign language teachers in Greece employ?
RQ4: What is the overall attitude of Greek teachers towards the integration of IT tools in the foreign language classroom?

RQ5: Is the attitude of Greek foreign language teachers towards the integration of educational technologies affected by their age, gender, level of confidence in using them, or any prior training?

A quantitative method was employed in order to approach the above research questions. Frequencies and correlation tests among the examined variables were conducted to process the data collected and draw conclusions about Greek foreign language teachers' practices in relation to the integration of educational technologies in their teaching. Although generalizations cannot be made based merely on this sample, the findings provide a rather indicative picture of FL teachers' perspective regarding the goals of this study.

In relation to the first research question, findings demonstrated that Greek foreign language teachers use educational technological tools to a great extent in their classroom and teaching, and that the majority of them integrate educational technologies in all their classes. According to the results, learning tools are mainly used to enhance students' Speaking and Listening skills. With reference to the second research question, out of the examined variables (i.e. teachers' age, gender, confidence in the use of technological tools and any previous training) the implementation of educational technologies was found to have a dependency relation only with their confidence in integrating learning technologies in their teaching routine. As anticipated, the more confident a language teacher is in using digital tools, the more often he/she integrates them in their teaching. On the other hand, the use of learning technologies tends not to be affected by the teachers' age, gender and training.

The third research question aimed to identify the most frequently used educational tools in FL teaching based on teachers' answers; video projection, audio play, interactive boards, online exercises and online games are those tools that were found to be massively used by Greek foreign language teachers. In relation to the fourth research question, the findings extracted confirmed that Greek FL teachers are very positive towards the use of educational technologies. It is noteworthy that—although some participants expressed their neutrality, none of them stated they were negative towards the integration of educational technologies in teaching. Additionally, the parameters impacting on teachers' attitudes are age and their level confidence in using technological tools, but not their prior training. As hypothesized, the younger and the more confident a teacher is, the more positive he/she appears towards the implementation of learning tools in their FL teaching.

To conclude, the findings of this research are expected to offer a better understanding of how educational technologies are used in the Greek environment and also to motivate educators to implement digital learning tools as these have proved to be beneficial for language learning and teaching. It is noteworthy that the findings of this study seem to deviate from those generated in other countries, mainly because they disconnect the integration of learning tools from any previous training taken by language teachers. It is also of great importance that the present study opens a window to teachers' practices in relation to the implementation of learning technologies in teaching and can find applications not only in Greece but also in other European language classrooms.

In terms of implications, the findings of this study can inform the fields of Foreign Language Teaching and Second Language Acquisition emphasizing the perspective of foreign language teachers towards educational technologies. The emerging results are expected to enhance FL teachers' awareness in relation to educational technological tools and help encourage teachers towards their integration, further facilitate language teaching and, more significantly, motivate students and teachers alike.

ACKNOWLEDGMENT

This research received no specific grant from any funding agency in the public, commercial, or not-for-profit sectors.

REFERENCES

Abdykhalykova, A. (2019). Modern Technologies in Foreign Language Teaching: The Case of L.N. Gumilyov Eurasian National University. *Economics and Culture*, *16*(2), 39–45. doi:10.2478/jec-2019-0020

Al-Awidi, H. M., & Ismail, S. (2014). Teachers' Perceptions of the Use of Computer Assisted Language Learning to Develop Children's Reading Skills in English as a Second Language in the United Arab Emirates. *Early Childhood Education Journal*, *42*(1), 29–37. doi:10.100710643-012-0552-7

Albirini, A. (2006). Teachers' attitudes toward information and communication technologies: The case of Syrian EFL teachers. *Computers & Education*, *47*(4), 373–398. doi:10.1016/j.compedu.2004.10.013

Alizadeh, M., Mehran, P., Koguchi, I., & Takemura, H. (2019). Evaluating a blended course for Japanese learners of English: Why Quality Matters. *International Journal of Educational Technology in Higher Education*, *16*(1), 1–21. doi:10.118641239-019-0137-2

Anderson, R. S., & Speck, B. W. (2001). *Using Technology in K-8 Literacy Classrooms*. Merrill-Prentice Hall.

Bafōz, T. (2016). Pre-service EFL teachers' attitudes towards language learning through social media. *Procedia: Social and Behavioral Sciences*, *232*, 430–438. doi:10.1016/j.sbspro.2016.10.059

Bensalem, E. (2019). English as a Foreign Language (EFL) Teacher's Perceptions and Use of Mobile Devices and Applications. *English Studies at NBU*, *5*(2), 190–202. doi:10.33919/esnbu.19.2.1

Birnbaum, M. H. (2004). Human research and data collection via the Internet. *Annual Review of Psychology*, *55*(1), 803–832. doi:10.1146/annurev.psych.55.090902.141601 PMID:14744235

Bolandifar, S. (2013). The teachers' attitudes toward integrating internet technology in English language classes. *International Journal of Language and Applied Linguistic World*, *4*(3), 81–93.

Brown, C. (2020). Flipped learning wheel (FLW): A framework and process design for flipped L2 writing classes. *Smart Learning Environments*, *7*(1), 1–21.

Chen, R., Chan, K., & Beck, D. (2019). Using Augmented Reality Flashcards to Learn Vocabulary in Early Childhood Education. *Journal of Educational Computing Research*, *57*(7), 1812–1831. doi:10.1177/0735633119854028

Chen, Y. L. (2008). A mixed-method study of EFL teachers' Internet use in language instruction. *Teaching and Teacher Education*, *24*(4), 1015–1028. doi:10.1016/j.tate.2007.07.002

Darus, S., & Luin, H. W. (2008). Investigating teachers' use of computers in teaching English: A case study. *Teaching English with Technology*, *8*(1), 1–18.

Dörnyei, Z. (2003). *Questionnaires in Second Language Research: Construction, administration, and processing*. Lawrence Erlbaum Associates.

Dörnyei, Z. (2007). *Research Methods in Applied Linguistics: Quantitative, Qualitative and Mixed Methodologies*. Oxford University Press.

Edwards, J., & Roblyer, M. D. (2000). Integrating educational technology into teaching. Upper Saddler River, NJ: Merill.

Egbert, J., Paulus, T., & Nakamichi, Y. (2002). The impact of CALL instruction on classroom computer use: A foundation for rethinking technology in teacher education. *Language Learning & Technology, 6*(3), 108–126.

Faizi, R. (2018). Teachers' perceptions towards using Web 2.0 in language learning and teaching. *Education and Information Technologies, 23*(3), 1219–1230. doi:10.100710639-017-9661-7

Gruba, P. (2004). Understanding digitized second language videotext. *Computer Assisted Language Learning, 17*(1), 51–82. doi:10.1076/call.17.1.51.29710

Gruzd, A., Haythornthwaite, C., Paulin, D., Gilbert, S., & del Valle, M. E. (2018). Uses and gratifications factors for social media use in teaching: Instructors' perspectives. *New Media & Society, 20*(2), 475–494. doi:10.1177/1461444816662933

Hussein, G. (2011). The attitudes of undergraduate students towards motivation and technology in a foreign language classroom. *International Journal of Learning and Teaching, 2*(2), 14–24.

Jauregi, K., de Graaff, R., van den Bergh, H., & Kriz, M. (2012). Native/non-native speaker interactions through video-web communication: A clue for enhancing motivation? *Computer Assisted Language Learning, 25*(1), 1–19. doi:10.1080/09588221.2011.582587

Jung, Y. S. (2001). Toward an effective EFL teacher development program focusing on multimedia and the Internet. *English Teaching, 56*(4), 141–162.

Kabilan, M. K., Ahmad, N., & Abidin, M. J. Z. (2010). Facebook: An online environment for learning of English in institutions of higher education? *Internet and Higher Education, 13*(4), 179–187. doi:10.1016/j.iheduc.2010.07.003

Kessler, G. (2007). Formal and informal CALL preparation and teacher attitude toward technology. *Computer Assisted Language Learning, 20*(2), 173–188. doi:10.1080/09588220701331394

Kiernan, P., & Aizawa, K. (2004). Cell phones in task based learning: Are cell phones useful language learning tools? *ReCALL, 16*(1), 71–84. doi:10.1017/S0958344004000618

Kim, H. (2002). Teachers as a barrier to technology-integrated language teaching. *English Teaching, 57*(2), 35–64.

Lam, Y. (2000). Technophilia vs. technophobia: A preliminary look at why second-language teachers do or do not use technology in their classrooms. *Canadian Modern Language Review, 56*(3), 389–420. doi:10.3138/cmlr.56.3.389

Lam, Y., & Lawrence, G. (2002). Teacher-student role redefinition during a computer-based second language project: Are computers catalysts for empowering change? *Computer Assisted Language Learning, 15*(3), 295–315. doi:10.1076/call.15.3.295.8185

Lawrence, G. P. J. (2000). *Teacher belief systems towards computer-mediated language learning, college ESL instruction* (Unpublished doctoral dissertation). National Library of Canada.

Lazaraton, A. (2000). Current trends in research methodology and statistics in applied linguistics. *TESOL Quarterly, 34*(1), 175–181. doi:10.2307/3588103

Lee, L. (2005). Using web-based instruction to promote active learning: Learners' perspectives. *CALICO Journal, 23*(1), 139–156. doi:10.1558/cj.v23i1.139-156

Liu, Y., Theodore, P., & Lavelle, E. (2004). Experimental effects of online instruction on teachers' concerns about technology integration. *International Journal of Instructional Technology and Distance Learning, 1*(1).

Loewen, S., Isbell, D., & Sporn, Z. (2020). The effectiveness of app-based language instruction for developing receptive linguistic knowledge and oral communicative ability. *Foreign Language Annals, 53*(2), 209–233. doi:10.1111/flan.12454

Manca, S., & Ranieri, M. (2016). Facebook and the others. Potentials and obstacles of social media for teaching in higher education. *Computers & Education, 95*(1), 216–230. doi:10.1016/j.compedu.2016.01.012

Martins, C. B. M. J., Steil, A. V., & Todesco, J. L. (2004). Factors influencing the adoption of the Internet as a teaching tool at foreign language schools. *Computers & Education, 42*(4), 353–374. doi:10.1016/j.compedu.2003.08.007

Mathew, N. G., & Alidmat, A. O. H. (2013). A study on the usefulness of audio-visual aids in EFL classroom: Implications for effective instruction. *International Journal of Higher Education, 2*(2), 86. doi:10.5430/ijhe.v2n2p86

Ndyay, M., Nguyen, W. H., & Grunina, E. O. (2020). Innovative technologies in teaching Russian as a foreign language. *Russian Language Studies, 18*(1), 7–38. doi:10.22363/2618-8163-2020-18-1-7-38

Park, N. C., & Son, J. B. (2009). Implementing computer-assisted language learning in the EFL classroom: Teachers' perceptions and perspectives. *International Journal of Pedagogies and Learning, 5*(2), 80–101. doi:10.5172/ijpl.5.2.80

Prasojo, L. D., Habibi, A., & Mukminin, A. (2017). Managing digital learning environments: Student teachers' perception on the social networking services use in writing courses in teacher education. *Turkish Online Journal of Educational Technology-TOJET, 16*(4), 42–55.

Punch, K. (2005). *Introduction to Social Research: Quantitative and Qualitative Approaches* (2nd ed.). Sage.

Russell, V. (2020). Language anxiety and the online learner. *Foreign Language Annals, 53*(2), 338–352. doi:10.1111/flan.12461

Shaffer, D. (2013). Language Teaching and Learning with Technology: Student Use, Teacher Beliefs. *Journal of US-China Public Administration*, *10*(9), 927–932.

Shin, H. J., & Son, J. B. (2007). EFL teachers' perceptions and perspectives on Internet-assisted language teaching. *CALL-EJ Online*, *8*(2), 8–2.

Sun, Y., & Dong, Q. (2004). An experiment on supporting children's English vocabulary learning in multimedia context. *Computer Assisted Language Learning*, *17*(2), 131–147. doi:10.1080/0958822042000334217

Taguchi, N. (2020). Digitally mediated remote learning of pragmatics. *Foreign Language Annals*, *53*(2), 353–358. doi:10.1111/flan.12455

Van Deusen-Scholl, N., Frei, Ch., & Dixon, E. (2005). Constructing learning: The dynamic nature of foreign language pedagogy in a CMC environment. *CALICO Journal*, *22*(3), 657–678. doi:10.1558/cj.v22i3.657-678

Wu. (2011). Using Online EFL Interaction to Increase Confidence, Motivation, and Ability. *Journal of Educational Technology & Society*, *14*(3), 118–129.

Yamauchi, M. (2009). Integrating Internet technology into the EFL classroom: A case study. *International Journal of Pedagogies and Learning*, *5*(2), 3–19.

Yang, S. C., & Chen, Y. J. (2007). Technology-enhanced language learning: A case study. *Computers in Human Behavior*, *23*(1), 860–879. doi:10.1016/j.chb.2006.02.015

Yang, Y. T. C., & Wu, W. C. I. (2012). Digital storytelling for enhancing student academic achievement, critical thinking, and learning motivation: A year-long experimental study. *Computers & Education*, *59*(2), 339–352. doi:10.1016/j.compedu.2011.12.012

Yunus, M. M. (2007). Malaysian ESL teachers' use of ICT in their classrooms: Expectations and realities. *ReCALL*, *19*(1), 79–95. doi:10.1017/S0958344007000614

ADDITIONAL READING

Abdous, M. H., Camarena, M. M., & Facer, B. R. (2009). MALL technology: Use of academic podcasting in the foreign language classroom. *ReCALL: The Journal of EUROCALL*, *21*(1), 76–95. doi:10.1017/S0958344009000020

Arvanitis, P., Krystalli, P., & Panagiotidis, P. (2016). Tablets as instructional tools in the foreign language classroom: The teacher perspective. In *INTED2016 Proceedings* (pp.7645-7651). Valencia: IATED Academy.

Bhatti, Z. (2020). A qualitative exploration of teachers' perspective on smartphones usage in higher education in developing countries. *International Journal of Educational Technology in Higher Education*, *17*(1), 1–16.

Blake, R. J. (2013). *Brave new digital classroom: Technology and foreign language learning*. Georgetown University Press.

Golonka, E. M., Bowles, A. R., Frank, V. M., Richardson, D. L., & Freynik, S. (2014). Technologies for foreign language learning: A review of technology types and their effectiveness. *Computer Assisted Language Learning*, *27*(1), 70–105. doi:10.1080/09588221.2012.700315

Kavoshian, S., Ketabi, S., Tavakoli, M., & Koehler, T. (2020). Construction and validation of Mobile Social Network Sites Utility Perceptions Inventory (MUPI) and exploration of English as foreign language teachers' perceptions of MSNSs for language teaching and learning. *Education and Information Technologies*, *25*(4), 2843–2869. doi:10.100710639-019-10078-2

Nikolopoulou, K., & Gialamas, V. (2016). Barriers to ICT use in high schools: Greek teachers' perceptions. *Journal of Computers in Education*, *3*(1), 59–75. doi:10.100740692-015-0052-z

Rüschoff, B., & Ritter, M. (2001). Technology-enhanced language learning: Construction of knowledge and template-based learning in the foreign language classroom. *Computer Assisted Language Learning*, *14*(3-4), 219–232. doi:10.1076/call.14.3.219.5789

Wiebe, G., & Kabata, K. (2010). Students' and instructors' attitudes toward the use of CALL in foreign language teaching and learning. *Computer Assisted Language Learning*, *23*(3), 221–234. doi:10.1080/09588221.2010.486577

Xu, Z., Chen, Z., Eutsler, L., Geng, Z., & Kogut, A. (2020). A scoping review of digital game-based technology on English language learning. *Educational Technology Research and Development*, *68*(3), 877–904. doi:10.100711423-019-09702-2

KEY TERMS AND DEFINITIONS

Computer-Assisted Language Learning (CALL): The study or integration (to a considerable extent) of applications of the computer (e.g., laptops, desktops, tablets, iPads, etc.) to support the language teaching and learning process.

Digital Tools: Software, programs, applications, platforms, and (online or offline) resources that can be used with computers, mobile devices or other digital devices, and which incorporate text, audio and visual stimuli.

Educational Context: The environment where instruction/teaching takes place; this may involve the people engaged in the learning/teaching process, the setting (e.g. school, facilities, community etc.), the object of study (namely, the unit/subject or curriculum), as well as more general factors influencing the educational experience such as society, parents' body, etc.

Educational Technologies: Digital/Technological tools designed and created to be integrated in the teaching and learning process; they aim to enhance learning, better engage learners, and help both instructors and students to achieve the desired educational objectives in an innovative and digital manner.

Foreign Language (FL): A language which is different from the native language of a speaker/learner.

Information Technology: The use or study of computers and telecommunications for purposes related to the creation, storage, retrieval, processing, and transmission of electronic data or information.

Teachers' Perceptions: Thoughts, opinions, and beliefs that instructors hold based on their personal experiences; the term usually refers to how teachers conceptualize their professional activity and behavior, as well as their teaching practices and experiences.

Compilation of References

Abdulwaheed, A., Paul, O. T., & Alu, F. (2016). The Complimentary Role of Information Communication Technology (ICT) in Agricultural Knowledge Management in Nigeria. *Journal of Agricultural Sciences*, *6*(5), 173–179.

Abdykhalykova, A. (2019). Modern Technologies in Foreign Language Teaching: The Case of L.N. Gumilyov Eurasian National University. *Economics and Culture*, *16*(2), 39–45. doi:10.2478/jec-2019-0020

Abeysekera, I. (2006). The project of intellectual capital disclosure: Researching the research. *Journal of Intellectual Capital*, *7*(1), 61–77. doi:10.1108/14691930610639778

Abhishek, N., Ashok, M.L., & Divyashree, M.S. (2018). A conceptual study on XBRL implementation in India: issues and challenges. *Open Journal of Economics and Commerce, 1*(4).

Abhishek, N., & Ashok, M. L. (2019). Role of XBRL in promoting the integrated reporting in indian scenario. *Indian Journal of Accounting*, *51*(1).

Abu, S. T., & Tsuji, M. (2012). The development of ICT for envisioning cloud computing and innovation in south Asia. In Grid and cloud computing: concepts, methodologis, tools and applications, IGI Global. doi:10.4018/978-1-4666-0879-5.ch207

Accenture (2016). Getting to equal: How digital is helping close the gender gap at work. *Digital Fluency Indonesia Report.* Retrieved from https://www.accenture.com/t20160506T060137__w__/id-en/_acnmedia/Accenture/Conversion-Assets/DotCom/Documents/About-Accenture/PDF/3/Accenture-IWD-2016-Digital-Fluency-Indonesia-Report.pdf

Acs, Z. J., Audretsch, D. B., Lehmann, E. E., & Licht, G. (2017). National systems of innovation. *The Journal of Technology Transfer*, *42*(5), 997–1008. doi:10.100710961-016-9481-8

Adediwura, A. A., & Tayo, B. (2007). Perception of teachers' knowledge, attitude and teaching skills as predictor of academic performance in Nigerian secondary schools. *Educational Research Review*, *2*(7), 165–171.

Adkins, B. A., Foth, M., Summerville, J. A., & Higgs, P. L. (2007). Ecologies of innovation: Symbolic aspect of cross-organizational linkages in the design sector in an Australian innercity area. *The American Behavioral Scientist*, *50*(7), 922–934. doi:10.1177/0002764206298317

Afacan, Ö., & Demirbaş, M. (2013). The problems that science and technology teachers face in science laboratory. *Balkan Physics Letters*, *21*(211006), 51–64.

Aggrawal, A., Dongre, A., Jafri, A., Shrivastava, S., Tripathi, V. N., & Overseas Development Institute. (2002). *Information communication technologies and governance: The Gyandoot experiment in Dhar District of Madhya Pradesh, India.* ODI. http://www.odi.org.uk/publications/wp160.pdf

Agustina, D., & Fajar, D. A. (2018, July). Learner Autonomy as a Challenge in English Language Education 4.0 in Indonesia. *English Language and Literature International Conference (ELLiC) Proceedings, 2*, 155–159.

Ahmad, N. H., Halim, H. A., Ramayah, T., Popa, S., & Papa, A. (2018). The ecosystem of entrepreneurial university: The case of higher education in a developing country. *International Journal of Technology Management, 78*(1-2), 52–69. doi:10.1504/IJTM.2018.093935

AICPA. (2017). *Benefits and potential uses of XBRL.* Retrieved from https://www.aicpa.org/InterestAreas/FRC/AccountingFinancialReporting/XBRL/Pages/BenefitsandPotentialUsesofXBRL.aspx

AiGroup. (2016). *STEM programme index 2016.* Retrieved from http://www.chiefscientist.gov.au/wpcontent/uploads/SPI2016_release.pdf

Al-Awidi, H. M., & Ismail, S. (2014). Teachers' Perceptions of the Use of Computer Assisted Language Learning to Develop Children's Reading Skills in English as a Second Language in the United Arab Emirates. *Early Childhood Education Journal, 42*(1), 29–37. doi:10.100710643-012-0552-7

Albirini, A. (2006). Teachers' attitudes toward information and communication technologies: The case of Syrian EFL teachers. *Computers & Education, 47*(4), 373–398. doi:10.1016/j.compedu.2004.10.013

Al-Fraihat, D., Joy, M., Masa'deh, R., & Sinclair, J. (2017). Identifying success factors for e-learning in higher education. In *International conference on e-learning* (pp. 247-255). Academic Conferences International Limited.

Al-Fraihat, D., Joy, M., Masa'deh, R., & Sinclair, J. (2020). Evaluating e-learning system success: An empirical study. *Computers in Human Behavior, 102*, 67–86. doi:10.1016/j.chb.2019.08.004

Al-Hattami, A. A., Muammara, O. M., & Elmahdi, I. A. (2013). The need for professional training programs to improve faculty members teaching skills. *European Journal of Research on Education, 1*(2), 39–45.

Ali, S., Uppal, M. A., & Gulliver, S. R. (2018). A conceptual framework highlighting e-learning implementation barriers. *Information Technology & People, 31*(1), 156–180. doi:10.1108/ITP-10-2016-0246

Alizadeh, M., Mehran, P., Koguchi, I., & Takemura, H. (2019). Evaluating a blended course for Japanese learners of English: Why Quality Matters. *International Journal of Educational Technology in Higher Education, 16*(1), 1 21. doi:10.118641239-019-0137-2

Aljuhani, K., Sonbul, M., Althabiti, M., & Meccawy, M. (2018). Creating a Virtual Science Lab (VSL): The adoption of virtual labs in Saudi schools. *Smart Learning Environments, 5*(1), 1–13. doi:10.118640561-018-0067-9

Allen, M., Witt, P. L., & Wheeless, L. R. (2006). The Role of Teacher Immediacy as a Motivational Factor in Student Learning: Using Meta-Analysis to Test a Causual Model. *Communication Education, 55*(1), 21–31. doi:10.1080/03634520500343368

Ambusaidi, A., Al-Mosawi, A., Al-Balushi, S., & Al-Balushi, K. (2018). The impact of virtual lab learning experiences on 9th grade students' achievement and their attitudes towards science and learning by virtual lab. *Journal of Turkish Science Education, 15*(2), 13–29.

Andersen, J. F., Andersen, P. A., & Jensen, A. D. (1979). The measurement of immediacy. *Journal of Applied Communication Research, 7*(2), 153–180. doi:10.1080/00909887909365204

Anderson, L. W., Krathwohl, D. R., Airasian, P. W., Cruikshank, K. A., Mayer, R. E., Pintrich, P. R., Raths, J., & Wittrock, M. C. (Eds.). (2001). A taxonomy for learning, teaching, and assessing: A revision of Bloom's Taxonomy of Educational Objectives (Complete edition). New York: Longman.

Anderson, R. S., & Speck, B. W. (2001). *Using Technology in K-8 Literacy Classrooms.* Merrill-Prentice Hall.

Anderson, T. (2003). Modes of Interaction in Distance Education: Recent Developments and Research Questions. In M. G. Moore & W. G. Anderson (Eds.), *Handbook of Distance Education* (pp. 129–144). Lawrence Erlbaum Associates, Publishers.

Anderson, T., & Garrison, D. R. (1998). Learning in a networked world: New roles and responsibilities. In C. Gibson (Ed.), *Distance Learners in Higher Education* (pp. 97–112). Atwood Publishing.

Andersson, P., & Mattsson, L. G. (2018). Digital transformation supporting public service innovation–business model challenges and sustainable development opportunities. In P. Andersson & ... (Eds.), *Managing DigitalTransformation, The Stockholm School of Economics Institute for Research (SIR)*. Stockholm: Stockholm School of Economics.

APJII. (2019). *Penetrasi & Profil Perilaku Pengguna Internet Indonesia*. https://www.apjii.or.id/survei

Area, M. (2010). ¿Por qué formar en competencias informacionales y digitales en la educación superior? *RUSC, Revista de Universidad y Sociedad del Conocimiento*, *7*(2), 2-5. Retrieved from http://rusc.uoc.edu/rusc/ca/index.php/rusc/article/download/v7n2-area/976-1011-1-PB.pdf

Arkorful, V., & Abaidoo, N. (2015). The role of e-learning, advantages and disadvantages of its adoption in higher education. *International Journal of Instructional Technology and Distance Learning*, *12*(1).

Arrieta-Reales, N., Gaviria-García, G., & Consuegra-Machado, J. (2017). Papel del capital intelectual en la calidad de las Instituciones de Educación Superior en Colombia. *Educación y Educadores*, *20*(3), 419–433. doi:10.5294/edu.2017.20.3.5

Artdej, R. (2012). Investigating Undergraduate Students' Scientific Understanding of Laboratory Safety. *Procedia: Social and Behavioral Sciences*, *46*, 5058–5062. doi:10.1016/j.sbspro.2012.06.385

Astrachan, O., Hambrusch, S., Peckham, J., & Settle, A. (2009). The present and future of computational thinking. In *Proceedings of the 40th ACM Technical Symposium on Computer Science Education - SIGCSE '09* (pp. 549–550). New York, NY: Association for Computing Machinery. Retrieved from 10.1145/1508865.1509053

Atmoko, B. D. (2020). *Tantangan Transformasi Digital Dunia Pendidikan di Indonesia*. Retrieved from https://gizmologi.id/news/tantangan-transformasi-digital-dunia-pendidikan-di-indonesia/

Aubusson, P. (2002). An ecology of Science education. *International Journal of Science Education*, *24*(1), 27–46. doi:10.1080/09500690110066511

Autor, D. H. (2015). Why Are There Still So Many Jobs? The History and Future of Workplace Automation. *The Journal of Economic Perspectives*, *29*(3), 3–30. doi:10.1257/jep.29.3.3

Autor, D. H., & Dorn, D. (2013). The Growth of Low-Skill Service Jobs and the Polarization of the US Labor Market. *The American Economic Review*, *103*(5), 1553–1597. doi:10.1257/aer.103.5.1553

Autor, D. H., Levy, F., & Murnane, R. J. (2003). The Skill Content of Recent Technological Change: An Empirical Exploration. *The Quarterly Journal of Economics*, *118*(4), 1279–1333. doi:10.1162/003355303322552801

Axaopoulos, P. J., Moutsopoulos, K. N., & Theodoridis, M. P. (2012). Engineering education using a remote laboratory through the Internet. *European Journal of Engineering Education*, *37*(1), 39–48. doi:10.1080/03043797.2011.644764

Bailey, A., Vaduganathan, N., Henry, T., Laverdiere, R., & Pugliese, L. (2018). *Making digital learning work: success strategies from six leading universities and community colleges*. Arizona State University.

Bakos, J. Y., & Treacy, M. E. (1989). Tecnologia dell'informazione e strategie aziendale. In R. Filippini (Ed.), Pianificare e gestire l'information technology. Tonino, Italy: Isedi.

Balbo, J., Pacheco, M., & Rangel, Z. (2015). Medición de las competencias investigativas en los docentes adscritos al Departamento de Ciencias Sociales de la Universidad Nacional Experimental del Táchira. *Revista de investigación en administración e ingeniería, 3*(2), 26 – 35. Retrieved from http://service.udes.edu.co/revistas/index.php/aibi/article/view/0302/030204.pdf

Baldwin, A. A., Brown, C. E., & Trinkle, B. (2006). Xbrl: An impacts framework and research challenge. *Journal of Emerging Technologies in Accounting, 3*(1), 97–116. doi:10.2308/jeta.2006.3.1.97

Balid, W., Abdulwahed, M., & Alrouh, I. (2014). Development of an educationally oriented open-source embedded systems laboratory kit: A hybrid hands-on and virtual experimentation approach. *International Journal of Electrical Engineering Education, 51*(4), 340–353. doi:10.7227/ijeee.0006

Balliu, V., & Belshi, M. (2017). Modern Teaching versus Traditional Teaching-Albanian Teachers between Challenges and Choices. *European Journal of Multidisciplinary Studies, 2*(4), 20–26. doi:10.26417/ejms.v4i4.p20-26

Baltes, P. B., Smith, J., & Staudinger, U. (1992). Wisdom and successful aging. In T. B. Sonderegger (Ed.), *Psychology and aging* (pp. 123–167). University of Nebraska Press.

Banks, J., Carson, B. N., & Nicol. (2001). Discrete-Event System Simulation. Prentice Hall.

Baranyai, K., Bowles, J., Hassan, S., Prinsley, R., Smith, P., & Walter, C. (2016). *Australia's STEM Workforce.* Retrieved from http://www.chiefscientist.gov.au/wp-content/uploads/Australias-STEMWorkforce_for-distribution.pdf

Barrios, A., & Fajardo, G. (2017). El ecosistema educativo universitario impactado por las TIC. *Anagramas, 15*(30), 101–120.

Barros, B., & Verdejo, M. (2001). Entornos para la realización de actividades de aprendizaje colaborativo a distancia. *Revista Iberoamericana de Inteligencia Artificial, 5*(12), 39-49. Retrieved from https://www.redalyc.org/pdf/925/92551205.pdf

Baföz, T. (2016). Pre-service EFL teachers' attitudes towards language learning through social media. *Procedia: Social and Behavioral Sciences, 232*, 430–438. doi:10.1016/j.sbspro.2016.10.059

Battisti, G., & Stoneman, P. (2010). How innovative are UK firms? Evidence from the fourth UK community innovation survey on synergics between technological and organizational innovations. *British Journal of Management, 21*(1), 187–206. doi:10.1111/j.1467-8551.2009.00629.x

Bauman, Z. (2008). *Los retos de la educación en la modernidad líquida.* Gedisa.

Bawden, D. (2008). Origins and concepts of digital literacy. *Digital literacies: Concepts, policies and practices, 30*(2008), 17-32.

Beamish, N., Armistead, C., Watkinson, M., & Armfiled, G. (2002). The development of e-learnig in UK/European corporate organization. *European Business Journal, 14*(3), 105–115.

Becerra, J. (2017). *Innovación, estrategia digital y Cuarta Revolución Industrial.* México: Colegio de Contadores Públicos de México. Disponible en https://www.ccpm.org.mx/avisos/innovacion-estrategia-digital.pdf

Becher, T., & Trowler, P. R. (2001). *Academic Tribes And Territories.* SRHE and Open University Press.

Bell, S. (2010). Project-based learning for the 21st century: Skills for the future. *The Clearing House: A Journal of Educational Strategies, Issues and Ideas, 83*(2), 39–43. doi:10.1080/00098650903505415

Beneitone, P., Esqueti, C., González, J., Marty, M., Siufi, G., & Wagenaar, R. (2007). *Reflexiones y perspectivas de la educación superior en América Latina. Informe final–proyecto Tuning–América Latina 2004-2007.* Universidad de Deusto–Universidad de Groningen.

Bennett, S., Maton, K., & Kervin, L. (2008). The 'digital natives' debate: A critical review of the evidence. *British Journal of Educational Technology, 39*(5), 775–786. doi:10.1111/j.1467-8535.2007.00793.x

Bensalem, E. (2019). English as a Foreign Language (EFL) Teacher's Perceptions and Use of Mobile Devices and Applications. *English Studies at NBU, 5*(2), 190–202. doi:10.33919/esnbu.19.2.1

Berenguer, A., Goncalves, J., Hosio, S., Ferreira, D., Anagnostopoulos, T., & Kostakos, V. (2017). Are Smartphones Ubiquitous? An in-depth survey of smartphone adoption by seniors. *IEEE Consumer Electronics Magazine, 6*(1), 104–110. doi:10.1109/MCE.2016.2614524

Berge, Z., & Huang, Y. (2004). A model for sustainable student retention: A holistic perspective on the student dropout problem with special attention to e-learning. *DEOSNEWS, 13*(5).

Bergeron, B. (2003). Essentials of Xbrl. Financial reporting in the 21st century. Wiley.

Berge, Z. L. (2002). Active, Interactive and Reflective eLearning. *Quarterly Review of Distance Education, 3*(2), 181–190.

Bergh, D. D., Connelly, B. L., Ketchen, D. J. Jr, & Shannon, L. M. (2014). Signalling theory and equilibrium in strategic management research: An assessment and a research agenda. *Journal of Management Studies, 51*(8), 1334–1360. doi:10.1111/joms.12097

Berkeley A. R., Donahue D. F., Moyer P. D., & Bolgiano M. C. (2009). Xbrl reaches tipping point. *Journal of Securities Operations & Custody, 2*.

Berlyne, D. E. (1960). *Conflict, arousal, and curiosity*. McGraw-Hill. doi:10.1037/11164-000

Berman, P. (2006). *E-Learning Concepts and Techniques*. Bloomsburg University of Pennsylvania.

Bertschek, I., Briglauer, W., Hüschelrath, K., Kauf, B., & Niebel, T. (2016). The Economic Impacts of Broadband Internet: A Survey. *Review of Network Economics, 14*(4), 201–227.

Best, M. L., & Maier, S. (2007). Gender, Culture and ICT Use in Rural South India. *Gender, Technology and Development, 11*(2), 137–155. doi:10.1177/097185240701100201

Bezhani, I. (2010). Intellectual capital reporting at UK universities. *Journal of Intellectual Capital, 11*(2), 179–207. doi:10.1108/14691931011039679

Bharadwaj, A., El Sawy, O., Pavlou, P., & Venkatraman, N. (2013). *Digital business strategy: Toward a next generation of insights*. Academic Press.

Bikanga Ada, M., Stansfield, M., & Bayter, G. (2017). Using mobile learning and social media to enhance learner feedback. *Journal of Applied Research in Higher Education, 9*(1), 70–90.

Birnbaum, M. H. (2004). Human research and data collection via the Internet. *Annual Review of Psychology, 55*(1), 803–832. doi:10.1146/annurev.psych.55.090902.141601 PMID:14744235

Bisogno, M., Citro, F., & Tommasetti, A. (2014). Disclosure of university websites. Evidence from Italian data. *Global Business and Economics Review, 16*(4), 452–471. doi:10.1504/GBER.2014.065365

Blašková, M., Blaško, R., & Kucharcíková, A. (2014). Competences and Competence Model of University Teachers. *Procedia: Social and Behavioral Sciences, 159*, 457–467. doi:10.1016/j.sbspro.2014.12.407

Blau, I., & Shamir-Inbal, T. (2017). Digital competences and long-term ICT integration in school culture: The perspective of elementary school leaders. *Education and Information Technologies, 22*(3), 769–787. doi:10.100710639-015-9456-7

Bloch, C., & Bugge, M. M. (2013). Public sector innovation—From theory to measurement. *Structural Change and Economic Dynamics*, 27.

Blundell, C., Lee, K. T., & Nykvist, S. S. (2016). Digital learning in schools: Conceptualizing the challenges and influences on teacher practice. *Journal of Information Technology Education*, *15*, 535–560. doi:10.28945/3578

BMVIT. (2014). *Breitbrandstrategie 2020*. https://www.bmk.gv.at/.../breitbandstrategie2020_ua.pdf

BMVIT. (2019). *Breitbrandstrategie 2030, Österreichs Weg in die Gigabit-Gesellschaft*. https://www.bmk.gv.at/.../breitbandstrategie2030_ua.pdf

Bock-Schappelwein, J., Famira-Mühlberger, U., & Leoni, T. (2017), Labour market opportunities through digitization. WIFO study.

Böheim, M., & Firgo, M. (2018). Effects of digitisation on the development of economic areas. *WIFO-Monthly Reports*, *91*(12), 881–890.

Bolandifar, S. (2013). The teachers' attitudes toward integrating internet technology in English language classes. *International Journal of Language and Applied Linguistic World*, *4*(3), 81–93.

Bologa, R., Lupu, A. R., Sabau, G., & Bologa, A. (2007). Digital fluency and its importance in educating young students for the knowledge age. In L. Congyan (Ed.). *Proceedings of the 7th WSEAS Int. Conference on Distance Learning and Web Engineering* (pp. 354-457). Stevens point, WI: World Scientific and Engineering Academy and Society (WSEAS).

Bonin, H., Gregory, T., & Zierahn, U. (2015). *Transfer of the study from Frey/Osborne (2013) to Germany*. ZEW Short Expert Report No. 57. https://www.bmas.de/DE/Service/Medien/Publikationen/Forschungsberichte/Forschungsberichte-Arbeitsmarkt/forschungsbericht-fb-455.html

Bonk, C. J., & Zhang, K. (2006). Introducing the R2D2 Model: Online learning for the diverse learners of this world. *Distance Education*, *27*(2), 249–264. doi:10.1080/01587910600789670

Bonsòn, E. (2009). The role of Xbrl in Europe. *The International Journal of Digital Accounting Research*, *1*(2).

Bösch, P. M., Becker, F., Becker, H., & Axhausen, K. W. (2018). Cost-based analysis of autonomous mobility services. *Transport Policy*, *64*, 76–91. doi:10.1016/j.tranpol.2017.09.005

Bose, D., Pakala, K., & Grover, L. (2017). *Learner perceptions of increase in digital fluency after participation in a living learning community based mobile learning community: A progress report*. Pacific North West American Society for Engineering Education (PNW-ASEE). Retrieved from https://www.researchgate.net/publication/318470232_Learner_perceptions_of_increase_in_digital_fluency_after_participation_in_a_Living_Learning_Community_based_Mobile_Learning_Community_A_progress_report

Bostock, S., & Lizhi, W. (2005). Gender in Students' Online Discussions. *Innovations in Education and Teaching International*, *42*(1), 73–86. doi:10.1080/14703290500048978

Boulton-Lewis, G. M. (2010). Education and learning for the elderly: Why, how, what. *Educational Gerontology*, *36*(3), 213–228. doi:10.1080/03601270903182877

Bovee, M., Ettredge, M. L., Srivastava, R. P., & Vasarhelyi, M. A. (2002). Does the year 2000 Xbrl taxonomy accommodate current business financial-reporting practice? *Journal of Information Systems*, *16*(2), 165–182. doi:10.2308/jis.2002.16.2.165

Bowden, J. L. H., & D'Alessandro, S. (2011). Co-creating value in higher education: The role of interactive classroom response technologies. *Asian Social Science*, *7*(11), 35–49. doi:10.5539/ass.v7n11p35

Bowman, C., & Ambrosini, V. (2000). Value creation versus value capture: Towards a coherent definition of value in strategy. *British Journal of Management, 11*(1), 1–15. doi:10.1111/1467-8551.00147

Bowonder, B., Prasad, B. R. R., & Kotla, A. (2005). ICT application in a dairy industry: The e-experience of Amul. *International Journal of Services Technology and Management, 6*(3/4/5), 241.

Boyd, D. M., & Ellison, N. B. (2007). Social network sites: Definition, history, and scholarship. *Journal of Computer-Mediated Communication, 13*(1), 210–230. doi:10.1111/j.1083-6101.2007.00393.x

Braun, V., & Clarke, V. (2006). Using thematic analysis in psychology. *Qualitative Research in Psychology, 3*(2), 77–101. doi:10.1191/1478088706qp063oa

Briggs, C., & Makice, K. (2012). *Digital fluency: Building success in the digital age.* Sociolens. Retrieved from http://www.socialens.com/blog/wp-content/uploads/downloads/2012/01/SociaLens_Digital_Fluency_Sample1.pdf

Brougham, D., & Haar, J. (2018). Smart technology, artificial intelligence, robotics and algorithms (STARA): Employees' perceptions of our future workplace. *Journal of Management & Organization, 24*(2), 239–257. doi:10.1017/jmo.2016.55

Brown, C. (2020). Flipped learning wheel (FLW): A framework and process design for flipped L2 writing classes. *Smart Learning Environments, 7*(1), 1–21.

Brown, J. S., & Duguid, P. (2000). Balancing act: How to capture knowledge without killing it. *Harvard Business Review, 78*(3), 73–73. PMID:11183980

Brown, R. E. (2001). The process of community-building in distance learning courses. *Journal of Asynchronous Learning Networks, 5*(2).

Brown, W., & Brown, I. (2008). Next generation ICT policy in South Africa: Towards a human development-based ICT policy. In C. Avgerou, M. L. Smith, & P. van der Besselaar (Eds.), *Social Dimensions Of Information And Communication Technology Policy* (Vol. 282, pp. 109–123). doi:10.1007/978-0-387-84822-8_8

Brüggemann & Bizer. (2016). Laboratory experiments in innovation research: a methodological overview and a review of the current literature. *Journal of Innovation and Entrepreneurship, 5*, Article number 24.

Brynjolfsson, E., & McAfee, A. (2014). *The Second Machine Age: Work, Progress, and Prosperity in a Time of Brilliant Technologies*. W.W. Norton & Company.

Buckler, C., & Creech, H. (2014). *Shaping the future we want: UN Decade of Education for Sustainable Development; final report*. UNESCO.

Burdick, A., & Willis, H. (2011). Digital learning, digital scholarship and design thinking. *Design Studies, 32*(6), 546–556. doi:10.1016/j.destud.2011.07.005

Burns, T. E., & Stalker, G. (1961). *The Management of Innovation*. Tavistock.

Burrows, P. (2005). The role of the teacher-enactor and author-publisher. In M. Kalantzis & B. Cope (Eds.), *Learning by Design* (pp. 197–216). Victorian Schools Innovation Commission.

Bushman, R., Chen, Q., Engel, E., & Smith, A. (2004). Financial accounting information, organizational complexity and corporate governance systems. *Journal of Accounting and Economics*, 37.

Business Dictionary. (2019). *Research methodology. Web Finance*. Retrieved from http://www.businessdictionary.com

Butcher, N. (2015). *A basic guide to open educational resources (OER)*. Vancouver: Commonwealth of Learning (COL).

Butland, M. J., & Beebe, S. A. (1992). *A Study of the Application of Implicit Communication Theory to Teacher Immediacy and Student Learning*. Paper presented at the Annual Meeting of the International Communication Association, Miami, FL. Retrieved from ERIC database. ED 346 532.

Cabra, F., & Marciales, G. (2009). Nativos digitales: ¿ocultamiento de factores generadores de fracaso escolar? *Revista Iberoamericana de Educación*, *50*, 113–130. doi:10.35362/rie500665

Caffarella, R. S. (1988). *Program Development and Evaluation: Resource Book for Trainers*. John Wiley and Sons.

Caffarella, R. S. (2002). *Planning programs for adult learners: A practical guide for educators, trainers, and staff developers* (2nd ed.). Jossey-Bass.

Caffarella, R. S. (2002). *Planning programs for adults: A comprehensive guide* (2nd ed.). Jossey-Bass.

Calvani, A., Cartelli, A., Fini, A., & Ranieri, M. (2008). Models and Instruments for assessing Digital Competence at School. *Journal of e-Learning and Knowledge Society*, *4*(3), 183-193. Retrieved February 7, 2020 from https://www.learntechlib.org/p/43442/

Campanella, F., Della Peruta, M. R., & Del Giudice, M. (2013). The role of sociocultural background on the characteristics and the financing of youth entrepreneurship. An exploratory study of university graduates in Italy. *Journal of the Knowledge Economy*, *4*(3), 244–259. doi:10.100713132-013-0157-4

Campanelli, A. S., & Parreiras, F. S. (2015). Agile methods tailoring-A systematic literature review. *Journal of Systems and Software*, 110.

Camussone, P. F. (2000). *Informatica organizzazione e strategie*. McGraw-Hill.

Carayannis, E. G., & Campbell, D. F. (2010). Triple Helix, Quadruple Helix and Quintuple Helix and how do knowledge, innovation and the environment relate to each other? A proposed framework for a trans-disciplinary analysis of sustainable development and social ecology. *International Journal of Social Ecology and Sustainable Development*, *1*(1), 41–69. doi:10.4018/jsesd.2010010105

Carayannis, E. G., & Meissner, D. (2017). Glocal targeted open innovation: Challenges, opportunities and implications for theory, policy and practice. *The Journal of Technology Transfer*, *42*(2), 236–252. doi:10.100710961-016-9497-0

Cardoso, E., & Cerecedo, M. (2011). Propuesta de Indicadores para Evaluar la Calidad de un Programa de Posgrado en Educación. *Revista Electrónica de Investigación Educativa*, *13*(2), 68–82. http://redie.uabc.mx/vol13no2/contenido-cardosocerecedo.html

Cardoso, E., Cortés, J., & Cuevas, I. (2018). La formación de las competencias profesionales 4.0 a nivel posgrado. In M. González & J. Cortés (Eds.), *Tendencias de la cuarta revolución industrial* (pp. 171–200). Colofón.

Carlino, J. (2001). Knowledge spillovers: cities' role in the New Economy. *Business Review*, *4*, 17- 26.

Carpentieri, J. D., Elliott, J., Brett, C. E., & Deary, I. J. (2017). Adapting to aging: Older people talk about their use of selection, optimization, and compensation to maximize well-being in the context of physical decline. *The Journals of Gerontology: Series B*, *72*(2), 351–361. PMID:28364519

Castaño, J., Redecker, C., Vuorikari, R. & Punie, Y. (2014). Open Education 2030: planning the future of adult learning in Europe. *Open Learning: The Journal of Open, Distance and e-Learning*, *28*(3), 171-186.

Castell, M. (2000). *La era de la información. La sociedad red*. Alianza.

Castro, M., Ruiz-Mezcua, B., Sánchez-Pena, J. M., Garcia Crespo, A., Iglesias, A., & Pajares, J. L. (2011). Tablets Helping Elderly and Disabled People. In *Partnerships for Social Innovation in Europe: Proceedings of the AAL Forum 2011 Lecce* (pp. 237–244). Lecce: Ambient Assisted Living Joint Programme Forum.

Centeno, Cl., Vuorikari, R., Punie, Y., O'Keefe, W., Kluzer, S., Vitorica, A., Lejarzegi, R., Martinez de Soria, I., & Bartolomé, J. (2019). *Developing digital competence for employability: Engaging and supporting stakeholders with the use of DigComp, DigComp: The European Digital Competence Framework*. https://publications.jrc.ec.europa.eu/repository/bitstream/JRC118711/jrc118711_digcomp4empl_stakeholders_consultation_ws_report_v1.0_in_pubsy_final_v0.pdf

Central Statistic Agency. (2016). *Jumlah Pulau di Indonesia Menurut Provinsi*. Retrieved from https://databoks.katadata.co.id/datapublish/2018/10/16/berapa-jumlah-pulau-di-indonesia

Central Statistic Agency. (2018a). *Kependudukan*. Retrieved from https://www.bps.go.id/subject/12/kependudukan.html#subjekViewTab3

Central Statistic Agency. (2018b). *Pendidikan*. Retrieved from https://www.bps.go.id/subject/28/pendidikan.html#subjekViewTab3

Central Statistic Agency. (2018c). *Indeks Pembangunan Manusia*. Retrieved from https://www.bps.go.id/subject/26/indeks-pembangunan-manusia.html#subjekViewTab3

Central Statistic Agency. (2019). *Indeks Pembangunan Teknologi, Informasi, dan Komunikasi 2018*. Retrieved from https://www.bps.go.id/publication/2019/11/29/0328ba9a85b461816e917291/indeks-pembangunan-teknologi--informasi--dan-komunikasi-2018.html

CEPAL. (2008). *Espacios Iberoamericanos: La economía del conocimiento*. CEPAL. Retrieved from http://www.cepal.org/publicaciones/xml/9/34459/EspacioIiberoIII.pdf

Cevik, A. A., Aksel, G., Akoglu, H., Eroglu, S. E., Dogan, N. O., & Altunci, Y. A. (2016). Social media, FOAMed in medical education and knowledge sharing: Local experiences with international perspective. *Turkish Journal of Emergency Medicine, 16*(3), 112-117.

Chaka, C. (2010). E-learning 2.0: Web 2.0, the semantic web and the power of collective intelligence. In Handbook of research on practices and outcomes in e-learning: Issues and trends (pp. 38-60). IGI Global.

Chakraborty, D., Dhara, S. K., & Santra, A. (2018). Effectiveness of ICT in Strengthening the Process of Higher Education System in India, *Amity. Journal of Management Research, 3*(1), 40–53.

Chan, C., & Fok, W. (2009). Evaluating learning experiences in virtual laboratory training through student perceptions: A case study in Electrical and Electronic Engineering at the University of Hong Kong. *Engineering Education, 4*(2), 70–75. doi:10.11120/ened.2009.04020070

Chassignol, M., Khoroshavin, A., Klimova, A., & Bilyatdinova, A. (2018). Artificial Intelligence trends in education: A narrative overview. *Procedia Computer Science, 136*, 16–24. doi:10.1016/j.procs.2018.08.233

Chavdoulas, A., Pavlis Korres, M., & Leftheriotou, P. (2019). Investigating Asynchronous Interaction between MOOC Learners through Forum Use and Peer Review. In *P. Ordóñez de Pablos, M. D. Lytras, X. Zhang & K.T. Chui (Eds.), Opening Up Education for Inclusivity across Digital Economies and Societies*. IGI-Global. doi:10.4018/978-1-5225-7473-6.ch005

Chehidi, T. (2012). *Tunisia's ICT in education policy: Engaging teachers*. Retrieved from http://siteresources.worldbank.org/EDUCATION/Resources/TarekChehidi_TunisiasICTinEducationPolicyEngagingTeachers.pdf

Chen, C.J. & Huang, J.W. (2009). Strategic human resource practices and innovation performance. The mediating role of knowledge management capacity. *Journal of Business Research*, *62*, 104-114.

Chen, I-S., & Chen, J-K. (2013). Present and future: a trend forecasting and ranking of university types for innovative development from an intellectual capital perspective. *Quality and Quantity*, *47*(1), 335-352.

Cheng, Y. M. (2011). Antecedents and consequences of e-learning acceptance. *Information Systems Journal*, *21*(3), 269–299. doi:10.1111/j.1365-2575.2010.00356.x

Chen, R., Chan, K., & Beck, D. (2019). Using Augmented Reality Flashcards to Learn Vocabulary in Early Childhood Education. *Journal of Educational Computing Research*, *57*(7), 1812–1831. doi:10.1177/0735633119854028

Chen, Y. L. (2008). A mixed-method study of EFL teachers' Internet use in language instruction. *Teaching and Teacher Education*, *24*(4), 1015–1028. doi:10.1016/j.tate.2007.07.002

Chou, C., Peng, H., & Chang, C. Y. (2010). The technical framework of interactive functions for course-management systems: Students' perceptions, uses, and evaluations. *Computers & Education*, *55*(3), 1004-1017. https://www.learntechlib.org/p/66863/

Chou, R., Valdés, A., & Sánchez, S. (2017). Programa de formación de competencias digitales en docentes universitarios. *Revista Universidad y Sociedad*, *9*(1), 81-86. Retrieved from http:// rus.ucf.edu.cu/

Chun, H., Kim, J.-W., & Lee, J. (2015). How does Information Technology improve aggregate Productivity? A new Channel of Productivity Dispersion and Reallocation. *Research Policy*, *44*(5), 999–1016. doi:10.1016/j.respol.2014.11.007

Cillo, V., Garcia-Perez, A., Del Giudice, M., & Vicentini, F. (2019). Blue-collar workers, career success and innovation in manufacturing. *Career Development International*, *24*(6), 529–544. doi:10.1108/CDI-11-2018-0276

Cillo, V., Rialti, R., Bertoldi, B., & Ciampi, F. (2019). Knowledge management and open innovation in agri-food crowdfunding. *British Food Journal*, *121*(2), 242–258. doi:10.1108/BFJ-07-2018-0472

Claro, M., Salinas, A., Cabello-Hutt, T., San Martín, E., Preiss, D. D., Valenzuela, S., & Jara, I. (2018). Teaching in a Digital Environment (TIDE): Defining and measuring teachers' capacity to develop students' digital information and communication skills. *Computers & Education*, *121*, 162 174. doi:10.1016/j.compedu.2018.03.001

Cocozza, A. (2012). *Comunicazione d'impresa e gestione delle risorse umane. Valorizzare le persone nelle imprese innovative e nelle pubbliche amministrazioni virtuose*. Franco Angeli.

Cohen, L., Manion, L., & Morrison, K. (2000). *Research Methods in Education* (5th ed.). Routledge Falmer.

Cohen, L., Manion, L., & Morrison, K. (2013). *Research methods in education* (7th ed.). Routledge. doi:10.4324/9780203720967

Comisión Europea (2013). *Education and Training Monitor*. Bruselas: Oficina Publicaciones de la Comunidad Europea.

Comisión Europea (2018). *IA para Europa. Comunicación de la Comisión al Parlamento Europeo*. Bruselas: COM.

Commission of the European Communities. (2001). The eLearning Action Plan: Designing tomorrow's education. Brussels: Author.

Conboy, K., & Fitzgerald, B. (2004). Toward a conceptual framework of agile methods: A study of agility in different disciplines. *Proceedings of the 2004 ACM Workshop on Interdisciplinary Software Engineering Research*. 10.1145/1029997.1030005

Connelly, B. L., Certo, S. T., Ireland, R. D., & Reutzel, C. R. (2011). Signalling theory: A review and assessment. *Journal of Management*, *37*(1), 39–67. doi:10.1177/0149206310388419

Conrad, R. M., & Donalson, J. A. (2004). *Engaging the online learner, Activities and resources for creative instruction*. Jossey-Bass.

Consejo Superior de Investigaciones Científicas (CSIC). (n.d.). *Ranking Web of Universities*. Retrieved from http://www.webometrics.info/en

Corr, A. C. (2006). *Children and Technology: A Tool for Child Development*. Barnardos' National Children's Resource Centre.

Cosco, T. D., Prina, A. M., Perales, J., Stephan, B. C., & Brayne, C. (2014). Operational definitions of successful aging: A systematic review. *International Psychogeriatrics*, *26*(3), 373–381. doi:10.1017/S1041610213002287 PMID:24308764

Costa, P. B., Prado, C., Oliveira, L. D. F. T. D., Peres, H. H. C., Massarollo, M. C. K. B., Fernandes, M. D. F. P., ... and Freitas, G. F. D. (2011). Digital fluency and the use of virtual environments: the characterization of nursing students. *Revista da Escola de Enfermagem da USP, 45*(SPE), 1589-1594.

Cram, W. A., & Newell, S. (2016). Mindful revolution or mindless trend? examining agile development as a management fashion. *European Journal of Information Systems*, *25*(2), 154–169. doi:10.1057/ejis.2015.13

Cranfield, D. J., & Taylor, J. (2008). Knowledge management and higher education: A UK case study. *Electronic Journal of Knowledge Management*, *6*(2).

Cranton, P. (2000). *Planning Instruction for Adult Learners* (2nd ed.). Wall & Emerson Inc.

Cranton, P., & Carusetta, E. (2004). Perspectives on authenticity in teaching. *Adult Education Quarterly*, *55*(1), 5–22. doi:10.1177/0741713604268894

Creswell, J. W. (2015). *Educational Research. Planning, Conducting, and Evaluating Quantitave and Qualitatine Research*. Pearson Education Inc.

Cricelli, L., Greco, M., Grimaldi, M., & Dueñas, L. P. (2018). Intellectual capital and university performance in emerging countries. *Journal of Intellectual Capital*, *19*(1), 71–95. doi:10.1108/JIC-02-2017-0037

Crittenden, V. L., Crittenden, W. F., & Ajjan, H. (2019). Empowering women micro-entrepreneurs in emerging economies: The role of information communications technology. *Journal of Business Research*, *98*, 191–203. doi:10.1016/j.jbusres.2019.01.045

Cross, A., & Lucas, E. (2019). *Getting into Medical School 2020 Entry*. Trotman Education.

Cross, K. P. (1981). *Adults as Learners: Increasing Participation and Facilitating Learning*. Jossey-Bass.

Crouzier, T. (2015). *Science Ecosystem 2.0: how will change occor?* Luxemburg: Publications Office of the European Union.

Cuadrado-García, M., Ruiz-Molina, M. E., & Montoro-Pons, J. D. (2010). Are there gender differences in e-learning use and assessment? Evidence from an interuniversity online project in Europe. *Procedia: Social and Behavioral Sciences*, *2*(2), 367–371. doi:10.1016/j.sbspro.2010.03.027

Cuddy, A. J., Norton, M. I., & Fiske, S. T. (2005). This old stereotype: The pervasiveness and persistence of the elderly stereotype. *The Journal of Social Issues*, *61*(2), 267–285. doi:10.1111/j.1540-4560.2005.00405.x

Cvetković, B. N., & Stanojević, D. (2018). Integrating digital technologies into teaching process. *TEME: Casopis za Društvene Nauke, 12*(4).

Czaja, S. J., Guerrier, J. H., Nair, S. N., & Landauer, T. K. (1993). Computer communication as an aid to independence for older adults. *Behaviour & Information Technology, 12*(4), 197–207. doi:10.1080/01449299308924382

Dalvi-Esfahani, M., Wai Leong, L., Ibrahim, O., & Nilashi, M. (2020). Explaining students' continuance intention to use Mobile web 2.0 learning and their perceived learning: An integrated approach. *Journal of Educational Computing Research, 57*(8), 1956–2005. doi:10.1177/0735633118805211

Dardanou, M., & Kofoed, T. (2019). It is not only about the tools! Professional digital competence. In G. Colette & I. Palaiologu (Eds.), *Early learning in the digital age* (pp. 61–76). SAGE Publications.

Darkenwald, G. G., & Merriam, S. B. (1982). *Adult education: Foundations of practice*. Harper & Row.

Darus, S., & Luin, H. W. (2008). Investigating teachers' use of computers in teaching English: A case study. *Teaching English with Technology, 8*(1), 1–18.

Davies, A., Fidler, D., & Gorbis, M. (2011). *Future Work Skills 2020*. Instituto de Investigación de la Universidad de Phoenix.

Davis, F. D., Bagozzi, R. P., & Warshaw, P. R. (1989). User acceptance of computer technology: A comparison of two theorical model. *Management Science, 35*(8), 982–1003. doi:10.1287/mnsc.35.8.982

De Cesare, S., Lycett, M., Macredie, R. D., Patel, C., & Paul, R. (2010). Examining perceptions of agility in software development practice. *Communications of the ACM, 53*(6), 126–130. doi:10.1145/1743546.1743580

De Freitas, S., & Conole, G. (2010). The influence of pervasive and integrative tools on learners' experiences and expectations of study. In R. Sharpe, H. Beetham, & S. de Freitas (Eds.), *Rethinking learning in the Digital Age*. Routledge.

De Graaf, E., & Kolmos, A. (2003). Characteristics of problem-based learning. *International Journal of Engineering Education, 19*(5), 657–662.

Debreceny, R., Felden, C., Ochocki, B., & Piechocki, M. (2005). *Xbrl for interactive data. Engineering the information value chain*. Springer-Verlag.

Dede, C. (2005a). Planning for neomillennial learning styles. *EDUCAUSE Quarterly, 28*(1), 7–12.

Del Giudice, M., Carayannis, E. G., & Maggioni, V. (2017). Global knowledge intensive enterprises and international technology transfer: Emerging perspectives from a quadruple helix environment. *The Journal of Technology Transfer, 42*(2), 229–235. doi:10.100710961-016-9496-1

Del Giudice, M., Garcia-Perez, A., Scuotto, V., & Orlando, B. (2019). Are social enterprises technological innovative? A quantitative analysis on social entrepreneurs in emerging countries. *Technological Forecasting and Social Change, 148*, 119704. doi:10.1016/j.techfore.2019.07.010

Del Giudice, M., & Maggioni, V. (2014). Managerial practices and operative directions of knowledge management within inter-firm networks: A global view. *Journal of Knowledge Management, 18*(5), 841–846. doi:10.1108/JKM-06-2014-0264

Del Giudice, M., & Straub, D. (2011). Editor's comments: IT and entrepreneurism: an on-again, off-again love affair or a marriage? *Management Information Systems Quarterly, 35*(4), iii–viii. doi:10.2307/41409961

Delello, J. A., & McWhorter, R. R. (2017). Reducing the digital divide: Connecting older adults to iPad technology. *Journal of Applied Gerontology, 36*(1), 3–28. doi:10.1177/0733464815589985 PMID:26084479

Demir, K. & Odabaşı, H. F. (2016). Dijital akıcılık kavramına eleştirel bir bakış. In *4. Uluslararası Öğretim Teknolojileri ve Öğretmen Eğitimi Sempozyumu* (pp. 373-376). Elazığ. Retrieved from http://www.ittes2016.org/belge/oku/37

Demir, K., Aydin, B., Ersoy, N. S., Kelek, A., Tatar, I., Kuzu, A., & Odabasi, H. F. (2015). Visiting digital fluency for pre-service teachers in Turkey. *World Journal on Educational Technology, 7*(1), 01-08.

Demircioglu, M. A., Audretsch, D. B., & Sloper, T. F. (2019). Sources of innovation and innovation type: Firm-level evidence from the United State. *Industrial and Corporate Change*, *28*(6), 1365–1379. doi:10.1093/icc/dtz010

Demir, E. B. K., Çaka, C., Tuğtekin, U., Demir, K., İslamoğlu, H., & Kuzu, A. (2016). Üç boyutlu yazdırma teknolojilerinin eğitim alanında kullanımı: Türkiye'deki uygulamalar. *Ege Eğitim Dergisi*, *17*(2), 481–503. doi:10.12984/egeefd.280754

Dengler, K., & Matthes, B. (2018). The impacts of digital transformation on the labour market: Substitution potentials of occupations in Germany. *Technological Forecasting and Social Change*, *137*, 304–316. doi:10.1016/j.techfore.2018.09.024

Denis, B., Watland, P., Pirotte, S., & Verday, N. (2004). *Roles and Competencies of the e-tutor.* Retrieved on 13 March, 2020 from https://orbi.uliege.be/bitstream/2268/12722/1/DENIS_WATLAND_PIROTTE_VERDAY_Roles_and_competencies_of_the_tutor_30_03_2009.pdf

Dianeosis. (2019, January). *Low fertility in Greece, demographic crisis and family support policies.* Dianeosis-Research and Policy Institute. Retrieved from https://www.dianeosis.org/wp-content/uploads/2019/01/ekke_family_policies.pdf

Dietz-Uhler, B., & Hurn, J. E. (2013). Using learning analytics to predict (and improve) student success: A faculty perspective. *Journal of Interactive Online Learning*, *12*(1), 17–26.

Digital competence: the vital 21st-century skill for teachers and students. (2020, January 17). Retrieved February 13, 2020, from https://www.schooleducationgateway.eu/en/pub/resources/tutorials/digital-competence-the-vital-.htm

Dillenbourg, P., & Fischer, F. (2007). Basics of Computer-Supported Collaborative Learning. *Zeitschrift für Berufs- und Wirtschaftspädagogik*, *21*, 111-130.

Diwakar, Kumar, Radhamani, Nizar, Nair, & Sasidharakur. (2015). Role of ICT-enabled virtual laboratories in biotechnology education: Case studies on blended and remote learning. *International Conference on Interactive Collaborative Learning (ICL)*, 915-921. 10.1109/ICL.2015.7318149

Diwakar, A. S., & Noronha, S. B. (2016). The Effectiveness of Virtual Labs in Engineering Education-what do we Measure? *Journal of Engineering Education Transformations*, *30*(1), 73. doi:10.16920/jeet/2016/v30i1/97425

Dommett, E. J. (2019). Understanding student use of twitter and online forums in higher education. *Education and Information Technologies*, *24*(1), 325–343. doi:10.100710639-018-9776-5

Dönmez, O., Simsek, Ö., & Arikan, Y. D. (2010). How can we make use of learner interaction in online learning environments? *Procedia: Social and Behavioral Sciences*, *9*, 783–787. doi:10.1016/j.sbspro.2010.12.234

Dörnyei, Z. (2003). *Questionnaires in Second Language Research: Construction, administration, and processing.* Lawrence Erlbaum Associates.

Dörnyei, Z. (2007). *Research Methods in Applied Linguistics: Quantitative, Qualitative and Mixed Methodologies.* Oxford University Press.

Drnevich, P. L., & Croson, D. C. (2013). Information technology and business – level strategy: Toward an integrated theoretical perspective. *MIS Quarterly*, *37*(2), 483–509. doi:10.25300/MISQ/2013/37.2.08

Dumay, J., & Cai, L. (2015). Using content analysis as a research methodology for investigating intellectual capital disclosure: A critique. *Journal of Intellectual Capital*, *16*(1), 121–155. doi:10.1108/JIC-04-2014-0043

Dumay, J., & Guthrie, J. (2017). Involuntary disclosure of intellectual capital: Is it relevant? *Journal of Intellectual Capital*, *18*(1), 29–44. doi:10.1108/JIC-10-2016-0102

Durán, M., Gutiérrez, I., & Prendes, M. (2016). Análisis conceptual de modelos de competencia digital del profesorado universitario. *RELATEC: Revista Latinoamericana de Tecnología Educativa*, *15*(1), 97–114. doi:10.17398/1695-288X.15.1.97

Dyrberg, N. R., Treusch, A. H., & Wiegand, C. (2016). Virtual laboratories in science education: Students' motivation and experiences in two tertiary biology courses. *Journal of Biological Education*, *21*, 1–17.

Earnhardt, M. P., Newcomer, J. M., Watkins, D. V., & Marion, J. W. (2014). An inquiry into the aviation management education paradigm shift. *International Journal of Aviation, Aeronautics, and Aerospace*, *1*(4), 7.

Education Endowment Foundation. (2019). *Using digital technology to improve learning*. https://educationendowmentfoundation.org.uk/public/files/Publications/digitalTech/EEF_Digital_Technology_Guidance_Report.pdf

Edvinsson, L. (2013). Reflections from 21 years of IC practice and theory. *Journal of Intellectual Capital*, *14*(1), 163–172. doi:10.1108/14691931311289075

Edwards, J., & Roblyer, M. D. (2000). Integrating educational technology into teaching. Upper Saddler River, NJ: Merill.

Egbert, J., Paulus, T., & Nakamichi, Y. (2002). The impact of CALL instruction on classroom computer use: A foundation for rethinking technology in teacher education. *Language Learning & Technology*, *6*(3), 108–126.

Eid, M. I., & Al-Jabri, I. M. (2016). Social networking, knowledge sharing, and student learning: The case of university students. *Computers & Education*, *99*, 14–27. doi:10.1016/j.compedu.2016.04.007

Elahi, E., Weijun, C., Zhang, H., & Nazeer, M. (2019). Agricultural intensification and damages to human health in relation to agrochemicals: Application of artificial intelligence. *Land Use Policy*, *83*, 461–474. doi:10.1016/j.landusepol.2019.02.023

Eletsonline. (2010). *Digital Learning*. https://digitallearning.eletsonline.com/2012/02/virtual-labs-project-launched-by-mhrd-under-nmeict/

Elliott, R. K., & Pallais, D. M. (1997). Know your market. *Journal of Accountancy*, 1.

Elsharnouby, T. H. (2015). Student co-creation behavior in higher education: The role of satisfaction with the university experience. *Journal of Marketing for Higher Education*, *25*(2), 238–262. doi:10.1080/08841241.2015.1059919

Engelhardt, H., Buber, I., Skirbekk, V., & Prskawetz, A. (2010). Social involvement, behavioural risks and cognitive functioning among older people. *Ageing and Society*, *30*(5), 779–809. doi:10.1017/S0144686X09990626

Enochsson, A. (2019). Teenage pupils' searching for information on the Internet. *Information Research*, *24*(1). Retrieved from http://www.informationr.net/ir/24-1/isic2018/isic1822.html

Ernst, E. W. (1983). A New Role for the Undergraduate Engineering Laboratory. *IEEE Transactions on Education*, *26*(2), 49–51. doi:10.1109/TE.1983.4321598

Esfijani, A. (2018). Measuring quality in online education: A meta-synthesis. *American Journal of Distance Education*, *32*(1), 57–53. doi:10.1080/08923647.2018.1417658

Eshet-Alkalai, Y. (2004). Digital literacy: A conceptual framework for survival skills in the digital era. *Journal of Educational Multimedia and Hypermedia*, *13*(1), 93.

Esteve, F., & Gisbert, M. (2013). Competencia digital en la educación superior: Instrumentos de evaluación y nuevos entornos. *Enl@ce Revista Venezolana de Información. Tecnología y Conocimiento, 10*(3), 29–43.

Ettredge, M. L., Kwon, S. Y., Smith, D. B., & Zarowin, P. A. (2005). The impact of SFAS N. 131 business segment data on the market's ability to anticipate future earnings. *The Accounting Review, 80*(3), 773–804. doi:10.2308/accr.2005.80.3.773

Etzkowitz, H. (2003). Innovation in innovation: The triple helix of university-industry-government relations. *Social Sciences Information. Information Sur les Sciences Sociales, 42*(3), 293–337. doi:10.1177/05390184030423002

European Commission. (2010). *A Digital Agenda for Europe.* https://www.kowi.de/Portaldata/2/Resources/fp/2010-com-digital-agenda.pdf

European Commission. (2018). *Digital Transformation 2021-2027.* https://ec.europa.eu/commission/sites/beta-political/files/budget-june2018-digital-transformation_en.pdf

Eurostat. (2018, August 17). *Proportion of population aged 65 and over.* Retrieved from https://ec.europa.eu/eurostat/tgm/table.do?tab=table&init=1&language=en&pcode=tps00028&plugin=1

Fagerstrøm, A., & Ghinea, G. (2013). Co-creation of value in higher education: Using social network marketing in the recruitment of students. *Journal of Higher Education Policy and Management, 35*(1), 45–53. doi:10.1080/1360080X.2013.748524

Faizi, R. (2018). Teachers' perceptions towards using Web 2.0 in language learning and teaching. *Education and Information Technologies, 23*(3), 1219–1230. doi:10.100710639-017-9661-7

Fellagara, A. M. (2008). *Governo, controllo e informazione societaria nei gruppi aziendali.* McGraw-Hill.

Fernández, E., Leiva, J., & López, E. (2017). Formación en competencias digitales en la universidad. Percepciones del alumnado. *Campus Virtuales, 6*(2), 79-89. Retrieved from http://uajournals.com/ojs/index.php/campusvirtuales/article/view/249/203

Fernández, E., Leiva, J., & López, E. (2017). Competencias digitales en docentes de educación superior. *Revista Digital de Investigación en Docencia Universitaria, 12*(1), 213–231. doi:10.19083/ridu.12.558

Ferrari, A. (2013). *DIGCOMP: A framework for developing and understanding digital competence in Europe.* Academic Press.

Ferrari, A. (2013). *DIGCOMP: A Framework for Developing and Understanding Digital Competence in Europe.* Joint Research Centre, Institute for Prospective Technological Studies., doi:10.2788/52966

Figerl, J., & Okropiridse, A. (2018). *The job miracle on the labour market? A (long-term) look behind the scenes of the rapid increase in job vacancies at AMS.* A&W Blog. https://awblog.at/offene-stellen-beim-ams/

Finkelstein, J. (2006). *Learning in Real Time Synchronous Teaching and Learning Online.* Jossey-Bass.

Firgo, M., Mayerhofer, P., Peneder, M., Grabmayer, P., & Reschenhofer, P. (2018). *Employment effects of digitisation in the federal states as well as in town and country.* Economic Research Institute. https://www.wifo.ac.at/jart/prj3/wifo/resources/person_dokument/person_dokument.jart?publikationsid=61633&mime_type=application/pdf

Firman Ramadhan, M., & Irwanto. (2017). Using virtual labs to enhance students' thinking abilities, skills, and scientific attitudes. In *Proceedings of International Conference on Educational Research and Innovation,* (*vol 1*, pp 494-499). Academic Press.

Fisk, P. (2017). *Education 4.0 … the future of learning will be dramatically different, in school and throughout life.* Retrieved from http://www.thegeniusworks.com/2017/01/future-education-young-everyone-taught-together

Foroudi, P., Yu, Q., Gupta, S., & Foroudi, M. M. (2019). Enhancing university brand image and reputation through customer value co-creation behaviour. *Technological Forecasting and Social Change*, *138*, 218–227. doi:10.1016/j.techfore.2018.09.006

Foster, L., & Walker, A. (2015). Active and successful aging: A European policy perspective. *The Gerontologist*, *55*(1), 83–90. doi:10.1093/geront/gnu028 PMID:24846882

Fradeani, A. (2005). *La globalizzazione della comunicazione economico-finanziaria. IAS/IFRS e Xbrl*. Giuffrè.

Fradeani, A. (2009). *Xbrl. Il presente e il futuro della comunicazione economico-finanziaria*. Giuffrè.

Frey, C. B., & Osborne, M. A. (2017). The future of employment: How susceptible are jobs to computerization. *Technological Forecasting and Social Change*, *114*, 254–280. doi:10.1016/j.techfore.2016.08.019

Friebe, J., & Schmidt-Hertha, B. (2013). Activities and barriers to education for elderly people. *Journal of Contemporary European Studies*, *64*(1), 10–27.

Frydrychova Klimova, B. (2012). Impact of ICT on foreign language learning. *AWER Procedia Information Technology and Computer Science*, *2*, 180–185.

Fullan, M. (2013). *Stratosphere: Integrating technology, pedagogy, and change knowledge*. Pearson Canada.

Fung, A., Graham, M., & Weil, D. (2007). *Full disclosure: the perils and promise of transparency*. Academic Press.

Gallagher, S. (2019). *Online education in 2019: a synthesis of the data*. Center for the Future of Higher Education and Talent Strategy, Northeastern University.

Gallego-Alvarez, I., Rodríguez-Domínguez, L., & García-Sánchez, I. M. (2011). Information disclosed online by Spanish universities: Content and explanatory factors. *Online Information Review*, *35*(3), 360–385. doi:10.1108/14684521111151423

García, A., & Tejedor, F. (2017). Percepción de los estudiantes sobre el valor de las TIC en sus estrategias de aprendizaje y su relación con el rendimiento. *Educación XXI*, *20*(2), 137–159. doi:10.5944/educxx1.19035

García-Sánchez, I., Frías-Aceituno, J., & Rodríguez-Domínguez, L. (2013). Determinants of corporate social disclosure in Spanish local governments. *Journal of Cleaner Production*, *39*, 60–72. doi:10.1016/j.jclepro.2012.08.037

Garrick, B., Pendergast, D., & Geelan, D. (2017). *Theorising personalised education: Electronically mediated higher education*. Springer. doi:10.1007/978-981-10-2700-0

Gasser, U., & Palfrey, J. (2008). *Born digital-connecting with a global generation of digital natives*. Perseus.

Gautam, M. (2016). Education System in Modern India. *International Journal of Scientific Research and Education*, *4*(1), 4876–4879.

Gayol, Y., & Boubsil, O. (2009). Digital fluency of faculty at distance education university. In Y. E. Ioannidis, D. L. Lee, & R. T. Ng (Eds.), *Proceedings of the ICDE: International Conference of Open and Distance Education*. Shanghai, China: IEEE Computer Society. Retrieved from https://www.ou.nl/Docs/Campagnes/ICDE2009/Papers/Final_Paper_396Gayol.pdf

Gegenfurtner, A. (2019). Reconstructing goals for transfer of training in faculty development programs for higher education teachers: A qualitative documentary method approach. *Heliyon*, *5*(11), 1–7. doi:10.1016/j.heliyon.2019.e02928 PMID:31844771

Gekara, V., & Snell, D. (2018). Designing and Delivering Skills Transferability and Employment Mobility: The Challenges of a Markent-Driven Vocational Education and Training System. *Journal of Vocational Education and Training*, *70*(1), 107–129. doi:10.1080/13636820.2017.1392996

Gelmereanu, C., Morar, L., & Bogdan, S. (2014). Productivity and cycle time prediction using artificial neural network. *Procedia Economics and Finance*, *15*, 1563–1569. doi:10.1016/S2212-5671(14)00626-1

Gershenfeld, N., & Vasseur, J. (2014). *As Objects Go Online: The Promise (and Pitfalls) of the Internet of Things*. Retrieved from https://www.foreignaffairs.com/articles/2014-02-12/objects-go-online

Ghavifekr, S., & Rosdy, W. A. W. (2015). Teaching and learning with technology: Effectiveness of ICT integration in schools. *International Journal of Research in Education and Science*, *1*(2), 175–191. doi:10.21890/ijres.23596

Ghezzi, A., Cortimiglia, M. N., & Frank, A. G. (2015). Strategy and business model design in dynamic telecomunications industries: A study on Italian mobile network operators. *Technological Forecasting and Social Change*, *90*.

Gian Paolo Cimellaro, & Domaneschi. (2018). Development of Dynamic Laboratory Platform for Earthquake Engineering Courses. *Journal of Professional Issues in Engineering Education and Practice*, *144*(4), 18–26.

Gibbs, G., & Coffey, M. (2004). The impact of training of university teachers on their teaching skills, their approach to teaching and the approach to learning of their students. *Active Learning in Higher Education*, *5*(1), 87–100. doi:10.1177/1469787404040463

Glewa, M., & Bogan, M. B. (2007). Improving children's literacy while promoting digital fluency through the use of blogs in the classroom: Surviving the hurricane. *Journal of Literacy and Technology*, *8*(1), 40–48.

Glynn, R. J., Bouchard, G. R., LoCastro, J. S., & Laird, N. M. (1985). Aging and generational effects on drinking behaviors in men: Results from the normative aging study. *American Journal of Public Health*, *75*(12), 1413–1419. doi:10.2105/AJPH.75.12.1413 PMID:4061714

Gnanadass, E., & Sanders, A. Y. (2019). Gender still matters in distance education. In M. G. Moore & W. C. Diehl (Eds.), *Handbook of distance education* (4th ed., pp. 70–90). Routledge.

Goh, E., Sigala, M. (2020). Integrating Information & Communication Technologies (ICT) into classroom instruction: teaching tips for hospitality educators from a diffusion of innovation approach. *Journal of Teching in Travel & Tourism*. doi:10.1080/15313220.2020.1740636

Göktalay, S. B., & Özeke, S. (2105). Essential for 21st Century Teachers in Turkey: Uludag University Example. *An Independent Scientific Journal for Interdisciplinary Research in Pedagogy, 19*(6), 100-121. doi:10.5507/epd.2015.020

Goldberg, L. R., Parham, D., Coufal, K., Maeda, M., Scudder, R. R., & Sechtem, P. R. (2010). Peer Review: The Importance of Education for Best Practice. *Journal of College Teaching and Learning*, *7*(2), 71–84. doi:10.19030/tlc.v7i2.91

Goldstein, J., & Sadhana, P. (2004). The Brink of Change: Gender in Technology-Rich Collaborative Learning Environments. *Journal of Science Education and Technology*, *13*(4), 505–523. doi:10.100710956-004-1471-1

González. (2018). Turning a traditional teaching setting into a feedback-rich environment, *International Journal of Educational Technology in Higher Education*, *15*, Article number: 32.

Goodyear, P., Salmon, G., Spector, J. M., Steeples, C., & Tickner, S. (2001). Competencies for online teaching. *Education Training & Development*, *49*(1), 65–72.

Goos, M., Manning, A., & Salomons, A. (2014). Explaining Job Polarization: Routine-Biased Technological Change and Offshoring. *The American Economic Review*, *104*(8), 2509–2562. doi:10.1257/aer.104.8.2509

Goos, M., Manning, A., & Solomons, A. (2009). Job polarization in Europe. *The American Economic Review*, *99*(2), 58–63. doi:10.1257/aer.99.2.58

Gorard, S., & Smith, E. (2007). Do barriers get in the way? A review of the determinants of post-16 participation. *Research in Post-Compulsory Education, 12*(2), 141–158. doi:10.1080/13596740701387437

Gorham, J. (1988). The relationship between verbal teacher immediacy behaviors and student learning. *Communication Education, 37*(1), 40–53. doi:10.1080/03634528809378702

Gray, W., & Gerrand, B. (1977). *Learning by doing: Developing teaching skills.* Addison-Wesley Publishing Company.

Greenhow, C., & Lewin, C. (2016). Social media and education: Reconceptualizing the boundaries of formal and informal learning. *Learning, Media and Technology, 41*(1), 6–30. doi:10.1080/17439884.2015.1064954

Green, R. M. (2005). *Predictors of digital fluency [Yayımlanmamış doktora tezi].* Northwestern Üniversitesi.

Gros, B., & Garcia-Penalvo, F.J. (2016). Future trend in the design strategies and technological affordances of e-learning. In M. Spector, B.B. Lockee, & M.D. Childress (Eds.), Learning and Technology. An International Compendoium of Theory, Research, Practice ad Policy (pp.1-23). Springer International Publishing.

Grosseck, G. (2009). To use or not to use web 2.0 in higher education? *Procedia: Social and Behavioral Sciences, 1*(1), 478–482. doi:10.1016/j.sbspro.2009.01.087

Gruba, P. (2004). Understanding digitized second language videotext. *Computer Assisted Language Learning, 17*(1), 51–82. doi:10.1076/call.17.1.51.29710

Gruzd, A., Haythornthwaite, C., Paulin, D., Gilbert, S., & del Valle, M. E. (2018). Uses and gratifications factors for social media use in teaching: Instructors' perspectives. *New Media & Society, 20*(2), 475–494. doi:10.1177/1461444816662933

Guàrdia, L., Maina, M., & Baztán, P. (2018). Digital competence assessment framework for primary and secondary schools in Europe: the CRISS project. *Towards Personalized Guidance and Support for Learning*, 229.

Guàrdia, L., Maina, M., & Julià, A. (2017). Digital competence assessment system: supporting teachers with the CRISS platform. In *Central European Conference on Information and Intelligent Systems* (pp. 77-82). Faculty of Organization and Informatics Varazdin.

Guitert, M., Romeu, T., & Baztàn, P. (2017). Conceptual framework on digital competences in primary and secondary schools in Europe. *Proceedings of ICERI, 2017*, 5081–5090. doi:10.21125/iceri.2017.1336

Gummesson, E., Mele, C., Polese, F., & Díaz-Méndez, M. (2012). Value co-creation and university teaching quality. *Journal of Service Management, 23*(4), 571–592. doi:10.1108/09564231211260422

Gunawan Gunawan, Sahidu, & Herayanti. (2017). Virtual laboratory to improve students' problem-solving skills on electricity concept. *Journal Pendidikan IPA Indonesia, 6*(2), 257-264.

Gunn, C. (2010). Sustainability factors for e-learning initiatives. *ALT-J: Research in Learning Technology, 18*(2), 89–103. doi:10.1080/09687769.2010.492848

Gunter, G. A. (2007). The Effects of the Impact of Instructional Immediacy on Cognition and Learning in Online Classes. *International Journal of Social, Behavioral, Educational, Economic. Business and Industrial Engineering, 1*(11), 729–735.

Gupta. (2019). Role of ICT on the Teaching and Learning Process. *Paripex - Indian Journal of Research, 8*(4), 49-50.

Gupta, P., Jain, S., & Vashishth, N. (2017). e-governance in India: A Case study of Leveraging Information & Communication technology (ICT) for Women empowerment under MgnRegA in the state of Rajasthan. *Journal of Governance & Public Policy, 7*(1), 78–105.

Gutiérrez, A., & Tyner, K. (2012). Educación para los medios, alfabetización mediática y competencia digital. *Comunicar, 19*(38), 31–39.

Gutiérrez, I. (2014). Perfil del profesor universitario español en torno a las competencias en tecnologías de la información y la comunicación. *Pixel-Bit. Revista de Medios y Educación, 44*, 51–65. doi:10.7821/naer.2016.1.152

Gu, X., Shao, Y., Guo, X., & Lim, C. P. (2015). Designing a role structure to engage students in computer-supported collaborative learning. *The Internet and Higher Education, 24*, 13–20. doi:10.1016/j.iheduc.2014.09.002

Hague, C., & Payton, S. (2010). *Digital literacy across the curriculum.* Bristol: Futurelab. Retrieved from https://www.nfer.ac.uk/publications/FUTL06/FUTL06.pdf

Hämäläinen, R., De Wever, B., Malin, A., & Cincinnato, S. (2015). Education and Working Life: Vet Adults' Problem-Solving Skills in Technology- Rich Environments. *Computers & Education, 88*(1), 38–47. doi:10.1016/j.compedu.2015.04.013

Hamid, S., Waycott, J., Kurnia, S., & Chang, S. (2015). Understanding students' perceptions of the benefits of online social networking use for teaching and learning. *The Internet and Higher Education, 26*(1), 1–9. doi:10.1016/j.iheduc.2015.02.004

Hammond, M. (2014). Introducing ICT in schools in England: Rationale and consequences. *British Journal of Educational Technology, 45*(2), 191–201. doi:10.1111/bjet.12033

Harel, I. (2016). *American schools are teaching our kids how to code all wrong.* Retrieved from https://qz.com/691614/american-schools-are-teaching-our-kids-how-to-code-all-wrong/

Haridza, R., & Irving, K. E. (2017). The Evolution of Indonesian and American Science Education Curriculum: A Comparison Study. *Educare (San José), 9*(2).

Harrington, C. L., Bielby, D., & Bardo, A. R. (2014). *Aging, Media, and Culture.* Lexington Books.

Harris, A. L., & Rea, A. (2019). Web 2.0 and virtual world technologies: A growing impact on IS education. *Journal of Information Systems Education, 20*(2), 3.

Harryson, S. J., Dudkowski, R., & Stern, A. (2008). Transformation networks in innovation alliances–the development of Volvo C70. *Journal of Management Studies, 45*(4), 745–773. doi:10.1111/j.1467-6486.2008.00768.x

Hattinger, M., & Eriksson, K. (2020). Mind the Gap: a collaborative competence e-learning model between University and industry. *Proceedings of the 53rd Hawaii International Conference on System Sciences.* https://hdl.handll.net/10125/63750978-0-9981331-3-3

Hayashi, A., Chen, C., Ryan, T., & Wu, J. (2004). The role of social presence and moderating role of computer self efficacy in predicting the continuance usage of e-learning system. *Journal of Information Systems Education, 15*(2), •••.

Hayes, H. (2010). *Curriculum 21: Essential education for a changing world.* ASCD.

Haywood, J. (2018). Leading innovation: digital education in a traditional university, Higher Education in the Digital Age. Edward Elgar Publishing.

Healy, P. M., & Palepu, K. G. (2001). Information asymmetry, corporate disclosure, and the capital markets: A review of the empirical disclosure literature. *Journal of Accounting and Economics*, 31.

Hendarman, A. F., & Cantner, U. (2018). Soft skills, hard skills, and individual innovativeness. *Eurasian Business Review, 8*(2), 139–169. doi:10.100740821-017-0076-6

Henderson, M., Selwyn, N., & Aston, R. (2017). What works and why? Student perceptions of 'useful'digital technology in university teaching and learning. *Studies in Higher Education, 42*(8), 1567–1579. doi:10.1080/03075079.2015.1007946

Herfindahl, O. C. (1950). *Concentration in the Steel Industry* [Unpublished Ph. D. thesis]. Columbia University.

Herga, N. R. (2016). Virtual Laboratory in the Role of Dynamic Visualisation for Better Understanding of Chemistry in Primary School, *Eurasia Journal of Mathematics. Science & Technology Education*, *12*(3), 593–608.

Herscovici, A. (2011). Economic Growth, technical progress and labor productivity: Knowledge economics and new forms of technical progress. *International Journal of Innovation in the Digital Economy*, 2.

Heyward, M., & Sopantini. (2011). *Indonesia, the challenges of quality and equity in education.* doi:10.15730/books.7

Hidayat, A., & Utomo, V. G. (2015). Virtual Laboratory Implementation to Support High School Learning. *International Journal of Computers and Applications*, *120*(16), 14–18. doi:10.5120/21310-4283

Hilbert, M. (2011). Digital gender divide or technologically empowered women in developing countries? A typical case of lies, damned lies, and statistics. *Women's Studies International Forum*, *34*(6), 479–489. doi:10.1016/j.wsif.2011.07.001

Hillman, D. C., Willis, D. J., & Gunawardena, C. N. (1994). Learner-interface interaction in distance education: An extension of contemporary models and strategies for practitioners. *American Journal of Distance Education*, *8*(2), 30–42. doi:10.1080/08923649409526853

Hirschman, A. O. (1958). *The Strategy of Economic Development.* Yale University Press.

Hirumi, A. (2002). A framework for analyzing, designing, and sequencing planned e-learning interactions. *Quarterly Review of Distance Education*, *3*(2), 141–160.

Hlasna, P., Klímová, B., & Poulova, P. (2017). Use of information and communication technologies in primary education–A case study of the Czech Republic. *International Electronic Journal of Elementary Education*, *9*(3), 681–692.

Hodge, F. D., Kennedy, J. J., & Maines, L. A. (2004). Does search-facilitating technology improve the transparency of financial reporting? *The Accounting Review*, 79.

Hogarth, R. (1980). *Judgment and choice.* John Wiley & Sons.

Homan, G., & Macpherson, A. (2005). E-learning in the corporate university. *Journal of European Industrial Training*, *29*(1), 75–90. doi:10.1108/03090590510576226

Hootsuite. (2020). *Global Report: Indonesia.* Retrieved from https://hootsuite.com/id/pages/digital-2020

Hope, A., Schwaba, T., & Piper, A. M. (2014, April). Understanding digital and material social communications for older adults. In *Proceedings of the SIGCHI Conference on Human Factors in Computing Systems* (pp. 3903-3912). ACM. 10.1145/2556288.2557133

Horton, W., & Horton, K. (2003). *E-learning Tools and Technologies: A consumer's guide for trainers, teachers, educators, and instructional designers.* Wiley Publishing.

Howard, S. K., & Mozejko, A. (2015). Teachers: technology, change and resistance. *Teaching and digital technologies: Big issues and critical questions*, 307-317.

Hrastinski, S. (2008). Asynchronous and synchronous e-learning: A study of asynchronous and synchronous e-learning methods discovered that each supports different purposes. *EDUCAUSE Quarterly*, *31*(4), 51–55. http://net.educause.edu/ir/library/pdf/EQM0848.pdf

HSA. (2014, September 12). *Demographic and social characteristics of the Resident Population of Greece according to the 2011 Population - Housing Census revision of 20-3-2014.* Hellenic Statistical Authority. Retrieved https://www.statistics.gr/en/statistics/-/publication/SAM03/2011

Hsi, S. (2007). Conceptualizing learning from the everyday activities of digital kids. *International Journal of Science Education*, *29*(12), 1509–1529. doi:10.1080/09500690701494076

Hsu, R. C., & Liu, W. C. (2005, June). Project based learning as a pedagogical tool for embedded system education. In *ITRE 2005. 3rd International Conference on Information Technology Research in Education, 2005*, 362–366.

Huang, H. M. (2002). Toward constructivism for adult learners in online learning environment. *British Journal of Educational Technology*, *33*(1), 27–37. doi:10.1111/1467-8535.00236

Hunton, J.E., & McEwen, R., (1997). An assessment of the relation between analysts earnings forecast accuracy, motivational incentives and cognitive information search strategy. *Account Review*, *72*(3).

Hurrell, S. A. (2016). Rethinking the soft skills deficit blame game: Employers, skills withdrawal and the reporting of soft skills gaps. *Human Relations*, *69*(3), 605–628. doi:10.1177/0018726715591636

Hussein, G. (2011). The attitudes of undergraduate students towards motivation and technology in a foreign language classroom. *International Journal of Learning and Teaching*, *2*(2), 14–24.

Hussin, A. A. (2018). Education 4.0 made simple: Ideas for teaching. *International Journal of Education and Literacy Studies*, *6*(3), 92–98. doi:10.7575/aiac.ijels.v.6n.3p.92

Hwang, H. G., Chang, I. C., Chen, F. J., & Wu, S. Y. (2008). Investigation of the application of KMS for diseases classifications: A study in A taiwanese hospital. *Expert Systems with Applications*, *34*(1), 725–733. doi:10.1016/j.eswa.2006.10.018

Ibarra, A. (2000). Formación de recursos humanos y competencia laboral. *Boletín Cinterfor*, *149*, 95–107.

Ilias, A., & Ghani, E. K. (2015). Examining the adoption of extensible business reporting language among public listed companies in Malaysia. *Procedia Economics and Finance*, 28.

Illeris, K. (2006). Lifelong learning and the low-skilled. *International Journal of Lifelong Education*, *25*(1), 15–28. doi:10.1080/02601370500309451

Ilomäki, L., Kantosalo, A., & Lakkala, M. (2011). What is digital competence. Linked portal. Brussels: European Schoolnet (EUN), 1-12.

IMD World Competitiveness Center. (2019). *IMD World Digital Competitiveness Ranking 2019*. IMD World Competitiveness Center.

Indian Institute of Technology Delhi. (2020). *Virtual Labs*. http://www.vlab.co.in/

Indonesian Constitution. Law No. 12 of 2012 concerning Higher Education Institutions. Retrieved January from https://unnes.ac.id/wp-content/uploads/uu-12-2012/

Indonesian National Accreditation Body. (2017). *National Higher Education Accreditation System*. Indonesian University National.

Instefjord, E. J., & Munthe, E. (2018). Educating digitally competent teachers: A study of integration of professional digital competence in teacher education. *Teaching and Teacher Education*, *67*, 37–45. doi:10.1016/j.tate.2017.05.016

Institute for the Future for Dell Technologies. (2017). *The next era of human/machine partnerships: Emerging technologies' impact on society and work in 2030*. Retrieved from http://www.iftf.org/fileadmin/user_upload/downloads/th/SR1940_IFTFforDellTechnologies_Human-Machine_070717_readerhigh-res.pdf

Ionita, A., Visan, M., Niculescu, C., & Popa, A. (2015). Smart Collaborative Platform for eLearning with Application in Spatial Enabled Society. *Procedia: Social and Behavioral Sciences*, *191*, 2097–2107. doi:10.1016/j.sbspro.2015.04.676

Iordache, C., Mariën, I., & Baelden, D. (2017). Developing Digital Skills and Competences: A QuickScan Analysis of 13 Digital Literacy Models. *Italian Journal of Sociology of Education*, *9*(1), 6–30. doi:10.14658/pupj-ijse-2017-1-2

Ismail, S., & Bakar, N. B. A. (2011). Reporting practices of Malaysian public universities: The extent of accountability disclosure. *African Journal of Business Management*, *5*(15), 6366–6376.

ISTE. (2019). *ISTE Standards for Students.* Retrieved from September 22, 2019 from https://www.iste.org/standards/for-students

Iswanto, Y. (2016). Menciptakan Lingkungan Pembelajaran yang Memperkuat Teknologi. In *Institusi Pendidikan Tinggi di Era Digital: Pemikiran, Permodelan dan Praktek Baik* (pp. 7–24). Universitas Terbuka, Tangerang Selatan.

Ito, M., Baumer, S., Bittanti, M., boyd, d., Cody, R., & Herr-Stephenson, B. (2009). Hanging out, messing around, and geeking out: Kids living and learning with new media. Cambridge: The MIT Press.

ITU. (2019). *ICT Development Index 2017.* Retrieved from https://www.itu.int/net4/ITU-D/idi/2017/index.html

James, S. A. (2019). Valuation of ICT proficiency of teachers in actualizing E-learning in home economics education, Ogun State, Nigeria. International Journal for Infonomics, 12(3).

Jauregi, K., de Graaff, R., van den Bergh, H., & Kriz, M. (2012). Native/non-native speaker interactions through video-web communication: A clue for enhancing motivation? *Computer Assisted Language Learning*, *25*(1), 1–19. doi:10.1080/09588221.2011.582587

Jenkins, H. (2007). *Reconsidering digital immigrants.* Message posted to http://www.henryjenkins.org

Jones, P., Packham, G., Miller, C., Davies, I., Jones, A., & Roberts, D. (2003). e-Retention: An Initial Evaluation of Student Withdrawals within a Virtual Learning Environment. In R. Williams, (Ed.), *Proceedings of the 2nd European Conference on E-learning (ECEL)* (pp. 239-248). Academic Conferences and Publishing International, Sonning Common.

Jones, P., Pickernell, D., & Welsh Enterprise Institute. (2004). *Student and tutor perspectives of online moderation.* Pontypridd: University of Glamorgan, Welsh Enterprise Unit.

Jones, B., & Flannigan, S. L. (2006). Connecting the digital dots: Literacy of the 21st century. *EDUCAUSE Quarterly*, *29*(2), 8–10.

Judson, K. M., & Taylor, S. A. (2014). Moving from marketization to marketing of higher education: The co-creation of value in higher education. *Higher Education Studies*, *4*(1), 51–67. doi:10.5539/hes.v4n1p51

Jules, T. (2017). *Public Policy and Governance. The Global Educational Policy Environment in the Fourth Industrial Revolution: Gate, Regulated and Governed.* Emerald Group Publishing Limited.

Julie, D., & Barry, R. (2010). Improving the Undergraduate Laboratory Learning Experience Through Redesigned Teaching and Assessment Strategies Integrating Transferable Skills and Focusing on Feedback. Learning, Teaching & Technology Centre, Dublin Institute of Technology, Paper 21, 1-8.

Jumaat, N. F., & Tasir, Z. (2013). Students' types of online interaction through Facebook discussion. *Procedia: Social and Behavioral Sciences*, *97*, 353–360. doi:10.1016/j.sbspro.2013.10.245

Jung, E. H., Walden, J., Johnson, A. C., & Sundar, S. S. (2017). Social networking in the aging context: Why older adults use or avoid Facebook. *Telematics and Informatics*, *34*(7), 1071–1080. doi:10.1016/j.tele.2017.04.015

Jung, I. (2012). Asian learners' perception of quality in distance education and gender differences. *The International Review of Research in Open and Distributed Learning*, *13*(2), 1. Advance online publication. doi:10.19173/irrodl.v13i2.1159

Jung, Y. S. (2001). Toward an effective EFL teacher development program focusing on multimedia and the Internet. *English Teaching*, *56*(4), 141–162.

Jyothi, V. E., & Rao, K. N. (2012). Effective implementation of agile practices - incoordination with lean Kanban. *International Journal on Computer Science and Engineering*, *4*(1).

Kabilan, M. K., Ahmad, N., & Abidin, M. J. Z. (2010). Facebook: An online environment for learning of English in institutions of higher education? *Internet and Higher Education*, *13*(4), 179–187. doi:10.1016/j.iheduc.2010.07.003

Kaminski, K., Switzer, J., & Gloeckner, G. (2009). Workforce readiness: A study of university students' fluency with information technology. *Computers & Education*, *53*(2), 228–233. doi:10.1016/j.compedu.2009.01.017

Kaplan, A. M., & Haenlein, M. (2016). Higher education and the digital revolution: About MOOCs, SPOCs, social media, and the Cookie Monster. *Business Horizons*, *59*(4), 441–450. doi:10.1016/j.bushor.2016.03.008

Karaca, O., Demir, K., & Caliskan, S. A. (2018). Virtual, Augmented and Mobile Learning in Health Education. In Computer-Mediated Learning for Workforce Development (pp. 168-195). IGI Global.

Karalis, T., & Koutsonikos, G. (2003). Issues and Challenges in Organising and Evaluating Web based Courses for Adults. *Themes in Education, 4*(2), 177-188.

Kattel, R., & Mazzucato, M. (2018). Mission-oriented innovation policy and dynamic capabilities in the public sector. *Industrial and Corporate Change*, *27*(5), 787–801. doi:10.1093/icc/dty032

Katz, R. (2015). *El ecosistema y la economía digital en América Latina*. Ariel – Telefónica.

Kavis, M. (2015). *The four stages of cloud competence*. Retrieved from https://www.forbes.com/sites/mikekavis/2015/10/21/the-four-stages-of-cloud-competence/#2fb55322183a

Kearsley, G. (2000). *Online education: Learning and teaching in cyberspace* (Vol. 91). Wadsworth.

Kemshal-Bell, G. (2001). *The Online Teacher. Final report prepared for the Project Steering Committee of the VET Teacher and Online Learning Project, ITAM, ESD*. TAFENSW.

Kennedy, G. E., Judd, T. S., Churchward, A., Gray, K., & Krause, K. L. (2008). First year students' experiences with technology: Are they really digital natives? *Australasian Journal of Educational Technology*, *24*(1). Advance online publication. doi:10.14742/ajet.1233

Keser, H., & Semerci, A. (2019). Technology trends, Education 4.0 and beyond. *Contemporary Educational Researches Journal*, *9*(3), 39–49. doi:10.18844/cerj.v9i3.4269

Kessler, G. (2007). Formal and informal CALL preparation and teacher attitude toward technology. *Computer Assisted Language Learning*, *20*(2), 173–188. doi:10.1080/09588220701331394

Khlifi, F., Bouri, A., (2007). Determinants of internet financial reporting. *Investment Research and Analysis Journal, 1.*

Kiernan, P., & Aizawa, K. (2004). Cell phones in task based learning: Are cell phones useful language learning tools? *ReCALL*, *16*(1), 71–84. doi:10.1017/S0958344004000618

Kim, H. (2002). Teachers as a barrier to technology-integrated language teaching. *English Teaching*, *57*(2), 35–64.

Kim, S., Chung, K., & Yu, H. (2013). Enhancing digital fluency through a training program for creative problem solving using computer programming. *The Journal of Creative Behavior*, *47*(3), 171–199. doi:10.1002/jocb.30

King, K., & Palmer, R. (2010). *Planning for Teachnical and Vocational Skills Development*. Unesco International Institute for Educational Planning.

Kirschner, P. A., & Meester, M. A. M. (1988). The laboratory in higher science education: Problems, premises and objectives. *Higher Education, 17*(1), 81–98. doi:10.1007/BF00130901

Klein, J., & Eseryel, D. (2006). The Corporate Learning Environment. In M. Lytras & A. Naeve (Eds.), *Intelligent Learning Infrastructure for Knowledge Intensive Organizations A Semantic Web Primer* (pp. 1–38). Information Science Publishing. doi:10.4018/978-1-59140-503-0.ch001

Knowles, M. S. (1980). The modern practice of adult education. New York: Cambridge.

Knowles, M. S. (1970). *The modern practice of adult education: Andragogy versus pedagogy*. New York Association Press.

Kock, N. (2015). *WarpPLS 5.0 User Manual*. Script Warp Systems. Retrieved from http://www.scriptwarp.com/warppls/UserManual_WarpPLS_V3_Redirect.pdf

Kolko, J. (2012). Broadband and Local Growth. *Journal of Urban Economics, 71*(1), 100–113. doi:10.1016/j.jue.2011.07.004

Kominfo. (2019). *Digitalisasi Sekolah Percepat Perluasan Akses Pendidikan Berkualitas di Daerah 3T.* https://kominfo.go.id/index.php/content/detail/22211/digitalisasi-sekolah-percepat-perluasan-akses-pendidikan-berkualitas-di-daerah-3t/0/artikel_gpr

Kompas. (2014). *"Nawa Cita", 9 Agenda Prioritas Jokowi-JK.* https://nasional.kompas.com/read/2014/05/21/0754454/.Nawa.Cita.9.Agenda.Prioritas.Jokowi-JK

Koppell, J. G. S. (2005). Pathologies of accountability: ICANN and the challenge of multiple accountabilities disorder. *Public Administration Review, 65*(1), 94–108. doi:10.1111/j.1540-6210.2005.00434.x

Kreijns, K., Kirschner, P. A., Jochems, W., & Van Buuren, H. (2007). Measuring perceived sociability of computer-supported collaborative learning environments. *Computers & Education, 49*(2), 176–192. doi:10.1016/j.compedu.2005.05.004

Kress, G. (2003). *Literacy in the New Media Age*. Routledge.

Krivickas, R. V., & Krivickas, J. (2007). Laboratory Instruction in Engineering Education, *Global. Journal of Engineering Education, 11*(2).

Ku, H.-Y., Tseng, H. W., & Akarasriworn, C. (2013). Collaboration factors, teamwork satisfaction, and student attitudes toward online collaborative learning. *Computers in Human Behavior, 29*(3), 922–929. doi:10.1016/j.chb.2012.12.019

Kühn, C. (2017). Are students ready to (re)-design their personal learning environment? The case of the e-dynamic.space. *Journal of New Approaches in Educational Research, 6*(1), 11–19. doi:10.7821/naer.2017.1.185

Kull, L., Miller, L. E., Clair, J. A., & Savage, M. (2007). Interactive data Xbrl: A revolutionary idea. *Journal of Government Financial Management*, 2.

Kupczynski, L., Mundy, M. A., Goswami, J., & Meling, V. (2012). Cooperative Learning in Distance Learning: A Mixed Methods Study. *International Journal of Instruction, 5*(2), 81–90.

Kurt, A.A., Dönmez, F.İ., Ersoy, M., Dindar, M., Mısırlı, Ö. ve Akçay, T. (2013). Teknoloji ışığında okuryazarlıklar. *Eğitim Teknolojileri Araştırmaları Dergisi (ETAD), 4*(2).

Kvavik, R. B., Caruso, J. B., & Morgan, G. (2004). *ECAR Study Of Students And Information Technology 2004: Convenience, Connection, and Control.* EDUCAUSE Center for Applied Research. http://www.educause.edu/ir/library/pdf/ers0405/rs/ers0405w.pdf

Laal, M., & Laal, M. (2012). Collaborative learning: What is it? *Procedia: Social and Behavioral Sciences, 31*, 491–495. doi:10.1016/j.sbspro.2011.12.092

Lambert, J., & Cuper, P. (2008). Multimedia technologies and familiar spaces: 21st century teaching for 21st Century Learners. *Contemporary Issues in Technology & Teacher Education*, *8*(3), 264–276.

Lam, Y. (2000). Technophilia vs. technophobia: A preliminary look at why second-language teachers do or do not use technology in their classrooms. *Canadian Modern Language Review*, *56*(3), 389–420. doi:10.3138/cmlr.56.3.389

Lam, Y., & Lawrence, G. (2002). Teacher-student role redefinition during a computer-based second language project: Are computers catalysts for empowering change? *Computer Assisted Language Learning*, *15*(3), 295–315. doi:10.1076/call.15.3.295.8185

Lankshear, C. J., & Knobel, M. (2008). *Introduction: digital literacies: concepts, policies and practices*. Peter Lang Publishing.

LaRose, R., & Whitten, P. (2000). Re-thinking Instructional Immediacy for Web Courses: A social cognitive exploration. *Communication Education*, *49*(4), 320–338. doi:10.1080/03634520009379221

Larraz, V. (2012). *La competencia digital a la Universitat*. Tesis: Universitat d'Andorra.

Larraz, V., Espuny, C., & Gisbert, M. (2012). *La presencia de la competencia digital en la universidad*. Retrieved from http://hdl.handle.net/123456789/3212

Laut, J. T. (1995). *The identification of critical teaching skills and their relationship to student achievement: A quantitative synthesis* (Doctoral dissertation). The Ohio State University. Retrieved from https://search.proquest.com/docview/304199329/142656967665CED9957/1?accountid=38885

Lawrence, G. P. J. (2000). *Teacher belief systems towards computer-mediated language learning, college ESL instruction* (Unpublished doctoral dissertation). National Library of Canada.

Lawton Smith, H., & Leydesdorff, L. (2014). The Triple Helix in the context of global change: Dynamics and challenges. *Prometheus*, *32*(4), 321–336. doi:10.1080/08109028.2014.972135

Lazaraton, A. (2000). Current trends in research methodology and statistics in applied linguistics. *TESOL Quarterly*, *34*(1), 175–181. doi:10.2307/3588103

Lee, B., Godbey, G., & Sawyer, S. (2003). SeniorNet, v. 2.0. *Parks & Recreation (Ashburn)*, *38*(10), 22–28.

Lee, L. (2005). Using web-based instruction to promote active learning: Learners' perspectives. *CALICO Journal*, *23*(1), 139–156. doi:10.1558/cj.v23i1.139-156

Lee, Y. H., Hsieh, Y. C., & Hsu, C. N. (2011). Adding Innovation Diffusion Theory to the Technology Acceptance Model: Supporting Employees' Intentions to use E-Learning Systems. *Journal of Educational Technology & Society*, *14*(4).

Legon, R., Garrett, R., & Fredericksen, E. (2019). *The Changing Landscape of Online Education (CHLOE): Behind the Numbers*. Quality Matters. Retrieved from https://www.qualitymatters.org/qa-resources/resource-center/articles-resources/CHLOE-3-report-2019

Lehr, U., & Kruse, A. (2006). Verlängerung der Lebensarbeitszeit-eine realistische Perspektive? *Zeitschrift für Arbeits- und Organisationspsychologie A&O, 50*(4), 240-247.

Leist, A. K. (2013). Social media use of older adults: A mini-review. *Gerontology*, *59*(4), 378–384. doi:10.1159/000346818 PMID:23594915

Leko, A. (2019). Learning and evaluation with the support of digital technologies in the Science and Society subject in Croatia. In K. Bilić Meštrić & A. Mudrinić (Eds.), *Teachers and head teachers as the agents of change in their own educational contexts: action research on new technologies as a challenge, stimulation and support to learning and teaching* (pp. 72–106). CARNET.

Leonard-Barton, D. (1992). Core capabilities and core rigidities: A paradox in managing new product development. *Strategic Management Journal, 13*(S1), 111–125. doi:10.1002mj.4250131009

Lestari, N. T. (2015). *Tantangan Masa Depan Pendidikan di Indonesia dan Pendidikan Global.* Retrieved from https://www.kompasiana.com/noviana-trilestari/5511408ba333116642ba8084/a-tantangan-masa-depan-pendidikan-di-indonesia-dan-pendidikan-global

Levano, L., Sánchez, S., Guillén, P., Tello, S., Herrera, N., & Collantes, Z. (2019). Competencias digitales y educación. *Propósitos y Representaciones., 7*(2), 569–588. doi:10.20511/pyr2019.v7n2.329

Levy, B. R. (2017). Age-stereotype paradox: Opportunity for social change. *The Gerontologist, 57*(suppl_2), S118-S126.

Leydesdorff, L. (2012). The triple helix, quadruple helix,…, and an N-tuple of helices: Explanatory models for analyzing the knowledge-based economy? *Journal of the Knowledge Economy, 3*(1), 25–35. doi:10.100713132-011-0049-4

Leymonié, J. (2015). Nativos e inmigrantes digitales: ¿cómo aprendemos y enseñamos? *Dixit, 12*, 10–19.

Liaw, S. S., Huang, H. M., & Chen, G. D. (2007). Surveying instructor and learner attitudes towarde-learning. *Computers & Education, 49*(4), 1066–1080. doi:10.1016/j.compedu.2006.01.001

Lim, J., & Newby, T. J. (2019). Preservice teachers' Web 2.0 experiences and perceptions on Web 2.0 as a personal learning environment. *Journal of Computing in Higher Education, 32*(2), 234–260. doi:10.100712528-019-09227-w

Link, A. N., & Siegel, D. S. (2007). *Innovation, entrepreneurship, and Technological Change.* Oxford University Press. doi:10.1093/acprof:oso/9780199268825.001.0001

Liu, A., Li, Y., & Ye, H. (2018). *Digital fluency and social media use: An empirical investigation of WeChat use. In Proceedings of the 51st Hawaii International Conference on System Sciences | 2018.* Curran Associates. Retrieved from https://scholarspace.manoa.hawaii.edu/bitstream/10125/49952/1/paper0065.pdf

Liu, C., Yao, L. J., Hu, N., & Liu, L. (2011). The impact of IFRS on accounting quality in a regulated market: An empirical study of China. *Journal of Accounting, Auditing & Finance, 26*(4), 659–676. doi:10.1177/0148558X11409164

Liu, D., Valdiviezo-Díaz, P., Riofrio, G., Sun, Y.-M., & Barba, R. (2015). Integration of Virtual Labs into Science E-learning. *Procedia Computer Science, 75*, 95–102. doi:10.1016/j.procs.2015.12.224

Liu, Y., Theodore, P., & Lavelle, E. (2004). Experimental effects of online instruction on teachers' concerns about technology integration. *International Journal of Instructional Technology and Distance Learning, 1*(1).

Llorens, F., & Capdeferro, N. (2011). Facebook's Potential for Collaborative e-Learning. *Revista de Universidad y Sociedad del Conocimiento, 8*(2), 197–210.

Loewen, S., Isbell, D., & Sporn, Z. (2020). The effectiveness of app-based language instruction for developing receptive linguistic knowledge and oral communicative ability. *Foreign Language Annals, 53*(2), 209–233. doi:10.1111/flan.12454

Lomelí, L. (2019). Educación superior y desarrollo: Los desafíos de México. *Economía UNAM, 16*(47), 3–11. http://www.economia.unam.mx/assets/pdfs/econunam/47/01Lomeli.pdf

Lopukhova, J., & Makeeva, E. (2019). University Teacher Professional Development in the Digital World. In The Challenges of the Digital Transformation in Education. ICL 2018. doi:10.1007/978-3-030-11935-5_49

Loup-Escande, E., Frenoy, R., Poplimont, G., Thouvenin, I., Gapenne, O., & Megalakaki, O. (2017). Contributions of mixed reality in a calligraphy learning task: Effects of supplementary visual feedback and expertise on cognitive load, user experience, and gestural performance. *Computers in Human Behavior*, *75*, 42–49. doi:10.1016/j.chb.2017.05.006

Low, M., Samkin, G., & Li, Y. (2015). Voluntary reporting of intellectual capital: Comparing the quality of disclosures from New Zealand, Australian and United Kingdom universities. *Journal of Intellectual Capital*, *16*(4), 779–808. doi:10.1108/JIC-03-2015-0022

Lubbe, J. C. I. (2016). Digital fluency of faculty members at an ODL institution. *Progressio*, *38*(2), 63–83.

Ludwig-Hardman, S., & Dunlap, J. C. (2003). Learner support services for online students: Scaffolding for success. *International Review of Research in Open and Distance Learning*, *4*(1). Advance online publication. doi:10.19173/irrodl.v4i1.131

Lundberg, H., & Andresen, E. (2012). Cooperation among companies, universities and local government in a Swedish context. *Industrial Marketing Management*, *41*(3), 429–437. doi:10.1016/j.indmarman.2011.06.017

Lyle, Feisel, & Rosa. (2005). The Role of the Laboratory in Undergraduate Engineering Education. *The Research Journal for Engineering Education*, *94*(1), 121-130.

Magni, D., Pezzi, A., & Vrontis, D. (2020). Towards a framework of students' co-creation behaviour in higher education institutions. *International Journal of Managerial and Financial Accounting*, *12*(2), 119–148. doi:10.1504/IJMFA.2020.109129

Mahmud, M. M., & Wong, S. F. (2018). Facebook and Collaborative Learning: An Empirical Study on Online Assessment. *International Journal of Learning and Teaching*, *4*(2), 107–113. doi:10.18178/ijlt.4.2.107-113

Makhaiel, N. K. B., & Sherer, M. L. J. (2018). The effect of political-economic reform on the quality of financial reporting in Egypt. *Journal of Financial Reporting and Accounting*, *16*(1), 245–270. doi:10.1108/JFRA-05-2016-0035

Makransky, G., Mayer, R. E., Veitch, N., Hood, M., Christensen, K. B., & Gadegaard, H. (2019). Equivalence of using a desktop virtual reality science simulation at home and in class. *PLoS One*, *14*(4), e0214944. doi:10.1371/journal.pone.0214944 PMID:30973900

Manca, S., & Ranieri, M. (2016). Facebook and the others. Potentials and obstacles of social media for teaching in higher education. *Computers & Education*, *95*(1), 216–230. doi:10.1016/j.compedu.2016.01.012

Mangal, S. K., & Mangal, U. (2009). *Essentials of educational technology*. New Delhi, India: PHI Learning Private Limited

Manyika, J., Chui, M., Bughin, J., Dobbs, R., Bisson, P., & Marrs, A. (2013). *Disruptive technologies: Advances that will transform life, business, and the global economy* (Vol. 180). McKinsey Global Institute.

Mao, J., Ifenthaler, D., Fujimoto, T., Garavaglia, A., & Rossi, P. G. (2019). National Policies and Educational Technology: A Synopsis of Trends and Perspectives from Five Countries. *TechTrends*, *63*(3), 284–293. doi:10.100711528-019-00396-0

Ma, Q., Chan, A. H., & Chen, K. (2016). Personal and other factors affecting acceptance of smartphone technology by older Chinese adults. *Applied Ergonomics*, *54*, 62–71. doi:10.1016/j.apergo.2015.11.015 PMID:26851465

Marcovitch, J. (2002). *La universidad (im)posible*. Cambridge University Press.

Maria, L. (2011). The professional competence of teachers: Which qualities, attitudes, skills and knowledge contribute to a teacher's effectiveness? *International Journal of Humanities and Social Science*, *1*(21), 66–78.

Mariappan, J., Shih, A., Schrader, P. G., & Elmore, R. (2004, January). Scenario-based learning and multimedia in improving engineering education. In *ASME 2004 International Design Engineering Technical Conferences and Computers and Information in Engineering Conference* (pp. 521-525). American Society of Mechanical Engineers Digital Collection. 10.1115/DETC2004-57704

Marr, B., Schiuma, G., & Neely, A. (2015). Intellectual capital – defining key performance indicators for organizational knowledge assets. *Business Process Management Journal*, *10*(5), 551–569. doi:10.1108/14637150410559225

Martin, A. (2009). Digital literacy for the third age: Sustaining identity in an uncertain world. *eLearning Papers, 12*, 1–15. Retrieved from https://pdfs.semanticscholar.org/c7e3/ee4aee40aa07718a7f5d1123ba074a604e78.pdf

Martin, A. (2005). DigEuLit – a European framework for digital literacy: A progress report. *Journal of ELiteracy*, *2*, 130–136.

Martini, E., & Vespasiano, F. (2015). University Services to the Students: Analysis of the Main Satisfaction Indices. *Italian Sociological Review*, *5*(3), 293–321.

Martins, C. B. M. J., Steil, A. V., & Todesco, J. L. (2004). Factors influencing the adoption of the Internet as a teaching tool at foreign language schools. *Computers & Education*, *42*(4), 353–374. doi:10.1016/j.compedu.2003.08.007

Martin, W., Strother, S., Beglau, M., Bates, L., Reitzes, T., & McMillan Culp, K. (2010). Connecting instructional technology professional development to teacher and student outcomes. *Journal of Research on Technology in Education*, *43*(1), 53–74. doi:10.1080/15391523.2010.10782561

Marzal, M. (2010). La evaluación de los programas de alfabetización en información en la educación superior: Estrategias e instrumentos. *Revista de Universidad y Sociedad del Conocimiento*, *7*(2), 28–37.

Marza, M., & Cruz, E. (2018). Gaming como Instrumento Educativo para una Educación en competencias Digitales desde los Academic Skills Centres. *Revista General de Información y Documentación*, *28*(2), 489–506. doi:10.5209/RGID.60805

Masanet, M., Contreras, P., & Ferrés, J. (2013). Highly qualified students? Research into the media competence level of Spanish youth. *Communicatio Socialis*, *26*(4), 217–234.

Massey University. (2016). *Scenario-based learning*. Retrieved March 3, 2020, from https://www.massey.ac.nz/massey/fms/AVC%20Academic/Teaching%20and%20Learning%20Cenrtres/Scenario-based-learning.pdf

Masud, M. (2016). Collaborative e-learning systems using semantic data interoperability. *Computers in Human Behavior*, *61*, 127–135. doi:10.1016/j.chb.2016.02.094

Matamala, C. (2014). Factores predictivos de las competencias TIC en alumnos chilenos de secundaria. *Revista Iberoamericana de educación*, *67*(1), 121-136. doi:10.35362/rie671267

Mathew, N. G., & Alidmat, A. O. H. (2013). A study on the usefulness of audio-visual aids in EFL classroom: Implications for effective instruction. *International Journal of Higher Education*, *2*(2), 86. doi:10.5430/ijhe.v2n2p86

McClure, P. K. (2018). "You're fired," says the robot: The rise of automation in the workplace, technophobes, and fears of unemployment. *Social Science Computer Review*, *36*(2), 139–156. doi:10.1177/0894439317698637

McKnight, S. T., Maniam, B., & Robertson, J. (2019). Effects of Technology Innovations on Business. *Journal of Business and Behavioral Sciences*, *31*(1), 84–101.

Media Indonesia, Enam Program Pendidikan di Nawacita Jadi Prioritas, Minggu 20 Oktober. (2019). https://mediaindonesia.com/read/detail/266451-enam-program-pendidikan-di-nawacita-jadi-prioritas

Mehra, B., Merkel, C., & Bishop, A. P. (2004). The internet for empowerment of minority and marginalized users. *New Media & Society*, *6*(6), 781–802. doi:10.1177/146144804047513

Mehrabian, A. (1967). Orientation behaviors and nonverbal attitude communication. *Journal of Communication*, *17*(4), 324–332. doi:10.1111/j.1460-2466.1967.tb01190.x

Mehrabian, A. (1971). Nonverbal communication. *Nebraska Symposium on Motivation*, *19*, 107–161.

Mehta, D. M. (2011). Comparative study of teaching competancy of c.b.s.e & g.b.s.c higher secondary school teacher. *International Referred Research Journal*, *3*(31), 23–24.

Melancon, B. (2006). *Testimony of Barry Melancon, President and CEO*. AICPA.

Merchant, G. (2009). Literacy in virtual worlds. *Journal of Research in Reading*, *32*(1), 38–56. doi:10.1111/j.1467-9817.2008.01380.x

Merriam, S. B. (2001). Andragogy and self-directed learning: Pillars of adult learning theory. In S. B. Merriam (Ed.), The new update on adult learning theory (pp. 3-13). New Directions for Adult and Continuing Education, No. 89. San Francisco: Jossey-Bass.

Miklos, A., Vasarhelyi, D.Y., Chan, J. P., & Krahel. (2012). Consequences of Xbrl standardization on financial statement data. *Journal of Information Systems*, *26*(1).

Miller, C., & Bartlett, J. (2012). 'Digital fluency': Towards young people's critical use of the internet. *Journal of Information Literacy*, *6*(2), 35–55. doi:10.11645/6.2.1714

Ministry of Education and Culture of the Republic of Indonesia. (2018). *Pembiayaan Operasional Non Personalia untuk Optimalisasi Mutu Lulusan SMK. Directorate of Vocational High School Development*. Directorate General of Primary and Secondary Education, and Ministry of Education and Culture, Republic of Indonesia.

Ministry of Education and Culture. (2019). *Coordination of Private Universities Edition XII*. Retrieved from: https://www.kemdikbud.go.id/main

Ministry of Research, Technology and Higher Education of the Republic of Indonesia. (2019). *Higher Education Institution*. Retrieved from: https://ristekdikti.go.id

Mira, J. (2008). Aspectos conceptuales de la Inteligencia Artificial y la Ingeniería del Conocimiento. In J. Palma & R. Marín (Eds.), *Inteligencia Artificial* (pp. 72–85). Mc Graw Hill.

Misanchuk, M., & Anderson, T. (2001). Building Community in an Online Learning Environment: Communication, Cooperation and Collaboration. *Proceedings of the Annual Mid-South Instructional Technology Conference*. Retrieved from http://www.mtsu.edu/-itconf/proceed01/19.pdf

Mishkin, F. S., & Eakins, S. (2008). *Financial markets and Institutions. Boston, USA: Addison Wesley*. Cambridge University Press.

Moore, M. (1989). Three types of interaction. *American Journal of Distance Education*, *3*(2), 1–6. doi:10.1080/08923648909526659

Moore, M. G. (2007). The theory of transactional distance. In M. G. Moore (Ed.), *Handbook of distance education* (pp. 89–103). Lawrence Erlbaum Associates.

Moore, M. G., & Kearsley, G. (1996). *Distance education: A systems view*. Wadsworth Publishing.

Morariu, C. M. (2013). The determinants of intellectual capital disclosure: Evidence from Romania. *Research in Accounting in Emerging Economies, 13*, 163–186.

Morin, E. (2003). *Geleceğin eğitimi için gerekli 7 bilgi*. İstanbul Bilgi Üniversitesi Yayınları.

Morrell, R. W., Mayhorn, C. B., & Bennett, J. (2000). A survey of World Wide Web use in middle-aged and older adults. *Human Factors, 42*(2), 175–182. doi:10.1518/001872000779656444 PMID:11022878

Morse, N. S., & Kocharian, A. (2014). Model Standard of ICT Competence of University Teachers in the Context of Improving the Quality of Education. *Information Technologies and Learning Tools, 43*(5), 27–39.

Mortera, F. (2016). Utilizar tecnologías de la información y de las comunicaciones: La alfabetización digital. In *J. R. Valenzuela (Comp.), Competencias transversales para una sociedad basada en conocimiento* (pp. 124–147). Cengage.

Moseley, J. L., & Heaney, M. J. (1994). Needs assessment across disciplines. *Performance Improvement Quarterly, 7*(1), 60–79. doi:10.1111/j.1937-8327.1994.tb00617.x

Mota, R., & Scott, D. (2014). *Education for innovation and independent learning*. Elsevier.

Muilenburg, L. Y., & Berge, Z. L. (2005). Student barriers to online learning: A factor analytic study. *Distance Education, 26*(1), 29–48. doi:10.1080/01587910500081269

Munir. (2017). *Pembelajaran Digital*. Bandung: Alfabeta, CV.

Murphy, M. D. (2016). A modular virtual laboratory quadrotor control simulation. *IFAC-Papers on Line, 49*(6), 93–98. doi:10.1016/j.ifacol.2016.07.159

Mutalib, M. A., Halim, N. D., & Yahaya, N. (2016). *Meta-analysis on Interaction in Online Learning*. Retrieved from https://www.semanticscholar.org/paper/Meta-analysis-on-Interaction-in-Online-Learning-Mutalib-Halim/1647b4ba14260089900ab06291cd5a76a153db45

Nadar, R. N. (2018). Contemporary Issues and Challenges In The Indian Education System. *Journal of Business and Management*, 86–91.

Nadhifah, A. (2019). *Bagaimana Edtech Indonesia Mudahkan Akses Pendidikan bagi Pengguna*. Retrieved from https://id.techinasia.com/bagaimana-edtech-permudah-akses-pendidikan

Nagl, W., Titelbach, G., & Valkova, K. (2017). *Digitisation of work: Substitutability of occupations in the course of automation by industry 4.0*. Studie des IHS im Auftrag des Sozialministeriums.

Nakamura, L.I. (2000, July). Economics and the New Economy: the invisible hands meets creative destruction. *Federal Reserve Bank of Philadelphia Business Review*.

Nath, B. K. (2009). *Revising teaching skills for professional empowerment*. Retrieved from https://files.eric.ed.gov/fulltext/ED507652.pdf

National Research Council, Committee on Information Technology Literacy. (1999). *Being fluent with information technology*. National Academies Press.

Nazarenko, A. (2015). Blended learning vs traditional learning: What Works? *Procedia: Social and Behavioral Sciences, 200*, 77–82. doi:10.1016/j.sbspro.2015.08.018

Ndyay, M., Nguyen, W. H., & Grunina, E. O. (2020). Innovative technologies in teaching Russian as a foreign language. *Russian Language Studies, 18*(1), 7–38. doi:10.22363/2618-8163-2020-18-1-7-38

Nef, T., Ganea, R. L., Müri, R. M., & Mosimann, U. P. (2013). Social networking sites and older users–a systematic review. *International Psychogeriatrics*, *25*(7), 1041–1053. doi:10.1017/S1041610213000355 PMID:23552297

Newcomer, K. E., Hatry, H. P., & Wholey, J. S. (2015). Conducting semi-structured interviews. Handbook of practical program evaluation, 492.

Nguyen, H., Tapanainen, T., & Obi, T. (2014). A Review of Information Communication Technology (ICT) Training for Elderly People – Toward Recommendations for Developing Countries. *Proceedings of the Pacific Asia Conference on Information Systems (PACIS 2014)*, 267.

Nickerson, J. V., Corter, J. E., Esche, S. K., & Chassapis, C. (2007). A model for evaluating the effectiveness of remote engineering laboratories and simulations in education. *Computers & Education*, *49*(3), 708–725. doi:10.1016/j.compedu.2005.11.019

Nicotra, M., Romano, M., Del Giudice, M., & Schillaci, C. E. (2018). The causal relation between entrepreneurial ecosystem and productive entrepreneurship: A measurement framework. *The Journal of Technology Transfer*, *43*(3), 640–673. doi:10.100710961-017-9628-2

Noble, H., & Smith, J. (2015). Issues of validity and reliability in qualitative research. *Evidence-Based Nursing*, *18*(2), 34–35. doi:10.1136/eb-2015-102054 PMID:25653237

O'Neil, S., Scott, M., & Conboy, K. (2010). A Delphi study on collaborative learning in distance education: The faculty perspective. *British Journal of Educational Technology*, *42*(6), 939–949. doi:10.1111/j.1467-8535.2010.01132.x

O'Reilly, T. (2005). *What Is Web 2.0? Pattern Recognition*. Retrieved from https://www.oreilly.com/pub/a/web2/archive/what-is-web-20.html

Obayelu, A., & Ogunlade, I. (2006). Analysis of the uses of information communication technology (ICT) for gender empowerment and sustainable poverty alleviation in Nigeria. *International Journal of Education and Development Using ICT*, *2*(3), 45–69.

Ocaña, Y., Valenzuela, L., & Garro, L. (2019). Inteligencia artificial y sus implicaciones en la educación superior. *Propósitos y Representaciones*, *7*(2), 536–568. doi:10.20511/pyr2019.v7n2.274

Odabaşı, H. F. (2000). Akademik eskimişlik ve sürekli mesleki gelişim. *Anadolu Üniversitesi Eğitim Fakültesi Dergisi*, *10*(2), 161–166.

OECD. (2016). *Trends shaping education spotlight15: A brave new world: technology & education*. Paris: OECD Publishing. Retrieved from http://www.oecd.org/education/ceri/Spotlight-15-A-Brave-New-World-Technology-and-Education.pdf

OECD. (2018). *Bridging the Rural Digital Divide*. OECD Digital Economy Papers No. 265. https://www.sipotra.it/wp-content/uploads/2018/03/BRIDGING-THE-RURAL-DIGITAL-DIVIDE.pdf

OECD. (2018). Emerging trends, challenges and opportunities. In *Valuing our teachers and raising their status: How communities can help*. OECD Publishing. doi:10.1787/9789264292697-3-

Oliver, B., & Goerke, V. (2007). Australian undergraduates' use and ownership of emerging technologies: Implications and opportunities for creating engaging learning experiences for the Net Generation. *Australasian Journal of Educational Technology*, *23*(2). Advance online publication. doi:10.14742/ajet.1263

Oluic, A., & Mamic Sacer, I. (2019). Information technology and accounting information systems' quality in Croatian middle and large companies. *Journal of Information and Organizational Sciences*, *43*(2).

Online Indonesian Dictionary. (2019). *Autonomy Ministry of Education and Culture*. Retrieved from: https://kbbi.kemdikbud.go.id

Ordonez, T. N., Yassuda, M. S., & Cachioni, M. (2011). Elderly online: Effects of a digital inclusion program in cognitive performance. *Archives of Gerontology and Geriatrics*, *53*(2), 216–219. doi:10.1016/j.archger.2010.11.007 PMID:21131070

Organisation for Economic Cooperation and Development (2003b). *Los desafíos de las tecnologías de la información y las comunicaciones en la educación*. España: Ministerio de Educación, Cultura y Deporte. doi:10.1787/9789264103429-es

Organisation for Economic Cooperation and Development. (1998). Human Capital Investment. An International Comparison. París: OECD.

Organisation for Economic Cooperation and Development. (2005). La definición y selección de las competencias clave. Resumen ejecutivo. Retrieved from http://www.deseco.admin.ch/bfs/deseco/en/index/03/02.parsys.78532.downloadList.94248.DownloadFile.tmp/2005.dscexecutivesumm ary.sp.pdf

Organisation for Economic Cooperation and Development. (2012). Better Skills, Better Jobs, Better Lives: A Strategic Approach to Skills Policies. París: OECD. Retrieved from doi:10.1787/9789264177338-en

Organization for Economic Cooperation and Development. (2017). *Education at a glance 2017: OECD indicators*. OECD.

Ott, L. E., Kephart, K., Stolle-McAllister, K., & La Course, W. R. (2018). Students' Understanding and Perceptions of Assigned Team Roles in a Classroom Laboratory Environment. *Journal of College Science Teaching*, *47*(4), 83–91. doi:10.2505/4/jcst18_047_04_83 PMID:29681667

Oyarzun, B., Stefaniak, J., Bol, L., & Morrison, G. R. (2018). Effects of learner-to-learner interactions on social presence, achievement and satisfaction. *Journal of Computing in Higher Education*, *30*(1), 154–175. doi:10.100712528-017-9157-x

Palloff, R. M., & Pratt, K. (2003). *The virtual student: A profile and guide to working with online learners*. Jossey-Bass.

Pallof, R. M., & Pratt, K. (2005). *Collaborating online: learning together in community*. Jossey-Bass.

Paluch, S., Brettel, M., Hopp, C., Piller, F., Salge, & Wentzler, D. (2017). Innovation in the Digital Age: From Stage-Gate to an Agile Development Paradigm? *Journal of Business Research*. Available at: https://www.journals.elsevier.com/journal-of-business-research/call-for-papers/innovation-in-the-digital-age-from-stage-gate-to-an-agile-a

Pan, S., & Jordan-Marsh, M. (2010). Internet use intention and adoption among Chinese older adults: From the expanded technology acceptance model perspective. *Computers in Human Behavior*, *26*(5), 1111–1119. doi:10.1016/j.chb.2010.03.015

Pappas, I. O., Mikalef, P., Giannakos, M. N., Krogstie, J., & Lekakos, G. (2018). Big data and business analytics ecosystems: Paving the way towards digital transformation and sustainable societies. *Information Systems and e-Business Management*, *16*(1), 479–491. doi:10.100710257-018-0377-z

Parahita, G. D. (2017). Mapping digital fluency in diverse socio-economic status of citizens of DKI Jakarta 2017. *INFORMASI*, *47*(2), 213–228. doi:10.21831/informasi.v47i2.16224

Parente, D. H., Stephan, J. D., & Brown, R. C. (2012). Facilitating the acquisition of strategic skills: The role of traditional and soft managerial skills. *Management Research Review*, *35*(11), 1004–1028. doi:10.1108/01409171211276918

Park, N. C., & Son, J. B. (2009). Implementing computer-assisted language learning in the EFL classroom: Teachers' perceptions and perspectives. *International Journal of Pedagogies and Learning*, *5*(2), 80–101. doi:10.5172/ijpl.5.2.80

Parlby, D., Taylor, R. (2002). *The power of knowledge: a business guide to knowledge management*. Academic Press.

Parveen, B. (2020). Multimodality and ICT in empowering Muslim women. *An evaluation of Government of India Schemes*, *40*(48), 10.

Pasaribu, R. D., Kartini, D., Oesman, Y. M., & Padmadisastra, S. (2016). The effect of customer demand and supplier performance in competitive strategy and business performance (Case of fixed broadband in Indonesia). *International Journal of Scientific & Technology Research*, *5*(2), 123–129.

Passi, B. K. (1976). *Becoming Better Teacher: Microteaching Approach*. Sahitya Mudranalaya.

Patterson, N. (2012). Distance education: A perspective from Women's Studies. *International Women Online Journal of Distance Education*, *1*(2), 1–14.

Pattnayak, J., & Pattnaik, S. (2016). Integration of Web Services with E-Learning for Knowledge Society. *Procedia Computer Science*, *92*, 155–160. doi:10.1016/j.procs.2016.07.340

Pavlis Korres, M. (2010). *Development of a framework for the e-education of educators of special groups aiming to improve their compatibility with their Learners* (PhD Thesis). University of Alcalá, Spain.

Pavlis Korres, M. (2012). The Role of the Communication Tools in the Development of the Learning Group in an Online Environment. *International Journal of Engineering Education*, *28*(6), 1360–1365.

Pavlis Korres, M. (2015). Promoting Interaction in an Asynchronous E-Learning Environment. In P. Ordonez, R. Tennyson, & M. Lytras (Eds.), *Assessing the Role of Mobile Technologies and Distance Learning in Higher Education* (pp. 154–175). IGI Global. doi:10.4018/978-1-4666-7316-8.ch007

Pavlis Korres, M. (2018). *Design and Implementation of E-Learning Programs*. Hellenic Open University.

Pavlis Korres, M., Karalis, Th., Leftheriotou, P., & García Barriocanal, E. (2009). Integrating Adults' Characteristics and the Requirements for Their Effective Learning in an E-Learning Environment. In M. Lytras (Ed.), *Best Practices for the Knowledge Society. WSKS* (pp. 570–584). Springer.

Pavlis Korres, M., & Leftheriotou, P. (2016). Building Interaction in Adults' Online Courses: A Case Study on Training E-Educators of Adults. In L. Kyei-Blankson, E. Ntuli, & C. Agyeman (Eds.), *Handbook of Research on Strategic Management of Interaction, Presence and Participation in Online Courses* (pp. 185–215). IGI-Global. doi:10.4018/978-1-4666-9582-5.ch008

Pavlis-Korres, M., & Garcia Barriocanal, E. (2013). Promoting Multiculturalism in Technology Based-Education: A Framework for the Improvement of Compatibility between Educators of Special Groups and their Learners and a Case Study on Educators of Roma in Greece to Prove its Efficiency. In F. Garcia-Penalvo (Ed.), Multiculturalism in Technology Based Education: Case Studies on ICT-Supported Approaches (pp. 100-124). University of Salamanca. doi:10.4018/978-1-4666-2101-5.ch007

Peidró, A., Tendero, C., Marín, J. M., Gil, A., Payá, L., & Reinoso, Ó. (2018). m-PaRoLa: A Mobile Virtual Laboratory for Studying the Kinematics of Five-bar and 3RRR Planar Parallel Robots. *IFAC Papers on Line*, *51*(4), 178–183.

Peneder, M., Firgo, M., & Streicher, G. (2019). Digitalisierung in Österreich: Eine Standortbestimmung (Digital Transformation in Austria: A Status-Quo Analysis). *WIFO-Monatsberichte*, *92*(6), 447–457.

Peng, S., & Bewley, K. (2010). Adaptability to fair value accounting in an emerging economy: A case study of China's IFRS convergence. *Accounting, Auditing & Accountability Journal*, *23*(8), 982–1011. doi:10.1108/09513571011092529

Perez-Escoda, A., Castro-Zubizarreta, A., & Fandos-Igado, M. (2016). Digital Skills in the Z Generation: Key Questions for a Curricular Introduction in Primary School. *Comunicar. Media Education Research Journal, 24*(2).

Pérez-Escoda, A., & Rodríguez-Conde, M. J. (2015, October). Digital literacy and digital competences in the educational evaluation: USA and IEA contexts. In *Proceedings of the 3rd International Conference on Technological Ecosystems for Enhancing Multiculturality* (pp. 355-360). 10.1145/2808580.2808633

Permatasari, A., & Anggadwita, G. (2019). Digital Entrepreneurship Education in Emerging Countries: Opportunities and Challenges. In Opening Up Education for Inclusivity Across Digital Economies and Societies (pp. 156-169). IGI Global.

Pinho, I. D. C., & Lima, M. D. S. (2013). Teacher's digital fluency: A new competence for foreigh language teaching. *Revista Brasileira de Lingüística Aplicada, 13*(3), 711–739. doi:10.1590/S1984-63982013005000014

Plumlee, R. D., & Plumlee, M. A. (2008). Assurance on XBRL for Financial Reporting. *Accounting Horizons*, 3.

Pluta, W. J., Richards, B. F., & Mutnick, A. (2013). PBL and beyond: Trends in collaborative learning. *Teaching and learning in medicine, 25*(sup1), S9-S16.

Porter, M. E., & Kramer, M. R. (2006). The link between competitive advantage and corporate social responsibility. *Harvard Business Review, 84*(12), 78–92. PMID:17183795

Portnoi, L., Rust, V., & Bagley, S. (2010). *Higher education, policy and the global competition phenomenon*. Palgrave MacMillan. doi:10.1057/9780230106130

Potkonjak, V., Gardner, M., Callaghan, V., Mattila, P., Guetl, C., Petrović, V. M., & Jovanović, K. (2016). Virtual laboratories for Education in Science, Technology and Engineering: A Review. *Computers & Education, 95*, 309–327. doi:10.1016/j.compedu.2016.02.002

Pozos Pérez, K. V., & Mas Torelló, O. (2012). The digital competence as a cross-cutting axis of higher education teachers' pedagogical competences in the European higher education area. *Procedia: Social and Behavioral Sciences, 46*, 1112–1116. doi:10.1016/j.sbspro.2012.05.257

Pozos, K. V. (2010). La competencia Digital del Profesorado Universitario para la sociedaddel Conocimiento: Aproximacion a un Model y Validacionde unCuestionario de Necesidades de Formcion Continua. Bellaterra: Departamento de Pedagogia Aplicada- UAB. (Unpublished)

Prasetio, A. (2014). Understanding knowledge sharing and social capital in social network sites. *International Journal of Science and Research, 3*(3), 760–766.

Prasojo, L. D., Habibi, A., & Mukminin, A. (2017). Managing digital learning environments: Student teachers' perception on the social networking services use in writing courses in teacher education. *Turkish Online Journal of Educational Technology-TOJET, 16*(4), 42–55.

Premuroso, R. F., & Bhattacharya, S. (2008). Do early and voluntary filers of financial information in Xbrl format signal superior corporate governance and operating performance? *International Journal of Accounting Information Systems*, 9.

Prendes, M., Castañeda, L., & Gutiérrez, I. (2010). Competencias para el uso de TIC de los futuros maestros. *Comunicar, 35*(18), 175–182.

Prensky, M. (2001). Digital Natives, Digital Immigrants. On the Horizon, 9(5).

Prensky, M. (2001). Digital natives, digital immigrants. *On the Horizon, 9*(5). http://www.marcprensky.com/writing/Prensky-DigitalNatives,DigitalImmigrants-Part1.pdf

Prensky, M. (2001). The games generation: How learners have changed. In *Digital game-based learning*. McGraw-Hill.

Prestridge, S. (2014). A focus on students' use of Twitter–their interactions with each other, content and interface. *Active Learning in Higher Education, 15*(2), 101–115. doi:10.1177/1469787414527394

Prihastuti, A.H., Wahyuni, S., & Ramadhani, S.(2018). The use of social media as a learning media in improving students' motivation in the management accounting course. *International Journal of Education Best Practices, 2*(2).

Principi, A., & Lamura, G. (2009). Education for older people in Italy. *Educational Gerontology, 35*(3), 246–259. doi:10.1080/03601270802611349

Punch, K. (2005). *Introduction to Social Research: Quantitative and Qualitative Approaches* (2nd ed.). Sage.

Rahayuningtas, D. P. A., & Triana, E. (2017). Intellectual capital and higher education competitiveness. *Journal of Accounting and Investment, 16*(1), 154–157.

Rajasthan Population (2019/2020). (n.d.). Retrieved June 20, 2020, from http://www.populationu.com/in/rajasthan-population

Ram'ırez, J., Soto, D., Lopez, S., Akroyd, J., Nurkowski, D., Botero, M. L., Bianco, N., Brownbridge, G., Kraft, M., & Molina, A. (in press). A. (2020). Virtual Laboratory to support Chemical Reaction Engineering courses using real-life problems and industrial software. *Education for Chemical Engineers.*

Ramaswamy, V., & Gouillart, F. (2010). Building the co-creative enterprise. *Harvard Business Review, 88*(10), 100–109. PMID:20929195

Ramírez Córcoles, Y., Santos Peñalver, J., & Tejada Ponce, A. (2011). Intellectual capital in Spanish public universities: Stakeholders' information needs. *Journal of Intellectual Capital, 12*(3), 356–376. doi:10.1108/14691931111154689

Ramírez-Córcoles, Y., Tejada, A., & Manzaneque, M. (2016). The value of disclosing intellectual capital in Spanish universities: A new challenge of our days. *Journal of Organizational Change Management, 29*(2), 176–198. doi:10.1108/JOCM-02-2015-0025

Ramón-Jerónimo, M. A., Peral-Peral, B., & Arenas-Gaitan, J. (2013). Elderly persons and Internet use. *Social Science Computer Review, 31*(4), 389–403. doi:10.1177/0894439312473421

Rana, E. (2001). Take initiative on online learning, trainers urged. *People Management, 25.*

Rangel, A., & Peñalosa, E. (2013). Alfabetización digital en docentes de educación superior: Construcción y prueba empírica de un instrumento de evaluación. *Píxel-Bit. Revista de Medios y Educación, 43*, 9–23. doi:10.12795/pixelbit.2013.i43.01

Rathod, S. S., & Kalbande, D. R. (2016). Improving Laboratory Experiences in Engineering Education. *Journal of Engineering Education Transformations, 29*(4), 51–60.

Ray, S., Koshy, N. R., Diwakar, S., Nair, B., & Srivastava, S. (2012). Sakshat Labs: India's Virtual Proteomics Initiative. *Journal of Engineering Education Transformations, 10*(7), e1001353. PMID:22802723

Redecker, C., & Punie, Y. (2013). The future of learning 2025: Developing a vision for change. *Future Learning, 1*, 3–17.

Rigby, D. K., Sutherland, J., & Takeuchi, H. (2016). Embracing agile. *Harvard Business Review, 94*(5).

Rizza, C. (2014). Digital Competences. Encyclopedia of Quality of Life and Well-Being Research, 1614-1619.

Rodgers, T. L., Cheema, N., Vasanth, S., Jamshed, A., Alfutimie, A., & Scully, P. J. (2020). Developing pre-laboratory videos for enhancing student preparedness. *European Journal of Engineering Education, 45*(2), 292–304. doi:10.1080/03043797.2019.1593322

Rodríguez, L., Serra, R., Lasaga, M., & Miranda, L. (2020). Impacto social del desarrollo de habilidades informacionales en doctorandos. *Universidad y Sociedad, 12*(2), 38–47. https://rus.ucf.edu.cu/index.php/rus/article/view/1478

Rogers, A. (2007). *Teaching Adults* (3rd ed.). Open University Press.

Roohani, S., Furusho, Y., & Koizumi, M. (2009). Xbrl: Improving transparency and monitoring functions of corporate governance. *International Journal of Disclosure and Governance*, *6*(4), 355–369. doi:10.1057/jdg.2009.17

Roosmaaa, E. L., & Saar, E. (2011). *Barriers to and in participation in lifelong learning*. Retrieved March 20, 2020 from http://lll2010.tlu.ee/folder.2006-02-22.7534376022/subproject-2/sp2-national-reports/sp2_nr_estonia_b-3.pdf

Rosen, A. (2009). *E-Learning 2.0 Proven Practices and Emerging Technologies to Achieve Results*. AMACOM.

Ross, P. (2015). Digital fluency, social enterprise and why they are ımportant for HR. *Huffpost Business*. Retrieved from http://www.huffingtonpost.com/pam-ross/digital-fluency-social-en_b_7148050.html

Rossi, F. M., Nicolò, G., & Polcini, P. T. (2018). New trends in intellectual capital reporting. *Journal of Intellectual Capital*, *19*(4), 814–835. doi:10.1108/JIC-09-2017-0119

Rossiter, & Pasik-Duncan, Dormido, Vlacic, Jones, & Murray. (2018). A Survey of Good Practice in Control Education. *European Journal of Engineering Education*, *18*, 1–22.

Ross, J. (2017). Speculative method in digital education research. *Learning, Media and Technology*, *42*(2), 214–229. do i:10.1080/17439884.2016.1160927

Rovai, A. (2002). Building Sense of Community at a Distance. *International Review of Research in Open and Distance Learning*, *3*(1). Retrieved 21/4/2020 from http://www.irrodl.org/index.php/irrodl/article/view/79/153

Rubenson, K., & Desjardins, R. (2009). The impact of welfare state regimes on barriers to participation in adult education: A bounded agency model. *Adult Education Quarterly*, *59*(3), 187–207. doi:10.1177/0741713609331548

Rumeser, D., & Emsley, M. (2018). A systematic review of project management serious games: Identifying gaps, trends, and directions for future research. *Journal of Modern Project Management*, *6*(1), 48–59.

Rural Subscriber Base of Internet Users as on 31.01.2016. (n.d.). *Open Government Data(OGD) Community*. Retrieved April 29, 2020, from https://community.data.gov.in/rural-subscriber-base-of-internet-users-as-on-31-01-2016/

Russell, V. (2020). Language anxiety and the online learner. *Foreign Language Annals*, *53*(2), 338–352. doi:10.1111/flan.12461

Ryerson University. (n.d.). *Teaching Scenarios*. Retrieved March 14, 2020, from https://www.ryerson.ca/digital-media-projects/teaching-scenarios/

SAEA. (2012). *Report on Educational Program for Third Age People*. Scientific Adults' Educators Association.

Sagasti, F. (2001). *The knowledge explosion and the knowledge divide*. United Nations Development Programme: Human Development Reports. Retrieved from http://hdr.undp.org/sites/default/files/sagasti-1-1.pdf

Salmerón-Manzano, E., & Manzano-Agugliaro, F. (2018). The higher education sustainability through virtual laboratories: The Spanish University as case of study. *Sustainability*, *10*(11), 1–22. doi:10.3390u10114040

Salmon, G. (2004). *E-moderating. The Key to Teaching and Learning Online* (2nd ed.). Routledge Falmer. doi:10.4324/9780203465424

Samani, M. (2018, July). Vocational Education in the Era of Industry 4.0: An Indonesia Case. In *International Conference on Indonesian Technical Vocational Education and Association (APTEKINDO 2018)*. Atlantis Press. 10.2991/aptekindo-18.2018.10

Sambrook, S. (2003). E-learning in small organization. *Education + Training*, *45*(8/9), 506–516. doi:10.1108/00400910310508892

Samson, V., & Vyjayanthi, S. (2013). Pre-University Teachers' Teaching Skills. *Journal of Education and Practice, 5*(4), 90–96.

Sánchez, M. P., Elena, S., & Castrillo, R. (2009). Intellectual capital dynamics in universities: A reporting model. *Journal of Intellectual Capital, 10*(2), 307–324. doi:10.1108/14691930910952687

Sang, G., Valcke, M., Van Braak, J., & Tondeur, J. (2010). Student teachers' thinking processes and ICT integration: Predictors of prospective teaching behaviors with educational technology. *Computers & Education, 54*(1), 103–112. doi:10.1016/j.compedu.2009.07.010

Santoro, G., Vrontis, D., Thrassou, A., & Dezi, L. (2018). The Internet of Things: Building a knowledge management system for open innovation and knowledge management capacity. *Technological Forecasting and Social Change, 136*(1), 347–354. doi:10.1016/j.techfore.2017.02.034

Sari, P. K., & Prasetio, A. (2017). Knowledge sharing and electronic word of mouth to promote information security awareness in social network site. In *2017 International Workshop on Big Data and Information Security (IWBIS)* (pp. 113-117). IEEE. 10.1109/IWBIS.2017.8275111

Sasongko, W. D., & Widiastuti, I. (2019). Virtual Lab for Vocational Education in Indonesia: A Review of the Literature. *AIP Conference Proceedings, 2194*, 020113. doi:10.1063/1.5139845

Savin-Baden, M. (2015). *Rethinking Learning in an Age of Digital Fluency: Is Being Digitally Tethered a New Learning Nexus?* Routledge. doi:10.4324/9781315718910

Saxton, G. D., & Guo, C. (2011). Accountability online: Understanding the web-based accountability practices of non-profit organizations. *Voluntary Sector Quarterly, 40*(2), 270–295. doi:10.1177/0899764009341086

Schlesinger, W., Cervera, A., & Iniesta, M. Á. (2015). Key elements in building relationships in the higher education services context. *Journal of Promotion Management, 21*(4), 475–491. doi:10.1080/10496491.2015.1051403

Schumpeter, A. (1942). *Capitalism, Socialism and Democracy.* Harper & Brothers.

Schumpeter, A. J. (1911). *Theorie der wirtschaftlichen Entwicklung. Eine Untersuchung über Unternehmergewinn, Kapital, Kredit, Zins und den Konjunkturzyklus.* Duncker & Humblot.

Schutt, M., Allen, B. S., & Laumakis, M. A. (2009). The Effects of Instructor Immediacy Behaviors in Online Learning Environments. *Quarterly Review of Distance Education, 10*(2), 135–148.

Schwab, K. (2015). *The Fouth Industrial Revolution: What It Means and How to Respond.* Retrieved from https://www.foreignaffairs.com/articles/2015-12-12/fourth-industrial-revolution

Scuotto, V., Ferraris, A., Bresciani, S., Al-Mashari, M., & Del Giudice, M. (2016). Internet of Things: Applications and challenges in smart cities. A case study of IBM smart city projects. *Business Process Management Journal, 22*(2), 1–11. doi:10.1108/BPMJ-05-2015-0074

Seaman, J. E., Allen, I. E., & Seaman, J. (2018). *Grade Increase: Tracking Distance Education in the United States.* The Babson Survey Research Group.

Secundo, G., Dumay, J., Schiuma, G., & Passiante, G. (2016). Managing intellectual capital through a collective intelligence approach: An integrated framework for universities. *Journal of Intellectual Capital, 17*(2), 298–319. doi:10.1108/JIC-05-2015-0046

Secundo, G., Elena-Perez, S., Martinaitis, Ž., & Leitner, K. H. (2015). An intellectual capital maturity model (ICMM) to improve strategic management in European universities: A dynamic approach. *Journal of Intellectual Capital*, *16*(2), 419–442. doi:10.1108/JIC-06-2014-0072

Seiler, S., Ptasik, D., & Sell, R. (2011). Remote and Virtual Labs in a Distance Learning Environment. In *Proceedings of 22nd International Daaam Symposium* (vol. 22, no. 1, pp. 1-12). Academic Press.

Selim, H. M. (2007). Critical success factor for e-learning acceptance: Confirmatory factor models. *Computer Education*, *49*(2), 396–413. doi:10.1016/j.compedu.2005.09.004

Selingo, J. (2017). *The future of the degree: how colleges can survive in the new credential economy.* Washington, DC: The Chronicle of Higher Education.

Selvi, K. (2010). Teachers' Competencies Culturass. *International Journal of Philosophy of Culture and Axiology*, *7*(1), 167–175. doi:10.5840/cultura20107133

Selwyn, N. (2012). Making sense of young people, education and digital technology: The role of sociological theory. *Oxford Review of Education*, *38*(1), 81–96. doi:10.1080/03054985.2011.577949

Serrano-Cinca, C., Gutiérrez-Nieto, B., & Molinero, C. M. (2012). Social and financial Efficiency of Microfinance Institutions. In B. Armendariz & M. Labie (Eds.), *The Handbook of Microfinance*. World scientific publishing.

Shaffer, D. (2013). Language Teaching and Learning with Technology: Student Use, Teacher Beliefs. *Journal of US-China Public Administration*, *10*(9), 927–932.

Shapira, N., Barak, A., & Gal, I. (2007). Promoting older adults' well-being through Internet training and use. *Aging & Mental Health*, *11*(5), 477–484. doi:10.1080/13607860601086546 PMID:17882585

Sharabati, A., Jawad, S., & Bontis, N. (2010). Intellectual capital and business performance in the pharmaceutical sector of Jordon. *Management Decision*, *48*(1), 105–131. doi:10.1108/00251741011014481

Sharan, S., Sharan, Y., & Tan, I. G. (2013). The Group Investigation approach to cooperative learning. In C. E. Hmelo-Silver, A. M. O'Donnell, C. Chan, & C. Chinn (Eds.), *The International Handbook of Collaborative Learning* (pp. 351–369). Taylor & Francis.

Sheeja N.K., Susan, M. K., & Cherukodan, S. (2018). Impact of scholarly output on university ranking. *Global Knowledge, Memory and Communication*, 1-8.

Shepard, L. (2000). The role of assessment in a learning culture. *Educational Researcher*, *29*(7), 4–14. doi:10.3102/0013189X029007004

Shepherd, C. (2000). *Competence Frameworks-Online tutors*. Institute of IT Training.

Shin, H. J., & Son, J. B. (2007). EFL teachers' perceptions and perspectives on Internet-assisted language teaching. *CALL-EJ Online*, *8*(2), 8–2.

Shulman, L. S. (1986). Those Who Understand: Knowledge Growth in Teaching. *Educational Researcher*, *15*(2), 4–14. doi:10.3102/0013189X015002004

Shyr, W. J. (2010). Multiprog virtual laboratory applied to PLC programming learning. *European Journal of Engineering Education*, *35*(5), 573–583. doi:10.1080/03043797.2010.497550

Siboni, B., Nardo, M. T., & Sangiorgi, D. (2013). Italian state university contemporary performance plans: An intellectual capital focus? *Journal of Intellectual Capital*, *14*(3), 414–430. doi:10.1108/JIC-03-2013-0033

Siemens, G. (2014). *Digital Learning research network.* Retrieved from:www.elearspace.org/blog/2014/11/18

Siemens, G. (2005). Connectivism: A learning theory for the digital age. *International Journal of Instructional Technology and Distance Learning*, *2*(1), 3–10.

Simpson, O. (2002). *Supporting students in online, open and distance learning*. Kogan Page.

Simpson, R., & Galbo, J. (1986). Interaction and learning: Theorizing on the art of teaching. *Interchange*, *17*(4), 37–51. doi:10.1007/BF01807015

Singh, A. (2015). Challenges in Indian Education Sector. *International Journal of Advance Research in Commerce and Management*, *1*(3), 54–58.

Sitterding, M. C., Raab, D. L., Saupe, J. L., & Israel, K. J. (2019). Using Artificial Intelligence and Gaming to Improve New Nurse Transition. *Nurse Leader*, *17*(2), 125–130. doi:10.1016/j.mnl.2018.12.013

Skilton, M., & Hovsepian, F. (2017). *The 4th Industrial Revolution: Responding to the Impact of Artificial Intelligence on Business*. Springer.

Skobelev, P. O., & Borovik, S. Y. (2017). On the way from Industry 4.0 to Industry 5.0: from digital manufacturing to digital society. *Industry 4.0, 2*(6), 307-311.

Slaper, T. F., Hart, N. R., Hall, T. J., & Thompson, M. F. (2011). The index of Innovation: A new tool for regional analysis. *Economic Development Quarterly*, *25*(1), 36–53. doi:10.1177/0891242410387592

Smythe, A., Jenkins, C., Galant-Miecznikowska, M., Bentham, P., & Oyebode, J. (2017). A qualitative study investigating training requirements of nurses working with people with dementia in nursing homes. *Nurse Education Today*, *50*, 119–123. doi:10.1016/j.nedt.2016.12.015 PMID:28043078

Soanes, C., & Stevenson, A. (2003). *Oxford Dictionary of English* (2nd ed.). Oxford University Press.

Solikhin, F., Ikhsan, J., & Sugiyarto, K. H. (2019). A need analysis in developing virtual laboratory according to the chemistry teachers, IOP Conf. Series. *Journal of Physics: Conference Series*, *1156*, 012020. doi:10.1088/1742-6596/1156/1/012020

Solimun, F.A.A.A., & Nurjannah. (2017). Multivariate Statistics Method - Structural Equation Modelling (SEM) Warp-PLS Approach. Indonesia: UB Press.

Somekh, B. (2007). *Pedagogy and learning with ICT: Researching the art of innovation*. Routledge. doi:10.4324/9780203947005

Song, L., Singleton, E. S., Hill, J. R., & Koh, M. H. (2004). Improving online learning: Student perceptions of useful and challenging characteristics. *Internet and Higher Education, 7*(1), 59-70. https://www.learntechlib.org/p/102596/

Soo, K. S., & Bonk, C. J. (1998). *Interaction: What Does It Mean in Online Distance Education?* Retrieved from https://eric.ed.gov/?id=ED428724

Sork, T., & Caffarella, R. (1989). Planning Programs for Adults. In Sh. Merriam & Ph. Cunningham (Eds.), *Handbook of Adult and Continuing Education* (pp. 233–245). Jossey-Bass.

Sosa, M. (2007). Inteligencia artificial en la gestión financiera empresarial. *Pensamiento y Gestión*, *23*, 1-34. Retrieved from http://rcientificas.uninorte.edu.co/index.php/pensamiento/article/viewFile/3518/2252

Sosa, M., & Palau, R. (2018). Flipped Classroom para adquirir la competencia digital docente: Una experiencia didáctica en la educación superior. *Pixel-Bit. Revista de Medios y Educación*, *52*, 37–54. doi:10.12795/pixelbit.2018.i52.03

Sousa, M. J., & Rocha, Á. (2019). Digital learning: Developing skills for digital transformation of organizations. *Future Generation Computer Systems, 91*, 327–334. doi:10.1016/j.future.2018.08.048

Sousa, M. J., & Rocha, Á. (2019). Skills for disruptive digital business. *Journal of Business Research, 94*, 257–263. doi:10.1016/j.jbusres.2017.12.051

Southwell, G. (2005). *Global alliances and changes in financial reporting: how can XBRL help? In Fifth annual XBRL international academic competition 2004-2005*. State University.

Sparrow, J. (2018). Digital fluency: Preparing students to create big, bold problems. *New Horizons*. Retrieved from https://er.educause.edu/articles/2018/3/digital-fluency-preparing-students-to-create-big-bold-problems

Spencer, K. (2015). *What is digital fluency?* Retrieved from https://www.blog.core-ed.org/blog/2015/10/what-is-digital-fluency.html/

Spilker, H. S. (2017). *Digital music distribution: The sociology of online music streams*. Routledge. doi:10.4324/9781315561639

Spivakovskiy, O., Kushnir, N., Kushnir, N., & Vinnyk, M. (2017). ICT Advanced Training of University Teachers. *13th International Conference on ICT in Education, Research and Industrial Applications: Integration, Harmonization and Knowledge Transfer*, 176-190.

Statistik Austria. (2018). *Average annual job vacancies according to the Job Vacancy Survey and the Labour Market Service*. http://www.statistik.at/web_de/statistiken/menschen_und_gesellschaft/arbeitsmarkt/offene_stellen/118100.html (29.4.2019)

Stojcic, N., & Hashi, I. (2014). Firm productivity and type of innovation: evidence from the community innovation survey 6. *Croatian Economic Survey, 16*(2).

Stokes, P. (2015). *Higher education and employability: new models for integrating study and work*. Harvard.

Sun, Y., & Dong, Q. (2004). An experiment on supporting children's English vocabulary learning in multimedia context. *Computer Assisted Language Learning, 17*(2), 131–147. doi:10.1080/0958822042000334217

Surendran, P. (2012). Technology acceptance model: A survey of literature. *International Journal of Business and Social Research, 2*(4), 175-178.

Suryani, A. (2010). ICT in education: Its benefits, difficulties, and organizational development issues. *Jurnal Sosial Humaniora, 3*(1), 13–33. doi:10.12962/j24433527.v3i1.651

Sutton, L. A. (2000). *Vicarious Interaction: A Learning Theory for Computer-Mediated Communications*. Presented at American Educational Research Association Annual Meeting 2000. Retrieved 21/4 2020 from https://www.learntechlib.org/p/87645/

Suvarna, V. S. (2020). *Leveraging ICT for Intellectual Growth and For Women Empowerment*. Academic Press.

Symonds, Q. (n.d.). *QS World University Ranking*. Retrieved from: https://www.topuniversities.com

Taguchi, N. (2020). Digitally mediated remote learning of pragmatics. *Foreign Language Annals, 53*(2), 353–358. doi:10.1111/flan.12455

Tavana, M., Abtahi, A. R., Di Caprio, D., & Poortarigh, M. (2018). An Artificial Neural Network and Bayesian Network model for liquidity risk assessment in banking. *Neurocomputing, 275*, 2525–2554. doi:10.1016/j.neucom.2017.11.034

Tawfik, A. A., Giabbanelli, P. J., Hogan, M., Msilu, F., Gill, A., & York, C. S. (2018). Effects of success v failure cases on learner-learner interaction. *Computers & Education*, *118*, 120–132. doi:10.1016/j.compedu.2017.11.013

Tchoubar, T., Sexton, T. R., & Scarlatos, L. L. (2018, July). Role of digital fluency and spatial ability in student experience of online learning environments. In *Science and Information Conference* (pp. 251-264). Springer.

Tejado, I., González, I., Pérez, E., & Merchán, P. (2019). Introducing systems theory with virtual laboratories at the University of Extremadura: How to improve learning in the lab in engineering degrees. *International Journal of Electrical Engineering Education*, *20*, 1–26.

Teller, P. (2008). The use of a formal representation of accounting standards. *International Journal of Computer Science and Applications*, *5*(3b).

Thomas, J. W. (2000). *A review of research on project-based learning*. The Autodesk Foundation. https://tecfa.unige.ch/proj/eteach-net/Thomas_researchreview_PBL.pdf

Thompson, J. D. (2010). *Organizations in Action: Social Science Bases of Administrative Theory* (7th ed.). Transaction Publishers.

Thurmond, V., & Wambach, K. (2004). Understanding Interaction in Distance Education, A review of the literature, *International Journal of instructional Technology & Distance Learning*. Available http://www.itdl.org/journal/Jan_04/article02.htm

Thweatt, K. S., & McCroskey, J. C. (1996). Teacher Nonimmediacy and Misbehavior: Unintentional negative communication. *Communication Research Reports*, *13*(2), 198–204. doi:10.1080/08824099609362087

Tippins, M., & Ravipreet, S. (2003). IT competency and firm performance: Is organizational learning a missing link? *Strategic Management Journal*, *24*(8), 745–761. doi:10.1002mj.337

Tirado-Morueta, R., Hernando-Gómez, Á., & Aguaded-Gomez, J. I. (2016). The capacity of elderly citizens to access digital media in Andalusia (Spain). *Information Communication and Society*, *19*(10), 1427–1444. doi:10.1080/1369118X.2015.1111401

Tobon, S. (2008). *La formación basada en competencias en la educación superior. El enfoque complejo*. Magisterio.

Tójar, J., & Mena, E. (2015). Desarrollo de la competencia comunicativo – investigativa en la educación superior. Investigación con métodos mixtos y educación por competencias en Perú. In AIDIPE (Ed.), *Investigar con y para la sociedad*, (vol. 2, pp. 609 – 616). Cádiz: Bubok Publishing. Retrieved from http://avanza.uca.es/aidipe2015/libro/volumen2.pdf

Torun, E. D. (2013). Synchronous Interaction in Online Learning Environments with Adobe Connect Pro. *Procedia: Social and Behavioral Sciences*, *106*, 2492–2499. doi:10.1016/j.sbspro.2013.12.286

Touger, G. E. (2018, August 3). *What's the Difference between Artificial Learning (AI), Machine Learning, and Deep Learning?* Prowesscorp. Retrieved from www.prowesscorp.com/whats-the-difference-between-artificial-intelligence-ai-machine-learning-and-deep-learning

Traxler, J. (2018). Digital literacy: A palestinian refugee perspective. *Research in Learning Technology*, 26.

Trentsios, P., Wolf, M., & Frerich, S. (2020). Remote Lab meets Virtual Reality – Enabling immersive access to high tech laboratories from afar. *Procedia Manufacturing*, *43*, 25–31. doi:10.1016/j.promfg.2020.02.104

Trilling, B., & Fadel, C. (2009). *21st Century Skills: Learning for Life in Our Times*. Jossey-Bass/John Wiley & Sons, Inc.

Tsovaltzi, D., Weinberger, A., Scheuer, O., Dragon, T., & McLaren, B. M. (2013). Collaborative learning in Facebook: Can argument structure facilitate academic opinion change? In N. Rummel, M. Kapur, M. Nathan, & S. Puntambekar (Eds.), Conference Proceedings Volume II of the *10th International Conference on Computer Supported Collaborative Learning (CSCL 2013)* (pp. 177-180). International Society of the Learning Sciences.

Tularam, G. A. (2018). Traditional vs Non-traditional Teaching and Learning Strategies – the case of E-learning! *International Journal for Mathematics Teaching and Learning*, *19*(1), 129–158.

Twigg, C. A. (2003). Improving learning and reducing costs: New models for online learning. *EDUCAUSE Review*, *38*(5), 28–38.

Tyner, K. (1998). *Literacy in a Digital World*. Lawrence Erlbaum.

United Nations Education Scientific and Cultural Organization (UNESCO). (2011). *EFA Global Monitoring Report 2011: Regional Overview East Asia and the Pacific*. http://unesdoc.unesco.org/images/0019/001917/191719E.pdf

United Nations Educational Scientific and Cultural Organization. (2009). Conferencia Mundial sobre la Educación Superior. La nueva dinámica de la educación superior y la investigación para el cambio social y el desarrollo. París: UNESCO.

United Nations Educational Scientific and Cultural Organization. (2010). *Desafíos de la educación*. Buenos Aires: IIPE-UNESCO.

United Nations Educational Scientific and Cultural Organization. (2014). *Políticas TIC en los sistemas educativos de América Latina*. París: UNESCO.

United Nations Educational, Scientific and Social Cultural Organization (UNESCO). (2006). *Education for all: Literacy for life. Global monitoring report 2006*. Retrieved from http://unesdoc.unesco.org/images/0014/001442/144270e.pdf

United States National Commission on Technology. (1966). *Automation and Economic Progress: America's industrial and occupational manpower requirements, 1964-1975*. U.S. Government Printing Office.

Valica, M., & Rohn, T. (2013). Development of the Professional Competence in the Ethics Teachers. 4th International Conference on New Horizons in Education. *Procedia: Social and Behavioral Sciences*, *106*, 865–872. doi:10.1016/j.sbspro.2013.12.099

Van Deursen, A. J., & Helsper, E. J. (2015). A nuanced understanding of Internet use and non-use among the elderly. *European Journal of Communication*, *30*(2), 171–187. doi:10.1177/0267323115578059

Van Deusen-Scholl, N., Frei, Ch., & Dixon, E. (2005). Constructing learning: The dynamic nature of foreign language pedagogy in a CMC environment. *CALICO Journal*, *22*(3), 657–678. doi:10.1558/cj.v22i3.657-678

Van Laar, E., Van Deursen, A. J., Van Dijk, J. A., & De Haan, J. (2017). The relation between 21st-century skills and digital skills: A systematic literature review. *Computers in Human Behavior*, *72*, 577–588. doi:10.1016/j.chb.2017.03.010

van Laar, E., van Deursen, A. J., van Dijk, J. A., & de Haan, J. (2019). Determinants of 21st-century digital skills: A large-scale survey among working professionals. *Computers in Human Behavior*, *100*, 93–104. doi:10.1016/j.chb.2019.06.017

Varela, S., & Valenzuela, J. (2020). Uso de las tecnologías de la información y la comunicación como competencia transversal en la formación inicial de docentes. *Revista Electrónica Educare*, *24*(1), 1–20. doi:10.15359/ree.24-1.10

Vargas-Vera, M., Nagy, M., & De Pablos, P. O. (2013). A framework for detecting and removing knowledge overlaps in a collaborative environment: Case of study a computer configuration problem. *Journal of Web Engineering*, *12*(5), 422–438.

Vásquez Macías, F. S. (2019). *Memoria del proceso de Design Thinking realizado en el modelo de negocios "Centro de educación inicial Little Genius"*. Universidad Casa Grande. Retrieved from http://dspace.casagrande.edu.ec:8080/handle/ucasagrande/1865

Veletsianos, G. (2016). Digital learning environments. Wiley Handbook of Learning Technology, 242-260.

Vera, F. (2018). Percepción de estudiantes respecto de la calidad educativa y organizacional de la carrera de enfermería de una universidad privada chilena. *Revista Electrónica Educare*, *22*(3), 1–25. doi:10.15359/ree.22-3.1

Vošner, H. B., Bobek, S., Kokol, P., & Krečič, M. J. (2016). Attitudes of active older Internet users towards online social networking. *Computers in Human Behavior*, *55*, 230–241. doi:10.1016/j.chb.2015.09.014

Vuopala, E., Hyvönen, P., & Järvelä, S. (2016). Interaction forms in successful collaborative learning in virtual learning environments. *Active Learning in Higher Education*, *17*(1), 25–38. doi:10.1177/1469787415616730

Wallace, C. S., & Kang, N. H. (2004). An investigation of experienced secondary science teachers' beliefs about inquiry: An examination of competing belief sets. *Journal of Research in Science Teaching*, *41*(9), 32–41. doi:10.1002/tea.20032

Walled, M.A., Yahaya, N., Aldraiweesh, A.A., Alamri, M.M., Aljarboa, N.A., Alturki U., & ALjerraiwi, A.A. (2019). Integrating technology acceptance model with innovation diffusion theory: an empirical investigation on students' intention to use e-learning system. *Integrating TAM with IDT, 7.*

Waltonen-Moore, S., Stuart, D., Newton, E., Oswald, R., & Varonis, E. (2006). From Virtual Strangers to a Cohesive Online Learning Community: The Evolution of Online Group Development in a Professional Development Course. *Journal of Technology and Teacher Education*, *14*(2), 287–311.

Wang, E., Myers, M. D., & Sundaram, D. (2012). Digital natives and digital immigrants – Towards a model of digital fluency. *Proceedings of the European Conference on Information Systems (ECIS 2012)*. Retrieved from https://aisel.aisnet.org/ecis2012/39

Wan, G., & Gut, D. (2011). *Bringing Schools into the 21 st Century. Explorations of Educational Purpose, 13. Dordrechet, (Países Bajos)*. Springer. doi:10.1007/978-94-007-0268-4

Wang, R., Liu, C., & Ma, T. (2018). Evaluation of a virtual neurophysiology laboratory as a new pedagogical tool for medical undergraduate students in China. *Advances in Physiology Education*, *42*(4), 704–710. doi:10.1152/advan.00088.2018 PMID:30431325

Wang, R., Wiesemes, R., & Gibbons, C. (2012). Developing digital fluency through ubiquitous mobile devices: Findings from a small-scale study. *Computers & Education*, *58*(1), 570–578. doi:10.1016/j.compedu.2011.04.013

Wartman, S. A., & Combs, C. D. (2018). Medical education must move from the information age to the age of artificial intelligence. *Academic Medicine*, *93*(8), 1107–1109. doi:10.1097/ACM.0000000000002044 PMID:29095704

Wartman, S. A., & Combs, C. D. (2019). Reimagining medical education in the age of AI. *AMA Journal of Ethics*, *21*(2), 146–152. doi:10.1001/amajethics.2019.146 PMID:30794124

Waymel, Q., Badr, S., Demondion, X., Cotten, A., & Jacques, T. (2019). Impact of the rise of artificial intelligence in radiology: What do radiologists think? *Diagnostic and Interventional Imaging*, *100*(6), 327–336. doi:10.1016/j.diii.2019.03.015 PMID:31072803

Wedman, J., & Diggs, L. (2001). Identifying barriers to technology-enhanced learning environments in teacher education. *Computers in Human Behavior*, *17*(4), 421–430. doi:10.1016/S0747-5632(01)00012-7

Weng, F., Yang, R. J., Ho, H. J., & Su, H. M. (2018). A TAM-Based Study of the Attitude towards Use Intention of Multimedia among School Teachers. *Applied System Innovation*, *1*(36), 1–9. doi:10.3390/asi1030036

White, G. K. (2013). *Digital fluency: Skills necessary for learning in the digital age*. Australian Council for Educational Research.

White, G. K. (2013). *Digital fluency: Skills necessary for learning in the digital age. Australian Council for Educational Research*. ACER.

WHO. (2002, April). *Active ageing. A policy framework*. World Health Organization. Retrieved from https://www.who.int/ageing/publications/active_ageing/en/

WIBIS. (2020). *Bezirksprofil Graz (Stadt)*. https://wibis-steiermark.at/fileadmin/user_upload/wibis_steiermark/regionsprofile/2020-04/B601_PROFIL_2_Daten_17.04.2020.pdf

WIBIS. (2020a). *Bezirksprofil Deutschlandsberg*. https://wibis-steiermark.at/fileadmin/user_upload/wibis_steiermark/regionsprofile/2020-04/B603_PROFIL_2_Daten_17.04.2020.pdf

WIBIS. (2020b). *Bezirksprofil Graz-Umgebung*. https://wibis-steiermark.at/fileadmin/user_upload/wibis_steiermark/regionsprofile/2020-04/B606_PROFIL_2_Daten_17.04.2020.pdf

WIBIS. (2020c). *Bezirksprofil Leibnitz*. https://wibis-steiermark.at/fileadmin/user_upload/wibis_steiermark/regionsprofile/2020-04/B610_PROFIL_2_Daten_17.04.2020.pdf

WIBIS. (2020d). *Bezirksprofil Leoben*. https://wibis-steiermark.at/fileadmin/user_upload/wibis_steiermark/regionsprofile/2020-04/B611_PROFIL_2_Daten_17.04.2020.pdf

WIBIS. (2020e). *Bezirksprofil Liezen*. https://wibis-steiermark.at/fileadmin/user_upload/wibis_steiermark/regionsprofile/2020-04/B612_PROFIL_2_Daten_17.04.2020.pdf

WIBIS. (2020f). *Bezirksprofil Murau*. https://wibis-steiermark.at/fileadmin/user_upload/wibis_steiermark/regionsprofile/2020-04/B614_PROFIL_2_Daten_17.04.2020.pdf

WIBIS. (2020g). *Bezirksprofil Voitsberg*. https://wibis-steiermark.at/fileadmin/user_upload/wibis_steiermark/regionsprofile/2020-04/B616_PROFIL_2_Daten_17.04.2020.pdf

WIBIS. (2020h). *Bezirksprofil Weiz*. https://wibis-steiermark.at/fileadmin/user_upload/wibis_steiermark/regionsprofile/2020-04/B617_PROFIL_2_Daten_17.04.2020.pdf

WIBIS. (2020i). *Bezirksprofil Murtal*. https://wibis-steiermark.at/fileadmin/user_upload/wibis_steiermark/regionsprofile/2020-04/B620_PROFIL_1_FactText_24.04.2020.pdf

WIBIS. (2020j). *Bezirksprofil Bruck-Mürzzuschlag*. https://wibis-steiermark.at/fileadmin/user_upload/wibis_steiermark/regionsprofile/2020-04/B621_PROFIL_2_Daten_17.04.2020.pdf

WIBIS. (2020k). *Bezirksprofil Hartberg-Fürstenfeld*. https://wibis-steiermark.at/fileadmin/user_upload/wibis_steiermark/regionsprofile/2020-04/B622_PROFIL_2_Daten_17.04.2020.pdf

WIBIS. (2020l). *Bezirksprofil Südoststeiermark*. https://wibis-steiermark.at/fileadmin/user_upload/wibis_steiermark/regionsprofile/2020-04/B623_PROFIL_2_Daten_17.04.2020.pdf

Widyaningdyah, Y. A. U., & Aryan, A. (2015). Intellectual capital and competitive advantage. *Journal of Accounting and Finance*, *15*(1), 3–5.

Wijnhoven, F., Amrit, C., & Dietz, P. (2014). Value-Based file retention. *Journal of Data and Information Quality*, *4*(4), 1–17. doi:10.1145/2567656

Wikipedia. (2020). *Virtual Laboratory.* https://en.wikipedia.org/wiki/Virtual_Labs_(India)

Williams, C. (2002). Learning On-Line: A review of recent literature in a rapidly expanding field. *Journal of Further and Higher Education*, *26*(3), 263–272. doi:10.1080/03098770220149620

Williams, D. L., Crittenden, V. L., Keo, T., & McCarty, P. (2012). The use of social media: An exploratory study of usage among digital natives. *Journal of Public Affairs*, *12*(2), 127–136. doi:10.1002/pa.1414

Williams, S. P., Scifleet, P. A., & Hardy, C. A. (2006). On-line business reporting: An information management perspective. *International Journal of Information Management*, 26.

Wilson, B. G. (1995). Metaphors for instruction: Why we talk about learning environments. *Educational Technology*, *35*(5), 25–30.

Wilson, B. G. (2004). Designing e-learning environments for flexible activity and instruction. *Educational Technology Research and Development*, *52*(4), 77–84. doi:10.1007/BF02504720

Wolf, M. A. (2009). Older Adulthood. In P. Jarvis (Ed.), *The Routledge International Handbook of Lifelong Learning* (pp. 56–64). Routledge, Taylor & Francis Group.

Woods, R., & Baker, J. (2004). Interaction and immediacy in online learning. *The International Review of Research in Open and Distance Learning*, *5*(2). Retrieved 10-1-2018 from http://www.irrodl.org/index.php/irrodl/article/view/186/268

Woods, R. H. (2002). How much communication is enough in online courses? Exploring the relationship between frequency of instructor-initiated personal email and learners' perceptions of and participation in online learning. *International Journal of Instructional Media*, *29*(4), 377–394.

World Economic Forum. (2017). *Project Plan Overwiew: 21st Century Curriculum Project.* Sydney: WSU.

World Economic Forum. (2017). *The global competitiveness report 2016–2017.* Author.

World Economic Forum. (2019). *The Global Competitiveness Report 2019.* Retrieved from http://www3.weforum.org/docs/WEF_TheGlobalCompetitivenessReport2019.pdf

Wu, J., & Koon, L. C. (2012, July). Tangible social-media application for the elderly. In *Proceedings of the 6th International Conference on Rehabilitation Engineering & Assistive Technology* (article no 37, pp. 1-4). Singapore Therapeutic, Assistive & Rehabilitative Technologies (START) Centre.

Wu. (2011). Using Online EFL Interaction to Increase Confidence, Motivation, and Ability. *Journal of Educational Technology & Society*, *14*(3), 118–129.

Wu, B., & Chen, X. (2017). Continuance intention to use MOOCs: Integrating the technology acceptance model (TAM) and task technology fit (TTF) mode. *Computers in Human Behavior*, *67*, 221–232. doi:10.1016/j.chb.2016.10.028

Wu, D. D. (2015). *Online learning in postsecondary education: a review of the empirical literature (2013-2014).* Ithaka S & R. doi:10.18665r.221027

Yahya, F. H. (2020). Teaching innovation with ICT. *Proceding Internasional Seminar of Primary Education*, *2*, 7–9.

Yalcin-Celik, A., Kadayifci, H., Uner, S., & Turan-Oluk, N. (2017). Challenges faced by pre-service chemistry teachers teaching in a laboratory and their solution proposals. *European Journal of Teacher Education*, *40*(2), 210–230. doi:10.1080/02619768.2017.1284792

Yamauchi, M. (2009). Integrating Internet technology into the EFL classroom: A case study. *International Journal of Pedagogies and Learning, 5*(2), 3–19.

Yang, S., Zhu, X., & Liu, F.C, (2016). An exploratory study of financial reporting structures: A graph similarity approach using XBRL. *SSRN*, 9.

Yang, S., Zhu, X., & Liu, F.C, (2018). The impact of XBRL on financial statement structural comparability. *Lecture Notes in Information Systems and Organisation*, 1.

Yang, H. H., & Yuen, C. Y. (2010). *Collective Intelligence and E-Learning 2.0 Implications of Web-based Communities and Networking*. Information Science Publishing. doi:10.4018/978-1-60566-729-4

Yang, S. C., & Chen, Y. J. (2007). Technology-enhanced language learning: A case study. *Computers in Human Behavior, 23*(1), 860–879. doi:10.1016/j.chb.2006.02.015

Yang, Y. T. C., & Wu, W. C. I. (2012). Digital storytelling for enhancing student academic achievement, critical thinking, and learning motivation: A year-long experimental study. *Computers & Education, 59*(2), 339–352. doi:10.1016/j.compedu.2011.12.012

Yeh, S.-P., & Fu, H.-W. (2014). Effects of Cooperative E-Learning Outcomes. *Eurasia Journal of Mathematics. Science & Technology Education, 10*(6), 531–536.

Yoon, H., Zo, H., & Ciganek, A. (2011). Does XBRL adoption reduce information asymmetry. *Journal of Business Research, 64*(2), 157–163. doi:10.1016/j.jbusres.2010.01.008

Yunus, M. M. (2007). Malaysian ESL teachers' use of ICT in their classrooms: Expectations and realities. *ReCALL, 19*(1), 79–95. doi:10.1017/S0958344007000614

Zainab, B., Bhatti, M. A., & Alshagawi, M. (2017). Factors affecting e-training adoption: An examination of perceived cost, computer self-efficacy and the technology acceptance model. *Behaviour & Information Technology, 36*(12), 1261–1273. doi:10.1080/0144929X.2017.1380703

Zambon, S., Chatzkel, J., Sánchez, M. P., & Elena, S. (2006). Intellectual capital in universities. *Journal of Intellectual Capital, 7*(4), 529–548. doi:10.1108/14691930610709158

Zempoalteca, B., Barragán, J., González, J., & Guzmán, T. (2017). Formación en TIC y competencia digital en la docencia de instituciones públicas de educación superior. *Apertura (Guadalajara, Jal.), 9*(1), 80–96. doi:10.32870/Ap.v9n1.922

Zhao, J., Qi, Z., & De Pablos, P. O. (2014). Enhancing enterprise training performance: Perspectives from knowledge transfer and integration. *Computers in Human Behavior, 30*, 567–573. doi:10.1016/j.chb.2013.06.041

About the Contributors

Patricia Ordóñez de Pablos is a professor in the Department of Business Administration in the Faculty of Business and Economics at The University of Oviedo (Spain). She completed her education in The London School of Economics (UK). Her teaching and research interests focus on the areas of strategic management, knowledge management, organizational learning, human resource management, intellectual capital, information technologies, with special interest in Asia (Bhutan, China, Laos, Myanmar). She is Editor-in-Chief of the International Journal of Learning and Intellectual Capital (IJLIC) and International Journal of Asian Business and Information Management (IJABIM), respectively. She has edited books for IGI-Global, Routledge and Springer.

Miltiadis D. Lytras is Associate Professor at Deree- ACG with a research focus on semantic web, knowledge management and e-learning, with more than 100 publications. He has co-edited more than 45 special issues in International Journals (IEEE Transaction on Knowledge and Data Engineering, IEEE Internet Computing, IEEE Transactions on Education, Computers in Human Behaviour, Interactive Learning Environments, Journal of Knowledge Management, Journal of Computer Assisted Learning) and has authored/[co-]edited 42 books [e.g. Open Source for Knowledge and Learning Management, Ubiquitous and Pervasive Knowledge Management, Intelligent Learning Infrastructures for Knowledge Intensive Organizations, Semantic Web Based Information Systems, China Information Technology Handbook, Real World Applications of Semantic Web and Ontologies, Web 2.0: The Business Model, etc]. He (has) serves(ed) as the (Co) Editor in Chief of 8 international journals [e.g. International Journal on Semantic Web and Information Systems, International Journal of Knowledge Society Research, International Journal of Knowledge and Learning, International Journal of Technology Enhanced Learning].

* * *

Grisna Anggadwita is a full time lecturer at the Business Management of Telecommunications and Informatics Department, School of Economics and Business, Telkom University, Indonesia. She teaches courses in entrepreneurship, small business management, e-commerce and business processes. Her research interests include entrepreneurial intention, technology management, women entrepreneurship, business incubator, and innovation management. She is an active researcher and published more than 100 articles in leading international and national journals as well as international proceedings.

Giovanni Bronzetti is associate professor in Business Economics within the Department of Business and Law of University of Calabria. His main research interests are related to intellectual capital, no-profit sector and accounting. One these research themes he has published books, book chapters, journal articles and presented papers at national and international conferences.

Edgar O. Cardoso, PhD, is Professor - Researcher since 2009 on Sección de Estudios de Investigación de Posgrado e Investigación en la Escuela Superior de Comercio y Administración (ESCA) of the Instituto Politécnico Nacional (IPN), Mexico City. In his position conducts research projects focused on the management and development of education in educational programs at senior level. He teaches courses Methodological Seminar I, II, III and Statistics for Educational Research to Master's and Research Seminars I, II and III as well as Research Visits I, II, III and IV to PhD level. Dr. Cardoso earned his doctorate at the IPN. He has a master of science in management and development of education in the ESCA-IPN. His research includes evaluation of educational programs and executive education. He has directed several research projects in the area of educational management. He has conducted thesis addresses at the master's and doctoral level in the educational area.

Trinidad Cerecedo, PhD, is Professor - Researcher on la Sección de Estudios de Posgrado e Investigación of the Escuela Superior de Comercio y Administración (ESCA) of the Instituto Politécnico Nacional (IPN), Mexico City. PhD in Administrative Sciences from the Higher School of Commerce and Administration. She is a specialist in leadership educational and has been the author of chapters of dissemination books, as well as various articles in research journals. Her systemic training and dedication to the knowledge society has allowed her to teach in the Master in Administration in Management and Development of Education.

Jésica Alhelí Cortés Ruíz, PhD, is Professor - Researcher since 2018 on la Sección de Estudios de Posgrado e Investigación of the Escuela Superior de Comercio y Administración (ESCA) of the Instituto Politécnico Nacional (IPN), Mexico City. PhD in Administrative Sciences from the Higher School of Commerce and Administration, Master of Science in Systems Engineering from the Higher School of Mechanical and Electrical Engineering. She is a specialist in transdisciplinary systemic and has been the author of chapters of dissemination books, as well as various articles in research journals. Her systemic training and dedication to the knowledge society has allowed her to teach In the International Business Degree, the Master in Administration in Management and Development of Education, The Master in Business Administration for Sustainability And the Master of Science in Business Administration.

Manlio del Giudice is a Professor at Link Campus University. He holds a PhD in Management from the University of Milano Bicocca and he has taught in a number of universities worldwide, including Grenoble Graduate School of Business, Twente University, and Jonkoping University. Professor Del Giudice has more than 100 publications in mainstream journals and publishers, such as Springer, Palgrave MacMillan, Nature Publishing Group and Elsevier. Professor Del Giudice serves on the editorial boards of prestigious peer reviewed academic journals; at the same time he has promoted and managed several academic spin-offs and technology transfer activities. His research interests focus on knowledge management, cross-cultural management, family business management, and entrepreneurship.

Kadir Demir is a researcher in the Department of Computer Education & Instructional Technology at Dokuz Eylul University, Turkey. He also serves as the coordinator of Instructional Technology Research & Development Laboratory where graduate students and academicians research and develop with emerging technologies such as 3d printing, modelling and scanning, hologram, virtual and augmented reality and robotic development kits. He has an M.A. in Computer Education & Instructional Technology at Dokuz Eylul University with emphasis on mobile learning, and a Ph.D. in Computer Education & Instructional Technology at Anadolu University, Turkey with investigation of digital fluency of teacher candidates. Dr. Demir lists her primary research interests as mobile learning, digital fluency, computational thinking and technology integration.

Saarce Elsye Hatane is a lecturer in the Accounting Department of Universitas Kristen Petra, Indonesia. She is majoring in Management Accounting and holding Certified Management Accountant from International Certified Management Accountant, Australia. She also has a Chartered Accountant designation from Indonesia Accountant Body. She is a trainer for Certified Management Accountant course in East Java, Indonesia. Besides, she also gives training in finance and cost accounting for the small enterprises in Surabaya, Indonesia. She has experiences in publishing research articles in some reputable journals which are indexed by Scopus. Her research areas are corporate governance, intellectual capital, social responsibility, and knowledge management. Besides, Ms Saarce also a reviewer in some reputable international journals indexed by Scopus. She became the head of Business Accounting Program in Universitas Kristen Petra since 2013 until now, 2020. She also gives business consultation for some small and medium enterprises in Indonesia.

Ferry Jie is the Associate Professor in Supply Chain and Logistics Management, in the School of Business and Law. In addition, Ferry is a Deputy Director, Centre for Innovative Practice. Ferry has graduated his doctorate study from The University of Sydney in 2008. His PhD thesis is Supply Chain Analysis in the Australian Beef Industry. Previously, he was a Senior Lecturer and taking a program coordinator role in Logistics and Supply Chain Management (LSCM) at RMIT University. He was managing and coordinating the undergraduate program in LSCM at RMIT from 2015 to 2016. Associate Professor Ferry Jie has maintained a high quality of research throughout his academic career including international scholarly leadership in the areas of supply chain management and logistics, including being invited to be keynote speaker and to give public lectures at symposiums and international conferences in Indonesia, Malaysia, Vietnam, China, UK and Australia. From 2014 to now, Dr Jie has published 55 refereed journal articles—including 18 (eight) articles in A/A* Ranked Journal - ABDC Journal Lists—and 18 refereed conference papers. Furthermore, Dr Jie has received research grants/awards adding up to over $1.5 million between 2010 and 2019. Dr Jie has professional and community engagement activities to contribute significantly to improve the university's reputation through contribution to the wider community. They are active participation in professional or governmental organisations at the Local, State, National, or International level; professional engagement, e.g. Senior Advisor for Supply Chain Indonesia (SCI); member of Supply Chain and Logistics Association of Australia (SCLAA), Chartered Institute Purchasing and Supply in Australia (CIPSA), Project Management Institute (PMI); Media Star (speaking to national/international participants, professional agency, including international guest lecturer at universities).

Venetis Kanakaris was born in Komotini, Greece. He received the B.Eng. degree in Electronic Engineering from Lamia Technical University, Greece, the B.Eng. degree in Electrical Engineering from Kavala Technical University, Greece, in 2004, and the M.Sc. degree in Telecommunications and Technologies from Technical University of Gabrovo, Bulgaria, in 2006. Also, received his PhD from

University of Portsmouth in 2012, U.K. as well as the M.Ed. from Open University of Greece in 2013. Since October of 2016, is adjunct Lecturer at International Hellenic University, Dept. of Computer Science, Kavala, Greece. His current research interests lie in energy ad hoc routing protocols and low-power underwater wireless sensor protocol architecture OSINT techniques, LORA infrastructures, BlockChain technologies in farming and agriculture. Besides the engineering research interests, he focuses on lifelong learning sector as well as the adult education. At the present he is postdoctoral student at School of Early Childhood Education, Aristotle University of Thessaloniki in Greece.

Eleni Karakolidou is a teacher of Philology in secondary public education with over twenty years of experience in both the private and the public sector. She studied Classical Literature at the Aristotle University of Thessaloniki (1993-1997) and took postgraduate studies in Adult Education at the Hellenic Open University (2015-2019). She has participated in many educational seminars and training programs and has been officially certified for the specialized pedagogical use of new technologies in the teaching practice. Her research interests focus primarily on distance learning and group education, as well as on the pedagogical methods and practices that support teaching and learning.

Piera Leftheriotou obtained one bachelor's degree in French Literature and one in Early Childhood Education in Athens. In 2005 she obtained a Master's degree and in 2014 a PhD from the Hellenic Open University. The subject of her PhD is "Planning adult education programs in Greece: the case of General Secretariat for Lifelong Learning". She has been working on Adult Education in the Greek Ministry of Education since 1984. She is a member of the scientific staff of Hellenic Open University and she teaches in "Adult Education" and "Education Science" postgraduate programs. She has published articles and chapters on adult education and e-learning. Her research interests mainly focus on topics related to adult education and educators' training in face to face and e-learning environments.

Domitilla Magni is Post-Doctoral Research Fellow in Strategic Management at Department of Business Studies at RomaTre University and a Visiting Professor at various top tier universities across the world (e.g. New York University, Montpellier Business School, South-Western University of Finance and Economics). She is also Lecture Assistant at RomaTre University for the classes of Management and Business Planning. She obtained her Ph.D. in "Management, Banking and Commodity Sciences" at Sapienza University of Rome. Research interests include, among others, Innovation Management, Knowledge Management, and Open Innovation, with a specific focus on the Value Co-Creation in Higher Education. She has participated as a presenter at many international conferences and author of many national and international publications. Domitilla is also reviewer for several top-tier management International Journals such as Journal of Knowledge Management (Emerald) and Journal of Intellectual Capital (Emerald).

Kapilan N. is working as Professor and Head, Department of Mechanical Engineering, Nagarjuna College of Engineering and Technology, India. He has more than 22 years of teaching, research and industrial experience. He has published more than 75 papers in journals and conferences. He authored one book and five book chapters. H has filed three patents. He has received US$ 100,000 worth sponsored projects from various government and professional organizations. He is the member of several professional societies such as ASHRAE, ISHRAE, IE, ISTE and CI(I).

H. Ferhan Odabasi is a faculty member of Department of Computer Education and Instructional Technology. She has an MA in English language education and a Ph.D. in educational technology. She has offered several undergraduate and graduate courses on English language education and educational technology. She has supervised several PhD dissertations, published many articles in both national and international peer-reviewed periodicals, supervised and actively took part in national and international research projects, and prepared educational software. She developed "Hypervocab" with Steve Neufeld, and received the European Academic Software Award: Best Software in the Field of Language. She has been the pioneer in Turkey to integrate educational technology into special education. She conducts research on safe, responsible and effective use of ICTs by children and families; parental awareness on Internet; professional development of teachers and higher education faculty; transformations stemming from the digital world; digital citizenship and ICT integration at K-12 and higher education institutions. She has been the primary national figure to resort to regarding safe, effective and ethical use of ICTs among children.

Eric Oktavianus is a graduate from International Business Accounting, Petra Christian University. He is currently working developing his own family business. He did ACCA accounting qualification program during his study at Petra.

Beatrice Orlando completed her Ph.D in Business Management and Corporate Finance at Sapienza University of Rome, where she also finished her Master in Finance. Currently, she is Senior Researcher at University of Ferrara. Her research areas cover topics such as innovation adoption, open innovation, and firm's strategy. She has published numerous articles in leading scholarly journals, such as Production, Planning and control, Technology Analysis and Strategic Management, Corporate Social Responsibility and Environmental Management, Journal of Intellectual Capital, and Technology Forecasting and Social Change.

Vidhya P. is working as assistant professor in Department of Computer Science, SRSMN Government First Grade College. She has more than 15 years of teaching and research experience. She published several papers in journals and conferences. She delivered few guest lectures in various colleges and filed a patent. She authored a one textbook.

Nicole Palan is a post-doc researcher at the university of Graz. She has worked in a number of research projects studying the structural convergence of European countries and regions, inequality and concentration patterns, the development of globalization, as well as the impact of digitalization on economies.

Rina D. Pasaribu is an experienced practitioner in ICT industry and also a lecturer of Telkom University at the Business Management of Telecommunications and Informatics Department, School of Economics and Business. Her fields and interests in academic environment are in Strategic Management, Marketing Management, Human Capital Management and Coaching. She has lots of strategic positions experiences that very useful to be given in her class regarding real industry illustration. Her previous strategic positions were in PT Telkom and Telkom Education Foundation. Currently, besides carry on her lecturer assignments, she is also a Vice Rector of Telkom University in Resources & IT.

Paschalia Patsala holds a PhD in Theoretical and Applied Linguistics, an MA in Lexicography, a PGCert in Learning and Teaching in Higher Education, and a BA in English Language and Literature. She is the International Partnerships and Engagement Manager of the Arts and Humanities Research Council, UK, where she is heavily involved in the development, management and delivery of a range of funding schemes, partnerships and strategic activity across the entire AHRC international portfolio. Her research interests include Corpus Linguistics, Second Language Acquisition, Lexicography, Learning, Teaching and Assessment in HE, and Educational Technologies.

Maria Pavlis-Korres obtained a university degree in Political Science in Athens. From 1983 until 2018 she worked on Adult Education in the Greek Ministry of Education. Since 2005 her research interests are focused on e-learning and she became a PhD student in the University of Alcalá, Spain. In 2008 she obtained her Advance Studies Degree from the Computer Science Department of the University of Alcalá and in 2010 she obtained her PhD with honors. Since 2012 she is a member of the scientific staff of Hellenic Open University and teaches in "Adult Education" and "Education Science" postgraduate programs. In June 2017 she has been elected Associate Professor in the Pedagogical Sector of the Aristotle University of Thessaloniki to teach "Lifelong Learning and non-Formal Education". She has published several articles, chapters and books on Roma, adult education and e-learning. Her current interests are focused on design, development and evaluation of educational projects for adults, face to face and e-learning, as well as the group dynamics in an online environment and the appropriate use of communication tools in order to promote interaction in an online environment.

Kristina Posavec received her master's degree in Journalism from the Faculty of Political Science in Zagreb in 2008. In 2009 she received her second master's degree in Museology from Faculty of Humanities and Social Sciences in Zagreb. In March 2017 she received her Ph.D. in Information and Communication Science from the Faculty of Humanities and Social Sciences, University of Zagreb. From 2008 till 2012 she worked at Open University Infokatedra in Zagreb where she was the lecturer of ICT courses. From 2013 she works at the Open University Algebra in Zagreb where she actively participates in conducting and teaching ICT courses. From 2014 she works at the Faculty of Education and Rehabilitation Sciences as a lecturer of Computer Science. From 2018 till 2019 she works at The Croatian Academic and Research Network – CARNET as an expert associate at the Education Support Department. From 2020 she works at the University Computing Center as IT project manager on science projects. She writes and presents widely on issues of e-learning, new technologies in education and rehabilitation, educational ICT platforms and application for improving the quality of learning process.

Adhi Prasetio is a full time lecturer at the Business Management of Telecommunications and Informatics Department, School of Economics and Business, Telkom University, Indonesia. He teaches courses in E-commerce, Management Information System, and Data Management. His research interests include e-commerce, online consumer behavior, and social CRM. He is an active researcher and published many articles in leading international and national publication and books.

Maurizio Rija is Associate Professor of Auditing whitin the Department of Business and Low of the University of Calabria. His main research interests concern internal and external control, accounting and auditing of companies. On these research topics he has published books, magazine articles and presented articles at national and international conferences.

Andreas Schober is a researcher at the University of Graz at the Department of System Sciences, Innovation and Sustainability Research. He is an expert on data mining for the labour market.

Amira Sghari is Assistant Professor in Management studies at the Faculty of Economics and Management of Sfax in Tunisia. She received a Ph.D. degree in management science, in 2013, from the Aix-Marseille University, France. Dr. Sghari is member of a Research Unit on Management Studies. Her research interests include strategy and organizational structure, organizational change and information management.

Vandana Singh brings over ten years of hands-on- experience in the academic sphere. An MBA in Finance and Marketing, Vandana brings unique skills in bridging theory into practice, core academic delivery, relationship management, and multitasking ability. Having worked with prestigious academic institutions such as Maharaja College of Management, Rajasthan Institute of Engineering and Technology, Jaipur. Radcliffe, St Wilfred Group, Tree House and Asian World School; she has, in past, successfully displayed her teaching capabilities with well-established academic institutions and corporate entities such as HDFC Bank and Reliance Mutual fund. Presently, pursuing a Ph.D. from Bhartiya Skill Development University.

Josua Tarigan has experience more than fifteen years in Accounting Education. Besides that almost two years experience in ERP related (Siemens Company) and also several years in freelance consulting. Have been interacting directly with several companies in Indonesia, Singapore, Malaysia, Bangkok, Vietnam, Myanmar, Korea, Japan, Hongkong, Macau, Shenzen, Dubai, Europe (Germany, Chezh, Austria, Spain, Netherland, Belgium, France & Switzerland) and United States of America (USA). Have strong knowledge and skill in the area of Strategic Management Accounting, Finance & Auditing Information System. Serve also as a visiting lecturer in Germany (Berlin & Munich) for Financial Management course and a reviewer for Journal of Asia Business Studies (Q1-Emerald); International Journal of Emerging Markets (Q2-Emerald) & Nankai Business Review International (Q3-Emerald). He also become Editorial Board for ASEAN Journal of Management & Innovation (AJMI) and Jurnal Akuntansi Keuangan (JAK). He has been recently invited as keynote speakers at Rangsit University (Thailand) international conference. Additionally, proficient in both written and spoken English, computer literate with excellent interpersonal, communication and intercultural skills.

Index

F

G

H

I

J

L

M

N

O

P

R

S

T

U

V

W

X

Purchase Print, E-Book, or Print + E-Book

IGI Global's reference books are available in three unique pricing formats:
Print Only, E-Book Only, or Print + E-Book.
Shipping fees may apply.

www.igi-global.com

Recommended Reference Books

ISBN: 978-1-5225-9348-5
© 2019; 454 pp.
List Price: $255

ISBN: 978-1-5225-7763-8
© 2019; 253 pp.
List Price: $175

ISBN: 978-1-5225-7531-3
© 2019; 324 pp.
List Price: $185

ISBN: 978-1-5225-7802-4
© 2019; 423 pp.
List Price: $195

ISBN: 978-1-5225-6246-7
© 2019; 610 pp.
List Price: $275

ISBN: 978-1-5225-2998-9
© 2018; 352 pp.
List Price: $195

Do you want to stay current on the latest research trends, product announcements, news and special offers?
Join IGI Global's mailing list today and start enjoying exclusive perks sent only to IGI Global members.
Add your name to the list at **www.igi-global.com/newsletters.**

Publisher of Peer-Reviewed, Timely, and Innovative Academic Research

IGI Global
DISSEMINATOR OF KNOWLEDGE

www.igi-global.com Sign up at www.igi-global.com/newsletters facebook.com/igiglobal twitter.com/igiglobal linkedin.com/igiglobal

Ensure Quality Research is Introduced to the Academic Community

Become an IGI Global Reviewer for Authored Book Projects

The overall success of an authored book project is dependent on quality and timely reviews.

In this competitive age of scholarly publishing, constructive and timely feedback significantly expedites the turnaround time of manuscripts from submission to acceptance, allowing the publication and discovery of forward-thinking research at a much more expeditious rate. Several IGI Global authored book projects are currently seeking highly-qualified experts in the field to fill vacancies on their respective editorial review boards:

Applications and Inquiries may be sent to:
development@igi-global.com

Applicants must have a doctorate (or an equivalent degree) as well as publishing and reviewing experience. Reviewers are asked to complete the open-ended evaluation questions with as much detail as possible in a timely, collegial, and constructive manner. All reviewers' tenures run for one-year terms on the editorial review boards and are expected to complete at least three reviews per term. Upon successful completion of this term, reviewers can be considered for an additional term.

If you have a colleague that may be interested in this opportunity, we encourage you to share this information with them.

IGI Global Proudly Partners With eContent Pro International

Receive a 25% Discount on all Editorial Services

Editorial Services

IGI Global expects all final manuscripts submitted for publication to be in their final form. This means they must be reviewed, revised, and professionally copy edited prior to their final submission. Not only does this support with accelerating the publication process, but it also ensures that the highest quality scholarly work can be disseminated.

English Language Copy Editing

Let eContent Pro International's expert copy editors perform edits on your manuscript to resolve spelling, punctuaion, grammar, syntax, flow, formatting issues and more.

Scientific and Scholarly Editing

Allow colleagues in your research area to examine the content of your manuscript and provide you with valuable feedback and suggestions before submission.

Figure, Table, Chart & Equation Conversions

Do you have poor quality figures? Do you need visual elements in your manuscript created or converted? A design expert can help!

Translation

Need your documjent translated into English? eContent Pro International's expert translators are fluent in English and more than 40 different languages.

Hear What Your Colleagues are Saying About Editorial Services Supported by IGI Global

"The service was very fast, very thorough, and very helpful in ensuring our chapter meets the criteria and requirements of the book's editors. I was quite impressed and happy with your service."

– Prof. Tom Brinthaupt, Middle Tennessee State University, USA

"I found the work actually spectacular. The editing, formatting, and other checks were very thorough. The turnaround time was great as well. I will definitely use eContent Pro in the future."

– Nickanor Amwata, Lecturer, University of Kurdistan Hawler, Iraq

"I was impressed that it was done timely, and wherever the content was not clear for the reader, the paper was improved with better readability for the audience."

– Prof. James Chilembwe, Mzuzu University, Malawi

Email: customerservice@econtentpro.com **www.igi-global.com/editorial-service-partners**

IGI Global
DISSEMINATOR OF KNOWLEDGE
www.igi-global.com

Celebrating Over 30 Years of Scholarly Knowledge Creation & Dissemination

InfoSci®-Books

A Database of Over 5,300+ Reference Books Containing Over 100,000+ Chapters Focusing on Emerging Research

InfoSci®-Books Database

The **InfoSci®-Books** database is a collection of over 5,300+ IGI Global single and multi-volume reference books, handbooks of research, and encyclopedias, encompassing groundbreaking research from prominent experts worldwide that span over 350+ topics in 11 core subject areas including business, computer science, education, science and engineering, social sciences and more.

Open Access Fee Waiver (Offset Model) Initiative

For any library that invests in IGI Global's InfoSci-Journals and/ or InfoSci-Books databases, IGI Global will match the library's investment with a fund of equal value to go toward **subsidizing the OA article processing charges (APCs) for their students, faculty, and staff** at that institution when their work is submitted and accepted under OA into an IGI Global journal.*

INFOSCI® PLATFORM FEATURES

- No DRM
- No Set-Up or Maintenance Fees
- A Guarantee of No More Than a 5% Annual Increase
- Full-Text HTML and PDF Viewing Options
- Downloadable MARC Records
- Unlimited Simultaneous Access
- COUNTER 5 Compliant Reports
- Formatted Citations With Ability to Export to RefWorks and EasyBib
- No Embargo of Content (Research is Available Months in Advance of the Print Release)

**The fund will be offered on an annual basis and expire at the end of the subscription period. The fund would renew as the subscription is renewed for each year thereafter. The open access fees will be waived after the student, faculty, or staff's paper has been vetted and accepted into an IGI Global journal and the fund can only be used toward publishing OA in an IGI Global journal. Libraries in developing countries will have the match on their investment doubled.*

To Learn More or To Purchase This Database:
www.igi-global.com/infosci-books
eresources@igi-global.com • Toll Free: 1-866-342-6657 ext. 100 • Phone: 717-533-8845 x100

IGI Global
DISSEMINATOR OF KNOWLEDGE
www.igi-global.com

IGI Global
DISSEMINATOR OF KNOWLEDGE
www.igi-global.com

Publisher of Peer-Reviewed, Timely, and Innovative Academic Research Since 1988

IGI Global's Transformative Open Access (OA) Model: How to Turn Your University Library's Database Acquisitions Into a Source of OA Funding

In response to the OA movement and well in advance of Plan S, IGI Global, early last year, unveiled their OA Fee Waiver (Read & Publish) Initiative.

Under this initiative, librarians who invest in IGI Global's InfoSci-Books (5,300+ reference books) and/or InfoSci-Journals (185+ scholarly journals) databases will be able to subsidize their patron's OA article processing charges (APC) when their work is submitted and accepted (after the peer review process) into an IGI Global journal. *See website for details.

How Does it Work?

1. When a library subscribes or perpetually purchases IGI Global's InfoSci-Databases and/or their discipline/subject-focused subsets, IGI Global will match the library's investment with a fund of equal value to go toward subsidizing the OA article processing charges (APCs) for their patrons.

   ***Researchers:* Be sure to recommend the InfoSci-Books and InfoSci-Journals to take advantage of this initiative.**
2. When a student, faculty, or staff member submits a paper and it is accepted (following the peer review) into one of IGI Global's 185+ scholarly journals, the author will have the option to have their paper published under a traditional publishing model or as OA.
3. When the author chooses to have their paper published under OA, IGI Global will notify them of the OA Fee Waiver (Read and Publish) Initiative. If the author decides they would like to take advantage of this initiative, IGI Global will deduct the US$ 2,000 APC from the created fund.
4. This fund will be offered on an annual basis and will renew as the subscription is renewed for each year thereafter. IGI Global will manage the fund and award the APC waivers unless the librarian has a preference as to how the funds should be managed.

Hear From the Experts on This Initiative:

"I'm very happy to have been able to make one of my recent research contributions, "Visualizing the Social Media Conversations of a National Information Technology Professional Association" featured in the *International Journal of Human Capital and Information Technology Professionals*, freely available along with having access to the valuable resources found within IGI Global's InfoSci-Journals database."

– **Prof. Stuart Palmer,**
Deakin University, Australia

For More Information, Visit: www.igi-global.com/publish/contributor-resources/open-access/read-publish-model or contact IGI Global's Database Team at eresources@igi-global.com.

www.ingramcontent.com/pod-product-compliance
Lightning Source LLC
LaVergne TN
LVHW060418300926
849162LV00006B/1458
* 9 7 8 1 7 9 9 8 4 9 7 2 8 *